# The Post-Soviet Handbook

*A Guide to Grassroots Organizations
and Internet Resources*

# The Post-Soviet Handbook

*A Guide to Grassroots Organizations*
*and Internet Resources*

## REVISED EDITION

M. Holt Ruffin
Alyssa Deutschler
Catriona Logan
Richard Upjohn

*Foreword by S. Frederick Starr*

Center for Civil Society International
*Seattle*

IN ASSOCIATION WITH

University of Washington Press
*Seattle and London*

Ruffin, M. Holt.
    The post-Soviet handbook : a guide to grassroots organizations and Internet resources, revised edition / by M. Holt Ruffin ... [et al.] ; foreword by S. Frederick Starr. — Rev. [2nd] ed.
        p.    cm.
    Rev. ed. of: Post-Soviet Handbook / M. Holt Ruffin, 1996.
    Includes indexes.
    ISBN 0-295-97794-9 (alk. paper)
    1. Associations, institutions, etc.—Former Soviet republics—Directories. 2. Economic assistance—Former Soviet republics—Directories. 3. Pressure groups—Former Soviet Republics—Directories. 4. Internet (Computer network)—Former Soviet Republics—Directories. 5. Former Soviet republics—Computer network resources—Directories.   I. Ruffin, M. Holt. II. Ruffin, M. Holt. Post-Soviet handbook. III. Center for Civil Society International.
HS71.F6P67 1999
067'.025—dc21
                                                                    98-54115
                                                                        CIP

The paper used in this publication meets the minimum requirements of American National Standard for Information Sciences—Permanence of Paper for Printed Library Materials, ANSI Z39.48-1984.

*Cover illustration:* St. Petersburg, 1991. Photograph by Holt Ruffin.

*For Lucy Dougall*

Free institutions, public service and active civic spirit deployed
to social ends are the lifeblood of the properly-ordered
commonwealth, the fundamental preconditions for
peace, harmony and material progress.

—Edward Gibbon
*The Decline and Fall of the Roman Empire*

# Contents

# Foreword

This volume, prepared by Holt Ruffin and his staff at the Center for Civil Society International, is in many respects remarkable. On the one hand, *The Post-Soviet Handbook* is the best available practical guide to the independent sector in the countries carved from the former Soviet Union. It consists of two parts, the first profiling "third sector" organizations in the newly independent states and American organizations interacting with them, and the second consisting of a useful compendium of Internet resources in those same countries.

Soaring far above these issues in importance is this volume's second identity, namely, as an insightful report on the state of civil society in Russia and other countries of the former Soviet Union, developed by an organization devoted to fostering and monitoring developments in this area. Thanks to this dual identity, *The Post-Soviet Handbook* offers something for everyone, no matter how practical and specific or how theoretical and general one's interest may be.

It need scarcely be said that the editors have had to be highly selective. *The Post-Soviet Handbook* describes only a few hundred of the tens of thousands of NGOs active in the NIS today. Only a small fraction of not-for-profit groups in Western Europe and Japan, which have found their own points of interaction in the newly independent states, are listed here. Most difficult to document are the many independent groups in Russia and elsewhere that are not interacting with Western counterparts. It is hoped that indigenous researchers will soon begin detailing such groups. But until then, this volume will remain the standard reference.

Anyone connected with the Internet is ipso facto part of the new societal sector worldwide that exists outside the ready control of governmental organs; any guide to independent sector activity in the former Soviet Union must therefore include Internet users. Like airline pilots' associations or ham radio operator networks, Internet users constitute a kind of supranational society in "cyberspace" whose links with one another are often as close as their ties with their local communities. Inevitably, even as substantial a guide to Internet resources as *The Post-Soviet Handbook* will not be comprehensive, so rapidly are these resources growing. The editors have wisely provided for regular updating through e-mail and through CCSI's World Wide Web site. In keeping with the democratic and participatory character of civil society, readers are encouraged to help update this site and perfect this compendium.

As the independent sector in the NIS grows and comes to include an ever greater number of increasingly diverse organizations, it would be very helpful if *The Post-Soviet Handbook* spawned additional, more specialized guides to important subsectors. Four possibilities stand out.

ix

First are scientific and technical fields. Highly organized and interactive, such disciplines have moved swiftly to participate both in third sector activity generally and in the Internet. Second and third are the many religious and ethnic-based organizations that exist within Russia and other newly independent states and which in many cases maintain close ties with kindred groupings abroad. It is worth noting that in Soviet times the vast majority of so-called dissident writings emerged form religious and national groups. Since the fall of the USSR, such groups have greatly expanded their activity and have extended their reach into the political realm as well.

The fourth sphere that deserves a special compendium consists of local and provincial organizations. Relatively few such bodies maintain links with Moscow or St. Petersburg, let alone with counterpart organizations abroad. Having grown up "from below," these essential elements of civil society are the hardest to document. It is to be hoped that over time some readers will carry *The Post-Soviet Handbook* idea forward in all four of these areas.

⌀

It is impossible to overstate the importance of the present guide to third sector organizations and Internet users in Russia and the other newly independent states. The astonishing proliferation of businesses and financial institutions in the former Soviet Union is well documented elsewhere, thanks to reports by the U.S. Department of Commerce, Deutsche Bank and various business groups. The independent sector has been far less accessible, however.

Perhaps it is too much to be hoped that those researching the rise of civil society in the former Soviet Union will adequately utilize a handbook like this. They should do so, however, for *The Post-Soviet Handbook* provides as revealing an index to this phenomenon as any in existence. More than three decades ago the MIT political scientist Karl Deutsch assessed the likelihood of political community embracing North America and Western Europe by counting the number of telephone calls and the amount of first-class mail between those two regions. The present volume provides the raw material for a similar study of civil society, and it is worth drawing here some of the obvious conclusions.

So rapidly does the past slip from our consciousness that we must pause to recall the situation as it existed only a decade ago. Soviet law permitted no truly independent organizations whatsoever. True, nominally "societal" (*obshchest-vennyi)* groups existed, but only under the tutelage of a governmental or Communist Party patron. Even in the case of these governmentalized entities, the state exercised a monopoly of communication, both domestic and international. Unauthorized communications both within the USSR and with independent entities abroad was banned. The receipt of funds from foreign bodies, whether public or private, was grounds for stern legal action.

The political underpinnings of this unnatural order traced directly to Marxism-Leninism, with its ideal of the totally organized society, and also to notions of autarky that permeated the official ideology. All these traced in turn to an earlier era when the major channels of communication—the printed word, mail, and film—were readily controlled by the state. Such control was all the easier if the state was prepared to use force, as was certainly the case in the USSR.

Beginning in the 1960s, however, the willingness of the Soviet state to employ force to achieve its ends diminished. Meanwhile, the spread of education in the USSR created a growing number of men and women who were eager to participate directly in the leading cultural movements worldwide. Beginning in the realm of religion and movements for national identity and rapidly extending into such diverse realms as popular culture, jazz, ecology, and the arts, truly self-organized and independent initiatives sprouted throughout Soviet society. Long before the Internet, these hearty bands of enthusiasts exploited 35-mm film, tape recordings, telephones, and photocopiers to advance their cause and forge links with like-minded groups both locally and abroad.

By this process, a true civil society began to reemerge even during the "golden age" of Brezhnev's rule. *Glasnost'* existed long before Gorbachev's *glasnost'*, and voluntary associations existed long before the state acknowledged them as legal.

Whence came this effervescence of independence in the very heart of the Marxist-Leninist state? Contrary to the claims of Soviet officialdom and Western kremlinology, Russians, Ukrainians, and many other peoples of the USSR possessed a strong tradition of self-organization. The progenitors of today's not-for-profits in the newly independent states are the thousands of self-help and philanthropic societies that existed prior to the Bolshevik revolution. The fact that the Soviet government had to exert so much brutal force in order to wipe out these groups in the 1920s and 1930s attests to their vitality. Nor did the spirit of self-initiative stay dead for long. Obliterated by 1937, the volunteeristic urge in Russia reappeared like Lazarus in the 1960s, a mere quarter-century later. As the spirit of self-initiative came once more to the fore, it revealed the absolute limits of absolute power in the USSR, thus contributing directly to the system's downfall.

What, then, is the state of volunteerism and the independent sector in Russia today? Besides the mere fact of their reappearance after so many years, the two most important features of the present situation are, first, that the new associations and groupings are far more closely interlinked with counterpart groups in Europe and America than were their predecessors, and second, that they are yet to obtain the solid legal basis that is essential if they are to be viable for the long term.

It is easy to be cynical about American and Western aid to the independent sector in Russia. Far too much of that aid—estimates range up to 90 percent—has ended up in the pockets of American and European organizations rather than of the

Russian groups they purport to champion. Nonetheless, wherever the money ends up, American assistance under USAID has helped forge close personal links between independent sector activists in the NIS and the U.S. Such ties are more enduring than any financial support, and over time they are bound to affect the "culture" and mentality of the third sector in Russia and neighboring countries.

Yet, for all the vitality of voluntary initiatives in Russia and elsewhere, they have yet to gain the firm basis in law that is essential for their long-term viability. Only in May 1995 did the first body of legislation in this area pass the Duma. Supplementary legislation validating foundations and political parties has, at this writing, yet to be approved.

Skeptics may find evidence in this of a kind of "Soviet hangover," i.e., the resistance of the new Russian government to true voluntarism and pluralism. For the time being, however, the evidence does not support this conclusion. On the contrary, the legislative delays are attributable not to opposition but to the serious effort of Russian legislators to "get it right," i.e., to produce legislation that is solid, enduring, and grounded in the best experience of other countries. The first section of the new Civil Code, approved early in 1995, is a solid piece of legislation based on the Napoleonic tradition. There is every reason to expect that subsequent legislation based on volunteerism will have an equally serious character, and will meet the needs of a modern society as Russians perceive them.

This leaves unanswered only one question, but a crucially important one. Already, there are many men and women of wealth in Russia. Thousands of other fortunes are bound to be made in the vast and increasingly privatized energy sector, the burgeoning service sector, banking, and even in the manufacturing sphere. Will those who possess such fortunes use them for the public good? Will they, in other words, adopt a philosophy akin to Andrew Carnegie's *Gospel of Wealth*, which would obligate them to devote the fruits of their good fortune to civic uplift and the public's welfare?

It is too early to judge whether this will occur. However, public discussion of this issue within Russia henceforth will no longer be a purely Russian affair. Thanks to the channels of communication with many organizations described herein, and to the great river of transnational dialogue that is the Internet, this issue can be thoroughly aired not only by Russians alone, but by friends of the independent sector everywhere. If this dialogue fosters the further effervescence of volunteerism in Russia, as one might hope and even expect, then the present volume will soon be obsolete. One can pay no higher compliment to it than this!

*S. Frederick Starr*
Chairman
Central Asia-Caucasus Institute
Johns Hopkins University

# *Acknowledgments*

**M**any people and organizations assisted Center for Civil Society International (CCSI) in producing this revised edition of *The Post-Soviet Handbook*. We would first like to thank the scores of individuals based in Armenia, Azerbaijan, Belarus, Georgia, Moldova, Russia, and Ukraine who e-mailed us information about their projects and updates on their organizations during 1998. We received more than 200 such e-mails and used virtually all of them. They enrich the book with their immediacy and level of detail. They also further demonstrate the power of the Internet for communication and collaborative projects between citizens of the U.S. and the newly independent states of Eurasia.

Catriona Logan traveled to Russia and Ukraine in the first months of 1998 to collect data for the revised edition of the *Handbook* (and her thesis). Amy Taylor of ISAR-Siberia and Svetlana Rubashkina of the Southern Russian Resource Center were particularly helpful during that trip. So also were the offices of the Agency for Social Information, Moscow; the Siberian Civic Initiatives Support Center, Novosibirsk; ISAR-Kyiv; and the American Information Center, Ekaterinburg. The Henry M. Jackson School of International Studies at the University of Washington helped pay for that trip; we are grateful for that support.

During the summer of 1998, Stanford student Regine Spector spent two months in the Republic of Georgia, where she voluntarily collected information on scores of Georgian NGOs and sent her write-ups to us. Regine's material was an unexpected and highly useful contribution to the *Handbook*. Brendan Bell, a Seattleite now studying at Macalester College, gave us part of his summer vacation to help research and write several parts of the *Handbook*. Likewise Maria Kozhevnikova, a graduate student at the Jackson School, interned with us that summer and contributed to the book.

Dennis McConnell, retired professor of finance at the University of Maine in Orono, CCSI advisor, and administrator of the Central and East European Management Development Association electronic mailing list (CEEMAN)—one of the Internet's best public services—made important contributions to our Internet section.

Without the support of the Center for International Neworking Initiatives, whose Friends and Partners site on the World Wide Web is the platform for both our CivilSoc electronic mailing list and our Web site, this book would have been much more difficult to produce. The same must be said for The Eurasia Foundation, which has funded a considerable amount of CCSI's work on the Internet in recent years.

Finally, CCSI wishes to acknowledge the thousands of "civil society builders" in the NIS, of all nationalities, only a small fraction of whose creative work we could document in *The Post-Soviet Handbook*. History too seldom recognizes the important contributions of such people.

Needless to say, Center for Civil Society International alone is responsible for any shortcomings in this revised edition of *The Post-Soviet Handbook*.

*The Authors*

# Guide to Foreign Words and Special Terms

## Russian and Other Foreign Words

| | |
|---|---|
| *A/ya (abonementnii yashchik)* | Post Office Box |
| *Bulvar, bul.* | Boulevard |
| *Dom, d.* | Building |
| *Etazh* | Floor |
| *Indeks* | Zip code |
| *Kabinet, kab.* | Office |
| *Komnata, kom., k.* | Room |
| *Korpus, korp.* | Section |
| *Krai* | Territorial area, comparable to *oblast* |
| *Kvartira, kv.* | Apartment |
| *Naberezhnaia, nab.* | Embankment |
| *Oblast, obl.* | Province (more or less equivalent to a U.S. state) |
| *Pereulok, per.* | Lane or alley |
| *Ploshchad, pl.* | Square |
| *Pochtamt, Glavnii Pochtamt* | Post Office, General Post Office (GPO) |
| *Podezd, pod.* | Entrance, doorway |
| *Prospekt, pr.* | Avenue |
| *Proyezd* | Passageway, thoroughfare |
| *Raion* | Municipal district |
| *Shosse* | Highway |
| *Ulitsa, ul.* | Street |
| *Vulytsya, vul.* | Street, in Ukrainian |

## Special Terms

| | |
|---|---|
| CEE | Central and Eastern Europe |
| CIS | Commonwealth of Independent States, the political association that succeeded the USSR. It includes Armenia, Azerbaijan, Belarus, Georgia, Kazakhstan, Kyrgyzstan, Moldova, Russia, Tajikistan, Turkmenistan, Ukraine, and Uzbekistan. No Baltic states are in it. |
| Eurasia | Roughly speaking, the geographic region of the CIS |
| FAQ | Frequently Asked Questions. The name given to a type of document, written in question-and-answer form, commonly found on World Wide Web sites. |
| FSU | Former Soviet Union |

| IDP | Internally displaced person. E.g., a refugee who has fled one part of a country for another because of civil war. |
| ODA | Official development assistance |
| NIS | Newly Independent States of the former Soviet Union. The term is used interchangeably with CIS; it may or may not include the three Baltic states. |
| NGO | Non-governmental organization |
| NPO | Nonprofit organization |
| PVO | Private voluntary organization, interchangeable with NGO |
| RF | Russian Federation |
| RFE | Russian Far East |
| TACIS | Technical Assistance to the CIS—a program of the European Union. |
| UNHCR | United Nations High Committee on Refugees |
| USAID | United States Agency for International Development |
| USIA | United States Information Agency |
| USIS | United States Information Service, used when referring to the overseas offices of USIA |
| URL | Uniform Resource Locator, the address of a file on the Internet |

## Notes to *Handbook* users

1.   Organizations in each country are sorted alphabetically by city, but the national capital is always the first city listed. If an organization is in a small town that is part of a larger region identified with a large city, e.g. the Kaluga *oblast*, it is classified by that larger city's name.

2.   There are no hyphens inserted in the line breaks that occasionally affect e-mail or Web site addresses in the *Handbook*. If you see a hyphen in an e-mail or Web site address, it is supposed to be there.

3.   Addresses in Russia and the NIS are written in the reverse order from that in the U.S. Russians first give the zip code, or *indeks*, then the city, then street, then an individual's name. The building (*dom*) number follows the street name, after a comma. After the building number, there may be a section (*korpus*) number, followed by an apartment *(kvartira)* or room (*komnata*) number.

Thus, a typical Russian address might read:   194156 St. Petersburg
Nevski pr., d. 93, korp. 4, kv. 203

Alternatively, the street address could be written:   Nevski pr., 93-4-203
or, Nevski pr., 93/4, kv. 203

4.   If you intend to send "snail mail," i.e., a letter, to an organization and have a choice between a post office box and a street address, use the post office box.

5.   A few telephone numbers have a special area code. Use the prefix that is given. It may represent a special line being leased from a telecommunications service provider.

Map 1. Western NIS

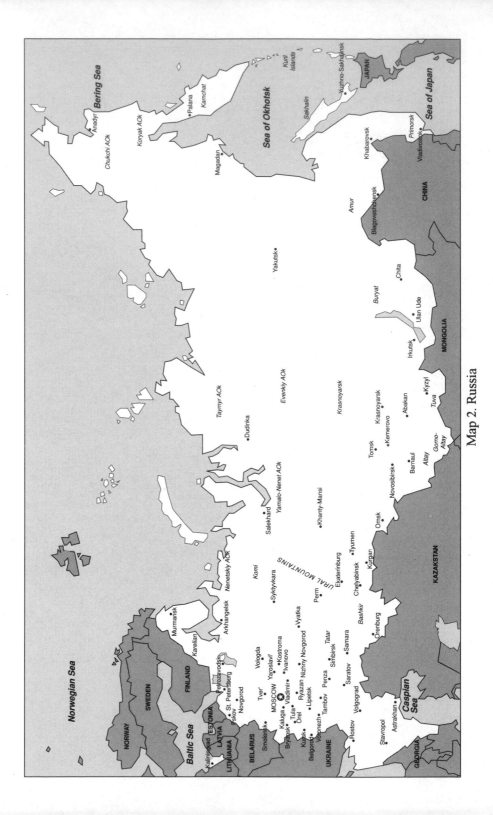

Map 2. Russia

# The Post-Soviet Handbook

*A Guide to Grassroots Organizations*
*and Internet Resources*

# Introduction

*Where institution building (and not mere constitution
writing) is concerned, time is measured in decades. This
was true of the German Länder, it has been true of the
Italian regions and of the communal republics before
them, and it will be true of the ex-Communist states of
Eurasia, even in the most optimistic scenarios.*[1]

—Robert Putnam
Harvard University

*It is easier to make fish soup from an aquarium, than to
make an aquarium out of fish soup.*

—Popular Eastern European aphorism

1998 was the fiftieth anniversary of the Marshall Plan. Over the course of four
years, 1948–52, the United States provided 16 nations in Europe with more than
$13 billion—90 percent of it as grants, not loans. In today's dollars, this is a sum
greater than $90 billion. In 1948, the $4 billion spent on the plan during its first year of
operation represented 13 percent of the total federal budget. Paul Hoffman, who was
the Marshall Plan administrator in Europe, would later describe it as "one of the most
truly generous impulses that has ever motivated any nation anywhere at any time."[2]

Perhaps this history helps explains why public opinion surveys repeatedly show
Americans believing our foreign economic assistance programs are as much as 20
times greater than they actually are.[3] The fact is that U.S. official foreign economic

---

[1] Robert D. Putnam, *Making Democracy Work: Civic Traditions in Modern Italy*
(Princeton, 1993), p. 184.

[2] See Curt Tarnoff, *The Marshall Plan: Design, Accomplishments, and Relevance to the
Present* (Congressional Research Service Report For Congress, January 6, 1997) for
an excellent summary and analysis of the plan, known formally as the European
Recovery Act. The paper is online at: www.usia.gov/topical/pol/marshall/crstoc.htm.

[3] A poll done in 1993 showed that the public believed 20 percent of government
spending went to foreign aid, a figure 20 times higher than the actual amount. These
numbers have not changed significantly over time. See "Public Believes Government
Spends as Much on Foreign Aid as on Social Security and Health Care," Harris Poll
#55, conducted November 1, 1993, by Louis Harris and Associates, New York, NY.

assistance was less in 1998, in real dollar terms, than in any of the past 50 years.[4] We are far indeed from the Marshall Plan.

The sense that the U.S. is not exercising international leadership today on a scale commensurate with the crisis in the post-Soviet world is undoubtedly behind the intermittent calls one hears for "a new Marshall Plan."[5] Those who compare the collapse of the USSR in 1991 to the end of World War II, as a "hinge point" in world history, look in vain for policies by the U.S. which match in scope and vision those of the postwar period. But there are important reasons why intermittent appeals for a "new Marshall Plan," despite the manifest seriousness of the post-Soviet crisis, have not generated a strong response. A brief review of these reasons will help illuminate what is both distinctive and problematic in the situation of the post-Soviet or so-called "transition" countries, as compared to the countries which were beneficiaries of the Marshall Plan 50 years ago.

Among the most distinctive differences between now and the postwar period is the general international situation. When the Marshall Plan was conceived, Europe was in effect a pile of rubble. If the U.S. had not provided assistance, there was no other source. At the same time, indigenous Communist movements and Stalin's actions in Germany were threatening the post-war order. It was not terribly difficult to appeal to Americans in these circumstances and ask for a large investment in Europe's future. Added to this was the fact that Americans identified closely with the plight of West Europeans and had fought side by side with them against Hitler. We had seen firsthand the devastation wrought by war. Thus concerns of national interest, plus empathy, altruism, and world order, all converged to form support for the Marshall Plan.

And it was neither totally altruistic nor totally unilateral, either. Ninety percent of Marshall Plan money was in the form of grants, but 83 percent of it came back to the U.S. in purchases of goods or services by grantees. European governments also matched the U.S. commitment of $13 billion in their own currencies, so that every project was a 50-50 partnership. Within a few years of the plan's inception, and largely owing to its massive scale and well-coordinated nature, Western European factories had been rebuilt, scarcities of urgently needed raw materials had been eliminated, and European recovery, economically and politically. was assured. Again in the words of Paul Hoffman, not only were "truly generous impulses" involved, but the United States also "derived enormous benefits from the bread it figuratively cast upon the international waters."

---

[4]    Advisory Committee on Voluntary Foreign Aid, *An Assessment of the State of the USAID/PVO Partnership* (USAID, June 1997), p. 7.

[5]    One of the most recent was Alexander Yanoff's "Western Policies Have Generated Only Misery: Have We Forgotten the Constructive Lessons of the Marshall Plan?", *Los Angeles Times*, December 23, 1998.

Today, of course, the countries of the European Union are as wealthy as the U.S. and have at least as much political incentive to assist the post-Soviet world; in fact, Germany and other EU countries have extended billions of dollars in soft loans and grant assistance to Russia and its neighbors. But the financial default by Russia in the summer of 1998 put billions of these dollars in jeopardy of never being repaid—and pointed to the aspect of the "new Marshall plan" idea which is most problematic.

It is this: Whereas in Europe after World War II, the institutional framework of market-oriented democracies was more or less in place, and mainly capital was needed to "prime the economic pump," this was not at all the situation in the post-Soviet world in the nineties. In the post-Soviet states, it is the institutional legacy of the USSR that is the problem and it requires enormous changes *before* large sums of capital can be invested productively. If recovery was the slogan after World War II, radical re-structuring of virtually all enterprises and institutions has been the need in the post-Soviet world since 1991. Far from advising large investments in capital-short ex-Soviet firms and industries, many economists have concluded that it would be better to shut many of these behemoths down while implementing reforms that would stimulate job growth in other ways.[6]

The same holds true at the macroeconomic level. In order for there to be growing, productive economies in Russia and other post-Soviet countries, profound institutional changes are needed, such that: citizens' acquire the ability to own and transfer property[7]; the banking system can function in a normal manner, gathering public savings and using them to finance housing and similar investments; public officials can rely on adequate and regular salaries, derived from a fair and reasonable tax code; judges can render decisions independent of administrative "guidance" and protected from intimidation by criminals. To list just some of the changes required is to recognize how large the task is.

But institutions must, of course, reflect a society's thinking and values. Thus the task is made even greater by the fact that these new social institutions require new public understandings and new public behavior. Unfortunately, significant sectors of the "new" ruling elites in Russia and other countries of the post-Soviet world are recycled members of the Communist nomenklatura, former servants of a system that offered better training in Marxist theory than in business administration or democratic governance. As a result, much remains at root unchanged in the post-Soviet world. The

---

[6] See Clifford Gaddy and Barry Ickes, "Russia's Virtual Economy," *Foreign Affairs*, September/October 1998, which makes the argument that most large Soviet firms are "value-subtracting" instead of value-adding enterprises.

[7] At the end of 1998, the Russian Duma was still blocking legislation that would allow the private ownership of farmland with full rights of individuals to buy and sell it.

lawlessness of the KGB has become the lawlessness of new "entrepreneurs" running protection rackets or extortion rings. The tight controls on citizens of the security-obsessed Soviet state have not all been thrown out; many remain in use by unreformed bureaucracies in the new Russia.[8] The culture of the communist era has given way to a culture of casinos and fast cars, as coarse in its own way as its proletarian predecessor. Where are concerns for the poor, the elderly, the disabled, and the sick? Where are concerns for reforming the system of justice, improving public security, eliminating corruption in high places, protecting a free press, or removing the red tape and regulatory thicket that prevents free enterprise from working in today's post-Soviet societies? Where are concerns for the spiritual and non-material sides of life, for education and true culture which can deepen human relationships and enhance personal growth?

### *A Sustained and Broad Engagement for Institutional Change*

The answer to these questions is to be found in the organizations profiled in *The Post-Soviet Handbook*. What do they represent? Not a Marshall Plan, if this means billions of dollars being spent to rebuild factories and industries. The sums of money involved are much smaller, and the tasks are very different. But they do represent, in the aggregate, a creative phenomenon that may be a contemporary equivalent of the Marshall Plan. Most fundamentally, the work of the organizations profiled in the pages that follow represents a long-term effort to build the new values and institutions that must ultimately underlie any successful democracy or market economy in the new independent states (NIS).

After the fall of the Berlin Wall and the retreat of communism from East Europe, many Americans heard for the first time the expression: "It is easier to make fish soup from an aquarium, than to make an aquarium out of fish soup." The aphorism referred to the difficulty of rebuilding noncommunist societies after decades of communism. As this understanding has penetrated more deeply in the West, it has shifted our expectations about the time line of reform in the NIS to more realistic terms. It remains to be seen what the long-term effects will be of the Russian financial default of 1998, but at this time it does not appear that there is any wholesale abandonment of reform efforts in Russia and other countries of the NIS by the organizations profiled in *The Post-Soviet Handbook*. Although there have been some closures of organizations, terminations of projects, and shifts of emphasis among countries in the NIS—much of this of a routine nature—the remarkable fact that emerges from this revised edition of

---

[8]  For example, the *propiska* system, which controls the city in which one can live in Russia, still operates in Moscow, despite having been ruled unconstitutional by the Russian Supreme Court.

*The Post-Soviet Handbook* is how much of the activity profiled three years ago in the first edition continues and has even expanded. A large number of projects now have been operating for more than five years—longer than the formal duration of the Marshall Plan!

Another noteworthy fact about this edition of *The Post-Soviet Handbook* lies in the breadth and comprehensiveness it reveals in the engagement between societies which until 10-15 years ago were almost totally isolated from each other. There is an approach to international relations, known as "political economy," that emphasizes trade and commercial relations as primary forms of interaction between nations. There is a good deal to be said for this approach, of course, but nowhere are its limits more obvious than with respect to the countries of the former Soviet Union. For here our economic relations are minimal, yet interactions on many other fronts are intense. Nearly ten years since the fall of communism, U.S. trade with the 15 countries that were once the USSR is still less than one percent of our total international trade. The U.S. exports three times as much to Hong Kong as we do to all of Russia. Our level of investment in the region ranks even lower than our trade relations.

But economics is not everything, and *The Post Soviet Handbook* demonstrates the many forms of interaction that other interests—environmental, security, cultural, and humanitarian—can generate between nations. In effect, citizens on both sides, East and West, have said that they will not wait for the economic ties of self-interest to bind our countries together. Such a process could take 20, 30 or more years…especially if the institutional changes that must precede the rapid growth of such ties do not materialize in the NIS soon. In these circumstances, which would surely be regrettable, the good news nonetheless is that relations across many other parts of the spectrum would still go forward. After all, the hundreds of projects described in the pages that follow, involving thousands of citizens from East and West, have been established and have succeeded despite an environment of great economic instability and stagnation for most people of the NIS, particularly Russians and Ukrainians.

There are limits, needless to say, as to what any nation or collection of nations outside the region can do to help ease institutional reform inside Russia and the NIS. But these limits are not nearly as narrow as most people think; and nowhere is the wide panorama of institutional-reform projects under way in the NIS more visible than in *The Post-Soviet Handbook*. It describes a multitude and variety of programs which would surprise most Americans greatly, if they knew they existed. These include:

- *Academic preparation, language study, and policy research.* Academic programs at major universities, as well as specialized programs such as Harvard's Ukrainian Research Institute, the Kennan Institute in Washington, DC, or the Institute for International Education (which organizes study abroad programs), all sponsor area studies and student exchanges, ensuring that the U.S. has a pool of well-

trained citizens who can either analyze correctly developments in the region or
work effectively in it.

- *Humanitarian programs.* Programs like Children of Chornobyl or Big
  Brothers/BigSisters represent a humanitarian response to real and often acute
  social problems. At the same time these programs show that American interest in
  relations with the NIS goes beyond protecting our security or other strategic
  concerns.

- *Technical assistance and training.* There are many technical assistance and
  training programs, such as Internews's media development programs, the
  Financial Services Volunteer Corps work with central banks and other financial
  institutions, and the American International Health Alliance's numerous hospital
  and medical partnerships. Together these provide well-focused and important
  transfers of skills and know-how taken for granted in modern "market
  democracies."

- *Major institutional reform.* Among the most challenging and ambitious efforts
  have been those directed to the reform of major institutions. These efforts have
  included projects such as the Central and East European Law Initiative (CEELI),
  a broad-ranging program involving everything from constitution-drafting to law
  school curriculum reform, and the Urban Institute's creative work in housing
  privatization.

- *Strengthening of civil society.* Much of this work has focused on the development
  and training of grassroots organizations which may either provide important
  human services or act as advocates for important social causes. (They sometimes
  do both, as in the case of the Committees of Soldiers' Mothers, which provides
  services to the families of soldiers and also advocates military reforms.) This can
  be no less a challenge than the reform of large institutions, primarily because of
  the cynical way that communism manipulated the concept of independent,
  voluntary initiative during the Soviet period—leaving a residue of skepticism
  toward any purportedly public-spirited activity.

Examples of projects of each of the types above will be found in *The Post-Soviet
Handbook*. Some of these projects are being carried out totally independently by
indigenous organizations, others are being carried out in partnership with local
governmental institutions or quasi-governmental organizations, and still others are the
result of partnerships with organizations based in the U.S., Canada, or elsewhere in the
West. For reasons of space, the *Handbook* largely omits a great number of projects that
occur under the auspices of religious institutions—Orthodox, Protestant, Jewish,
Catholic and Muslim. These make important contributions to the growth of civil
society in the region, but really deserve a directory of their own, they are so numerous.

## *Forms of Partnership*

The 140 projects described in the North American Organizations section that follows illustrate the astonishing range of activities being undertaken through East-West partnerships despite significant barriers of language, culture, geography, and inadequate financial resources. Together they add up to an engagement between broad sectors of society, and not just the political or business elites. The true number of projects and partnerships that exists is much higher than represented in the book—and we regret having to omit so many. But our hope is that those selected represent some of the most important and far-reaching, as well as the most creative.

Consider the medical field. The American International Health Alliance has forged 32 partnerships with major health care providers or educational institutions in 11 countries of the NIS. Add to these ongoing and active partnerships the work of projects such as the Overseas Medical Advisory Group based in Kyiv, Magee Womancare International in Pittsburgh, the Tolstoy Foundation in New York, plus the scores of occasions in which medical training and exchanges have been part of a sister-city relationship—and there emerges a quantity of work which, taken together, is contributing significantly to the transformation of medicine and health care in the NIS.

Or consider the field of culture. New York-based CEC International Partners is involved in an extended and exciting series of arts exchanges culminating in the celebration of St. Petersburg's 300th birthday in the year 2003. Add to this the work of an organization such as the Fund for Arts and Culture, based in McLean, VA, which has been helping museums, symphonies, and other major cultural institutions in post-Soviet countries adjust to conditions in which full subsidies from the state are no longer possible. Here is a field in which conditions were better in some ways under communism than during the current transition. But there is no returning to the past for artists, museums, and their publics in the NIS; and organizations like the Fund for Arts and Culture are sharing the West's expertise in arts marketing, user-friendly cultural facilities, and fund-raising to ease the pain of the transition.

The partnerships are many, various and productive. USAID funded an Institutional Partnerships Project through IREX which involved 22 discrete projects between organizations as different as the American Road and Transportation Builders Association and the Russian Association of Territorial Bodies of Highway Administration (RADOR); the World Institute on Disability, based in Oakland, CA, and the All-Russian Society of the Disabled, based in Moscow; and the Carl Vinson Institute of Government at the University of Georgia and Ukraine's Uzhgorod State University Center for Public Administration Reform and Assistance. Many of these partnerships, and others like them, have continued and will continue beyond the time when USAID funding terminates.

Sister-city relationships, already mentioned, have been an arena for many fruitful partnerships between local institutions in the NIS and the U.S. There are upwards of 200 U.S.-NIS sister-city relationships. Again, we regret not being able to do justice to them all, but we selected a few to give a sense of their variety. The reader interested in seeing how much can be done through one of these relationships should visit the Web site of the Cincinnati-Kharkiv Sister City Project. It has won prizes for its work four years in succession, and deservedly.[9]

It must be remembered that the international collaborations described in this revised edition of the *Handbook* describe almost exclusively projects between American and Canadian organizations and the NIS. It would require another book to do justice to the hundreds of citizen collaborations occurring between the UK, Germany, the Netherlands, other European countries, South Korea, Japan, and countries of the NIS. There, too, is an exciting story of grassroots partnerships between sister cities, educational institutions, professional associations, hospitals, NGOs, and the like.

### *Funding, Foundations and Volunteering*

Virtually all of the organizations in *The Post-Soviet Handbook* wanted us to acknowledge their sources of funding. Unfortunately, for reasons of space, we could not accommodate them all. So if a donor reads the profile of an organization it has supported but does not see itself acknowledged, please understand that the fault is ours, not the organization's. In limited cases we have identified some of the funders of "third sector"[10] activities in the region, if only to remind ourselves and our readers how important this side of the story is, too.

The most visible U.S. government funder of projects in the NIS is USAID (U.S. Agency for International Development). USAID might operate in a less costly manner—eliminating a wedding-cake style of grant-making which sometimes involves two or more intermediary organizations administering part of a grant, and taking their percentage, before any funds reach their ultimate goal. Nevertheless, the agency— along with USIA and other federal departments—is still funding many important projects in the NIS…as the examples in the *Handbook* will demonstrate.

Private foundations are another key source of funding. Again, the *Handbook* has not been able to profile every private American foundation supporting grassroots,

---

[9]  The Cincinnati-Kharkiv Web site is at http://www.queencity.com/Kharkiv/  The first U.S.-USSR sister city relationship was established between Seattle and Tashkent in 1972 and it continues to thrive.

[10]  The term "third sector" refers to voluntary organizations, associations, and other nonprofit enterprises, such as religious, service and charitable institutions. The two other sectors are business firms and government agencies.

civil-society-building projects in the NIS. But their work is significant and their presence, large or small, in this recently opened region is very welcome.

Foundations as well as government agencies can sometimes look a bit like slaves of fashion, showering a few "hot" nonprofit organizations (e.g., the Memorial organization a few years ago) with a lot of money, all at the same time. When this happens, other local nonprofit organizations not in the "hot" category begin to question the process used by Western philanthropic organization to make grants. It would be an interesting question for further investigation to ask how often projects and organizations in the NIS receive funds simultaneously from two or more U.S. foundations or government agencies; and to ask whether a broader distribution of such funds might be desirable.

Be this as it may, we have profiled in the *Handbook* some of the foundations which stand out as being among those with serious, long-term commitments to the region. After leading for many years in the sheer volume of resources dedicated to philanthropy in the post-communist world, the Soros foundations (mostly known as Open Society Institutes) recently announced intentions to scale back their involvement significantly in the next two-three years. Even with cutbacks, however, the Open Society Institutes will continue to have a very large impact in the region.

The work of other foundations such as MacArthur and Ford, and smaller "regional" foundations such as the Jackson Foundation in Seattle, also deserve mention. With the exception of Ford and a few other large foundations such as those already mentioned, the great majority of American foundations until recent years have tended not to be active overseas. This pattern may be changing as more foundations with strong commitments to certain issues (the environment, human rights, media freedom) think of giving where the needs are greatest—in global terms and not merely national ones.

But for all the funding provided by the U.S. government and private foundations, a fundamental strength of the hundreds of nonprofit projects and organizations profiled in the *Handbook* derives from the noncommercial, voluntary spirit that drives many of the participants. If the world of nonprofit organizations can be divided into just two kinds, those which are *grant-driven* and those which are *cause-* or *mission-driven*, the NIS probably has its fair share of both. But what strikes one after collecting all the data about the multitude of projects reflected in the *Handbook* is how many of them are genuinely cause- or mission-driven in their motivation. This is what explains projects such as Serendipity or the American Institute for Business and Economic Education, for example. The fundamental reason these are so successful is not because of their skills at responding to RFPs ("requests for proposals" in bureaucratese), or their good political contacts, but because of the interest, initiative, and commitment of the individuals who lead them.

This spirit is also what allows organizations like the Financial Services Volunteer Corps, based in New York, or the American Bar Association's CEELI project to find hundreds of otherwise highly compensated and skilled professionals to forgo income in the U.S. and volunteer their time on short- or long-term assignments in the NIS. Such organizations not only accomplish a great deal in their projects, they also truly leverage millions of USAID dollars by using so many highly qualified volunteers.

## Civil Society and the NIS

It cannot be denied that for some years now, the American media's "spin" on Russia and other post-Soviet countries has been that of crime, corruption, economic collapse, and general disorder. Of course, these phenomena are a real part the story of the very difficult conditions of countries which have abandoned communism but not yet achieved "market democracies. But crime-and-chaos are not the whole story. The repetition of this one theme in so many news treatments of the NIS unfortunately feeds misconceptions some Americans might have that law-abiding, honest, hard-working people are scarcely found outside our borders and those of a handful of other countries.

This becomes sheer chauvinism, and it is unjustified. An equally compelling aspect of the "transition" story is represented by the ten of thousands of indigenous, socially motivated, grassroots organizations that have sprung up in the NIS in the past decade—only a small fraction of which could be profiled in *The Post-Soviet Handbook*. This is the story of myriad independent groups and organizations, staffed by altruistic individuals, that are working to meet the needs of the old, the sick, and the disabled; attempting to repair environments devastated by decades of mindless industrialization and the lack of democratic controls on the military or large industrial enterprises; helping to create the conditions for an independent print and electronic media; and ultimately, building new values of personal responsibility and civic-mindedness after decades of a collectivist philosophy based on lies and compulsion.

According to a statement drafted at a 1993 meeting in Moscow by leaders of 50 charitable and nonprofit organizations, Russia's third sector contained more than 50,000 organizations at that time.[11] A recent e-mail to Center for Civil Society International from an NGO leader in Novosibirsk claimed that in that city alone there are now more than 700 NGOs. Directories of the nonprofit sector now exist for many cities or regions in the NIS and typically each directory profiles hundreds or thousands of organizations. Without a doubt, there are among these organizations a certain percentage of frauds and scam artists—just as there are in America's nonprofit world. But the great majority of the people who work in the groups profiled in *The Post-Soviet Handbook* are public-spirited individuals, giving part of their lives for service to

---

[11] Interlegal International Foundation (Moscow), *Third Sector*, no. 1, 1994, p. 4.

their communities and to individuals less fortunate than they. In short, they are builders of civil society.

It is regrettable that this story rarely reaches the American public. There is no dearth of material or sources. The Agency of Social Information, based in Moscow, issues a weekly bulletin by e-mail, full of interesting stories about developments in Russia's nonprofit sector. Were more of these stories known to Americans—not only about Russians, but also Ukrainians, Armenians, Azerbaijanis and others—we might come to see these nations as more like ourselves, and be more willing to help them. Yes, they are passing through a difficult period, but they are capable of surmounting their difficulties and becoming law-governed, stable, democratic countries—not very different basically from Taiwan, South Korea, Argentina, Greece, or us. For this reason, Nina Belyaeva, president and founder of Interlegal, the nonprofit Moscow legal consulting group whose statement was cited above, has praised *The Post-Soviet Handbook* as "a wonderful source of practical knowledge... [it gives to those] who want to look beyond the 'horror stories' on Headline News a view of organized society in Russia."[12]

## *Can Social Capital Be Developed in a Decade?*

At root, the question posed by the thousands of citizen organizations now active in the NIS is whether, and how, they are contributing to prospects for democratization, the rule of law, and economic reform in Russia and neighboring countries? As a vehicle for discussing such a question, the concept of "social capital" has become fashionable in recent years. It can refer to social norms as well as to organizations and institutions. Basically it represents those intangible elements of accumulated know-how, belief and custom that make modern democratic societies cohere and work well. The concept's great appeal is that it points to those things outside of politics—in the culture, in the beliefs and habits of citizens, or in the non-governmental sectors of society—that make important contributions to the successful working of democracies. Debate societies and student councils might be considered a form of social capital. So would virtually any public association that brings people together to pursue collective ends. The set of beliefs that prevent public officials from accepting bribes would be another form of social capital.

Social capital can be lost or destroyed, just as cultures can change and civilizations decline. Close down the American Bar Association (ABA) and all independent organizations of lawyers for 70 years, or hold no real elections for that

---

[12] E-mail message to CCSI, November 27, 1998.

period of time, and you have destroyed important assets of a society as surely as if you had burned down a library or bombed an office building.

Social capital tends to grow and accumulate over time. Physical capital can be either a public good (a park) or a private good (a yacht), but social capital is by its nature a public good. Lawyers derive personal benefit from belonging to the ABA, it is true, but ultimately the association's value is to the legal profession and the rule of law in the United States. As the association grows in size and the number of services it provides, so does its value to the society.

Trust and cooperation between citizens are important aspects of social capital. If trust and cooperation are low in a society, people will not join voluntary organizations to pursue shared goals. If the general opinion is that all nonprofit organizations are only scams, or tools of special interests, few people will take them seriously or want to participate in them. Vice versa, participation in the activities of public organizations tends to build trust and respect for cooperative endeavors, both for participants and non-participants. A work camp that builds a clinic in a barrio of Mexico not only satisfies the volunteers who build it and benefits the ultimate users of the clinic; it also sends a message to onlookers as to the power of voluntary, cooperative action.

A vibrant third sector, composed of many independent public organizations, is assumed to be a key feature of civil society, and the repository of much social capital. Total autonomy or independence from government are not required in order for such organizations to be considered genuine members of the third sector. But when all or most of their funding derives from government, the question arises whether it is more appropriate to view such entities as "non-governmental organizations," or as a special subset of government contractors. Such ambiguities dog many third sector organizations, especially those with multiple programs, some of which are funded privately, others with government grants. In many cases, third sector organizations are pragmatic and accept government funds as long as it appears that this won't compromise their mission. In other cases, complete financial independence is really essential if the organization is to maintain its credibility. A case in point is the non-governmental Underwriters' Laboratories (UL), whose product certification program makes a major contribution to household and consumer safety in the U.S. UL funds and governs itself independently of government, and this plus a long track record of highly professional work are the reasons why the UL insignia is respected widely as a mark of integrity.[13]

These, then, are some aspects of social capital. If we grant that it is a meaningful concept, the question becomes: What was communism's legacy in social capital? Is "new" social capital being created in Russia and other post-Soviet societies? In

---

[13] Putnam's *Making Democracy Work* devotes a chapter to the idea of social capital, including a refutation of the charge that "associationism" is anti-democratic. See pp. 163–185.

particular, is it being created by the organizations described in *The Post-Soviet Handbook*? Can support for their activities help create a democratic and stable set of countries in that region of the world known today as Eurasia? The assumption that it can prompted Vice President Al Gore to state in 1995 that by the year 2000 the U.S. government would be channeling nearly half of its foreign aid through private voluntary organizations rather than governments.[14]

If this is indeed to be the case, it would seem important for the U.S. government to have good research on which to base such a decision. But in fact not much substantial or conclusive research on social capital or civil society, at least with respect to the countries of the NIS, appears to exist. One of the better examples of such research was a report on "Russian Civil Society," prepared for the World Bank in 1996 by Leonid Polishchuk. It asserted that "a high degree of dependency on the state sector is a fundamental feature of the Russian third sector."[15] This made sense intuitively, in view of the low levels of personal wealth in Russia, the suppression over many decades of religiously-based and private philanthropy, and the tradition, inherited from the communist era, of the state being responsible for all social services and all dimensions of human care.

But data collected in early 1998 in Russia by Catriona Logan, researching her masters thesis for the University of Washington, provided a different picture. "Upon closer examination," wrote Logan, "it is clear that at the local level, many civil society groups are making considerable progress towards healthy interaction with local government—interaction based upon increasing autonomy and the ideas of popular democracy rather than patron-client relations." Logan interviewed 37 NGOs in four Russian regional cities: Ekaterinburg, Krasnodar, Novosibirsk and Pskov. She found that:

> In fact, the only NGOs that rely on the government for the majority of their funding are the eight government-affiliated groups. The remaining 29 grassroots organizations receive no significant funding from the state, yet most have continued to find ways to survive and serve their missions—a considerable feat for an organization in Russia today. While the majority of groups (18 total) have been successful in obtaining foreign grants, none of them has been able to survive on these alone, and [all] have had to find additional local sources of funding. In

---

[14] See "President's Letter" in COUNTERPART Foundation's 1994–1995 Program Summary and Annual Report.

[15] Polishchuk, p. 32.

fact, even government-affiliated groups have made efforts to diversify funding sources in order to expand services beyond the level the state can subsidize.[16]

Logan's findings are intriguing and invite a more extended investigation of the important question of how NGOs in fact are interacting with governments—local, regional, and national—in post-Soviet societies.

Polishchuk's study also emphasized instances in Russia of nonprofit organizations being used by corrupt or criminal elements (e.g., to avoid tariffs by importing goods through a charitable front organization). Yet offsetting this criminalization of NGOs, Polishchuk found that the wave of crime which had overcome Russia had also

> stimulated a powerful grassroots reaction which involves more than 800 NGOs. These organizations' activities could be broken down into two major categories: (a) to assist (supplement) the state law-enforcing bodies in the prosecution of criminals, deterrence of crime and maintenance of law and order and (b) to prevent criminal actions through outreach to those social groups with a high propensity for criminal behavior.[17]

Thus, Russia's criminal culture has damaged some NGOs by corrupting them, but it has also caused the formation of more than 800 NGOs concerned with the reduction of crime! This was a fascinating discovery. It would be interesting to know much more about this phenomenon.

There are other aspects of the growth of civil society in the NIS which invite deeper investigation. Regionalism is a powerful force in Russia and Lilia Shevtsova has suggested that recently formed inter-regional economic associations will become increasingly important influences, serving both as counterforces to Moscow-based authoritarian elites as well as to disintegrative tendencies in the federation.[18]

Polishchuk's study also included among his 10 case studies the organization *KonfOP*, or Confederation of Consumer Societies. This organization was established in 1990 to coordinate the work of regional consumer associations. It is nonpolitical, derives all its income from fees and dues, and refuses commercial advertisements in its publications. It has strong outreach efforts that make good use of the media, and it has facilitated a large number of out-of-court settlements between consumers and retailers throughout Russia. It has modeled some of its work on the Better Business Bureaus of

---

[16] "Civil Society Development in Russia's Regions: A Survey of Local NGOs" Masters Thesis of Catriona Logan, University of Washington, Jackson School of International Studies, 1998, p. 63.

[17] Polishchuk, p. 40.

[18] Examples of these associations include *Sibirskoe soglashenie* (Siberian Agreement), *Bolshaya Volga* (Big Volga), *Severo-Zapad* (North-West), *Tsentralnaya Rossia* (Central Russia), and *Chernozemye* (Black Earth Zone). See Shevtsova, *Yeltsin's Russia: Challenges and Constraints* (Moscow: Carnegie Moscow Center, 1997), p. 17.

the U.S. and is part of an international consumer protection federation. In other words, KonfOP is precisely the kind of NGO that represents the growth of civil society and social capital in Russia and other countries of the region. What prevents the American media from running a few stories about this type of development in the NIS? Again, it would have been interesting if Polischuk could have written more about this organization and its network of affiliates in Russia.

In short, even if research has been limited to date and not always as conclusive as one might hope, there is considerable evidence to indicate that the emergence of organized civil society in Russia is at least as important a phenomenon as its well-publicized opposite, i.e., crime and disorder. More research is needed, and not only for Russia but all the countries of the former Soviet Union. Certainly the challenges that public-spirited, active people in those countries face are daunting; and it would be well worth learning more about the strategies they use to overcome them, what prompted them to try in the first place, why some succeed while others fail, and what are the prospects for the more successful ones, such as KonfOP.

Indeed, if one reviews the work of the organizations profiled in *The Post-Soviet Handbook*, keeping in mind the difficult historical and economic context in which all their activity is taking place, the question of real interest becomes how to explain the existence of so many grassroots organizations with important civic purposes through-out most of the former Soviet Union. Some of their work may be naïve or flawed in one way or another, some of it may ineffective. Yet it exists, and seems to be growing. Certainly this is the impression gleaned from a comparison of the data in this edition of *The Post-Soviet Handbook* with the data for the first edition, published in 1996.

## *Borrowing 1.5 Percent of the Marshall Plan*

We began this introduction by suggesting that the multi-billion-dollar model of the Marshall Plan is not appropriate to the situation faced by the countries which emerged from the breakup of the Soviet Union. But there is one element of the Marshall Plan which holds great relevance and deserves being emulated today. This is the technical assistance (TA) part of the plan.

The International Technical Assistance program of the Marshall Plan cost a total of $300 million for 15 countries over its 12-year duration—a sum equal to only 1.5 percent of the total Marshall Plan's cost. Instead of sending U.S. consultants to Europe, the TA program organized hundreds of so-called productivity tours which ultimately brought a total of 24,000 Europeans to the U.S. on six-week tours. Each tour group consisted of 12-17 individuals and these teams' itineraries were carefully planned to expose them to American work place environments that corresponded to their firm or industry at home. Teams were exposed to everything from marketing and accounting to factory floor production lines and inventory control. At the end of the tour each team wrote a technical report, which was disseminated among co-workers back home. Follow-up services ensured that contacts developed during the study tours were able to fulfill requests for additional information or assistance once a team had returned to Europe. According to an architect of the Marshall Plan's Independent Technical Assistance program, the effect of the productivity tours was to raise the annual rate of increase of labor productivity in West European industry from one percent a year to four percent or more.[19]

To be sure, the challenge of transition in nations of the former Soviet Union is much broader and more difficult than that of raising labor productivity in enterprises. As we stated at the beginning, it requires changing a very wide range of institutions—not only factories and firms, but also schools and universities, branches of the military, municipal governments, courts, banks, etc.—and habits of thought and behavior associated with them. But there is no reason to think that the same model of six-week tours that worked so well with factory managers and engineers under the Marshall Plan could not have a similarly powerful impact today, especially if it reached out to an expanded list of professions and participants, and not just to those in business.

Indeed programs of this kind already exist, and their track record is excellent. The Center for Citizen Initiatives, based in San Francisco, runs a successful and cost-effective program called PEPS (Productivity Enhancement Program), modeled explicitly on the Marshall Plan technical assistance program. With strong support form Rotary Clubs and similar community groups nationwide, CCI has organized study tours for more than 1,000 Russian business leaders since 1996. By requiring the Russians to pay a program fee and their own travel expenses, and offering no per diems, CCI is able both to ensure that participants are personally invested in the program and to keep costs in the range of $5,000-$10,000 per participant. The Foundation for Russian-American Economic Cooperation (FRAEC) runs a similar program under the USIA-funded Community Connections program. By early 1999, FRAEC had organized 15 five-week study tours in the Pacific Northwest for Russian business managers. Nationwide, the Community Connections programs in fiscal year 1999 is bringing 1,600 participants from five countries of the NIS (Russia, Belarus, Ukraine, Moldova, and Georgia) to 39 cities in the U.S. The total cost of this program, which involves not only business persons but also legal professionals, NGO leaders, farmers, educators, and public administrators, is approximately $13 million.

Such programs have been highly successful, to judge from the participants' evaluations and analysis of the programs' long-term effects on their alumni. What is

---

[19] For this and a general review of the technical assistance program, see James M. Silberman, Charles Weiss, Jr., and Mark Dutz, "Jump-Starting Ex-Communist Economies," *Foreign Affairs*, January/February 1994, pp. 21-26. Silberman was responsible for the Productivity Assistance Program of the Marshall Plan.

needed, however, is an expansion of programs like PEP and Community Connections to a significantly larger scale: more participants, from more NIS countries, representing a wider range of occupations and professions. It has been estimated that a technical assistance program for just the Russian Federation modeled on that of the Marshall Plan's TA program would require 7,500 study tours totaling 100,000 participants at a cost of $1-2 billion over a ten-year period.[20] (That is, 750 study tours a year involving about 10,000 Russians each year.) Since Russia's population is half that of the NIS, a program for the entire NIS might be assumed to involve twice as many participants and cost roughly twice as much: $2-4 billion over a ten-year period. In annual terms, such a program would cost the taxpayer a total of $200-400 million/year. The sum is about $1 per American citizen per year, or about ten percent of the annual allocation to USAID—not a great amount of money, especially when compared to what it buys.

Such estimates might err on the high or low side. The point is that it is this order of magnitude that is needed. With careful planning going into the selection of participants and the design of itineraries in the U.S., a program of study tours on this scale could help create the preconditions in the NIS for rapid movement toward market democracies in ways that no other programs could achieve. There may be a phenomenon at work here that reflects a law of "increasing marginal returns to scale." In other words, by involving sufficiently large numbers of participants in such programs, it may be that impulses for institutional change would be generated in Russia and other NIS countries that might never gather force as long as our technical assistance and exchange programs continue at current levels. As three experts on the Marshall Plan TA program wrote in an article for *Foreign Affairs*, any effort to emulate that program in relation to the NIS today must expose "huge numbers of people...to new ideas on an unprecedented scale and within a very few years."

Support for essentially the same idea has been expressed by the Librarian of Congress and distinguished historian of Russia, James Billington. In a speech delivered in Seattle in early 1998, Billington stated that the funds spent "on bringing young Germans over after World War II...proved to be far more important than many of the more expensive activities of the Marshall Plan. It allowed a whole new generation of Germans not just to see for themselves how a free society works but to adapt our experience to their situation." (It was, of course, a "free society" whose benefits then did not extend to its African-American citizens.)

Billington called for the U.S. to make "a comparable investment in bringing young Russians over to America." As a first step, he suggested bringing "a genuinely large number...say, 25,000 in one summer—for exposure to the rich variety of institutions and regional experiences that make up our continent-wide democracy and

---

[20] Silberman, Weiss and Dutz, p. 22.

particularly our civil society. We are still at the stages of tokenism in our exchange programs…"[21]

This is not an overstatement. The seriousness of the ongoing crisis in the NIS, the intractable difficulties of the transition from communism to market democracies, call for programs by the U.S. which are orders of magnitude more responsive to that crisis than those which are now in place. The models for these programs exist, whether in the technical assistance part of the Marshall Plan 50 years ago, or in programs developed in more recent years. Examples of the latter will be found on many of the pages of the *The Post-Soviet Handbook*. To be sure, much of the creative activity described in the *Handbook* will go forward whether or not the U.S. government recognizes how fragile and uncertain are the democratic "transitions" of Russia, Belarus, and other nations of the post-Soviet world. Many of the organizations to be found in the *Handbook* represent a solid core of commitment; they will continue to work in many ways, big and small, to promote the growth of civil society in the NIS.

In stressing the importance of exposing a much larger number of NIS citizens to Western institutions, it is also important to remember that the great majority of democratic civic organizations established in the NIS in the past decade were started and are staffed by Russians, Ukrainians, and other citizens of the newly independent states. Their commitment to this work is based on principles and values found in themselves, their own cultures, and their own societies. It was not exchange programs with the West that gave rise to the thousands of NGOs now active in the NIS.

However, the prospects for democracy and social stability in Russia and the NIS could be considerably more assured if the U.S. adopted the more ambitious policies proposed by Billington and James Silberman and his colleagues. Cost is not really the issue, since American citizens, working through a variety of local organizations, have demonstrated their willingness to help make citizen exchanges remarkably economical undertakings, through home stays and other contributions. The issue is really whether American leaders appreciate the seriousness of the problems in the post-Soviet world and have weighed carefully the consequences of failing to ratchet up substantially the level of assistance that is now being offered—while the opportunity to offer that assistance still exists.

January 1999                                      *M. Holt Ruffin*
Seattle, Washington              Center for Civil Society International

---

[21] James H. Billington, The Henry M. Jackson Memorial Lecture, delivered April 14, 1998, p. 16. Reprint available from the Henry M. Jackson Foundation, Seattle, WA.

# North American Organizations

# North American Organizations

## Academy for Educational Development

1875 Connecticut Avenue, Suite 900
Washington, DC 20009-1202
**Tel:** (202) 884-8000
**Fax:** (202) 884-8400
**E-mail:** admin@aed.org
**Web:** www.aed.org
**Contact:** Stephen F. Moseley, CEO and President

AED implements USAID-funded training to support the Agency's objectives for development in the NIS, and also provides training services on a fee basis to public and private sector organizations. The goal of the training is NIS leaders with the knowledge and technical skills needed to create policies, programs, and institutions for the transition to democratic governance and free market economies. Since 1993, AED has provided training to more than 10,000 mid- and senior-level professionals from the NIS. Training is generally three to six weeks in duration in such fields as: energy, agriculture, business development, democratic initiatives, economic restructuring, health, housing, and NGO development and management.

AED has four offices in the NIS.

## Access Exchange International

112 San Pablo Avenue
San Francisco, CA 94127
**Tel:** (415) 661-6355
**Fax:** (415) 661-1543

**E-mail:** globalride-sf@worldnet.att.net
**Contact:** Tom Rickert, Executive Director

Founded in 1990 by Tom Rickert, AEI promotes accessible transportation for the disabled. Rickert played a key role in developing accessible transit in San Francisco in the 1980s. AEI has held workshops with individuals from the Moscow transportation agency (Mosgortrans) and is consulting informally with it on how to make the bus service more accessible. AEI has published a guide, *Mobility for All: Accessible Transportation Around the World*, with funding from the United Methodist Church. Cost is $3.00.

## ACDI/VOCA

50 F Street NW, Suite 1075
Washington, DC 20001
**Tel:** (202) 383-4961
**Fax:** (202) 783-7204
**E-mail:** pletson@acdivoca.org
**Web:** www.acdivoca.org
**Contact:** Mike Deegan, President and CEO; Perry Letson, Director of Communications

ACDI/VOCA is a private, nonprofit organization that has been providing training, management assistance, and technical development expertise to farmers worldwide since the early sixties. It is active in 33 countries and has 12 projects in the NIS.

The organization's membership includes 40 regional agricultural-supply, marketing and manufacturing cooperatives, national farmer associations, and farm credit banks. It is affiliated with the National Council of Farmer Cooperatives and the Farm Credit Council.

ACDI/VOCA's seven core competencies are:

- Volunteer services
- Agricultural production, processing, and marketing systems
- Co-op and association development
- Rural finance
- International agribusiness partnerships
- Natural resource management
- Food for development (using the PL 480 program to deepen agricultural markets overseas)

The organization is the chief implementer of the USAID-funded Farmer-to-Farmer Program. Under this program, ACDI/VOCA is fielding more than 130 volunteers throughout the NIS in 1999. In the past, these volunteers helped to strengthen agricultural credit institutions, assisted farmers in implementing better systems of record-keeping, and contributed to the development of legislation on cooperatives and on land title registration, among other things.

Volunteers are normally mid-career or retired persons with considerable experience in their field of expertise. An average assignment is from two weeks to two months. ACDI/VOCA will typically cover travel and living expenses. Language skills may be required, depending on the assignment. Programs exist throughout the region, but the largest number of volunteer opportunities are in Russia.

ACDI/VOCA has also administered a "reverse Farmer-to-Farmer" pilot project: bringing NIS nationals to the U.S. to study in more depth what they have learned through the Farmer-to-Farmer project.

## Advocates International
9691D Main Street
Fairfax, VA 22031
**Tel:** (703) 764-0011
**Fax:** (703) 764-0077

**E-mail:** advonet2@aol.com
**Web:** www.advocatesinternational.org
**Contact:** Samuel E. Ericsson, President and CEO

The mission of AI is "to work with judges, lawyers, clergy and national leaders" to promote three themes: personal and professional ethics; finding common ground within ethnic and religious diversity; and conflict resolution—reconciliation through mediation. AI's president has extensive experience in corporate law and litigation. He was also for a time executive director of the 4,500-member Christian Legal Society. Current countries of emphasis are Albania, Bulgaria, China, Mongolia, South Africa, Zambia, and Russia.

## American Association for the Advancement of Slavic Studies
8 Story Street
Cambridge, MA 02138
**Tel:** (617) 495-0677
**Fax:** (617) 495-0680
**E-mail:** aaass@hcs.harvard.edu
**Web:** www.fas.harvard.edu/~aaass/index.html

AAASS describes itself as "the leading private organization dedicated to the advancement of knowledge about Russia, Central Eurasia, and Eastern and Central Europe." Its quarterly journal, *The Slavic Review*, is the major scholarly journal in the field. *News Net*, the bimonthly newsletter, is an excellent source of information on language-study programs and academic exchange and travel opportunities. It sometimes carries information about organizations in the NIS that are looking for staff and volunteers. Likewise, its *Directory of Programs* and *Directory of Members*, each published biannually, are useful resources for locating academic centers engaged in projects in the NIS.

## American Bar Association
### Central and East European Law Initiative (CEELI)
740 15th Street, NW
Washington, DC 20005-1022
**Tel:** (202) 662-1950
**Fax:** (202) 662-1597
**E-mail:** ceeli@abanet.org
**Web:** www.abanet.org/ceeli
**Contact:** Mark S. Ellis, CEELI Executive Director; Molly Stephenson, Outreach Coordinator

CEELI is a public service project of the 370,000-member ABA, which supports the process of legal reform in Eastern Europe and the former USSR. CEELI began working in CEE in 1990 and in the NIS in 1992. With little other technical legal assistance flowing into the regions from Western Europe or the U.S., CEELI initially focused on issues such as constitutional law, judicial restructuring, and criminal law. Assistance quickly expanded to an array of additional legal issues such as media law, nonprofit law, civil codes, property, and land use law. In 1992, CEELI started its Commercial Law Program, which focuses on the fundamental legal principles necessary for a functioning market economy. In 1995, CEELI began a joint program on criminal law reform with the U.S. Department of Justice. Currently CEELI is addressing media law reform.

CEELI relies on the large network of attorneys available to it through the ABA and related international organizations. From this pool, it selects lawyer "liaisons" who agree to reside in a host country for a period of at least one year. Liaisons work with the host country to identify legal reform priorities and coordinate CEELI's assistance. In response to requests for assistance in

specialized areas of law, CEELI also provides U.S. legal experts for extended visits. CEELI currently has liaisons stationed in most countries of the NIS. It has provided approximately 200 legal specialists to date.

All of CEELI's assistance adheres to three principles:
- Programs are responsive to the needs and priorities of the countries of Central and Eastern Europe and the NIS, not those of the U.S. participants or sponsors. Thus programs are developed in close consultation with host country institutions and representatives.
- CEELI recognizes that various legal models and traditions, including those of many civil law countries, are also valuable sources of law. Consequently, CEELI includes other perspectives besides an American one in its programs.
- CEELI is a public service project and not a device for developing business opportunities. Accordingly, CEELI has adopted strict conflict-of-interest rules that seek to avoid any of its programs being undertaken for private gain.

Beyond the work of liaisons and specialists, CEELI's assistance can take the form of in-country technical workshops and training seminars, legal assessments, and concept papers. By circulating draft laws for comment within and outside the U.S. and using ABA sections with appropriate expertise, CEELI has been able to provide expert assessments of more than 300 draft laws, including those addressing key issues such as antitrust, tax, foreign investment, criminal law, and land use, as well as the constitutions of 15 countries. Concept papers discuss issues of law prior to any drafting process. They analyze issues raised by a particular set of problems and provide information regarding current trends in the law.

CEELI has assisted the process of legal reform in the NIS in several other areas: through judicial training centers, development of voluntary bar associations, clinical legal education, legislative assistance, and criminal law reform, as well as commercial and environmental law reform. In the first seven years of its work, more than 4,000 American lawyers, judges, and professors volunteered in 24 countries through CEELI.

## The American Center for International Labor Solidarity (Solidarity Center)

1925 K Street, NW, Suite 410
Washington, DC 20006
**Tel:**      (202) 778-4500
**Fax:**      (202) 778-4525
**E-mail:**   psomogyi@acils.org
**Web:**      www.ned.org/page_3/
center.html
**Contact:** Paul Somogyi, Regional Coordinator for European Programs

The Solidarity Center represents a merger of four international institutes of the AFL-CIO. Its purpose is to "foster the development of viable free democratic and independent trade unions." Through programs of democratic and civic education, institution building, worker rights protection, and trade union exchanges, the Solidarity Center promotes free trade unionism worldwide.

The Solidarity Center inherits from its predecessor institutes a network of field offices located in every region of the world, with contacts reaching tens of thousands of unions and other indigenous civic organizations at the national, regional, and local levels. These organizations have a combined

membership in the tens of millions and often represent the largest grassroots institutions in their respective countries.

## American Councils for International Education: ACTR/ACCELS

1776 Massachusetts Avenue, NW
Suite 700
Washington, DC 20036
**Tel:**      (202) 833-7522
**Fax:**      (202) 833-7523
**E-mail:**   general@actr.org
**Web:**      www.actr.org
**Contact:** Dan E. Davidson, President

American Councils used to be ACTR/ACCELS, or the American Council of Teachers of Russian/American Council for Collaboration in Education and Language Study. It continues to operate as ACTR in Russia and as ACCELS in the remaining 11 countries of the new independent states.

American Councils is an "educational association and exchange organization devoted to improving education, professional training, and research within and about the Russian-speaking world, including the many scores of non-Russian cultures and populations in the regions of central and eastern Europe and Eurasia." Specifically, it:

- administers more than 20 exchange programs, ranging from three months to two years in duration, with the countries of the former Soviet Union;
- manages student advising centers in Russia, Tajikistan, Turkmenistan, Ukraine, and Uzbekistan;
- administers standardized testing in the NIS for the Educational Testing Service;
- publishes textbooks and materials for the teaching of Russian and English as foreign languages.

The organization has 42 offices in 12 countries of the NIS, a staff in excess of

250, an annual budget approaching $45 million, and ongoing relationships with more than 500 U.S. and NIS schools, institutions of higher learning, and NGOs.

## American Federation of Teachers
### Education for Democracy/ International Project
555 New Jersey Avenue, NW, Suite 880
Washington, DC 20001-2079
**Tel:** (202) 879-7484
**Fax:** (202) 879-4502
**E-mail:** iad@aft.org
**Web:** www.aft.org
**Contact:** David Dorn, International Affairs Department Director

The AFT represents 985,000 teachers, school support staff, health care professionals, and public employees. It conducts international activities in four main areas: technical and material assistance to democratic teachers' unions; materials development, consultation, and teacher training workshops on civic education abroad under the Education for Democracy/ International Project; defense of human and trade union rights for teachers and others; representation at international conferences and other programs.

AFT established ED/I in 1989 "to provide teacher unions and educators in newly emerging democracies with assistance in the development of curriculum materials and teacher training." ED/I has three main activities: teacher training and curriculum development, democratic skills and leadership training, and publications on democracy and education. In 1994 ED/I co-sponsored a National Conference on Civics Education in Russia with *Uchitelskaja Gazeta* ("Teachers' Newspaper"). A result of the con-

ference was the creation of a Russian civic educators' association, the Civic Education Union. ED/I continues to work with *Uchitelskaja Gazeta* on a variety of projects, including the creation of an electronic network for Russian civic educators. Most ED/I training programs are undertaken by U.S. volunteers.

ED/I has a database of several hundred organizations and individuals in 50 countries working to improve civics education. The Education for Democracy/International Database is available in both print and electronic media. ED/I also sponsors a Classroom-to-Classroom program, which to date has linked more than 900 U.S. classrooms with counterparts in developing democracies throughout the world.

## American Institute of Business and Economics
216 Bliss Lane
Great Falls, VA 22066
**Tel:** (703) 759-2507
**Tel/Fax:** (703) 759-3389
**E-mail:** aibec@knight-hub.com
**Web:** www.knight-hub.com/aibec
**Contact:** Edwin G. Dolan, President

AIBEc is a nonprofit corporation formed in Virginia in 1992 in order to raise funds and develop a first-class school of business administration in Moscow. Its founder splits his time between Moscow and Virginia, so if there is no answer at the telephone above, try the Moscow number. (See AIBEc under Moscow organizations.)

## American International Health Alliance
1212 New York Avenue, NW, Suite 750
Washington, DC 20005
**Tel:** (202) 789-1136
**Fax:** (202) 789-1277

**E-mail:**  aiha@aiha.com
**Web:**     www.aiha.com, www.friends-
partners.org/aiha/

AIHA establishes and manages partnerships between health care institutions in
the U.S. and the NIS. There are currently
32 such partnerships with health care
providers or educators in 11 nations of
the NIS. The partnerships are contributing to the improvement of health care
delivery in these areas, among others:
health administration, breast cancer,
nursing, diabetes, emergency care,
infection control, and neonatal resusci-
tation. AIHA has a very useful Web site,
in English and in Russian. For example,
its Health Resources section describes
more than 400 documents that have been
translated into one or more of the
languages of the NIS and tells how to
obtain them.

AIHA's regional NIS offices are in
Moscow, Almaty, and Kyiv. The
organization operates under a
cooperative agreement with USAID.

## American Russian Center

University of Alaska Anchorage
BEB 203
3211 Providence Drive
Anchorage, AK  99508-8356
**Tel:**      (907) 786-4300
**Fax:**      (907) 786-4319
**E-mail:**   ayarc@uaa.alaska.edu
**Web:**      www.arc.uaa.alaska.edu/arc
**Contact:**  Russell B. Howell, Director

ARC operates in a territory that covers
one-third of Russia: its Far East. ARC's
principal mission is "to bring awareness
of American governmental practice and
business methods to a resource rich
area that will play a key role in Russia's
future."

The American Russian Center, a part
of the University of Alaska Anchorage,
has been operating since 1993. With

funding from USAID and in each case
with a Russian partner, it has opened
and operated four business training
centers in Khabarovsk, Magadan,
Yakutsk, and Yuzhno-Sakhalinsk. Also,
USIA has underwritten 33 cultural and
educational exchange programs run by
ARC, involving local government,
women's groups, natives, educational
institutions, and specialized agencies.
More than 600 Russians and Americans
have taken part in those programs.

A partnership program managed by
ARC has created continuing linkages
between the University of Alaska and
educational institutions in Sakhalin,
Yakutsk, and Magadan, all focused on
business programs. Additionally, ARC
has established a joint program in
Khabarovsk that graduates 20 Russians
a year with both American and Russian
business degrees.

ARC estimates that its training and
technical assistance programs have
benefited more than 16,000 Russian
clients. Its exchange activities have
involved citizens of 9 RFE cities and 10
Alaskan cities and towns. The organization has helped to establish three new
national parks in Russia and has also
helped 21 NGOs get started. An ARC
program in Yakutsk introduced educational authorities to nonresident adult
educational models.

In the future, the keystone of ARC's
program will continue to be the four
business centers. In addition, ARC will
offer U.S.-based advanced practicums
for approximately 100 RFE entrepreneurs a year, and more tailored
programs for businesses involved in
trade or investment opportunities with
U.S. firms.

ARC calculates that its programs
have created 4,000 new jobs and an
estimated 826 new companies in the
Russian Far East. They believe they

have helped five times as many RFE companies stay in business. All of ARC's partner regional universities now have functioning business colleges and ARC believes its programs have "significantly sped up the pace of transition" in the regions where it has centers. Finally, ARC has promoted the Alaska Sakhalin Working Group, an entity that is evolving into "a primary conduit for U.S. management and technical expertise to the RFE." ARC laid the groundwork for the creation of a joint UAA/Academy of Sciences training institute on Sakhalin that will prepare local workers for skilled jobs in the oil fields.

## Amiq Institute

276 Three Sisters Drive
Canmore, Alberta T1W 2M7, Canada
or
660 West 89th Avenue
Anchorage, AK 99515
**Tel:** (403) 678-5027
**Fax:** (403) 678-2879
**E-mail:** hcorbett@web.net
**Contact:** Helen Corbett, Susanne Swibold

Amiq seeks to protect and enhance the biological and cultural diversity of the Bering Sea region. Amiq recognizes the bioregional partnership of Russia and America in the Bering Sea and works to foster small, self-sustaining economies at the local level while preserving the environment at the regional and national levels. The Pribilof Islands, Alaska, and the Commander Islands, Kamchatka, have been the focus of the institute's work since 1981. Both island groups were settled by Aleut populations in conjunction with the Russian-American fur trade and are marine sanctuaries for globally significant wildlife populations.

Swibold and Corbett have worked extensively with Bering Sea Aleut communities over the past 18 years on "participatory research projects" focusing on conservation, human ecology, and community development. They produced four award-winning films on the Pribilof culture and environment, and set up the framework for five conservation programs. Their activities led to the creation of the Amiq Institute in 1993.

Amiq is currently working with the local community of the Commander Islands on three levels:
- Informal science education that focuses on conservation and biodiversity of the Bering Sea
- Development of cottage industries appropriate to Bering Sea island communities (kelp, educational tourism, and alternative energy)
- Biodiversity protection through cooperative partnerships between the local nature reserve and native population

Amiq is a registered NGO in Kamchatka and also works with the Arctic Institute of North America, University of Calgary, 2500 University Drive NW, Calgary, Alberta T2N 1N4, Canada.

## ARD/Checchi Rule of Law Consortium

1899 L Street NW, Suite 800
Washington, DC 20036
**Tel:** (202) 861-0351
**Fax:** (202) 861-0370
**E-mail:** 102262.3176@compuserve.com
**Web:** www.checchiconsulting.com, www.ardinc.com
**Contact:** Garber Davidson, Project Manager

The Rule of Law Consortium (ROLC) is a joint venture formed in 1993 between two consulting groups, Associates in Rural Development and Checchi and Company Consulting. The objective of the ROLC is to collaborate with public and private organizations in the NIS countries to develop or strengthen the laws, legal institutions, and civic structures that support democratic, market-based societies.

Currently, under several USAID contracts, ROLC is involved in legal reform projects in Ukraine, Armenia, Georgia, Kazakhstan, Kyrgyzstan, and Tajikistan. Field offices exist in Ukraine, Kazakhstan, and Kyrgyzstan.

The major areas of activities are as follows:

- *Legislative drafting*. The ROLC is working with ministries of justice and legislatures in NIS on drafting legislation.
- *Judicial training*. The ROLC has worked to support institutionalization of judicial training. Through training centers, the ROLC has worked to modernize teaching methods and to improve the curriculum for judges in newly developing areas such as commercial law, as well as in areas new to judges in NIS countries such as the role of the judge in a demo-cratic country, judicial ethics, and similar topics.
- *Court reform*. The ROLC has worked with organizations both in the U.S. and in Western Europe and with policy makers from all branches of government to formulate plans to develop the court systems. These policy workshops have included strategic planning for the courts, the relationship of the judiciary with other branches of government, court administration, and court automation.
- *Attorney training*. The ROLC has worked with bar associations and law schools to organize and conduct

continuing legal education for practicing lawyers and government lawyers.

- *Law schools*. The ROLC has worked with various law schools to galvanize support for law school associations. The ROLC is working to develop curricula for emerging areas of the law and has provided material assistance to law schools to print and disseminate new materials.
- *Procuracy*. The ROLC has worked with trainers of procurators to institutionalize training, particularly in new areas of the law, including new substantive areas such as white-collar crime.
- *Civil society*. The ROLC has provided small grants to local, indigenous advocacy groups to enable such organizations to bring public interest cases to local courts and has linked the media with such efforts so that the general public can be informed of such litigation.

## Armenian Assembly of America

122 C Street NW, Suite 350
Washington, DC 20001
**Tel:** (202) 393-3434
**Fax:** (202) 638-4904
**E-mail:** info@aaainc.org
**Web:** www.aaainc.org/
**Contact:** Ross Vartian, Executive Director; Joan Ablett, Public Affairs Director

## Western Region Office

50 North La Cienega Blvd., Suite 202
Beverly Hills, CA 90211
**Tel:** (310) 360-0091
**Fax:** (310) 360-0094
**E-mail:** aaawr@idt.net
**Contact:** Peter Abajian, Western Region Director

The Armenian Assembly of America promotes public understanding and awareness of Armenian issues through research, education, humanitarian, development, and advocacy programs. It also assists in development and humanitarian aid programs in the Republic of Armenia and sponsors Armenian-American youth for professional internships in Washington, DC. Founded in 1972, the assembly is a national nonprofit, nonpartisan in both the Armenian and American contexts, but serves as a legislative advocate to Congress on behalf of Armenian-American interests. The assembly is headquartered in Washington, DC, with offices in Los Angeles, California; Yerevan, Armenia; and Stepanakert, Nagorno Karabagh. The community of Armenian-Americans in Southern California is the largest in the U.S., and much of the Western Region Office's recent work has been with new immigrants.

### Armenian National Committee of America
888 17th Street, NW, Suite 904
Washington, DC 20006
**Tel:** (202) 775-1918
**Fax:** (202) 775-5648
**E-mail:** ancu-dc@ix.netcom.com
**Web:** www.anca.org
**Contact:** Aram Hamparian, Executive Director

ANCA is the largest and most influential Armenian-American grassroots political organization. It has 45 chapters in 25 states in the U.S. and regional offices in Watertown, MA, and Glendale, CA. There are also affiliates in 20 other countries.

The committee engages in a wide variety of political and educational activities, including

- supporting legislation
- strengthening Armenia as a secure, prosperous and democratic state

- supporting Nagorno Karabagh's right to self-determination
- securing direct U.S. aid for Nagorno Karabagh
- ensuring the appropriate commemoration of the Armenian Genocide
- encouraging Turkey and Azerbaijan to lift their blockades

The committee publishes *The TransCaucasus: A Chronology* on its Web site, as well as various press releases and issue papers.

### Azerbaijani-American Educational Cultural and Economic Center, Inc.
4501 Connecticut Avene, NW
Suite 103
Washington, DC 20008
**Tel:** (202) 537-3774
**Fax:** (202) 537-3735
**Contact:** Dr. Mahir Ibrahimov, President

Azerbaijan is an important producer of oil and gas and has significant strategic importance in the Transcaucasian region. As a traditionally Moslem country, it is also an important bridge between the Western democracies and the Islamic world. The purpose of the center, founded in 1997, is to organize conferences and seminars in both the United States and Azerbaijan, to assist scholars in their travels between the two countries, and to publish occasional papers written by cooperating academics from both countries. The center aims to facilitate joint research projects in the fields of international relations, science and technology, economics, democracy, and the history, culture, and traditions of the two countries.

### Biointensive for Russia
831 Marshall Drive

Palo Alto, CA  94303-3614
**Tel:**      (415) 856-9751
**Fax:**      (415) 424-8767
**E-mail:**   cvesecky@igc.apc.org
**Web:**      www.igc.org/biointensive
forrussia/
**Contact:**  Carol Vesecky, Director

The organic farming and gardening
methods promoted by Biointensive for
Russia have been developed over the
past two decades by Ecology Action, a
nonprofit organization based in Willits,
California which conducts research into
methods of agriculture that are
economically and environmentally
sustainable. Biointensive's "textbook"
is John Jeavons's *How to Grow More
Vegetables*. Since degradation of soils
and inefficient food production are
unfortunate realities of agriculture in
the lands of the former Soviet Union,
Biointensive for Russia is implementing a program, called "Biointensive
Sustainable Mini-Farming," that seeks
to provide a sufficient food supply
while using available local resources.
The project includes training sessions
for Russians who are now teaching
biointensive methods to gardeners and
farmers in Russia, and exchanges with
representatives of Ecodom, Inc., based
in Akademgorodok (near Novosibirsk)
in Siberia.

   Ecodom is a project of Russian
architects, engineers, and scientists,
which builds self-sufficient single-
family dwellings that have "minimum
impact on the local environment"
outside of existing towns and cities in
Russia. Ecodom's educational director,
Larissa Avrorina, traveled to California
in late 1994 to study resource-
conserving biointensive gardening
techniques, which are now being
incorporated into the Ecodom program.
(For more on Ecodom, see the
Novosibirsk section in *Russia: East of*

*the Urals*.) In 1998 Biointensive for
Russia sponsored workshops in St.
Petersburg, Russia, and Tashkent,
Uzbekistan

## Canada-Russia Partnership Fund, University of Calgary

2500 University Drive, NW
Calgary, Alberta  T2N 1L4, Canada
**Tel:**      (403) 220-7702
**Fax:**      (403) 282-0683
**Contact:**  Bill Warden, Executive
Director, The International Centre

The fund works through the University
of Calgary to support small-scale
technical cooperation projects between
Canadian and Russian institutions in
four priority sectors: democratic
development, northern studies, joint
investment and natural resources
development. The Gorbachev
Foundation in Moscow is a principal
partner.

## Canadian Bureau for International Education
### Civil Society Community Roots Project (Ukraine)

1100-220 Laurier Avenue West
Ottawa, Ontario  K1P 5Z9, Canada
**Tel:**      (613) 237-4820
**Fax:**      (613) 233-2379
**E-mail:**   tberezowecki@cbie.ca
**URL:**      www.cbie.ca
**Contact:**  Anthony Berezowecki

The Civil Society Community Roots
(CSCR) project is a four-year, C$3.9
million dollar project which began in
July 1998. Funded by the Canadian
International Development Agency, the
goal of CSCR is "to contribute to the
democratic reform process in Ukraine
by strengthening the capacity of the
NGO sector to manage itself effectively." According to CSCR, the number
of voluntary non-governmental

organizations in Ukraine has risen from none at independence to 18,000 today.

A major project goal is to engage ordinary citizens in "participatory development processes, which contribute to substantive improvements in the quality of their lives." Major Ukrainian partners include the West Ukrainian Resource, Lviv State University, Odessa Council for Civic Interaction, and Plast (a youth organization). Major Canadian partners in the CSCR project are the University of Calgary, Four Worlds Centre for Development Learning and Grant MacEwan Community College.

CBIE is a national organization established in 1966 and "dedicated to international education: the free movement of ideas and learners across national boundaries." It has a membership of 110 universities, colleges and other organizations, departments and corporations with an interest in international education.

## Canadian Cooperative Association

275 Bank Street, Suite 400
Ottawa, Ontario K2P 2L6, Canada
**Tel:** (613) 238-6711
**Fax:** (613) 567-0658
**Contact:** Olivia Enns

CCA is assisting Ukraine in a five-year project to develop a countrywide network of 100 "viable, soundly governed credit unions operating according to the principles of the World Council of Credit Unions." CCA is managing this project in collaboration with the Council of Ukrainian Credit Unions of Canada.

The project is currently in its second phase, which involves creating 20 model credit unions in all regions of Ukraine. Twenty-four Ukrainian credit union leaders will experience two-

month internships with Canadian credit unions, as well as training in Ukraine. The model credit unions will be responsible for the design and implementation of credit union promotion and training action plans, with technical and logistical support from the project. Small-business lending will also be encouraged through a credit union Enterprise Development Fund.

One Canadian professional is posted in Ukraine for the duration of the project. Long-term linkages and commercial possibilities between Ukrainian and Canadian credit union movements will be established through twinning arrangements with seven credit union.

## Canadian Feed the Children
174 Bartley Drive
Toronto, Ontario M5A 1E1
**Tel:** (416) 757-1220
**Fax:** (416) 757-3318
**E-mail:** 75363.1412@compuserve.com
**Contact:** Emmanuel Mankumah, Director of Programs

CFTC has developed a program in the Ekaterinburg region of Russia, working with the NGO The Healthy Family, designed to foster an active civil society and promote health sector reform. The Healthy Family provided resources and training programs for local NGOs to address the complex environmental, social, and economic problems of the Sverdlovsk region and their health effects, paying special attention to childbearing women and infants.

## Canadian International Development Agency (CIDA)
200 Promenade du Portage
Hill, Quebec K1A 0G4, Canada
**Tel:** (819) 997-5006

**Fax**: (819) 953-6088
**Email**: info@acdi-cida.gc.ca
**Web**: www.acdi-cida.gc.ca/europe-e.htm

CIDA is a federal agency, analogous to USAID in the U.S., responsible for the majority of Canada's international assistance and cooperation programs, which provide development assistance to countries in Africa, Asia, and the Americas. CIDA has administered assistance programs to the former Soviet Union since 1989 with the objectives of supporting the transition to market-based economies, increasing Canadian trade and investment links with the region, and promoting democratic development.

CIDA programs are implemented in cooperation with a wide range of partners, including non-governmental organizations, the private sector, universities and colleges, cooperatives, international organizations, and local and national governments. CIDA's contribution is never paid in cash to the government of a country. It is provided in the form of programs and projects that respond to the developing country's requests and are planned in cooperation with that country.

## Carnegie Endowment for International Peace

1779 Massachusetts Avenue, NW
Washington, DC 20036-2103
**Tel**: (202) 483-7600
**Fax**: (202) 483-1840
**E-mail**: info@ceip.org
**Web**: www.ceip.org

The endowment, founded in 1910 by industrialist Andrew Carnegie, is a tax-exempt operating (not a grant-making) foundation. It conducts its own programs of research, discussion, publication, and public education.

Associates of the Carnegie Endowment bring to their work substantial firsthand experience in government, journalism, universities, international organizations, and the law. Through media appearances, consulting, and conference participation worldwide, CEIP staff address the major policy issues of the day in ways that reach both expert and general audiences. The endowment publishes books, monographs, and *Foreign Policy*, a leading U.S. international affairs magazine.

In 1993 the endowment established the Carnegie Center in Moscow. The Moscow Center holds seminars, workshops, and study groups at which international participants from academia, government, journalism, the private sector, and non-governmental institutions gather to exchange views. The Carnegie Moscow office, together with IREX, has produced a *Directory of Foreign Affairs Research Organizations in Russia*.

## CEC International Partners

12 West 31st Street, Suite 400
New York, NY 10001-4415
**Tel**: (212) 643-1985
**Fax**: (212) 643-1996
**E-mail**: cecny@igc.apc.org
**Web**: www.cecip.org
**Contact**: Michael Brainerd, President

CEC International Partners is in its fourth decade of work to improve understanding and cooperation between the U.S., the NIS, and countries in Central and Eastern Europe. CEC's new mission is to facilitate and create partnerships in the arts.

CEC develops partnerships by providing regional expertise, contacts, logistical support and program consultation to both sides and by cooperating in fundraising efforts. Their ArtsLink exchange program for artists and art managers offers grants to U.S. artists and organizations to facilitate a Residency program and a Collaborative Projects program.

The Residency program selects 50 artists and art managers annually from Eastern/Central Europe and the NIS for six-week residencies at a U.S. host site. Residency grants are awarded to U.S. organizations. The Collaborative Projects give grants of up to $10,000 to approximately 25 U.S. artists (individuals or groups) for work with partners in Eastern/Central Europe and the NIS. Applications for both programs are available in the fall.

CEC's St. Petersburg 2003 project supports professional exchanges and art projects with partners in St. Petersburg. Currently museum professionals, specialists in contemporary visual arts, 20th-century ballet, and St. Petersburg's *Avangard* theater are participating in the program. CEC also supports the "American Committee for St. Petersburg 2003," a national effort to stimulate U.S. participation in St. Petersburg's tercentennial celebrations.

## Center for Citizen Initiatives

Presidio of San Francisco
Building 1008, 1st floor
General Kennedy Ave.
P.O. Box 29912
San Francisco, CA 94129
**Tel:** (415) 561-7777
**Fax:** (415) 561-7778
**E-mail:** cci@igc.org
**Web:** www.igc.org/cci
**Contact:** Sharon Tennison, President; Amy Vossbrinck, Chief Operating Officer

CCI began in 1983 as an organization that pioneered "citizen diplomacy," taking thousands of Americans to the USSR to create "irreversible human links" between our two societies. The Soviet Meet Middle America program also brought 400 Soviet citizens to 265 American cities in the late eighties.

In the nineties, a central program of CCI has been its Productivity Enhancement Program (PEP). This program brings non-English-speaking Russian manufacturers and business owners to U.S. firms and plants for one-month management training internships. All training is provided pro bono by U.S. companies. Between 1995 and 1998, more than 850 Russian businesspeople came to the U.S. under this program.

Other programs run by CCI in Russia include:

- The Russian Initiative for Self Employment (RISE) is a micro-enterprise development center that supports start-up businesses in St. Petersburg. RISE runs a "business incubator" for 19 microenterprises and a small loan program, and offers classes in business development and self-employment.

- The Agricultural Initiative works with agricultural colleges and the Ministry of Agriculture to provide technical assistance to Russian private farmers. The model used is U.S. agricultural extension services, and offices have been established in seven cities in Russian agricultural regions.

- The Schultz Fund for Russian Entrepreneurship and Related Philanthropy is designed to "stimulate the development of a socially responsible Russian private business sector." Entrepreneurs are offered funds to purchase modern equipment in exchange for donations of their professional services to the Russian needy. This fund operates through six of the eight CCI offices in Russia.

- St. Petersburg State University School of Management. CCI is overseeing a $4-million renovation of a historic building in St. Petersburg, which will become the university's first School of Management, to be operated in a partnership with the University of California at Berkeley.
  CCI is funded by USAID, a range of U.S. foundations and private member-ships. CCI has eight Russian offices: St. Petersburg, Volgograd, Voronezh, Dubna, Ekaterinburg, Rostov-on-Don, Moscow, and Vladivostok. Thirty employees work for the organization in the U.S., half of whom speak and write both English and Russian.

## Center for Civil Society International

2929 NE Blakeley Street
Seattle, WA 98105-3120
**Tel:** (206) 523-4755
**Fax:** (206) 523-1974
**E-mail:** ccsi@u.washington.edu
**Web:** www.friends-partners. org/~ccsi/
**Contact:** Holt Ruffin, Executive Director; Richard Upjohn, Associate Director

CCSI promotes the growth of civil and democratic societies by publishing materials both in print and electronically, intended to assist citizen organizations in the West to engage in collaborative projects with partner organizations in the NIS. It makes this information available at its large multilingual Web site, which receives several hundred visits a day from around the world. CCSI also produces a free daily e-mail service, CivilSoc. This consists of job announce-ments, news of funding opportunities, briefs from organizations in the field, and occasional translations of selections from the newsletters of its partner orga-nizations in Moscow, Agency for Social

Information (ASI), and in Almaty, Central Asian Sustainable Development Information Network (CASDIN).

## Center for Democracy

1101 15th Street, NW, Suite 505
Washington, DC 20005
**Tel:** (202) 429-9141
**Fax:** (202) 293-1768
**E-mail:** center@centerfordemocracy. org
**Web:** www.centerfordemocracy.org
**Contact:** Allen Weinstein, President; Erin Hammel Skootsky, Deputy Director, European Programs

The center has organized a series of conferences and informal dialogues designed to encourage exchange among parliamentarians, government officials, jurists, and other leaders from Europe, the Republics of the former Soviet Union, and North America on issues related to the democratization process. Many of these activities have occurred in cooperation with the Council of Europe, the Strasbourg Conferences on Parliamentary Democracy, and the European Parliament.

## Center for Economic Initiatives

P.O. Box 234
Terrace Park, OH 45174
**Tel/Fax:** (513) 831-6771
**E-mail:** cei@ukrainebiz.com
**Web:** www.ukrainebiz.com
**Contact:** Leland M. Cole, President

CEI is an outgrowth of the Cincinnati-Kharkiv Sister City Project whose mission is to promote economic development within Ukraine and other countries of the post-Soviet world. It provides industry with the training and technical information to produce high-quality, low-cost consumer goods for domestic and export markets. CEI's Web site is intended to link Ukrainian and Western business enterprises and to locate trading and investment partners. In 1997 CEI was awarded a grant from USAID to fund two pilot "Marshall Plan–type" study tours from Kharkiv, Ukraine. These study tours took place in mid-1998.

## Center for International Networking Initiatives

The University of Tennessee System
UT Conference Center, Suite 313
Building 600, Henley Street
Knoxville, TN 37996-4137
**Tel:** (615) 974-2908
**Fax:** (615) 974-6508
**E-mail:** gcolc@solar.rtd.utk.edu
**Web:** www.friends-partners.org/friends/
**Contact:** Greg Cole, Director

The center was established in 1995 by the University of Tennessee to further the work that Greg Cole, formerly with the university's Research Services, has done together with Natasha Bulashova of Pushchino State University in Russia. Cole and Bulashova are responsible for the widely-visited World Wide Web site "Friends and Partners," often cited as a model for how the Internet can assist U.S.-Russian citizen collaborations. Through CINI they are now extending their work in Russia to China and other nations.

In 1998, CINI was awarded a $6.5-million grant from the National Science Foundation and the Russian Ministry of Science for establishing the MirNET project, a jointly funded initiative to establish high speed Internet2 connectivity between the U.S. and Russian scientific and academic communities. It is a grant for five years of activity ($4 million from NSF and $2.5 million from the Russian Ministry of Science).

## Center for International Private Enterprise

1155 15th Street, NW, Suite 700
Washington, DC 20005
**Tel:** (202) 721-9200
**Fax:** (202) 721-9250
**E-mail:** cipe@cipe.org
**Web:** www.cipe.org
**Contact:** John D. Sullivan, Executive Director

The Center for International Private Enterprise is funded by the National Endowment for Democracy, USAID, and private donors and is affiliated with the U.S. Chamber of Commerce. It works directly with foreign business organizations, think tanks, and other business-oriented private sector organizations, assisting them to function as national entities supportive of free enterprise. Since its inception in 1983, CIPE has funded more than 500 projects in more than 70 countries and has conducted business-association and management-training programs throughout the world. Through USIA, it distributes the monthly *Economic Reform Today* to policy makers in governments around the world. CIPE's Internet-based Forum on Economic Freedom received the "Business Web Site of 1997" award from the *Financial Times* of London.

## Center for Russian and Eurasian Studies (CRES) and Center for Nonproliferation Studies (CNS)

**Monterey Institute of International Studies (MIIS)**
425 Van Buren Street
Monterey, CA 93940
**Tel:** (831) 647-4154, 647-6688 (CRES)
**Fax:** (831) 647-3519
**E-mail:** msevcik@miis.edu, cres@miis.edu, cns@miis.edu

**Web:**     cns.miis.edu/
**Contact:** Dr. William C. Potter,
Director; Allene Thompson (CNS);
Margarita Sevcik, CRES Library
Manager

The Center for Russian and Eurasian
Studies (CRES) at MIIS was established in 1986. Its director, William Potter,
an expert on NIS security issues,
nonproliferation, and nuclear safety,
has written and edited numerous books
and articles on these issues.

Current projects at CRES include a
series of special Web-based reports on
the present situation in Russia written
by Elena Sokova, a CRES Senior
Research Associate and former CRES
librarian currently living in Moscow.
CRES also jointly hosts a seminar
series with CNS and the Russian
Studies Program at MIIS, headed by
MIIS professor Anna Scherbakova.

The Center for Nonproliferation
Studies at the Monterey Institute of
International Studies is the world's
largest non-governmental organization
devoted to combating the spread of
weapons of mass destruction. With a
full-time staff of more than 35
specialists located in offices in
Monterey, Washington, DC, and
Almaty, Kazakhstan, the center's six
research programs examine all aspects
of nonproliferation, publish online
databases, and train graduate students.
The center also publishes *The
Nonproliferation Review*, a journal
featuring the latest research on
nonproliferation.

One of the primary functional units
and areas of research at the CNS is the
NIS Nonproliferation Project (NISNP).
Its goals are:

- to combat the proliferation of
  weapons of mass destruction in and
  from the former Soviet Union;

- to train a new generation of
  nonproliferation specialists in the
  NIS;
- to develop self-sustaining communities of NIS nonproliferation experts;
- to collect data and distribute timely
  analysis regarding NIS proliferation
  problems.

Its activities include training
programs for NIS government officials,
scholars, journalists, and scientists;
maintenance of computer databases on
NIS nuclear and missile facilities and
developments; and the publication of
research and periodicals, including
*Nuclear Successor States of the Soviet
Union.*

Currently, the NISNP supports five
NGOs in the NIS: the Center for Policy
Studies in Russia (PIR Center) in
Moscow; the Committee for Critical
Technologies and Nonproliferation in
Moscow; the International Institute for
Policy Studies (IIPS) in Minsk; the
Nonproliferation Association of
Kazakhstan (NAK) in Almaty; and the
Scientific and Technical Center for
Export and Import of Special
Technologies, Hardware, and Materials
(STC) in Kyiv. All five are making
important contributions to the
nonproliferation field.

In August 1998, CNS opened a
branch office in Almaty, Kazakhstan.
Contacts for the NISNP Almaty Office
are Martin and Emily Ewell Daughtry,
Co-Directors <daughtry@kaznet.kz>.

Contacts for the NIS Nonproliferation Project are:

- Project Director: Dr. James Clay
  Moltz <cmoltz@miis.edu>
- Nuclear Database Supervisor and
  Senior Scholar: Dr. John Lepingwell
  <jlepingwell@miis.edu>
- Contact Person: Sheri Deeter, NISNP
  Program Coordinator
  <sdeeter@miis.edu>

## Center for War, Peace, and the News Media—New York University

418 Lafayette Street, Suite 554
New York, NY 10003
**Tel:** (212) 998-7960
**Fax:** (212) 995 4143
**E-mail:** war.peace.news@nyu.edu
**Contact:** Robert Karl Manoff, Director;
Julie Raskin, Assistant Director

Since 1985 the NYU Center for War, Peace, and the News Media has been undertaking research and program activities "devoted to ameliorating international and substate conflict by means of the media." Their current programs include the National Press Institute of Russia (the "major comprehensive media NGO in that country"), the Global Reporting Network (the principal midcareer educational program for journalists covering international issues), and the Media and Conflict Program. The latter undertakes research on questions related to media and conflict issues; publishes manuals, training materials, and programmatic research; and undertakes pilot projects with a wide range of partner organizations in the interest of developing effective media-based conflict-intervention strategies.

For a description of the National Press Institute, see that organization's entry in the Russia section.

## Chamber of Notaries of Québec

Tour de la Bourse
800 Place Victoria, Suite 700
Montréal, Québec H4Z 1L8 Canada
**Tel:** (514) 879-1793
**Fax:** (514) 879-1923
**Contact:** Ms. Nathalie Parent, Director,
Ukraine Program

The Chamber of Notaries of Québec is working with the Ministry of Justice

and the Order of Notaries of Ukraine to create a strong and self-governing association of notaries having the characteristics of organizations in western European countries.

## ChildLife International, Inc.

2716 LeClair
Davenport, IA 52803
**Tel:** (319) 324-5797
**E-mail:** CLSiefken@aol.com
**Contact:** Connie Siefken

CLI brings children, mostly orphans, from Russia to the U.S. for short-term stays with families and needed medical care. (In 1998 three received open-heart surgery in the U.S.) Some of the children have been musically gifted individuals who perform in the U.S. and take home donations to further their musical careers. CLI also received a million-dollar catheterization lab from Genesis Health in Davenport, Iowa, which was donated to the Acturin group in Moscow.

## Children of Chornobyl Relief Fund

272 Old Short Hills Road
Short Hills, NJ 07078
**Tel:** (973) 376-5140
**Fax:** (973) 376-4988
**E-mail:** info@ccrf-icef.org
**Web:** www.ccrf-icef.org
**Contact:** Nadia Matkiwsky, Executive Director

CCRF was established in 1989 to aid children in Ukraine affected by the 1986 nuclear accident in Chornobyl, Ukraine. Since its founding, CCRF, which now has numerous chapters in the U.S. and an office in Kyiv, has organized 19 airlifts and six sea shipments of medicine and medical equipment, valued at more than $40 million. CCRF has sponsored hospitals in Chernihiv,

Donetsk, Kyiv, Lviv, Luhansk, Kharkiv, and Vynnytsia; provided fellowships for Ukrainian health professionals to study in the U.S.; and sent more than 100 American volunteer physicians to Ukraine to train local doctors in Western medical techniques.

In 1991 officials in Lviv transferred the administration of a former Communist Party hospital to CCRF. With contributions of equipment from corporations and expertise from volunteer health care professionals, CCRF has transformed the hospital into a modern 160-bed facility that specializes in treating children with leukemia, Hodgkins disease, and other illnesses. CCRF volunteers have also installed a dental clinic at the hospital. The hospital is governed by a joint Ukrainian-American board of directors and has become the region's official teaching hospital.The "finest regional biochemistry laboratory in Eastern Europe" was certified in 1997, and Children of Chornobyl has also developed the "best-equipped treatment center for children with leukemia in the region."

## Cincinnati-Kharkiv Sister City Project

3620 Carew Tower
441 Vine Street
Cincinnati, OH 45202
**Tel/Fax:** (513) 241-8833
**E-mail:** cinkhars@pol.com, hmess@pol.com
**Web:** www.queencity.com/kharkiv
**Contact:** David Brokaw, Office Manager; Helen Mess, Vice President

The Cincinnati-Kharkiv Sister City Project has received four consecutive awards for outstanding achievement from Sister City International/Reader's Digest and the prestigious Post Corbett Award for its work. Since its inception in 1989 more than 1,100 people—

Ukrainians and Americans—have traveled back and forth as part of various exchange programs. Over 65 different types of exchanges, from pen pals to human resources specialists, have taken place. Highlights of past accomplishments include:

- Provision of humanitarian aid, including vaccine and medical supplies to fight an outbreak of diphtheria among children and young adults in Kharkiv, and over $130,000 worth of medical equipment
- In cooperation with the Cincinnati Salvation Army, providing a model for human services which resulted in the opening in Kharkiv of an adult day-care center, 13 soup kitchens, six social service centers, a homeless shelter and a halfway house for ex-prisoners
- Promotion of youth and educational exchange activities that have resulted in highly successful programs involving students and faculty at the University of Cincinnati and various other elementary and secondary schools
- Establishment of a landmark Municipal Training Program for Kharkiv-area public administrators in cooperation with the International Executive Service Corps (IESC) and the United States Information Agency (USIA)
- Development of a Memorandum of Understanding between Cincinnati and Kharkiv, which is negotiated and signed periodically and which has served as a model for other sister-city pairs worldwide
- Establishment of the Kharkiv-Cincinnati Sister City Association in 1992, the first NGO of its kind in the NIS

CKSCP, working with Ecumedia of Greater Cincinnati, has also helped produce *Springtime of Hope*, a video about the rebirth of religion in Kharkiv. This video aired on public television and other stations.

Under a USIA grant, CKSCP recently completed the Community Connections program. This series of training programs, each lasting from three to four weeks, was for Ukrainian legal professionals (including lawyers and judges), public administrators, entrepreneurs, and NGO leaders. Each Community Connections group of about 10 Kharkivites stayed in host homes and participated in Cincinnati training programs entirely organized by the CKSCP. Under another grant from Sister Cities International (funded by USIA), CKSCP recently completed a pilot project—the Municipal and Community Problem Solving Program. This activity focused on exchange of municipal administrators tasked with human resource development and revision of the structure of municipal administration.

The next major activity will be the Community Partnerships Project, funded by USAID through the U.S.-Ukraine Foundation. Cincinnati and Kharkiv will choose an area in need of development by the Kharkiv city administration and develop joint projects to address the need with practical solutions.

## Citizens Democracy Corps
1400 I Street, NW, Suite 1125
Washington, DC 20005
**Tel:** (202) 872-0933
(800) 394-1945
**Fax:** (202) 872-0923
**E-mail:** info@cdc.org
**Web:** www.cdc.org
**Contact:** Teresa Andrus Cochran, Manager, Volunteer Coordination

CDC was established in 1990 with major support from USAID. It recruits senior-level entrepreneurs and executives as short-term volunteers to advise their clients: local companies and business-support organizations in the CEE/NIS. Specific volunteer opportunities are listed at their Web site. Assignments are typically two to three weeks in duration. CDC advisors and staff also may assist clients—during and after assignments—to find financing and to develop relationships with potential U.S. partners, buyers, and suppliers.

## Citizens Network for Foreign Affairs
1111 19th Street, NW, Suite 900
Washington, DC 20036
**Tel:** (202) 296-3920
**Fax:** (202) 296-3948
**E-mail:** cohend@cnfa.org
**Web:** www.cnfa.com
**Contact:** John Costello, President and CEO; David S. Cohen, Director of Marketing and Public Outreach

Established in 1985, CNFA is a not-for-profit "intermediary development organization" dedicated to stimulating economic growth and development in the world's emerging economies. Since 1992 it has generated more than $120 million in ODA (official development assistance) resources. More than 250 U.S. organizations (agribusiness firms, lenders, governments, and associations) participate in global initiatives through the Citizens' Network Agribusiness Alliance.

CNFA was part of the Civic Initiatives Program, which, among other things, established technical assistance centers in Krasnodar, Stavropol, and Rostov to help more than 150 Russian grassroots organizations in those regions become more effective. Under CIP, CNFA designed and managed a

$600,000 micro-grant program to foster development of new grassroots organizations in southern Russia.

CNFA believes that the opportunity and incentive to earn a profit inherent in private enterprise is one of the most potent and sustainable engines of development. By leveraging private sector investment, technology and know-how with public funds through public-private partnerships, CNFA helps to create market-oriented, economically viable enterprises where none or few existed before. CNFA's projects include Russia, Ukraine, Kyrgyzstan, Moldova, Zimbabwe, and Mozambique. It has 75 employees and field offices in the capitals of each of these countries.

## Civic Education Project

P.O. Box 205445, Yale Station
New Haven, CT 06520
1140 Chapel Street, Suite 2A
New Haven, CT 06511
**Tel:**     (203) 781-0263
**Fax:**    (203) 781-0265
**E-mail:**  cep@cep.yale.edu,
             sasbury@cep.yale.edu
**Automated info:** info@cep.yale.edu
**Web:**     www.cep.yale.edu
**Contact:** Donna Culpepper, Executive Director; Shayne Asbury

The Civic Education Project (CEP), founded in 1991, believes that critical-minded and informed individuals are fundamental to a thriving democratic society. To this end, CEP strives to develop the capacity of faculty and students in the post-Soviet region to teach and carry out research in the social sciences, law, and the humanities. CEP's Visiting Lecturer Program places and supports Western scholars for at least one academic year in social science departments at universities in central and Eastern Europe and Eurasia. There they teach, supervise research,

initiate outreach activities, and serve as a resource for the host university. The Eastern Scholar Program identifies academics from the region with substantial training from a Western or Western-accredited institution who may be assigned back to the region.

CEP lecturers receive air transportation, health insurance, a shipping allowance, teaching materials, local language lessons, and a modest living stipend. The host university provides housing and a local-currency salary.

For the 1998–99 academic year, CEP had 186 Fellows (Visiting Lecturers and Eastern Scholars) teaching students at 97 universities in Albania, Armenia, Belarus, Bulgaria, the Czech Republic, Estonia, Georgia, Hungary, Kazakhstan, Kyrgyzstan, Latvia, Lithuania, Moldova, Poland, Romania, Russia, Slovakia, Ukraine, and Uzbekistan.

Partner organizations are the Central European University in Budapest, Hungary, and Yale University and the Civic Education Project Trust in London, England.

## Committee to Protect Journalists

330 Seventh Avenue
New York, NY 10001
**Tel:**     (212) 465-1004
**Fax:**    (212) 465-9568
**E-mail:**  europe@cpj.org
**Web:**     www.cpj.org
**Contact:** Ann K. Cooper, Executive Director; Chrystyna Lapychak, Program Coordinator, Central Europe and the former Soviet Republics

CPJ was founded in 1981 to monitor abuses of the press and to promote freedom of the press internationally. A group of U.S. foreign correspondents created CPJ in response to the often brutal treatment of their foreign colleagues by authoritarian governments and other enemies of independent journalism. By publicizing abuses against the press and acting on behalf of imprisoned and threatened journalists, CPJ effectively identifies where attacks on press freedoms are likely to occur. CPJ also organizes vigorous campaigns at all levels—ranging from local governments to the United Nations—and, when necessary, works behind the scenes through other diplomatic channels to effect change.

The Eurasia program coordinator visited Ukraine in 1998 to help fragmented journalists' associations there to protest increasing violence against journalists and a proliferation of libel suits that have bankrupted many opposition publications. CPJ is also conducting a study of libel laws and practices across the FSU.

CPJ has the only full-time staff (of 15) in the U.S. dedicated exclusively to reporting attacks against journalists and the press around the world. Its five area specialists track press conditions in their regions through independent research, reports from the field and fact-finding missions. The committee's activities are directed by a board of prominent U.S. journalists. An annual benefit dinner, where CPJ presents its International Press Freedom awards to prominent international journalists, has attracted greater numbers of donations every year. Over 1,000 prominent journalists and media personalities attended the 1997 awards dinner at the Waldorf-Astoria.

CPJ is one of more than 30 groups concerned with press freedom that make up the so-called IFEX clearinghouse, or International Freedom of Expression network, which is based in Toronto, Canada.

## Corvallis Sister Cities Association

P.O. Box 176
Corvallis, OR 97339
**Tel:**     (541) 754-9394
**E-mail:**  rrackham@proaxis.edu
**Web:**     osu.orst.edu/~corvuzh/
**Contact:** Bob Rackham, President

Corvallis established a relationship with Uzhgorod, Ukraine, in 1988. During the 1996–97 academic year, 12 high school students and three teachers traveled each way for extended stays in each city. There have also been two shipments (20- and 40-foot containers) of medical equipment and supplies from Corvallis to Uzhgorod; five delegates accompanied the shipments to oversee the distribution. The association received an award for Best Assistance Program at the Sister Cities International (SCI) convention in 1998. They have also received a USIA grant (through SCI) under the Municipal and Community Problem Solving Program. Corvallis will focus on the needs of children with physical disabilities in Uzhgorod. The association also intends to expand cultural contacts.

## Council on International Educational Exchange

205 East 42nd Street
New York, NY 10017-5706
**Tel:**     (212) 822-2600
**Fax:**     (212) 822-2699
**E-mail:**  Info@ciee.org
**Web:**     www.ciee.org

CIEE, founded in 1947, offers study and work camp experiences in the NIS for high school students and undergraduates. Twenty thousand students from 12 countries participate in these experiences annually. CIEE offers international voluntary work camps in Lithuania, Russia, and Ukraine. Typically two to four weeks in duration, they bring together 10–20 volunteers from different countries to work on a variety of projects: e.g., renovation work in the historical center of Kyiv, excavation of ancient burial grounds in the Urals, and renovation of an old cathedral in Siberia. The work camp program is open to anyone over the age of 18, and most participants are between 20 and 25 years old.

CIEE charges a $275 placement fee for each individual. Besides the CIEE placement fee, work camp participants must pay their own airfare. In-country room and board are provided.

CIEE also organizes school-to-school partnerships and study abroad programs, and publishes many useful resources.

## Counterpart International, Inc.

910 17th Street, NW, #328
Washington, DC 20006
**Tel:**      (202) 296-9676
**Fax:**      (202) 296-9679
**E-mail:**   info@counterpart.org
**Web:**      www.counterpart.org
**Contact:** Stanley W. Hosie, Executive Director; Karen L. Sherman, Vice President, Programs

Founded in 1965 as the Foundation for the Peoples of the South Pacific, Counterpart International has "supported the creation and development of strong local institutions, non-governmental networks and locally owned and operated small enterprises to meet community needs."

Since1992, with support from USAID, Counterpart has been deeply involved in the NIS, seeking to strengthen indigenous NGO capacity and service delivery and to foster partnerships between U.S. PVOs and indigenous NGOs. In recent years its emphasis has shifted somewhat to the development of the small business

sector and the development of women entrepreneurs in particular.

Counterpart Service Centers serve as regional resources for local and international NGOs, and provide training in management and leadership, strategic planning, fiscal management, fund-raising, and project design. The first CSC was established in Kyiv, Ukraine, in 1993 and the program has expanded since then. See the Ukraine section for more information on Counterpart's work there.

The Counterpart Alliance for Partnership (CAP) program in Ukraine and Belarus has awarded more than $1.3 million in "seed grants" to 71 NGO partners; conducted almost 50 training workshops; provided training and consultation to more than 1,300 NGOs (with 150 of these receiving "priority intensive assistance"); and raised US$125,000 in corporate contributions to 25 local NGOs through the Corporate Challenge Grant program—98 percent from indigenous corporations.

The Working Capital Russia program in Khabarovsk is another microcredit program, this one funded by The U.S.-Russian Investment Fund (TUSRIF).

Counterpart's Humanitarian Assistance Program (CHAP) coordinates the provision of U.S. Department of Defense excess property for humanitarian purposes to vulnerable groups in the region. Counterpart estimates that the program has provided several million dollars in aid to a broad range of social service providers in the NIS since 1992. Excess property includes medical supplies, clinical furniture, school furniture and supplies, sleeping bags, bedding, clothing, appliances, and vehicles. CHAP staff also maintain a stock of emergency relief supplies.

## Développement International Desjardins

150 Avenue des Commandeurs
Lévis, Québec G5V 6P8, Canada
**Tel:** (418) 835-2400
**Fax:** (418) 833-0742
**Contact:** Yves Boily, Program Officer, Central and Eastern Europe

Working with the Russian Credit Union League in Moscow, this project aims to establish a network of credit unions in the province of Volgograd, based on the Canadian credit union model. Components of the project include support for the development of a legal and regulatory framework, technical assistance for the Russian Credit Union League, and establishment of a cooperative banking system

## Doctors without Borders/ Médecins Sans Frontières USA

6 East 39th Street, 8th floor
New York, NY 10016
**Tel:** (212) 679-6800
**Fax:** (212) 679-7016
**E-mail:** dwb@newyork.msf.org
**Web:** www.dwb.org

West Coast Office
2040 Avenue of the Stars, 4th floor
Los Angeles, CA 90067
**Tel:** (310) 277-2793
**Fax:** (310) 277-1667

Founded in 1971, Doctors without Borders/Médecins Sans Frontières USA (MSF), has achieved global recognition for its assistance to victims of armed conflict or natural disasters and to residents of refugee camps. MSF delivers medical relief to populations in danger due to war, civil strife, epidemics, or natural disasters. Annually, more than 2,000 volunteers representing 45 nationalities work in some 80 countries in front-line hospitals, refugee camps, disaster sites, towns, and villages.

Teams from Doctors Without Borders provide primary health care, perform surgery, vaccinate children, rehabilitate hospitals, operate emergency nutrition and sanitation programs and train local medical staff.

MSF's program in Russia focuses on HIV/AIDS education, tuberculosis in a Siberian prison hospital, and doctor education and training. MSF also works with the Russian NGO, Committee for Citizens' Rights, on health care problems of the homeless. In Azerbaijan, MSF has continuing programs in camps for displaced persons. In Armenia the organization's work focuses on the problem of sexually transmitted diseases, especially syphilis and gonorrhea. In Georgia, MSF concentrates on various problems of public health in the province of Abkhazia.

## E. F. Schumacher Society

140 Jug End Road
Great Barrington, MA 01230
**Tel:** (413) 528-1737
**E-mail:** efssociety@aol.com
**Web:** www.schumachersociety.org
**Contact:** Robert Swan, President; Susan Witt, Executive Director

Representatives of the Schumacher Society have helped the Olkhon Center for Sustainable Agriculture (in the Baikal area) develop a program of small loans for local businesses. Recently the Schumacher Society helped a team of Buryats associated with Olkhon to visit two environmental NGOs in Central Europe, one in the White Carpathian mountain area, the other in the Tatras. This is part of an ongoing project of training and education toward the goal of establishing a "community land trust" in the Baikal area. Under a community land trust, land is held in common, but buildings and equipment can be owned privately.

For further information, request the Society's booklet, *Land: the Challenge and the Opportunity.*

### Earth Island Institute
300 Broadway, Suite 28
San Francisco, CA 94133
**Tel:**      (415) 788-3666
**Fax:**      (415) 788-7324
**E-mail**:   baikalwatch@igc.apc.org
**Web**:      www.earthisland.org/
**Contact:**  Gary Cook, Director

Earth Island has over 20,000 private members, a staff of 150, and offices in San Francisco, Moscow, Irkutsk, Seattle, Colorado, and elsewhere. Expenditures in1997 amounted to $5,000,000. In 1998, Earth Island received a $1,000,000 award from the Goldman Environmental Prize for its work around the world.

EII was founded in 1982 by David Brower to support the work of creative individuals engaged in environmental projects with a minimum of bureaucracy. Its more than 30 projects worldwide have had major impacts on rainforest protection, habitat protection for whales and dolphins, protection of sea turtle nesting beaches, the emerging Russian environmental movement, protection for indigenous sacred lands, promotion of organic agriculture, development of urban multicultural environmental leadership, promotion of ecological paper-fiber alternatives, and involvement in the UN's sustainable development efforts. The quarterly *Earth Island Journal* has won numerous awards for its pioneering coverage.

In Russia, EII works with the Baikal Environmental Wave and Baikal Center, the Baikal Fund, EcoJuris Institute, ISAR, and Novib.

### Earthwatch
680 Mount Auburn Street

P.O. Box 403
Watertown, MA 02272
**Tel:**      (800) 776-0188
**Fax:**      (617) 926-8532
**E-mail:**   info@earthwatch.org
**Web:**      www.earthwatch.org

Earthwatch supports research on a variety of environmental projects that monitor global change, study the possibilities for the conservation of endangered species and habitats, explore the heritage of humankind, and foster world health and international cooperation. Earthwatch sponsored more than 150 scientific research projects in 1998 and recruited more than 4,200 volunteers.

Earthwatch funds scientific research with volunteers' contributions of time, labor, and money. It solicits proposals for research projects that can use the help of nonspecialist volunteers. Once proposals are chosen for funding, the cost of the project is divided by the number of volunteers needed for the project, and that cost is passed on to those volunteers who sign up for it.

Most projects last between two to three weeks. There are a limited number of scholarships available for teachers and high school students over age 16. They are awarded according to the applicants' merits, including the abilities they bring to the project and what they plan to do with knowledge gained from the experience.

On average there are six to eight projects in the NIS annually. The cost to volunteers includes room and board and the volunteer's contribution to project financing but does not include travel expenses. Projects in the NIS cost about $1,600–$1,800, exclusive of travel.

### ECOLOGIA
P.O. Box 142

1 Main Street
Harford, PA 18823-0142
**Tel:** (717) 434-9588
**Fax:** (717) 434-9589
**E-mail:** ecologia@igc.apc.org
**Web:** www.ecologia.org,
www.virtualfoundation.org
**Contact:** Randall Kritkausky, President

ECOLOGIA (Ecologists Linked for Organizing Grassroots Initiatives and Action) was founded in 1989 and provides information, training, and support for grassroots environmental groups in the former Soviet Union, the Baltic states, and Central and Eastern Europe. ECOLOGIA has offices in Vilnius, Moscow, Minsk, and Kolkhozobad, Tajikistan.It also works in partnership with the Central European University and operates a program on the CEU campus in Budapest.

ECOLOGIA's work focuses on fostering the growth of independent environmental institutions in Eurasia and Central/Eastern Europe. The organization's current programs include:

- Providing air- and water-quality monitoring equipment and training to NGOs
- The Environmental Technical Information Project (E-TIP), a bilingual program designed to help the environmental community in Russia and other "countries in transition" generate integrated environmental information about their region
- the Virtual Foundation (VF)

VF is an on-line philanthropy project carried out by ECOLOGIA and a partner organization in Japan. Project proposals are submitted to the VF by NGO consortiums across Eurasia and Central/Eastern Europe. Donors review project proposals and budgets at the VF

Web site and select a project to fund. In turn, funding recipients provide donors with progress reports and opportunities to become involved as advisors or in other capacities. A VF project in Nepal matched a local solar energy provider with a Buddhist monastery to bring electricity to monks who had studied by candlelight for centuries.

## Economics America
1140 Avenue of the Americas
New York, NY 10036
**Tel:** (212) 730-7007
**Fax:** (212) 730-1793
**E-mail:** cconintl@eaglobal.org
**Web:** www.economicsintl.org
**Contact:** Patricia Elder, Vice President, Economics International

The National Council on Economic Education was founded in 1949 as a partnership of leaders from education, business, and labor dedicated to improving economic literacy. A network of 48 state councils and 270 university centers for economic education delivers training, materials, curriculum and evaluation assistance, and other services to teachers, students, schools, and communities throughout the U.S.

In 1992, with significant funding from the Soros and Amoco foundations, the NCEE began developing training programs to introduce innovative teaching strategies and high-quality materials to educators in the former Soviet Union. Since 1995, with funding from the U.S. Department of Education, NCEE has conducted the economic education component of the International Education Exchange Program which helps international partners reform their educational systems and educate their citizens for the transition to a market economy. By mid-1998, NCEE estimated the program had an impact on more than 450,000 students annually in 16 countries.

In the former Soviet Union, the greater part of NCEE's work has been done in Latvia, Russia and Ukraine.

## Environmental Law Institute

1616 P Street, NW
Washington, DC 20036
**Tel:**      (212) 939-3800
**E-mail:**   mcmurrin@eli.org
**Web:**      www.eli.org
**Contact:**  J. William Futrell, President

ELI is an internationally recognized independent research and education center focused on improving environmental law, policy, and management. ELI researches pressing problems, educates professionals and citizens about the nature of these issues, and involves all sectors in forging effective solutions. One of ELI's ongoing programs is to develop a CEE/NIS regional network of public interest lawyers through information exchanges and joint projects in Europe. The institute also runs an annual Study Tour for public interest lawyers and other advocates from abroad, allowing them to visit the U.S. and observe firsthand how lawyers in the U.S. use citizen suits, right-to-know laws, and involvement in the legislative and rule-making process.

In 1996, ELI, in cooperation with EcoPravo–Ukraine, received a grant to:
- train Ukrainian judges, lawyers, and government officials;
- compile and publish laws and legal analyses for an audience of citizen groups, policymakers, and practicing lawyers;
- assist the Ukrainian government with law-drafting and implementation for pending and future legislation;
- continue to provide legal consultation to individuals and citizen groups.

ELI's work in Ukraine continues; institute staff visited the country in 1998 on a variety of projects to assist the country in implementing a democratic environmental protection system.

## The Eurasia Foundation

1350 Connecticut Avenue, NW
Suite 1000
Washington, DC 20036
**Tel:**      (202) 234-7370
**Fax:**      (202) 234-7377
**E-mail:**   eurasia@eurasia.org
**Web:**      www.eurasia.org
**Contact:**  Charles William Maynes, President; Jennifer Stuart, Program Associate

The Eurasia Foundation is a privately managed, grant-making organization "dedicated to funding programs that build democratic and free market institutions" in the 12 new independent states of the former Soviet Union. The foundation was incorporated in the District of Columbia in 1992 and began making grants in June 1993. Those who launched the Eurasia Foundation hoped to create a vehicle for public-private partnerships. Approximately 20 percent of the foundation's funding is from non–U.S. government sources.

In fiscal 1997 alone the foundation awarded 805 grants worth more than $15.6 million, bringing the total since 1993 to $70 million awarded in 3,000 grants.

The Eurasia Foundation makes grants in the following eight priority areas: business development, business education and management training, economics education and research, electronic communications, media, NGO development, public administration and local government reform, and rule of law.

Headquarters are in Washington, DC
Regional offices are located in Almaty,
Kyiv, Moscow, Saratov, Tashkent,
Tbilisi, Vladivostok, and Yerevan. The
foundation also has branch offices in
Ashgabat, Baku, Bishkek, Chisinau,
Dushanbe, Gyumri, and Minsk and
works with local NIS representatives in
other NIS cities.

Field office addresses are listed on
their Web site, which also includes a
searchable database of the foundation's
grants and information on current
competitions and projects.

## Financial Services Volunteer Corps

10 East 53rd Street, 24th floor
New York, NY 10022
**Tel:**     (212) 771-1400
**Fax:**    (212) 421-2162
**E-mail:**  fsvc@fscv.org
**Contact:**  J. Andrew Spindler,
Executive Director

FSVC "mobilizes the expertise of
financial professionals to assist
countries making the transition to
market economies." It does this by
recruiting senior bankers, lawyers,
accountants, and other professionals to
serve as volunteers on carefully
designed assistance missions. It is a
nonprofit organization supported by
grants from USAID, private foundations, corporations and individuals.
Founded in 1990 by Cyrus Vance and
John C. Whitehead, it has since then
carried out hundreds of projects in more
than 23 countries.

FSVC activities focus on these
primary areas:
- Commercial banking
- Central banking
- Capital markets
- Bank supervision and regulation
- Payments systems
- Credit fundamentals
- Risk management
- Legislation relating to capital
  markets, commercial and central
  banking, and foreign investment

FSVC provides assistance only after
staff members working overseas and at
the New York headquarters have
received requests from host institutions
and helped them clearly define their
needs. These requests are then carefully
reviewed, and a determination is made
as to the urgency of the need and the
viability of the project. FSVC's years
of experience and its relationships with
a wide network of professionals in the
financial services community allow it
to find and send out volunteers with the
required skills and experience in very
short order.

FSVC projects are designed to be
practical and results-oriented. Among
hundreds of projects to date, FSVC has:
- worked with key Polish legislators
  and Russian Labor Ministry officials
  on pension reform;
- provided management training to
  Hungarian executives in the
  fundamentals of Employee Stock
  Ownership Plans, which have played
  a key role in the privatization process
  in Hungary;
- advised the Russian and Ukrainian
  central banks on developing laws
  establishing a deposit insurance
  system and governing the resolution
  of troubled and insolvent banks;
- participated with the International
  Monetary Fund, the World Bank, the
  European Union, and Central Banks
  of several major Western countries as
  a member of the International
  Steering Committee for the
  Improvement of the Payment System
  in the Russian Federation.

FSVC owes its success to the
experience of professionals it has been
able to recruit as volunteers from

commercial and investment banks, law and accounting firms, and public financial institutions. By relying on these pro bono experts, FSVC is able to leverage its funding in a highly cost-effective manner. Since 1990, more than 1,000 volunteers have served on projects in 23 countries, and the value of their pro bono services has exceeded $80 million.

Those interested in volunteering or providing other support are invited to contact FSVC's New York office. Assignments usually range from one to several weeks, following which volunteers may be asked to maintain ongoing involvement, if warranted.

Once FSVC approves a project, volunteers are selected and briefed on the details and goals of the assignment and the expectations of the host institutions. FSVC reimburses project-related travel costs, including transportation, hotel, and meal expenses.

FSVC also sponsors U.S.-based training for qualified professionals from the financial sectors of host countries.

## For the Children of the World
P.O. Box 718
Milton, WA 98354
**Tel:** (253) 946-9241
**Fax:** (253) 839-6375
**E-mail:** nsneal@aol.com
**Web:** www.geocities.com/rainforest/canopy/1158/
**Contact:** Nancy S. Neal

For the Children of the World (FCW) is a nonprofit corporation in the state of Washington that sponsors Belarusian children for "health respites" in the U.S. It works with the organization For the Children of Chernobyl in Belarus. In 1998, For the Children of Chernobyl arranged family stays for 27 Belarusian children over a period of six weeks.

Seventy percent of the radiation from the Chernobyl nuclear disaster fell on Belarus. According to FCW, the children it hosts suffer from a "breakdown of their immune system due to constant bombardment by radiation." During the six-week stay each summer, the children undergo a nutritional program, extensive diagnostic blood testing (provided by Smith Kline Laboratories), and other medical and dental check-ups.

## The Ford Foundation
320 East 43rd Street
New York, NY 10017
**Tel:** (212) 573-5283
**Fax:** (212) 856-9330
**E-mail:** office-communications@fordfound.org
**Web:** www.fordfound.org
**Contact:** June H. Zeitlin, Director, Governance and Civil Society Program

The Ford Foundation is a private philanthropic institution dedicated to international peace and the advancement of human welfare throughout the world. Following WWII, the foundation sponsored a range of education and cultural exchange activities involving the Soviet Union and East Europe. After 1989, the foundation refocused its work in the region and began making grants in direct support of indigenous institutions. In the period 1989–95, the foundation spent over $30 million on projects related to this endeavor. See the Moscow section for more information about Ford-Russia.

## Foundation for International Professional Exchange, Inc.
1246 W. Caida Del Sol Drive
Pueblo West, CO 81007
**Tel:** (719) 547-7510
**Tel:** (602) 275-2966 Arizona office (part-time)

**Fax:** (719) 547-2720
**E-mail:** wjwfipe1@juno.com
**Contact:** W. Jackson Wilson, R.Ed.D., President

FIPE was created in 1990 by a small group of Russian and American professionals and businesspeople to facilitate the exchange of professional persons, information, equipment, and students between the U.S. and the NIS. They focus on the fields of medicine, education, government, and church.

In medicine their activities include a program for NIS physicians at the famed Mayo Clinic branch in Scottsdale, AZ, and the placement of NIS physicians in U.S. medical schools for short-term intensive study in their specialties. With the support of the Ukraine Ministry of Health, FIPE works with the International Medical Equipment Collaborative in Seabrook, NH, to renovate facilities and provide state-of-the-art medical equipment to hospitals in Ukraine. One new clinic has been completed and three more are in process.

FIPE's work in education includes providing American teachers of English to NIS schools. FIPE helped an English magnet school in Ukraine create a computer center for their 1,600 students, all of whom use the English language. Vice Principal Volodymyr Bondarenko credits FIPE with helping his students develop "an understanding of themselves as citizens of the world, absolutely essential if they are going to lead Ukraine into the 21st century." FIPE also has a "Books-in-English" program, which provides otherwise unaffordable English language textbooks to NIS schools from two collection points in the U.S. and four distribution points in the NIS. The books are donated by American school systems and publishers.

FIPE also created a Resident Municipal Government Intern Program with the American Graduate School of International Business Management (Thunderbird School) and the city of Scottsdale, AZ.

With the endorsement of the leadership of the Episcopal Church in the U.S. and the Russian Orthodox Church, FIPE developed a Parish Partnership Project that links congregations of the two churches at the local level. Active, ongoing partnerships now exist between more than 20 Episcopal congregations in the U.S. and Orthodox congregations in the NIS. Each partnership involves a visit to the other's community by clergy and laity on both sides. Although some American congregations do make financial gifts to their NIS partners, such support is neither required nor expected. "Love is the medium of exchange."

FIPE has a Medical Director and Associate for Education living in the U.S., and resident representatives in Russia and Ukraine. President Jack Wilson states, "FIPE is not a funding organization, we are facilitators, brokers of people and resources. No American in our organization is paid. We operate on a bare-bones budget and a lot of loving goodwill and help from a lot of people. We think this is very much worth doing."

## Foundation for Russian/ American Economic Cooperation

1932 First Avenue, Suite 803
Seattle, WA 98101
**Tel:** (206) 443-1935
**Fax:** (206) 443-0954
**E-mail:** fraec@fraec.org
**Web:** www.fraec.org
**Contact:** Carol Vipperman, President; Brian Jones, Administrative Manager

FRAEC is a nonprofit organization established in 1989 with the goal of meeting the day-to-day needs of member firms conducting business in Russia and to foster a better business environment in the Russian Far East.

FRAEC has conducted programs in cross-cultural training for over 140 participants and is scheduled to host another 60 by July 1999. Twenty Russian and American companies have participated in FRAEC's cross-cultural training, and 100 managers of the Boeing Company received cross-cultural consultation. Additionally, 97 Russian Far East officials have received specialized training in areas such as taxation, customs, fisheries, education, and regional administration.

FRAEC operates two American Business Centers (ABCs) in the Russian Far East, in Khabarovsk and Yuzhno-Sakhalinsk. The ABCs have assisted over 275 companies and numerous U.S. and state government officials to find footing in the RFE.

CLEAR-PAC, a project to expedite customs clearance, successfully completed its pilot phase in the beginning of 1998, having processed nine shipments (159 containers with 4,000 tons of cargo worth $6.2 million) in two days or less each, which resulted in a savings of $100,000 to the importers. Because of this concrete result, CLEAR-PAC is now addressing the issues of expanding the project into other ports, the creation of a Russian brokerage industry, and the need for continued work with—and integration of—the Russian regional certifying agencies in the project, including training and exchanges.

FRAEC was appointed and continues to operate as the U.S. Executive Secretariat to the U.S. West Coast–Russian Far East Ad Hoc Working Group

(AHWG). The AHWG has conducted bilateral meetings in both Russia and the U.S. attended by over 1,200 American and Russian business representatives. The Fisheries Sector of AHWG, working with the Immigration and Naturalization Service, created a list of recommended practices for processing Russian fishing crews in U.S. ports. Implementation of those proposals reduced the time required to clear immigration by 50 percent.

In addition to its offices in Russia, FRAEC has 15 full-time staff in Seattle.

## Freedom House/National Forum Foundation

1319 18th Street, NW
Washington, DC 20036
**Tel:**      (202) 296-5101
**Fax:**     (202) 296-5256
**E-mail:**  nff@nff.org
**Web:**    www.nff.org,
             www.freedomhouse.org
**Contact:** Adrian Karatnycky, Chairman; Jim Denton, Executive Director

Freedom House (FH) was founded in 1941 by Eleanor Roosevelt and Wendell Wilkie, as a nonpartisan human rights organization dedicated to promoting political rights and civil liberties internationally. Since WWII, FH has been a watchful monitor of human rights around the world, advocate of an "engaged American foreign policy," and publisher of useful resources such as its magazine *Freedom Review* and its annual survey, *Freedom in the World*.

In 1997 Freedom House merged with National Forum Foundation. Since the late eighties, NFF has pursued creative programs designed to strengthen democratic leadership and institutions in the CEE and NIS regions. Its Central and

East European Internship Program—the "first of its kind, the largest and most successful"—has brought more than 500 "emerging leaders" to the U.S. to participate in three-month professional internships, working side by side with partners in the media, government, nonprofit organizations, and business firms. The program is open to participants from certain countries in the NIS (e.g., Russia, Ukraine, and the Kyrgyz Republic) as well as from Eastern Europe.

NFF's American Volunteers in International Development (AVID) program is described as a Democracy Corps style initiative. The program is "driven by the applications submitted by prospective host organizations in the emerging democracies" and the great majority of the more than 90 AVID assignments to date have been in media management, nonprofit, governance, public administration, or business management (with an emphasis on financial and strategic planning). The foundation provides most of the transportation and housing costs for volunteers. In addition, there is an expense stipend based on local living standards, approximately $250–300/month. Assignments may be anywhere in Eurasia or Eastern Europe.

Under a USAID-sponsored Habits of the Heart program, Freedom House is working closely with a number of NGOs in Ukraine. Please see Freedom House entry under Kyiv for details.

## The Fund for Arts and Culture in Central and Eastern Europe

817 Mackall Avenue
McLean, VA 22101
**Tel:** (703) 893-6016
**Fax:** (703) 448-1270
**E-mail:** jhpoole@erols.com

**Contact:** Jillian Poole, President; Frank S. Johnson, Jr., Corporate Secretary

Founded in 1991, the fund is a nonprofit corporation governed by four officers in consultation with a 26-member board of advisors. There are no paid full-time staff members and officers and consultants who represent the fund do so without compensation. The fund provides assistance upon request to selected major arts and cultural institutions in Central and Eastern Europe and Russia, to "support their efforts to adjust to a free market economy."

Assistance is primarily provided through consultations by experts in the fields of nonprofit organization and planning, public relations, marketing, fundraising, administration, management, and governance. After the fund receives a formal invitation from an arts or cultural institution in its territory, a fund director makes an initial visit to more narrowly define needs and identify experts who are capable and might be willing to provide the needed assistance as unpaid consultants. These experts then travel to the region and provide whatever services are needed—lectures, training courses, roundtable discussions or seminars, individual consultations, etc. After such a visit, follow-up is maintained, usually by fax or e-mail.

Since the fund began work, 39 consultants have made numerous individual trips to four countries in the region; together, they have spent 922 days with host arts and cultural institutions. In Russia, the fund has worked with the Russian State Museum in St. Petersburg, but they have also provided seminars on management, marketing and fundraising for regional museums in Irkutsk, Omsk, Yaroslavl, and Pyatigorsk. A description of this aspect of the fund's work, found in an appendix to their 1997 annual report, is of exceptional interest. In 1998 they held similar seminars in Khabarovsk and Dudinka (Taymir peninsula).

## Fund for Democracy and Development
1501 M Street, NW, Suite 1175
Washington, DC 20005-1702
**Tel:** (202) 466-4700
**Fax:** (202) 223-4826
**E-mail:** ffdd@erols.com
**Web:** www.cbi.co.ru/homepages/fdd/index.html
**Contact:** Lewis Townsend, Executive Director

FDD was founded in 1991 "to aid the economic and political transformation of the NIS...to democratic market economies." Initially FDD managed a project, funded by the U.S. State Department, which shipped more than 9,000 containers of donated materials to 300 cities in the NIS.

In 1994 FDD established the New Russian Small Business Investment Fund to extend loans to small and medium-sized businesses on reasonable terms. The initial funds came from the sale of commodities from the U.S. Agriculture Department. In its first two years of operations, FDD's Russian Bank Training Program conducted 26 seminars for over 550 Russian bankers representing 130 banks operating in all parts of Russia. Seminars were offered in cooperation with the Moscow International Finance and Banking School, the International Banking Institute in St. Petersburg, and other leading training institutions.

In addition to its seminar offerings, FDD provided in-bank consulting and technical assistance to a diverse group of large and medium-sized banks in various parts of Russia, including

Moscow, St. Petersburg, Zelenograd, Pushkino, Tomsk, Izhevsk, Kostroma, and Voronezh. Over 200 Russian bankers participated in FDD in-bank training sessions.

Building on expertise gained from analyzing the 11 "partner banks" of the New Russia Small Business Investment Fund (NRsbiF), FDD has developed a specialized methodology for analyzing and monitoring the performance of Russian banks. FDD claims that its model of bank analysis, developed following extensive on-site work inside Russian banks, sets "a new standard" for both qualitative and quantitative analysis of bank performance in the Russian market. These services are available through:
FDD Banking Advisory Services
Vasilevsky Mal. per., 14/23, Suite 17
121002 Moscow
Tel: 241-5747, -4489, -5324
Fax: 241-5877
E-mail: fddcis@sovam.com

## The Global Earth
2759 Mill Avenue, 1st Floor
Brooklyn, NY 11234
**Tel:** (718) 241-5842
**Fax:** (718) 491-5505
**E-mail:** tge@road2new.com
**Web:** www.road2new.com
**Contact:** Elvira Souleymanova

Founded in 1998, The Global Earth is organizing a year-long Arctic Circle expedition to commemorate the advent of the new millennium. The focus of the expedition will be the everyday life, customs and traditions of the northern indigenous people who have lived along the Arctic Circle for generations. Members of the expedition will visit the lands traditionally inhabited by Komi, Karel, Saami, Eskimos, Chukchi, Hanty-Manci, Yakuti, and Nentsi tribes.

The expedition will address issues of environment and development: how to preserve the Arctic wilderness and traditional indigenous habitats from the destructive influence of modern industrial development. Additionally, the expedition will pay tribute to a legion of heroic Arctic explorers of the past, including: Willem Barents, Henry Hudson, Martin Frobisher, William Baffin, Alexander Mackenzie, Ivan Dezhnev, Vitus Bering, John Franklin, Fritjof Nansen, Roald Amudsen, Robert Peary, Frederick Cook, and Ivan Papanin.

The expedition is scheduled to start in January 2000 and will cross through eight countries: Finland, Sweden, Norway, Iceland, Denmark (Greenland), Canada, the U.S. (Alaska) and Russia. Wherever possible, means of transportation will include traditional ones, such as dog and reindeer sledges, skis, snowshoes, and native wooden boats. A film crew will accompany travelers en route, documenting the most memorable encounters and events.

A highlight of the year-long journey will be a celebration of the eve of the new millennium at the North Pole. Members of the expedition, representatives of the northern indigenous people and distinguished guests will be transported to the North Pole by icebreaker. A "gala celebration" will be broadcast around the world from a TV studio built on the ice.

Three full-time office staff are working on this project. The Russian partner is an organization in Moscow named Zemlya-2000.

## Global Volunteers

375 E. Little Canada Road
St. Paul, MN 55117-1628
**Tel:**      (800) 487-1074
**Fax:**      (651) 482-0915

**E-mail:** email@globalvolunteers.org
**Web:**     www.globalvolunteers.org
**Contact:** Michele Gran, Communications Director

Founded in 1984 with the goal of "building a foundation for peace through mutual international understanding," Global Volunteers sends some 120 teams of North American volunteers each year to work on human and economic development projects in 20 countries. Projects originate from the invitation of a local host organization and volunteers work alongside local people under the direction of local leaders. Volunteers pay all program and travel costs for these one-, two-, and three-week programs.

GV sponsors programs teaching English and business in Zaporizhia, Ukraine. The Znanie Society is their local partner. Business volunteers give two to three lectures a day in a university setting or they consult with local businesses. The service program fee for participants is $1,995 for two weeks, exclusive of airfare. Four teams of approximately 15 people each are planned for Ukraine in 1999.

## Goodwill Industries International, Inc.

9200 Wisconsin Avenue
Bethesda, MD 20814
**Tel:**      (301) 530-6500
**Fax:**      (301) 530-1516
**E-mail:**  internat@goodwill.org
**Web:**      www.goodwill.org/internat/europe.htm

Founded in 1912 by Edgar J. Helms, a Methodist minister in Boston, Goodwill Industries International (GII) has evolved into a federation of 187 autonomous, community-based organizations in the United States and

Canada with a network of 48 overseas associate members located in 34 countries outside North America.

Goodwill "strives to achieve full participation in society of people with disabilities and other individuals with special needs by expanding their opportunities and occupational capabilities." To achieve this goal, Goodwill trains people with disabilities and vocational disadvantages, such as illiteracy, a history of criminal behavior, or a lack of work experience to meet labor needs of the community. Goodwill provides four vocational services: (1) vocational evaluation, (2) vocational adjustment, (3) development of job-seeking skills and placement, and (4) transitional employment for those who cannot be competitive in the labor market in the short term.

Since 1989, private and governmental agencies in Eastern Europe and the NIS have requested direct assistance from GII in creating domestic Goodwill-style programs. Currently Goodwill organizations exist in the Czech Republic, Hungary, Poland, Russia, and Ukraine.

A key element in GII's international growth is its International Partnership Program, which matches North American Goodwill organizations with counterparts overseas. Partnerships encompass trade and informational exchanges, consultancy visits by North American executives and staff to overseas locations, and internships for overseas Goodwill staffers at American Goodwills.

GII is a founding member of the U.S. Council in International Rehabilitation and a member of Rehabilitation International.

## Gray Doves International Inc.

4109 S. Laredo Way
Aurora, CO  80013
**Tel/Fax:** (303) 680-3504
**E-mail:** Graydoves@aol.com, getpjm@aol.com
**Web:** members.aol.com/graydoves/index.html
**Contact:** Barbara Johnston, Executive Director; Phil McPeck, Chairman

Gray Doves International Inc. was formed in January 1997 out of a concern that the elderly, particularly elderly women, "fall through the cracks of international aid." It has grown to a worldwide network of volunteers committed to providing dignity and hope for elderly women who "are left to struggle desperately when their spouses die or when they have no extended family upon which to rely." Gray Doves was formed to address this issue and promote the values of volunteerism in societies where it traditionally has not been a part of the culture.

Gray Doves' provides needy elderly women with essentials that improve their quality of life. These range from personal hygiene products to vitamins, decent clothing, sewing supplies, handheld magnifying glasses for reading, garden hand tools, and the like. Furthermore, Gray Doves is developing a curriculum suitable to upper middle school and high school students, as well as civic organizations, which will promote volunteerism and coordinated aid to needy elderly women.

Gray Doves has published *The Open Cupboard*, a small but charming book that combines drawings and wisdom of elderly women in Belarus with a "robust" collection of authentic Russian and Eastern European recipes.

Projects to date have largely concentrated on Russia and the former Soviet Union but include India and Mexico. In the NIS, Gray Doves shipments of essentials have reached needy women in Minsk, Kyiv, Semipalatinsk, Petropavlosk and Pskov.

Staff is all volunteer. Numerous corporations have supported Gray Doves work with in-kind contributions and shipping supplies.

## Harvard Ukrainian Business Initiative

Ukrainian Research Institute
Harvard University
1583 Massachusetts Avenue
Cambridge, MA 02138
**Tel:**        (617) 496-6002
**E-mail:**   hubi@fas.harvard.edu
**Web:**      www.sabre.org/huri/
hubi.html
**Contact:** Janet Hunkel, Director of the Cambridge office

HUBI, formerly Project for Economic Reform in Ukraine, was created in 1990 in response to requests for assistance by Ukrainian policymakers. HUBI publishes the monthly *Ukrainian Economic Monitor*, which it describes as "the leading authority on economics, politics and legislation in Ukraine..."

In addition to publishing *UEM*, the organization performs the following services:

- Organizes seminars for business people that provide current information about economic and political events in Ukraine
- Disseminates information on opportunities in Ukraine for targeted industries
- Participates with the Commonwealth of Massachusetts in global business programs such as the Sister State program and the Partners for Trade series
- Provides U.S. businesses with access to information about industries and key business transactions, and sponsors opportunities to interact

with Ukraine's officials and business and economic leaders

## Heartland International

1033 West VanBuren Street
Chicago, IL  60607-2919
**Tel:**        (312) 413-8591
**Fax:**       (312) 413-8151
**E-mail:**   kegere1@uic.edu
**Web:**      www2.uic.edu/orgs/heartland
**Contact·** Karen A. Egerer, President

Heartland International is a "women-managed, nonprofit organization" established in 1989 to manage international educational exchange programs and promote social, economic, and political development worldwide. Through its programs, Heartland International seeks to:

- bring to bear the "traditionally underutilized resources of the Midwestern United States" on international programs;
- act as a catalyst in strengthening emerging democratic institutions;
- provide training and technical assistance to encourage microenterprise development;
- support the role of women in economic, political and social affairs in emerging democracies.

The organization has worked with the USIA-sponsored Community Connections Program for entrepreneurs, government officials, and NGO leaders from Russia and Belarus. Through Heartland's programs, more than 100 participants have developed new skills in NGO management, running a small business, or enhancing the effectiveness of local government.

## Henry M. Jackson Foundation

1001 Fourth Avenue, Suite 3317
Seattle, WA  98154
**Tel:**        (206) 682-8565
**Fax:**       (206) 682-8961

**E-mail:** HMJackson@aol.com
**Web:** www.hjf.org
**Contact:** Lara Iglitzin, Executive Director

The foundation was established after the death in 1983 of Senator Jackson, a strong supporter of human rights around the world. It supports funding for new initiatives in four areas: education and advanced research in international affairs, public service, environment and natural resources management, and human rights. In recent years the foundation, seeking to assist "groups that are involved in Russia's transition to democracy," committed approximately $300,000 to organizations with programs that focus on Russia. These include Human Rights Watch and the Lawyers Committee on Human Rights (both in New York) and in Russia, Panorama Information & Research Center, Moscow Anti-Fascist Center, the Independent Publishing House, and two sections of Memorial, the Moscow center as well as a Perm affiliate.

## Infoshare International

584 Castro Street, Suite 671
San Francisco, CA 94114
**Tel:** (415) 437-1873
**Fax:** (510) 843-4066
**E-mail:** Infoshare1@aol.com
**Contact:** Julie Stachowiak, Executive Director

This organization was formed in October 1993 under the name AIDS Infoshare Russia. They work in conjunction with their Moscow office to provide Russian individuals and organizations with the tools that they need to fight HIV/AIDS and STDs. Current emphasis is on the provision of HIV/AIDS information, human rights and public health advocacy, and NGO

technical support. Infoshare's work is primarily in Russia where they help to distribute food, clothing, and medications to people affected by HIV/AIDS through Russia AIDS Relief, an HIV support program they developed.

Infoshare International has established a 4,000-volume library devoted to HIV/AIDS and STDs, the largest of its kind in Russia, which is open to the public on weekdays. They have also established SPIDNET, an e-mail conference in Russian on HIV/AIDS and STDs; created an electronic database containing information on individuals and institutions working in the fields of HIV/AIDS; conducted seminars on NGO management and development for NGOs working in the field of HIV/AIDS; produced fact sheets on topics related to HIV/AIDS; and conducted various outreach events.

## Institute for Democracy in Eastern Europe

2000 P Street, NW, Suite 400
Washington, DC 20036
**Tel:** (202) 466-7105
**Fax:** (202) 466-7140
**E-mail:** idee@idee.org
**Contact:** Irena Lasota, Director; Eric Chenoweth, Treasurer

IDEE was established in 1986 to support the growing independent opposition movements in Eastern Europe seeking peaceful democratic change and an end to communism. IDEE provides financial and technical assistance and also publishes *Uncaptive Minds*, an English-language forum in the West for a broad range of East European independent opinion. IDEE has administered over $5 million in assistance to nearly 2,000 independent publications, civic organizations, human rights groups, and opposition movements in the Caucasus, Central and Eastern Europe, the Baltics, Russia and Ukraine. Among the organizations it works with are Karta/Memorial in Ryazan, Russia; Supolnosc in Minsk, Belarus; Inam in Baku, Azerbaijan; Center for Development and Cooperation in Tbilisi, Georgia; the Helsinki Association in Yerevan, Armenia; Rebirth of Crimea in Bakchisaray, Ukraine; and several others in Crimea itself.

In 1992, IDEE began its Centers for Pluralism Program. The hub of the program is the IDEE office in Warsaw: P. O. Box 311, Warsaw 00950, Poland. Tel: (48 22) 627-1845; Fax: (48 22) 627-1846; E-mail: idee@plcarn.edu.pl Contact Malgorzata Nainska, CfP Program Coordinator.

IDEE-Warsaw publishes the quarterly *Centers for Pluralism Newsletter*, which is distributed to more than 4,000 individuals and groups in English, Azeri, Russian, and Ukrainian. It provides basic information on the activities and needs of democratic and independent organizations in the region, helping these organizations to communicate and cooperate within and across borders. For more information, see Print Resources. To order *Uncaptive Minds*, contact the IDEE office in Washington, DC. ($30/year for four issues).

## Institute for East-West Christian Studies

Wheaton College
Wheaton, IL 60187-5593
**Tel.** (630) 752-5917
**Fax.** (630) 752-5916
**E-mail:** iewcs@wheaton.edu, melliott@wheaton.edu
**Web:** www.wheaton.edu/bgc/iewcs
**Contact:** Dr. Mark Elliott, Executive Director

Founded in 1986 by professor Elliott, the institute's purpose is "to provide the church, academia, and the media with an informed understanding of Christianity in the former Soviet Union and East Central Europe and to facilitate Christian ministry in these regions." Besides contributing to the academic program at Wheaton, the institute sponsors conferences, puts together orientation sessions and materials for prospective missionaries, and develops a wide variety of print and audio resources. It publishes the quarterly, *East-West Church & Ministry Report.* See Print Resources for more information about the newsletter.

## Institute for East-West Studies

700 Broadway
New York, NY 10003
**Tel:** (212) 824-4100
**Fax:** (212) 824-4149
**Web:** www.iews.org
**Contact:** John E. Mroz, President

The institute was founded in 1981 to "challenge, bridge and transform the security, economic and social situation in Central Europe and Eurasia." It is a policy research center whose focus is in the areas of security, economics and community development, and democratic institution building. It publishes a weekly *Russian Regional Report.*

## Institute for Sustainable Communities

56 College Street
Montpelier, VT 05602
**Tel:** (802) 229-2900
**Fax:** (802) 229-2919
**E-mail:** isc@iscvt.org
**Web:** www.iscvt.org
**Contact:** George Hamilton, Executive Director

The mission of ISC is to promote environmental protection and economic and social well-being through integrated strategies at the local level. ISC projects emphasize participating actively in civic life, developing stronger democratic institutions, and engaging diverse interests in decision making.

Since 1990, ISC has undertaken or completed more than 28 projects in 13 countries of Central and Eastern Europe and Eurasia that are intended to advance the aims of "sustainable development and civil society through community-based action." In 1998, ISC had ongoing projects in eight countries and a total budget of $5.7 million (approximately 50 percent of which was awarded as grants to other organizations). ISC has offices in Russia, Macedonia, and Bulgaria, besides the U.S.

Since 1993 ISC has worked with several Russian organizations to address the pollution problems in Nizhny Tagil. Out of 81 cities considered, a Russian health study ranked the central Urals city first in incidence of carcinogenic diseases, third in respiratory diseases, and ninth in skin diseases. ISC and its project partners worked to identify and rank more than 4,700 sources of air pollution. Using a comparative risk analysis, a multi-stakeholder committee identified PM10 particulate pollution as the pollutant responsible for the most adverse public health impacts. (PM10 are "dust" particles less that 10 microns in size. Because of their small size they travel deeper into the respiratory system and are more dangerous to humans.) Opportunities to reduce particulate pollution were identified and remediation measures have begun.

In 1998, ISC and its Nizhny Tagil partner organization, Clean Home, began a new project to coordinate a participatory process to develop and implement a new solid waste management plan for Nizhny Tagil. A broadly representative, community solid-waste-management advisory committee has been formed and is driving the process to improve waste management and make the city a cleaner place to live.

ISC helped establish environmental training centers in Volgograd and Ekaterinburg that have delivered dozens of courses to representatives of government, business, and non-governmental organizations.

From its office in Moscow, ISC manages the USAID-funded Replication of Lessons Learned (ROLL) Activity. ROLL is a four-year environmental project designed to provide financial assistance to Russian organizations, enabling them to spread best practices and lessons learned throughout the country. The project is managed with the help of six regional centers. In 1998, ISC launched a new grants program focused on promoting environmentally sound business development in the Russia Far East.

In Ukraine, through its public awareness project, ISC supported the development of one of the first national television programs focused on environmental issues and the first Environmental Journalist Association. ISC also coordinates a community-based environmental education demonstration project that emphasizes the development of locally relevant curricula and materials. The two pilot communities are Ivano-Frankivsk and Khmelnitsky in western Ukraine.

## International Center for Journalists

1616 H Street, NW, 3rd floor
Washington, DC 20006
**Tel:**    (202) 737-3700
**Fax:**    (202) 737-0530
**E-mail:**  editor@icfj.org
**Web:**    www.icfj.org
**Contact:** David Anable, President;
Whayne Dillehay, Vice President;
Margaret Fleming Glennon,
Communications Director

ICFJ was established in 1984 to strengthen journalism worldwide through professional training and exchanges. Since it opened its doors, ICFJ has worked with more than 8,000 journalists from 172 countries. It is the only nonprofit orga-nization in the United States dedicated exclusively to developing overseas print media, radio, and television. Besides supporting the continuing professional development of journalists worldwide, ICFJ also serves as a resource for policymakers, business executives, academics, and others who need reliable information on the international media.

ICFJ provides professional development programs, administers fellowships and exchanges for journalists in the U.S. and abroad, and publishes resources for journalists, including an *Environmental Sourcebook, Interviewing Techniques, Tips on Editing*, and the *Newsroom Management Handbook*. (The center's most popular training publication is *Ten Tips for Business and Economic Reporting in Developing Countries*, available in Arabic, English, French, Portuguese, Romanian and Spanish.) Among the exchange programs ICFJ administers is the Knight International Press Fellowship Program, which sends American journalists overseas on long-term media assistance projects.

ICFJ has recently established the International Journalists' Network (IJN) on the World Wide Web. Building on the former Clearinghouse on the Central and East European Press, the network tracks media assistance efforts and training opportunities around the world. The page titled Online Journalism Resources is especially worth a visit: www.icfj.org/onelinere/resources7.html

## International Center for Not-for-Profit Law

1511 K Street, NW, Suite 723
Washington, DC 20005
**Tel:**    (202) 624-0766
**Fax:**    (202) 624-0767
**E-mail:**  infoicnl@icnl.org
**Web:**    www.icnl.org
**Contact:** Dr. Leon Irish, President;
Prof. Karla W. Simon, Executive Vice
President; Natalia Bourjaily, Program
Director

ICNL was registered in 1993. Its purpose is to assist "in the creation and improvement of laws and regulatory systems that permit, encourage, and regulate the not-for profit sector in countries around the world." ICNL provides technical assistance for writing laws and regulations that will enable the growth of a "vital, yet accountable and sensibly regulated, independent sector."

Technical assistance projects coordinated by ICNL are staffed by lawyers and other experts who volunteer their time. ICNL provides preparatory materials, in-country support, and follow-through. Airfare and out-of-pocket expenses are reimbursed when a project requires travel, and modest stipends may be available in some circumstances.

ICNL enjoys strong in-country relationships with governmental authorities, parliamentarians, NGOs, lawyers, and academics. Working from this base of contacts, ICNL conducts training on issues related to the regulation of the not-for-profit sector, sponsors and conducts research, and organizes conferences and workshops in different regions of the world.

Under a contract with the World Bank, ICNL developed the *Handbook on Good Practices for Laws Relating to Non-Governmental Organizations* (available in Russian, Arabic, Spanish, French, and Chinese, in addition to English). This has been published as a Discussion Draft by the bank, which is currently holding a series of meetings to critique it in various forums around the world.

As part of the research effort to produce the *Handbook,* ICNL has created a unique documentation center of laws, regulations, and reports from over 100 countries. Summaries of the available materials are being placed in the documents file at ICNL's Web site. ICNL also worked with CIVICUS, the global alliance for citizen participation, to assist in the development of *Principles for Citizen Participation*, published in August 1997. In 1998 ICNL began publishing the *International Journal of Not-for-Profit Law* online.

ICNL has published a survey of laws governing the not-for-profit sector in Central Europe and a comprehensive study of the current laws governing NPOs in Russia. In cooperation with the Open Society Institute, it developed *Guidelines for Laws Governing Civic Organizations* (published in December 1997 and now available in Russian and Farsi in addition to English).

## International Executive Service Corps

P.O. Box 10005
Stamford, CT 06904-2005

**Tel:** (203) 967-6000
**Fax:** (203) 324-2531
**E-mail:** nisiesc@well.sf.ca.us,
62054816@eln.attmail.com
**Web:** www.interaction.org/
mb/iesc.html

Since its founding in 1964, the IESC has helped place volunteer business executives in technical assistance projects in about 100 countries around the world. IESC maintains a database of thousands of retired executives who can be matched with requests for assistance from overseas client companies, governments and organizations.

In the NIS, IESC Volunteer Executives (VEs) are used in technical assistance projects, business planning workshops, industry restructuring projects, and public administration seminars. VEs develop and implement training programs with government officials, work with former defense industry enterprises making the transition to market economies, and assist companies to develop viable business plans to attract U.S. partners and/or sources of financing. Since the NIS program's inception in 1992, IESC has sent several hundred VEs to the NIS, providing volunteer service to more than 1,000 enterprises. The average length of stay for a technical assistance volunteer in the NIS is two months. IESC covers travel and living expenses as well as spouse accompaniment for projects over 28 days. IESC has offices in various locations throughout the NIS.

## International Exchange Council

3160 Hall Street, S.E.
Grand Rapids, MI 49506
**Tel:** (616) 949-1826
**Fax:** (616) 954-1864
**E-mail:** bhof@ix.netcom.com
**Web:** site under development

**Contact:** Barbara Van't Hof, President; Bonnie Miller, Board Chair

Formerly the West Michigan/St. Petersburg International Exchange Council, IEC organizes educational, economic, and cultural exchanges for improved understanding between the people of West Michigan and Russia. (Founded in 1993 with a focus on St. Petersburg, it has expanded its area of work to include all of Russia.) IEC is a volunteer-driven organization and has no paid employees. All funds received (approximately $90,000 in 1997) are used for program development and implementation.

Since 1994, when IEC entered into a partnership with the Society for Cultural and Business Contacts "Russia-USA" in St. Petersburg, programs have included:

- *Bank exchanges*. Russian bankers were trained in banking law, finance, accounting and commercial services by seven West Michigan banks, and West Michigan bankers traveled to St. Petersburg to lecture on U.S. bank practices. (This project was funded by USAID and Eurasia Foundation.)
- *Faculty exchanges*. Business school faculty lectured in St. Petersburg on topics of economics, finance, marketing, entrepreneurship, etc., and professors from St. Petersburg lectured in West Michigan universities and colleges.
- *Scholarships*. IEC raised funds to provide an MBA candidate with a partial scholarship to a local business school. The candidate was selected through fair and impartial competition, graduated with honors, and now works with Arthur Anderson in St. Petersburg.
- *Coordination*. Helped the Center for Citizen Initiatives Productivity Enhancement Program for 10

furniture manufacturing executives from five Russian cities. Training was provided by West Michigan furniture manufacturers such as Steelcase, Baker, Nucraft, area universities etc. Trainers, host families, transportation, cultural events, etc., were arranged by IEC.

IEC has received in-kind support from West Michigan universities, corporations, and funds from foundations and individuals. Current emphases are the Cultural Exchange Program and a Health Care Management Program for the directors of polyclinics and hospitals in the northwest region of Russia. IEC is interested in connecting with other Russian NGOs, such as the Society for Cultural and Business Contacts "Russia USA," in order to expand exchanges and develop programs.

## International Foundation for Electoral Systems

1101 15th Street, NW, 3rd floor
Washington DC 20005
**Tel:** (202) 828-8507
**Fax:** (202) 452-0804
**E-mail:** juliana@ifes.org
**Web:** www.ifes.org
**Contact:** Richard W. Soudriette, President; Julian G. Pilon, Director, Europe and Asia Programs

IFES was established in 1987 to "support electoral and other democratic institutions in emerging, evolving, and experienced democracies." It has worked in more than 90 countries providing pre-election technical assessments, on-site technical support, training of election workers, voter and civic education, and election observation.

In 1989 IFES began work in Eastern Europe and the NIS, where it played a key role in the establishment of the Association of Central/Eastern

European Election Officials. It has field offices in Armenia, Russia and Ukraine.

IFES contracts with election officials, computer professionals, lawyers, public relations professionals, academics, and other specialists from over 80 countries to take part in its project, conference, and observation activities. It maintains a database of consultant candidates from which program staff select appropriate individuals for various project activities. Most consultants have years of direct experience in elections administration, in the technical aspects of election administration (such as voter education, civic education, etc.), or in database programming and information technology management.

## International League for Human Rights

432 Park Avenue South, 11th floor
New York, NY 10016
**Tel:**      (212) 684-1221
**Fax:**      (212) 684-1696
**E-mail:**   ilhr@perfekt.net
**Web:**      www.ilhr.org
**Contact:** Catherine Fitzpatrick, Executive Director

The league has four program areas. The core program relates to the United Nations, and the league carries out a number of activities on behalf of its affiliates and partners abroad. The league has a network of about 300 human rights activists, journalists, and officials around the world with which it is in regular communication. Under the Countries in Transition program, the league puts special emphasis on countries experiencing upheavals or change that may pose special threats to human rights. The league's Belarus Project—designed to raise awareness as to the threat posed to human rights by

the Lukashenko regime—falls under this program. The Women's and Children's Rights program covers a third area. Finally, the Human Rights and Business program focuses on incorporating human rights standards into management and financial reporting, with a focus on accounting firms.

The league issues a series of regional reports. In 1997 it issued a report on trafficking in women from the former USSR. In 1998 it issued a report on the failure of Azerbaijan to comply with the recommendations of the UN Committee on the Elimination of Discrimination Against Women and another on Racism in Russia. These reports are normally based on the work of local ILHR affiliates (in these cases, the Human Rights Center of Baku and Moscow's Memorial organization).

## International Orthodox Christian Charities

711 West 40th Street, Suite 306
Baltimore, MD 21211
**Tel:**      (410) 243-9820
**Fax:**      (410) 243-9824
**E-mail:**   iocc@igc.apc.org
**Web:**      www.ioc.org
**Contact:** Constantine M. Triantafilou, Executive Director and CEO; Alexis Troubetzkoy, Representative for Russia; Mark Hodde, Public Relations Officer

The IOCC, founded in 1992, works in partnership with Orthodox churches to deliver humanitarian aid programs around the world. Much has recently gone to people affected by war in Kosovo and the surrounding area, but some assistance has gone to Georgia and other countries.

## International Republican Institute

1212 New York Avenue NW, Suite 900
Washington, DC 20005
**Tel:** (202) 408-9450
**Fax:** (202) 408-9462
**E-mail:** iri@iri.org, web@iri.org
**Web:** www.iri.org

IRI began its efforts in 1984, following congressional authorization of the National Endowment for Democracy, the umbrella organization for the IRI (as well as the National Democratic Institute for International Affairs, the Free Trade Union Institute, and the Center for International Private Enterprise).

IRI conducts programs outside the United States to promote democracy and strengthen free markets and the rule of law. The programs are tailored to the needs of pro-democracy activists in over 30 countries and include, for example, grassroots political organizing, campaign management, polling, parliamentary training, judicial reform, and election monitoring.

In the former Soviet Union, IRI's efforts focus on Russia, Ukraine, Belarus, Georgia, and Azerbaijan, "nations whose democratic transitions are of paramount importance to the United States." In Russia, where IRI has a field office, it conducts a program designed to improve the ability of the national and local legislators to govern, enhance democratic party organizational skills and support the development of Russian NGOs. In Ukraine (also a field office location), IRI works to improve the governance skills of democratic legislators and the campaign skills of democratic parties. IRI has a program in Belarus to assist in the development of a coalition of democratic political parties. In addition, IRI is beginning party-building programs in Georgia and Azerbaijan.

**Internews**
P.O. Box 4448
Arcata, CA 95518-4448
**Tel:** (707) 826-2030
**Fax:** (707) 826-2136
**E-mail:** info@internews.org
**Web:** www.internews.org
**Contact:** David Hoffman, President; Kim Spencer, Managing Director

Internews Network was founded in 1982 to "support the independent broadcast media in the former Soviet Union and other parts of the world through training programs and equipment grants." The organization now has 13 affiliates in Europe, the former Soviet Union, the Middle East, and Africa, each an independent NGO. Together they are known as Internews International. For information on Internews projects in Russia and Ukraine, see the Moscow and Kyiv sections.

### IREX (International Research & Exchanges Board)
1616 H Street, NW
Washington, DC 20006
**Tel:** (202) 628-8188
**Fax:** (202) 628-8189
**E-mail:** irex@irex.org
**Web:** www.irex.org

IREX was founded in 1968 by a consortium of U.S. colleges and universities to administer academic and research exchanges between the U.S. and the Soviet Union. Since then IREX's activities have expanded greatly, as has their territory, which now includes countries of Central and Eastern Europe, Eurasia, and Northeast Asia. Today, in collaboration with partners in the public, private, and academic sectors, IREX sponsors educational exchanges, professional training and institutional development programs, and international seminars. These activities have three mutually reinforcing goals:

- To foster scholarship, strengthen university leadership, and improve policy analysis and development within the U.S.
- To help partner countries successfully develop their intellectual, social, economic, and political communities by improving research capabilities, expanding access to information resources, bolstering professional associations and civic institutions, and increasing corporate and media skills
- To forge partnership links between universities, policymakers, professional and civic associations, and corporate and media groups in the U.S. and abroad

Through a series of integrated programs, IREX:

- provides field research opportunities for American specialists and analysts;
- administers U.S.-based as well as on-site education and training for international leaders, professionals, and scholars;
- assists in the creative restructuring of overseas universities and their curricula, finding them committed U.S. university partners where possible;
- promotes the creation and development of institutional partnerships between U.S. universities and professional associations and their international counterparts;
- supports, through technical assistance, the development of self-sustaining, independent media in Central and Eastern Europe (CEE) and the NIS;

- promotes the use of the Internet for scholarly and professional communication;
- fosters cooperative programs of development for libraries, archives, and information systems;
- designs new courses and training programs for corporate and professional needs;
- organizes conferences and workshops addressing contemporary issues for policymakers, scholars, corporate representatives, and the media.

IREX receives funding and support from its member universities, major foundations, U.S. government sponsors, leading corporations, and committed individuals in the private sector. An extensive network of field offices overseas provides outreach for IREX programs and services to program participants and alumni in the regions they serve. More information regarding IREX's country-specific programs will be found under the appropriate offices.

## IRIS—Center for Institutional Reform and the Informal Sector

University of Maryland
2105 Morrill Hall
College Park, MD 20742
**Tel:** (301) 405-3110
(301) 405-3052 (Thorpe)
**Fax:** (301) 405-3020
**E-mail:** info@iris.econ.umd.edu,
thorpe@iris.econ.umd.edu
**Web:** www.inform.umd.edu/iris/iris.html
**Contact:** Robert Thorpe, Market Environment Project Director

IRIS was launched in 1990 with funding from USAID not only "to examine specific practical problems of institutional reform . . . but also [to] attempt to provide a better theory of institutions, so that institutional reforms can be guided by a sound general understanding of how institutions affect economic performance." IRIS is currently managing a five-year $28-million contract with USAID, the Market Environment Project, for work in Armenia, Georgia, Moldova, Russia and Ukraine. Project specifics vary by country. In Armenia and Georgia, IRIS has established the IRIS Center Caucasus, a center for policy research and analysis on economic matters. In Moldova and Ukraine, IRIS offices are working on various aspects of commercial law reform. In Russia, the Program on Natural Monopolies focuses on, among other issues, the need to develop independent monopoly regulation in country accustomed to a very high degree of centralization.

## ISAR: Initiative for Social Action and Renewal in Eurasia

1601 Connecticut Avenue, NW, #301
Washington, DC 20009
**Tel:** (202) 387-3034
**Fax:** (202) 667-3291
**E-mail:** postmaster@isar.org
**Web:** www.isar.org
**Contact:** Eliza Klose, Executive Director; Kate Watters, Director of Programs

Founded in 1983, ISAR promotes citizen participation and the development of the non-governmental sector in the countries of the former Soviet Union. ISAR's seven offices in the U.S. and Eurasia support citizen activists and grassroots NGOs in their efforts to create "just and sustainable societies."

Responsive to local needs, ISAR's programs emphasize information exchange, cooperative activities and networking. They facilitate links among activists and their counterparts, nurturing partnerships among NGOs in Eurasia and the United States. ISAR also educates the public in the U.S. and

Eurasia about the unique role that grassroots NGOs play in shaping a positive transformation in the countries of the former Soviet Union.

ISAR's Washington, DC, activities fall into four categories: coalition building and public education; partnerships and exchanges; publications and information; and advocacy for ISAR offices in the countries of the former Soviet Union. A key function of the D.C. office is to serve as a clearinghouse for the public on issues related to NGOs in former-Soviet countries. ISAR staff are knowledgeable about each region and are available to help those seeking information. The office offers the following:

- An NGO Forum Series that convenes area NGOs to discuss issues related to NGO work in the FSU
- Ongoing brown bag sessions on regional issues in the FSU
- A library that focuses on specific environmental and societal concerns (energy, sustainable development, alternative economics, etc.)
- Databases on U.S. NGOs working in the FSU and on local NGOs in each of the regions where ISAR offices are located
- Briefing packets on the regions where ISAR operates
- Issue files by region
- Organizational files profiling U.S. NGOs working on concerns relevant to the FSU
- A job folder with listings of job, fellowship and internship opportunities for both the U.S. and post-Soviet countries
Publications available through the DC office include:
- *Give & Take: A Journal on Civil Society in Eurasia,* a quarterly that profiles issues relevant to the NGO sector of the former Soviet Union

- *ISAR in Focus,* a newsletter that details the activities of ISAR's different offices

ISAR's Web site features program descriptions of each office, highlights from the NGO Forum series, articles from ISAR's publications, and job opportunities at ISAR.

## Junior Achievement International

2780 Janitell Road
Colorado Springs, CO 80906
**Tel:**     (719) 540-0200
**Fax:**     (719) 540-8770
**E-mail:**  jai@jaintl.com
**Web:**     www.jaintl.com

Founded in 1919 in the U.S., JA seeks to "educate and inspire young people to value free enterprise, business and economics to improve the quality of their lives." Junior Achievement International (JAI), created in 1994, is responsible for developing and serving Junior Achievement programs outside the U.S. Since its inception, JAI has administered grants totaling $7.4 million on behalf of its member nations worldwide. According to JAI, each year millions of primary, secondary, and university students in most of the world's countries take part in some kind of Junior Achievement program.

In 1991, Junior Achievement established its first program in the former Soviet Union with the launching of Junior Achievement of Russia. Today Junior Achievement programs and representatives exist in every nation of the former Soviet Union except Tajikistan and Turkmenistan.

## Kennan Institute for Advanced Russian Studies

The Woodrow Wilson International Center for Scholars

One Woodrow Wilson Plaza
1300 Pennsylvania Avenue, NW
Washington, DC 20523
**Tel:**     (202) 691-4100
**Fax:**     (202) 691-4001
**E-mail:**  popsonna@wwic.si.edu
**Web:**     wwics.si.edu/programs/region/kennan/kenmain.htm
**Contact:** Blair A. Ruble, Director; Nancy Popson, Senior Associate

Founded in 1974, the Kennan Institute is named after George Kennan "the Elder," a nineteenth-century explorer of Russia and Siberia. It offers residential research scholarships of three to six months to academic scholars and to specialists from government, the media, and the private sector. The institute also administers an active program of public lectures and meetings and issues publications that include meeting reports, occasional papers, and books. The meeting reports are available at their Web site and offer an excellent way to "attend" the institute's ongoing series of first-class lectures.

## Law and Liberty Trust/ International Law Group

333 Maple Avenue East, Suite 1085
Vienna, VA 22031
**Tel:**     (703) 319-3646
**Fax:**     (703) 319-3625
**E-mail:**  75050.3251@compuserve.com, lawandlibertytrust.org@ibm.net
**Contact:** Lauren B. Homer

Formed in 1990, LLT's purpose is "to assist the people of Russia and other formerly communist nations in attaining religious freedom and to teach about the relationship between faith and sound government and legal systems." LLT has worked intensively on religious freedom issues in Russia and other former Soviet republics, Eastern European countries, and Asian nations emerging from communism. It seeks to be a source of objective and informed analysis about changes in laws regulating religious organizations, as well as broader political, social, and religious issues

In Russia, LLT has sponsored publication of magazines and books, organized conferences, and provided commentary to governmental, religious, and legal leaders. It campaigned to inform the American and Russian people about the dangers of the 1997 Russian Federation Law on Religious Freedom and Religious Organizations, giving frequent testimony and media appearances on the issue and pivotal testimony before the Senate Foreign Relations Committee, the Helsinki Commission, and other governmental bodies. In October 1998, it was the only organization asked to testify on religious freedom issues at a Senate Foreign Relations Committee Hearing

Its partner in Moscow is the Institute for Religion and Law.

## League of Women Voters Education Fund

1730 M Street, NW, Suite 1000
Washington, DC 20036
**Tel:** (202) 429-1965
**Fax:** (202) 463-3692
**E-mail:** orna@lwv.org
**Web:** www.lwv.org
**Contact:** Carolyn Jefferson-Jenkins, Ph.D., Chair; Orna Tamches, Program Manager, International Relations

The League of Women Voters was founded in 1920 to educate and empower women after they won the right to vote. Founders of the league believed that "citizens who have access to the facts on public policy issues and who know how to participate effectively will make wise decisions for their communities and their countries."

The League of Women Voters Education Fund (LWVEF) is a nonpartisan public policy educational organization that works to encourage informed and active participation of citizens in government and to increase understanding of major public policy issues. The LWVEF complements the membership and political advocacy activities of its sister organization, the League of Women Voters of the United States (LWVUS). The LWVEF has ready access to a network of 1,100 local and state leagues across the United States, as well as partner NGOs in the Newly Independent States, Balkans, Central and Eastern Europe, Africa, the American Republics, and Asia.

LWVEF launched the Voices for Women–Forces for Change initiative in 1997. In 1998, LWVEF held two leadership workshops for Belarusan and Russian women in Tver and Ekaterin-burg, Russia. The workshops were designed to improve the leadership, networking and grassroots political skills of women in these countries and encourage the vision of participatory democracy and civic education.

The Global Community Dialogue Program responds to a number of requests for assistance from NGOs in emerging democracies worldwide Through this program, the league provides training in skills for effective grassroots organization, education, and advocacy. LWVEF training includes:

- Building consensus
- Citizen networking
- Coalition building
- Conflict management, community dialogue, and alternative dispute resolution
- Identifying and prioritizing issues
- Lobbying/advocacy
- Monitoring elections
- NGO capacity building

- Organizing candidate debates and issue forums
- Promoting open government
- Running for office
- Strengthening the role of women in politics
- Strengthening the rule of law
- Voter education and outreach

Grassroots Internship Programs provide civic leaders with an opportunity to live in U.S. communities and gain hands-on skills in nonpartisan grassroots citizen education, organization, participation and advocacy. Working with local and state Leagues of Women Voters and their grassroots community partners, interns attend public hearings, shadow candidates running for office, monitor elections, observe candidate debates, learn voter education techniques, work with local government officials and network with diverse citizen groups. Interns also have the opportunity to work on issues of common concern, such as environmental protection, minority rights, economic development, women's equality, and health care.

LWVEF technical assistance is provided to civic organizations around the globe through small-group training workshops and conferences, satellite videoconferences, speaker tours, mentor programs and personalized training activities. LWVEF assistance is based upon a train-the-trainers construct.

The LWVEF offers NGOs grants of financial and technical assistance. The Grassroots Assistance Grants Program is an excellent opportunity for non-profit, grassroots-based groups in new and emerging democracies to strengthen their role as active players in civil society and public life.

Among the league's partners in the NIS are Ariadna (Russia), the Ukrainian Center for Women's Studies, the League of Women Voters of St. Petersburg, the League of Women Voters of Armenia, and the League of Women Voters of Ukraine.

## Legal Training and Curriculum Development

Faculty of Law
University of Alberta
Edmonton, Alberta T6H 2H5, Canada
**Tel:**     (403) 492-3313
**Contact:** Walter Mis, Professor of Law

This project is training 18 Ukrainian law professors, each for a one-year period (including eight months in Canada). The trainees return to Ukraine to teach new courses, from a western perspective, at the Centre of Legal Studies, University of Kyiv. The Ukrainian Legal Foundation, a leading law reform organization in Ukraine, is a key sponsor of the new Centre of Legal Studies. Canadian partners are the University of Alberta, York University, and McGill University.

## Magee Womancare International

Magee-Women's Hospital
300 Halket Street, P.O. Box 144
Pittsburgh, PA  15213-3180
**Tel:**     (412) 641-1189
**Fax:**     (412) 641-4949
**Web:**     www.siecus.org/inter/
russia/magee/mage0000.html
**Contact:** Tanya Ozor, Director; Kristen Tsapis, Program Coordinator

Magee is the obstetrics and gynecology teaching hospital of the University of Pittsburgh School of Medicine and a national leader in both research and the delivery of "family-centered maternity care." See Moscow in Russia: West of the Urals, for further information.

## MEDA Trade and Consulting
**Mennonite Economic Development Associates**
155 Frobisher Drive, Suite 1-106
Waterloo, Ontario N2V 2EI, Canada
**Tel:** (519) 725-1633
**Fax:** (519) 725-9083
**Contact:** Ronald Braun, Vice President

MEDA has an office in Moscow, which has been administering the Zelenograd Small Business Development Program for about five years.

## MiraMed Institute
314 Occidental South
Seattle, WA 98104
**Tel:** (206) 632-5444
**Fax:** (206) 285-8216
**E-mail:** MiraMedUSA@aol.com
**Web:** www.miramed.com
**Contact:** Robert Aronson, Program Director; Dr. Yuri Puchkov, All-Russia Representative

MiraMed Institute was founded by Dr. Juliette Engel in 1991 to address health issues of pregnancy and birth. The institute started the first Western childbirth center in Moscow. Since then it has expanded activities to include educational programs in Russian orphanages conducted by American volunteers and a six-oblast program of direct education on the growing international practice of coercive sexual trafficking of Russian girls.

## National Academy of Sciences
**Office of International Affairs–**
**Central Europe and Eurasia**
2101 Constitution Avenue, NW
Washington, DC 20418
**Tel:** (202) 334-2644
**Fax:** (202) 334-2614
**E-mail:** ocee@nas.edu
**Web:** www2.nas.edu/oia/21e6.html
**Contact:** Glenn Schweitzer, Director

The Central Europe and Eurasia component of the Division for Development, Security, and Cooperation at the NAS organizes and manages collaborative activities relating to countries of the former Soviet Union and Central Europe. Its two main types of activities are (1) individual grants programs for American scientists to pursue joint collaborative projects with counterparts from the region, and (2) workshops and Young Investigator Programs to facilitate cooperation on problems at the intersection of science and public policy. Examples of past programs or workshops include the environmental risks of nuclear power and defense conversion at the enterprise level. This program has been particularly active in Western efforts to aid the best scientists and to help reform the scientific enterprise in the former Soviet bloc.

## National Democratic Institute for International Affairs (NDI)
1717 Massachusetts Avenue, NW
Washington, DC 20036
**Tel:** (202) 328-3136
**Fax:** (202) 939-3166
**Web:** www.ndi.org

NDI was founded in 1983 and is affiliated with the National Democratic Party. It runs seminars and workshops for political parties and civic organizers to help strengthen democratic institutions in the NIS. Programs are geared toward political leaders, civic activists, parliamentarians, officials from all levels of government, journalists, professionals, academics, and students. Trainers are usually professional political or parliamentary trainers and civic organizers (special interest group and NGO professionals).
    NDI's program activities include: political party training (techniques for organizing, communication with consti-

tuencies, etc.); technical assistance for election monitoring; civic education programs; legislative training (staffing, research, committee structuring); city management; civil-military relations; and voter education.

In addition, NDI arranges programs in the U.S. for civic organizers, political party activists and Parliamentarians. These programs provide on-site experience for activists, elected officials and others in the democratic process as practiced in the U.S.

## National Endowment for Democracy
1101 15th Street, NW, Suite 802
Washington, DC  20005
**Tel:**      (202) 293-9072
**Fax:**      (202) 293-6042
**E-mail:**   info@ned.org
**Web:**      www.ned.org
**Contact:**  Carl Gershman, President; Sydnee Guyer Lipset, Public Affairs Manager

NED is a grant-making organization created in 1983 to strengthen democratic institutions around the world through non-governmental efforts. Funded by an annual congressional appropriation, the endowment makes hundreds of grants annually to civic education, media, human rights, and other organizations dedicated to democratic principles. Endowment programs in the areas of labor, business and political party development are funded through four core institutes: the Free Trade Union Institute, the Center for International Private Enterprise, the International Republican Institute, and the National Democratic Institute for International Affairs. The endowment supports programs in more than 90 countries, including all the countries of the NIS.

Through its International Forum for Democratic Studies the endowment produces the *Journal of Democracy*, conducts analysis of the theory and practice of democratic development worldwide, and serves as a clearinghouse for information on that development.

## Network of East-West Women
1601 Connecticut Avenue, NW
Washington, DC  20009
**Tel:**      (202) 265-3585
**Fax:**      (202) 265-3508
**E-mail:**   eastwest@neww.org
**Web:**      www.neww.org
**Contact:**  Erin M. Barclay, Executive Director

Founded in 1990 by women from across the United States and the former Yugoslavia, NEWW "links over 2,000 women's advocates in more than 30 countries who work in partnership to promote tolerance, democracy, nonviolence, health and respect for the institutions of a civil society." Its major projects are:
- *NEWW Online*. One of the first women's electronic communication networks in the region, this links women's advocacy organizations and activists in the former Soviet Union (FSU), Central and Eastern Europe (CEE), Western Europe, and the United States.
- *East-East Legal Coalition*. Women's rights lawyers from 22 countries in the FSU and CEE organized this legal reform network in an effort to develop and enforce laws and policies that strengthen women's legislative status and sense of citizenship in their respective countries. Activities include the compilation of Legal Status of Women Reports in post-totalitarian countries, and short-term legal

fellowships for recent law school graduates from FSU/CEE.
- *Book and Journal Project*. This contributes books and journals from the now vast literature of modern women's movements to women's centers and to individuals in the NIS/CEE region.

## NIS-US Women's Consortium
Winrock International (Global Women's Leadership Program)
1611 North Kent Street, Suite 600
Arlington, VA 22209
**Tel:** (703) 525-9430
**Fax:** (703) 525-1744
**E-mail:** sscott@winrock.org
**Contact:** Sheila Scott, U.S. Coordinator

The NIS-US Women's Consortium works toward "increasing the participation of NIS women and women's NGOs in the political process of democracy-building by strengthening institutional capacity, fundraising capability and advocacy expertise." A membership organization administered by Winrock International, it was founded in 1992 at the request of women from Russia, Ukraine and the United States. Since then, it has developed into an active international coalition, uniting more than 250 women's NGOs in Armenia, Belarus, Moldova, Russia, Ukraine, the U.S., and Uzbekistan. It has officially registered local NGO affiliates in Russia and Ukraine.

Members conduct activities supporting women's initiatives through their own organizations and in concert with the NIS-US Women's Consortium. Consortium members represent a broad spectrum of interests including advocacy, agriculture, economic conversion, education, entrepreneurship, health, journalism, leadership, rule of law, environment, and violence prevention.

The planning and implementation of Consortium activities are guided by a strong belief in the principles of participation, equality for women of all cultures, self-help, respect for diversity of perspectives, and a focus on issues of women's rights and development.

Since 1994, the NIS-US Women's Consortium has awarded $365,000 in seed grants to women's NGOs in Russia and Ukraine under programs funded by USAID. Between 1996–1998 more than 3,000 women gained skills and knowledge through women's leadership and small business training programs. In January 1998, the NIS-US Women's Consortium hosted the Second International Membership Meeting, "Preparing for the 21st Century." Over 190 women's organizations attended, representing the NIS, U.S., and Eastern Europe.

The current emphasis of the consortium is on women's leadership development, small business and job skills, violence prevention training programs, information dissemination, technical assistance and seed grants to NIS women's NGOs.

## Open Society Institute–New York
400 West 59th Street
New York, NY 10019
**Tel:** (212) 548-0600
**Fax:** (212) 548-4679
**E-mail:** osnews@sorosny.org
**Web:** www.soros.org
**Contact:** George Soros, Chairman; Aryeh Neier, President

George Soros established his first foundation in 1979 in New York and his first Eastern European foundation in Hungary in 1984. His network of foundations—the great majority of which are named Open Society Institutes but are commonly referred to as Soros Foundations—spans 31 countries. Open Society Institutes operate in most countries of Central and Eastern Europe and the former Soviet Union, as well as in Southern Africa, Haiti, Guatemala, and the United States. These foundations are dedicated to "building and maintaining the infrastructure and institutions of an open society." Total spending by the foundations in a recent period was as follows (in millions):

| 1994 | 1995 | 1996 | 1997 |
| --- | --- | --- | --- |
| $300 | $350 | $362 | $428 |

The Soros foundations began operating in the NIS in 1987 with the establishment of the Cultural Initiative Foundation in Moscow (now the Open Society Institute–Russia). Each national institute or foundation operates independently with its own staff and board. However, all are "committed to certain common goals, such as the rule of law, a democratically elected government, a vigorous, diverse civil society, respect for minorities, and a free market economy."

The national foundations establish programs and support projects based on their own local board and staff preferences. There is also, however, a series of Soros Foundations Network programs that are carried out across a region, or in several countries simulta- neously. These projects are managed either from the Open Society Institute– New York or the Open Society Institute –Budapest. A page at the Soros Web site lists all the network programs and provides e-mail addresses for persons involved with each of them. It also gives the office addresses and telephone numbers for each of the national Soros foundations: www.soros.org/minidir.html

The names of the network programs indicates the breadth of the Soros Foundations' concerns. The following Network Programs are administered by the OSI-Budapest office:
- Constitutional and Legal Policy Institute
- Higher Education Support Program
- Local Government and Public Service Reform Initiative
- Network Library Program
- Network Media Program
- Network Publishing Center
- Network Roma Participation Program

## Organization Promoting Everlasting Neighbors (O.P.E.N.)

P.O. Box 253
1109 E. 16th Street S.
Newton, IA  50208
**Tel:**      (515) 792-6049
**Fax:**      (515) 791-1236
**E-mail:**   open@pcpartner.net
**Web:**      www.midiowa.com/newton-sister-city
**Contact:**  Jane Ann Cotton, Chair

O.P.E.N is a sister-city organization for Newton, Iowa, but—apart from $1,000 in seed money received when it organized in 1991—it is independent from the city government. Between 1995–97 the organization brought about 10 high school students from Smila, Ukraine. The organization pays for the students' insurance and finds home stays for them.

There have been three humanitarian aid programs that include taking "CARE" packages to Smila. Newton sent $240,000 of medical equipment and supplies and a delegation to assist in setting up the equipment. This included bringing a physician from

Ukraine to Iowa. O.P.E.N invited Dr. Valentina Zirnyk to visit their hospital in Newton; the University of Iowa Medical School in Iowa City, Iowa; and Blank Children's Hospital in Des Moines.

O.P.E.N also brought the Verbena trio (a famous group of Bandura players from Cherkassy) to the U.S. The three-woman trio performed in several venues, including the state capitol in Des Moines, and spoke to the Iowa legislature. There was also an exchange of artists—a Ukrainian graphic artist and his high school art programs came to Iowa, and an Iowa artist had three one-man shows in Kiev, Cherkassy, and Smila.

In late 1998 a delegation took clothing to an orphanage, including $1,200 in assistance to the regional hospital in the form of sheets (300) and medicines. They also left $5,300 for the orphanage's use.

O.P.E.N has hosted the governor of Cherkassy *oblast* and his delegation as well as business, education, govern-ment and legal interns from Ukraine. Iowa has a Sister State relationship with Cherkassy *oblast* in Ukraine.

## Overseas Medical Aid Group

P.O. Box 14341
Tampa, FL 33690-4341
**Tel:** (813) 417-2290
**Fax:** (813) 839-0557
**E-mail:** omag@bandit.net, docdonald@worldnet.att.net
**Web:** www.omaghq.com
**Contact:** Dr. Donald Houston
President and Medical Director

OMAG is dedicated to the "restoration, re-building, and the upgrading of the integrated medical and healthcare delivery systems of the republics of the former Soviet Union" and other countries that were part of the old Soviet bloc. It works with the ministries of health, institutes of medicine, hospitals, polyclinics, organizations, and medical-health professionals to develop seminars, conferences and workshops, continuing education, public education programs, and a wide range of other programs.

The keystone to assisting is the joint-partnership program, OMAG believes. After learning of a need or needs, the organization meets with the people involved in the relevant country, performs a needs assessment, delineates projects, and locates the Western joint-partner or partners to accomplish the goals and fulfill the needs of the project.

OMAG is based in Kyiv and has offices in Tampa, St. Petersburg (Russia), Tallinn, Almaty, and Vladivostok. It is active in every country of the former USSR and several others in the Balkans area. OMAG offers various opportunities for medical professionals to serve in the countries where it is active.

## Pacific Environment and Resource Center

1055 Fort Cronkhite
Sausalito, CA 94965
**Tel:** (415) 332-8200
**Fax:** (415) 332-8167
**E-mail:** perc@igc.apc.org
**Web:** www.pacenv.org
**Contact:** David Gordon, President

PERC is a policy research, public education, and advocacy organization that seeks to "protect biodiversity around the Northern Pacific Rim through the empowerment of citizens." Among recent achievements it has:

- created several new protected areas in Siberia and the Russian Far East;
- successfully halted the importation of raw logs from Russia and other

countries which posed a severe threat of pest invasion;
- successfully implemented higher environmental standards with U.S.-based international lending institutions;
- conducted a variety of exchanges between Russia and the U.S. on sustainable practices in mining, fisheries, forestry, and oil drilling.

The Siberian Forests Protection Project has been working since 1991 with Russian environmentalists, forest scientists, government officials, and indigenous peoples to implement cooperative forest protection strategies that protect the Siberian taiga. PERC partner Misha Shishin in the Altai Republic won the Conde Nast Traveler Environmentalist Award.

PERC's work with Vladivostok-based Zov Taigi has been one of its most successful subprojects. According to PERC, their work together saved two biodiverse forests in Olginsky Raion (near Vladivostok) from logging, and strengthened Primorksy Region's wildlife regulations to clamp down on Siberian-tiger poaching.

Other PERC partners in Russia are the Wildlife Foundation, Khabarovsk; Magadan Center for the Environment; Sakhalin Environment Watch; Fund for the 21st Century, Altai (Barnaul); and Friends of the Siberian Forests, Krasno-yarsk.

PERC has satellite offices in Washington, DC, and Anchorage, AK, and a staff of 10.

## Partners for Democratic Change

823 Ulloa Street
San Francisco, CA  94127
**Tel:**       (415) 665-0652
**Fax:**      (415) 665-2732
**E-mail:**  info@partners-intl.org

**Web:**     www.partners-intl.org
**Contact:**  Raymond Shonholtz, President

PDC, established in 1989, claims to be one of the largest "training organizations" in Central and Eastern Europe. In a recent year it trained more than 3,000 government, civic, labor, and business leaders in conflict management and democracy-building skills. According to PDC, "Mediation, negotiation, facilitation of meetings, effective communication, and cooperative planning are components of conflict resolution." PDC's work is primarily in the countries of Central and Eastern Europe, but it has a project in Georgia.

## PATH (Program for Appropriate Technology in Health)

4 Nickerson Street
Seattle, WA  98109
**Tel:**       (206) 285-3500
**Fax:**      (206) 285-6619
**E-mail:**  hgeorges@path.org
**Web:**     www.path.org
**Contact:**  Gordon W. Perkin, M.D., President; Helen Georges, Assistant to the President

PATH's mission is to improve health, especially the health of women and children. It emphasizes improving the quality of reproductive health services and preventing and reducing the impact of widespread communicable diseases. Working in partnership with government agencies, community groups and funders, PATH finds "appropriate and innovative solutions to public health problems."

International and national health and family planning agencies, governments, foundations, corporations, and individuals support PATH's efforts. Since 1977, when PATH was founded, it has managed more than 800 health and family planning projects in 85 developing countries. Most of its work currently is in Southeast Asia, but it also has projects in Kenya and Ukraine.

The work in Ukraine currently emphasizes two areas:

- The Breast Cancer Assistance Project seeks to improve screening, diagnosis, treatment, and rehabilitation in breast cancer services. This involves training of health professionals, provision of equipment, increasing patient understanding and public awareness of breast cancer, and promoting dialogue on policies and practices.
- The Health Information Systems and Management Reform Program is working to improve the capacity of health officials to monitor and manage infectious disease prevention and control programs.

## Peter Deyneka Russian Ministries

P.O. Box 496
Wheaton, IL 60189
**Tel:** (630) 462-1739
**Fax:** (630) 690-2976
**E-mail:** rmusa@mcimail.com,
rmmoscow@mcimail.com
**Web:** www.russian-ministries.org
**Contact:** Peter Deyneka, Jr., President

Deyneka, son of a Russian immigrant, served for 17 years as head of Slavic Gospel Association before he and wife Anita founded this organization in 1992. Since then, Russian Ministries has helped train more than 1,400 national evangelists who have started more than 1,000 independent Christian churches. Headquarters in Moscow supports 24 "Evangelism and Church Planting Centers" in Belarus, Georgia, Latvia, Russia, and Ukraine. A major emphasis currently is organizing Christian summer camps for orphans.

RM works with numerous other Christian organizations active in the former Soviet Union, most of which are non-denominational.

## Petro Jacyk Educational Foundation

1260 Eglinton Avenue East
Mississauga, Ontario L4W 1K8
Canada
**Tel:** (905) 238-0467
**Fax:** (905) 625-8445
**E-mail:** pjrc@vax.library.utoronto.ca,
oiatsyk@chass.utoronto.ca
**Contact:** Oxana Iatsyk

Petro Jacyk is a Canadian businessman and philanthropist who has contributed a great deal of his wealth to support scholarship about Ukraine around the world. In 1986 the foundation was created with the following objectives: to advance Ukrainian scholarship at academic institutions in the West, to promote knowledge of Ukraine, and to foster better understanding and cooperation between Ukraine and the world community. Since Ukraine became an independent country the foundation has been actively supporting a number of educational projects there. The Petro Jacyk Resource Center at the University of Toronto is a major resource for Ukrainian studies.

## Planned Parenthood of Northern New England

51 Talcott Road
Williston, VT 05495-8116
**Tel:** (802) 878-7232
**Fax:** (802) 878-8001
**E-mail:** judyw@ppnne.org
**Contact:** Judy Wechsler, Director of The International Program

The International Program of PPNNE takes the knowledge gained from its experience throughout northern New

England and applies it globally, offering facilitation, education, and technical, medical, and managerial training to family planning professionals worldwide. Through several partnership projects with NGOs abroad, PPNNE trainers have facilitated workshops in clinical skills and management, board development, sexuality education and training, peer education, fund-raising, and marketing.

In Yaroslavl, PPNNE helped the Center for the Formation of Sexual Culture, a secondary school that provides week-long sexuality education programs to students from 20 schools, to develop a peer education program, enhance their teaching style, and increase their capacity to manage and sustain their organization. The peer education program, "From Heart to Heart," trains and supports approximately 30 teens each year. These students then staff a hotline, act as peer counselors in their schools, and create and perform teen theater in schools and other sites where young people congregate.

In Novosibirsk, PPNNE trainers have worked with ARIADNA, the women's club of FINIST, an advocacy organization for people with disabilities. With training and support from PPNNE, ARIADNA women now facilitate support and sexuality education groups for women with disabilities, provide counseling at a trauma center and a polyclinic in Novosibirsk, staff a resource center, and advocate for services for the disabled.

Also in Novosibirsk, at a World Learning conference for women NGO leaders, PPNNE facilitated an advocacy workshop where participants designed their own advocacy campaigns and developed a workbook for use in their communities.

In Ukraine, PPNNE has facilitated workshops about the importance of advocacy and fund-raising at two conferences for NGO leaders. The director of PPNNE's International Program also worked with Project Kesher to co-facilitate workshops for young women leaders on reproductive health, client-centered care, and consumer activism.

Throughout Russia, PPNNE has worked with the Russian Family Planning Association (RFPA), the International Planned Parenthood Federation affiliate in Russia. RFPA and PPNNE staff developed management systems and skills appropriate to Russia so that the six regional centers and 50 affiliates work together productively. PPNNE also assisted the six regional centers as they developed training sites and resource centers to provide contraceptive information to doctors and midwives.

## Project Harmony

6 Irasville Common
Waitsfield, VT 05673
**Tel:** (802) 496-4545
**Fax:** (802) 496-4548
**E-mail:** ph@projectharmony.org
**Web:** www.projectharmony.org
**Contact:** Jared Cadwell, Charlie Hosford, and Barbara Miller, Co-Directors

Project Harmony (PH) was founded in March 1985 by on the belief that "active citizenship and community involvement strengthen the international community." PH programs emphasize interactive projects, hands-on training and home stays in each country. In the past 13 years, PH has organized over 350 programs, including 190 secondary school exchanges between U.S. and NIS schools. Participants have included students, teachers, police officers, doctors, attorneys, ecologists, musicians, dancers, athletes, and city planners.

To date, over 5,000 American and 5,000 NIS participants have taken part in Project Harmony programs. The organization has a community volunteer network of over 1,000 individuals throughout the U.S.

Current programs include:

- *Community Connections.* This program provides training and internship opportunities for professionals from Russia, Ukraine, Georgia and Moldova at sites in Vermont, Maine, and Massachusetts. For the 1998–99 program, Project Harmony recruited 345 professional and business participants from across Ukraine.
- *Law Enforcement Exchange Programs (LEEP).* Since 1995, PH has managed training and education programs for police, law enforcement officials, and criminal justice experts from the United States and the NIS. With funding from the U.S. State Department, the LEEP program includes four components: Law Enforcement Exchange Programs, Criminal Justice University Partnerships, Fellowship and Internship Programs, and a Professional Development Workshop Series.
- *Domestic Violence Community Partnership Program.* This program has enlisted teams of American specialists to train NIS organizations and professionals in the fields of law enforcement, health care, education, legal advocacy, and social services in techniques used to combat domestic violence through a train-the-trainers component. It has established a Victim Support Network and Resource Center to provide outreach and counseling for victims and their families within the target NIS

communities (Petrozavodsk and Volgograd in Russia and Lviv and Odessa in Ukraine).

- *Baikal Women's Leadership Program.* This program works with women's groups served by the Angara Women's Union in Irkutsk and the Women's Union of Buryatia in Ulan-Ude to provide them with the leadership skills and resources needed to access government, shape policy, and assume decision-making positions in the emerging democratic system.
- *Internet School Linkage Program (ISLP).* The ISLP, supported by the Soros Open Society Institute, applies telecommunications technology to new and existing partnerships between secondary schools in the U.S. and NIS. Teachers and students use the Internet to communicate with partners via electronic mail and use on-line resources to conduct joint educational projects. The ISLP network has grown to include approximately 250 schools from 10 countries around the world.
- *Project Harmony Academic Study Term.* Since 1994, with funding from USIA, Project Harmony has brought 325 students from remote areas of Russia, Ukraine, Belarus, and Georgia to the U.S. to live with American families and study for one academic semester.
- *Teacher Intern Program.* This program offers an opportunity for recent college graduates and experienced educators to teach English in Russia and Ukraine. PH arranges the teaching positions at one of its partner schools or organizations for six months or a full academic year. Since 1992, 35 interns have been placed.
- *School Linkage Program.* This program has grown from three school

pairings in 1989 to more than 75 in 1997–98.

PH offers a variety of other exchange programs oriented to university students, high school students and teachers. Staff size is 38, including 14 Russian-speaking Americans and 9 English-speaking Russian and Ukrainian nationals. Grant funding to the organization in the period 1995–98 totaled approximately $12 million.

## Project HOPE
Health Sciences Education Center
Carter Hall
Millwood, VA  22646
**Tel:**      (703) 837-2100,
              (800) 544-4673
**Fax:**      (703) 837-1813
**Web:**      www.projhope.org

Project HOPE was established in 1958 to bring improved medical care to developing areas of the world. It is best known for its hospital ship SS *HOPE* which sailed around the world from 1960 to 1974.

In 1989, the Russian medical staff at Moscow Children's Hospital No. 9 expected children with burns on more than 30 percent of their bodies to die. Today, trained by Project HOPE in the latest burn treatment skills and basic infection control practices, they have reduced the mortality rate by 29 percent and are now saving children with burns on 65 percent of their bodies. In the past five years, over 8,000 children have been treated at the hospital's burn unit and more than 400 Russian medical professionals, from throughout the Russian Republic have received formal training. The burn unit has become the principal referral center for severely burned children from not only Russia but Ukraine, the Caucasus, the Far North, Siberia, and Central Asia. Since 1994 HOPE has also expanded its educational efforts at Children's Hospital No. 9 to include rehabilitation therapy to combat the effects of scarring so common to burn victims.

In 1995, the Dean of the Faculty of Basic Medicine at Moscow State University invited Project HOPE to assist in strengthening the medical school and facilitate medical education reforms. To date, Project HOPE has donated more than 11,000 volumes of modern medical textbooks. It has also recruited a voluntary faculty of approximately 20 physicians and allied health professionals presently working in Western medical facilities in Moscow. These volunteers have agreed to give lectures and/or act as preceptors for Moscow State students undertaking clinical training at these Western facilities. Another American volunteer is providing an English language course for the medical school students, to enable them to communicate on a professional level with their colleagues around the world. Within the Dean's Council itself, Project HOPE's Medical Education Advisor has initiated a series of discussions and seminars on developments in medical education, as well as an introductory management course. These activities will enhance the organization and management of the medical school as a whole.

Project HOPE has signed an agreement with the Russian Ministry of Education to implement a substance abuse prevention program in Russian primary schools.

In Ukraine, Project HOPE has implemented a tuberculosis diagnosis and treatment program in Odessa, which has TB rates five times as high as the U.S. The goal is to identify and treat 400 TB patients in a year and demonstrate the effectiveness of new therapies.

In Georgia, Project HOPE offers maternal and child health consultancy services to the government.

## Project Kesher
1134 Judson Avenue
Evanston, IL 60202
**Tel:**      (708) 332-1994
**Fax:**     (708) 332-2134
**E-mail:** projectkesher@compuserve.com
**Web:**    ourworld.compuserve.com/homepages/projectkesher
**Contact:** Sallie Gratch, President; Karyn Gershon, Executive Director

Project Kesher was founded in 1989 by Sallie Gratch after she met Svetlana Yakimenko while participating in a peace walk from Leningrad to Moscow. Svetlana helped Sallie realize the need for grassroots training among women in the former Soviet Union as well as the need for a renewed Jewish presence. Over the next few years, Sallie spent a great amount of time in the NIS and further developed the vision of Project Kesher to unite women at a global level.

In 1994 Project Kesher organized the International Conference of Jewish Women in Kyiv, Ukraine. The conference brought together 300 Jewish women from around the world to support Jewish women in the NIS. Since that conference the Kesher network in the NIS has grown to over 1,500 women in 124 locations throughout Russia, Belarus, Ukraine, and Moldova.

Project Kesher has led 17 women's exchanges in the NIS. During these exchanges, Western delegates travel to the NIS and lead workshops on community organizing, women's health care issues, democratic group process, and Judaism. The emphasis is not on teaching facts but on teaching skills. Because of this, the NIS participants

are able to return to their communities and lead similar programs for other women. There are 45 local Project Kesher groups in the NIS that meet to develop Jewish, humanitarian, and women's programs.

Project Kesher is currently focusing on the development of grassroots leadership in Belarus, Moldova, Russia, and Ukraine. Project Kesher's American operations are based in Evanston, Illinois. Its NIS operations are directed from Povarovka, Russia (a suburb of Moscow), and Cherkassy, Ukraine.

## Québec Institute for International Research and Education (QIIRE)
455-3680 Rue Jeanne Mance
Montreal, Québec H2X 2K5
**Tel:**      (514) 982-6606
**Fax:**     (514) 982-6122
**Contact:** Robert David, Coordinator

QIIRE has developed programs in Russia that aim to strengthen the labor movement through training programs for labor educators and union members.

## REAP International
1427 4th Street, SW
Cedar Rapids, IA 52404
**Tel:**      (319) 366-4230
**Fax:**     (319) 366-2209
**E-mail:** reap@reapintl.com
**Contact:** William Mueller, Director

The Rural Enterprise Adaptation Program International (REAP) grew out of a program to aid private farmers in Latvia. Since its inception in 1992, REAP International has worked with local partners in Russia (Moscow, Irkutsk, and Ulan-Ude), Latvia, and Lithuania. The mission of REAP is to promote diversification and sustainability among rural populations. REAP has administered in excess of $1 million in grants from USIA, USAID, Eurasia, SABIT, Soros, International Foundation, and Academy of Educational Development. REAP was registered as a tax-exempt nonprofit organization in March 1993.

The strategy is a two-tier system with REAP as administrative and service provider; foreign national NGOs are partners and operants of the strategy at the local level. The partnerships have conducted training, information distribution, exchanges, and internships, and established demonstrations and development projects.

The current emphasis is on rural schools, and the theme is "The Rural School as Center for Sustainable Development of the Village." The goal is to use multiple resources in schools so they can better serve their communities. This includes school-to-school linkages with strong agriculturally oriented American schools, establishment of micro-enterprises in schools, volunteers and service organizations for business consultation, youth organizing, adult training, assistance with civic leadership, distance learning, and new information. Most of this work has been conducted in Buryatia at Lake Baikal.

REAP operates a for-profit limited liability company, Rural Enterprises International, LC, which engages in export-import and tourism. Rural Enterprises was established to better serve the target populations where it already operates. Rural Enterprises provides countertrade opportunities to clients for sales of their goods in the U.S.

REAP welcomes volunteers and collaboration with other NGOs also interested in rural stabilization.

## The Rule of Law Foundation

1001 G Street, NW, Suite 250
Washington, DC 20530
**Tel:** (202) 307-0511
**Fax:** (202) 307-2217
**E-mail:** chapkey@rol.org
**Web:** www.justinfo.net
**Contact:** Sergey Chapkey, President and CEO; Charlie Cochran, Vice President for Programs

The Rule of Law Foundation was established in January 1996 to promote the rule of law in the NIS and other emerging democracies using new technologies, primarily the Internet, to facilitate communications among legal professionals worldwide. The foundation's primary accomplishments in 1996 and 1997 were the establishment of the United Nations Online Crime and Justice Clearinghouse (UNOJUST) and the creation of an online database of crime- and justice-related Web sites through the Rule of Law Online project. This received support from the National Institute of Justice of the U.S. Department of Justice, and the Bureau for International Narcotics and Law Enforcement Affairs of the U.S. Department of State.

In July 1998 the Rule of Law Foundation brought the World Justice Information Network, or JUSTINFO. NET, online as an Internet-based system for sharing open source information on crime, justice, and the rule of law among policy makers, executives, criminal justice and law enforcement officials, international organizations, researchers and other academics, students, civic activists, journalists, and concerned citizens worldwide. It is designed to be a truly independent, global research forum operated by representatives of the international community.

The Rule of Law Foundation is currently managing the content acquisition process for the World Justice Information Network in co-operation with the National Institute of Justice. In addition, with the support of the Bureau for International Narcotics Affairs of the U.S. Department of State, we are establishing Internet Studios at criminal justice-related sites in Ukraine.

The foundation currently has four permanent staff members, and received grants in 1998 totaling over $500,000. Partnerships overseas include the Rule of Law Foundation, Kyiv, Ukraine; the Suprematia Legii Foundation, Chisinau, Moldova; and the Scientific Center for Legal Information, Moscow, Russia.

### Rural Development Institute

4746 11th Avenue NE, #504
Seattle, WA 98105
**Tel:**     (206) 528-5880
**Fax:**    (206) 528-5881
**E-mail:** rdi@u.washington.edu
**Web:**   www.law.washington.edu/rdi
**Contact:** Roy L. Prosterman, President;
Tim Hanstad, Executive Director

RDI was founded in 1981 by Roy Prosterman, a professor of law at the University of Washington. Its mission is to "design and promote needed land reform measures that will alleviate rural poverty and develop the rural econo my." The organization has decades of experience in 29 nations around the world.

RDI's current activities in the NIS center on Russia, the Kyrgyz Republic, and Moldova. Recent accomplishments include:

- Working with federal and regional Russian policymakers on legislation establishing and protecting citizens' right to own, use, and transfer agricultural land
- Establishment and management of legal aid centers in the Russian provinces of Vladimir and Samara, which aid farmers and rural citizens in exercising their land rights
- Providing ongoing advice to senior officials in the Kyrgyz government on key issues of agricultural land re-form, such as the draft basic law on land and procedures for land auctions
- Providing legal advice to a USAID-financed project in Moldova, which has distributed land ownership certificates to more than 65,000 Moldovan citizens who formerly worked on collective farms

RDI's staff consists of 15 lawyers and administrative personnel. It has an office in Moscow and a lawyer station-ed in Chisinau. The organization works closely with the Centers for Land Re-form Support in Vladimir and Samara. Support for RDI's work comes from private individuals, foundations, and international donor organizations such as USAID.

### Russia and West Virginia: A Partnership for Exchange Foundation, Inc.

2106 Kanawha Boulevard East,
Unit B-217
Charleston, WV 25311
**Tel:**     (304) 558-0160
**Fax:**    (304) 558-0048
**E-mail:** vsimmons@access.k12.wv.us
**Web:**   www.friends-partners.org/
~ericd/index.htm
**Contact:** Virginia Simmons, Ph.D.,
President

The foundation was created in 1993 when it brought the Presidential Orchestra of the Russian Federation to West Virginia and then to the Kennedy Center in Washington, DC. Most of the exchange activity has been with the city of Korolev, which has a sister-city relationship with Charleston. Korolev, named after the "father of the aerospace industry" in Russia, is about 15 miles northeast of Moscow. It is home to Russian Mission Control, which gave one group of students and teachers from West Virginia the opportunity to talk live to the cosmonauts on the space station Mir. (Many of Russia's famous cosmonauts are now considered "best friends" in West Virginia.)

Eight Russian students attend West Virginia institutions of higher education because of the foundation. Two students are part of a special scholarship program at Fairmont State College called "Aerospace Scholars." This allows top Russian students and top West Virginia students to study and learn together in the fields of aerospace technology.

The Russia School in America program actually lifted part of a school in Russia—students and teachers—and placed them at West Virginia State College for a semester. There they continued their Russian studies with computers, American culture, and ESL as part of their curriculum. The students stayed in American homes for the weekends and were immersed in the culture. The Russia School in America will return for another semester of learning in West Virginia in 1999.

Teachers from Ft. Gay Elementary School visited Russia and met with Russian teachers. They intend to take their students to Russia in 1999.

The organization has a mailing list of 2,000 and has involved 16 states in its exchange activities. Their main contact in Korolev is Alexey Tcheremnykh. There are six West Virginia directors and four Russian directors on the foundation's board.

## Russian Children's Welfare Society
200 Park Avenue South, Suite 1617
New York, NY 10003

**Tel:** (212) 473-6263
**Fax:** (212) 473-6301
**E-mail:** main@rcws.org
**Web:** www.rcws.org
**Contact:** Jennifer J. Kaplan, Executive Director

RCWS was founded in 1926 by Russian immigrants. The organization's mission is to provide financial aid and other help to needy Russian children in the United States, South America, Europe, and other regions throughout the world. RCWS also gives grants to organizations working with children in Russia, such as schools, orphanages, summer camps, and hospitals. Financial aid and grants are monitored by volunteer representatives from around the world.

## Russian Medical Fund
1862 Brothers Road
Vienna, VA 22182
**Tel:** (703) 255-0827
**Fax:** (703) 255-0682
**E-mail:** mcintosh@mida.com
**Contact:** Susan G. McIntosh

The Russian Medical Fund was started in 1997 with the goal of "reducing mortality and morbidity in Russia and the newly independent states." The fund provides medical equipment and supplies and medical education and training. It also promotes public health research. St. Petersburg is the current focus of its activities. Its annual budget is around $200,000.

## Sabre Foundation
872 Massachusetts Avenue, Suite 2-1
Cambridge, MA 02139
**Tel:** (617) 868-3510
**Fax:** (617) 868-7916
**E-mail:** sabre@sabre.org
**Web:** www.sabre.org
**Contact:** Tania Vitvitsky, Director

Sabre Foundation was established in 1969 by a small group of Americans interested in the philosophy and practice of free institutions. During its first 15 years, the foundation engaged in a variety of public policy projects.

In the late 1970s, one of Sabre's projects generated requests for new English-language reference books and texts from researchers, teachers, students, physicians and other professionals in Poland who had no access to hard currency. Thus was born the Scientific Assistance Project, deriving its name from the common Eastern European use of "science" to refer to any disciplined branch of knowledge. Launched experimentally in Poland and Hungary in 1985–1987, the project had, by the end of 1997, received 3 million books from some 200 donating publishers, with an appraised value of $85 million, for distribution in 52 countries —many of them in the former Soviet bloc.

Through the Library and Information Technology Services (LITS) project, Sabre provides training in Internet and related information technologies to people from transitioning countries and works on library development overseas. In 1997, Sabre's reference librarian conducted a detailed assessment of the computer and library needs at a secondary school in Ukraine. In 1998, Sabre opened its own computer lab at its headquarters in Cambridge, MA.

Sabre's Information Technology Seminars program, which provides training in the Internet and related information technologies to people from transitioning countries, is growing. The content and materials of the seminars are customized to the backgrounds and goals of each trainee. Sabre's computer lab is available for hands-on training of individuals and groups.

## The Sacred Earth Network

267 East Street
Petersham, MA 01366
**Tel:** (978) 724-3443
**Fax:** (978) 724-3436
**E-mail:** sacredearth@igc.apc.org
**Web:** www.igc.apc.org/sen/
**Contact:** Bill Pfeiffer, Executive Director

Bill Pfeiffer founded SEN in 1985 to help people he had met in the then-USSR working against difficult odds on various environmental issues. Fundraising through the network, Pfeiffer began supplying activists with computers and modems. Since then, SEN has played a major role in the creation of a computer network of environmentalists spanning over 100 cities in 14 of the 15 former Soviet republics.

Through its Environmental Telecommunications Project (ETP), SEN has provided equipment and training that have directly enabled more than 150 Eurasian environmental groups to communicate via electronic mail.

Once the e-mail connection is in place, SEN also provides information and professional exchanges to strengthen organizations' contacts with similar groups operating regionally, nationally, and internationally.

The Toxic Monitoring Network was started by the U.S. environmental organization ECOLOGIA, which has been able to coordinate its activities and create a database of toxins in Eurasia via the e-mail network put in place by the ETP.

In 1998 SEN published the fifth edition of its *Directory of Environmental Electronic Mail Users in Northern Eurasia*. The *Directory* lists 875 environmental e-mail stations in 15 nations and has maps showing their locations. The directory profiles scores of ecological groups and lists over 300 e-mail users and their addresses. For more information on the *Directory*, including prices, see Resources.

## Save the Children Federation
54 Wilton Road
Westport, CT  06880
**Tel:**      (203) 221-4000
**Fax:**     (203) 221-3799
**E-mail:**  kpecceri@savechildren.org
**Web:**     www.savethechildren.org
**Contact:** Kate Peccerillo, Administrative Assistant for the NIS

SC administered the $30-million Russian Civic Initiatives for Democratic and Economic Reform Program between 1994 and 1998. This resulted in the creation of NGO resource centers in six regions of Russia; 1,200 "trainings" on NGO management, "social marketing," and computer skills; more than 10 publications on the NGO sector in Russia; increased local government-NGO collaboration in the regions; and "dramatically increased" media coverage of NGO activities.

Today SC's involvement centers on the Caucasus region. In Nagorno-Karabakh it is administering a humanitarian relief initiative focused on housing, health, and income-generating projects. It is carrying out similar humanitarian relief activities in Azerbaijan, with the added element of AzerWeb, an e-mail network linking 40 relief agencies working in Azerbaijan.

In Georgia, SC started a UNHCR-funded "group-guaranteed lending and savings" (GGLS) program. Working with a local NGO named Constanta, SC had created 64 lending groups by the end of 1997 and made 585 loans—with a 100 percent on time repayment rate.

This program has since expanded to other urban centers in Georgia.

## Search for Common Ground
1601 Connecticut Avenue, NW,
Suite 200
Washington, DC  20009
**Tel:**      (202) 265-4300
**Fax:**     (202) 232-6718
**E-mail:**  ghuebner@sfcg.org
**Web:**     www.sfcg.org
**Contact:** John Marks, President;
Gillian Huebner, Project Coordinator

Search for Common Ground (SCG) believes that "conflict resolution can have a transformative impact on a country." The organization has carried out its work in several regions of the world and maintains a European office in Brussels. The organization's Ukrainian Mediation Group (UMG) has regional centers in Donetsk, Kharkiv, Kyiv, Lugansk, Odessa, and Crimea. The UMG's mission is to promote mediation and dispute resolution in Ukraine and, in the process, strengthen civil society and democratic reform. Major activities include:

- A training program to certify conflict resolution specialists. Graduates mediate labor, family, commercial, and consumer disputes. In 1997, the training program involved nearly 100 participants including judges, lawyers, psychologists, teachers, and students.
- Promoting alternative dispute resolution in the legal system. The UMG has been working with a core of Ukrainian judges who understand mediation and are outsourcing cases to UMG mediators. In Donetsk and Odessa, UMG mediators have established a presence in the district courts and have gained the support of local judges.

- Conflict resolution in enterprise restructuring. The UMG has worked to provide consulting services for enterprises in various stages of the privatization process.
- Conflict and the mass media. The UMG has carried out programs designed to encourage media operators to consider the range of ways in which television, newspapers, and radio can "affect and change conflict situations."
- Dialogue on Crimea. The Crimea is threatened by tensions among various national and ethnic groups, notably Russians, Ukrainians and the recently returned Crimean Tatars. With two mediation centers in Crimea, the UMG is planning to build an intergroup dialogue between civil society leaders representing each of the ethnic groups.

## Serendipity: Russian Consulting and Development

1403 Kingsridge Drive
Normal, IL 61761
**Tel:** (309) 454-2364
**Fax:** (309) 452 6332
**E-mail:** ruskii_dom@msn.com,
73123.3543@compuserve.com,
a_home@met vpti.vladimir.ru.
(Vladimir e-mail)
**Web:** www.serendipity-russia.com/default.html
**Contact:** Dr. Ronald Pope, President

With a team of Russian and American volunteers, Ronald Pope, a professor of political science at Illinois State University (ISU) in Bloomington-Normal, constructed a ranch-style American home in the center of Vladimir during the summer of 1992. The following year a local newspaper, *Molva*, paid tribute to the *Amerikanskii Dom* project in an editorial titled, "The American Home Has Stood for a Year and Not

Collapsed." *Molva* called special attention to the Serendipity attitude: "to complete in Russia small but concrete projects. The professor's motto: It isn't necessary to wait until everything here is in order—we need to work now."

Since 1992 Serendipity has spawned a number of creative, ongoing programs, including some small businesses.

- *American English Program.* The program, initiated in 1992, remains in strong demand in Vladimir. (Enrollment is 250 and there is a long waiting list.) It offers English classes from native speakers—usually recent college grads. Serendipity hires several teachers every year, typically for an eight-month period. Teachers pay their own air fare and some incidentals, but expenses in Russia are covered by the program.
- *Cultural and professional exchanges.* Photographers, police officers, art gallery curators, Girl Scouts, high school students—these are some of the participants in a rich pattern of ongoing citizen exchanges that Serendipity has catalyzed.
- *Remodeling business.* This offshoot of the American Home building project has become a very professional business which will soon add new construction (home and office) to its capabilities.
- *Tour business.* Serendipity has organized local stays for several groups, prepared a Visitor's Guide to Vladimir, and seeks to expand this business.
- *Small business, trade, and investment.* Serendipity has found wholesale outlets for small businesses in Vladimir and consulted with companies examining investment opportunities in the region. (A good hotel for out-of-town business people is one such need.)

## Sister Cities International
1300 Pennsylvania Avenue, NW,
Suite 250
Washington, DC 20004
**Tel:**      (202) 312-1200
**Fax:**      (202) 312-1201
**E-mail:**   rfrye@sister-cities.org
**Web:**      www.sister-cities.org/
**Contact:**  Juanita M. Crabb, Executive
Director; Roma Frye, Executive
Assistant

SCI is the coordinating body for more
than 1,000 U.S. communities that are
paired with nearly 2,000 partner cities
around the world. There are more than
150 U.S.-NIS sister-city relationships.
SCI operates two listservs, scilist-
announce@sci.sister-cities.org, scilist-
general@sci.sister-cities.org.

## Sister Schools International, Inc.
3422 NW 187 Street
Miami, FL 33056
**Tel:**      (305) 621-5681, ext. 332
**Fax:**      (305) 624-9317
**E-mail**:   WINFREF@mail.firn.edu
**Web:**      schools.techno.ru/sch1269/
index.htm
**Contact:**  Dr. Fran Winfrey, Project
Director

SSI has paired more than 100 schools
to date, some of them through e-mail.
The current focus is on school pairings
between Florida and Russia, Belarus,
and Azerbaijan.  In Russia, the Sister
Schools Coordinator is Natalya
Dmitrieva, whose e-mail address is
<natalya@school.aie.msk.su> and
whose telephone number in Moscow is
7 (095) 368-57-25.

   In Belarus, the Sister Schools Coordinator is Svetlana Mischenko, telephone number 375 (172) 36-60-54. The
project's partner in the NIS is the International Movement of Educators for

Peace and Understanding, headed by
Dr. Mikhail Kabbatchenko.

## Small Business and Economic Development Project
Confederation College of Applied Arts
and Technology
P.O. Box 398
Thunder Bay, Ontario P7C 4W1
Canada
**Tel:**      (807) 473-3751
**Fax:**      (807) 623-9165
**Contact:**  Don Domansky, Project
Director

A consortium of Canadian institutions
is working to support growth of small
businesses in the Ivano-Frankivsk
region of Ukraine through an entrepre-
neurial training program and a small-
business loan fund. (See program
description under Ivano-Frankivsk in
Ukraine section.) The consortium of
Canadian institutions is led by Confederation College. Other consortium
members include the School of Urban
and Regional Planning of the University of Waterloo, the Centre for Second
Language Instruction of the University
of Saskatchewan, and the Parkland
Community Futures Corporation of
Manitoba. The city and *oblast* governments of Ivano-Frankivsk and a local
financial institution are the principal
Ukranian partners.

## Special Olympics International
1350 New York Avenue, NW,
Suite 500
Washington, DC 20005
**Tel:**      (202) 628-5431
**Fax:**      (202) 628-0068
**Contact:**  Gregory S. Rehkopf,
Director, Eastern European and
Eurasian Programs

Special Olympics International (SOI)
was founded in 1968 by Eunice Ken-

nedy Shriver to support the creation and expansion of sports programs for individuals with mental retardation by providing year-round training and competition opportunities. The organization estimates that 156 million people, or 3 percent of the world's population, are mentally retarded, and that about 87 percent of this number are affected with mild retardation.

Soviet Special Olympics was established in 1989 and during its first two years trained more than 400 coaches from throughout the Soviet Union. Costs for the training seminars were covered entirely by proceeds from the sale of "A Very Special Christmas," a record created through donated services of singers, musicians, and producers. In July 1992, Special Olympics–Eurasia was legally recognized by 12 former Soviet republics. Later that year, 125 athletes participated in the first Eurasian Winter Special Olympic Games in Petrozavodsk, Russia. Today SOI has offices in all of the new independent states.

### Street Law, Inc.

918 16th Street, NW, Suite 602
Washington, DC 20006
**Tel:** (202) 293 0088
**Fax:** (202) 293-0089
**E-mail:** korenstein@streetlaw.org
**Web:** www.streetlaw.org
**Contact:** Edward L. O'Brien, Executive Director; Karen Orenstein, Administrative Assistant, International Programs

Street Law (formerly the National Institute for Citizen Education in the Law) began in the District of Columbia public schools in 1972, in response to what some Georgetown University students and law professors saw as a need in the community: knowledge about practical law. They began designing and teaching lessons in District of Columbia high schools to inform students about how the law works and how to protect their legal rights.

Over the past 27 years, Street Law's programs have spread across the U.S. and to more than 30 countries. The content of their programs has also broadened to include human rights, democracy, and conflict resolution.

All of Street Law's programs are designed by local educators, lawyers, and human rights activists and reflect each country's unique laws and culture. In Eastern and Central Europe and Central Asia, the organization is partnering with the Soros Foundation in the formation of the Open Society Institute Street Law Network Program, which involves 14 countries in those regions.

This program provides expertise in the fields of teacher training, program design, curriculum development, and evaluation of law instruction, human rights, and democracy in schools and community settings. Emphasis is placed on interactive methodologies and the organization of special events (such as mock trial competitions and youth summits).

This project collaborates with the Constitutional Legal Policy Institute (COLPI) in Hungary. (COLPI supports the development of legal clinics as well as conferences, training seminars, and technical assistance for law school projects that create clinics for law students to teach Street Law in secondary schools.) In Russia, Street Law, works with the St. Petersburg School of Law.

Street Law publications, some of which have been translated into other languages, include:
- *Law in Your Life* (1998)
- *Teens, Crime and the Community* (3rd ed., 1998)

- *Human Rights for All* (South African version, 1991; U.S. version, 1995)
- *Street Law: A Course in Practical Law* (5th ed., 1994)
- *Democracy for All* (1994)
- *We Can Work It Out! Problem Solving through Mediation* (1993)
- *When Justice Is Up to You* (1992)
- Street Law staff consists of 25 educators, lawyers, and administrators. Total expenditures in a recent year were $1.6 million.

## Theodosian Ministries
30 Old Orchard Lane
Princeton, NJ 08540
**Tel:** (609) 921-8068
**Fax:** (609) 921-8298
**E-mail:** Teriwebb@aol.com
**Web:** crc.iugm.org/theod.html
**Contact:** Mary Webb

Theodosian Ministries develops and supports indigenous Christian leadership abroad in alcohol and other drug addiction treatment, encouraging community-based prevention and 12-step recovery. It has supported two Orthodox Temperance Fellowships and is supporting the OPORA Program in Moscow. It provides small grants for humanitarian aid and organizes mission trips.

Theodosian Ministries is also active in the training of addiction professionals and clergy in Russia and the U.S. It publishes a newsletter, *The Legacy*, twice a year.

## Tolstoy Foundation, Inc.
104 Lake Road
Valley Cottage, NY 10989
**Tel:** (914) 268-6722
**Fax:** (914) 268-6937
**E-mail:** thfq@aol.com
**Web:** www.tolstoyfoundation.com
**Contact:** Xenia Woyevodsky, Executive Director

The Tolstoy Foundation (TF) was founded and incorporated in New York in 1939 by Alexandra Tolstoy, daughter of Leo Tolstoy. The foundation's original purpose was to assist Russian refugees fleeing Communism to resettle in North and South America and Europe. In fact, it has assisted in resettling over 100,000 refugees, including Afghans, Armenians, Bulgarians, Cambodians, Circassians, Czechs, Ethiopians, Hungarians, Iranians, Iraqis, Laotians, Poles, Rumanians, Tibetans, and Ugandans.

TF extended its operations into Russia and the NIS in 1992. It has provided financial and social assistance to the elderly and others who have been hurt in the economic restructuring in Russia. It also provided medical treatment for children from the NIS.

The Alexandra Tolstoy Alliance for Continuing Education works with the Community Health Plan (CHP), a not-for-profit health maintenance organization with headquarters in Albany, N.Y. In 1996 in Tula, Albany's Russian sister city, CHP helped to inaugurate Russia's first Health Maintenance Organization and has been instrumental in organizing the exchange and the training of Tulan physicians in primary and specialty care at its health centers in upstate New York. (The Tula region is the birthplace and family home of Alexandra Tolstoy.)

The new training program is improving physicians' technical and practical skills in areas that are immediately adaptable and relevant to their home environment. The initial focus is on women's health, advanced primary care, public health and health management, education (English-language immersion courses) and gerontology—an area in which the Tolstoy Foundation, with its many years of experience working with the elderly, can play a significant role.

Each course—a combination of seminars and practical training—instructs 20 physicians and runs for six weeks. Each aspect of the course is taught by qualified professionals from New York medical schools and hospitals. The visitors are housed at the CHP International Programs headquarters in Albany and at the Tolstoy Foundation Center in Valley Cottage, NY. The goal of the project is a partnership with the ministries and the universities of the participating countries, which eventually can become self-supporting. For the first year, however, because of economic hardship in the NIS, the participating countries provided only transportation costs for the visiting physicians.

## Ukrainian American Bar Association

4 Avon Court
Chatham, NJ 07928-1765
**Tel:** (888) 822-2529
**E-mail:** BohdannaP@aol.com
**Web:** www.brama.com/uaba
**Contact:** Donna Pochoday, President

Founded in 1977, the Ukrainian American Bar Association (UABA) is composed of several hundred American lawyers of Ukrainian heritage. In the past the UABA focused on human rights issues in Ukraine. More recently it has worked to support the development of the rule of law in Ukraine, especially in the areas of economics and business. With its many contacts in Ukraine, UABA is a good resource for American attorneys interested in volunteering their services in Ukraine.

On occasion the UABA has provided technical assistance to the Verchovna Rada (the parliament of Ukraine) on matters of legal reform.

The fourth world congress of Ukrainian lawyers was held in Lviv in September 1998, and the UABA was allocated a quota of 20 delegates; Canada's quota was 30!

## Ukrainian Canadian Congress

456 Main Street
Winnipeg, Manitoba R3B 1B6 Canada
**Tel:** (204) 942-4627
**Fax:** (204) 947-3882
**Contact:** Oleh Romaniw, President

This is the major organization of Ukrainian-Canadian citizens and it plays an important role in networking people at both ends of exchanges with technical assistance projects in Ukraine.

## Ukrainian National Association

30 Montgomery Street
Jersey City, NJ 07302
**Tel:** (201) 451-2200
**Fax:** (201) 451-2093
**Contact:** Prof. Zirka Voronka, Director

For more than 100 years the Ukrainian National Association (UNA) has served the needs of Ukrainian-Americans in the U.S. Its newspapers, *Svoboda*, the longest running Ukrainian daily in the world, and *The Ukrainian Weekly* contain news of activities in the Ukrainian-American community, and are among the best sources of information in English on the current situation in Ukraine.

In the summer of 1992, the UNA, under the direction of Prof. Voronka, launched its Teaching English in Ukraine program. Over the next four years, more than 300 volunteer teachers from the United States, Canada, Europe, and Africa taught over 4,000 students in more than 80 cities throughout Ukraine. The UNA supplies the textbooks and teaching materials.

UNA invites volunteers with teaching experience or a very high aptitude for teaching. Experience in teaching English as second language is preferred. Volunteers should expect difficult living conditions and be in good physical health. Some knowledge of Ukrainian is helpful but not required.

## Ukrainian Student Association in the USA (USA/USA)
P.O. Box 250093
Columbia University Station
New York, NY 10025-1531
**Tel:** (212) 475-5326
**E-mail:** usa.usa@ibm.net
**Contact:** Bohdan Oryshkevich, President

The purpose of the Ukrainian Student Association in the USA (USA/USA) is to recruit and advise a selected number of Ukrainian students who are considering pursuing an American college education. A select group of applicants who have demonstrated their scholastic and English skills are invited to attend a weeklong workshop in Kyiv. The workshop teaches them about the American educational system and helps the students prepare for the TOEFL, the SAT, and the SAT IIs. Students also receive college counseling and advice on scholarship programs.

## U.S.-Azerbaijan Council
1010 Vermont Avenue, NW, Suite 814
Washington, DC 20005
**Tel:** (202) 662-1343
**Fax:** (202) 662-1353
**E-mail:** 75403.2004@compuserve. com
**Web:** ourworld.compuserve.com/ homepages/usazerb/
**Contact:** Jayhun Mollazade, President

The U.S.-Azerbaijan Council is a non-partisan, nonprofit organization serving the development of U.S.-Azerbaijani relations. It was created in 1995. Its goal is to foster greater interest in and knowledge about Azerbaijan as well as about the whole Caspian region. It publishes a quarterly magazine, *The Caspian Crossroads*, and a biweekly newsletter, *The Caspian Business Report.* The organizations also hosts seminars and cultural events.

## U.S. Civilian Research and Development Foundation for the Independent States of the former Soviet Union
1800 North Kent Street, Suite 1106
Arlington, VA 22201
**Tel:** (703) 526-9720
**Fax:** (703) 526-9721
**E-mail:** information@crdf.org
**Web:** www.crdf.inter.net/
**Contact:** Gerson S. Sher, Ph.D., Executive Director; Charles T. Owens, Associate Director

CRDF is a private, nonprofit foundation created in August 1995 by the National Science Foundation in response to the dramatic decline of resources for science and engineering research in the former Soviet Union. The CRDF's initial endowment of $10 million derived from a $5 million contribution from the U.S. Department of Defense's Nunn-Lugar program to promote demilitarization in the FSU, and from a $5 million gift from philanthropist George Soros to the U.S. National Science Foundation.

All research activities funded by CRDF must be carried out in a civilian environment and directed toward non-defense uses. The three major assignments of CRDF are:

- To provide productive research and development opportunities within the independent states of the FSU that offer scientists and engineers alternatives to emigration and help prevent the dissolution of the scientific and technological infrastructure of the independent states

- To advance defense conversion by funding civilian collaborative research and development projects between scientists and engineers in the United States and in the independent states of the FSU
- To assist in the establishment of a market economy in the independent states of the FSU by identifying and partially funding joint R&D ventures between U.S. and FSU businesses, scientists, engineers and entrepreneurs; to provide a mechanism to promote understanding of commercial business practices; and to provide opportunities to develop mutually beneficial trade with the countries of the FSU based on the products of advanced scientific and technological research

Among the more creative of the CRDF's programs is its Closed Cities program, designed to promote collaborations between Americans and Russian researchers living in so-called "closed cities" (e.g., Sarov or Snezhinsk, formerly Arzamas-16 and Chelyabinsk-70). There were dozens of such cities in the Soviet Union, all involved in defense research. Today, according to CRDF, "the facilities have become somewhat less restricted, but access remains tightly controlled. Researchers working in closed cities have few contacts with foreigners and only limited communication with their own civilian research community."

The premise of the Closed Cities program is that civilian research opportunities won't materialize for scientists in these closed cities until,

through international collaborations, they are exposed to industry and better understand some of the markets that may exist for their skills.

## Union of Councils for Soviet Jews

1819 H Street, NW, Suite 230
Washington, DC 20006
**Tel:** (202) 775-9770
**Fax:** (202) 775-9776
**E-mail:** 4201773@mcimail.com, mail15895@alterdial.uu.net
**Web:** www.fsumonitor.com/
**Contact:** Yosef I. Abramowitz, President; Micah H. Naftalin, National Director

The Union of Councils for Soviet Jews (UCSJ), also known simply as the Union of Councils, was founded in 1970 as a coalition of local grassroots "action" councils supporting freedom for Jews in the Soviet Union. As the Soviet Jewry movement gathered steam in the 1970s, more councils were formed, more individuals became involved, and UCSJ grew to become the largest independent grassroots Soviet Jewry movement in the world.

Today, UCSJ comprises 23 councils in the United States, with affiliates in Canada, England, Norway, and Australia. UCSJ is headquartered in Washington, DC, but also maintains an additional office in Highland Park, IL. Currently, UCSJ sponsors human rights bureaus in seven cities throughout the former Soviet Union: Moscow, St. Petersburg, Lviv, Riga, Tbilisi, Almaty, and Bishkek. Funding and supervision of the St. Petersburg bureau are provided by the Bay Area Council for Jewish Rescue and Renewal. The UCSJ Web site is a rich source of information about the programs and network the Union of Councils maintains in the NIS and also offers good links to topics of special interest, e.g., politics, religion, human rights, etc.

## United Way International
701 North Fairfax Street
Alexandria, VA 22314-2045
**Tel:**       (703) 519-0092
**Fax:**      (703) 519-0097
**E-mail:**  uwi@unitedway.org
**Web:**      www.unitedway.org
**Contact:** Robert M. Beggan, President and Chief Executive Officer; Gregory Berzonsky, Program Director

The first United Way outside of the United States was founded in 1928 in South Africa, but United Way International was first officially registered in 1974. Although UWI was founded by United Way of America, it is a completely separate legal entity, with its own independent board of directors, staff, and funding. United Way International now has affiliates in 35 countries and territories on six continents. Together they raise approximately US$550 million annually for local health and human service needs.

   UWI was formed to respond to requests for assistance from international United Ways, Community Chests and other community-wide fundraising organizations, and to assist communities outside of the U.S. in forming new United Way organizations or improving existing ones. Its mission statement is "Helping Build Community Capacity for a Better Quality of Life Worldwide through Voluntary Giving and Action"
   UWI's current focus of activities includes:
- Providing ongoing technical assistance and consultation for existing affiliates
- Facilitating the exchange of information and establishing links between community-based fundraising institutions, voluntary social service agencies and other international organizations
- Delivering presentations to foreign officials regarding the potential of a single community-wide fundraising appeal to provide funding for health and human service organizations
- Serving as a resource for corporations seeking to expand their philanthropy initiatives in overseas communities

There are United Way offices in Moscow and Minsk.

## Urban Institute
2100 M Street NW
Washington, DC 20037
**Tel:**       (202) 261-5709
**Fax:**      (202) 466-3982
**E-mail:**  paffairs@ui.urban.org
**Web:**      www.urban.org
**Contact:** Jeffrey P. Telgarsky, Director, International Activities Center

The Urban Institute, a nonprofit, policy research and educational organization in Washington, DC, has assisted Russia in its housing privatization program. The materials developed under this program, "Papers on Housing in Russia," are available in English or Russian. The institute consults in a number of areas—e.g., social safety-net reform, capital financing for urban infrastructure, intergovernmental fiscal relations—in connection with projects in the NIS/CEE region.

## U.S.-Ukraine Foundation
733 15th Street, NW, Suite 1027
Washington, DC 20005
**Tel:**       (202) 347-4264
**Fax:**      (202) 347-4267
**E-mail:**  usuf@usukraine.org
**Web:**      www.usukraine.org
**Contact:** Nadia McConnell, President

The foundation is a nonprofit non-governmental organization established in 1991 to facilitate democratic development, encourage free market reform, and enhance human rights in Ukraine. It creates and sustains channels of communication between the U.S. and Ukraine for the purpose of building peace and prosperity through shared democratic values. The foundation aspires to a Ukraine that is a cornerstone of regional stability and a full partner in the community of nations.

In 1992 the foundation established the Pylyp Orlyk Institute for Democracy in Kyiv. The institute is an independent public policy research organization that provides information to Ukrainian policy-makers, NGOs, academia, and media on issues pertaining to the development of civil society. (See Ukraine section.)

In Washington, DC, the U.S.-Ukraine Foundation distributes *Update from Ukraine*, a periodic analysis of political trends and events in Ukraine, to important American policymakers and experts on Ukrainian affairs. The foundation is currently directing several major projects, including the "US-Ukraine Community Partnerships for Local Government Training and Education Project" and "Integrating the Constitutional Court into Ukraine's Civil Society." In 1995 it became a subcontractor to Indiana University's USAID-funded "Parliamentary Development Project."

The Community Partnerships Project is a three-year, USAID-funded program designed to link 18 U.S. communities with 18 Ukrainian communities in mutually beneficial partnerships to establish education and training programs in public administration for local governments in Ukraine. The USIA-funded Constitutional Court Project, through a series of seminars, aims to inform the populace about the critical importance of the newly created Constitutional Court and its role as final interpreter of the Constitution and ultimate guarantor of the rule of law in Ukraine. Under the Parliamentary Development Project, staff work with Ukrainian legislators to develop the institutional mechanisms of the national parliament, including commission structure and operations, transparency, legislative-executive relations, and legislative processes.

## VOICE International
Voluntary Organizations Initiative in Central and Eastern Europe/Eurasia
1511 K Street, NW, Suite 663
Washington, DC 20005
**Tel:** (202) 737-2870
**Fax:** (202) 737-2872
**E-mail:** voice@voiceinternational.org
**Web:** www.voiceinternational.org/
**Contact:** Nancy Pettis, President

VOICE International was incorporated in 1992 after working informally for a year and a half to provide needed information to civic organizations in Central and Eastern Europe, the Baltics, and the NIS. The founders of VOICE traveled in the region and repeatedly were asked by NGOs for models of policies, programs, and practices overseas that might be adapted to local or national circumstances.

Since incorporation, VOICE International has sent thousands of documents and books to the region in response to requests for information. It has also:
- Linked a number of groups from the region to like organizations in North America so that information sharing can continue over the long-term.
- Provided technical assistance to the Independent Forum of Albanian Women to strengthen its organization

and to put on a conference for legal literacy on women's human rights.

- Provided technical assistance and materials to the ICCF in Ukraine to develop the basic, local language manual on how to start and operate an NGO in Ukraine.
- Published *Funding for Civil Society: A Guide to U.S. Grantmakers Giving in Central/Eastern Europe and the Newly Independent States* (1998). Local versions of this guide are being re-published in 16 countries in the region. It is also available online at the VOICE Web site.
- Published *To Promote and Protect Women's Rights: Strategies and Resources for Women's Nongovernmental Organizations in Central and Eastern Europe, the Baltics, and the Newly Independent States* (1998).

Also in 1998, VOICE implemented its Resources for Civil Society project that reviews materials (books, audiovisual materials) helpful to the institutional development, public policy concerns, and programs of civic groups in the CEE/NIS region. Working through partners in the region, VOICE offers any NGO abroad a lower-cost method of purchasing materials; its office staff is also able to serve as a liaison to U.S. or other publishers to obtain translation rights.

VOICE's Information Clearinghouse responds to requests for educational materials from individual civic organizations and libraries in the region. If VOICE receives a number of requests for the same information and appropriate materials cannot be found, it will develop projects to produce them.

Among the groups VOICE works with in the region are United Way Belarus, Minsk; Civic Development International Center, Tbilisi; English Teachers Association of Georgia, Tbilisi; Siberian Civic Initiatives Support Center, Novosibirsk; Foundation to Support Civic Initiatives, Dushanbe; GURT Resource Center for NGO Development, Kyiv; Innovation and Development Center, Kyiv; and The Philanthropy Center, Kyiv.

## Volunteers for Peace International Work Camps

43 Tiffany Road
Belmont, VT  05730
**Tel:**      (802) 259-2759
**Fax:**     (802) 259-2922
**E-mail:**  vfp@vfp.org
**Web:**    www.vfp.org
**Contact:** Peter Coldwell, Executive Director

Volunteers for Peace (VFP) offers organized travel experiences, language study, and work camps in the NIS and around the world. It was founded in 1981. VFP is a member of the Executive Committee of the Coordinating Committee for International Voluntary Service (CCIVS) at UNESCO in Paris. CCIVS is an umbrella organization for all non-governmental voluntary service organizations on our planet. More than 70,000 volunteers are exchanged in work-camp programs every year. Most of VFP's foreign partner organizations receive government support equal to 50 percent or more of their annual budgets. VFP is totally membership supported. In 1997 VFP administered the exchange of 1,200 volunteers on combined staff salaries of only $43,000.

Work camps originated in Europe over 75 years ago. Generally 10–20 people from four or more countries arrive on a given day in a host community. They may be housed in a school, church, private home, or community center. The work is unskilled and casual, and there are cultural and recreational programs during leisure time.

VFP's online International Work Camp Directory lists more than 1,000 programs in more than 50 countries. A volunteer pays transportation and visa fees plus $195 for a two- to three-week work-camp experience. This may involve maintaining a natural park, working in an orphanage or children's hospital, renovating historical buildings, etc. VFP work camps exist in most countries of the NIS.

## Whirlwind Wheelchair International

2233 California Street
Berkeley, CA 94703
**Tel/Fax:** (510) 548-3652
**E-mail:** krizack@sfsu.edu
**Web:** whirlwind.sfsu.edu
**Contact:** Marc L. Krizack, Russia Project Manager

Whirlwind Wheelchair International, formerly the Wheeled Mobility Center, ran two major projects in Novosibirsk, Russia from 1993 to 1996. The common goal of these projects was the integration of people with disabilities into society. Major funding for these projects came from USAID. As a result, a disabled sports club was transformed into an independent living center (FINIST), which is a non-residential service and advocacy organization run by and for people with disabilities.

An essential characteristic of the independent living center lies in its philosophy of uniting people of many different disabilities. There is now a wheelchair factory and a disabled-community health clinic. FINIST also has its own law firm, KONSUL, which provides representation for people with disabilities. WWI and FINIST are currently seeking funding for two major projects. The first is a year-long project

to promote collaborative relationships between disability NGOs and various government agencies in the Novosibirsk region. The second is a five-year project to make Novosibirsk State Technical University accessible to people with disabilities. WWI and FINIST are also collaborating in the development of FINIST's Web site.

## World Information Transfer, Inc.

444 Park Avenue South, Suite 1202
New York, NY 10016
**Tel:** (212) 686-1996
**Fax:** (212) 686-2172
**E-mail:** wit@un-wit.org
**Web:** www.worldinfo.org
**Contact:** Dr. Christine K. Durbak, Chair and CEO

WIT was formed in 1987 in reaction to the Chernobyl nuclear disaster in Ukraine. A small group of international professionals who recognized the long-term health implications of the Chernobyl accident established an international not-for-profit organization for the general purpose of promoting environmental health. The underlying premise was recognition of "the pressing need to provide accurate actionable information about our deteriorating global environment and its effect on human health" to leaders and concerned citizens around the world.

WIT produces a quarterly newsletter, *World Ecology Report*, which is a digest of important current information related to environment and health. The newsletter, published in English, Arabic, Russian, Spanish, and Ukrainian, is circulated around the world by WIT's regional directors and its headquarters in the U.S.

WIT organizes an annual international conference on Health and the Environment: Global Partners For Global Solutions. It has been held at

UN headquarters in New York since 1992. The world's leading authorities in the field of environmental medicine share their latest findings and discuss possible solutions with leaders in governments, business, organizations and the media. Two hour-long video tapes of the conferences are available and more information is available at WIT's Web site.

Since 1995, WIT has been providing and promoting humanitarian relief to areas devastated by environmental degradation. Supplies and equipment have been sent to hospitals and orphanages in areas contaminated by the Chernobyl fallout. This program has been rapidly spreading to other regions of the former Soviet Union.

WIT has opened two Centers for Sustainability and Health Communication. One is in Lviv and the other in Beirut. One of WIT's seven Regional Directors is also based in Lviv.

WIT works with other U.S.-based organizations and with local groups in the areas to which its medical aid is delivered. As a member of the Board of the Conference of Non-Governmental Organizations (NGOs) in Consultative Relationship with the UN (CONGO), and with WIT's Chairperson serving as Vice Chair of the Executive Committee of NGOs associated with the UN Department of Public Information, WIT is involved, beyond its own mandate, with NGOs from around the world in many other activities related to the work of the UN.

## World Learning Inc.
Democracy Fellows Program
1015 15th Street, NW, Suite 911
Washington, DC 20005-2605
**Tel:**      (202) 408-5427
**Fax:**      (202) 408-5397
**E-mail:**   dfp.info@worldlearning.org

**Web:**      www.worldlearning.org

World Learning Inc., founded in 1932 as The U.S. Experiment in International Living, is one of the oldest, international educational exchange services in the world and the oldest of its kind in the U.S. It manages numerous programs, including a Democracy Fellows Program, awarded to approximately 15 persons annually. Candidates must be U.S. citizens with at least an M.A. or J.D. degree. Upon being awarded the fellowship, they develop an assignment together with a USAID agency. Fellowships are based upon the programs of sponsoring USAID missions and may involve activities such as providing policy analysis and advice, developing program indicators or methodologies, strengthening the capacities of local civil society organizations, providing electoral and constitutional assistance, etc.

## Yeltsin Democracy Fellowship Program
University of Saskatchewan International
117 Science Place
Saskatoon, SK S7N 5C8, Canada
**Tel:**      (306) 966-5548
**Fax:**      (306) 966-8736
**Contact:** Gordon Barnhart, Associate Director and Senior Programs Officer

Under this 10-year program, scheduled to expire in 2003, approximately 100 Russians a year are receiving training relevant to their country's reform process. The program combines short-term training with internships in Canadian public and private sector organizations. The project is financed from the investment proceeds of a $20-million repayable loan by the government of Canada. The Russian partner is the Moscow Public Science Foundation.

# NIS-Based Organizations

# *Armenia*

## Country Code: 374

### *Yerevan (2)*

#### AMNIC Network Information Center of Armenia

Yerevan
**E-mail:** imkrtoum@aua.am,
edd@aic.net
**Web:** www.amnic.net
**Contact:** Dr. Igor Mkrtoumian, President, Armenian Internet Users; Edgar V. S. Der-Danieliantz, Group Manager, AM Network Information Center

AMNIC was established by Dr. Igor Mkrtoumian of the American University of Armenia and Edgar V.S. Der-Danieliantz of Arminco Network Solutions on behalf of the Armenian Internet Users Group in Yerevan. It receives free equipment and network connection from Arminco, Ltd.

AMNIC serves as a national Internet registry for domain name registrations in Armenia. The primary goal of AMNIC is to enhance the integration of Armenia into the international information infrastructure by fostering the open interchange of information between Armenia and other parts of the world.

The Armenian Internet Users Group publishes a monthly bulletin, which is distributed in both print and electronic forms and is also available on AMNIC's Web page.

#### Apaga-2000

pr. Mets Tigran 59, k. 60
Yerevan
**Tel:** 55-51-65
**Contact:** Laurens Gasparian, President; Sirean Khlakhian, Vice President

Apaga-2000's mission is to promote population growth in Armenia. Through public education, it encourages families to have more children. It also sponsors clubs for single persons and newborn health care.

#### Armenian Agricultural Academy and Agribusiness Center

ul. Teryan 74/2, etazh 1
375009  Yerevan
**Tel:** 56-74-11
**Fax:** 15-19-30
**E-mail:** agacad@arminco.com
**Contact:** Hrachik Gavadyan, Director of ABC; Professor Sergey Meloyan, Deputy Director of ABC

Established in July 1998, AAA-ABC seeks to strengthen ties with farmers and promote the application of its agricultural research in order to improve production techniques.

#### Armenian Assembly of America

pl. Republic 2, k. 105
375010  Yerevan
**Tel:** 15-10-60
**Fax:** 15-10-69
**Web:** www.aaainc.org/

The Armenian Assembly of America, founded in 1972 and headquartered in Washington, D.C., promotes public awareness of Armenian issues, encourages greater Armenian-American cooperation, and assists in humanitarian and development programs in Armenia. The group also runs a resource and training center in Yerevan in support of NGOs.

The assembly has an office in Stepanakert, Nagorno-Karabakh at ul. Azatamartikneri 28.

## Armenian Assembly of America–NGO Training and Resource Center

23 Sevastopolian St.
375033  Yerevan
**Tel:** 27-42-66, 27-87-32, 15-19-19
**Fax:** 15-17-95
**E-mail:** ngoc@arminco.com
**Web:** ngoc.yerphi.am/
**Contact:** Nouneh Doudoyan, Director

This center is a project of the Armenian Assembly of America, funded by USAID through Save the Children. It was founded in 1994 to provide assistance and support to Armenia's NGO sector. With offices in Yerevan and Gyumri, the center currently works with over 600 NGOs through the following activities:

- Advanced Management and Leadership Training program combines in-class training with on-site consulting for NGOs
- Open Dialogue Program encourages cooperation between the NGO sector, the government, media, and private sector through round table meetings and other events
- Public relations training aims to raise public awareness about NGOs
- Free access for NGOs to the center's electronic mail system, computers, databases and a library of print materials

The center's NGO-TV project aims to familiarize the general public with the work of social organizations. An eight-part documentary film series, The Third Power, was broadcast on prime time television beginning July 1998. The series profiles thirty NGOs working in the fields of social rehabilitation, social services, education, culture, housing, environment, and legal awareness, and includes an introductory description of NGOs in an international and local context, explaining their role in public life.

The center has published 10 handbooks covering key topics for NGO development, available in both English and Armenian. It also has distributed the *NGOC Newsletter* since 1995, providing information about third sector news and events. An electronic version of the newsletter is available at the center's Web site.

## The Armenia Center for Alternative Education and the Arts

ul. Baghramyan 23
Yerevan
**Tel:** 27-37-24
**Fax:** 15-10-48
**E-mail:** charmar@relaypoint.net
**Web:** ngoc.yerphi.am/ngos/acaea.htm

The center began working in 1992 to create alternative means of education for women, children, and minorities in Armenia. The group engages in advocacy work, research, educational programs, and publications in the mass media to raise the awareness of the general public on issues of gender equality and human rights. ACAEA established a Resource and Publishing Center for Women and Children in Yerevan, as well as an Environmental Education Program for primary school children. Training seminars include an NGO leadership program for young women on topics of media use and fund-raising strategies, as well as gender training seminars for family planning practitioners. The Income Generation Project provided supplies and equipment for local craftsmen to make and sell crafts at ACAEA's Christmas crafts fair. ACAEA has assisted close to 150 refugee families in the Yerevan area.

## Armenian Electron Microscopy Society

**Fax:** 15-17-95
**E-mail:** ngo@moon.yerphi.am
**Web:** ngoc.yerphi.am/ngos/aems.htm
**Contact:** Karlen Hovnanyanis, President

One of the first non-governmental scientific societies in Armenia, AEMS was founded in 1991 to promote the science and practice of microscopy. It publishes the journal *The World of Microstructure* and encourages the participation of youth and women in its activities. AEMS was accepted as an Associate Member of the International Federation of Societies for Electron Microscopy in 1994.

## Armenian Federation of UNESCO Clubs and Associations

53 Mashtots Ave.
375009 Yerevan
**Tel:** 256-2601
**Fax:** 248-6210
**E-mail:** bars@arminco.com
**Web:** www.unesco-clubs.am
**Contact:** Arshak Banuchyan, President; Vardan Hovannisyan, Coordinator

AFUCA was established in 1993 in response to the degradation of local conditions brought about by the war in Nagorno-Karabakh. Specifically, AFUCA is concerned with the loss of Armenian culture, human rights abuses, and the state of the Armenian environment. The federation is a coordinating body for its nine full-member clubs and its six acting members and is also responsible for collaborations with international partners, other countries' UNESCO clubs, and NGOs.

AFUCA's member clubs are currently responsible for nine projects across the country, including:

- A center to help children heal the psychological wounds of war through therapy and art
- Three projects to maintain, clean and protect historical sites
- A program to create reserves for Armenia's dwindling eagle population
- A reforestation plan for Yerevan
- Computer classes and job training for teenagers and adults
- A film about the Armenian National Art Museum
- A program that encourages youth participation in sports

AFUCA maintains a network of 40 public libraries and has created a Youth Initiatives Supporting Center to provide job skills and foster youth creativity.

## Armenian Land and Culture Organization

Yerevan
**E-mail:** lcousa@aol.com, armlco@arminco.com
**Web:** www.lcousa.org, ngoc.yerphi.am/ngos/armlco.htm
**Contact:** Gevorg Yaghjyan, President; Hasmik Gazazyan, Assistant

LCO, headquartered in New York, began its work in Armenia after the 1988 earthquake. Its mission is to preserve Armenian historical monuments, restore villages and public centers, and help people of the Armenian Diaspora learn about their heritage. Projects such as the restoration of churches and cultural centers and assistance to small villages have been implemented in Yerevan, Gogaran, Saghmosaran, Dprevan, Tatev, and Shushi and Karintak in Karabakh.

## Armenian League of Women Voters

ul. Teryan 23/18
Yerevan
**Tel:** 53-10-53
**Fax:** 15-17-95
**E-mail:** ngoc@moon.yerphi.am
**Web:** ngoc.yerphi.am/ngos/
alwv.htm
**Contact:** Aida Topuzian, President;
Gohar Martikian, Narine Havhanessian,
Vice Presidents

ALWV began working in 1996 to
increase women's participation in
Armenian elections. The group seeks to
influence national policy on voter rights
and women's issues through education
and information dissemination. After
the 1995-96 elections, ALWV implemented the Women and Voters project
to determine how to ensure women's
participation in elections. The project
included a roundtable, Lessons from the
Previous Elections and Future Actions,
attended by women's NGO representatives and government authorities. The
group also publishes the bulletin *My
Vote Gives Me Strength* and a brochure
Towards Free and Fair Elections.
    Another project of ALWV is Women
and Community, which seeks to
promote the participation of women's
NGOs in community development. In
an effort to prioritize problems
identified by women, 350 telephone
interviews have been conducted in two
communities. A Women and
Development Center has also been
established to collect information on
the status of women in society.

## Armenian Technology Group

ul. Kuznetsoz 30
375018  Yerevan
**Tel:** 57-80-37
**Tel/Fax:** 15-17-96
**E-mail:** atgya@arminco.com

**Contact:** Roger Culver, In-Country
Director

ATG was founded in 1989 to help
deliver humanitarian aid and assist
farmers with crop development. The
group has focused its efforts on providing training to farmers in order to help
them increase the yield and quality of
their harvest. It has distributed wheat,
alfalfa seed, and medical supplies to
people in need. ATG's program staff
are local professionals who hold
university degrees. Last year, program
farmers planted and harvested 1,100
hectares of winter wheat throughout
Armenia.

## Association of Farmers of Armenia–Haifermer

ul. Nalbandian 8
Ministry of Trade
Yerevan
**Tel:** 52-63-70, 53-80-53

This is a German project that provides
fertilizers and equipment to farmers and
farming associations in 11 villages in
Armenia. They seek to advance
agricultural reforms and assist farmers
in defending their rights and interests.

## Bars Media Documentary Film Studio

a/ya 044
375009  Yerevan
**Tel:** 56-26-01
**E-mail:** bars@arminco.com
**Web:** www.barsmedia.am
**Contact:** Vardan Hovannisyan,
President

Founded in 1993 by journalist and
cameraman Hovannisyan, this studio
consists of a team of professional film-
makers dedicated to filming the social
dimensions of a region in transformation, addressing such issues as the

devastating consequences of war, environmental issues, ethnic struggles, and the population's struggle to retain their dignity in the midst of these crises. So far, the studio has produced films on human rights, environmental problems, and various cultural topics.

## Center for Development of Civil Society–Scientific Women's Council

ul. Nalbandyan 27/25, k. 7
375001 Yerevan
**Tel:** 58-56-77, 56-15-70
**Fax:** 58-56-77, 15-17-95
**E-mail:** aslanys@mhf.arminco.com, aslanys@freenet.am
**Contact:** Svetlana Aslanyan, Ph.D., President

The council was established in 1991 with a mission to protect women's rights, increase the role of women in public, social, cultural and political life, and foster international cooperation between women and women's organizations. Among the councils projects are an education program for voters, and the Training for Leaders of Women's NGOs program administered with the local group Youth for Armenia. The council has also published a brochure on the prevention of migration, Warning for Women, in cooperation with the Dutch group Religious Women Against Trafficking of Women. It is currently at work on a USIS-sponsored project, Village Women in Civil Society.

The council offers summer training courses in Armenian language and culture, as well as a summer camp for refugee children. The group has published a two-volume textbook, *Let's Speak Armenian*, for refugees and national minorities. It also published a multilingual illustrated dictionary for refugee children with USAID funding,

and runs Armenian language training courses for female refugee teachers from rural areas with support from UNICEF.

In 1996, the council established its Center for Development of Civil Society to promote the values of democracy and pluralism in Armenian society. The center has hosted round-tables and conferences, including Civil Society and Tolerance, held jointly with the Center for Democracy and Human Rights, and The Role of Women's Organizations in the Development of a Democratic Society. The center is currently working on programs to establish an Education Center for Women.

CDCS Director Svetlana Aslanian is the driving force behind the organization's activities. Ms. Aslanian holds a Ph.D. in Linguistics and has been researching the women's movement in Armenia since 1992. She was a participant at the Fourth World Conference on Women in Beijing, China, at which she conducted a workshop The Adaptation and Integration of Refugee Women and Children into Armenian Society.

## The Eurasia Foundation

ul. Isahakian 22, k. 9
375009 Yerevan
**Tel/Fax:** 15-18-24, 52 24 95, 58-55-98
**E-mail:** armenia@eurasia.am

See the profile for the foundation in the North American Organizations section.

## Hay Voskedzerikner Benevolent Union (Armenian Golden Hands)

8 Kuznetsov k. 42
Yerevan
**Tel:** 55-71-37, 62-01-25
**Fax:** 15-17-95
**E-mail:** ngoc@moon.yerphi.am

**Contact:** Louiza Hovhannisyan, President; Suzan Ghazaryan, Executive Director

The union was formed in 1995 to raise the professional level of local artists and craftsmen and alleviate the industry's rampant unemployment. The union holds art auctions and exhibitions of local crafts, which has assisted over 500 local artists and their families. A council of 12–15 experts evaluates local crafts and plans advertising and marketing for exhibitions. The union also holds individual workshops and consultations for craftsmen on topics of professional development.

Since 1996, the union has been working to stem refugee unemployment. A needs assessment project conducted in rural areas of Armenia revealed that 60–70 percent of the heads of refugee families travel outside Armenia for work, while 30–40 percent remain unemployed. Large communities of refugees have no appropriate shelter and rely primarily on humanitarian assistance for survival. The union provides refugees with manual-skills training for high-demand professions. For instance, a vocational training course in pottery making for 25 refugees was held in Ashtarak, a suburb of Yerevan. The union also works to encourage small business development. Through a network of small ventures, the union strives to expand production of the most marketable handicrafts, such as tapestry, jewelry making, embroidery and lace, carved wood, and pottery.

## Internews Armenia
Dom Kompositorov
Demirchian St. 25, First floor
375002   Yerevan
**Tel:**      58-36-20, 52-55-27, 56-55-06
**Tel/Fax:** 90-69-23

**E-mail:**  internews@internews.am,
             dbolger@interenws.am
**Web:**     www.internews.am
**Contact:** Daniel Bolger, Director;
Nouneh Sarkissian, Executive Director

Internews is committed "to the development of independent media because independent mass media represent the basis for a free society." It has programs in several post-Soviet countries. In Armenia, the focus of Internews has been on developing independent broadcast media by helping non-state-run radio and television stations with their programming, translating and distributing trade news, providing technical assistance and advice, and encouraging cooperation between independent broadcasters.

Internews has equipped seven non-governmental stations with computer stations capable of incorporating video graphics and titling and has installed phone lines and modems to allow stations to access e-mail and the Internet. The group has also coordinated a national weekly news program in the Armenian language for over 13 non-governmental TV stations and participates in a three-country news program linking Armenia, Azerbaijan, and Georgia, which is now shown on over 30 non-governmental stations in the region. The first video-conferencing "tele-bridge," linking persons via satellite between Yerevan and Baku, was conducted by Internews.

## IREX Office and Education Information Center
Marshal Baghramian 17
Union of Armenian Architects, etazh 2
375019   Yerevan
**Tel:**     56-12-15
**Fax:**     15-11-16
**E-mail:**  irex@irex.arminco.com
**Web:**     www.irex.am,

www.irex.am/eic
**Contact:** Zara Oganessian,
IREX/Armenia Representative

See the profile of IREX in the North
American Organizations section.

## "Khachatour Badalian's" Children Stomatologists and Maxillofacial Surgeons Association of Armenia

ul. M. Sarian 40-A, k. 4
375002  Yerevan
**Tel:**       53-00-68
**Fax:**       15-17-95
**E-mail:**   kbadal@yahoo.com
**Web:**      ngoc.yerphi.am/ngos/
stamatology.htm

The association was founded in 1994 to
improve medical services in Armenia.
The group researches major health
problems in Armenia, provides surgical
support in rural areas, and offers medical training, seminars and exchange
opportunities to medical students.

## Mission Armenia

22 Eghbairutian, k. 68
375039  Yerevan
**Tel:**       42-76-08, 42-76-58
**Fax:**       15-19-54
**E-mail:**   mission@ripsik.arminco.com
**Web:**      ngoc.yerphi.am/ngos/mal.htm
**Contact:** Hripsimeh Kirakossian,
President

Mission provides medical assistance to
42 refugee communal centers, runs a
local TV series to increase social
knowledge and acceptance of people
with disabilities, and provides personal
home care to 900 elderly people. The
group also provides food to the
Vardenis Neurological Internment and
Psychological Hospital. It receives
funding from UNCHR.

## Sakharov Armenian Human Rights Foundation

Yerevan
**E-mail:**   root@nerses.arminco.com
**Contact:** Levon Nersisyan, Director

## Union for Cultural Development of Childhood/Youth Creativity

ul. Aigestan 11, d. 49
375025  Yerevan
**Tel:**       57-84-68
**Fax:**       53-88-86
**E-mail:**   nadrav@hotmail.com
**Contact:** Vardan Vardanyan, President

Founded in November 1997, the union
organizes concerts, artistic tours, and
festivals for youth in Armenia and
abroad. It is prepared to work with
similar groups to organize joint events
and exchanges.

## Union of Armenian Government Employees

ul. Komitas 3
375033  Yerevan
**Tel:**       22-15- 65
**Fax:**       15-17-95
**E-mail:**   ngoc@moon.yerphi.am
**Web:**      ngoc.yerphi.am
**Contact:** Vacheh Kalashyan, President

The mission of the union is to "support
the creation and development of a
national statehood of Armenia through
the establishment of rule of law in the
sphere of government service, and
protection of government employees'
rights and interests." The group works
to create a code of ethics for government employees, specifically for local
self-governance bodies, and is drafting
the Law on Government Service for
consideration by Parliament. It also
sponsors professional development
programs for government employees
including, information services,
seminars and roundtable discussions,

and access to a library of materials on government administration and management.

## Women's Council of the Republic of Armenia

ul. Moskovian 35
Yerevan
**Fax:** 15-17-95
**E-mail:** ngoc@moon.yerphi.am
**Web:** ngoc.yerphi.am/ngos/women.htm
**Contact:** Nora Hakobian, President

The council researches the situation of women in Armenia's political, economic and social sectors and lobbies legislative and executive authorities on behalf of women. It publishes a weekly newspaper, *Aragast* (Sail), which contains information on national and international women's issues. The council's Women Leaders of the Twenty-First Century program offers training to 60 young women on the history of the women's movement, women's issues and conditions in Armenia, and organizational management and leadership skills. The group has translated and distributed copies of the 1979 *UN Convention on the Elimination of Female Discrimination*, a publication that was previously unavailable to Armenian women.

## Women Economists Union

3 Norki Zangvats, d. 53
375056 Yerevan
**Tel:** 63-59-06, 47-46-84, 52-15-51
**Fax:** 15-17-03, 56-55-02
**Contact:** Petrosian Armine, President; Boyakchyan Karine, Vice President

The WEU was founded in 1997 to promote the participation of women in the structural reforms currently being undertaken by the Armenian government. It works to help women realize their abilities in the sphere of economics, support the cooperation of women economists engaged in theoretical and practical activities, organize and conduct seminars, and establish relationships with local and foreign organizations and individuals.

## Yerevan Press Club

pr. Mesrop Mashtots 39/12
Yerevan
**Tel:** 52-92-06, 52-29-26
**Contact:** Boris Navasardian, President; Michael Diloyan, Executive Director

The club promotes the formation and development of a free press in Armenia. It publishes press bulletins, conducts seminars on parliamentary and presidential elections, and maintains a database called Armenia in Faces and Figures.

## Young Lawyer's Union

ul. Gusan Sherami 27 k. 49
Yerevan
**Tel/Fax:** 72-38-97
**E-mail:** root@ylu.arminco.com
**Contact:** Karen Zadoyan, Chairman; David Abgaryan, Vice Chairman; Narine Karapetyan, Secretary

YLU was formed in 1995 by a group of students and young lawyers from Yerevan State University. The union seeks to raise public awareness of the rule of law and citizen rights through the dissemination of information, legal consultation, and programs to improve the quality of education in law schools.

In collaboration with the British Armenian Lawyers Association, YLU implemented a Legal Advice project to provide legal assistance to public organizations and practical experience to law students. About 220 organizations received free legal advice from 130 law students from four law schools in

Armenia. The union also drafted a law with local NGO representatives, On Public (Non-Governmental) Organizations, and presented it to the National Assembly.

In 1998, YLU conducted the Suspension of Migration in Support of Defense of the Motherland project in collaboration with the Armenian Republican Committee Zinvori Mayr (Soldiers' Mother). As part of the project, changes in legislation for military service were drafted and disseminated in order to promote repatriation of military conscripts. A booklet on the rights and obligations of conscripts, entitled *Our Son and Our National Army,* was published and distributed among conscripts free of charge. YLU is a member of the European Young Bar Association and has a regional branch in Sunik province, with headquarters in Meghri.

## Youth for Armenia

Baghramian 54-2
375019  Yerevan
**Tel:**      27-13-31
**Fax:**      15-17-68 (c/o ACCELS)
**E-mail:**   yfa@accels.arminco.com
**Contact:** Gurgen Hakopian, President; Nelson Petrosyan, Vice President

The association was established in 1994 by alumni of the Freedom Support Act Secondary School Program, an educational exchange program sponsored by the U.S. government. Its mission is to promote ideas of democracy, freedom, and humanism. Membership in the association is limited to those who have spent at least six months in an American high school. This requirement is based on the premise that such experience contributes to a better understanding of democratic processes.

Recent projects include recruitment and orientation assistance for ACCELS

and World Learning's high school exchange programs, English-language courses, a tree-planting project, and fund-raising for orphanages. The group helped organize the youth conference Trancaucasus in Transition as well as a regional conference, Shifting The Paradigm of Democracy. It has carried out three major projects on democracy development: the Vote For Voting youth campaign, a young voters education program, and the Face the Democracy program on civic education. Two regional branches are located in Gyumri and Vanadzor.

## Vanadzor (88557)

### Armenian Constitutional Right Protective Center

ul. Narekatsi 3/1
Vanadzor
**Tel/Fax:** 2-65-24
**E-mail:**   ngoc@moon.yerphi.am
**Web:**      ngoc.yerphi.am

This center works to promote and defend human rights in Armenia through educational programs, the mass media, and election monitoring. ACRPC organized the work of independent observers during the 1989 and 1990 elections. The center's seminars have included a two-week teaching course on human rights at the Vanadzor Teachers' Training Institute, a seminar Teaching Human Rights in Armenian schools with the Norwegian Refugee Council in 1996, and the joint project NGOs in the Building of Civil Society and Democracy in 1997. The center established a human rights library in the town of Vanadzor in 1996 and has been publishing the newspaper *For the Sake of Justice* since 1989.

# Azerbaijan

## Country Code: 994

## Baku (12)

### Association Design of Invalids
8th 96 Sharifly Str., k. 87
Baku
**Tel:** 23-28-49, 96-59-63
**Contact:** Solmaz Azizova

ADI was founded in 1992 to unite citizens to help the disabled community in Azerbaijan. It provides vocational training for people with disabilities and conducts public education programs on the rights of the disabled. The association has a program which teaches disabled women, children, and their families to create artwork and handicrafts.

### Azerbaijan Atlantic Cooperation Association
pr. Azerbaijan 37
370000  Baku
**Tel:** 98-31-76
**Fax:** 98-31-65
**Contact:** Sulhatdin Akberov

Founded in 1997, the association works to strengthen Azerbaijan's international relations, particularly its integration with Europe and incorporation into NATO. It conducts research and public education toward this end.

### Azerbaijan "Buja" Humanitarian Children's Foundation
ul. Gala Side 26/4
Icheri Shahar  Baku
**Tel:** 92-64-80
**Contact:** Tarlan Gorchy

The foundation provides aid, health care, and educational programs for refugee children, orphans, and children from low-income families.

### Azerbaijan Children's Organization
ul. 28th Mai 4
370000  Baku
**Tel:** 98-50-86
**E-mail:** avaz@hca.baku.az
**Contact:** Guler Ahmedoova, Chairwoman; Rushara Mamedova

Established in January 1996, this organization provides assistance to Azeri children, focusing specifically on orphans, refugees, and the disabled. The group offers recreational activities and educational programs, and conducts research on the psychological effects of war and economic hardship on children.

### Azerbaijan Committee for Democracy and Human Rights
pr. Azerbaijan 37, k. 203
370000  Baku
**Tel:** 98-31-50
**Tel/Fax:** 98-35-71
**Contact:** Chingiz Ganiyev

Founded in 1993, the committee works to defend citizens who have been illegally imprisoned or otherwise had their rights violated, assist the families of victims, and monitor the human rights situation in Azerbaijan. It organized a campaign in 1995–6 for the release from prison of several journalists of the satirical newspaper, *Cheshme*. It operates a walk-in center where citizens seek legal help.

### Azerbaijan Foundation for the Development of Democracy
Khagani 33
Baku

**Tel/Fax:** 98-07-94
**E-mail:** ayna@anm.baku.az
**Contact:** Ali Masimov, President; Dr. Assim Molladze, Vice President

The AFDD was established in 1994 to "spread democratic values and implement a civil society in Azerbaijan based upon the experience of highly developed countries." Through the mediation of the AFDD, a dialogue was established between the Azerbaijan government and opposition parties. The foundation has established seven centers to carry out its activities, including:

- The Economic Research Center studies the Azerbaijan market economy during its transitional period. The center works on issues such as the privatizing state industries, stabilizing national currency, and fostering free enterprise.
- The Legal Research Center works on constitutional issues and economic regulation, and offers guidance concerning parliamentary elections.
- The Humanitarian Research Center researches the effects of the transitional economy on formerly state-subsidized programs such as science and art.
- The Public Opinion Poll Center provides public opinion polls, taken mostly in Baku, to political parties, newspapers, and embassies. Most of the polls deal with political and economic issues.
- The Human Rights and Democracy Protection Center monitors and documents human rights abuses. The center publishes a weekly bulletin during parliamentary elections.
- The newspaper *Chaq* publishes articles dealing with political, economic, and social issues. It collaborates with popular radio stations, the BBC, and Voice of America.

## Azerbaijan Green Movement
Istiglaliyyet Str.31, etazh 5
370001 Baku
**Tel:** 93-09-51
**Contact:** Bahar Hadjy-zadeh

Founded in 1990, the Green Movement works to preserve and restore the natural environment. Its projects include monitoring the environment, preparing policy briefs for members of Parliament and informing the public about the environmental situation in the country. It has organized numerous environmental restoration projects.

## Azerbaijan Humanitarian Issues Fund
Baku
**Tel:** 38-63-30, 38-49-67
**Fax:** 32-20-26
**E-mail:** museih@prognoz.baku.az

The fund studies humanitarian problems in Azerbaijan and prepares draft laws and reports that outline strategies to overcome them. It has conducted around 100 opinion polls in Baku and 15 nationwide since it was founded in 1994. Recently AHIF conducted a survey of the family planning requirements of doctors, nurses, and midwives and prepared a 300-page report on how to deal with family planning needs in Azerbaijan. Other research projects have focused on how to cope with disasters, women and development, and young families.

## Azerbaijan National Democracy Foundation
1 A. Aliev St.
370004 Baku
**Tel/Fax:** 92-74-56
**E-mail:** andf@ulvi.baku.az

## Azerbaijan Women's Rights Protection Society

ul. Indjasanat 1
370073   Baku
Tel:       92-14-83, 92-78-28, 92-74-56
Fax:      98-90-84, 94-24-71, 94-15-50
E-mail:  root@chag.baku.az
Contact: Novella Jafarova

Founded in 1988, the society now has more than 20,000 members. It works to protect social and civic rights of women and to organize and implement a wide variety of educational and assistance programs for women. Its projects include monitoring conditions of women's prisons, assisting refugees from Iran and Nagorno-Karabakh, and establishing a newspaper which focuses on problems women face.

## Azerbaijan Women's Society

Boyuk Gala St. 6
370004   Baku
Tel:       92-74-87, 93-65-00
Contact: Zemfira Verdiyeva

The society defends the rights of women and provides humanitarian assistance to refugees and orphans.

## Center for Modernization of Azerbaijan

pr. Byulbyula 11/5
370000   Baku
Tel:       95-45-42, 98-31-79
Contact: Niyazi Mehdi

The center was established in 1996 by a group of philosophy and sociology scholars and journalists to gather and publicize information about how other countries have dealt with the same kind of social and political problems facing Azerbaijan. In 1996 it launched a project entitled In Search of Adequate Awareness of Azerbaijan's Problems, which involved conducting opinion polls and research, publishing the results of this research, and organizing conferences.

## Conflict Research Center

E-mail:  gulshan@research.baku.az
Web:     www.geocities.com/capitolhill/lobby/9754
Contact: Gulshan M. Pashayeva, Director

The center was established in 1996 to promote conflict resolution among the people of Azerbaijan and to "enhance their understanding and participation in a peaceful and responsible civil community." It organizes training programs and has made a special effort to reach refugees and minority populations. It works in partnership with the Center for International Development and Conflict Management at the University of Maryland.

## Ecoil-Ruzgar

Sector of Radiation Researches
H. Javid Ave. 31-a
370143   Baku
Tel:       39-41-13, 94-06-18
Tel/Fax: 76-98-01
E-mail:  ruzmk@rad.dl.ab.az,
             ssx@azun.baku.az
Contact: Islam Mustafayev, President

Ecoil-Ruzgar is an environmental association founded in February 1998 after the merger of two groups, Ruzgar and Ecoil. The association is composed of scientists, engineers, doctors, sociologists, lawyers, economists, and journalists working on various aspects of environmental protection. The main goals of Ecoil-Ruzgar are to carry out public monitoring of the ecological situation in Azerbaijan and to organize civic and educational activities to protect and improve the environment.

The group's monitoring activity includes cataloging toxic emissions and substances used in industry, setting standard levels for factory air pollution, studying radiation levels, and developing recommendations to reduce industrial pollution. Ecoil-Ruzgar also organizes conferences, seminars, and meetings on environmental topics; publishes articles and brochures; and participates in the drafting of environmental laws.

Before its merger with Ecoil, Ruzgar organized a workshop on the environmental impact of oil pipelines with support from the World Bank in July 1997. Research projects conducted by Ecoil-Ruzgar in 1998 include:

- An inventory of ozone depleting emissions by Baku factories
- Publication of *Anomalous Atmospheric Phenomena and Change of Climate*
- Public monitoring of the environmental effects of off-shore oil production
- A study of radiation levels in Azerbaijan
- Development of a strategy to support private agriculture.

The group has also organized training for environmental assessment of the oil industry for specialists and NGO leaders in Azerbaijan, Kazakhstan, Turkmenistan, and Georgia.

## ECORES

Tagizade St. 68/100
370134   Baku
**Tel:**      95-13-91, 95-12-23
**Fax:**     98-31-81, 92-99-61
**E-mail:**  irex@irex.org.az
**Contact:** Dr. Shahin M. Panahov, Founder and President

ECORES was established in 1995 to analyze and inform the public about the Azerbaijani and world environment. It publishes a monthly bulletin, *Green Azerbaijan*, and issues press releases to the mass media. ECORES also conducts seminars on environmental issues and is organizing an environmental library.

## Free Teachers Association of Azerbaijan

ul. Uzeyir Cajibekov 49
Baku
**Tel:**      94-90-64, 94-95-57
**Contact:** Malahat Murshudli

FTAA is a voluntary association of teachers founded in 1992 to democratize the educational system in Azerbaijan and protect the rights of teachers. It organizes student competitions, prints textbooks, and conducts conferences and training workshops on new methods of teaching.

## Human Rights Center of Azerbaijan

Bashir Safaroglu St. 165-3
370000   Baku
**Tel:**      97-32-33, 94-75-50
**Fax:**     94-24-71, 94-75-50
**E-mail:**  eldar@hrcenter.baku.az
**Web:**     www.koan.de/~eldar
**Contact:** Eldar E. Zeynalov, Director

HRCA was created in 1993 by a group of journalists concerned about the restoration of political censorship in Azerbaijan. It has published more than 300 reports on human rights violations since 1993 and recently began publishing a bulletin on women's rights. Its reports have been cited in the publications of large international human rights groups such as Amnesty International and Human Rights Watch.

## "Inam" Association

11/5 Bulbul Ave.
Baku

**Tel:** 98-31-79
**Tel/Fax:** 98-45-42
**E-mail:** merkez@baku.az,
merkez@inam.baku.az
**Contact:** Vahid Gazijev

Inam, meaning "trust," was established in 1992 to promote the study of democracy and the development of civil society in Azerbaijan. The association educates the public about a market economy and local self-government institutions, translates and publishes books about democracy, and organizes civic education programs. In 1996–97, it established the School for Young Political Leaders, which consisted of ten monthly seminars for 40 young politicians from eight political parties. Pamphlets based on the seminars and brochures about democracy were published for public distribution. In 1997–98, the school was expanded to include a civic education program for teachers and representatives of independent unions.

### Independent Consumers' Union
ul. Mai 28 18/25
370000  Baku
**Tel:** 93-69-79
**E-mail:** gulnara@arj.baku.az
**Contact:** Eyyub Guseynov, Director

Founded in January 1997, ICU works to defend and promote consumers' rights and to provide a channel for consumer representation. Their goals are to improve the standards of goods and services and to educate both consumers and government authorities about consumer laws.

### Institute of Peace and Democracy
Shamsi Badalbeily St. 38-2
370014  Baku
**Tel/Fax:** 94-14-58

**E-mail:** root@ipd.baku.az
**Contact:** Dr. Leila Yunusova, Director

IPD was formed in 1994 as a humanitarian project of the Azerbaijan Council of Dialogue of Women of the Transcaucasus for Peace and Democracy. IPD seeks to educate citizens about the rule of law, a market economy, fair elections, and conflict resolution. It is divided into five departments: Human Rights Protection, State and Society, Conflict Resolution Studies, Women's Issues, and Youth Issues. Each department conducts research and disseminates its findings. IPD is currently publishing five books concerning the state of human rights in Azerbaijan.

### Internews Azerbaijan
ul. Khagani 18, k. 56
370000  Baku
**Tel/Fax:** 98-37-27, 93-73-75
**E-mail:** office@internews.azeri.com,
internews@azeri.com
**Contact:** Andrea Stallknecht, Director;
Ilham Safarov, Managing Director

Internews was established in Baku in January, 1997 with a mission to support non-governmental broadcasters in Azerbaijan. The group conducts seminars for TV journalists on topics such as journalism skills, TV management, computer skills, and legal aspects of non-governmental TV. It produces a weekly countrywide news exchange program for non-governmental TV stations, *Hayat* ("Life"). Since March 1998, Internews has participated in a three-country program *Perekrestok* ("Crossroads"), linking Azerbaijan, Armenia, and Georgia. Its other projects include legal support for non-governmental broadcasters, an e-mail network of non-governmental TV stations, and two satellite links between Armenia and Azerbaijan.

## IREX/Azerbaijan

Malaia Krepostnaia 8/1
370004 Baku
**Tel/Fax:** 92-99-61
**E-mail:** roxana@irex.baku.az

See the profile of IREX in the North
American Organizations section.

## RSEP/CI Alumni Coordinator

ul. Tagizade 68/100
370134 Baku
**Tel:** 95-12-23
**Fax:** 98-31-81
**E-mail:** shahin@irex.baku.az
**Contact:** Shahin Panahov

## ISAR–Azerbaijan

ul. Shamil Azizbekov 157, k. 23
370014 Baku
**Tel/Fax:** 95-83-68
**E-mail:** ngo@isar.baku.az
**Web:** www.isar.org/isar/
azerbaijan.html
**Contact:** Craig McCook, Director

Established in December 1995, ISAR's
office in Baku runs an NGO support
and resource center to stimulate new
NGOs and to promote and strengthen
the activities of existing ones. ISAR's
client NGOs work in the fields of
environment, assistance to Azerbaijan's
700,000+ refugee population, culture,
women's issues, human rights, public
health information, journalism,
legislative reform, and others. ISAR
provides training in strategic management, proposal writing/budgeting,
financial management/fundraising,
computers, and public, media, and
government relations. Major support
for ISAR– Azerbaijan is provided by
USAID and Save the Children. For
more information about ISAR, see the
profile in the North American
Organizations section.

## "Meeting of Religions" Center

ul. uzeyir Hajibayov 27
370000 Baku
**Tel/Fax:** 93-81-49

The center was founded in 1996 as a
place where representatives of different
religions could come together to find
ways to promote pluralism and the
development of democracy. It conducts
research, organizes conferences, and
publishes analytical bulletins, including
*Islam in the Post-Soviet State.*

## NGO Resource and Training Center

ul. S. Askerova 85, etazh 7
Baku
**Tel:** 97-34-30
**Tel/Fax:** 97-34-72
**E-mail:** kabir@nrtc.baku.az
**Contact:** Lutful Kabir, Chief Technical
Advisor, UNDP/UNDESA; Jafar
Jafarov, National Project Coordinator

This project is funded by UNDP and
implemented by UNDESA in close
collaboration with the government of
Azerbaijan. Its objective is to promote
the growth and development of
indigenous NGOs in Azerbaijan in
support of civil society. The project
was initiated in September 1997 within
the framework of UNDP's Democracy,
Governance, and Participation program.
The resource center began operating in
June 1988 with a full-time staff of
seven and a project budget of about
US$600,000 and currently works with
approximately 90 local NGOs.

## Open Society Institute–Baku

Prospect Azadlyg 39, k. 52
370010 Baku
**Tel/Fax:** 93-40-79, 98-18-44, 93-26-39
**E-mail:** office@soros.baku.az
**Web:** www.soros.org/azerbjan.html

See the profile for the Open Society Institute in the North American Organizations section.

## Relief International

203 S. Rahimov St., k. 2/12
370009  Baku
**Tel:**      98-87-78
**Fax:**     98-05-67
**E-mail:**   riaz@ri.org
**Contact:** Dr. Magdi Kassem, Deputy Country Director; Dr. Kevin Kelly, Country Director

Relief International (RI) is a humanitarian non-profit agency that provides emergency relief, rehabilitation, and development assistance services to vulnerable communities worldwide. RI is dedicated to reducing human suffering and is non-political and sectarian in its mission.

The group has implemented programs to house over 1,925 displaced families, foster community and economic development, improve and protect livestock and agriculture, provide health care to those who need it, and educate children whose schools have been destroyed.

## "SANIYA" Information Analytical Agency

ul. Zardabi 80, etazh 5
Baku
**Tel:**      93-26-11, 93-48-98, 71-11-41
**E-mail:**   elchin@isar.baku.az

SANIYA began working in 1994 to provide information and legal services to unemployed sectors of the population, specifically targeting refugees and displaced persons. The agency conducts research on labor issues and the mass media, and works with the press to publicize issues of migration, refugees, and unemployment. With support from ISAR, SANIYA

published a bulletin on displaced persons and unemployment issues in 1997 as well as the bulletin *Emergency Migration in the CIS*. It also conducted a seminar entitled Role of Information Means in Labor Rehabilitation of Refugees and IDPs.

## Support Center for Democratic Elections

Rashid Behbudov 3
Baku
**Tel:**      98-31-79
**Fax:**     98-31-65
**Contact:** Ali Guliyev

The main goal of the center is to mobilize public opinion for democratic elections. It organizes conferences, works with political parties on practical election issues, and publishes booklets on election topics.

## Union of Azerbaijan Journalists

18 Bul-Bul av.
370000  Baku
**Tel:**      93-18-38, 93-63-42
**Fax:**     93-18-38
**Contact:** Gaji Gajiyev

The union works to defend the rights of journalists to receive and distribute information freely.

## Youth and Democracy Research Center

28th May St. 4, k. 34
Baku
**Tel:**      69-02-46, 98-50-86
**Fax:**     94-24-71
**E-mail:**   avaz@hca.baku.az
**Web:**     www.friends-partners.org/ ~ccsi/azerbaijan/azyfd.html
**Contact:** Avaz Hasanov, Director; Mahriban Mamedova

YDRC was created in 1997 to monitor and research the situation of youth, refugees, women, and children in Azerbaijan. The group writes briefs and proposals in an attempt to steer national legislation affecting youth. YDRC organizes conferences and seminars focusing on human rights and publishes newsletters, books, and magazines. Currently the group is writing articles related to state youth policy and compiling information on youth organizations in Azerbaijan in order to produce a booklet and directory.

# Belarus

**Country Code: 375**

## Minsk (172)

### ACCELS Minsk
pr. Skaryny 35, k.21
220005  Minsk
**Tel:**      36-68-83
**E-mail:**  netb@netb.minsk.by

See the profile for American Councils
for International Education in the North
American Organizations section.

### "April 26" Minsk Foundation
Sudmalisa 10-18
220033  Minsk
**Tel/Fax:** 61-21-21
**Contact:** Mikhail Obrazov, President

The nuclear reactor at Chernobyl
exploded on April 26, 1986. The April
26 Minsk Foundation was founded five
years later to help the people still
suffering from the disaster. With
assistance from its partners abroad, the
foundation has arranged for 100
children to be rehabilitated in France
and numerous adults in Germany. Its
partner in Japan has provided drugs and
medical equipment that the foundation
has distributed to local health facilities.
It also has helped organize training
abroad for local health officials.

### Assembly of Belarusian Pro-Democratic Non-Governmental Organizations
K. Marks St. 6, k. 36
220050  Minsk

**Tel/Fax:** 20-73-74
**E-mail:**  ngo@home.by
**Contact:** Vladimir Rovdo, Chairman of
the Executive Bureau

The assembly's first congress was held
on February 22, 1997, when 250 organizations decided to unite their efforts to
strengthen and develop Belarus's
democratic civic sector. Congresses are
held at least once a year. To coordinate
the activity of member NGOs between
congresses, the assembly has established a Working Group, which
facilitates the exchange of information
both among Belarusian NGOs and
between these NGOs and international
organizations, organizes roundtables to
discuss problems affecting the third
sector, defends the rights of NGOs, and
informs the public about their work.

### Belarus Association of Think Tanks (BATT)
a/ya 68
220030  Minsk
ul. Moskovskaya 18, k. 424
**Tel:**      45-29-19
**Fax:**      22-80-49
**E-mail:**  minskedu@user.unibel.by,
            vasel@user.unibel.by
**Web:**     www.cacedu.unibel.by/batt
**Contact:** Mr. Vassily Selishchev,
Executive Director; Prof. Oleg Manaev,
Chairman of Coordinating Board

"Professionalism and Civil Responsibility" is the motto of BATT. The
association was established in June
1997 by 15 leading non-state research
and analytical centers from Minsk and
most of the provinces of Belarus. It
unites dozens of leading scholars in
sociology, economics, law, psychology,
and political science, along with well-
known policymakers. BATT's mission

is "to promote the formation of civil society, democracy, the free market economy, and national sovereignty of Belarus." The founders of BATT were inspired by the success of Charter 77 and KOS-KOR's "invisible universities" in Czechoslovakia and Poland in 70s, which created independent and trusted sources of information and analysis about public policy in states whose governments sought monopoly control over public opinion.

BATT organizes quarterly briefings in Minsk and regions of Belarus, where important research results and analysis are presented to the public and diplomatic corps, as well as regional seminars for scholars and public policymakers. In June 1998 the association began publishing a quarterly *BATT Analytical Bulletin,* which is widely distributed in Belarus and abroad. BATT's plan of action includes an Internet-based communication network among members, development of a joint database of information, joint research projects, and various publications.

## Belarus Democratic Reforms Support L Sapieha Foundation

V. Khoruzhaya St. 416-13
220123   Minsk
**Tel:**      34-84-70
**Tel/Fax:** 34-37-91, 76-97-11
**E-mail:** Kobasa@sapieha.belpak. minsk.by
**Contact:** Miroslaw Kobasa, President

The foundation was established in 1992. Its members include deputies of the Belarus parliament, local town-council members, academics, journalists, and businessmen. It has participated in the work of the Congress of Local and Regional Authorities in Europe. It has organized conferences and issued papers on such topics as local government reform in Belarus. self-government in Poland and Germany, and municipal privatization programs. The foundation has regional branches in Grodna (tel/fax 0152-72-03-11), Gomel (0232-52-41-70), Brest (0162-66-569), Mogilev (0222-22-89-77), and Vitebsk (0212-22-49 25).

## Belarus Entomological Society

ul. Academicheskaya 27
220072   Minsk
**Tel:**      84-21-92
**Fax:**      84-10-36
**E-mail:** khotko@biobel.bas-net.by
**Contact:** Igor Lopatin, President; Eleonora Khotko, Vice President

The society unites entomologists from across Belarus to collaborate on research and share ideas. The group has published several of its members' works, including *Invertebrates of Priapyatskii National Park* and *Beetles of Belarus.*

## Belarus Science and Industry Association

ul. Lenina 19
220030   Minsk
**Fax:**      27-15-29
**Contact:** Vladimir Sobolev, Director of Overseas Economic Relations

## Belarusian-American Educational Project on Radiation Monitoring

pr. Gazety Pravda 58/2, k. 40
220116   Minsk
**Tel:**      36-35-81
**E-mail:** root@pchela@by.glas.apc.org
**Contact:** Olga V. Klimanovich

The project is active in environmental education and NGO development work.

## Belarusian Association for the Victims of Political Repression
ul. F. Skorina 1, k. 308
220072  Minsk
Tel:      39-58-89, 55-47-21
Contact: Valentina Vergei,
Coordinator

## Belarusian Association of Journalists
pr. Pravda 22, k. 672
220016  Minsk
Tel:      68-28-22, 68-29-23
Fax:      36-95-73
E-mail:   baj@user.unibel.by
Web:      www.baj.unibel.by
Contact: Zhanna Litvina, President;
Mikhail Pastukhov, Director; Serge
Komlatch, External Relations

BAJ works to strengthen the social, economic, and professional positions of journalists and to provide them legal assistance. The association has launched a new project to raise international awareness of the violations of journalists' rights in Belarus. Monthly reports monitor violations such as restricted access to information and harassment and intimidation of journalists. Events and activities of BAJ are included in the reports.

The BAJ Monitoring Network began working in 1998 as a joint endeavor of the BAJ central office in Minsk and its affiliated branches throughout Belarus, which gather and report information for the monthly reports. BAJ seeks ties to international associations of journalists in order to exchange information and obtain support for its activities.

## Belarusian Association of UNESCO Clubs
a/ya 432
220050  Minsk
Tel:      46-25-55, 46-41-73
Fax:      55-21-21
E-mail:   belau@user.unibel.by
Contact: Alexander Karankevich,
President

Founded in 1989, the association unites 46 UNESCO clubs of Belarus with a focus on education and culture. It organizes educational programs for teachers, youth club leaders, and UNESCO club members on such issues as peace education, AIDS prevention and safe sex, and leadership training. Since 1995, the association has held the National Conference on Peace Education in Minsk. It also organizes youth exchange programs, including the Cultural Triangle project, which involved exchanges with young people from Belarus, Germany, and Italy.

## Belarusian Congress of Democratic Trade Unions
Zakharova St. 24
220005  Minsk
Tel:      84-59-54
Fax:      84-31-82
E-mail:   khanhres@kanhres.
belpak.minsk
Contact: Gennady A. Bykov,
President; Anatoliy V. Gurinovich,
Executive Director

BCDTU was created in 1993 as a select group of Belarusian Trade Unions. It was forced to reorganize and expand the number of member organizations in 1996 due to political repression. BCDTU is still not officially recognized by the government of Belarus, but it continues to fight for the rights of its members. Currently it is focusing on training its members in an effort to organize the various national trade unions working to protect the rights of Belarusian labor. Seeking guarantees of health and labor safety, social guarantees, and adequate pay, BCDTU and its member organizations represent 20,000 Belarusian workers.

## Belarusian Fund "Liberty and Democracy"
a/ya 499
220050  Minsk-50
E-mail:  B_F_L_D@hotmail.com
Fax:  37-64-09
Web:  www.fund.minsk.by
Contact: Victor V. Gertsik

## Belarusian Helsinki Committee
ul. Gikalo 20-52
220071  Minsk
Tel:  36-06-08
Tel/Fax: 39-68-28
E-mail:  bhc@user.unibel.by
Web:  helsinki.home.by/
Contact: Tatyana Protko, President; Svetlana Kuro, Press Relations; Pavel Kurza, Secretary

The committee was registered in November 1995 and joined the International Helsinki Federation the next year. It has more than 100 members including, doctors, journalists, jurists, and scientists, as well as the heads of the Belarus PEN center, the head of the national journalists' association, and leaders of movements such as the Belarusian Popular Front.

The committee has organized numerous public events, including a Human Rights: Youth and Law seminar series. It documents violations of the Helsinki Accords in Belarus. In mid-1997 it published a long analysis of the situation in Belarus, *Crushing Civil Society*, which is available at their Web site.

## Belarusian Hospice for Children
Общественная благотворительная организация "Белорусский детский хоспис"
pr. Rokossovskogo, 63/2
220094  Minsk
Tel:  38-85-51
Fax:  38-85-31
E-mail:  hospice@user.unibel.by
Contact: Gorchakova Anna, Director; Petrovskaia Elena, Coordinator of the Program of Social Assistance

The Hospice for Children was founded in 1994 at the initiative of the republican onco-hematological center for children in order to provide professional medical help, counseling, legal advice, and financial assistance to terminally ill children and members of their families.

During its first four years of existence, hospice employees have helped 103 families and offered free counseling to more than 400 children who had lost a relative or a family member. Children receive medical care while parents and siblings are taught how to cope with psychological stress and care for the child. The hospice provides material help to low-income families with terminally ill children. It also pays for funeral services and requests religious services on behalf of some families.

The hospice has 20 employees including a pediatrician, a pharmacist, onco-hematologists, nurses, counselors, teachers, social workers, and a lawyer. It is financed through grants from local and foreign organizations and donations from commercial organizations, state agencies and individuals.

The hospice plans to open a training center within the next two years to train medical workers in methods of palliative medicine. It also plans to open a number of branches in Belarus's regions.

The hospice has the following partners: Children's Hospice in Warsaw, Charitable organization Hifswerk-Osterreich (Austria), Healthprom (Great Britain), TACIS, Christian Children's Foundation (U.S.), Healthcare Development Association (CIS), Counterpart Alliance (U.S.), Soros Foundation (U.S.), and UNICEF.

### Belarusian Library Association
49 F. Skoriny prospect
220005  Minsk
**Tel/Fax:** 31-66-90
**E-mail:** root@bibsport.minsk.by
**Web:** www.kolas.bas-net.by
**Contact:** Vladimir Soroko, President

BLA was founded in 1992 and unites institutional libraries and individual library members. Members of the association hold over 20 million printed publications and 19 million invention descriptions, which are kept on microfiche in the Republican Public Science and Technical Library. Recently BLA has been involved in new legislation concerning librarians, libraries, and the distribution of information. They have also conducted seminars covering the electronic media's role in libraries.

### Belarusian National Council of Youth and Children's Associations
K. Marx St. 40
220030  Minsk

**Tel:**     21-81-79
**Fax:**     22-30-05
**E-mail:**  rada.by@usa.net

The council unites 27 national youth organizations. It works to coordinate the activities of its members, defend the interests of young people, and cooperate with national youth councils in other countries. It also organizes training programs for young leaders.

### "Belarusian Perspective" Non-Governmental Center for Analysis and Research
ul. Plekhanov 52-1-136
Minsk
**Tel/Fax:** 26-87-99
**Contact:** V. Ivashkevich, Executive Director

The center was created in 1995 with a mission to support the development of democracy, human rights, and a transition to a market economy in Belarus. It conducts seminars, conferences, and discussions and contributes to the drafting of national legislation. In 1995-96, the center conducted four international conferences: Problems of Attracting Foreign Investors to the Economies of Eastern European Countries, Problems of Market Reforms in Agriculture in Eastern Europe, Leadership and Its Role in Post-Communist Society, and Problems of National and Cultural Identification in Belarus. In the autumn of 1996 the center conducted a number of regional conferences in Grodna, Brest, Vitebsk, and Mogilev on the problems of democratic transformations at the local level.

### Belarusian Popular Front
**E-mail:**  BPF@bpf.minsk.by

## Brest Independent Sociological and Psychological Center

2-338 Gorovtsa St.
220094   Minsk
**Tel:**   49-95-53
**Contact:** Dr. Sergey Shein, Director;
A. Mushnitski, Executive Director

Founded in 1991, BISPC has organized "focus groups" and trained factory employees in the context of privatization programs, conducted public opinion surveys for the International Finance Corporation (World Bank), published articles in the *Brest Courier*, organized the Brest Business Club, and developed training programs for NGO and small business leaders. It has a staff of 7 full-time and 23 part-time persons and offices in Minsk, Brest, and Grodna.

## Bureau for Environmental Consulting (BURENCO)

Бюро по Экологическим Консультациям
a/ya 53
220027   Minsk
**Tel:**   31-30-52
**Fax:**   31-30-49
**E-mail:**   koltunov@ecodcpt.unibel.by
         polina@ecodept.unibel.by
**Contact:** Vladimir Koltunov, Director;
Polina Pimenova, Coordinator

BURENCO was established in 1996 as a result of a joint project, Sister City Efforts for a Healthy Environment, sponsored by Minsk and its sister city Eindhoven, Netherlands. It works to promote greater public awareness of environmental issues among the citizens of Minsk. The group sponsored a drawing competition for children on the theme "How would I encourage people to save energy and water?" Winners'

drawings were used on posters promoting conservation and placed in the Minsk subway. BURENCO also sponsors seminars on environmental themes for secondary school teachers and Belarusian NGOs.

## Charter '97

Pl. Svabody, 17-508
220061   Minsk
**Tel/Fax:** 39-62-89
**E-mail:**   charter@charter97.org
**Web:**   www.charter97.org,
www.ilhr.org/league/league_index.html
**Contact:** Andrei Sannikov, International Coordinator; Oleg Bebenin, Press Secretary

This is a popular movement modeled on the Charter '77 movement in Czechoslovakia, which united intellectuals against the communist regime. Charter '97 was formed in Minsk in December 1997 when 100 well-known Belarusian politicians, human rights activists, lawyers, artists and journalists signed the Charter '97 document, which called for a free and prosperous Belarus governed by democracy and the rule of law. Within a year, 100,000 Belarusian citizens had signed the Charter.

The main aim of Charter '97 is to unify the efforts of organizations and individuals who share the idea of democracy. It has provided financial and legal assistance to more than 300 people persecuted by the regime. It initiates protests and has organized numerous concerts of folk and rock singers to promote national Belarusian culture. The press office publishes a monthly bulletin about human rights violations in the country. With assistance from groups abroad, it has helped arrange visits for Belarusian journalists and politicians to democratic countries in the West. Charter '97 has representative offices in Brussels and New York and plans to open others in Kyiv, Moscow, Prague, and Warsaw.

The International League for Human Rights, based in New York, has an active program to support Charter '97. Information about the Charter is available at their Web site (www.ilhr.org). ILHR also issues a biweekly e-mail bulletin that includes news about Belarus and the activities of democratic organizations. To be added to the distribution list, contact: belarus@ilhr.org.

### "Discussion" Women's Club

c/o Ann Sergeeva or Vita Isaenko
a/ya 5 (postal address)
Karbysheva St. 11-48
220119   Minsk
**Tel:**        63-77-36
**Fax:**       30-80-54, 31-04-72
**E-mail:**   beluwi@minsk.sovam.com,
             beri@cwer.belpak.minsk.by
**Contact:** Anna Sergeeva, President

Discussion is an independent NGO founded in 1993. Its purpose is to strengthen women's influence in national life by means of partnerships, training activity, and informational exchanges and to develop contacts with women's organizations in Belarus and throughout the world.

The club has organized workshops and roundtable discussions on problems of women's NGOs and the status of women in Belarus. It has also developed psychology and language courses for women and collected information about women's NGO activity in Belarus and abroad, plus statistical and other materials related to different aspects of women's lives.

### East European Jewish Heritage Project

13b Dauman St.
220002   Minsk
**Tel/Fax:**  34-56-12, 34-33-60
**E-mail:**   root@eejhp.open.by
**Contact:**  Frank Swartz, Executive Director

The project was initiated in 1991 to provide assistance to victims of the Holocaust and to preserve and promote East European Jewish culture. The project has restored Jewish monuments, supplied eyeglasses to elderly Jews, established a Resource and Research Center for Jewish Culture, and supplied Yiddish libraries in two communities. Its current projects include restoring Jewish buildings and cemeteries, providing medical supplies and aid to 5,000 people, and compiling an oral history archive of pre-war Jewish life.

The project has offices in Minsk, London and Oxford, England, and Philadelphia.

### "Envila" Women's College

ul. Karla Marxa 25/78
220002   Minsk
**Tel:**        26-06-87
**Contact:**  Galina Shaton, Vice Rector

### Environmental Chemistry Society of Senior Students

Экологическое химическое общество старшеклассников и студентов (ЗХОСС)
a/ya 120
220027   Minsk
**Tel:**        39-92-14
**Fax:**       31-36-17
**E-mail:**   dov_zone19@infra.belpak.minsk.by
**Contact:**  Tatiana Dovbyisheva, Chair

Also known as the Ecological Chemical Society of High School and College Students, this organization was formed in 1991 to increase environmental awareness and conservation activity among Belarusian youth. Students of the society conduct environmental monitoring expeditions and publish information on specific environmental concerns. In 1994, the society conducted a research project, Drinking Water, in which it measured the levels of chlorine in city tap water as compared to natural water sources, and presented the results in local newspapers, TV and radio. From 1995 to 1997, the society studied pollution levels in Minsk through the Clean Air–Health for All project, the results of which were also presented in the mass media. The society is also concerned with health problems resulting from the Chernobyl nuclear accident in 1986, especially among children

## F. Skaryna National Scientific and Educational Center

vul. Revaliucyjnaja 15
220050   Minsk
**Tel/Fax:**   20-93-50, 20-76-04,
             20-51-57
**E-mail:**   mab@lingvo.minsk.by

The Skaryna Center of the Belarusian Ministry of Education and Science also houses the International Association for Belarusian Studies. Together they have organized international conferences and symposia such as Ideals in the Post-Communist Countries, and—with additional support from UNESCO— Non-Forcible Variants of Restitution: Joint Use of Disputed Cultural Objects.

Questions concerning membership in the International Association for Belarusian Studies can be addressed to

the IAB committee at the Skaryna Center at the e-mail address above.

## "FIALTA" Youth Education Center

pr. Skorinyi 65
220027   Minsk
**Tel:**        10-16-83, 48-13-32
**E-mail:**   fialta@user.unibel.by
**Contact:** Svetlana Papsui

Fialta was founded in 1995 and now operates on local, national, and international levels. It organizes educational and training programs for young people, aged 14 and older, on aspects of human relations, leadership empowerment, and team building. Fialta also organizes training programs on NGO development issues.

## For the Children of Chernobyl

ul. Starovilenskaya 14
220029   Minsk
**Tel:**        34-12-15, 34-21-53
**Fax:**       34-34-58
**E-mail:**   bbf@charity.belpak.minsk.by
**Contact:** Gennady Grushevoy, Ph.D., Chairman of the Board

For the Children of Chernobyl was founded in 1989 and legally registered in 1990. Dr. Grushevoy has been a professor of philosophy at Belarusian State University since 1973 and a member of the Belarus parliament since 1990. The organization claims to be one of the largest self-supported social organizations in Belarus. It has support teams in over 20 cities or regions of the country and over 40 long-term programs of charitable, medical, and humanitarian outreach.

Among other accomplishments, it has arranged for nearly 400 sick children to receive medical treatment abroad; provided direct material aid to thousands of evacuee families, Chernobyl invalids, and rescue workers; constructed a facility for producing organically grown food on a collective farm in the Brest district; created specialized nursery school programs for handicapped children; and facilitated direct relations between foreign partners of the fund and hospitals, schools, orphanages and other public organizations in 32 areas of Belarus.

### Independent Institute of Social, Economic and Political Studies (IISEPS)

a/ya 329 (postal address)
220101   Minsk
ul. Moskovskaya 18, k. 424
**Tel/Fax:**  22-80-49
**E-mail:**   iiseps@user.unibel.by
**Web:**      www.cacedu.unibel.
by/iiseps
**Contact:** Prof. Oleg Manaev, Director; Dr. Alexander Sosnov, Deputy Director; Dr. Yuri Drakokhrust, Head of IISEPS Center for Documentation

Founded in February 1992 by a group of academics, journalists, politicians, and private entrepreneurs, The mission of IISEPS is to promote the "formation of democracy, civil society, and free market economy in Belarus." Its main activities include research, consulting, organizing conferences and seminars, networking among civil society organizations, publishing and distributing analytical materials, and professional training. In six and a half years, it has organized 30 regional, national, and international conferences and seminars; conducted more than 30 research projects; and published more than 130 analytical papers and more than 800 articles in the mass media (including TV and radio broadcasting). Since 1996, the Institute has published (in Russian and English) a quarterly analytical bulletin *IISEPS News*.

IISEPS conducts two national polls annually and interviews public-policy leaders and experts on a quarterly basis. It regularly analyzes the Belarusian mass media, program documents of political parties and public associations, new legislation, and economic statistics and data.

IISEPS has collected numerous documents in its five years of activity, including profiles on 100 of "the most influential leaders of Belarus." These have been classified and cataloged, and now are stored in IISEPS's Center for Documentation, the first non-state center of its kind in the country. IISEPS has also created public access sites for its materials at the National Archives of the Republic of Belarus and at Belarusian State University. In 1997, IISEPS created the Belarus Association of Think Tanks (see separate entry). IISEPS has nine full-time and six part-time researchers, half of whom have a Ph.D.s in the social sciences.

In 1998, IISEPS's sources of funding were divided between international foundations (70%), international government organizations (15%), fees for services (10%) and sales of literature and materials (5%).

### IREX ProMedia Office

a/ya 90
220005   Minsk
**Tel/Fax:**  27-15-72
**Fax:**      29-29-87
**E-mail:**   110141.2076@compuserve.com

For an overview of IREX's ProMedia project, see the profile for ProMedia in the Ukrainian Organizations section.

## IREX RSEP/CI Alumni Coordinator

"Envila" Women's College
ul. Karla Marxa 25/78
220002 Minsk
**Tel:** 26-06-87
**Contact:** Galina Shaton, Vice Rector

## "Legislative Initiative" Foundation

a/ya 260
220098 Minsk
**Tel:** 21-58-68
**Fax:** 21-58-68
**E-mail:** fli@fli.minsk.by
**Contact:** Alexander F. Spiglazov, Executive Director

The foundation was established in 1996 by leading members of the Belarusian government and academia to change the laws of Belarus so that they would support and promote the rule-of-law, market economy, independent media, and human rights. It organizes lectures and seminars around Belarus on rule-of-law issues.

## Minsk Gender Center

Минский Гендерный Центр
a/ya 200 (postal address)
220002 Minsk
or
ul. Belozavodskaya 3
220033 Minsk
**Tel:** 26-04-19, 84-86-93
**Fax:** 26-06-87
**E-mail:** envila@user.unibel.by,
ira@tchikal.belpak.minsk.by
**Web:** www.geocities.com/
CapitolHill/Senate/5479

**Contact:** Irina Tchikalova, Executive Director

The Minsk Gender Center performs academic research on women's issues in contemporary Belarus and lobbies for equal rights for women. Current research projects of the center include a three-year study of women in economic disciplines, the Women and Politics: A Comparative Study project, and the Gender Interpretation in Pedagogics study. Since 1996, the center has worked on implementing the Economics for Women Through Computer Technologies project, financed by the Eurasia Foundation and the Open Society Institute. The center has organized a number of conferences and roundtables, including Women and Education (1996), Women and Education in the Changing World (1998), and Children's Rights–Women's Rights.

## National Center for Strategic Initiatives "East-West"

ul. Varvasheni 77, k. 601-603
220002 Minsk
**Tel:** 34-01-61, 34-69-88
**E-mail:** main@centre.minsk.by
**Contact:** Dr. Leonid Zaiko, President

Established in May 1992, the center organizes conferences and roundtables, and has issued an analytical journal, *Belarus Monitor*, since 1995. It also publishes occasional reports, including "Problems of Civil Society Formation in Belarus," issued in January 1996.

## Support Center for Associations and Foundations

ul. Korolys 16, k. 327-328
220004 Minsk
**Tel:** 29-19-31

**Fax:**　　34-71-29
**E-mail:**　izag@scaf.minsk.by,
　　　　　vasel@scaf.minsk.by
**Web:**　　www.scaf.minsk.by

SCAF was established in 1995 in order to promote "good practice and effective work" among Belarusian NGOs. The center distributes information about effective foundations and associations, funding practices, grant management, NGO governance, and legal and fiscal matters. In 1997, SCAF published *Guidelines for NGO and Grant Management in Belarus*. It also works with government and non-governmental organizations to increase public understanding of foundations and NGOs, and helps local and Western grant makers to identify potential partners in Belarus.

## United Way of Belarus

3 Uralskaya St., k. 30
220038　Minsk
**Tel:**　　30-32-76
**Tel/fax:**　30-80-54
**E-mail:**　uwb@user.unibel.by
**Web:**　　www.uwb.unibel.by
**Contact:** Anna I. Sergeyeva, Program Coordinator

United Way International began its activity in Belarus in 1993 with a research grant from World Learning. Funding from the Eurasia Foundation made it possible to establish United Way Belarus, a national organization. In 1994, United Way Belarus created a Belarusian Center for NGO Development, which offers the following services free-of-charge to newly created NGOs: use of computers, fax, e-mail, telephones and photocopier; a library of NGO development materials; quarterly seminars; monthly roundtables for both the PVO and NGO community;

publication of a monthly newsletter; consultations on how to prepare proposals; legal advice; a database of existing NGOs; and temporary office space for visiting NGOs. The office employs six full-time and three full-time employees as well as around 30 volunteers.

## Women's Christian-Democratic Movement of Belarus

Pr. Gasety Pravda 11
220116　Minsk
**Tel/Fax:**　72-20-98, 50-31-68
**E-mail:**　wcdmb@user.unibel.by
**Contact:** Liudmila Petina, President

WCDM began working in 1991 to conduct research, education and consulting on the status of women in Belarus. It organized the International Congress entitled Woman, Family and Society in 1994, attended by about 200 Belarusian women and representatives from 15 countries. The movement conducted an educational program for women NGO leaders and has held conferences such as Women and Poverty, Women and Violence, Women and Mass Media, and Women in Decision-Making. It has also participated in numerous international conferences on women's issues. WCDM has offices in six cities of Belarus and 380 registered members.

In March 1998, WCDM opened the Women's Education and Consulting Center with funding from Counterpart. Over 100 women have received assistance through the center, which provides professional development programs and encourages women's participation in public affairs. The center also maintains a database on legal issues and employment information and statistics, and provides consulting for victims of sexual abuse. The center publishes a monthly bulletin, *We Are Women*, and organized the seminar Women in Small Business: the First Steps and a workshop for journalists, Women and Mass-Media: Transformation of Gender Stereotypes.

## Youth Information Center
P.O. Box 493
220050  Minsk
**Tel/Fax:** 33-22-94
**E-mail:**  ylc@user.unibel.by
**Web:**  www.ned.org/page_3/yic/

The center was founded in 1994 to help young people gain the experience and knowledge for participation in non-governmental organizations. It organizes information exchanges with Belarusian and foreign youth groups, maintains a database, conducts research on state youth policy and the perspectives of youth movements in Belarus, promotes library and archival cooperation in the field of independent youth publishing, and conducts seminars for young leaders.

## Brest (0162)

### Info-Center
Blvd. Kosmonavtov 48
224016  Brest
**Tel:**  23-21-23, 23-42-29
**E-mail:**  info@ssw.belpak.brest.by,
valeri@ssw.belpak.brest.by
**Contact:** Valeri S. Fominski, Executive Director

The Info-Center in Brest was founded by local educators, "computer geeks," and human service professionals to make Internet resources available to local non-governmental organizations,

schools, hospitals, libraries, and others that need them.

## Gomel (232)

### Civil Initiatives
ul. M. Bogdanovicha 22-106
246010  Gomel
**Tel:**  54-60-05
**Fax:**  52-41-70
**E-mail:**  viktor@bsfdr.gomel.by
**Contact:** Viktor Korneenko, President

Civil Initiatives was created by leaders of citizen groups from Gomel and six nearby cities or towns, and was officially registered in 1996. Its goal is to support the "processes of democratic reforms in the Gomel region in the sphere of human rights, economic reforms, science, culture and ecology." (Gomel was very strongly affected by Chernobyl.) The association has branches in Zhlobin, Kalinkovichi, Loyev, Mozyr, Rechitsa, Rogachev, and Svetlogorsk.

### Green Class
ul. Sovetskaya 106, kv. 65
246028  Gomel
**Tel:**  56-99-17
**Fax:**  44-23-52
**E-mail:**  greenway@karopa.belpak.
gomel.by, gnkaropa@gsu.unibel.by
**Contact:** Dr. Gennadiy N. Karopa,

Green Class was established in 1993 to develop "modern systems of environmental education in Belarus." It has developed a curriculum about nuclear contamination that is used in schools in the Chernobyl region. It has also conducted many conservation projects in and around Gomel.

In 1998, it began publishing a newsletter, *Green Way*, which is dedicated to the human right to live in a healthy environment and to publicizing authentic information about environmental conditions. The project seeks to establish in Belarus "the international principle of a community's 'right to know.'" Green Class has more than 180 members and 16 regional branches.

## Gomel Regional Department of the Belarusian Committee "Children of Chernobyl"

Pushkin St., d. 34, k. 11
26400    Gomel
**Tel:**     53-78-08
**Fax:**    57-12-48
**E-mail:**  root@cherchild.
belpak.gomel.by
**Contact:** Eleonora Kapitonova, Chairman of the Presidium; Elena Levchenko, Deputy Chairman.

The organization was registered in 1995 and is one of seven regional departments of the Belarusian Committee "Children of Chernobyl." (The national office in Minsk is headed by Tamara Belookaya.) The organization's goal is to "protect the future and the health of the Belarusian children affected by the accident." GRDBC brings together many of the most active and well-informed experts on the Chernobyl disaster: members of the scientific and medical communities, teachers, psychologists, journalists, lawyers, and economists. The group's establishment nine years after the accident is attributed to the fact that before 1995 "there was no scientific medical manpower in [the Gomel] region." This changed with the establishment of the Gomel Medical Institute in the years 1990–92.

Among the accomplishments of GRDBC are:

- the creation of the Gomel NGO Resource Center
- publication of a quarterly information bulletin, *The NGO Establishment*
- production of a series of broadcasts and telecasts
- a permanent column on public health in a regional newspaper.

GRDBC has organized training seminars on NGO management, writing grant proposals, computer use and modern information technologies, legal and financial aspects of NGO activities, environmental law, children's rights, business ethics and psychology, youth and leadership development, and how to start a new NGO. It has published manuals or worksheets for most of these training programs. It has also published the *Gomel Province NGO Directory*, and provides local NGOs with access to its database, as well as the temporary use of office equipment.

## "ORACUL" Independent Sociological Center

ul. Lange 17
246050    Gomel
**Tel/Fax:** 55-14-54
**E-mail:**  anat@ora.gomel.by
**Contact:** Dr. Anatoly Kayanenko, Director

Oracul was created in 1989 as a non-governmental, educational, research, publishing, and training organization. Though independent of Gomel State University, it makes extensive use of its professional staff and facilities. Dr. Kasyanenko teaches at GSU, and many of the center's projects have been conducted through academic partnerships with, for example, Cornell and the University of Michigan. The Belarusian-Dutch Health Information

Center is a project organized in cooperation with the Utrecht Academic Hospital in the Netherlands. A project on the psychological consequences of the Chernobyl disaster is funded by European Community, and with experts from Russia and Ukraine.

In 1995, the center started a project together with ACDI/VOCA, (see profile in North American Organizations), aimed at promoting the development of private farming in Belarus.

### Grodna (152)

### Grodna Regional Center for Informational Support of Civic Initiatives "The Third Sector"
a/ya 54
230009   Grodna
**Tel:**   31-83-84
**Tel/Fax:** 33- 12-74
**E-mail:**   sektar@iname.com
**Contact:** Vitaut Rudnik, Chairman

Thir Sector was established in 1997 by a group of journalists, representatives of Belarusian NGOs, and civic education activists with the mission to create a system of information exchange for the third sector and independent mass media in Grodna oblast. The center acts as an information clearinghouse, maintains a resource library for local NGOs, and offers training in publishing and information management. Its newsletter, *Treci Sektar*, is distributed to approximately 300 local NGOs.

The center has also administered the School of Young Journalist for the past two years, and reports that the majority of its 60 graduates are currently employed in 18 Belarusian newspapers. Third Sector has partnerships with

IREX-Kyiv, EJN-Prague, Institute for Democracy in Eastern Europe in Warsaw, and the Foundation in Support of Local Democracy in Szczecin, Poland.

### Grodna Regional Council of Youth Organizations "RADA-23"
a/ya 233
230023   Grodna
**Tel:**   33-12-74
**Fax:**   33-12-74
**E-mail:**   vit@saleis.belpak.Grodna.by, rada-23@jansco.syslab.ceu.hu
**Web:**   www.syslab.ceu.hu/~rada-23
**Contact:** Siarhei Salei, Chairman

RADA-23 is an information resource center for youth organizations from Grodna and Grodna oblast. It was established by representatives of nine youth organizations in December 1996 to coordinate local NGO activities for youth. RADA-23 currently works with more than 20 youth groups and has held a series of seminars on NGO registration, NGO cooperation, and general development issues for youth organizations. It has affiliates in four small towns of Grodna oblast and partnerships with L'Espace Ressources Jeunes in Roubaix, France, and the Institute for Democracy in Eastern Europe in Warsaw, Poland.

### Mogilev (0222)

### Mogilev City Association "Humanitarian Initiative"
Prospekt Mira 20-32
121030   Mogilev
**Tel:**   22-04-82
**Contact:** Dr. Valeri Sivukha, Chairman of the Board

This organization, founded in late 1996, aims to "promote the institutions of civil society...and revival of the traditions of humanism and democracy" in Belarus. It is eager to promote "peoples' diplomacy" and participate in international programs.

### Youth Ecologogical Club "Hoosphera"
Молодёжный экоклуб "Ноосфера"
ul. Kashtanovaia 25-26
212008   Mogilev
**Tel:**      24-00-63
**Fax:**      31-06-00
**Contact:** Yulia Vorobyeva

Founded in 1998, the club has established an environmental-information center to educate youth on conservation issues.

## *Novopolotsk (0214)*

### Fund for Social Protection of Invalids and the Elderly
ul. Molodyezhnaya 111-21
211440   Novopolotsk
**Tel:**      42-28-01
**Contact:** Nikolai Lukashevich, President

This fund provides medical, social, legal, and psychological assistance to pensioners and invalids in the city of Novopolotsk and regions of Vitebsk oblast. Founded in 1996, the fund's main mission is to improve the standard of living for disadvantaged segments of the population. In cooperation with the Salvation Army, the Fund created the Rehabilitation Center for Invalids and Elderly of Novopolotsk through which it conducts several assistance projects.

The programs Home Services, Nutrition for the Elderly, and Psychological Assistance, for example, have reached over 800 people in the region.

The fund has received grants and humanitarian assistance from Counterpart Consortium and the Salvation Army. It is interested in fostering international partnerships in order to exchange experiences and information. It also plans to set up an international legal and information center for organizations involved in invalid and pensioner assistance projects.

## *Slutsk (1795)*

### "Children in Trouble" Regional Branch of Belarusian Society
Слуцкое отделение Белорусского общества "Дети в беде"
ul. Soligorskaia 6-159
223610   Slutsk
**Tel:**      2-08-85, 2-70-12
**Contact:** Irina Babaitseva

The society seeks to bring the problems and misfortune of children to the attention of local and national authorities. It is a member of the Soligorsk Regional Center of Public Initiative.

### Independent Trade Union of Railroad Workers
Независимый профсоюз Железнодорожников
ul. Chekhova 59-36
223610   Slutsk
**Tel:**      4-48-98, 4-25-22, 9-32-67
**Contact:** Aleksei Podubitsky

The union works to protect the economic and social rights of railroad workers. It has a membership of 70 and is a member of the Soligorsk Regional Center of Public Initiative.

## Vytoki Association
Слуцкая ассоциация содействия формированию демократического общества "Вытокі"
ul. 8 Marta 22a
223610 Slutsk
**Tel/Fax:** 2 09 04
**E-mail:** vytoki@user.unibel.by
**Contact:** Sergei Stankevich, Executive Director; Vladimir Protasevich, Executive Secretary

Vytoki was organized in 1995 on the initiative of city council deputies and representatives from the fields of education, medicine, and culture to promote civil society in Belarus. It organized the seminar, Problems of Power Decentralization in the Republic of Belarus: How It Was Done in Poland, and a seminar on student exchanges for local high school students. Vytoki also published a book on architectural monuments in the region, and trained members of NGOs to use e-mail and the Internet. The organization publishes a weekly newsletter, *Kis-Kurier.*

## Soligorsk (1710)

### "Ragneda" Women's Organization
Женская организация "Рагнеда"
Zheleznodorozhnaya 12
223710 Soligorsk
**Tel:** 5-30-91, 3-71-41
**Contact:** Tamara Egiyan, Natalia Chechykha

Founded in 1996, Ragneda is a union of Soligorsk women that works to defend the interests and rights of women. The union is a member of the Regional Center of Public Initiative (see profile below).

### Soligorsk Regional Center of Public Initiative
Солигорский региональный центр общественных инициатив
Zheleznodorozhnaya 12
223710 Soligorsk
**Tel:** 2-06-22, 2-31-53
**Fax:** 2-00-59, 2-02-34, 3-72-01
**Contact:** Alexander Dovnar, Director; Alexander Korolev, Irina Babaitseva, Coordinators

Founded in 1997, the center consists of 21 social organizations in the cities of Soligorsk (15 groups), Slutsk (3), Mozir (2) and Mikashevich (1), which work together in support of civil society development in Belarus. The largest supporting organization of the center is the independent *profsoyuz*, or trade union, in the Soligorsk region. SRCPI's members strive to increase citizen participation in public life, local and national elections, and community problem-solving. They also support local citizen initiatives to strengthen the country's third sector of independent, non-commercial organizations. They distribute information to the public on democracy, political and economic reform, and civil society, and encourage local NGOs to do the same. In 1998, SRCPI conducted a conference, Non-Governmental Organizations in the Provinces of Belarus: Problems and Solutions, attended by 96 regional NGO representatives.

## Vitebsk (0212)

### Jewish Human Relations Club
### The Friends' House
Chernichovskova Ave. 22-5-41
210027   Vitebsk
**Tel:**      22-40-49, 24-83-46 (home)
**Fax:**     25-43-21
**Contact:** Olga Isser, President

The club coordinates pen pals programs and student exchanges at the high school and university level.

### "Private Initiative" Voters' Club of Vitebsk
Витебский городской клуб избирателей "Частная инициатива"
pr. Cheryakhovskogo 20, 7-18
210027   Vitebsk
**Tel:**      21-26-15, 25-04-03, 25-20-56
**E-mail:** inform@vcm.belpak.vitebsk.by
**Contact:** Valerii Zhurakovsky, Chairman

The main goals of the Private Initiative club are to build a foundation for legal and political culture in Belarus, to form a positive public opinion of democratic and economic reforms, to encourage voters to take a more active role in elections, and to unify the efforts of voters and elected officials in solving civic problems.

Members of Private Initiative monitored local elections in Vitebsk during 1995 and 1996. Additionally, the club has organized a series of public seminars and lectures on topics such as consumers' rights, the importance of civic participation, and local self-government. It has recently established a school for young leaders.

Private Initiative has 42 members and an annual budget of around $10,000.

### Belarusian Center of Ecological Information and Biodiversity Conservation
Белорусский эколого-информационный центр охраны дикой природы
Lepelskii raion, Vitebskaia oblast
211188   Domzheritsy
**Tel:**      (02132) 2-64-59
**E-mail:** leadkash@ber_bio.belpak.vitebsk.by
**Contact:** Aleksandr P. Kashtalian, Chairman; Igor I. Byshnev, Co-Chairman

The center was founded in 1997 as the Belarusian branch of the Russian organization Center for Biodiversity. In June 1998, it registered in Belarus as a national organization. The center's main goal is to increase cooperation between environmentalists, intellectuals, and scientists in Belarus in order to protect the biological diversity of the country, support existing nature preserves, and create new ones. Some of the priorities of the center include:
- Environmental education
- Collection, analysis and distribution of information on environment in Belarus
- Development of recommendations on nature protection and the rational use of resources
- Research on biodiversity

It participated in "Parks March" in 1997 and 1998 to protect and clean-up city parks. It is also a member of the "Biodiversity 12" coalition and the Working Group for an Environmental Network in Northern Eurasia.

# Georgia

## Country Code: 995

### Tbilisi (32)

### A Call to Serve Georgia (ACTS–Georgia)
ul. Asatiani 7a
Tbilisi
**Tel/Fax:** 39-37-76
**E-mail:** acts@acts.ge
**Contact:** Gia Tsilosani

This organization, formed in August 1993 and affiliated with ACTS International in California, works with the Salvation Army, Georgian Red Cross and other relief organizations to provide food, medicine and shelter to refugees from civil conflict. It works closely with the Georgian Medical Association, the first private professional association in the country. With four regional offices, ACTS claims to have the only nationwide distribution system for medications and medical supplies. ACTS recently provided free examinations and treatment for 800 diabetics. The organization also sent a mission of physicians to examine prison patients and visits regional outpatient clinics.

### AIDS Foundation–XXI Century without AIDS
pr. Gamsakhurdia 14b, k. 47
Tbilisi
**Tel:** 38-19-12, 38-26-67
**Fax:** 00-11-53
**Contact:** David Kvaliashvili

Since 1996, the foundation has offered free educational and consulting services with physicians, lawyers and psychologists to people with AIDS. They also have created an information bank.

### Association for the Social Protection and Rehabilitation of Disabled Children
pr. Vazha Pshavela 18a
Tbilisi
**Tel:** 39-65-74
**Contact:** Maia Bibileishvili, Tamar Maglakelidze

The association has been working to persuade the state to fund medical treatment for disabled children. The association has:
- Distributed 500 language textbooks, specially written for disabled children, to the Tbilisi Disabled Children's School, with funding from ISAR.
- Started a bakery, with support from Save the Children, where nine fathers work to support their children and the association.
- Established a "psycho-pedagogical correction group" for children with mental development challenges, with funding from OXFAM.

### Biological Farming Association "Elkana"
ul. Delisi III 13
Tbilisi
**Tel:** 53-64-87, 53-64-85
**E-mail:** elkana@access.sanet.ge
**Contact:** Nana Nemsadze

Elkana was established in 1993 by a group of farmers and members of the Georgia Green party to promote organic and biological farming in Georgia. Nearly 30 farms across Georgia participate in Elkana. Each farm serves as an organic farming model for its area, and each farmer is required to contribute a percentage of his or her produce to a local charity. For example, one farm provided vegetables for a soup kitchen for pensioners in Tbilisi, and in return, the employees of the soup kitchen assisted the farmer during harvest.

Elkana is establishing an organic farming school and demonstration site near Tbilisi and provides courses on farming and ecology. The school will serve as an extension service and provide on-site consultation for local farmers. Elkana is also translating nearly 200 books and documents on organic farming into Georgian and, with a grant from ISAR, will publish a journal and brochures on a variety of organic farming methods and topics.

## Business Law Center
pl. May Square 26/2, k. 419
Tbilisi
**Tel:**      94-16-05
**Fax:**      94-15-04
**E-mail:**   vazha@gedi.org.ge
**Contact:** Vazha Salamadze

Established in 1996, the center aims to support the development of a strong legal basis for a market economy in Georgia and render assistance to entrepreneurs in business law issues. The center offers free consulting and seminars on legal and tax issues. In March 1998, it published a book, *Investor's Guide for Georgian Business Law*, with funding from USAID/Save the Children.

## Caucasian Institute for Peace, Democracy and Development
pr. David Agmashenebeli 89/24
Tbilisi
**Tel:**      95-47-23
**Fax:**      95-44-97
**E-mail:**   cipdd@access.sanet.ge
**Contact:** Gia Nodia

CIPDD, founded in August 1992, is involved in research and publishing activities. Its main objective is "to promote democratic and free-market values, publicize the major achievements of Western democratic thought, and encourage non-partisan theoretical analysis of problems related to the post-Communist transition process in Georgia and the Caucasus region."

The institute has:
- sponsored a survey of public attitudes toward law and legality in Georgia
- coordinated a project (for the UN Development Program) that resulted in the publication of *Human Development Report for Georgia*
- organized seminars and conferences on topics such as regional problems of the Caucasus and the socio-psychological problems of a post-communist transition
- Participated in a research project on "Ethnic Conflicts in the NIS, financed by the European Community and led by the London School of Economics.

CIPDD has translated and published:
- the Universal Declaration of Human Rights
- Montesquieu's *Spirit of the Laws*
- early-20th-Century essays by Russian philosophers on themes of democracy and revolution
- M. Mamardashvili's *Classic and Non-Classic Ideals of Rationality*
- Vaclav Havel's *Power of the Powerless*
- *Reason from Woe*, a collection of original essays on the problems of democratic transition in Georgia.

CIPDD issues a monthly bulletin in English, *The Georgian Chronicle*, which is available by e-mail or international mail upon request. It published an informational brochure on political parties in Georgia in October 1992 and another is forthcoming.

Besides CIPDD's permanent staff, 25–30 persons are associated with the institute on a contractual basis. It is loosely organized into four units: Publishing House, Video Studio, Information Unit, and Conference Unit.

## Center for Development and Cooperation

ul. Atoneli 31/2
380000   Tbilisi
**Tel/Fax:** 93-25-36
**E-mail:**   cdc@access.sanet.ge
             objective@iberiapac.ge
**Contact:** Otar Zoidze, Director; Ivlian Haindrava, Program Director; David Berdzenishivili, Board Member

CDC works to promote the development of the NGO sector in Georgia and to facilitate cooperation among Caucasian and East European NGOs on topics of human and civil rights. It publishes a weekly bulletin covering Georgian social and political events, which is available in print and electronically. It also translates and edits books and films on human rights and conflict resolution.

Founded in 1996, CDC is a member of the Centers for Pluralism, an informal network of civic education organizations in Central and Eastern Europe and the NIS, which is coordinated by the Institute for Democracy in Eastern Europe in Warsaw, Poland.

## Center for Enterprises Restructuring and Management Assistance

ul. Zubalashvili 12a
380008   Tbilisi
**Tel:**       92-03-69
**Tel/Fax:** 92-03-68
**E-mail:**   cerma@caucasus.net

**Contact:** Nana Adeishvili, Executive Director

Supported by TACIS and the World Bank, CERMA was established in June 1997 to facilitate the restructuring of newly privatized Georgian companies and to foster the development of private sector consulting services in Georgia. It utilizes the services of foreign specialists, who provide technical assistance and training to enterprise managers, to promote a market-oriented approach to business.

In its first year, CERMA implemented restructuring assignments for 14 medium-sized and large enterprises in Tbilisi, Kutaisi, Rustavi and Gori, engaged in agro-processing and power generation and the manufacturing of textiles, pharmaceuticals, and chemicals. Approximately 25 local consultants participated in formal training sessions and on-the-job training. In 1999 it plans to implement 12-15 additional restructuring projects. CERMA currently employs 38 local consultants and staff.

## Center for Strategic Research and Development of Georgia

ul. Zubalashvili 19
380002   Tbilisi
**Tel:**       95-70-30
**Tel/Fax:** 96-41-24
**E-mail:**   csrdg@iberiapac.ge
             CSRDG@caucaus.net
**Contact:** Eka Urushadze, Executive Director; Nana Karseladze

CSRDG was established in July 1995 as a research and policy center addressing the challenges of political, economic and social transition in Georgia. It seeks to combine the efforts of representatives from scientific institutions, NGOs, government and the media to draft optimal solutions to the various problems of transition in Georgia today. The policy topics of the center fall under the direction of five Working Groups (WG).

The Environmental Protection and Sustainable Development WG drafted a 1997 environmental law for Georgia after extensive discussion with members of the Parliamentary Committee on Environment Protection and local environmental groups. It drafts reports on biodiversity and natural resources for submission to parliamentary committees and is involved in a World Bank program to develop a "National Environment Action Plan" for Georgia.

The Society and Democracy WG, in collaboration with the Young Lawyers Association of Georgia, drafted a Law on "Political Organizations of Georgia" in 1996. The project involved consultation from German political experts and contributions from local NGOs. The WG has also drafted a law on "Territorial Arrangement of Georgia." In July 1998 it began a Local Democracy Development project in cooperation with NOVIB and Young Lawyers Association. The six-month project fosters public participation in local elections in two regions of Georgia.

Other Working Groups include the Economics, Finances, and Social Policy WG, which offers seminars on economic policy, and the Foreign Policy and National Security WG, which addresses Georgia's ethnic and territorial conflicts.

A new Georgia-Ossetia WG focuses on conflict resolution and has established a working relationship with the South Ossetia Center for Social and Political Research. It has organized conferences to discuss joint initiatives in the fields of local government, strategic management, economic and demo-

cratic reform, sustainable development, and environmental protection.

The center periodically publishes bulletins, distributed to over 1,000 subscribers. Bulletin topics have included problems of local self-governance, health-care reform, privatization, taxation and investment, energy resources, and the banking system of Georgia. English translations are distributed free-of-charge to foreign investors and government representatives working in Georgia.

## Child and Environment
ul. Gamsakhurdia 14, k. 51
**Tel:**      93-14-56, 93-38-70, 94-37-35
**Fax:**     00-11-53, 94-37-35
**Contact:** Nana Iashvili

The center was founded in 1995 and works to provide social activities, first aid, and educational assistance to orphans, handicapped children, and internally displaced persons in Tbilisi. It implemented a Street Children in Tbilisi project with funding from Soros. In the summer of 1997, the government gave the organization a building. With a grant from TACIS and OXFAM, it was renovated into a shelter which now houses 20 children at night and 50 during the day. Child and Environment has organized a benefit concert to raise money for homeless children, numerous art exhibitions, and published a children's book, *Your Rights*, with funds from USAID/Save the Children.

## Civic Development International Center
ul. Chavchavadze 39a
Tbilisi
**Tel:**       93-22-27
**Tel/Fax:** 29-22-19, 23-06-57
**E-mail:**   cdic@access.sanet.ge
**Web:**      www.geocities.com/Athens/

Parthenon/4304/
**Contact:** Levan Berdzenishvili,
Chairman; Irakli Sasania, Executive
Director

CDIC promotes the development of
civil society in Georgia through civic
education and participation. Specifically, the center focuses on defining the
concept of civic development, researching third sector problems and the
history and function of civil society,
and facilitating dialogue between
NGOs and the government. The center
has implemented a number of projects,
including the establishment of a Community Health Center in the Varketili
District (with the Curatio International
Foundation) and a program to provide
Internet access for professional journalists. It has a professional staff of
five, and more than 50 people who help
out occasionally on special projects.

## CLARITAS Foundation for Healthy Nutrition of Children

Tevs district 11
mcrn. Pediatric Clinic #3
Tbilisi
**Tel:** 94-34-48, 60-08-65
**Fax:** 94-00-09
**E-mail:** nemsadze@tmgph.kheta.ge
**Contact:** Medea Beleshadze

CLARITAS has a three-tiered mission:
to establish breast-feeding support
programs, to clarify milk-substitute
marketing strategies, and to instill
"baby friendly" hospital practices. The
foundation has implemented training
seminars for medical personnel and has
assessed hospitals for "baby friendli-
ness." It has offered free medical consulting for mothers, established a free
hotline for pregnant and lactating
mothers, and drafted a law for milk
substitute marketing practices.

## Curatio International Foundation

Curatio Medical Group
144 A. Tsereteli
380019  Tbilisi
**Tel/Fax:** 99-55-40
**E-mail:** curatio@caucasus.net
**Web:** www.curatio.com
**Contact:** Alexander Kvitashvili,
Director; Dr. George Gotsadze,
Program Coordinator; David Gzirishvili

Curatio International Foundation was
founded in 1994 by a group of young
doctors who comprised a for-profit
medical organization, Curatio Ltd. (The
for-profit organization has evolved into
one of Georgia's first health maintenance organizations.) The foundation
focuses on the development and implementation of pilot projects in health
care. Its projects have included: a set of
TV programs and publications on public health and social security, several
studies assessing health care conditions
in Georgia, and several public health
pilot projects. In 1998 it initiated a
research project to evaluate how hospitals are financed in Georgia and a pilot
project on Public Education Against
Drug Addiction. The foundation employs 4 permanent staff members and
coordinates 68 project staff. Its membership consists of experts in their own
field who volunteer as consultants

## Disabled Soldiers Society– Demetre Tavdadebuli

pr. Rustaveli 32
Tbilisi
**Tel:** 32-40-74, 93-29-98
**Contact:** Jemal Arkania

Established in 1997, the society aims to
engage veterans in an active social life
and thus support their psycho-social
rehabilitation. In March 1998, together
with the Children's Federation, the

society organized vacations for 70 children from families of handicapped veterans and soldiers killed in battle. In May 1998, the society held a conference with other organizations on the most urgent problems facing disabled soldiers.

## Ecological Law Club

pr. Rustaveli ave 1, V entr, etazh IV
Tbilisi
**Tel:** 99-76-56, 98-60-39 (h)
**Fax:** 95-48-70
**Contact:** Besik Barkalaia

Established in 1996, the club has three projects funded by ISAR. First, the club aims to translate into Georgian, publish, and distribute the international convention on biological diversity and climate changes. Second, the club has translated, published, and distributed 300 free copies of a collection of environmental protection laws. Finally, the club plans to create a databank for environmental protection legislation and is working on the Environmental Organizations in the Law-Making Process project to present to Parliament.

## The Eurasia Foundation

ul. Iraki Abashidze, k. 4
380064   Tbilisi
**Tel/Fax:** 22-56-88
**E-mail:** eftbilis@iberiapac.ge

See the profile for the foundation in North American Organizations.

## Feminist Club

3 Takaishvili Street
Tbilisi
**Tel:** 22-40-18
**E-mail:** femclub@yahoo.com

The club was founded in the spring of 1998 to promote gender equality in Georgia. It conducts research on the conditions and status of women in Georgian society. Every Friday from 6 to 9 pm, the club holds public discussion groups on topics related to feminism. It also publishes the *Feminist Club Newsletter,* which includes essays on feminist theory, discussions of issues such as sexual harassment, and extracts from feminist literature. The club houses a collection of literature on gender issues and feminism, which it makes available to interested persons.

## Gaia

ul. Sulkhan-Saba 4
Tbilisi
**Tel:** 99-45-41
**E-mail:** gaia@access.sanet.ge
**Contact:** Zaal Kikvidze, Guliko Mikeladze

Gaia implements new educational methodologies in Georgian schools, especially in the fields of environmental and human rights education. Gaia has established the Teachers Training Institute and opened the first two model grades in a Tbilisi public school. The group has also held training seminars in ecology for teachers in Kuzbegi and plans to hold the same for teachers in Batumi. In March 1998, the organization published the first Georgian environmental textbook. Gaia plans to open a library of educational and popular scientific videos.

## Georgian Art and Culture Center

pr. Rustaveli 3, etazh 3
Tbilisi
**Tel:** 93-56-85
**E-mail:** maka@iacgaa.ge,
gacc@access.sanet.ge
**Contact:** Maka Dvalishvili, Natia Trapaidze

Founded in 1995, the GACC's mission is two-fold: (1) to increase the economic viability and technological capability of Georgian artists and craftspeople, and (2) to ensure the continuation and preservation of Georgian art and culture. In conjunction with Aid to Artisans, an American nonprofit organization, the center provides assistance and training to approximately 300 artisans, many of whom are internally displaced persons.

The center has remodeled an area on the third floor of the Georgian State Museum, where it operates a gallery to display the work of contemporary Georgian artists as well as a gift shop that sells traditional Georgian crafts. The organization held a Charity Art Exhibition in April 1997 and published a catalogue of the participating artists and their accomplishments.

## Georgian Center for the Conservation of Wildlife

ul. Ambrolauri 4/2
380060  Tbilisi
**Tel:**    37-38-94
**E-mail:**  gccw@ip.osgf.ge,
        gccw@gccw.postnet.ge
**Contact:** Ramaz Gokhelashvili, Director; Alexander Gavashelishvili, Deputy Director

Established in 1994, GCCW's mission is to promote environmental conservation and establish the principles of sustainable environmental development in Georgia. It produces various publications about environmental issues, organizes camps and outdoor seminars for students, produces television programs about birds and the need for their protection, and sponsors training programs for young people interested in ornithology.

The center also conducts ornithological and ecological research in various habitats of Georgia and is building a database of Georgian fauna. It drafts recommendations for new legislation to protect various species and promotes the establishment of protected natural areas in Georgia.

In past years, GCCW has assisted the World Bank in the development of the Georgian Biodiversity Project. With support from the Open Society Institute, the center took an inventory of fauna in different regions of Georgia and broadcast a TV series about Georgia's wildlife. It has conducted surveys of waterfowl in southern Georgia, completed an ornithological survey and monitoring project along the oil pipeline in Georgia and implemented the TACIS-sponsored Black Sea Biodiversity Program.

The Georgian Ministry of Environment and the Department of Protected Areas recently hired GCCW to help establish a national parks network in Georgia. With a grant from Horizonti (see below), the center produces a monthly newspaper, *Khanchali*, for the population of Javakheti. The center has a staff of 10, with 200 volunteers and part-time workers scattered throughout the country.

## Georgian Constitutional Protection League

pr. Rustaveli 52
Tbilisi
**Tel:**    98-79-23, 98-53-36, 99-05-27
**Fax:**    98-79-24
**E-mail:**  league@gbpm.pvt.ge
**Contact:** Vakhtang Khmaladze, Pridon Sakvarelidze

GCPL is currently working on the project Legal Education for All, which will include a TV series intended to explain constitutional norms of human rights and freedoms to citizens of all ages, including children. GCPL also regularly translates laws passed by the Georgian parliament into English.

## Georgian Foundation for the Development of Political Science
ul. Vazha-Pshavela, etazh 12
380060   Tbilisi
**Tel/Fax:** 33-45-91
**E-mail:**   gfdps@altern.org,
gfdps@usa.net
**Contact:** Irakli Kuchuloria, President;
Ucha Nanuashvili, Vice President

Founded in January 1997, the foundation works to promote the development of political science and civic education in Georgia.

## Georgian Young Lawyers' Association
ul. Erekrell -II, 7
Tbilisi
**Tel:**      99-50-76, 98-95-60
**Tel/Fax:** 93-61-01
**E-mail:**   lawyer@access.sanet.ge,
lawyer@gyla.org.ge
**Contact:** Tinatin Khidasheli, Director

Since 1994 the association has supported the establishment of civil society based on law through seminars on legal issues, civic education in secondary schools, and free legal consulting for NGOs, refugees, the general public, and mass media representatives. GYLA has also helped draft nonprofit legislation for Georgia. In August 1998, with support from the Open Society Institute–New York and the American Bar Association, GYLA opened a Legal Training and Information Center. Currently, GYLA is working with the UNHCR on a year-long project with two objectives: (1) to develop legislative reforms on issues affecting refugees and internally displaced persons (IDPs) and (2) to popularize UN con-

ventions on refugees by training state authorities who deal with refugees and IDPs. GYLA has a membership of 40 and offices in Tbilisi, Batumi, Kutaisi, and Rustavi.

## Green Earth Foundation
ul. Mazniashvili 4/3
Tbilisi
**Tel:**      95-16-16
**Fax:**      95-84-20
**E-mail:**   nugzar@kheta.ge
**Contact:** Nugzar Meladze, Dodo Kereselidze

Since 1994, Green Earth has actively promoted solar energy in Georgia. It has a small center to exhibit solar technologies and the advantages of solar energy. The foundation is planning to hold a fee-based scientific and practical conference Nature and Energy and will publish a booklet of scientific articles based on the conference.

## Green Wave Association
ul. Vazha Pshavela 45, etazh 18
380077   Tbilisi
**Tel:**      93-62-74
**Tel/Fax:** 99-71-69
**E-mail:**   gwave@access.sanet.ge
**Contact:** Maka Jakhua, Chairman of the Board

Founded in 1995, the association's main project is Radio Green Wave, an independent, nonprofit, educational radio station dedicated to strengthening the NGO sector and promoting environmental protection. The radio's programs include economics lessons, "environmentalgrams," legal advice, discussions of ethnic conflicts, exploration of religious issues, presentations by NGO representatives, and English lessons. At present, Green Wave (FM 107.4) broadcasts for Tbilisi and a radius of about 60km. A February 1998 opinion poll conducted by the newspaper *Seven Days* reported Green Wave was the most popular radio in Tbilisi, according to association sources.

The group is a member of the World Association of Public Radios (AMARC) and the International Federation of Environmental Journalists. It has participated in a European AIDS prevention project, Play Safe in Europe, together with 40 European radio stations. Green Wave has also conducted environmental projects with AMARC Europe, the BBC, London Radio Service (broadcasting the serial "Big Ben iz Londona"), and various projects with the International Press Club in Baku, Azerbaijan.

Green Wave's other activities include promoting the NGO sector; facilitating cooperation between the government, NGOs and the business sector; developing an independent mass media; promoting environmental awareness; and establishing information networks within the Transcaucasus region. In 1998, the group organized a Rock Action Festival in Varke Park to celebrate the 50th anniversary of Human Rights and Environment Week, sponsored by the UNDP, TACIS, and Coca-Cola Bottlers of Georgia.

## Helsinki Citizens' Assembly Committee of Georgia

ul. Tsinamdzgvrishvili 31
380002   Tbilisi
**Tel/Fax:**  96-15-14
**E-mail:**  hcagc@access.sanet.ge

The Helsinki Citizens' Assembly is a transnational coalition of civic groups working for peace and democracy throughout Europe with an international secretariat headquartered in Prague. HCA-Georgia's current projects include:

- Training seminars for NGO leaders in Georgia
- Establishing the Independent Human Rights Library in Tbilisi, which includes a large collection of samizdat published in Georgia, Russia, Ukraine and the Baltic states prior to 1989
- Free legal consultation to vulnerable groups and national minorities living in Georgia
- Establishing a network of Civic Initiative Centers in eastern and western Georgia, which will offer civic education curricula, NGO training workshops, and Internet access, as well as publish NGO bulletins
- Organizing "Consent '98," a region-wide planting of trees and flowers as a symbol of peace and reconciliation in the South Caucasus
- Establishing the Terrorism and Political Violence Research Center in Tbilisi

In 1998 HCA-Georgia received funding from the Eurasia Foundation, Open Society-Georgia Foundation, the U.S. Embassy in Tbilisi, The Netherlands Embassy in Moscow, and the European Union's TACIS program.

## Horizonti, The Foundation for the Third Sector

ul. Gogebashvili 33
380079   Tbilisi
**Tel/Fax:**  29-29-55, 98-75-04
**E-mail:**  presscenter@horizonti.org,
**Web:**  www.horizonti.org

Horizonti began working in December 1997 as a support center for Georgian NGOs. (It took over the mission of ISAR–Georgia, which had begun work to develop the third sector in Georgia in 1993.) Horizonti helps local groups effectively identify and solve problems facing their communities by providing financial, informational, managerial, and technical assistance. It also supports initiatives to expand the number and influence of NGOs outside of Tbilisi through a network of contacts in Georgia's regions and promotes positive relations between NGOs and the government.

Horizonti's grants program offers funding of up to $3,000 for local groups and conducts grant competitions for the Virtual Foundation (see profile for the foundation in Internet Resources, under Funding). Its training and consulting services include NGO management and development courses, strategic planning, structural development, financial management NGO-media relations, NGO-government relations, and individualized consulting. The group's weekly *NGO News Bulletin*, in English and Georgian, is distributed to over 500 subscribers worldwide electronically and in print form, and its quarterly journal highlights developments in Georgia's third sector. Horizonti also publishes news updates and articles in local newspapers and magazines and produces documentary films and monthly programs about Georgian NGOs for television.

## Independent Society "Human Rights in Georgia"

ul. Dolidze 144
3380071 Tbilisi
**Tel:**    29-23-99, 33-10-04
**Fax:**    33-45-91
**E-mail:**  ishrg@altern.org
        ucha@altern.org
**Web:**    www.fly.to/ishrg
**Contact:** Ucha Nanuashvili

The society was established in December 1996 with a mission to promote the development of democratic institutions, the rule of law, and human rights education in Georgia. It publishes and distributes human rights education materials,

including information about international human rights laws and citizens' rights. The society also fosters civic education at the primary and secondary school level, preparing manuals and teacher training materials. The founders of the organization are primarily students of the International Law and International Relations Departments of Ivane Javakhishvili Tbilisi State University.

In 1998 the society founded the Human Rights Information Center in conjunction with the Helsinki Citizens' Assembly and the independent library Open Society. The center works to contribute to human rights education and to foster information and consulting networks on human rights issues in Georgia and the Caucasus region.

## International Center for Civic Culture

ul. Baku 20a
Tbilisi
**Tel:**    95-38-73, 38-18-63
**Fax:**    39-65-54
**E-mail:**  iccc_georgia@yahoo.com
**Contact:** Paata Gurgenidze,
Coordinator of International Programs

The ICCC began working in September 1996 to support the development of civil society and democracy in Georgia. One of its main activities is promoting electoral rights. In October 1997, with support from the Friedrich Ebert Foundation, ICCC organized a conference on the Basic Guarantees of Electoral Rights of Citizens. In December 1997, it received a grant from the Open Society Georgia Foundation to organize training programs for party monitors at local government elections.

ICCC states that previous elections in Georgia have seen extensive violations of election laws. By monitoring the upcoming elections in Tbilisi, ICCC hopes to gather sufficient evidence of election tampering to file successful lawsuits and thus to help set legal precedents for electoral reforms.

## International Center for Conflict and Negotiation

pr. Chavchavadze 16/3, etazh 1
Tbilisi
**Tel:** 22-36-18
**Tel/Fax:** 93-91-78
**E-mail:** iccn@access.sanet.ge
**Web:** members.tripod.com/~icon
www.chat.ru/~icon
**Contact:** George Khutshishvili

Established in 1995, the center monitors conflict in Georgia and the Caucasus region and publishes a monthly bulletin with the support of the MacArthur Foundation. Recently, ICCN has been working on a project to revive trust between Abkhazians and Georgians.

## International Fund of Medical Women

pr. Chavchadze 15
380079 Tbilisi
**Tel:** 39-32-31
**Tel/Fax:** 23-32-99
**E-mail:** grc@access.sanet.ge

Founded in 1996, IFMW works to support Georgian women and children with health care, social services, educational programs, and business training. The fund runs a Women's Center to provide assistance to refugees, teenagers, and young women. Its services include gynecological exams, psychological counseling, legal consulting, job counseling, family planning, and information about sexually transmitted diseases.

The fund offers classes in cooking, massage, sewing, computer skills, and lamp-shade. It has a training program How to Establish a Small Business.

## International Society for Fair Elections

pr. Agmashenebeli 89/24, etazh 5
Tbilisi
**Tel:** 96-72-89
**Tel/Fax:** 95-45-59
**E-mail:** isfe@nike.pvt.ge
**Contact:** Nugzar Ivanidze

The Society for Fair Elections was formed, with support from the National Democratic Institute for International Affairs (see profile in North American Organizations), at the initiative of a group of Georgia NGOs. It aims to help create a democratic political process and promote an active role by citizens in government affairs. During the 1995 elections, it deployed hundreds of trained poll watchers and election monitors to ensure the integrity of the democratic process and published a comprehensive report on the elections. The society also publishes a monthly paper, *Civil Society*, and has established a good-will Civic Advisers Committee in various regions to promote active citizenship.

## International Society for the Revival of Georgian Business

pl. Javakhishvili 1
380002 Tbilisi
**Tel:** 94-36-14
**Fax:** 94-36-15
**E-mail:** society@georgian-business.org
**Web:** www.georgian-business.org/

The society, founded in 1989, works to improve Georgia's business environment and assist members of the business community with integration into the global market. It has numerous corporate and individual members and representative offices in the U.S., Germany, Turkey, Romania, Azerbaijan, Armenia, and Russia. Golden Fleece International is the group's U.S. representative, tel: (202) 822-1722.

### International Society for Human Rights–National Group of Georgia

ul. Giorgi Tsabadze (Martskhena Sanapiro) 3-32
380012  Tbilisi
**Tel/Fax:** 34-86-51
**Fax:**      00-11-53
**E-mail:**   adupl@mmc.net.ge,
              levanu@hotmail.com,
              igfmgeorgia@lycosmail.com
**Web:**      members.delphi.com/levur
**Contact:** Dr. Levan Z. Urushadze, Chairman

ISHR's Georgia group was founded in January 1997 and now has 50 members —all activists in the Georgian human rights movement. The society is a member of ISHR–IGFM, a worldwide human rights organization, which has its headquarters in Frankfurt, Germany, and affiliates in 40 countries.

ISHR-Georgia publishes a news-paper, *Adamianis Uplebebi* (Human Rights), and issues press releases concerning freedom of the press and speech and social-economic and cultural rights in Georgia and the Caucasus. The society conducts research on conflicts in the Caucasus region, monitors human rights infringements, and organizes civic education programs. In 1997 the editorial staff of *Adamianis Uplebebi* received a grant from the Westminster Foundation for Democracy to organize in Tbilisi an international conference, The Genocide of Peoples in the Caucasus. ISHR-Georgia's local partners include the Tbilisi Working Group of the Netherlands Helsinki

Union, the Georgian Helsinki Union, and the Caucasian Information and Research Center for Human Rights and Conflictology.

### International Telecommunications and Information Center

pl. 26th May 2, etazh 6
380008  Tbilisi
**Tel:**      33-04-25;
**Tel/Fax:** 98-77-97
**E-mail:**   itic@itic.org.ge
**Web:**      www.friends-partners.org/partners/georgia/itic-1.htm
**Contact:** Valeri Nanobashvili, Executive Director

ITIC was established in March 1995 with a mission to provide technical and communications assistance to non-governmental organizations. The center provides free access to electronic resources to Georgia's NGO community and maintains an on-line database of around 400 local NGOs. It has created a network of eight regional partner NGO information centers around Georgia.

The center published the *Handbook of Donors, Development Agencies and Investment Funds in Georgia*, with support from USAID/Save the Children. Over 5,000 copies of the *Handbook* have been distributed, and more than 1,500 people have participated in ITIC's computer and Internet training seminars. ITIC has received financial support from USAID/Save the Children Federation, Eurasia Foundation, ISAR, and Sacred Earth Network.

### International Women's Center For Education And Information

Baratashvili 10
380005  Tbilisi
**Tel:**      38-89-25, 99-92-53
**Tel/Fax:** 98-92-17

**E-mail:** tamar@caucasus.net
**Contact:** Tamar Abramishvili, Coordinator; Dali Makhatadze

The center began work informally in 1991, when there was a "very strained situation" in Georgia. Its focus was cultural change. It organized an event in Hamburg, Germany, Women's Cultural Autumn. Two years later a joint exhibit by Georgian and German painters was organized in Tbilisi and Hamburg.

IWCEI was formally established in 1994 with the purpose of promoting an open, democratic society in Georgia. The center focuses on studying women's rights, preventing violence towards women, and providing computer and foreign language training for women.

Its main aim currently is to promote and ensure de facto gender equality by advocating its Platform for Action. Funded by the Heinrich Böll Foundation of Germany, the platform has the following objectives:

- To encourage women to participate actively in the political life of the country
- To raise women's political self-consciousness
- To make society sensitive toward women's problems
- To improve the economic condition of women by furthering their education
- To establish contacts with the international women's movement

The center organizes seminars and conferences focused on women's issues for psychologists, economists, lawyers, other professionals, and representatives of state agencies. It has published numerous books and pamphlets. The center says its advocacy work is responsible, in part, for the decision of the Georgian parliament to allocate 3.3 million lari to public health programs focused on cancer. An alternative address for the center is Kazbegi 8a, 380005 Tbilisi.

## Internet Center for a Wide Open World (WOW!)

ul. Chavchavadze 27
380079   Tbilisi
**Tel:**      25-05-90
**Tel/Fax:** 25-05-91
**E-mail:** wow@osgf.ge
**Web:**     www.soros.org/georgia.html

## Internews–Georgia

ul. Kakabadze 2, etazh 3
House of Cinematographers
380008   Tbilisi
**Tel/Fax:** 98-83-24, 98-83-25, 98-83-27, 93-50-66
**E-mail:** board@internews.org.ge
**Web:**     www.internews.org.ge
**Contact:** Genadi Uchumbegashvili, Director

Internews–Georgia began working in 1995 to promote freedom of information and to strengthen electronic media in Georgia. It provides advice, training, equipment grants, and programming for private TV stations in Georgia, as well as training for TV journalists, managers, and technicians. Over the past three years, Internews has trained more than 80 journalists and camera operators/tape editors in Georgia, and organized on-site training with a former CNN manager for Rustavi-2, a private TV station in Tbilisi.

The benefit of these activities for independent media coverage in Georgia are already evident in local broadcasting. According to Internews, the news program *Rustavi-2* enjoys an extremely high popularity rating in Tbilisi. Likewise, a weekly current affairs program established by Internews in conjunction with a local group, Kvira, now tops the national ratings list. Seven journalists trained by Internews are now working on Radio Liberty's Georgian language programs in Prague.

Furthermore, local journalists are now covering more controversial issues. For example, the postmaster in the town of Gori was fired following an investigative report revealing that he was using pensioners' money to finance his private business. The journalist heading the report had participated in advanced journalism training from Internews.

### IREX Office and Education Information Center
Ivane Shavakhishvili Sakhelmtsipo University
pr. Chavchavadze 1, Otakhi 231
380028   Tbilisi
**Tel/Fax:** 23-26-88
**E-mail:** irex@irex.ge

See profile of IREX in North American Organizations.

### Journalists International Press-Club "Forte"
Tbilisi
**Tel:**      93-99-77
**Fax:**     99-85-73
**E-mail:** sts@access.sanet.ge

Forte began working in 1996 to promote professional relations between Georgian and foreign media and to foster the development of an independent mass media and "open informational space" in the region. The club provides professional training for journalists through seminars and workshops and facilitates cooperation between local and foreign mass-media organizations on publishing, broadcasting, and distribution projects. Forte seeks to help develop a modern and

democratic society in Georgia, defend the rights of local journalists, guarantee free and timely access to objective and full information, and facilitate the integration of the Georgian press into the international information system.

### "Lomisa" Georgian Society for the Protection of Animals
ul. Sakanela 35
Tbilisi
**Tel:**      93-21-28, 36-01-13 (h)
**Fax:**     levan@nacres.ge
**Contact:** Mzia Lolishvili, Levan Butkhuzi

Lomisa protects domestic animals and encourages humane treatment of animals. It has worked with the World Society for the Protection of Animals and the Bridget Bardot Foundation to improve conditions for animals in the Tbilisi Zoo. With a grant from ISAR, the society opened a shelter for stray dogs in Tbilisi and has educated municipal agencies and urban citizens on the problem of stray dogs and the threat of rabies.

### Morioni–Speleologists Club
ul. Mardzhanishvili 46
Tbilisi
**Tel:**      96-15-38, 95-38-26
**Contact:** Mamuka Nikoladze

Morioni is a group of speleologists who organize expeditions and visits for visitors and children to underground grottoes. It has made photo and video presentations about how trash is circulated and how this pollutes the drinking water.

### Multiple Assistance for Georgia
pr. K. Gamsakhurdia 10
380060   Tbilisi
**Tel/Fax:** 37-19-18
**E-mail:** gia@mag.org.ge

**Contact:** Gia Mchedlisvili

MAG was established in May 1994 to bridge the gap between providing relief assistance and the development of an indigenous NGO community capable of responding to societal needs. It has conducted training programs on fundraising and provides free consultation to NGOs. It has worked in the health sector—supporting programs in maternal and child health; AIDS awareness, education and prevention; and the development of a local pharmaceutical industry. MAG works with local NGOs, governmental organizations, UN agencies, and international NGOs.

MAG is the national coordinator of a regional project sponsored by the International Organization for Migration to strengthen NGOs that deal with migration issues in the Caucasus. Through this program, MAG collaborates with the Armenian Sociological Association and Hayat in Azerbaijan.

## Noah's Ark Center for Recovery of Endangered Species

ul. Mtskheta 8/ V, etazh I
Tbilisi
**Tel/Fax:** 23-56-06
**E-mail:** pardus@nacres.ge
**Contact:** Jason Dadridze, Levan Butkhuzi

Noah's Ark has been involved in a number of projects to recover endangered species. Members went on an expedition to recover and reintroduce the hyena in Georgia and address the problem of overgrazing. Its project, Assessment Research for Brown Bear Recovery in Georgia, aims to collect data and plan for the recovery and welfare of the brown bear. The center worked with the Georgian Center for Wildlife Conservation to establish the NGO Bird Conservation Group. In

collaboration with ISAR and the Know How Fund, Noah's Ark is working on a six month project Rabies Control in Tbilisi.

## Open Society Georgia Foundation

ul. Irakli Abashidze 18 I
380079 Tbilisi
**Tel:** 22-23-46, 29-10-52, 22-61-72
**Fax:** (1-908) 888-9698
(satellite fax from USA)
**E-mail:** kartuli@osfg.ge
**Web:** www.soros.org/georgia.html
**Contact:** Mikhail Chachkhunashvili, Director

See the profile for Open Society Institute under North American Organizations.

## Poseidon Marine Association

Agmashenebeli 182
Tbilisi
**Tel:** 35-19-14
**Fax:** 35-16-74
**E-mail:** irisi@gmep.khcta.ge
**Contact:** David Nikoleishvili, Tika Akhvlediani

The association has brought together marine experts, farmers, and youths to study the Black Sea. With funding from the Georgian Saphosto Bank and the World Bank, Poseidon made the film *A New Wave* about the pollution and environmental degradation occurring in the Black Sea.

## Public Interest Protection League

ul. Marukhis Gmirebi 1
380079 Tbilisi
**Tel:** 25-01-38
**E-mail:** pipl1@hotmail.com, upleba@hotmail.com
**Web:** attend.to/pipl
**Contact:** Levan Khubulava, Chairman

#3 Kostava St., Apt 7, 3rd floor
384700  Zugdidi
**Tel:**     2 36 60
**Web:**    members.tripod.com/~pipl1/
home.html
**Contact:** Levan Khubulava, Chairman

PIPL, founded in January 1998, works
to raise awareness of human rights and
environmental issues and promote the
NGO sector. It runs an NGO development and support center and publishes
and distributes its newsletter, *Right to
Speech*, as well as other materials
donated by USIS, WWF, and NDI to
NGOs, government agencies, and
educational institutions in Zugdidi,
Kutaisi and Tbilisi. In June 1998, PIPL
made *Right to Speech* available via e-
mail. To request copies, use the contact
information above. PIPL would welcome materials related to human rights
or the environment, which it will
distribute for free.

### Society Varketili

Varketili-3, III m/r 181 kindergarden
Tbilisi
**Tel:**     73-59-21, 73-38-06 (home),
         73-99-11 (home)
**Contact:** George Dzamukashvili, Vano
Tsnobiladze

The society was founded in 1995 to
represent the 70,000 residents of the
Tbilisi suburb, Varketili. With over 300
members and 1,000 volunteers, the
organization aims to create better living
conditions for the suburb, which is
often cut off from water and electricity
and is one of the more rundown areas
around Tbilisi.

In the summer of 1997, the organization hosted a meeting of members of
Parliament, local department officials,
members of the Georgian Citizens'
Union, and the president of the Parlia-

ment, which resulted in an improved
water and energy situation for the area
and a resolution of emergency assistance, signed by the President. The
Social Investment Fund also agreed to
repair roads in the area. The society
continues to hold conferences on social
and environmental issues facing their
community.

With a grant from ISAR, it rebuilt a
park where a dump used to be. With
funding from the World Bank and the
assistance of Curatio Medical Services,
the society began a pilot community
health care program. It has also established a handicraft school that now
produces shoes, planted 250 trees for
Earth Day, created its own local TV
program, established a humanitarian
program to collect and distribute
clothes, founded a studio for public
concerts, and produced a collection of
ecological videos. The society's current
projects include:
- Vaccination and sterilization of dogs
  and the establishment of a shelter for
  dogs, with assistance from Veterans
  Without Borders
- Provision of door and window
  insulation for 500 families, with
  funding from the Open Society
  Foundation
- Creating a TV program to foster
  support for the local government,
  with funding from the Open Society
  Foundation
- Construction of a "garden town" for
  40 families and provision of seeds,
  with funding from the British Know
  How Fund
In May 1998, the society won an EU
and U.S. government grant of $20,000
for its Building Democracy and Civil
Society project.

### Studio "Re"

ul. M. Aleksidze 1

Institute of Geophysics, Meeting Room
Tbilisi
**Tel:** 33-12-56
**Fax:** 95-44-97
**E-mail:** studiore@caucasus.net
**Contact:** Mikheil Mirziashvili

Studio "Re" is a TV channel that airs
NGO programs, advertisements, and
other third sector announcements. The
studio has worked with the Caucasian
Institute for Peace, Democracy and
Development on documentaries and
other educational projects. In 1998, the
studio created a film, *Home Sweet
Home*, on the Georgian-Ossetian
conflict and the return of refugees.
Other film topics include third sector
issues, ethnic minorities, and
contemporary constitutional changes.

## Transition
87-3 Bagebi
380062 Tbilisi
**Tel:** 29-03-04
**Fax:** 99-60-54
**E-mail:** archlig@access.sanet.ge
**Contact:** Dr. Feride Zurikashvili,
Director; Iren Bakhtadze, Deputy
Director

Transition was founded in 1997 as a
gender research group. It researches
gender issues and state gender policy
and prepares recommendations for new
legislation. Recently, the group drafted
recommendations for the improvement
of gender statistics in Georgia.

## Udabno
pr. Rustaveli 52
380008 Tbilisi
**Tel/Fax:** 99-88-23
**E-mail:** mze@didi.org.ge
**Contact:** Temo Jojua

Founded in 1994, Udabno (Desert)
studies and preserves the historic region
of the Gareji Desert, which was formerly a firing ground and military training
site. It has published articles, prepared
and distributed five documentary films,
and published the second annual edition
of *Natural and Historic Monuments in
the David Gareji Desert*. Udabno
recently built protective shielding for
the walls and frescoes (X-XI century)
of a monastery. It has organized ecological lessons at the site for university
and high school students and is currently organizing the first international
conference in Georgia dedicated to
historic rock monuments.

## UN Association of Georgia
postal address:
c/o UN Country Office in Georgia
tr. Erisatvi 9
380079 Tbilisi

street address:
ul. Dolidze 2, etazh 4, k. 27
380015 Tbilisi
**Tel:** 99-35-16
**Fax:** (via U.S.) 908-739-3928,
ext. 131
**E-mail:** una@ltic.ge
**Contact:** Jaba Devdariani, George
Kalandadze, Alexander Vashakidze

On July 31, 1992, Georgia was
accepted as a member of the United
Nations. Formed in December 1995,
the UNA seeks to popularize the ideals
of the UN through civic education. The
association has two priorities: to inform
the population of the most important
ideals, principles, and procedures of the
international system; and to entrust the
population with adequate skills to contribute to its functioning and development.

In 1997, UNA implemented a project
called New Generation for the Better
World, which taught 150 high school
students over a two month period about

the UN, focusing on various, including international human rights and the UN family of organizations. In 1998, UNA's regional branch in Imereti established a Human Rights Educational Center, which offers lessons for students on the UN; discussions on drug addiction, AIDS and sexual issues; and training sessions for internally displaced persons on conflict resolution, cooperation, and competition.

### Union of God–Children of Georgia–Association of Disabled Persons
ul. Tsereteli 144
Tbilisi
**Tel/Fax:** 94-01-62
**E-mail:** iunona@iberiapac.ge
**Contact:** Zaza Sikharulidze

The association aims to revitalize and strengthen humanistic traditions and provide support for disabled persons. It attempts to integrate disabled people into society through employment opportunities and psycho-social or medical rehabilitation. Since 1993, the association has received five international grants.

UGCG has developed several databases, including one with personal files for 190,000 disabled persons in Georgia and another for 7,000 children institutionalized under state care. UGCG has produced two analytical reports on the status of disabled people and children and published a book for the disabled on their rights. It has also formed a shoe factory that employs 14 children and produces shoes for refugees and handicapped children in state institutions.

### Wild Plant Conservation Center
ul. Kojori 4
Tbilisi

**Tel:** 99-74-48, 22-24-33, 99-66-02
**E-mail:** dato@botany.kheta.ge
**Contact:** Tsira Pantsulaia

The center has established an ecological school and offered seminars for 11 to 14-year-old students, with support from ISAR.

### Women and Business
ul. Shanidze 1
Tbilisi
**Tel:** 23-40-96
**E-mail:** wcenter@itic.ge
**Contact:** Nino Elisbarashvili

Established in 1993, Women and Business's mission is to improve the role of women in a market-oriented economy. In 1997, it opened a small dry-cleaning business, with funding from the Norwegian Refugee Council, which now employs 21 internally displaced persons (IDPs). The German embassy provided the organization with sewing machines, which are used by nine IDPs. Later, in the same complex, a beauty salon was opened that now employs 21 IDPs. These businesses are self-sustaining and offer free services to the elderly, handicapped, and families with many children, and reduced fees for IDPs. The organization also began silkworm breeding in the Bolnisi region that created jobs for 15 families. Women and Business has about 300 members and volunteers active in Tbilisi, Kartli, Kakheti, Imereti, and Achara.

# Moldova

**Country Code: 373**

## Chisinau (2)

### 21st Century Youth Foundation
a/ya 206
2012MD Chisinau
**Tel:** 23-42-55
**Fax:** 23-24-03
**E-mail:** iorgu@infotin.moldova.net
**Web:** www.infotin.moldova.net
**Contact:** Iorgu Apostol, Executive Director

The foundation strives to raise awareness among the citizens of Moldova about freedom of speech, environmental protection, conservation, NGO development, the youth of Moldova, and Moldovan culture. As a member of the National Youth Council of Moldova, it hopes to work in collaboration with all youth organizations in Moldova and abroad. It was established in 1994 by a group of young journalists.

In 1994 the foundation, in collaboration with the Youth and Sport Department of Moldova, organized the Poesis camp to promote the literary work of young writers from both sides of the river Prut. It has also conducted a conference, Surviving Together, which brought together participants from the regions close to the rivers Nistru and Prut and prepared a report Main Environmental Organizations, which was later discussed at the European Conference of Ministers of the Environment in Sofia.

The foundation's InfoTin project, financed by the Eurasia Foundation, organized seminars and conferences on the development of youth organizations and prepared a catalog of youth NGOs of Moldova. The foundation's current project is the development of the youth center InfoTin.

### ADSISTO
ul. 31 August 1989, k.153
MD-2004 Chisinau
**Tel:** 23-72-10
**Fax:** 23 72-10
**E-mail:** office@acdi-voca.moldline.net
**Contact:** Vasile Munteanu, President

ADSISTO provides training and consulting to associations, organizations and enterprises engaged in the agricultural, agribusiness, and social sectors. Founded in 1995 with assistance from the U.S. group Volunteers in Overseas Cooperative Assistance (VOCA), ADSISTO offers training in agricultural production, post-harvest handling and storage, processing, marketing, packaging, distribution, natural resource management, and integrated pest management. In addition, the group offers technical assistance and legal consultation on business management and planning, association development, trade linkages, and joint-venture partnership development.

In December 1996, ADSISTO conducted a Local Needs and Capacity Study for the World Bank, as well as a Social Assessment Project for the World Bank in the spring of 1997. In the spring of 1998, ADSISTO managed the distribution of U.S. aid in the village of Leusheni after massive landslides rendered 1,158 persons homeless. The group also helped the World Bank conduct a pensions survey in June and July 1998.

ADSISTO keeps a database of over 20 experienced Moldovan specialists in various fields who are willing to offer consulting services. It also has 11 permanent members.

## Altair International Ecological Agency

a/ya 91
277012   Chisinau
**Tel:**      56-88-44
**E-mail:**   altair@ch.moldpac.md,
             altair@glas.apc.org
**Contact:** Larissa Petrovna Milovanova

Altair conducts environmental public education projects and monitors environmental hazards. It distributes a free monthly, electronic, English-language journal, *Heritage*, which contains news about the environment and third sector issues.

## "Anti-HIV" Association

Republican Clinical Hospital for Children "E. Cotsaga"
ul. V. Alecsandri 2
2009     Chisinau
**Tel:**      72-77-76
**Fax:**      72-77-74
**E-mail:**   antihiv@mic.moldova.net
**Contact:** Ruslan David, President

The association anti-HIV was founded in September 1997 to provide individuals and organizations in Moldova with the tools to fight HIV/AIDS, sexually transmitted diseases (STDs), and human rights violations in the health system. It conducts research, translates materials, and disseminates information to individuals and organizations.

Anti-HIV collects information from international sources on a wide range of topics, including the latest drugs and newest treatment methods for HIV/ AIDS, information for health professionals on counseling and communication, international organizations working in the field of HIV/AIDS, issues concerning organizational development and management, and human rights in the health care system,

Anti-HIV is working to establish the InfoShare Center to raise public awareness of medical issues such as hygiene, disease prevention, AIDS, STDs, and drug addiction. It is also working to establish a library and a database of the best teaching practices with regards to HIV/AIDS infection and its prevention and to create an information sharing networks among specialists who work on these issues. It hopes to develop health education curricula for schools, conduct periodic sociological studies to assess public understanding of health issues, and publish a monthly bulletin that would report on "best practices" in health education.

## BIOS

str. Ialoveni 98/1 #68
2070     Chisinau
**Tel/Fax:** 73-0522
**E-mail:**   valentin@bios.moldova.su
**Contact:** Elena Bivol, Project Coordinator

BIOS was established in 1995 to work in the fields of environmental protection, sustainable agriculture, and assistance to low-income people. It has completed four projects with support from the Eurasia Foundation, Counterpart, USAID, and the Dutch foundation Novib. It is currently working on a project in Cretoaia, in the Anenii-Noi district, to create a training site to educate the local farming community about soil rejuvenation.

## BIOTICA Ecological Society of Moldova

a/ya 570
2043     Chisinau

**Tel/Fax:** 24-32-74
**E-mail:** bio@mdearn.cri.md
**Web:** www.scils.rutgers.edu/
~olejka/biotica/biot.html,
mariner.rutgers.edu/~olejka/biotica/boo
k-ngo/
**Contact:** Piotr Gorbunenko, President
of the Board; Ilya Trombitsky, Deputy
President of the Board

BIOTICA was established in 1992 to
foster public participation in environmental decision-making. Currently the
group is concentrating on projects
concerning the preservation of biodiversity and a program to revitalize
Iagorlic, a Moldovan state reserve. It
has published two books recently, one
concerning the creation and purpose of
NGOs and another on the international
legal precedent for environmental
protection.

## Bluebird Charitable Fund European School

Independence 20/1-113
Chisinau
**Tel:** 56-20-42
**Fax:** 23 40 51
**E-mail:** bstheim@hotmail.com
(attention G. Moshcovitch)
**Contact:** Galina Moshcovitch, Director

The school was established in an
attempt to diversify the existing educational system. Bluebird is a non-profit
charitable organization financed
entirely by private investment money.
The curriculum includes five languages
(English, German, French, Moldavian,
Russian), arts and sciences, painting,
music, dance, and computer training. In
the higher grades, the main objective is
to master foreign languages. The
teachers come from Europe and teach at
least two languages. Bluebird prepares
students for a variety of professional

careers. The fund offers scholarships
for educational materials.

## Civil Society Development Institute

a/ya 4046
2001    Chisinau
**Tel:** 739-040, 440-835
**E-mail:** bstheim@hotmail.com,
bstheim@ññ.acad.md
**Contact:** Boris Steinman, Director-
Coordinator; Anna Cartaseva, Secretary

CSDI is a non-governmental research
institute, established in 1997 to support
social development and the creation of
a democratic society in Moldova. With
research focusing on social stability,
democratic regulation, and social development, CSDI hopes to promote the
development of constructive interaction
between the state, business, and non-
governmental sectors. It hopes to
facilitate Moldova's integration into the
European and global markets.

## CONTACT–National Assistance and Information Centre for NGOs

28 Bulgara St.
2001    Chisinau
**Tel/Fax:** 26-04-36
**E-mail:** contact@contact.md,
contacts@contact.md
**Web:** www.contact.md
**Contact:** Aliona Niculita, Director;
Doina Melnic, Public Relations
Coordinator

CONTACT was founded in November
1995 by the Soros Foundation–
Moldova in cooperation with the
International Foundation for Electoral
Systems–Moldova (see profile in North
American Organizations) and Centras-
Romania. It also received funding from
PHARE/TACIS. Its purposes are:

- Support democratic processes in the community
- Encourage civic initiatives
- Promote the development of an open society

CONTACT claims to be the biggest NGO in Moldova and to have "very good relations" with all funds in the country and the government. It has developed a "strong and viable network of NGOs" and has facilitated the exchange of information and open dialogue between the third sector and the government.

CONTACT provides a wide range of services to NGOs, including: consulting services; access to a database of Moldovan NGOs; training seminars; and office equipment, such as computers, telephones, and copiers. It maintains an Internet node which NGOs can use for e-mail and to post a Web page. In 1997, 200 NGOs received assistance from CONTACT. It has recently expanded its services to the northern and southern regions of Moldova (Balti and Cahul), as part of a plan to foster new NGOs in rural areas.

CONTACT's current projects include:

- The three-year Rural Development Project to strengthen NGOs in other regions of Moldova, especially the northeast (Soroca) and southeast (Comrat).
- Digital Synergy Project, which will assist donor organizations in Moldova by providing them with a single mechanism for distributing information to the development community in Moldova and provide information, e-mail and Internet services to NGOs, particularly those in rural areas.

The center has a resource library and publishes a regular bulletin, which has information about CONTACT and other Moldovan NGOs. It recently published the second edition of its catalogue of Moldovan NGOs.

## "Contranomia" Public Scientific Research Institute

ul. Pietrarilor 4, k. 55
2021      Chisinau
**Tel/Fax:** 73-50-13, 49-14-77
**Contact:** Sergie Voroshilov
or
ul. Drumul Viilor 40, k. 23
2021      Chisinau
**Tel:**      72-30-50
**E-mail:** office@contranomia.euro-apri-ori.com, gsteim@ce.acad.md
**Contact:** Irina Povar

## Coordination Center of Environmental NGOs of Moldova

St. Mateevici 60
2009      Chisinau
**Tel:**      24-00-43
**Fax:**      24-32-74
**E-mail:** duca@cinf.usm.md
**Contact:** Gheorghe Duca, President; Ilya Trombitsky, Member of the Board

CCENM was established in 1995 to coordinate the activities and fund-raising for twelve separate environmental NGOs. The group has begun a series of training seminars in environmental law, fund-raising, and capacity building. Its current projects include preservation of water quality and biodiversity of the Dniester River and publication of *Environment of Moldova: The Point of View of Some NGOs.*

## "DRUGS" Association

pr. Moscow 90, 13/3
2068      Chisinau
**Tel:**      73-83-48
**Fax:**      73-83-30

**E-Mail**: natalie@drugs.mldnet.com
**Contact:** Natalia Cebotarenco, Ph.D.,
Director; Salaur Marina, Program
Assistant

DRUGS, founded in 1995, works to
improve public health in Moldova
through research, education and
informational services on pharmaceutical and the use of drugs. According to Director Natalia Cebotarenco,
economic reforms in Moldova, including efforts to privatize medical services,
have resulted in a decentralization of
control and a deterioration of Moldo
va's health care system since 1991.
Reliable information about pharmaceuticals and their correct use is
virtually nonexistent and privatization
has encouraged unethical behavior by
pharmaceutical wholesalers and
pharmacies. Furthermore, pharmaceuticals donated by Western countries
are not always familiar to healthcare
professionals, contributing to
irresponsible use.

DRUGS runs the Information
Pharmacological Center to provide
independent, objective information
about pharmaceuticals to health care
professionals, pharmacists, and
consumers. It publishes a monthly
bulletin, *Medexpress*, which has been
distributed free-of-charge to 500
subscribers since 1996. The association
has carried out 34 seminars on responsible drug use at local and regional
hospitals and at the Medical and Pharmaceutical University of Moldova.
More than 1,500 people have taken part
in these seminars.

Other projects by DRUGS include:
- HIV/AIDS prevention programs in
  Moldova
- A 1996 survey of 158 adolescents on
  the use of contraceptives
- In collaboration with the group
  UNAIDS, DRUGS organized a

meeting in 1997, "Situation Among
Drug-Users in Moldova," that was
attended by government representatives, NGOs, and representatives of
the drug-using community
- In February 1997, with support from
  UNAIDS, DRUGS conducted a
  behavioral research study of intrave-
  nous drug-users in Chisinau, Tiraspol, and Belti, which became the
  basis for the Harm Reduction project,
  financed by UNAIDS and the
  Lindesmith Institute
- The project Safe Medicines in
  Moldova was launched in July 1998,
  to examine the side-effects of
  pharmaceuticals in five regions of
  Moldova.

DRUGS has also been cooperating
with the Counterpart Creative Center in
Kyiv since 1995 on third-sector support
projects in Moldova.

## Fundatia Viitorul

bul. Stefan cel Mare 123, kv. 16
2016     Chisinau
**Tel/Fax:** 24-74-83
**E-mail:** igorm@cc.acad.md
**Web:** www.iatp.md/viitorul/
**Contact:** Igor Munteanu

The Viitorul Foundation is comprised
of a group of young political scientists
and researchers who represent non-
governmental organizations in Moldova. Since June 1993, the group has
initiated several programs aimed at
developing a new sense of responsibility among politicians, public servants,
and citizens in the fields of public
administration and civic education. In
cooperation with the Foundation for
Political Culture, the group publishes a
journal, *Arena Politicii*, which focuses
on the process of political transition in
Moldova.

Viitorul is currently engaged in a
one-year project, Transparency of

Public Institutions, to assess the public need for greater transparency of state and public authorities. A special emphasis will be placed on promoting NGOs that serve as intermediaries and a source of dialogue between government officials and voters.

The foundation would like to learn about organizations and resources that might be helpful in its work on government transparency in Moldova.

## Gender in Development Project in Moldova

ul. 31 Avgusta 131
2012      Chisinau
**Tel:**      24-82-78
**Fax:**     24-82-77
**E-mail:**  saca@un.md
**Contact:** Silvia Saca, Head of Project

The United Nations Development Program's GID Project was established in 1994 to assist the women of Moldova. It has organized seminars for women and girls on business, gender roles, leadership, and violence. GID organized the Beijing Group, a coalition of NGOs in Moldova working with or for women. The coalition includes organizations which: educate women in business, work on the issue of violence toward women, organize gender training for women and girls and leadership seminars. The Beijing Group hopes to raise funds to set up a shelter for women and a legal center focused on domestic violence.

## Helsinki Citizens' Assembly of Moldova

a/ya 570
2043      Chisinau
**Tel/Fax:** 24-32-74
**E-mail:**  bio@mdearn.cri.md

**Contact:** Vladimir Solonari, MP, President of the Board; Tatiana Sineaeva, Member of the Board

HCAM was formed in 1993 in response to the development of nationalist extremism in Moldova. HCAM feels that, without standards and protection for national minorities, Moldova will never develop as a democratic state or become integrated into the European community. It has sponsored numerous international seminars and conferences dealing with such issues as, conflict resolution, interethnic relations, and the current state of Nazism and racism in Moldova.

## Independent Journalism Center

Scuisev 53
2012      Chisinau
**Tel:**      21-36-52, 22-75-39
**Fax:**     22-66-81
**E-mail:**  ijc@ijc.moldnet.md,
            director@ijc.moldnet.md
**Contact:** Corina Cepoi, Director; Angela Sirbu, Coordinator

IJC is a nonprofit, non-governmental organization focusing on media training. Presently, its two primary sources of funding are the Soros Foundation Moldova (SF-Moldova) and the Eurasia Foundation. It has also received many in-kind donations and program support from other organizations.

IJC has organized numerous seminars, workshops, and training programs, including:

- A 1995 seminar Cooperating on Public Information, which focused on the relationship between media, business, and government structures and was sponsored by PBN Company and SF-Moldova
- Management of Print Media seminar, organized by ODIHR, SF-Moldova

and IJC in 1995 and attended by 40 people from seven countries
- English language scholarships for journalists from Moldova sponsored by SF-Moldova
- TV news training
- Computer training for young journalists in 1995-1996
- Business and Economic Reporting workshop in 1996
- Public Relations for Journalists and Public Relations: Communications Skills workshops in 1996

IJC maintains a resource center with information on Moldovan media organizations, journalists, NGOs, political parties, government agencies, unions, printing facilities, foreign experts working in Moldova, embassies, and international media organizations. IJC's current projects include an 18-month program to train 84 Moldovan journalists in business and economic reporting through training seminars and internships in Ukraine and Romania.

IJC hosts a press club, in cooperation with the Moldovan Committee for the Freedom of Press. The club publishes a weekly information digest for Moldovan journalists, *Lumea Deschisa*, and a biannual research magazine, *Media in Moldova*, available in Romanian and in English, that reports on the mass media situation in Moldova. *Media in Moldova* is also distributed to around 500 international organizations in the West.

## The Independent Press Association

bul. Stefan cel Mare 123, k. 14
2004    Chisinau
**Tel/Fax:** 24-72-39
**E-mail:** pucketts@ch.moldpac.md
**Contact:** Dorina Osipov, Coordinator; Glenn Puckett, Peace Corps Volunteer

The association was formed in 1997 by a group of newspapers in Chisinau who meet regularly to exchange ideas and news information. This small network quickly attracted more newspapers and media representatives, who began working together to strengthen Moldova's free press.

Members have coordinated the purchase of newsprint, collaborating to find the best price and highest quality. Under a Eurasia Foundation grant, the association is holding a series of round table discussions in different regions of Moldova on an independent press, to which media representatives throughout the country are invited. The association also received a grant from the United States Information Service to provide digital cameras to all members.

In the future, the group plans to establish an e-mail system to facilitate greater communication between media representatives, and would like to produce a guide for journalists on how to start up and operate an independent newspaper.

## IREX Office—RSEP/CI Alumni Coordinators

Academy of Sciences of Moldova
bul. Stefan cel Mara 1, k. 303
Chisinau
**Tel:**       26-13-53
**Tel/Fax:** 76-88-23
**E-mail:**   dusk@irex.mldnet.com
**Contacts:** Yurii Datii, Alla Skvortsova

Office hours: Tuesday and Thursday 2:00 - 6:00 pm. See profile of IREX in North American Organizations

## Kishinev Rock–Club Krok

Кишиневский рок-клуб "Крок"
Chisinau
**Tel:**     52-26-41, 58-07-86
**Fax:**     52-16-46
**E-mail:**  vict@mer.un.md

**Contact:** Victor Kupershlak, President

Krok serves to unite young people in Moldova through rock music. It strives to propagate the ideas of nonviolence and a healthy lifestyle as well as the ideals of a free society, personal freedom and personal development. Krok has representatives in Sever-Beltsy, Drokiia, Comrat, Ungeshty, Chadyr-Lunga, and other regions of Moldova. It works in collaboration with the Youth Federation of Moldova and the Vremia Molodykh movement . Krok is looking for sponsors for the following projects: publication of *Rock-gazeta*, financial assistance for young, talented musicians, a recording studio, and a program on the local TV channel.

### "Moldova Open to the World"
ul. Plaiului 2, k.15
2002 Chisinau
**Tel/Fax:** 55-46-47
**E-Mail:** igers@moldnet.md
**Web:** harnet.nor.md
**Contact:** Sergiu Raileanu, President

This organization uses the Internet to publicize information about Moldova internationally.

### NGO Club of Moldova "Life and Society"
Renasterii 2
277012 Chisinau
**Tel:** 73-90-40, 22-51-37
**Fax:** 23-40-51
**E-mail:** bstheim@hotmail.com
**Contact:** Boris Steinman, NGO Club Coordinator

Life and Society is a volunteer union of more than 25 NGOs in Moldova, formed in 1997. Members are active in charity and children, national arts, ecology, social and economic processes in society, science and education, medicine, and international cultural connections. The focus of the club is developing the third-sector in Moldova, facilitating coordination between different club members for common projects, sharing information, and establishing cooperative relations between NGOs and government agencies in Moldova. The club was organized under the auspices of the newly established Social Innovations Center.

### Women's Organization of Moldova
ul. Kogalniceanu 36-a, kv. 11
2009 Chisinau
**Tel:** 26-58-93, 33-13-03
**E-mail:** wommoldova@yahoo.com
**Contact:** Irina Martiniuc, President

WOM is a non-governmental, non-political organization, founded in 1996. It has branches located in Chisinau, Hincesti, Tiraspol, Ceadir-Lunga, Straseni, and Balti, and has 600 members. Its works to promote democratic values by involving women in the democratization process, upholding and stimulating women's civic initiatives, and ensuring the protection of women's and children's civic, economic and social rights.

WOM's past and current activities include:
- Organizing seminars and training sessions on women's rights, women in business, and NGO development in six cities
- Establishing new women's NGOs in the regions of Moldova
- Consulting for professional women
- Aiding orphans with food
- Collaborating with the mass media.

WOM is supported through membership fees and private sponsors. In 1997, the branches in Hincesti and Tiraspol received short-term grants from the Eurasia Foundation to help women develop agribusinesses in the Hincesti region and create NGOs in the Trans-Dniester region of Moldova.

## Beltsy (31)

### National Medical Training Center
Pacii St. 55A
3100    Beltsy
**Tel:**    2-44-59
**E-mail:**  cim@bl.moldpac.md
**Contact:** Ion Reicu, Director

The center was established in March 1998, with support from the Soros Foundation. It provides first aid training for policemen, firemen, health care workers, employees of transport and security services, and other interested citizens. It also designs educational programs for specific areas of emergency medicine, such as CPR and poison control. The center is working to develop its own medical knowledge, technology and services to meet international standards. Its partners include the Initial Response Training Center in Smithfield, Virginia, and Lakeland Sisters Cities Committee in Florida.

**Contact:** Ms. Lilia Diaciuc, Director; John W. Baggaley, U.S. Peace Corps Volunteer

CESI works to promote social progress in southern Moldova, particularly in Gagauzia (a new autonomous region in Moldova with Comrat as its capital), by assisting with economic development and stimulating individual initiative. CESI views economic development as essential to achieving social change. It focuses on supporting private businesses and non-governmental organizations.

CESI activities include business and management consulting, training, education, and distributing information. The organization is also actively involved in gender issues and a free press. Funding and support has been provided by the local Gagauzian government, the U.S Peace Corps, the Soros Foundation and the Eurasia Foundation.

One of CESI's accomplishments has been publication of a cultural and investor's guide to Gagauzia. The guide includes a directory of all Gagauzian business enterprises and NGOs, as well as cultural and historical information To receive the guide, contact CESI.

## Comrat (38)

### Center for Economic and Social Initiative
Центр экономико-социальной инициативы
ul. Lenina 160
3805    Comrat
**Tel/Fax:**  2-37-87
**E-mail:**  baggaley@alum.mit.edu,
          bag@pc.moldpac.md
**Web:**     www.contact.moldnet.md/
cesi.html

# Russia: West of the Urals

**Country Code: 7**

## Moscow (095)

### Adventure Club—Charity Rehabilitation Foundation

Donskaya St. 37
117419  Moscow
**Tel:**      959-9940, 959-9936,
             959-9941
**Fax:**      952-0459
**E-mail:**   advclub@aha.ru
**Web:**      www.advclub.aha.ru
**Contact:** Dmitry Shparo, Ph.D,
Director; Matvey Shparo

Adventure Club was established in 1989 by Dmitry Shparo, a well-known Russian outdoorsman who led the first ski expedition to the North Pole in 1979. The club organizes mountain expeditions and wheel chair competitions for the disabled as a method of rehabilitation. In 1996, Shparo led a team of disabled sportsmen from Armenia, Azerbaijan, Georgia, Norway and Russia, all in wheel chairs, on an ascent of Mt. Kazbek (5,047 m.). In 1997, a team of disabled people, including deaf, blind and amputees, climbed Mt. Kilimanjaro in Africa (5,875 m.). Wheel chair marathons organized by the club have included the following: Moscow to Kiev to Krivoy Rog, 1991; Vladivostok to St. Petersburg, 1992; St. Petersburg to Almaty, Kazakstan, 1994; and Semipalatinsk to Chelyabinsk to Chernobyl, 1996.

The club also hosts activities for youth. For several years it has organized youth trips to the festival Children of the Arctic, held in different countries each year. It has also arranged kayak expeditions for youth in the U.S. and Canada, and in 1997 led youth on a scientific trip to Chita oblast to observe a total solar eclipse. The club's Youth Geographical School has been arranging outdoor activities and lectures for youth for more than seven years.

Shparo, age 56 with a Ph.D. in mathematics, has participated in numerous other club expeditions. On March 21, 1998, he and his son Matvey became the first people to cross the Bering Strait on skis. In 1996-1997, Shparo sailed a yacht built by the Adventure Club around the world. He participated in a Russian-Danish expedition to the Commander Islands in 1991, where the team discovered the grave of Vitus Bering. Shparo was also part of a Soviet-American expedition of dog sleds across the Bering Strait and Alaska in 1989, and in 1988, he led a Soviet-Canadian ski expedition across the Arctic Ocean, from Russia to the North Pole to Canada.

### Aesop Center

ul. Pokrovka 22/1
Moscow
**Tel:**      .928-2782
**Fax:**      234-3990
**E-mail:**   aesop@aesop.org
**Web:**      www.aesop.org
**Contact:** Andrei S. Sinelnikov,
Executive Director

A major project of Aesop has been to establish and operate SPIDNET, the first HIV/AIDS information network in Russia. The network includes an e-mail network, database, library, and bulletin on HIV/AIDS issues. Its primary goal is to reach civic groups and individuals, especially those outside of Moscow, with up-to-date information on HIV/AIDS and other sexually transmitted diseases.

It has also developed the Russian Sexual Health Coalition to promote education and information on STDs and reproductive health issues.

## Agency of Social Information

Агенство Социальных Информаций

Sivtsev Vrazhek 14
121019  Moscow
**Tel:**      241-6964
**Fax:**     241-8980
**E-mail:** asi@glas.apc.org
**Web:**     www.friends-partners.org/~ccsi/asi/asihome.htm
**Contact:** Elena Topoleva, Director; Andrei Topolev, Co-Director

ASI is a Moscow-based, independent information agency that works to support Russia's emerging third sector of non-governmental, nonprofit social organizations. Founded in 1994 through the initiative of Post Factum News Agency, two Russian charitable foundations (Dusha Cheloveka and NAN—"No to Alcoholism and Drug Addiction") and others, the agency disseminates news and information about third sector organizations, upcoming events, and social issues in an effort to publicize the work of Russian NGOs and foster social support for their initiatives.

ASI has 12 regional affiliates in St. Petersburg, Ekaterinburg, Nizhny Novgorod, Velikii Novgorod, Arkhangelsk, Kaluga, Voronezh, Krasnodar, Krasnoyarsk, Irkutsk, Novosibirsk and Barnaul. They are based on existing NGOs in each city, which support the work of ASI's central office.

ASI's services include:
- The *ASI Weekly Bulletin*, a digest in Russian that reports on a wide range of third sector activities, such as upcoming conferences, cooperation with government and commercial structures, and work with international foundations. The bulletin features information on grants and grant-making organizations, and presents brief profiles of third sector organizations. Reports on legislation impacting civil society in Russia are also included. The bulletin is distributed to a prestigious list of Russian media clients, various government structures, and both Russian and international nonprofit organizations and individuals. It is also sent by electronic mail to more than 300 organizations in Russia and abroad (approximately 90 percent of subscribers are in Russia).
- The *Analytical Bulletin*, produced in collaboration with the charitable foundation Soprichastnost since May 1996. This monthly topical bulletin addresses current social issues in Russia through interviews, essays, and statistical information.
- ASI also maintains an extensive database of Russian NGOs organized by area of activity and offers consulting services to new groups seeking guidance on such activities as media relations, publicity campaigns, and organizing PR events.

## AIDS Infoshare Russia

СПИД Инфосвязь
a/ya 51
105037  Moscow
**Tel/Fax:** 110-2460, 383-7553
**E-mail:**  infoshare@glas.apc.org
**Web:**     www.spiral.com/infoshare/
**Contact:** Julie Stachowiak, Executive Director; Alena Pyroshkina, Program Director

AIDS Infoshare Russia works in conjunction with AIDS Infoshare

International, a U.S.-based organization, to foster awareness of HIV/AIDS and sexually transmitted diseases in Russia. The group also works to expose human rights violations in the health system.

AIDS Infoshare oversees the STD/HIV/AIDS Prevention Among Women Project, which provides women's organizations in Russia with information and training to conduct AIDS awareness campaigns. This organization collaborates with others in more than 20 cities throughout Russia. For a listing of their partners by city, consult their Web site.

## All-National Fund for the Promotion of Individual Apartments

ul. Solyanka 1/2
109028   Moscow
**Tel:**      923-0220
**Fax:**      928-1719
**Contact:** Anatoly Basargin, President

The fund was created in 1989 to address the needs of local tenants in a residential complex in the Kitai Gorod neighborhood of Moscow. The tenants were frustrated with the government's failure to renovate their building. The founders, who had been running a small theater in the building, formed the residential association in order to promote the building's renovation and encourage "a spirit of community" among residents. ANF's primary goal now is the elimination of communal apartments.

In 1991, the courts granted ANF control of their landmark building. They have now completed the design work for capital renovation of the structure.They have also established their own maintenance and repair operation, created dozens of jobs for local residents, initiated social services

for the elderly and youth, and offered technical assistance to other housing organizations throughout Russia.

ANF published a manual for residents, *How to Get Out of a Communal Apartment*, and has taken the lead in promoting the concept of "housing partnerships" in Russia. To meet residents' need for banking services and to help finance their project, ANF established their own accredited bank on the premises. Their president, Anatoly Basargin, played a role in drafting the housing portion of the Russian Constitution.

The ANF cooperated with the Urban Homesteading Assistance Board in a two-year institutional partnership project, funded by USAID.

## All-Russian Society of the Disabled

Всероссийское Общество
Инвалидов
Kutuzovsky pr. 30/32
121165   Moscow
**Tel:**      241-2286, 241-1880,
            241-7825
**Fax:**      241-8180
**E-mail:**  voi@glas.apc.org
**Contact:** Aleksander Lomakin, Chair

ARSD is a national organization with 2,500 district and regional offices and 2.2 million members. Its primary goal is the integration of disabled people into society.

The society has become an active member of the international disabled community and frequently takes part in international conferences. As a result of management and leadership development training, several ARSD and regional affiliate members ran for office in Russia's December 1993 elections. The ARSD also lobbied successfully for the development of national legislation regarding the rights and protection of disabled citizens in Russia.

ARSD owns a large number of businesses whose profits support its regional and district branches. ARSD and the World Institute on Disability (WID) have collaborated to develop a model training and technical assistance project to ensure the viability of these businesses. The WID/ARSD partnership (which began in 1992) has been effective in educating the public about disability-related issues through regional, national, and international media. WID and ARSD have also collaborated to train more than 70 ARSD leaders in advocacy, accessibility, management, public education and media, disability legislation, and other issues related to the disability movement worldwide.

## American Institute of Business and Economics

Moscow State Geological Prospecting Academy
Miklukho-Miklaya 23, etazh 1
**Tel:** 438-0830
**Tel/Fax:** 438-1439
**E-mail:** aibec@co.ru, walberg@co.ru
**Web:** www.knight hub.com/aibec
**Contact:** Gretchen Walberg, Director of Development

AIBEc is an independent, not-for-profit American business school operating in Moscow since 1993. It offers a program of evening courses in all major areas of business, taught in English by American instructors. Students can earn an MBA in two to three years. More than 90 percent of students are Russian, but international students are also welcome. A competitive entrance examination for the MBA program is offered once a year in April. Financial aid is available to students with outstanding scores but limited financial means. Students

interested in taking only a few courses in their specialty may apply at any time.

AIBEc students develop an understanding of international business that makes them especially valuable to Western firms doing business in Russia, as well as Russian firms working with Western partners and clients. A 1997 study commissioned by the World Bank ranked AIBEc first among 20 business schools surveyed in Moscow.

## Andrei Sakharov Foundation

Фонд Андрея Сахарова
Zemlyanoi val 48b, kom. 62
107120 Moscow
**Tel:** 923-4401, 923-4420, 923-4115
**Fax:** 917-2653
**E-mail:** bela@sakharovfound.msk.su
**Web:** www.wdn.com/asf
**Contact:** Elena Bonner, Chair; Yuri Samodurov, Executive Director; Bela Koval, Director of Sakharov Archives

The foundation is also known as the Public Commission for the Preservation of the Legacy of Academician A. D. Sakharov. It oversees several organizations dedicated to furthering the work and memory of Andrei Sakharov, one of the Soviet Union's most prominent scientists and respected dissidents. The foundation maintains the Sakharov Archives in Moscow, which house thousands of documents related to Sakharov's life and human rights activities. It also operates the Andrei Sakharov Museum and Community Center.

The museum and community center was opened in 1996 with the goal of "educating the next generation of Russians about the USSR's totalitarian past" and serving as a resource for Russia's human and civil rights movements. It offers a research facility for historians and human rights activists, educational programs for children, and meeting space for non-governmental groups. It also frequently hosts lectures, concerts, and roundtable discussions related to the work of Sakharov and current human rights issues in Russia.

## Anti-Military Radical Association

Антимилитаристская Радикальная Ассоциация
ul. Trubnaia 25-2-49
103051   Moscow
**Tel/Fax:** 923-9127
**E-mail:**  ara@glasnet.ru
**Web:**       www.glasnet.ru/~ara

The ARA is an affiliate of the Transnational Radical Party, an international political movement that follows a Ghandian philosophy of non-violence and conscientious objection. The group is opposed to current Russian law requiring mandatory military service and is working to abolish the law and establish alternative service. ARA produces a monthly newsletter, *The Anti-Militarist*, (available on-line at the group's Web site) and holds weekly seminars in Moscow informing young men of legal methods to avoid the draft.

During the spring draft in April 1998, ARA members plastered Moscow subway trains with thousands of stickers reading "Call to Military Service? No, thanks!" that gave ARA's phone number and cited the article of the Russian constitution protecting conscientious objectors. ARA has offices in several cities across Russia, including Vladimir, Nizhny Novgorod, Severomorsk (in Murmansk oblast) and Yaroslavl.

## Association "Women in Science and Education"

Ассоциация Женщины в Науке и Образовании

Moscow State University
Biological Faculty
Biophysics Department
119899   Moscow
**Tel:**        939-1963
**Fax:**       939-1115
**E-mail:**  awse@mars.biophys.msu.ru
**Web:**       mars.biophys.msu.ru/awse
**Contact:** Galina Riznichenko, President; Dr. Evgenij Maevsky, Co-President

AWSE was founded in September 1994 with a mission to support the efforts of women working in the fields of science and education. The group currently has approximately 600 members in more than 40 cities across Russia.

AWSE organizes conferences, congresses, seminars and other events to discuss the professional and social problems facing women scientists and educators. It also provides women with information about grants, academic competitions, and educational events in Russia and abroad in an effort to help them develop their careers.

## Association of Young Leaders

Ассоциация Юных Лидеров
Prospekt Mira 184-2-118
129301 Moscow (postal address)
pr. 60-Letiya Oktobriya, d. 9, k. 1512
Moscow (street address)
**Tel/Fax:** 135-4247
**E-mail:**  ayl@glasnet.ru
**Web:**       www.glasnet.ru/~ayl/

In 1987 a visit to Moscow by six members of the California Association of Student Councils (CASC) prompted a group of Soviet students to create a similar organization in Russia. The result was the Association of Young Leaders, established in 1992. AYL is a nonprofit organization run by students that helps young people develop civic responsibility, leadership skills, and self-esteem. Using programs developed by CASC, AYL works with schools to provide leadership training courses for students and teachers and sponsors four-day workshops that train students to become "peer leaders" for their classmates.

Currently, there are AYL branches in Moscow, Murmansk, Orel, Volgograd, Volgodonsk, Magnitogorsk, Kemerovo, and Gorno-Altaisk. In 1994, the Kazakhstan Association of Young Leaders was established in Almaty with the direct assistance of AYL.

## Carnegie Moscow Center
ul. Tverskaya 16/2
103009  Moscow
**Tel:** 935-8904
**Fax:** 935-8906
**E-mail:** info@carnegie.ru
**Web:** www.carnegie.ru/
**Contact:** Alan Rousso, Director; Dmitri Trenin, Deputy Director

Foreign and Russian scholars at the center collaborate with staff of the Carnegie Endowment for International Peace in Washington, D.C., but carry on independent research on topics of political, economic and military affairs. Current research emphases are:
- Russian domestic politics and political institutions
- Post-Soviet economies in transition
- Nuclear non-proliferation
- Ethnicity and nation-building
- Migration and refugees
- Foreign and security policy
- CIS integration
- Rethinking U.S.-Russia relations
The Moscow Center publishes a quarterly journal in Russian, *Pro et Contra*.

## Center for Energy Efficiency
Центр по эффектиному использованию энергии
ul. Novocheremushkinskaya 54, korp. 4
117418  Moscow
**Tel/Fax:** 120-5147
**Fax:** 883-9563
**E-mail:** cenef@glas.apc.org
**Web:** www.glasnet.ru/~cenef

CENEf is a nonprofit, independent Russian-American organization founded in 1992 by a consortium of U.S. and Russian organizations to promote energy efficiency and environmental protection in Russia. The center's main objectives are:
- Developing legislation and policy proposals to implement more efficient use of energy resources in Russia
- Initiating energy-efficiency projects
- Developing potential opportunities for cooperation between Russian and foreign companies using energy-efficient equipment or production procedures
CENEf publishes two newsletters: *The Energy Efficiency Bulletin* (available in Russian and English), which contains news on energy policy and projects throughout Russia, and *The Russian Energy Picture* (in English only), which provides data on Russian energy consumption and other energy-related statistics, including prices and macroeconomic indicators.

## Center for Humanitarian Aid
ul. Novaia Basmanaia 11
109117  Moscow
**Tel:** 257-3010 ext. 176, 261-6654
**Fax:** 257-3211
**E-mail:** bezdna@imedia.ru
**Contact:** Namrud Negash, Julie MacDonald

The center began working in 1996 when a small group of volunteers from St. Catherine's Orthodox Church (U.S.) united to feed Moscow's homeless. Daniel Ogan of the U.S. and Alexander Kozhamyakin of Russia founded the center in order to revive the spirit of charity that characterized the pre-revolutionary Russian Orthodox Church. The two worked out of the Saints Peter and Paul Orthodox Church to cook food, store clothes, and serve meals two days a week to the homeless, pensioners, ex-convicts, and street children near Kazan Railway Station in Moscow.

The center currently operates six days per week, feeding up to 150 people daily. Volunteers and staff also distribute clothes and other items donated by foreign and Russian organizations and individuals. The center offers advice to the homeless on how to obtain personal documents and legal registration. In 1998, it founded a "homeless" newspaper, *Yest Vykhod*, to inform the public of the plight of Moscow's needy. Dozens of homeless people now earn money selling the newspaper.

## Center for Peacemaking and Community Development

ul. Usachova 29, korp. 7, k. 405
119048   Moscow
**Tel/Fax:** 245-4632
**E-mail:**   peacecentre@glasnet.ru
**Contact:** Chris Hunter, Director

CPCD was founded in 1995 to collect and distribute information concerning human rights violations from the war in Chechnya as well as to advocate an end to the conflict. It has provided education and training in non-violent conflict resolution and human rights, and humanitarian assistance to war victims in the North Caucasus. CPCD has set up the Little Star psychological rehabilitation facility in Grozny for children traumatized by the war. Little Star also trains local specialists in psychological rehabilitation for war victims.

Currently CPCD carries out postwar, humanitarian, physical reconstruction work and raises public awareness of the social and psychological effects of war. It has also begun to create an e-mail network for North Caucasus youth and women's groups and is hoping to create a prosthetics center in Grozny. Besides Grozny, CPCD has offices in Novgorod, Ingushetia, and Exeter, Great Britain (tel/fax in UK: +44 1392-219-022).

CPCD works with Mothers for Peace in Dusseldorf and the Kornhaug Norwegian Peace Center in Lillehammer. Its annual budget is US$200,000–$300,000 and the staff of 30 is mainly Russian.

## Charities Aid Foundation–Russia

Yakovoapostolsky per.10
103064   Moscow
**Tel:**        928-0557
**Fax:**       298-5694
**E-mail:**   lenay@glas.apc.org
                  caftacis@glas.apc.org
**Web:**      www.charitynet.org/
cafrussia/index.html
**Contact:** Jenny Hodgson, Olga Alexeeva, Co-Directors; Maria Klimova, Office Manager

CAF-Russia is a charitable organization registered as both a foreign representative office of Charities Aid Foundation (UK) and a Russian nonprofit group. Its mission is "to promote the sustainability of the nonprofit sector in Russia." It currently has a staff of 23 full-time employees and a yearly budget of over $500,000. CAF runs over 10 projects and has support from nearly as many donors. The group has a library, a wide range of consultation services, and a research and publications department. All information is available to the public in CAF-Russia's library, which they fairly describe as "the best-stocked NPO library in Russia." A magazine, *Money and Charity,* is published every two months (in Russian).

CAF-Russia opened in August 1993. Since then, it has created a wide range of services and programs for NGOs and donors as part of its three-point mission:

- To assist foreign and Russian donors and provide them with detailed information about the Russian nonprofit sector, legal and fiscal issues, funding opportunities, priorities and partnerships; effective project and money management services; and design of corporate sponsorship programs
- To assist democratic developments in Russia by encouraging legal awareness and respect for human rights, strengthening nonprofit management training, and helping NGOs improve their relations with the public, media and government
- To work as an intermediary to increase the flow of international resources to Russia.

Since the beginning of 1997, CAF-Russia has worked closely with the Association of Russian Banks and leading Russian and international companies to create the independent Donors' Forum in Moscow. A large seminar on corporate giving took place in May 1997 with the participation of representatives of the Moscow government, the federal parliament, leading NGOs, and 32 of the largest Russian banks.

Other CAF activities include training workshops, roundtables, lectures, conferences, legal and financial consultations (free to any Russian NGO), and legislative lobbying. CAF is involved in a working group of corporate representatives, which has proposed a revision to the Russian tax code whereby companies making donations to local charities that have received "charitable passports" from the Moscow Charitable Council can reduce their local tax obligations by up to 100 percent of the amount of their donations.

Currently, CAF-Russia is working to develop a Moscow Community Foundation along the lines of the New York Community Trust or similar institutions. NYCT, the first and largest community foundation in the world, hosted a CAF-organized study trip in September 1998 for 11 persons representing Moscow city government, the corporate sector, and NGOs.

CAF is also implementing a Local Community Cooperation Models program. Sponsored by the Ford Foundation, this program will look for and document "sustainable models of local community participation, corporate giving, and local government understanding" in five cities in Russia: four cities where there is already a healthy NPO sector—Moscow, St. Petersburg, Saratov, and Tyumen—and one city, Orel, where Communist influence is still strongly felt. Orel was chosen to see how a new approach to community development and cooperation can be introduced in a very conservative Russian region. The experience gathered there will provide strategies for working in similar Russian oblasts. After the investigative part of this project is concluded, the second component will be to develop and draft new legislation for local-level nonprofit work based on the results.

## Citizens Democracy Corps–Moscow

ul. Lyusinovskaya 36, etazh 11
119093　Moscow
**Tel:**　745-5043, 745-5046,
　　　　745-5067
**Fax:**　745-5059
**E-mail:**　bccoffice@bcc.ru,
　　　　wjensen@bcc.ru, all@bcc.ru
**Web:**　www.bcc.ru
**Contact:** William H. Jensen, Jr.,
General Director

The Moscow office of CDC was formed in 1998 as a sister organization of CDC, Inc., based in Washington, D.C. As a Russian entity, it is expected to seek funding from domestic Russian sources and provide Russian staff with the opportunity to work independently.

The main mission of CDC is to provide training, consulting, and information services in support of the development of business and non-governmental organizations in Russia, Central Asia, the Caucasus region, and Central and Eastern Europe. Since 1992, CDC has facilitated the travel and work of more than 500 volunteer consultants on more than 600 projects in companies and organizations throughout Russia. Over 60 percent of CDC's volunteers are entrepreneurs dedicated to assisting small and medium-sized enterprises to start, grow, and sustain themselves in Russia. CDC has a total staff of 55 and expenditures of approximately $6 million per year.

CDC's volunteer consulting and technical assistance program, begun in 1992, is administered through its seven regional field offices located in St. Petersburg, Novgorod, Khabarovsk, Vladivostok, Yakutsk, Magadan, and Yuzhno-Sakhalinsk. Examples of this program's success are its recent consulting projects for the city of St. Petersburg, which included project development for rebuilding of the Leningrad Zoopark, a feasibility study for a large amusement park, and a development plan for the Peterhof National Historical Site.

CDC's Business Collaboration Center, opened in 1995, maintains an informational Web site for USAID. The center has offices in Khabarovsk, Ekaterinburg, Moscow and St. Petersburg and roving reporters in Vladivostok, Rostov, and Stavropol.

Recent projects to extend Internet access and business consulting to local businesses have been implemented in collaboration with the Congress of Business in Stavropol; the International Investment Center in Yaroslavl, Kostroma, and Ivanovo; and the International Business Center in Ekaterinburg.

## Citizen's Foundation

Народный Фонд
Smolensky bulvar 17, 5
119121　Moscow
**Tel:**　244-0042
**Fax:**　230-2200
**Contact:** Dr. Igor Kokarev, President

Citizen's Foundation was founded by a group of Russian scholars and intellectuals in an effort to foster a culture of democracy based on grassroots initiatives and a "self-help" philosophy. In 1994, the foundation opened the Neopalimovka Center, a community center in Moscow that encourages citizens to work together on community development and coordinates activities of the foundation.

## Civic Assistance Committee for Refugees and Displaced Persons

Общественный комитет
помощи беженцам и

вынужденным переселенцам
"Гражданское содействие"
ul. Nizhegorodskaia 21a, podval 4
Moscow
**E-mail:** meminf@glasnet.ru
**Web:** www.openweb.ru/windows/
cca/htm/
**Contact:** Lidiia Grafova, Svetlana
Gannushkina

The committee was formed in 1990 to
aid Armenian refugees from Azerbaijan
seeking asylum in Moscow. Today, it
continues to provide legal and practical
assistance to refugees and displaced
persons in the Moscow region, helping
them obtain asylum and find jobs and
homes.

In 1996, the committee began operating a school in Moscow for the children
of refugees. The school, called the
Center for Adaptation and Study, provides both academic courses and
"social adaptation" classes for refugee
children who would otherwise be
unable to attend school in Moscow due
to lack of official residency (i.e., a
*propiska*).

## Committee of Soldiers' Mothers
## of Russia

Комитет солдатских матерей
России
per. Louchnikov 4/3, k. 5
101000   Moscow
**Tel:**      928-2506
**Fax:**      206-8958
**E-mail:** usm@glasnet.ru
**Web:**      www.hro.org/ngo/usm/
index.htm
**Contact:** Maria I. Kirbasova,
Chairwoman; Veronika A. Marchenko;
Valentina Melnikova, Press Secretary

Founded in 1989, the committee has
worked to expose human rights
violations within the Russian military,
including the high number of deaths

from hazing or severe punishment. It
gives legal help and material assistance
to the families of dead servicemen,
consults on legislation affecting military service, and publishes research on
service-related deaths in the military.
The committee advocates improved
living conditions in the military and a
true alternative service option for conscientious objectors. It also operates
barracks in Moscow for fugitive
soldiers.

Between January and March 1998,
the committee received 331 letters from
conscripts and servicemen reporting
human rights violations. More than six
percent were from parents of soldiers
killed in service, and 25 percent came
from servicemen citing hazing abuses,
including torture and extreme physical
violence. Three press conferences held
by the committee in the first half of
1998 addressed worsening conditions in
the Russian military and were widely
reported by Russian press, TV, and
radio. The group continues to actively
lobby the RF government for legislation to protect the rights of servicemen, reform the military, rehabilitate
veterans of regional conflicts, and
provide support to the families of dead
servicemen.

In early 1998, the committee worked
with the Moscow military prosecutor's
office to address appeals for amnesty
from military deserters. At the committee offices, military prosecutors heard
the testimony of several hundred
deserters regarding the human rights
violations that prompted their abandonment of military duties. After consultation with the committee, the prosecutor's office was able to dismiss criminal
charges against those servicemen with
legitimate claims of abuse.

Regional branches of the committee
are active throughout Russia. The

committee received the 1995 Sean MacBride Peace Prize, awarded by the International Peace Bureau, for its work in opposing the war in Chechnya as well as for its previous campaigns to end human-rights abuses within the Russian military.

## Downside Up Children's Center
19 Strelbishensky per., k. 3
123317   Moscow
**Tel/Fax:** 256-4525
**E-mail:** downsideup@matrix.ru

Downside Up is a UK-registered charity and a registered Russian charitable fund dedicated to improving the quality of life for children with Down's syndrome and their families in the Russia. The charity was established in 1996 in response to the lack of social and educational services for children with Down's syndrome in the Russian Federation. DU provides effective and comprehensive special education programs to enrich children's learning and lives so that they may reach their individual potentials. The charity also works to increase public awareness of Down's syndrome and to further opportunities for the inclusion of people with Down's syndrome in Russian society.

Downside Up's programs include home visits by specialists who work on development skills with parents and young children affected with Down's syndrome and specialized play groups that target specific needs for individual children (e.g., motor skills, speech, coordination). The organization co-sponsors the first integrated kindergarten in Moscow, where children with Down's syndrome are "mainstreamed" with nondisabled children.

## "ECOPRESS" Regional Center of Journalists and Experts Concerned with Environmental Problems
ul. Rogova 12-46
123479   Moscow
**Tel:**      947-1909, 947-7772
**E-mail:**   larin@glasnet.ru
**Contact:** Vladislav Larin, Senior Expert; Eugeny Tarakanov, Director

ECOPRESS was established in 1989 for the collection, evaluation, and distribution of reliable environmental information. The group uses an extensive network of well-known experts and professional journalists for implementation of the following projects:
- International public environmental impact assessment of natural gas drilling on the Yamal peninsula in Western Siberia
- Study of renewable energy utilization in Denmark
- Study of methods for environmental monitoring from space (ECOPRESS has published several articles and prepared an instruction manual)
- Participation in the international conference Environmental Impact Assessment–Situation and Perspectives in Europe, in Genoa, Italy
- Research projects on nuclear accidents in the Urals, including a book published in Russian in 1996 and in English in 1998, and the production of a video
- Study of methods used for application of environmental information to national policy formulation.

Th last involved preparation of a *Catalogue of Primary Sources of Environmental Information* and *A Review of the System of Environmental Monitoring and Related Environmental Policy Issues in the Russian Federation and the Former Soviet Union.*

Articles and photos prepared by ECOPRESS have been published in numerous Russian newspapers and journals, including *Energiya, Zeleny Mir, Radical, Komsomolskaya pravda, Chelovek i priroda*, and *Zhurnalist*.

## Ecosystem Association
Ассоциация "Экосистем"
a/ya 427
109072  Moscow
**Tel:**      959-0495
**Fax:**      354-3548
**E-mail:**  abogol@stk.mmtel.ru
**Web:**     www.ilstud.edu/~aggubin/bogol.htm
**Contact:** Aleksandr Bogolyubov, President

The association develops course materials on environmental science for use by school teachers in Russia and the NIS. Their philosophy is that environmental education should take place within nature itself; thus, the group organizes educational field trips and summer camps that take children into the wild to teach them about ecology and the natural sciences.

## The Eurasia Foundation
ul. Volkhonka 14, etazh 4, k. 403
119843   Moscow
**Tel:**      956-1235
**Fax:**      956-1239
**E-mail:**  etmoscow@eurasia.msk.su

See the profile for the foundation in the North American Organizations section.

## Expert Institute
Moscow
**Tel:**      206-0129
**Fax:**      206-0504
**E-mail:**  exin@glasnet.ru
           ilipsits@yahoo.com
**Contact:** Andrey Neshchadin, Executive Director

The institute conducts research in applied economics, addressing such topics as the challenges of transition to a market economy for Russian enter- prises and regional social and economic development. It has made policy re- commendations to the Ministry of Economy and Central Bank, and has received financial support from the Ford Foundation, Eurasia Foundation, and TACIS.

## Ford Foundation–Russia
Pushkin Plaza
ul. Tverskaya 16/2
Moscow
**Tel:**      935-7051
**Fax:**      935-7052
**E-mail:**  ford-moscow@fordfound.org
**Contact:** Mary McAuley, Representative; Christopher Kedzie, Program Officer

Four broad goals provide a thematic focus for Ford Foundation's program in Russia:
- To promote the economic reform process and to support efforts to address the social policy issues raised by the transition to market-oriented economies
- To help consolidate democracy through the reform of political and legal institutions and the integration of international human rights stan- dards in domestic law and practice
- To strengthen institutions of higher education and research in the social sciences
- To enhance Western capacity to understand events in the region.
  Ford strives to address both short- term and long-term needs, combining research and policy analysis with training and institution-building programs.
  The foundation's Russian office made 24 grants in 1997 amounting to

$1.8 million under the Governance and Civil Society program, and 22 grants totaling approximately the same amount under the Human Rights and International Cooperation program. Under its Education, Knowledge, and Religion program, it made seven grants totaling $1.4 million. The largest of these, for $606,000, was to the Moscow Public Science Foundation for a national fellowship competition in the social sciences and modern history. Another $118,000 in grants were made to arts and media projects.

## Foundation for Agrarian Development Research

Фонд Исследования Аграрного Развытия
Nauchnii Park MGU, Zd. 1
119899   Moscow
**Tel/Fax:** 932-9195, 932-9207
**E-mail:**   admin@fadr.msu.ru
**Web:**   www.fadr.msu.ru/
**Contact:** Dmitrii Durmanov, President; Aleksandr Makeev, General Director

FADR was formed in 1993 in conjunction with the U.S.-based Rodale Institute in response to growing concerns over the fate of Russia's agricultural sector. The primary objective of FADR is to promote efficient and sustainable land use systems in Russia by establishing networks for information exchange among groups and individuals within Russia, implementing environmental education programs, and helping people adapt to new forms of land use.

## Friends House Moscow

Zemlyanoi Val 25, k. 45
Moscow
**Tel/Fax:**   917-5013
**E-mail:**   fhm@glasnet.ru

**Web:**   webcom.com/peace/FHM/welcome.html
**Contact:** Erik Cleven, Clerk of the Governing Board; Galina Orlova, Sergei Nikitin

FHM emerged from discussions among American and British Quakers and Russians about the benefit of promoting the unique style of Quaker spirituality in Russia. Founded in 1996, a primary goal of the group is to foster communications between Russians interested in Quakerism and Western Quakers, and to contribute to the development of grassroots organizations in Russia focusing on traditional Quaker concerns. The following activities are carried out by FHM:

- Rehabilitation program for Chechen child refugees in Moscow, addressing their post-traumatic stress
- Alternatives to Violence communication workshop, which is part of an international network of programs offered in prisons and local communities
- Support for programs in Moscow and Novgorod assisting conscientious objectors to Russian military service
- Organization of gatherings across Russia for youth and adults interested in Quakerism
- Financial and moral support in the operation of a model group home for homeless children in Moscow

FHM also conducts on-going programs to teach skills to the physically handicapped in Chechnya, assist Moscow families with handicapped children, and provide emergency assistance to Moscow Quaker Meeting families in crisis.

FHM has a staff of two, and is supported by volunteers, interns, and Friends in Residence. Its annual budget is about $60,000. Support comes primarily from the Religious Society of Friends (Quakers).

## Gaia International Women's Center

Khlebnyi per. 2/3
121817 Moscow
**Tel:** 135-3207
**Fax:** 200-1207
**E-mail:** gaia@glas.apc.org
**Contact:** Elena Erskhova, Nadezhda Shvedova

The center works in the sphere of women's rights policy and advocacy. It provides courses on leadership training and small business development, as well as legal counseling. The group also is involved in women's health care.

## Glasnost Defense Foundation

Фонд защиты гласности
Zubovskii bul. 4, k. 432
Moscow
**Tel:** 201-4420
**Tel/Fax:** 201-4947
**E-mail:** simonov@fond91.msk.ru, aleks@sovamsu.sovusa.com
**Web:** 194.85.111.7/GDF/index.html
**Contact:** Aleksei Simonov

GDF was organized in February 1991 for "the defense of journalism and journalists" throughout the territory of the former Soviet Union. Its work includes large-scale monitoring projects and research as well as case-by-case investigations into violations of individual journalist's rights.

GDF conducts research into broad abuses of freedom of the press and mass media, especially in so-called hot spots across the region. The group plays the role of an information clearinghouse on the topic of Russian mass media and the legislation affecting journalistic work and press freedoms in Russia and abroad. GDF reports on freedom of the press in Russia and the NIS are regularly available at the organization's Web site. The foundation has produced an extensive number of publications, including:

- *A Journalist in Search of Information*, by Vladimir Avdeev (1997), which explores the issue of journalists' limited access to information in the Russian Federation and details citizens' legal rights to information
- *The Republic of Kalmykia vs. Sovetskaia Kalmykia*, by V. Rudnev (1997), which documents the ongoing political pressure and harrassment of the independent newspaper *Sovetskaia Kalmykia* by the government of the republic
- *Legislation and Practical Experience of the Mass Media*, a monthly bulletin

## "Golubka"– Center of Experimental Education for Social Change Democracy

ul. Garibaldi 117/313, k. 11, 76
Moscow
**Tel/Fax:** 134-0295
**E-mail:** golubka@glas.apc.org
**Contact:** Ivan Timofeev, Program Director

## Gorbachev Foundation

Leningradskii Prospekt 49
125468 Moscow
**Tel:** 943-9990
**Fax:** 943-9594
**Contact:** Svetlana Ukhtinam, University of Calgary Program Coordinator

Among other things, the Gorbachev Foundation works with the University of Calgary in support of technical-cooperation projects between Canadian and Russian institutions.

## Human Rights Foundation "For Civil Society"

Правозащитный Фонд "За Гражданское общество"
pr. Louchnikov 4-3-25
102982   Moscow
**Tel/Fax:**  206-0924
**E-mail:**  hrcenter@glas.pac.org
**Contact:** Natalia Taubina, Director

The foundation was created in 1995 at the initiative of several Moscow human rights organizations to provide a support center for local human rights groups. It currently conducts an educational program for NGOs on such topics as fund-raising, accounting, grant-writing, and press relations. In 1996–97, the foundation conducted eight seminars attended by 73 representatives of 57 human rights groups from around Russia. The group also administers a small grants program for regional NGOs with support from the Eurasia Foundation and publishes a weekly bulletin of news and events.

## Information Center of the Independent Women's Forum

Информационный Центр Независимого Женского Форума
a/ya 230
121019   Moscow
**Tel/Fax:**  366-9274
**E-mail:**  iciwf@glas.apc.org
**Contact:**  Liza Bozhkova, Zoya Khotkina

The center acts as an advocate for women's groups in Russia and the NIS. ICIWF helps establish support/resource centers for women's NGOs and promotes cooperation between groups and with government structures.

In 1996–97, ICIWF's national-scale project, New Opportunities for Women, provided women's groups across Russia with organizational assistance and training. Women's organizations in Karelia, Mirny, Voronezh, Pskov, and Chelyabinsk learned strategies for working with government agencies and winning public support for their projects. ICIWF also provided these groups with consultations on management and fundraising, and published a digest featuring updates on the New Opportunities project and related events. The digest also included articles on women's issues, such as the history of women-owned businesses in Russia.

ICIWF maintains an extensive library of international and Russian materials related to the women's movement, as well as a database of women's organizations.

## Institute for Perspectives and Problems of the Country

Vernadskii Prospekt 113-244
117571   Moscow
**Tel:**      126-7790
**Fax:**      434-5280
**Contact:** Dr. Boris Rakitskii

Working with the Québec Institute for International Research and Education (QIIRE) under a Canadian government grant, this organization has carried out a project to strengthen the democratic labor movement in Russia. The project involved development of a training program for labor educators and union members associated with the Workers' Democracy School.

## Institute for Sustainable Communities

a/ya 85
117312   Moscow
ul. Gubkina 14, k. 75-76

117312 Moscow
**Tel:** 937-5002
**Fax:** 937-5003
**E-mail:** isc@iscmoscow.glasnet.ru
**Web:** www.iscvt.org
**Contact:** Gary Burniske, Office Director; Oleg Fokin, Communications Coordinator

ISC Moscow was formed in 1996 as a representative office of the Vermont-based Institute for Sustainable Communities. The Moscow office was initially established to implement a national environmental grants and information program, Replication of Lessons Learned (ROLL). The goal of the project is to improve environmental management capability in order to promote sustainable development and economic growth in Russia. This project will continue through August 2000.

ISC Moscow has awarded 37 grants for a total of a million dollars in 46 different administrative units of the Russian Federation through the ROLL program. It has also helped to establish two environmental training centers, in Ekaterinburg and Volgograd.

In Nizhny Tagil, ISC worked with partners to complete a detailed analysis of air pollution problems using computer modeling and risk assessment, and implement a system of continuous environmental education in the 11th grade.

ROLL seeks to expand the impact of successful environmental programs beyond the original "pilot" sites. Regional Support Centers throughout Russia are responsible for the day-to-day coordination of local activities, applicant and grantee consulting, and dissemination of project information. Centers are located in Ekaterinburg, Moscow, Novokuznetsk, Nizhny Novgorod, Vladivostok, and Ulan-Ude.

## Institute of International Education

Prospekt Mira 36, k. 46
129010 Moscow
**Tel:** 280-3062
**Tel/Fax:** 280-3516
**E-mail:** asyaslv@glas.apc.org
**Web:** www.iie.ru
**Contact:** Asya Silaeva, Program Officer

## Interlegal: International Charitable Foundation for Political and Legal Research

Krupskaya St.19/17, k. 126
117331 Moscow
**Tel/Fax:** 133-6608
**E-mail:** interlegal@glas.apc.org
**Contact:** Nina Belyaeva, President

Interlegal was founded in 1989 "to promote the growth and development of the independent sector throughout the former Soviet Union." It provides legal consultations to government agencies and NGOs and conducts research on the third sector.

At the request of the Duma Committee on the Affairs of Public Associations and Religious Organizations, Interlegal drafted legislation covering the registration of NGOs and charitable activity. It has provided similar assistance to the Moscow City Government. It has also provided more than 400 consultations to NGOs.

Interlegal's research projects have included:

- Government Policy Toward the Voluntary Sector in Russia, Ukraine, Kazakhstan and Uzbekistan (1992-1994)
- Business and Charity (1994-1995)
- Interaction Between State Structures and NGOs on the Local Level: Legal Models (1996-1997)

It also compiles databases on NGO activity in regions where it has offices: St. Petersburg, Nizhnii Novgorod, Irkutsk, Odessa, and Almaty.

## International Assembly for Human Rights Protection

Международная правозащитная ассамблея
ul. Azovskaia 4-88
113149   Moscow
**Tel:**      126-1611
**Tel/Fax:** 310-1683
**E-mail:**  compatr.lot@g23.relcom.ru
**Contact:** Mikhail G. Arutiunov, President; Irina M. Baber

The assembly was formed in December 1997 with the objective to unite human rights organizations in post-Soviet Russia because "after the disintegration of the USSR, many human rights organizations were formed, but they did not coordinate their efforts. Hence, in most of the post-Soviet states the human rights protection movement did not become a mass movement and the image of a human rights activist was compromised."

The assembly was founded by individuals and legal entities such as the Public Center for Promoting Criminal Legislation Reform, the Association for Protection of the Handicapped, Interlegal, the Mercy and Healthcare Foundation of the Russian Federation, the Society for Promoting Human Rights Protection in Central Asia, Foundation for Development of Muslim Peoples, the Guild of Attorneys of the Russian Federation, and some others.

The assembly has branch offices and representatives in many regions of the Russian Federation as well as Kazakhstan, Kyrgystan, Uzbekistan, Belarus, and Ukraine. It collaborates with foreign and international public organizations such as the Open Society Institute and the International Migration Organization.

The assembly works to promote broad protection of human rights, including the rights of forced emigrants and political refugees and the social and economic rights of citizens. Activities conducted by the assembly in 1997-1998 include:

- A roundtable discussion on the residence registration regime and passport system in the Russian Federation and the rights of freedom of movement and residence
- A hot line service available weekly since September 1997 to provide consultation to refugees and forced emigrants on the territory of the CIS
- Legal assistance to citizens of cities with assembly representatives
- Assistance to political refugees from Uzbekistan, Turkmenistan and the Republic of Kalmykia
- Assistance to forced emigrants in replacing lost personal identification documents
- Help in obtaining Russian citizenship and residency registration
- Publication of two issues of the *Human Rights: Refugees, Forced Emigrants, Compatriots Abroad* magazine (64 pages each)
- Publication of a monthly bulletin *Dobrota bez granits* (Kindness without Borders).

## International Discussion Club

Московский международный дискуссионный клуб
Kashirskoe shosse 88/26-112
115551   Moscow
**Tel/Fax:** 200-2265
**E-mail:**  zarov@host.cis.lead.org, andrey_o@orc.ru
**Web:**     idc.cis.lead.org/
**Contact:** Andrei Ozharovsky, President

Established in 1989, IDC was among the first independent organizations established in the former Soviet Union. The goal of the club is to promote contact between young people in Russia and the West by organizing international exchanges, seminars, and projects. The club is based in Moscow, but has branch offices in Minsk, St. Petersburg, Murmansk, and Novorossiisk.

Since 1993, IDC has sponsored a program that brings international observers to Russia to oversee elections, and is currently organizing observation groups for the parliamentary elections in December 1999. Other club activities include a project to establish an arboretum in Novorossiisk and organization of an environmental youth camp at the Black Sea. The club is currently working with Glasnost Productions (a Washington, D.C. company) to develop a series of civic educational films for Russian and Kazakstani television.

## International Educational Foundation

a/ya 68
129515   Moscow
**Tel/Fax:** 216 7877, 219-9030
**E-mail:** icf@glasnet.ru
**Contact:** Professor Dr. Bronislav Bitinas, President; Mr. Robert Beebe

IEF was founded in 1993 by a group of scholars and teachers from the NIS, U.S. and UK following a series of conferences, Spiritual Renewal and School Education in Russia, held in Moscow in November 1992. Since then, it has published a series of textbooks and held workshops for thousands of teachers throughout the NIS. Its books have been translated into Mongolian, Tajik, Azeri, Estonian, and Armenian.

All IEF's projects are designed to foster "the spiritual and moral growth of young people so that they can inherit the traditions that are at the basis of any civilized society."

In 1998, IEF campaigned against the introduction of condom-based sex education in Russia and also held a conference, School Wide Character Education. The current focus of its activities includes:

- Publishing textbooks to foster the spiritual and moral education of schoolchildren
- Promoting pro-marriage and pro-family abstinence-based sex education
- Promoting character education programs in schools
- Holding teacher training workshops in new interactive methodologies

Among the textbooks it has published in Russian are *My World & I: The Way to Unification* (1993), *Living Religions* (1997), and *Love, Life, and Family* (1998). IEF states that it has published about 240,000 textbooks that are currently being used in approximately 4,000 schools throughout the NIS. Its partner organizations abroad include the International Educational Foundation of America in New York and the International Educational Foundation in London.

## International Institute for a Law-Based Economy

ul. Gasheka, 8-10, Ducat Place etazh 5
125097   Moscow
**Tel:**      258-3570
**Fax:**      258-3563
**Contact:** Sergei Shishkin, Deputy Director

The institute obtains expert legal advice and offers training for Russian lawyers involved in reforming Russia's civil code. It also provides assistance in drafting commercial legislation and conducts general training courses for Russian lawyers and jurists.

The institute has a civil code reform project with the law firm of Ogilvy Renault and the Institute of Comparative Law at McGill University in Canada. The contact at McGill is Dean of the law faculty, Stephen J. Toope, tel: (514) 398-6604, or fax: (514) 398-4659.

## International Relief Friendship Foundation

UN Non-governmental Organization of the ONU-DPI
Yaroslavskoe shosse 22-1-83
129348   Moscow
**Tel/Fax:**  234-3292
**E-mail:**   ffwpuod@orc.ru
**Contact:** Nina Ignatieva, Director

IRFF began working in Russia in 1996 to create and sponsor programs of agricultural development, humanitarian and technical education, medical work, and assistance projects for urban populations and victims of natural disasters. The group helped renovate the Children's Rehabilitation Center in Ufa, Bashkortostan in 1996-98. In Ekaterinburg, it led the full reconstruction of the Crippled Children's Rehabilitation Center and Orphanage House, donating $16,000 in material assistance. IRFF also constructed seven children's playgrounds on the site of the Children's House in Moscow in 1997. The group has offices in Ekaterinburg and Tver.

## International Society for Human Rights

Международное Общество
Прав Человека
a/ya 118
107078   Moscow
**Tel/Fax:**  924-4701

**Web:**      www.glasnet.ru/~hronline/ngo/ishr/index.htm
**Contact:** Vladimir Novitskii, Boris Miller

The society was created in 1972 in Germany. It promotes the implementation of the United Nation's Universal Declaration of Human Rights around the world, focusing on issues of freedom of opinion and expression, movement, religion, information, and association. ISHR currently operates offices in 30 countries, including Ukraine and Russia. The organization offers aid to individuals, social organizations, commercial ventures, and religious groups that feel that their rights have been violated; however, it maintains strict political neutrality and does not ally itself with any specific party or movement.

In Russia, ISHR established an "adopt-a-family" program in which German families were matched with financially-strapped Russian families. The German donor families provide their Russian counterparts with $20–50 monthly, which is used for necessities such as food, clothing and textbooks. Additionally, representatives of the Moscow ISHR office make periodic visits to prisons and camps around Russia to investigate prison conditions, consult with prisoners about potential human rights violations, and provide medical consultation and assistance for sick prisoners.

## Inter-Republic Confederation of Consumer Societies (KonfOP)

КонфОП
ul. Varvarka 14
103690   Moscow
**Tel:**      298-46-49
**Fax:**      298-47-18
**E-mail:**   hotline@spros.ru
**Web:**      www.spros.ru

**Contact:** Dr. Alexander A. Auzan, President; Anastasiia Baibakova, International Affairs Coordinator

KonfOP unites 48 regional and 8 national consumer organizations in NIS countries. The main objective of KonfOp is to protect consumer interests by providing them legal assistance through the services of independent lawyers, economists and journalists. KonfOP publishes a special consumer magazine, *Spros* (about 100, 000 copies per month), in which it informs consumers about the quality of products and services offered on the market. Ratings of various products ranging from food stuffs to home appliances are published in every issue.

KonfOP's Web site offers information on consumer rights and a large number of topical articles ranging from test results for certain products to ratings and consumer advice.

## IREX–Moscow
ul. Volkhonka 14/5
119842  Moscow
**Tel:**      203-9889, 203-9696
**Fax:**     203-5966
**E-mail:**  irexmos@irex.ru
**Web:**    www.irex.ru

See the profile for IREX in the North American Organization section.

## IREX Education Information Center
Library of Foreign Literature
ul. Nikolo-Yamskaia 1
109189  Moscow
**Tel:**      956-3022
**Fax:**     956-3262 (from NIS),
             1 (212) 479-19-41
             (from US and Europe)
**E-mail:**  eic@useic.ru
**Web:**    www.useic.ru

## IREX Partnerships and Training Office
Khlebnyi per. 1, k. 417-418
121069  Moscow
**Tel:**      203-64-38
**Fax:**     203-43-11
**E-mail:**  irexpart@glasnet.ru

## ISAR–Moscow
ИСАР–Москва
a/ya 210
121019  Moscow
**Tel/Fax:** 251-7617
**E-mail:**  clearh@glasnet.ru
             isarmos@glasnet.ru
**Web:**    cci.glasnet.ru/isar.html/
**Contact:** Mila Bogdan, Director

In 1992, ISAR's first office in the former Soviet Union was established in Moscow. The following year, the group began its Seeds for Democracy grant program with funding from USAID in support of environmental NGOs throughout Russia. Six years later, ISAR's offices in Ukraine, Siberia, the Far East, and Azerbaijan are working towards the same broad goal: the provision of technical, informational, and financial assistance to "green organizations" in order to contribute to an independent non-governmental sector in the former Soviet Union.

Today ISAR-Moscow focuses its activity on European Russia. The Seeds of Democracy Small Grants Program is the oldest of ISAR's grant-making initiatives, based on ISAR's concept that "small amounts of money in support of small, local projects—such as cleaning up a park, running a summer camp, monitoring local water sources and sharing the results with the community, or an environmental radio show every Saturday—plant a seed that helps nourish and foster the grassroots movement. We have found that small effective projects have a lasting ripple effect, galvanizing others to think and act locally to respond to the complex environmental problems of their communities."

This program has expanded over the years to include organizational support to environmental NGOs and funding to projects and groups that promote inter-regional cooperation. Since the Seeds of Democracy grant program began, more than 400 small grants, totaling over $1 million in funding, have been awarded. Typically, ISAR-Moscow holds between two and three grant rounds a year.

ISAR-Moscow also maintains a small library of nonprofit and environmental information. In 1997, it began publishing an NGO bulletin containing news and events for the environmental third sector. It also provides grants to produce printed Russian-language materials for environmental NGOs.

### Jewish Heritage Society

Общество "Еврейское Наследие"
ul. Novocheremushkinskaya 1/14-3-12
Moscow
**Tel:**       503-7845, 316-9930
**E-mail:**  heritage@glas.apc.org
**Web:**      www.glasnet.ru/~heritage/
**Contact:** Yohanan Petrovsky, Acting Director

The society is an independent scholarly institution dedicated to the development of cultural and historical research on the Jewish people in the Russian Empire and the former USSR. The society embraces a wide range of academic scholarship in the field of Jewish studies, including history, sociology, and ethnography. Its primary goal is to collect, preserve and share among scholars the "remnants of the remnants" — the documentary heritage of the Jewish people in Russia and the NIS.

Ongoing projects and publications of the society include:

- The Preprints and Reprints Series involves the publication and distribution of important research articles, monographs, bibliographies, and source studies that have not yet appeared in scholarly journals. The Society also accepts previously published scholarly works for reprint.
- The Depository of Sources for Jewish Scholars makes available archival inventories and records of Jewish communities, organizations, and individuals prepared by archivists, librarians and JHS members throughout the NIS.
- The Jewish Archive Program aims to to locate, describe, preserve, and make available to scholars the great number of Jewish historical sources in state repositories throughout the former Soviet Union. The program also investigates neglected historical collections in Jewish communities and synagogues.
- The *JHS Information Bulletin* includes current events and research in academic Judaic studies, focused primarily on Jewish history in Eastern Europe. Issued quarterly, the bulletin also publicizes conferences, exhibitions, academic programs, and research institutions specializing in Judaic studies.

### Lawyers of the 21st Century Association

Ассоциация "Юристы XXI Века"
a/ya 51
103006  Moscow
**Tel/Fax:** 126-1611
**E-mail:**  lawyer@openmail.irex.ru,
               pavlenko@mtu-net.ru
**Web:**     ns.openweb.ru/lawyers/
**Contact:** Aleksandr Pavlenko,

President

The association is composed of more than 5,000 practicing lawyers and law students from regions across the Russian Federation. Formed in 1992 by a group of law students, professors, and young lawyers, the association works to uphold the principle of rule-of-law and develop a "legal consciousness" in the new generation of young Russians.

The group is currently collaborating with the Rule of Law Institute in Washington, D.C., to operate an electronic discussion list focusing on the topic of Russian law and legal reform. The list is in English. To subscribe, send a message reading "subscribe ruslaw" to listserv@rol.org.

## MacArthur Foundation

Khlebnyi per. 8, k. 2
121069  Moscow
**Tel:**     290-5088
**Fax:**    956-6358 within NIS,
           (503) 956-6358 international
**E-mail:** macarthur@glas.apc.org
**Web:**    www.macfdn.org/programs/
fsu-guide.htm
**Contact:** Tatiana D. Zhdanova, Ph.D.,
Director; Noune Sargisian, Executive
Secretary

The MacArthur Foundation is one of the 10 largest in the U.S., with assets of more than $4 billion dollars. The foundation established a grant-making program in the NIS in 1992. Through the Program on Global Security and Sustainability, the MacArthur Foundation Initiative seeks:

- To support independent research and creative approaches to pressing societal issues
- To enhance the skills and capacities of scholar-practitioners

- To encourage links among scholar-practitioners in the independent states of the region
- To support interaction between those individuals and their colleagues abroad.

The MacArthur Foundation Initiative concentrates on four issue areas: law and society, seeking public understanding of legal procedures and public access to information; human rights, to protect civil liberties, the rights of women and minorities, and the monitoring of human rights violations; environment and society, to promote sustainable development, the preservation of biodiversity, and creative approaches to efficient energy production and consumption; and peace and security, to address the root causes and effects of conflict and encourage arms control and disarmament.

## Magee Womancare International

pr. Federativny 17, k.10
111399  Moscow
**Tel/Fax:** 918-4331
**E-mail:** moskva70@glasnet.ru
**Contact:** Pamela Deligiannis, Field
Administrator; Anna Syomena, Woman
and Family Education Center, tel: 301-
1502, Alexander Marachev, Magee-
Savior's Family Planning Clinic, tel:
176-3824

Magee-Women's Hospital began its program to improve health care conditions for women and infants in the former Soviet Union in 1992. Partnering with the second largest hospital in Moscow, Savior's Hospital for Peace and Charity (formerly Municipal Hospital #70), Magee-Women's Hospital is one of 21 American hospitals participating in USAID's health partnerships program of the American International Health Alliance

(AIHA). The mission of the Magee-Savior partnership is:

- To develop a culturally-sensitive model of improved obstetric care that can be easily and economically replicated throughout the former Soviet Union
- To develop a model consumer and community education program for women and their families
- To strengthen health care administration
- To encourage the growth of the Russian voluntary sector as it pertains to women's issues.

Magee's Woman and Family Center provides educational information and programs to Russian women and their families, including childbirth preparation, general health, family planning, infant massage, and sibling classes. Over 15,000 Russians have registered for the center's programs. The center also publishes and distributes educational materials and video productions on women's health issues and childcare to Russian women and families In 1994, Magee received a grant from World Learning to replicate its women's education center in 24 regions of Russia. Hilary Clinton and Naina Yeltsin visited Magee-Savior in 1994 to discuss health care reform efforts for women and children in Russia.

A Womancare Clinic Network (WON), with an emphasis on teen health, has also been established in 18 regions of Russia with funding from USAID/Save the Children and the Open Society Institute. In May 1995, Magee began collaborating with the United Nations Commission on Refugees in Russia to provide health services to the refugee population of the Moscow region. Nearly 7,000 refugee women and children currently receive medical care, family planning, and health education.

The group has also received an estimated $3 million in medical equipment distributed to the former Soviet Union through the U.S. State Department Provide Hope project. In 1996, Magee extended its activities to Belarus, working with a Minsk hospital on the development of women's health, pediatric care and nurse management and training programs. It also expanded its family planning services to include menopause and fertility education and treatment in 1997.

The Magee-Savior partnership is supported by the Moscow Main Medical Administration. The Ministry of Health for the Russian Federation provides transportation and accommodations for participants in Rural Outreach to Russia and Womancare Clinic Program through an in-kind annual donation of $75,000.

## Medical-Educational Pro-Life Center
ul. Krasnoarmeiskaya, d. 2/2
125414   Moscow
**Tel:**       211-1636
**E-mail:**   orthomed@glas.apc.org
**Web:**      www.stmichael.org/Zhizn/

The center was established in Moscow in April 1993 by Orthodox parishioners of the Annunciation Church. Its goal is to provide the public with reliable information about abortions, contraceptives, and their consequences. The center has a paid staff of 10 people and several hundred volunteers. Activities include publishing and distributing educational pro-life materials and delivering anti-abortion lectures at schools and hospitals.

## Memorial Historical, Educational, and Charitable Society

Историко-просветительское,
правозащитное и
благотворительное общество–
"Мемориал"
Malyi Karetnyi per.12
103051 Moscow

**Tel:**
299-1180
Human Rights Center: 200-6506
Educational Center: 209-7883
**Fax:**
Human Rights Center: 209-5779
Educational Center: 973-2094
**E-mail:** meminf@glasnet.ru
H.R. Center: memhrc@glasnet.ru
Ed. Center: memnipc@glasnet.ru
**Web:** ns.openweb.ru/windows/
memorial/
**Contact:** Yurii Afanasiev, Yurii
Karyakin, Sergei Kovalev, Co-
Directors

The Memorial Society was founded in 1988 by leading elements of Russia's democratic intelligentsia, such as Andrei Sakharov and Yury Afanasiev. Chapters spread to many cities of Russia, as well as other countries of the former Soviet Union. The central aim of the society in its early years was to recognize the millions of Soviet citizens whose lives passed through (and often ended) in the Gulag, to document their experiences, and to provide support for those still living and their families.

Today, Memorial has over 100 affiliates across Russia and the NIS. Its activities encompass three spheres: education and history, human rights, and charitable projects. Its education/history projects include:

- Research on anti-communist resistance during the Lenin and Stalin periods and the dissident movement of the post-Stalin period

- A museum containing more than 1,000 items from the Gulag
- The Memorial Archives containing nearly 50,000 documents and more than 5,000 photos.

Human rights and charitable projects include:

- Hotpoints, a human rights monitoring project in areas of conflict in the post-Soviet world, such as Azerbaijan, Moldova, and Chechnya
- Social, legal, and medical assistance to former political prisoners and current victims of political repression across the former Soviet Union. (Memorial staff fought for and won the release of Bozor Sobir, a Tajik poet imprisoned for political reasons)
- A weekly radio program, Vybor (Choice), broadcast on Radio Russia and dedicated to news from the human rights community
- Human rights monitoring throughout the Russian penitentiary system. The society lobbies for reform of the current penal system and provides legal assistance for the imprisoned. It also sponsors rehabilitation programs for juvenile offenders and newly released prisoners.

Memorial is a principal organizer of a national day honoring the victims of Soviet totalitarianism, which is observed annually on October 30. For a complete listing of Memorial affiliates in Russia, the Baltics and the NIS, see the group's Web site.

## Mennonite Economic Development Associates

Varshovskoye Shosse, dom 12-A
113105 Moscow
**Tel/Fax:** 952-2173
**Contact:** Christopher Shore, Regional Manager

MEDA has run a Small Business Development Program in the Moscow suburb of Zelenograd for several years, assisting Russian enterprises with training in western business methods and providing access to credit for equipment acquisition and production space for small businesses. The project includes the creation of a "business incubator" in Zelenograd. MEDA works closely with the Russian group Association of Christians in Business.

## Modern University for the Humanities

Современный Гуманитарный Университет
ul. Kozhevnicheskaya 3
113114   Moscow
**Tel:**     239-1240
**Fax:**     235-5764
**E-mail:**  olga@muh.ru
**Web:**     www.muh.ru/
**Contact:** Mikhail Karpenko, Rector

The Modern University for the Humanities was founded in 1993 as an independent nonprofit institution. It offers four-year bachelor's degree programs in economics, law, management, and foreign languages, as well as continuing education classes focused on specific areas of business education (such as marketing and human resource management). Day and evening classes are held, and correspondence courses are available.

## Moscow Media Law and Policy Center

a/ya 351 (postal address)
103009   Moscow
Mokhovaya 9 (street address)
Dept. of Journalism
Moscow State University
103009   Moscow
**Tel/fax:**  203-9388, 203-6571,
             737-3371
**E-mail:**   arichter@glasnet.ru,

mmlpc@glasnet.ru
**Web:**     www.medialaw.ru
**Contact:** Andrei Richter

The center maintains an extensive Web site on media law in Russia, which it updated and expanded in 1998, dramatically increasing the amount of information available. English pages were added as well. The site was developed with support of the Know How Fund in the UK and with technical assistance from Internews. In late1998, the center held a conference for lawyers, policymakers and professionals on the legal aspects of mass media licensing and communications organizations in Russia and in the West. A report of the conference's proceedings was published in early 1999.

## Moscow Public Science Foundation

Prospekt Mira 36, Suite 205
Moscow
**Tel/Fax:**  280-5204
**Fax:**     280-7016
**Contact:** Vladimir Benevolenski

This organization works with the University of Saskatchewan International under a grant from the Canadian government to administer the Yeltsin Democracy Fellows Program. Under this program, approximately 100 Russians each year receive training in Canada related to some aspect of the Russian reform process.

## Moscow Research Center for Human Rights

Louchnikov per. 4, k.1-6, 11, 19
103982   Moscow
**Tel:**     206-0923, 206-8836
**Fax:**     206-8853
**E-mail:**  hrmoscow@glas.apc.org
**Contact:** Alexei Smirnov, Executive Director

The center helps to coordinate a wide range of human rights organizations and activities in Russia. It seeks to develop a professional infrastructure for the human rights movement by enhancing communication networks among groups, providing assistance with funding opportunities, assisting with publishing projects, and serving as a central locus for information regarding human rights work.

## Moscow School of Human Rights

Московская Школа Прав Человека
Golovinskoye Shosse 8, d. 2, k. 302
125212   Moscow
**Tel/Fax:** 452-0513
**E-mail:** hrschool@redline.ru
**Web:** www.mshr.redline.ru
**Contact:** Anatolii Azarov, Director

MSHR seeks to improve the state of human rights and civil society in Russia through civic education. The school provides professional training courses for secondary school teachers and university professors to help them learn how to "teach democracy" and promote civic culture in the classroom. Since the school's creation in 1994, more than 7,000 teachers have attended these courses. Additionally, staff from MSHR consult with school administrators to devise curricula for civics courses and have published several textbooks and educational films on themes of human rights and government.

The school's board of directors includes several prominent figures from the Soviet dissident movement, such as Larisa Bogoraz and Ludmila Alexeeva. In December 1997, it was a co-organizer (with UNESCO and the Federation Ministry of Education) of the Seventh Annual Conference on Human Rights Education, where participants discussed problems confronting education reform in Russia and strategies for continued teacher training.

## Mothers' Rights Foundation

Фонд "Право Матери"
Luchnikov per. 4, pod. 3, k. 4
103982   Moscow
**Tel/Fax:** 206-0581 (for individuals),
206-8894 (for organizations or the media)
**E-mail:** mright@glasnet.ru
**Web:** www.glasnet.ru/-hronline/ngo/mright/indfr.html
**Contact:** Veronika Marchenko, Chairwoman

MRF conducts advocacy campaigns on behalf of parents whose sons were killed during peacetime military service in Russia and the CIS. The group was founded in 1990 by relatives of young soldiers who had died during peacetime. Similar difficulties in each case (such as problems in ascertaining information surrounding the deaths and difficulty in acquiring entitlements for the surviving family) suggested that a collective effort to expose problems in the military might improve the conditions of service for young men in the future and provide moral and practical support for surviving families.

One of the organization's primary activities is providing legal consultations and aid to the families of deceased soldiers. Staff from Mothers' Rights are also active in Duma committees working on military reform. The organization publishes a monthly news bulletin reporting on human rights violations in the military that is circulated to the media and to the various Mothers' Rights offices across Russia. Since 1992, Mothers' Rights has published three "yearbooks" dedicated to the memories of soldiers who died during peacetime. These yearbooks, which contain photos of the dead soldiers and commentary from their families, have had great social resonance in Russia. The group also published a brochure in 1995 entitled *What Kind of Army is This? Human Rights Violations in the Russian Military*, which exposes chronic abuses and problems in the military.

## National Press Institute

Национальный Институт Прессы
Novyi Arbat 2, a/ya 229
(postal address)
121019   Moscow
ul. Prechistenka 10
121019   Moscow
**Tel:**      202-9324, 202-5351,
             202-2314, 202-4187
**Fax:**      202-2307
**E-mail:**   npi@npi.ru
**Web:**      www.npi.ru/
**Contact:** Vladimir Svetozarov,
Executive Director

NPI, formerly known as the Russian-American Press and Informational Center, was established in 1992 as a joint project of New York University's Center on War, Peace, and the News Media and the Russian Academy of Sciences' Institute for the Study of Canada and the USA. In 1997, the organization changed its name and expanded its activities. Today, in addition to the main Moscow office, NPI has bureaus in St. Petersburg, Ekaterinburg, Nizhny Novgorod, Novosibirsk, and Rostov-on-Don.

The institute's projects and programs include:

- Regular press conferences, briefings, discussions and debates held at NPI's Press Center in Moscow
- The Commission on Free Access to Information, which monitors legislation and government acts regarding journalists' access to information and publishes a bulletin, *The Right to Know*
- The Center for Cyberjournalism, an educational resource that introduces new media technology to Russian journalists by providing them with Internet access and computer courses. The center holds an annual conference for domestic and foreign journalists on new developments in media technology
- Special projects directed at increasing media awareness of topics such as election campaigns, ethnic conflict, and nuclear proliferation.

## National Youth Council of Russia (NYCR)

ul. Maroseyka 3/13
101970   Moscow
**Tel:**      206-8934
**Fax:**      206-8012
**E-mail:**   nycr@morozov.ru
**Web:**      www.youth.nsu.ru

NYCR is an umbrella coalition of youth and student NGOs. Established in 1992, it has 78 members, including 27 regional youth councils representing social, political, trade union, children's, and cultural organizations. NYCR works with the Russian parliament, organizes seminars and training courses for youth groups, publishes bulletins, and helps its members with legal issues.

## Naukograd Development Union of Russia

Российский Союз Развытия Наукоградов
a/ya 4
Dolgoprudniy 4
141700   Moscow
**Tel:**      255-3374, 576-8782
**Fax:**      255-3197

E-mail: sazonov@aha.ru
Contact: Igor A.Sazonov, Executive
Director

Founded in 1996, the union works to
create the infrastructure for "nauko-
grads" (specialized scientific/technolo-
gical communities traditionally dedicated to research) in Russia. The
organization's membership consists of
16 naukograd administrations, 20 of
Russia's more prestigious scientific
institutions, and individual scientists.

## New Perspectives Foundation
Фонд Новые Перспективы
Malyi Kakovinskii per. 2/6
121099  Moscow
Tel/Fax: 232-3820
E-mail: nadia@glas.apc.org
Web: www.npf.ru/

The primary focus of New Perspectives
is civic education of youth and development of young leaders to popularize
ideas of democracy in Russia. The
foundation is currently active in 50 of
Russia's regions, ranging from Vladivostok to the Udmurt Republic. It
implements civic education programs
and leadership training courses, and
encourages civic and political participation of youth at the local level.

The foundation developed a year-
long civic education program that is
being used in several schools in Moscow and regional cities. The program
emphasizes the importance of civic
participation and features role-playing
games and mock parliamentary elections. The program also includes a
workshop session for teachers and
parents on the principles of civic
education.

## NAN–No to Alcoholism and Drug Addiction
НАН–Нет Алкоголизму и
Наркомании
ul. Shvernik 10-a
117449  Moscow
Tel: 126-3475
Fax: 310-7076
E-mail: rbfnan@got.mmtel.ru,
nan@mc313.medlux.msk.su
Contact: Oleg V. Zykov, MD, Ph.D.,
President

NAN was founded in 1987 and registered as an independent social organization in 1991. Its mission is to combat
alcoholism, drug addiction, and chemical dependency in Russian society. The
organization has been instrumental in
establishing chemical dependency
training and treatment facilities in
Russia, as well as shelter facilities for
youth. NAN also works to increase
public knowledge of chemical dependency and its social and health-related
issues.

The group provides education,
certification, and training in the field of
chemical dependency prevention and
treatment through the Social Science
Academy in Moscow. Students are
professionals in health care, psychology, and human services. In addition,
NAN developed the certified position
Specialist in Human Services. This
position was recognized by the Health
Ministry of Russia, allowing state
institutions to hire Human Services
Specialists.

NAN also established the Center of
Medical and Social Support and
Adaptation, a treatment facility that
adheres to the 12-Step Model of
Recovery. The center runs a 12-step-
based outpatient program called
"ZEBRA." The Professional Addiction
Information and Resource Center
houses and disseminates information

concerning drug and alcohol prevention and treatment, including 12-step literature, translated lectures, etc.

In 1992, NAN established the first Moscow shelter for abandoned children at ul. Profsoyuznaya 27-4 in Moscow. NAN's shelter was used as a model by the Russian Parliament's Committee of Women, Family, and Youth for a bill that addressed issues of child abandonment, youth crime prevention, and the rights of young people. NAN is also responsible for the creation of a network that links shelters founded by NAN's affiliates in other regions, including Saransk, Mordovia, Ivanovo, Ekaterinburg, and Kursk.

NAN works with Russian and foreign media to raise public awareness of nonprofit activity in Russia, especially with regard to prevention and treatment issues. It is also the author of the *sotsial'nye zakaz* initiative in Moscow, a draft regulation for the creation of a formal system of government contracting for social services.

### NIS-U.S. Women's Consortium

Olympiysky Prospekt 16, #2383
129090  Moscow
**Tel:**      288-7066
**Tel/Fax:** 288-9633
**E-mail:**  wcons@com2com.ru
**Web:**      www.winrock.org
**Contact:** Elena N. Ershova, Russian Coordinator; Karina Petrosan, Assistant Director

See description in North American Organizations section.

### Nonviolence International–NIS

Международное Ненасилие–
Новые независимые
государства
Luchnikov per. 4, k. 2
103982  Moscow
**Tel:**      351-4855, 206-8618

**Fax:**      336-5323
**E-mail:**  ninis@glas.apc.org
**Web:**      www.glasnet.ru/~ninis/
**Contact:** Andrei Kamenshikov, Vladimir Sukhov

An affiliate of the U.S. based organization Nonviolence International, NI-NIS was created in 1992 to increase public awareness of armed conflict and assist victims of military aggression.

The group's Peace-Info project aims to strengthen the role of individual activists and NGOs in preventing violence in areas of conflict or tension. In connection with this project, NI–NIS has created a database of peace-related activists, organizations, and programs in the former Soviet Union. The database (in Russian) is accessible from the group's Web site.

NI-NIS has worked extensively in areas of heavy conflict in the Transcaucasus. In Dagestan and Chechnya, it helped peace activists and NGOs develop project proposals and contact funding agencies. The group also helped peace activists in Dagestan obtain e-mail access.

### ORT-Russia (Educational Resources and Technological Training)

ul. Novoslobodskaya 57
103055  Moscow
**Tel:**      251-9275
**Tel/Fax:** 972-1410
**E-mail:**  irana@ort.ru
**Web:**      www.ort.ru
**Contact:** Irana Mojeiko, Director of ORT-Russia International Cooperation

ORT-Russia's mission is to "provide practical training in institutional development, professional skills, and modern technologies in order to enable individuals and institutions to earn income and contribute to the advancement and well-being of the Russian society." The group has participated in a number of projects such as *Computer Training and Information Support of NGOs* and *NGO Help-Desk* under the Civic Initiatives Program for Democratic and Economic Reform in Russia, funded by USAID. It has trained and provided technical support to over 3,000 NGO representatives in six different locations in Russia, designed an NGO database, and trained 30 Webmasters for NGOs.

Under a vocational training project funded by the Ministry of Labor and the World Bank, ORT rendered technical assistance to 34 regional training centers of the Federal Employment Center and trained 200 specialists in program development, labor market analysis, advanced instructional techniques, and use of computer technologies. ORT-Russia has 14 regional centers in the CIS. Its partner, World ORT Union, is based in London.

## Ozon Center

ul. Nizhnaya Krasnosyelskaya 45
Moscow
**Tel:** 265-0118
**Fax:** 265-2663
**E-mail:** chapf@vitcp3.itcp.ru

The Ozon Center was developed by the Russian organization Children Abuse Prevention Society to provide diagnostic exams and therapy for abused children and individualized counseling for families. The center's staff conducts sociological research regarding the roots of child abuse, and has developed educational programs for parents and children, including a program on sexual abuse designed for elementary school children. Training is also offered for counselors of abused children.

## Peace and Hope Center for Social Support

Мир и Надежда
Dokuchaev per. 17, k. 104
107078 Moscow
**Tel:** 207-6943
**E-mail:** tigran.yepoyan@g23.relcom.ru
**Contact:** Tigran Yepoyan, Chairman

CSS was founded in 1997 to provide health and community outreach programs for children in the Moscow area. Working with the Russian Nurses Association, CSS has completed a project to improve the quality of nursing care and strengthen the national federation of nurses' organizations. It has also begun an outreach program, the Orphaned Children Support Project, which provides psychological and medical rehabilitation services to underprivileged and orphaned children in an effort to reintegrate them into society. CSS has a staff of five.

## Pericles ANO

Tsentralnaya Hotel
Tverskaya Ulitsa 10, Suite 319
103009 Moscow
**Tel:** 292-5188, 292-6463
**E-mail:** pericles@glas.apc.org
**Contact:** Marion Dent

Pericles ANO (autonomous noncommercial organization) is a Russian registered group which conducts educational projects and training in the fields of economics and law. Its parent organization, Pericles International, was founded in France. Since 1992, Pericles International and Pericles ANO have worked together on various projects in Russia, including:
- Translating into Russian and publishing books on economics and banking law

- Assisting the Ministries of Justice of Russia and France with training projects for Russian judges
- Arranging for Russian law students to study international law topics in Europe
- Assisting the Moscow Mayor's office with conferences on safety in major cities
- Helping to establish Moscow as the 1998 host for the UN Sustainable Cities Program.

Pericles' first permanent project, the American Business & Legal Education Project (ABLE), is an intermediate-term training program founded by several American professors teaching in Moscow. The professors recognized the dire need for young professionals to get professional training quickly. Marion Dent, Dean of ABLE, notes that "there is nothing available in Moscow between expensive, one or two-day business seminars and full bachelors or MBA programs. Young professionals don't have the financial luxury of spending a year or two in school, and they can't afford and don't learn enough in short commercial seminars."

ABLE provides affordable six week seminars in business, legal and English language topics. Most courses are offered in a series of three so that students can study up to 18 weeks on one topic. For example, ABLE's Marketing series includes courses on Marketing Principles, Advertising and International Marketing, and Public Relations. Other course series are offered in Business English and Law. ABLE also runs a program to help students get into American Universities and Law or Business Schools.

Typically, seminars meet 6 hours per week, and are limited in size to 14 people (averaging 8-10). Classes are practically oriented and most are taught

in English. Tuition per course typically ranges from $400-$500. This fee included books, computer time, software, and other teaching materials. Pericles also offers scholarships, financial aid, and work study positions to students based on both merit and need. Dent estimates that about half the students in the ABLE program receive financial aid, with one or two studying on full scholarships.

## Project Harmony–Moscow

**Tel/Fax:**  234-1695
**E-mail:**   phmos@online.ru

See profile in North American Organizations section.

## Russian Children's Hospital

Детская больница России
Stoleshnikov per. 2
103009   Moscow
**Fax:**     123-7294
**E-mail:**  eryazan@iki.rssi.ru
**Web:**     www.space.ru/charity/
**Contact:** Lina Saltykova, Coordinator

RCH treats children with serious illnesses. The hospital's highly specialized pediatric medicine departments include oncology, immunology, and hematology. The hospital remains the only medical facility that performs pediatric kidney transplants in the regions of the former Soviet Union.

In 1989, Father Alexander Men founded a Christian charity group in collaboration with the Saints Cosmos and Damien Church to help find sponsors to support the RCH and its patients. The charity secures funding for medical equipment, operations, and treatment and assists families with traveling expenses, housing, and food while their children are being treated. Because many children have to remain in the hospital for months at a time, the charity group also raises money to pay for holiday celebrations and leisure activities.

## Russian Credit Union League

ul. Varvarka 14
103690  Moscow
**Tel:**     298-4542
**Fax:**     298-4718
**Contact:** Dr. Dina G. Plakhotnaya, General Director

Under a grant from the Canadian International Development Agency, the RCUL is working with Développement International Desjardins of Québec to establish a network of credit unions in Volgograd oblast based on the Canadian credit union model.

## Russian Orphan Opportunity Fund

ul. Novorogozhskaya 10, k. 57
109544  Moscow
**Tel/Fax:** 278-7637
**E-mail:**  roof@glasnet.ru
**Web:**     www.glasnet.ru/~roof

ROOF was formed in 1997 to increase the employment potential of children who are growing up in Russia's orphanages. It offers English language programs and donated computers to orphanages in Moscow and the Moscow region. Classes in computer literacy and professional development internship programs with local businesses are in the planning stages. ROOF would like to establish links with schools and other institutes in Russia and abroad in order to provide more supplemental education and vocational training to Russian orphans. The fund's headquarters are located in New York.

## Social Center for Reform of the Criminal Justice System

Общественный Центр содействия реформе уголовного правосудия
Luchnikov per. 4, k. 24, 26
101000  Moscow
**Tel:**     206-8684, 206-8276
**Fax:**     921-209, 206-8658
**E-mail:**  mcprinf@glasnet.ru
**Web:**     www.glasnet.ru/~hronline/ngo/mcprinf/
**Contact:** Valerii Abramkin, Coordinator

The center has been in operation since 1988. Its primary goal is to help create an effective, fair, and humane criminal justice system in Russia. It works together with local and federal criminal justice agencies in the Russian Federation on structural and legislative reform of the criminal justice system. The center also acts as an advocate for the imprisoned by visiting prisons and camps on a regular basis to provide legal and spiritual counseling. It also publishes educational materials about the penal system. More than 30,000 copies of the center's 1992 publication, *How to Survive in a Russian Prison*, have been distributed to prisoners and their families.

Since 1992, the center has produced a weekly program, *Oblaka*, for broadcast on Radio Rossiya. This popular hour-long program is aimed primarily at the prison population, providing information on prison reforms, legal issues affecting prison conditions and treatment of prisoners, stories from prisons and labor camps around Russia, general information on human rights groups and activity in Russia, and other material of practical value.

In 1996 the center began work with the Moscow Research Center for Human Rights Information Network

Project to develop an in-office library of materials relating to comparative criminal justice and issues facing the Russian penitentiary system. As part of this ongoing project, the center seeks to expand their use of information and communications technology (including e-mail and the Internet) to enhance their research in the field of criminal justice and increase regional and international contacts.

## Socio-Ecological Union
Социально-Экологический Союз
a/ya 211
121019   Moscow
**Tel:**      298-3087
**Tel/Fax:** 124-7934
**E-mail:**  soceco@glas.apc.org
**Web:**     cci.glasnet.ru/seu/

The SEU serves as an umbrella group for nearly 300 independent non-governmental organizations and groups from the NIS and the U.S. The goal of the organization is to utilize "the intellectual potential, material and financial means, and organizational possibilities of the union's members for the preservation of nature and the protection of living beings; for the protection and revival of mankind's natural and cultural heritage; for the protection of human physical and mental health; and for guaranteeing a safe environment and sustainable development."

SEU was established in 1988 as a voluntary association of environmental groups. The groups are extremely diverse, ranging from radical activist organizations to educational nature clubs for schoolchildren. Members are united by mutual devotion to environmental action, a spirit of cooperation, freedom of information, and the belief that the environment cannot be divided by national borders. The union operates

"without a vertical administrative structure" and its members are organizationally and financially independent. SEU has a Center for Coordination and Information in Moscow. Other SEU activities include:

- Environmental monitoring: SEU members monitor dioxin levels in the regions surrounding paper plants, measure industrial pollution levels in Russia and Uzbekistan, and evaluate the management of boreal forests by Russian and multinational timber companies.
- Biodiversity protection: the union's Biodiversity Conservation Center (BCC) was designed to ensure the survival of nature reserves in the CIS countries and establish new protected areas.
- Research and Monitoring of Nuclear Sites: SEU's Center for Nuclear Ecology and Energy evaluates the effects of nuclear sites on the environment and populations living in nuclear zones.

## Sympathy Humanitarian– Charitable Center
Гуманитарно-благотворительный центр "Сострадание"
a/ya 181
Moscow
**Tel:**     240-1828
**Web:**     www.glasnet.ru/~hronline/ ngo/sostr/index.htm
**Contact:** Marina Berkovskaia

The Sympathy Center was originally established in 1992 to help victims of Soviet-era political repression. Today, its efforts are primarily focused on aiding children in war-torn areas of the Russian Federation. During the war in Chechnya, the center sent medical personnel to Chechen hospitals under the auspices of its Children of War in the 21st Century program. It continues to send psychiatric specialists to the area and currently operates a training program in which Chechen medical professionals receive special instruction in Moscow.

## Ukrainian Library in Moscow

Библиотека Украинской Литературы
Velozavodskaya 11/1
109280  Moscow
**Tel:**      118-91-92
**E-mail:**  libukr@glas.apc.org
**Web:**     www.glasnet.ru/~libukr/

This library is the descendant of the Central Ukrainian Library, which was founded in Moscow in the 1920s and closed in 1938. The library reopened in December 1989 with the help of the Moscow Ukrainian Youth Club and a private firm, Ukrainian Publicity. The library contains more than 13,000 books and 8,500 periodicals, as well as audio and video recordings and music collections.

## Union for Chemical Safety

8-2-83 Profsojuznaja str.
117292  Moscow
**Tel/Fax:**  129-0596
**E-mail:**  lefed@glas.apc.org
**Contact:** Professor Lev A.Fedorov, President

The purpose of the union is "to help the people of Russia find an ecologically sound way out of the legacy of many years of chemical toxins proliferation and abuse." It is an interregional non-governmental organization working to eliminate the proliferation and widespread misuse of toxic chemicals in Russia, including biological and chemical weapons, dioxins, PCBs, liquid rocket fuels, and pesticides. Fedorov is a chemist by profession, and

the organization is governed by an Association Council.

The fundamental objectives of UCS are:

- Publishing articles in the mass media—in major media as well as the local press—on the topics of chemical safety and the ecologically safe disposal of chemical weapons
- Lobbying in governmental bodies
- Risk assessment in the field of chemical safety
- Ecological monitoring and rehabilitation of the many regions destroyed by chemical accidents and the process of preparing for chemical and rocket warfare
- Medical monitoring and assistance to people suffering from the consequences of the production, testing, and disposal/stockpiling of CWs and other chemical toxins (pesticides, etc.)
- Ecologically safe destruction of CWs and military and other toxins (dioxins, rocket fuel, old pesticides etc.)
- Conversion of the CWs industry.

Founded in 1993, UCS has many branches addressing the specific problems of their region: Bryansk (storage of CWs, pesticides); Chuvash Republic (production of modern CWs, dioxins, pesticides); Ivanovo region (old CWs production, liquid rocket fuels); Kemerovo (dioxins; emissions of chemical plants); Khabarovsk (pesticides); Kurgan (storage of modern CWs); Nizhny Novgorod (production of old CWs and new pesticides, dioxins, liquid rocket fuels, emissions of chemical plants); Penza (storage of modern CWs); Samara (production and disposal of old CWs, pesticide production, dioxins); Saratov (testing of CWs, storage of old CWs, liquid rocket fuels); Tula (old production of CWs, dioxins, emissions of chemical plants);

Udmurt Republic (storage of old and modern CWs, disposal of old CWs, dioxins); and Volgograd (production of old and modern CWs, pesticide production, dioxins, emissions of chemical plants).

UCS has published three books, *Dioxins as the Ecological Danger* (Moscow, 267 pp., 1993), *Chemical Weapons in Russia: History, Ecology, and Politics* (Moscow,120 pp., 1994), and *Undeclared Chemical War in Russia: Politics Against Ecology* (Moscow, 304 pp., 1995). UCS cooperates with ecological organizations and individuals of different countries.

### United Way International– Moscow

ul. Vilgelma Pika 4, korp. 2, kom. 215
129256   Moscow
**Tel/Fax:**   187-1780
**E-mail:**   uwi@igc.apc.org
**Contact:**   Mila Medina, Executive Director

See the profile for UWI in the North American Organizations section.

### Volunteer Center–Moscow Charity House

Центр Добровольцев - Московский Дом Милосердия
Novyi Arbat 11, k. 1728-1735
121099   Moscow
**Tel/Fax:**   291-1473, 291-2004

The Volunteer Center was created in 1991 with the goal of educating post-Soviet Russian society about the need for volunteers in a healthy civil society and the rewards of volunteerism. In December 1995, the group organized the Week of Volunteer Action and Moscow Volunteer Forum—the first such events to be held in Russia. The forum brought together more than 300

leaders from volunteer organizations to discuss strategies for further development of volunteerism and collaborative projects.

Since 1996, the center has been working to develop ties with Moscow's commercial sector and the local press to promote their activities. The Moscow Charity House works closely with the U.S.-based Points of Light Foundation.

### Women's Innovation Foundation "East-West"

Женского инновационного фонда "Восток-Запад"
a/ya 24
117607   Moscow
**Fax:**   952-2572
**E-mail:**   femrus@glas.apc.org
**Web:**   www.owl.ru
**Contact:**   Galina Grishina, Director

East-West works to promote cooperation, exchange, and partnerships between women's groups around the world. The group hosts a Web site, Open Women Line (OWL) that "seeks to provide women with easy access to new information and resources." (See Internet section for OWL profile.)

## *Apatity (81533)*

### "GAIA" Kola Coordinating Environmental Center

ul. Lenina 24, k. 54
184200   Apatity
**Tel:**   3-01-58
**E-mail:**   krugl@aprec.ru
**Contact:**   Elena Kruglikova
Murmansk department:
ul. Sofya Perovskaya 31/11, k. 14
183038   Murmansk
**Tel:**   (815) 55-67-52

## Arkhangelsk (8182)

### Center for Support of Non-Governmental Organizations (Young Lawyers' Union Regional Branch)
Центр поддержки
некоммерческих организаций
–Архангельское отделение
союза молодых юристов
Arkhangelsk
**Tel:** 44-15-23
**E-mail:** lawyer@lawyer.nordlink.ru
**Contact:** Fedor Loginov, Natalia Barabin

This organization is an affiliate of the Agency for Social Information in Moscow.

### "Conscience" Arkhangelsk District Organization
pr. Troickyi 49/130
a/ya 47
Arkhangelsk
**Tel:** 49-66-40
**Contact:** Yurii Budeev

## Bryansk (8322)

### "VIOLA" Bryansk Regional Non-Governmental Organization
ul. Oktyabrskaya 23a, k. 21
241000 Bryansk
**Tel:** 74-59-06
**E-mail:** viola@ecos.bryansk.ru
**Contact:** Ludmila Zhirina, Coordinator

VIOLA began working in 1993 to address issues of environmental conservation in the Bryansk region through public education and support to local environmental groups. It also works to solve children's health problems resulting from Chernobyl.

VIOLA is made up of university and schools teachers, students, scientists, journalists, and doctors.

## Kaluga (8439)

### French-Russian Institute of Business Administration
ul. Lenin 129
249020 Obninsk, Kaluga oblast
**Tel:** 73-351
**Fax:** 40-88
**E-mail:** fridas@obninsk.ru
**Contact:** Julia Nikolayevna Rastopchina, Deputy Rector

A coalition of French and Russian business schools established FRIBA in 1993 as a non-governmental, nonprofit higher education institution, which offers Russian students bachelor's and master's degree programs based on Western business practice. In 1995, FRIBA began offering training and consulting services to small and medium-sized local businesses. FRIBA currently has a faculty of 55 and enrolls 210 students.

### Kitezh Children's Community
Детская Община "Китеж"
Kaluzhskaya oblast
249650 Baryatino raion
**Tel:** 23-224
**E-mail:** kitezh@kaluga.ru
**Web:** communities.gaia.org/kitezh/
**Contact:** Dmitrii Morosov

Kitezh is a non-governmental, nonprofit home and school for orphaned children based on the concept of the Russian "obshchina," or peasant commune. Orphans are raised in a community of foster families who live together on a large piece of land in a rural area, located 300 km. south of Moscow in the Kaluga region. The community acts as an alternative to state-run children's homes or orphanages.

Education is the main focus of Kitezh; two-thirds of the community's 20 permanent residents work directly with the 25 children who live there. Kitezh residents adhere to the principle of "voluntary simplicity" and aim to live in harmony with nature. The community produces its own dairy products, vegetables, and honey, and residents live in peasant-style wooden houses without running water.

Visitors are always welcome at the community, and since the summer of 1998, Kitezh has offered classes on Russian folklore and history to foreign students. The program operates in conjunction with the U.K.-based organization Ecologia Trust. For more information on summer courses, contact Ecologia Trust at: The Park, Forres, Moray IV36OTZ Scotland, Tel/fax: +44-(0)1309-690995  E-mail: ecoliza@rmplc.co.uk  Contact: Liza Hollingshead

## Strategy Foundation
Фонд "Стратегия"
132-10 Grabchevskoe shosse
248009   Kaluga
**Tel:**       (095) 773-6433 (Moscow)
**Tel/Fax:** 24-27-82
**E-mail:**   strategy@serve.com
**Web:**      www.serve.com/strategy
**Contact:** Vitaly V. Matrosov, President

The foundation was created in 1995 with the goal of supporting the development of Kaluga's business community and third sector. Since 1997, it has been working on a project to establish information resource centers for NGOs in Kaluga.

## Kazan (8432)

### IREX Office–Kazan Center for Corporate and Cultural Development
Kazan State University
ul. Lenin 18
420008   Kazan
**Tel:**       8-79-90, 31-84-67
**Fax:**       38-74-18

See the profile for IREX in the North American Organizations section.

### Kazan Youth Political Club
a/ya 61
420141   Kazan
**Tel:**       38-73-21
**Fax:**       36-02-41
**E-mail:**   petrovd@open.ksu.ras.ru
**Contact:** Denis Petrov

## Kirov (8332)

### Civic Initiatives Support Foundation
ul. Krasno-Armeiskaia 17
610002   Kirov
**Tel:**       62-82-77
**Fax:**       62-89-58
**E-mail:**   fond@centr.vyatka.su
**Contact:** Aleksandr Fominikh

The foundation was established in July 1996 to provide moral and financial support for socially significant civic initiatives in Kirov oblast. Its main mission is to develop institutions of civil society and to support teaching and educational activities. Members of the organization have recently begun developing materials about local self-government and cooperation between government agencies, political parties, and NGOs.

The foundation's plans include sociological research on the local population's adaptation to the conditions of market transition, and the development of projects to revive the cultural traditions of Vyatskii krai.

## Krasnodar (8612)

### Association for the Protection of Consumer Rights
Краснодарская Краевая Ассоциация по Защите Прав Потребителей
ul. Pashkovskaya 65
350000   Krasnodar
**Tel:**      57-02-31, 57-64-53
**Tel/Fax:** 55-01-60
**Contact:** Lyubov Bakhmetova, President

Since 1990, the association has worked to develop consumer-oriented legislation and improved goods and services for consumers. The association conducts independent evaluations of products and services and disseminates this information to the public. The information is also used to lobby government agencies for better consumer protection and product safety. In addition, the association offers legal consultations to consumers who feel their rights have been violated and represents these consumers in court.

The group publishes a monthly newspaper, The Kuban Consumer, which contains articles ranging from reports of substandard housing conditions in Krasnodar to warnings about possible allergic reactions to cosmetic moisturizers. In 1997, the group published a handbook on how to protect your rights as a consumer; the booklet contained the full text of the Russian Federation's law on consu-

mers' rights, as well as practical advice from Lyubov Bakhmetova, the association's president.

### Chernobyl Union–Association of Invalids and Veterans of Chernobyl
Союз Чернобыль–
Общественная организация инвалидов и ветеранов чернобыля
ul. Ordzhonikidze 59, k. 8
350000   Krasnodar
**Tel:**      52-98-41
**Contact:** Mikhail Markyshin, President

The Chernobyl Union provides legal and psychological support to people in Krasnodar who have suffered injuries or medical complications from the Chernobyl nuclear accident in 1986. The union counsels victims and families of victims on their rights and lobbies the regional administration for improved services and legislation to protect this segment of the population. It has also published a directory of medical specialists and legal services in the region, which it distributes free-of-charge. The union also works to inform the public about the dangers of radiation through articles in the press, presentations on local TV and radio shows, and informational booklets.

### Education Consulting Center
Консультационный образовательный центр
ul. Tikhoretskaia 5/1, etazh 5
Krasnodar
**Tel:**      33-24-30
**Fax:**  ⸱   57-31-89
**E-mail:**  rubass@online.ru
**Contact:** Svetlana Rubashkina

This center offers educational testing and research services for students interested in studying abroad or participating in international exchange programs. The TOEFL test and TOEFL preparation classes are provided periodically through the center. Seminars and individual consulting sessions for students on the types of academic programs available abroad, the requirements for entry, and the application process are also provided. A resource library of directories and publications on U.S. and international academic institutions is open to the public.

In April 1996, the center hosted a Study Abroad Fair with Kuban State University to publicize opportunities to study abroad. The center receives support from IREX, ACTR, and the Open Society Institute.

## Krasnodar Regional Community Foundation Resource Center

a/ya 1157
350078 Krasnodar
**Tel:** 52-85-93, 52-69-54
**E-mail:** kuzmis@kuban.sbcorp.ru
**Web:** www.sbcorp.ru/krc
**Contact:** Sergei Kuzmin, President;
Irina Biryukova, Vice President

The resource center supports the growth of non-governmental organizations and civil society in Southern Russia by providing consulting services in the areas of public relations, computer technology and Internet use, law, fund raising, and accounting. It makes efforts to foster interaction between NGOs and local government officials through its discussion group, Club Vmeste (Club Together).

## Legal Youth Agency "Your-Inform"

Молодежное юридическое
агентство Юр–Информ
ul. Krasnaya 57, k. 24

350000 Krasnodar
**Tel:** 69-34-94
**Fax:** 69-32-42
**E-mail:** urinform@i-connect.ru
**Contact:** Evgenii Nizhnik, President

Founded in 1996, Your-Inform works to foster an understanding and respect for the rule of law among Krasnodar youth. The group has three main programs:

- The Youth and Law program provides lectures on human rights in schools and free legal consultations for minors
- The Third Sector program offers seminars and consulting sessions to social organizations on their legal status, rights and registration requirements
- The Law and Ecology program consists of roundtables and conferences on issues of environmental law.

The agency receives support from the city administration, the Kuban State Youth Union, and the Attorneys' Bar of Krasnodar.

## Modus-Veli Association for Children with Congenital Facial Defects

Ассоциация Детей-Инвалидов
с Врожденными Пороками
Лица Модус-Вели
ul. Kommunarov 221
350020 Krasnodar
**Tel:** 55-73-15
**Contact:** Natalia Baronova

Circumstances are often grim for children born with facial defects in Russia; they are frequently given up for adoption at birth and even simple reconstructive surgery is difficult to obtain. This association was founded in 1992 to help children born with facial defects overcome social and physical obstacles and to provide support for their families. The goals of the association include increasing access to necessary surgical procedures, securing needed medical equipment and qualified personnel for hospitals, and defending the rights of children with facial defects.

## "Personnel" Foundation of Assistance for Training of Staff in the Market Economy and Development of Market Infrastructure in the Krasnodar Region

"Персонал" Региональный фонд содействия подготовке кадров для рыночной экономики и развитию рыночной инфраструктуры в Краснодарском крае
ul. Garazhnaya 93
350000 Krasnodar
**Tel/Fax**: 54-83-32
**E-mail**: personal@mail.uraltel.com
**Contact**: Olga Pavlovna

The foundation, founded in 1991, works to develop the small business sector of the Krasnodar region through research projects and education for entrepreneurs and business personnel.

## Public Information Center

ul. Krasnoarmieskaya 53
350000 Krasnodar
**Tel**: 53-14-66
**Fax**: 53-48-34
**E-mail**: root@cnk.kuban.ru
**Web**: www.kuban.ru/users/cnk/erindex/shtml

## Russian Red Cross Society– Krasnodar City Committee

Краснодарский городской комитет Российского Общества Красного Креста
ul. Ugnatova 16
350063 Krasnodar
**Tel**: 37-54-95
**Contact**: Zhanna Berezhnaia, President

The Russian Red Cross has been working in the Kuban region since 1877, providing humanitarian aid and social support to the poor of southern Russia.

In 1992, five district-level Red Cross offices in the city of Krasnodar merged to form the Krasnodar City Committee to coordinate city-wide distribution of material aid. In addition to traditionally needy segments of the Russian population such as the elderly and disabled, the committee supports the rising number of refugees and internally displaced persons in southern Russia. It also addresses new sectors of poor spawned from radical economic and political transition, including single woman, families with many children, orphans, and a growing homeless population. The committee collects and donates old clothing, medicine and medical equipment, food, books, and toys to those in need. In 1995, it distributed food, clothes, and shoes to victims of the Chechen War, assisting nearly 1,000 refugees of that conflict. In 1996, the society was able to provide humanitarian assistance to 470 needy families of the region with support from the International Red Cross. Its Health program is a joint initiative with a local soy-production business, Assoya, in which free soy products are distributed to malnourished children and families.

The committee also works with local youth organizations to distribute educational information to schools on social issues such as AIDs, drug use, and sexual relations. It also fosters charitable giving within the local business community, analyzes donor trends in the region, and lobbies the regional administration for legislation to benefit charitable donors.

The Russian Red Cross has been in existence since 1863, and today has branches in 89 regions of the country. It is a member of the International Red Cross.

## Society in Defense of Intellectual Property Rights

Краевая общественная организация "Общество защиты интеллектуальной собственности"
ul. 40-let Pobedy 37/1, k. 114
350029  Krasnodar
**Tel:**       68-52-06
**Contact:** Irina Belova, Vice President

This organization works to improve legislation for protection of property rights in Russia. It lobbies national and regional level government for new copyright laws to prevent the illegal duplication and dissemination of publications, books, videos, and audio cassettes, which has become a lucrative business on the Russian black market since 1991. The organization also distributes information to the public on this growing problem, the need for new legislation, and the rights of individuals to protect their intellectual property.

## Southern Russia Resource Center

Южно-Российский Ресурс Центр
ul. Starokubanskaya 114
350058  Krasnodar
**Tel:**       319-144, 319-020
**Fax:**       310-989
**E-mail:**   srrc@online.ru
**Web:**      www.online.ru/people/srrc/
**Contact:** Svetlana A. Chernyshova, President; Emilia Rymina, Administrative Assistant;  Svetlana Rubashkina,

Editor of *Formula for Success* newsletter

Founded in 1995 and supported by USAID through the Civic Initiative Program, the resource center's goal is to "develop, strengthen and catalyze" non-governmental organizations in Southern Russia. The center seeks to influence local legislation, holds training seminars, offers consultations for NGO leaders, operates a library and information center, and publishes a monthly newsletter, *Formula for Success*. In 1997, the center published *Directory of Southern Russia NGOs* and the *NGO Self-Evaluation Tool and Self-Improvement Guide*. It also held an NGO Fair in April 1998 with the active participation of local officials and NGOs. Three interregional conferences were also convened in 1997–98: Conference of Southern Russia, Collaboration of NGOs with Government and Within the Sector, and Business and NGOs: From Dialog to Partnership.

SRRC program coordinators work in eight cities: Rostov, Novocherkassk, Taganrog, Sochi, Novorossiisk, Armavir, Kislovodsk, and Piatigorsk. There is also a SRRC affiliate office in Stavropol (see SRRC entry under Stavropol for contact information).

## Southern Wave Creative Union

Творческий Союз "Южная Волна"
ul. Krasnaia 57, k. 20
350000  Krasnodar
**Tel/Fax:** 69-32-42
**E-mail:**   ugvolna@online.ru
**Contact:** Evgeny Grekoff, Chairman of the Board

Southern Wave is a youth organization formed in 1993 as a result of a festival of independent artists held in Krasnodar, entitled Southern Wave '93. Since its inception, the group has held more than 100 events for youth throughout the Kuban region. 1997 programs included:

- Choose and Vote!–students participated in a mock parliament to learn about democratic values and processes. A mobile voting station also traveled to various student and youth clubs for these groups to hold elections and gain an understanding of the electoral process.
- Say No to Drugs!–using pop culture as a medium to reach youth, Southern Wave held a series of anti-drug events that featured local rock bands, DJs, and actors from a popular television show. The events also included a public debate on tobacco advertising and an art exhibition, entitled Art Against AIDS.

## Women and Families Center

ul. Gimnazicheskaya 93
Krasnodar
**Tel:** 52-28-18
**Contact:** Irina B. Kotelevits

The center is associated with the Russian-American Women and Families Center in Moscow. One of its projects is the creation of a birth clinic based on Western models, where husbands can remain with their wives during delivery. It has also established a learning center for women, with a library and a meeting place for women.

## Union of Young Leaders

Объединение Юных Лидеров
ul. Krasnaia 57, k. 52
350000 Krasnodar
**Tel:** 69-34-54
**E-mail:** oyl@chat.ru
**Contact:** Dmitry Kosyakov, President

The union was established in 1995 and is affiliated with the Association of Young Leaders in Moscow. It organizes activities for teenagers to develop self-esteem, build character, and teach the basic principles of leadership.

## Youth Association for the Development of National Cultures of the Kuban

Молодежная Ассоциация Развития Национальных Культур Кубани
ul. Krasnoarmeiskaya 53, k. 9
350000 Krasnodar
**Tel:** 69-33-23, 69-34-54
**Tel/Fax:** 52-40-18
**Contact:** Natalia Nazarenko, Director

This association supports the right of young people to learn about their national heritage as well as the cultures of others in order to help develop their creative potential. The association promotes interregional communication and exchanges between young people; in 1997, the group developed the Friendship Bridge - North & South program that brought together youth from the St. Petersburg area, Krasnodar krai, and the Adygei Republic. The association also established a National Cultures Club dedicated to the diverse cultural heritage of Russia. The club hosts ethnic dance performances, cooking demonstrations, holiday celebrations, and other cultural events.

## *Lipetsk (0742)*

## Socio-Ecological Union– Lipetsk Branch

Липецкое Отделение Российского Социально-Экологического Союза
ul. Vodopyanova 11, k. 80
398046 Lipetsk
**Tel:** 45-28-82, 31-62-07, 25-54-89

**E-mail:** root@grenn.lipetsk.su
**Contact:** Aleksandr Federov

This SEU branch defends the rights of citizens to live in a clean environment.

## Lipetsk Society for Human Rights

Липецкое Общество Прав
Человека
ul. Filipchenko 9/2-7
398035   Lipetsk
**Tel:**     25-64-20
**Fax:**     72-01-67
**E-mail:**  hrlipetsk@glas.apc.org
**Web:**     www.glasnet.ru/~hrlipetsk/
**Contact:** Mark Goldman

The society coordinates the efforts of various smaller human rights organizations in Lipetsk oblast. It monitors regional human rights and provides both material and professional support for organizations and individuals. Since 1996, the society has maintained a database of human rights violations in local military units and operated a program on farmers' rights.

## Murmansk (8152)

## GAIA Environmental Center

Гая
**E-mail:**  krugl@aprec.ru
**Contact:** Elena Kruglikova

GAIA was established in Murmansk in 1992 and now also has a branch in Apatity. It conducts an energy project addressing four broad issues:

- Renewable resources of the north
- Energy conservation
- Energy education
- Antinuclear activity
  Its forest project focuses on preservation of protected territories, reforestation, and "model forests."

GAIA also conducts environmental education through a Youth Ecological Club and a resource center. It offers support to other enviromental NGOs, and works with state officials and organizations.

## Nizhny Novgorod (8312)

## Agency for Volga Ecological Information (AVE-Info)

Агенство Волжской
Экологической Информации
(АВЭ-Инфо)
ul. Kostina 2, kv. 145
603134   Nizhny Novgorod
**Tel:**      34-31-42
**Fax:**      39-11-91
**Tel/Fax:** 30-28-90
**E-mail:**  Yury@aveinfo.sci-nnov.ru
**Web:**     www.sci-nnov.ru/massmedia/
papers/nnpapers/aveinfo/
**Contact:** Yury L. Rodygin

AVE-Info is an independent news agency that provides Russian and international environmental information to local newspapers and journals. The agency produces a bulletin that features news stories on local environmental topics, ranging from reports of anthrax outbreaks in Siberia to longer essays that explore issues of solar energy or waste disposal. Archived bulletins are available at the AVE-Info Web site.

## Cadres Training Foundation

Нижегородский
региональный фонд
подготовки финансовых и
управленческих кадров
Kreml, korp. 2, k. 8
603082   Nizhny Novgorod
**Tel:**      39-94-97
**Tel/Fax:** 39-16-78

**Contact:** Vasily D. Kozlov, General Director

Responding to the dire need for a professional, market-oriented class of private and public sector leaders in Russia today, this foundation provides professional training to managers in the energy, transportation and manufacturing industries, as well as representatives of privatized companies, state sector companies and small-scale businesses. Its mission is the following:

- To develop effective training programs for people working in management and finance
- To provide financial support for broad-scale education and training programs
- To assist in the development of new cadres for economic reform.

The foundation organized a conference, Strategy for Employee Development, and supports the weekly publication *Biznes Plus Kariera*. It was instrumental in the creation of the Delovaya Kniga (Business Book) club and an association for professors of economics and business in Nizhny Novgorod.

## Chance

Шанс
GSP-1005
Pamirskaya Street 11, k. 210
603600   Nizhny Novgorod
**Tel:** 52-54-97, 52-35-31, 52-69-54
**Fax:** 52-77-17
**E-mail:** chance@vozm.sci-nnov.ru
**Contact:** Olga Voroshilova

Chance training center was created in January of 1996 by the organization Opportunity through a one-year grant from the Eurasia Foundation. During its first year of operation, Chance trained over 200 individuals for positions as secretaries, bookkeepers and accountants and provided free vocational

courses in sewing and computers. Students at the training center included teenagers entering the workforce, recently discharged soldiers, and unemployed workers from closed factories.

Today, the center provides courses in management and business for professionals who are seeking to upgrade their skills. Chance is currently working to create an employment center with a job bank in Nizhny Novgorod.

## Dront Environmental Center Press Service

a/ya 34
630163   Nizhny Novgorod
**Tel:**        30-28-81
**Fax:**       39-11-91
**E-mail:**   dront@glas.apc.org
**Contact:** Elena Shirokova

The press service is a regional support center for the ROLL Project. (See the profile for the Institute for Sustainable Communities in the Moscow section.)

## Human Rights Society of Nizhny Novgorod

Нижегородское Общество Прав Человека
a/ya 80
603122   Nizhny Novgorod
**Tel:**        39-08-95
**Tel/Fax:** 30-07-14, 30-39-98
**E-mail:**   hrnnov@glasnet.ru,
                 rights@vineyard.nnov.ru
**Contact:** Sergei Shimovolos, President

When it formed in 1990, the society was the first independent human rights organization in the Volga region. Today, it focuses its efforts on prison reform and has established a committee to monitor human rights abuses in local penitentiaries. Since 1992, the society has collaborated with the Center for Reform of the Criminal Justice System in Moscow. In 1995, these two groups formed the Penal Monitoring Council. Council members visit prisons and penal colonies and interview prisoners with the goal of exposing rights abuses and providing inmates with legal and material aid.

The society also collects books, medical supplies, and writing materials for prisoners. It maintains a database of prisoners in need of urgent help and attempts to find them (and their families) necessary legal or financial resources.

## "Invatur" Regional Voluntary Organization for Rehabilitation of the Disabled
Nizhny Novgorod
**Tel:** 36-80-85
**E-mail:** invatur@sandy.ru
**Contact:** Rafik Roganyan

## Journalists Union of Nizhny Novgorod
Нижегородский Союз Журналистов
ul. Vavarskaia 32
603006 Nizhny Novgorod
**Tel:** 38-94-49
**Tel/Fax:** 35-62-53
**E-mail:** nnrapic@glas.apc.org
**Contact:** Natalya Skvortsova, Coordinator; Marina Stepanenko, Assistant

The union has been in operation for more than 40 years. Today, it has over 1,000 voluntary members from the newspaper and television industry who represent a full spectrum of different political orientations and viewpoints. The union holds press conferences and organizes training seminars for its members.

## "Kariatida" Center of Contemporary Art
"Кариатида" Нижегородский центр современной культуры
V. Volzhskaia Naberezhnaya 2
Nizhny Novgorod
**Tel:** 39-03-58, 39-05-03
**Contact:** Liubov M. Saprykina, President

Kariatida's goal is to preserve and develop contemporary Russian art and culture. The center has conducted a series of exhibitions entitled "The Different Generation," and held an international conference "Center-Periphery: Cultural Interaction." It collaborates with the State Center of Contemporary Art in Moscow, the Department of Culture in Novgorod, and the Goethe Institute in Germany.

## Kurgan Society
"Курган" Нижегородское поисковое объединение
pr. Gagarina 23, korp. 2, k. 423
The Museum of Nizhny Novgorod State University
603022 Nizhny Novgorod
**Tel:** 65-84-61
**Contact:** Tamara I. Kovaleva, President

The Kurgan Society researches Russia's history during World War II and works with state and public organizations to find, preserve and restore the monuments of the war. It organizes search parties to find and properly bury the remains of Soviet soldiers killed in the Great Patriotic War, as WWII is commonly known in Russia. Kurgan has reburied the remains of 480 soldiers and officers, and published five articles on the history of the war. The society's members also educate young people about the war.

## "Nizhegorodskaia Zemlia" Public Foundation

Общественный фонд Земля Нижегородская

per. Kozhevennyi, dom 10/13
603001   Nizhny Novgorod
**Tel:**      34-38-86
**Contact:** T. I. Semenova

The foundation aids low-income families and participates in the restoration of local historical and architectural monuments. It provides help to the Makarievskii monastery, offers stipends for gifted children, and supports children's sports.

## Opportunity

Возможность

GSP-1005, Pamirskaya 11
603600   Nizhny Novgorod
**Tel:**      52-54-97
**Fax:**      52-74-17
**E-mail:**  opportuntiy@glas.apc.org
**Web:**      prime.cbi.co.ru/partners/
opportunity/vozmozhnost.htm
**Contact:** Galina Popova, Director

Opportunity is an umbrella organization that comprises both for-profit financial companies and nonprofit training and service organizations. It created the local organizations Service, now an independent NGO resource center, and Chance, which still works closely with Opportunity to provide practical training and business skill courses, often in high demand by local companies. See separate entries for Service and Chance.

## Russian Foundation of Disabled Afghanistan War Veterans–Nizhny Novgorod City Branch

a/ya 66
ul. Magistratskaia 11
603001   Nizhny Novgorod
**Tel:**      33-03-72

**Tel/Fax:**  33-82-05
**Contact:** Gennadii Chernyshev

This foundation branch was established in March 1996 to protect the civil, economic, social, and cultural interests of disabled veterans. It also supports the families and relatives of soldiers killed in military service.

In 1996–97, the group began a program to help veterans obtain medical treatment for conditions incurred in Afghanistan and Chechnya, and has created a database of patients needing medical attention. It also works to find jobs for disabled veterans, and has twice lobbied the Nizhny Novgorod City Duma for better employment opportunities for the handicapped.

## "Sluzhenie" Association

Служение

Markina Square 3
603001   Nizhny Novgorod
**Tel:**      31-35-64
**Fax:**      34-28-06
**E-mail:**  sluzh@pop.sci-nnov.ru,
              sluzh@pent.sci-nnov.ru
**Web:**      www.sci-nnov.ru/socio/
public/sluzhenie/index.html
**Contact:** Evgenia Verba, Executive Director; Olga Makhova, Program Assistant; Elena Belyaeva

Sluzhenie, meaning "service," began in 1994 as an informal club within the organization Opportunity. It has since developed into an NGO information and resource center for the Nizhny Novgorod region, serving about 20 member organizations ranging in focus from the arts to charity, children, and the disabled. Activities of Sluzhenie include:

- A monthly NGO bulletin of local and national third sector news, available on Sluzhenie's Web site

- A resource library with over 1,000 third sector publications
- Internet access and training in Web design for local NGOs
- A volunteer program to encourage participation in charitable work— 130 people volunteered at a June 1998 fund raising event for children with tuberculosis
- A regional NGO conference attended by over 60 organizations
- Monitoring of changes in local, regional, and federal legislation and consulting local NGOs on legal and taxation issues
- Development of centers in the cities of Cheboksary, Saransk and Ioshkar-Ola in the Volga-Vyatka region to support local NGO communities.

## "Social Rehabilitation"

Нижегородская Обществен-
ная организация "Общественная Реабилитация"
ul. Arkhitekturnaya 10
603032   Nizhny Novgorod
**Tel:**       52-59-31
**Fax:**      52-48-68
**Contact:** A. U. Zlatov, Executive Director

According to Social Rehabilitation, 189,000 people–five percent of the population–are registered as disabled in Nizhny Novgorod and its surrounding area of 3.74 million. The organization was founded in 1996 to protect the rights of this often-neglected sector and enable the integration of disabled persons into society. It also lobbies for legislative reforms to prevent discrimination of the disabled.

The organization sponsors free legal consultations for local disabled citizens with lawyers, social workers, and medical/orthopedic specialists. It is in the process of forming a Center for the

Protection of the Rights of the Disabled. The center will:

- Maintain a databank of disabled organisations and individuals, employment opportunities and publications
- Train the leaders of disabled organizations
- Improve outreach to disabled people in rural areas
- Develop computer courses for the disabled at Nizhny Novgorod Economic College
- Provide Internet access through the Internet Center of N. Novgorod State University
- Foster regional and international links with local groups
- Organize meetings of regional and urban leaders with representatives of disabled social organisations
- Issue *Your Right*, a monthly supplement to the newspaper *Nizhegorodsky Invalid.*

## Sokol Youth Organization

Общественное молодежное
объединение "Сокол"
ul. Chaadaeva 9
603035   Nizhny Novgorod
**Tel:**       29-31-55, 46-19-55
**Fax:**      46-71-77
**Contact:** Oleg Posdnyakov, President; Sergei Ermakov, Vice President

This organization strives to provide an alternative to crime, alcoholism, and substance abuse for teenagers and young people. Its members patrol schoolyards and streets and lecture children on the dangers of drug and alcohol abuse. The group also organizes after-school sports programs and tournaments for teens.

## UNESCO Center of Nizhny Novgorod

Нижегородский Центр
ЮНЕСКО
pr. Gagarina 23, korp. 2, k. 320
Nizhny Novgorod State University
Nizhny Novgorod
**Tel:**      65-77-45
**Contact:** Y. Marchenkov, President

Founded in 1994, the center strives to
strengthen peace and security by
establishing communication between
peoples of the world in the spheres of
education, science, and culture. It
supports UNESCO programs in world
culture, women's issues, ethnic arts and
crafts development, and youth movements. The center organized a regional
conference, Theory and Practice of
Sustainable Development, and a seminar, Women, Spiritual Values, the
World, and the 21st Century.

## "Women Mathematicians"– Regional Branch

Нижегородское отделение
Российской ассоциации
"Женщины-математики"
GSP-20
pr. Gagarina 23, korp. 2, k. 216
603600  Nizhny Novgorod
**Tel:**      65-78-83, 33-00-43
**Fax:**     65-85-20
**E-mail:**  yemel@nncnit.unn.ac.ru
**Contact:** Inna S. Yemelianova,
President

Established in 1994, the association
assists women mathematicians in their
research and teaching activities through
consultation and financial support. It
has organized a number of conferences
in different regions of Russia, including
Puschino, Voronezh and Suzdal, and
has published four volumes of material
from these conferences. The association
seeks new investment so that modern

technology can be incorporated into the
education system.

Partners of the association include
the Foundation of the Russian Federa-
tion for Support of Legal Initiatives, the
Mathematical Society and the U.S. and
European branches of the association
Women in Mathematics.

## Young Lawyers Union–Nizhny Novgorod Regional Branch

Нижегородское региональное
отделение "Молодежного
союза юристов"
ul. Tropinina 14-59
Nizhny Novgorod
**Tel:**      66-12-97
**Fax:**     66-50-20

Established in 1995, the union seeks to
educate a new generation of demo-
cracy-oriented lawyers. It provides
consultation and training through its
Consultative Legal Center, and helps its
members find employment. The union
has worked with the Committee of
Soldiers' Mothers, the regional Bar
Association, and the U.S.-based
National Democratic Institute.

## Zabota-Hesed-Sara Jewish Charitable Center in Nizhny Novgorod

Забота-Хесед-Сара,
Нижегородский еврейский
благотворительный центр
ul. Ilinskaia 43b
Nizhny Novgorod
**Tel:**      34-18-81
**Contact:** Susanne D. Turova,
Chairperson

The center provides medical assistance
and social support to elderly residents
of the city. It rents medical equipment
for home use and organizes concerts
and festivities.

## Novgorod (8162)

### Citizens Democracy Corps
Bolshaya Sankt-Peterburgskaya St. 41,
k. 3402
173003   Novgorod
**Tel:**      13-17-05
**E-mail:**   elena@cdc.novsu.ac.ru
**Contact:** Elena Efremova, Regional
Director

See the profile of CDC in the North
American Organizations section.

### "Doveriye" Psychological-Educational Center
ul. Popova, 5A
173021   Novgorod
**Tel:**      22-14-00, 22-56-50
**Contact:** Nadezhda Lisitsina, Director

Doveriye, meaning "trust," offers
psychological services and counseling
for troubled youth and women. The
center runs numerous telephone help
lines, a shelter for battered women,
provides psychological counseling in
local schools, and supports a women's
entrepreneurship center in Staraya
Rusa, a smaller city in Novgorod
Oblast.

### IREX–Partnerships for Civil Society and Economic Development Project (PCSED)
ul. Germana 3, k. 2
Novgorod
**Tel:**      13-19-56
**Fax:**      23-17-07
**E-mail:**   irex@telecom.nov.ru

See the profile of IREX in the North
American Organizations section.

### Novgorod Oblast Association of Women Entrepreneurs
Novgorod
**Tel:**      27-00-11

**Fax:**      13-19-67
**Contact:** Olga Sergeyeva, President

The association links various organizations in the region that support women
entrepreneurs, and works with local
officials to improve conditions for
small business. Sergeyeva is an entre-
preneur herself. In June 1998, she
opened a *blini* (Russian pancakes) cafe
in Novgorod.

### Russian Orphanage Association
ul. Sushanskaya, 7
174400   Borovichi
Novgorod Region
**Tel:**      (64) 34-505
**Tel/Fax:** (64) 34-112
**E-mail:**   rusor@rusor.org,
             orphan@telecom.nov.ru,
             orphan@novgorod.net
**Web:**      www.geocities.com/~rusor
**Contact:** Mikhael M. Airumyan, MD,
President

RusOR was established in 1995 by a
coalition of 200 orphanages seeking to
change the structure of the Russian
orphanage system to focus on helping
families stay together. It provides
professional training for orphanage
employees and assistance to charitable
organizations aiding orphans and low-
income families. RusOR is currently
advocating the rights of children in
opposition to legislation that is antago-
nistic to orphans. RusOr currently
represents 257 orphanages in 87
regions of the Russian Federation.

## Novocherkassk (86352)

### Union of Don Women
Союз Донских Женщин
ul. Kalinin 88
346427   Novocherkassk

**Tel:** 31-936
**Fax:** 34-107
**Contact:** Valentina Cherevatenko

This organization was formed out of the first Women of the Don Forum, held in Novocherkassk in April 1993 and attended by 101 women from 13 towns of Rostov oblast. The union focuses on protecting the rights of women and enhancing their role in public, economic and cultural affairs.

In 1996, the union organized an international conference, Women for Life Without War and Violence!, sponsored by the Open Society Institute. More than 250 people representing 85 NGOs from Russia, Armenia, Georgia and the U.S. attended the conference.

## "Zeleny Don" Regional Environmental Movement
ul. Dachnaia 1, k. 2
346408　Novocherkassk
**Tel:**　27-239
**E-mail:**　zedon@novoch.ru
**Contact:** Vladimir Lagutov, President;
Peter Kolpack

Founded in 1990 as a city-wide environmental society in Novocherkassk, Zeleny Don, meaning "Green Don", formally registered in 1996 as a regional environmental association serving the southern Don.

The group is primarily concerned with preservation of fish stocks in the Azov Sea and improving legislation on fishing rights. In 1997, Zeleny Don helped to create an interparliamentary commission on the Azov, consisting of deputies from both the Russian and Ukrainian parliaments. The commission has met several times to discuss international fishery legislation and the problems of illegal harvesting of fish in the Azov Sea.

Zeleny Don also runs an information center, Azovbas, with resources for local environmental groups, and holds seminars to discuss regional environmental issues and opportunities for joint cooperation among local groups.

The group has six branch offices in the Rostov and Volgograd oblasts located in the cities of Rostov, Shakhty, Sulin, and Aksai. It is a member of the Socio-Ecological Union.

## Novorossiysk (86134)

## "Journalist" Novorossiysk Union of Journalists
"Журналист" Новороссийская городская организация Союза журналистов
ul. Leta Shmidta 9A
353510　Novorossiysk
**Tel:**　33-125
**E-mail:**　AQUATORIA@glasnet.ru
**Contact:** Valerii Timochenko, Director

The union has set up an e-mail network of environmental organizations in southern Russia, through which it disseminates information on mass media and environmental issues and encourages discussion and exchange between activists and organizations.

## Perm (3422)

## "New Home" Regional Public Organization for Defense of Citizens' Housing Rights
ul. Mekhahoshisa 29, k. 4
614016　Perm
**Tel:**　49-60-12
**Contact:** Natalia Averichieva, President

New Home works to protect the rights of both tenants and private property owners in the city of Perm and the surrounding region. It has contributed to government discussions on regional housing reform and took part in a Clean Water program for better-quality drinking water and increased supplies of hot water to the city. The group distributes legal information for renters and is interested in developing a homeowners association.

## "Charitable Work" Regional Public Association of Invalids
ul. Revolutsii 58
614010   Perm
**Tel:**        45-48-32
**Fax:**        69-52-47
**Contact:** Rostislav Timiriazev

This group provides educational, material, and psychological support to the disabled. It conducts seminars and distributes information on legal rights for the disabled and organizes outings and recreational activities for local children with disabilities.

## Union of Women's Organizations of Perm
ul. Lenina 23/1
614000   Perm
**Tel:**        92-70-20
**Fax:**        34-94-91
**Contact:** Nina Chebikina, President

The union works to develop a strong community of women's organizations in the city of Perm. It has created a Leadership School for NGOs in order to contribute to women's professional development.

## *Petrozavodsk (8142)*

## Karelian Center for Gender Research
Карельский Центр Гендерских Исследований
a/ya 199
185035  Petrozavodsk
**Tel:**        52-53-40
**Tel/Fax:** 55-70-89
**E-mail:**   gender@onego.ru
**Web:**       ns.onego.ru/gender/
**Contact:** Larisa Boichenko, Chairperson

The center was founded in 1995 on the principle that "women's rights are inseparable from human rights." In 1997, it held a series of seminars for women in Karelia. Seminar topics included violence against women, the role of women in contemporary society, and strategies for lobbying local government structures for anti-discriminatory policies. The center maintains a database of women's organizations in Russia and abroad.

## Karelian Society for the Protection of Animals
Карельское Общество Защиты Животных
a/ya 1377
185034  Petrozavodsk
**Tel:**        52-75-77, 76-02-66
**E-mail:**   nvtsnchoz@karelia.ru, max@students.soros.karelia.ru
**Web:**       students.soros.karelia.ru/~nickolay/homepagea.html
**Contact:** Max Olenichev, Irina Bondarenko, Vlad Rybalko, Co-Presidents

The society works to prevent cruelty to animals by promoting public awareness of animal testing, the humane treatment of strays, the importance of neutering pets, and vegetarianism. It is currently working to establish a shelter for homeless animals in Petrozavodsk.

## Project Harmony–Petrozavodsk

**Tel/Fax:** 77-33-61
**E-mail:** pharmony@petrodtd.
karelia.ru

See the profile for Project Harmony in the North American Organizations section.

## *Pskov (8112)*

## Ecological Coordination Fund (Eco Fund)

ul. Kommunalnaia 46-55
180024 Pskov
**Tel:** 15-49-36
**E-mail:** ecofund@pskov.teia.org,
ecofund@teia.org
**Contact:** Dmitry Antonuk

EcoFund seeks to strengthen NGO activity in Pskov, foster cooperative links between local groups, and promote citizen participation in local environmental protection efforts. The group disseminates information about the environmental movement to the local population and publishes the *Nota Bene Nonprofit Bulletin*, which reports on NGO activities and issues impacting the nonprofit sector in Pskov.

EcoFund works in close collaboration with the Lake Peipsi Project.

## Lake Peipsi Project

ul. Kommunalnaia 46-55
180024 Pskov
**Tel:** 15-49-36
**Fax:** 44-02-04
**E-mail:** lppinfo@lake-peipus.net,
tanya @lake-peipus.net
**Web:** www.lake-peipus.net
**Contact:** Tatiana Maximova, Russian Projects Coordinator

Lake Peipsi (Chudskoe in Russian) occupies two-thirds of the Russian-Estonian border region and is the fourth largest lake system in Europe. Commercial fishing and recreational activities on the lake have historically played an important role in the economic and social life of local communities, which are an ethnic mix of Estonian, Russian, and Setu (a unique cultural mixture of the two).

Estonian independence and new border regulations have interrupted old norms of cooperation between government agencies, economic enterprises, and local communities in Russia and Estonia regarding the lake and its environs. Unemployment and deep economic recession are now major problems on both sides of the lake, and fishing rights have become a point of contention.

In 1993, a group of environmental activists, scientists, and community leaders from Tartu, Estonia, St. Petersburg, and Pskov met to discuss the environmental, social, and economic problems of the Lake Peipsi region, forming a citizens' group called The Lake Peipsi Project. The project works to foster communication and exchange between specialists, local authorities, and interested citizens of Russia and Estonia on the future of the lake and its surrounding communities. It also promotes environmental protection of the lake and watershed, and regulation of its natural resources.

In 1996, LPP organized a series of seminars and conferences in both countries, including the program Civil Forum in Pskov. Civil Forum involved the preparation of discussion brochures targeting specific local problems for distribution to Pskov residents. The project also established the Pskov Information Center in 1996 with assistance from Transboundary Education and Information Agency in St. Petersburg, Volny University, and St. Petersburg University. The center provides Internet access to six NGOs in Pskov.

LPP publishes a bulletin, *The Lake Peipsi Quarterly*, containing Russian and Estonian essays and news reports on the lake's environment and communities, available on the project's Web site. LPP's main office is located in Tartu, Estonia: Lai 24, EE2400 Tartu, fax: (372) 7 441-481.

## "Renaissance" Rehabilitative Center for Adolescents
"Возрождение"
**Tel:**　22-33-29, 28-33-29
**Fax:**　22-30-00
**E-mail:**　vestnik@pskov.teia.org
**Contact:** Lev Schlossberg, Director

## Russian Children's Fund– Pskov Branch
Псковское Областное Отделение Российского Детского Фонда
ul. Sovetskaia 15a, k. 12
180000　Pskov
**Tel/Fax:** 22-07-92
**Contact:** Tatiana Bodrova, Vice Chairwoman

The Pskov branch of the Russian Children's Fund provides material, psychological, medical, and social support to disabled children, children from needy families, orphans, and former residents of orphanages in the city of Pskov and the surrounding region. The fund's programs include:
- Career Support Program. Helps young adults raised in orphanages or children's homes to find jobs and housing and provides them with them psychological, legal, and material aid
- Warm House Program. Children's institutions are provided with equipment and material aid. The program

has already donated school buses and trucks to five children's homes and secured funds for an orphanage to make badly needed repairs
- Programs for the Disabled. In cooperation with the Association of Parents with Disabled Children, the Children's Fund established a school for children with cerebral palsy in 1997; other programs have provided blind children with "talking books" and obtained glucometers for young diabetics.

## "Veche" Public Movement
Общественное Движение "Вече"
a/ya 16
180007　Pskov
**E-mail:**　veche@ellink.ru
**Contact:** Sergei Afanasiev

Veche originally began in Pskov in 1989 as an association agitating for reform and civil rights. ("Veche" were the name of small town assemblies in medieval Russia). The informal group was responsible for organizing several protest marches and collecting signatures in support of Andrei Sakharov and other dissidents.

In 1996, the group revived and officially registered. Today, Veche works to increase citizen participation in national and local elections. It organized meetings with mayoral candidates in 1996 and engaged in a campaign to encourage voter turn-out. Veche regularly sponsors public lectures on topics such as economic reform and human rights and gives legal consultations to young men seeking alternatives to mandatory military service.

## Volny University of Pskov
Nab. Reki Velikoi 6
18000　Pskov
**Tel/Fax:** 23-37-29, 24-39-59,

28-33-29
**Web:**  www.know.com/volny/
pvu_hp.htm
**Contact:** Edward Moppel, Executive
Director; Igor Savitsky, Chairman of
the Board; Lev Schlossberg, Vice-
Chairman of the Board

Pskov Volny ("Independent") University was established in 1992 as one of
the first independent institutions of
higher education in Russia. The university's founders are leaders of local state
institutions, private enterprises, and
research and cultural organizations who
came together to form a joint-stock
company and direct all dividends
toward the university. The administration includes leading specialists in
various fields of education who develop
curriculum and teaching methods for
the university's B.S., M.S., and foreign
language programs.

The university consists of five
academic faculties:

- Social Sciences: sociology and
  several schools of psychology
- Law
- Business: banking, accounting,
  foreign trade, commerce, marketing,
  strategic planning, and personnel
  management
- Art Studies: music and management
  of cultural institutions
- Information Systems
- English for Business Management.

Each academic program involves
professional internships and mandatory
English language study. French, Dutch,
and German are offered as electives.
There are currently about 200 students
at Volny, most of whom have received
scholarships that the university arranges
with various sponsoring organizations.

Volny has partnered with the U.S.
nonprofit Interweave in Olympia, WA,
since 1992 to conduct faculty and
student exchanges. It also has close

relations with Tacoma Community
College, Tacoma, WA, which granted
two scholarships to Volny students in
1993. In the summers of 1993 and
1995, the university hosted a group of
American students for a summer
language program.

## "Woman of Pskov" Independent Social Women's Center
Независимый Социальный
Женский Центр
"Псковитянка"
ul. Yubileinaia 34
180024   Pskov
**Tel:**   46-77 16, 15-89-12
**Contact:** Natalia Vasileva

This center works to end discrimination
against women in the workplace and in
society. It organizes seminars on feminist topics and has established partnerships with several women's organizations abroad, such as the Association of
Women's Crisis Centers in Sweden,
since its formation in 1995. The center
operates a women's crisis hotline and
publishes a monthly newsletter that
reports on public policy and legislation
in Russia that impacts women, as well
as news from the local women's
movement.

## Rostov-on-Don (8632)

## Christians Against Torture and Child Slavery
Христане Против Пыток и
Детского Рабства
Grechesky per. 3, k. 17
344006   Rostov-on-Don
**Tel:**   65-14-55
**E-mail:**  hrrostov@glasnet.ru
**Web:**   www.glasnet.ru/~hronline/
ngo/rostov/christ.htm

**Contact:** Stanislav Velikoredchanin

This organization was formed in 1996 by a group of young evangelical Baptists who were concerned about the state of human rights in the Don area. Despite its name, the group focuses its efforts primarily on soldiers' rights, and is active in exposing human rights violations in the Russian military and providing legal help for young men who desert their military units because of mistreatment.

## IREX–Rostov-on-Don
ul. Ivanovskogo 38, k. 28-29
344012   Rostov-on-Don
**Tel/Fax:**  32-69-78
**E-mail:**   irexros@irexros.rnd.su

See the profile for IREX in the North American Organizations section.

## "Most" Charitable Foundation
Мост
20-aya Liniya 25, k. 5
344030   Rostov-on-Don
**Tel/Fax:**  51-62-34, 51-76-37
**E-mail:**   moct@icomm.ru
**Contact:** Maureen Diffley, Coordinator of Education Department; Ekaterina Molchanovna, Office Manager

In 1996, the Russian Ministry of the Interior estimated that there were two million drug addicts in Russia, but that treatment was available for only ten percent of them. Salvation Army officers Geoff and Sandra Ryan's work in Rostov-on-Don and Kuleshovka of Rostov Oblast confirmed this report. High rates of drug use in these cities is due in part to local trading points for narcotics from Asia. However, sniffing of legal toxic narcotics, use of home-grown opium and marijuana, and heavy alcohol consumption are also rampant.

Today the Russian AIDS Center for Southern Russia and Caucasus estimates that there are 10,000 IV drug users in Rostov-on-Don. At the close of 1996, there were 176 HIV-positive persons in Rostov oblast—mostly infected children at the Rostov-on-Don Children's Hospital in 1991. At the end of July 1998, there were 1,053 infected persons, making Rostov's HIV-positive population the third largest in Russia.

Upon reviewing these conditions, the Ryans wrote a proposal for the opening of a drug rehabilitation program that would also work with HIV-positive people and submitted it to Salvation Army Headquarters in London. The Rufford and Laing Foundation donated the original grant for the initiative, and Most, meaning "bridge," was registered as a separate charitable social organization in August 1998.

Since September 1997, Most has provided free individual counseling, visiting lessons to local schools, brochures, and educational materials to the Rostov community. In February 1998, a third department, Youth Programming, was added to supplement Most's existing departments of Education and Counseling. This involved the creation of a youth drop-in center at a dormitory of the Donskoi Government Technical University. The center is frequented by many students each night and features lessons and discussions about narcotics, AIDS, and personal difficulties.

Most has developed a "healthy decision-making" curriculum with workbook, posters, and video cassettes and secured approval to train Azov and Kuleshovka teachers/psychologists in this program. They have also started a weekly radio program on the station Echo Rostov. The show deals with public health issues and responds to callers who ask for advice from 6 to 7 p.m.

Titles of brochures produced and distributed by Most include: AIDS Sexually Transmitted Diseases, The Abstinence Option, Smoking, Marijuana, Hallucinogens, Heroin, Cocaine, Toxinogens, Alcohol, Pregnancy and Smoking, and Pregnancy and Alcohol.

Most's staff consists of one part-time and five full-time employees, plus two part-time volunteers. Expenditures for a recent year were $60,000.

Partner organizations abroad and within Russia include the Salvation Army, the Azov and Rostov Narcological Dispensaries, Doctors without Borders, and AIDS centers in Rostov oblast and Southern Russia.

### Rostov Charitable Association of Families with Many Children
Ростовская Городская Благотворительная Ассоциация Многодетных Семей
a/ya 6494
344004   Rostov-on-Don
**Tel/Fax**: 24-42-70
**E-mail**: rghams@icomm.ru
**Web**: icomm.ru/home/rghams/
**Contact**: Sergei Goncharov, Chairman

This association was founded in 1993 by a group of parents who united to defend the rights and interests of families with many children. The association works not only to provide needy families with aid but to encourage a sense of accountability and responsibility.

In May 1998, the association held a telethon to raise money for needy children in Rostov oblast. The group is also planning a long-term fund raising project (1998–2000) to raise money for overburdened families. The association is collaborating with the Rostov oblast government to realize this project.

### Russian-British Consulting Center
Российско-Британские Консалтинговые Центры
ul. Pushkinskaia 140, k.109
344006   Rostov
**Tel**:      65-53-60
**Tel/Fax**: 65-52-24
**E-mail**:   usatyuk@gin.global-one.ru
**Contact**: Vladimir Usatyk, Vice President

Founded in 1997, the center is a project of the Know How Fund (UK) that provides consulting services for the restructuring of Russia's coal-mining industry. It offers technical advice on the safe operation and maintenance of mines for optimal output, assists in business-plan development and investment decisions, and has created a department for miners who have lost their jobs. The center has 28 employees and an affiliate office in Kemerovo, Siberia.

## *Ryazan (0912)*

### Araks Armenian Cultural Society
Армянское Культурное Общество "Аракс"
ul. Esenin 53/13, k. 6
390046   Ryazan
**Tel**.      11-50-46
**Web**:     ngo.ryazan.ru/ngo/araks/
araks.htm
**Contact**: Gyulyab Martirosian, Director

The Araks Society is dedicated to the study and preservation of Armenian language, literature, and cultural traditions. It unites people of Armenian ancestry from the Ryazan area but also welcomes others with an interest in Armenian culture.

Since 1994, the society has operated an Armenian language school in

Ryazan and has published materials in Armenian.

## Artists' Union of Ryazan
Рязанский Союз Художников
Pervomaiskii per. 42/2
390000   Ryazan
**Tel:**      77-29-55
**Contact:** Boris Gorbunov

The Artists' Union supports artists in the Ryazan area by organizing exhibitions and shows and offering educational art programs. The group is also active in preserving traditional folk arts from the region.

## Jewish Religious Society of Ryazan
Рязанская Еврейская религиозная община
ul. Dzerzhinskogo 61, kv. 34
390005   Ryazan
**Tel:**      76-26-36
**Tel/Fax:** 93-03-49
**Web:**     ngo.ryazan.ru/relig/evrei/
evrei.htm
**Contact:** Leonid Rezink, Chairman

The society operates programs for Jewish people of all ages—a Sunday school for children, a youth club and Jewish student organization, and a support network for elderly Jews. The society has also organized a library of books and videotapes on topics related to Judaism and Jewish culture and history.

## Memorial–Ryazan
Рязанское региональное отделение "Мемориал"
pl. Kostyushko 3
390000   Ryazan
**Tel:**      77-51-17, 75-40-20
**E-mail:**  karta@glasnet.org
**Web:**     ngo.ryazan.ru/memorial/
index.htm

Memorial–Ryazan was one of the first NGOs to start up in the oblast, working to expose human rights violations committed during the Soviet era and support former political prisoners and other victims of repression.

During the war in Chechnya, Memorial-Ryazan members accompanied the former Russian presidential commissioner on human rights, Sergei Kovalev, on human-rights monitoring missions and reported on rights abuses taking place in the war zone. The group campaigns for the construction of monuments to victims of Soviet-era prison camps in the oblast, including the numerous Polish, German, and Czech prisoners who died in the Ryazan-Dyagilevo camp. It also works with local NGOs to develop a human rights curriculum for schools in Ryazan.

In 1996, Memorial collaborated with Open Society/Ryazan and the Center for Pluralism to create an on-line database of local NGOs, and helped with the construction of Human Rights Online, a Web site dedicated to the Russian human rights movement.

In 1998, the group began working with the Center for Pluralism to publish a human rights bulletin, *Karta*, focusing on both the history of totalitarian Soviet regimes and the activities of today's human rights activists.

## Open Society–Ryazan
Открытое общество/Рязань
a/ya 20
390000   Ryazan
**Tel:**      79-04-02, 77-51-17
**E-mail:**  karta@galsnet.ru
**Web:**     www.ngo.ryazan.ru/
authors/open/open-w.htm
**Contact:** Yulia Sereda, Vladimir Sivakov

This branch of the Soros Foundation's Open Society Institute sponsors a local

NGO club for the exchange of information and experience. It also operates a human rights consultation center, offering free legal information and support for citizens who feel their rights have been violated. Recently, the consultation center aided a woman in her attempts to reopen investigations of her son's death. The young man was killed under suspicious circumstances by a fellow soldier while serving in North Ossetia.

## Ryazan Initiative Group for the Implementation of the Helsinki Accords

Рязанская инициативпая группа «За выполнение Хельсинкских соглашений»
a/ya 20
390000   Ryazan
**Tel:**      76-82-42
**E-mail:**   hrryas@glasnet.ru
**Web:**      www.glasnet.ru/~hronline/ngo/helr/helr.htm
**Contact:** Viktor Lozinskii

This organization was formed in 1992 by a group of deputies from the Ryazan city council. It seeks to educate the local populace on civil rights and international human rights standards and laws. To this end, the group developed an educational program on human rights for local high schools during the 1996–97 school year.

## Waldorf Initiative Pedagogical Center

Педагогический центр "Вальдорфская Инициатива"
Ryazan
**Tel:**      77-00-21
**Web:**      www.ngo.ryazan.ru/ngo/walfdor/walf.htm
**Contact:** Roman Borisov

The center operates an elementary school and kindergarten that use the Waldorf teaching method. The center also offers Waldorf training for teachers and child-care workers and supports a club for parents of children attending Waldorf schools.

## St. Petersburg (812)

### "Alexandra" Legal Aid Society for Domestic Violence and Sexual Assault Cases

a/ya 604
191002   St. Petersburg
**Tel:**      445-1257
**Fax:**      112-3948
**E-mail:**   ruslen@admiral.ru

Alexandra works to defend women's civil, economic, and cultural rights. It provides legal assistance to women who have been victims of domestic violence and sexual assault. Founded in 1995, the group conducted a two-year project to analyze the issues of domestic and sexual violence and devised a strategy for meeting the needs of abused women. Lawyers, psychologists, and social workers participated in the project.

Alexandra now runs a crisis hot line for women, and assists abused women in court and in dealings with the police. Training programs for representatives of law enforcement agencies are also offered, and the group publishes pamphlets on legal rights for abused women. It also recruits and trains volunteers to work on the hotline and assist women in courts.

## Baltic Nature Foundation of the St. Petersburg Society of Natural Scientists

Балтийский Фонд Природы
Санкт-Петербургского
Общества
Естествоиспитателей
Universitetskaia nab. 7/9, k. 112
199034   St. Petersburg
**Tel:**       218-9620
**Fax:**      324-0885
**E-mail:**   baltic@teia.org
**Web:**      www.teia.org/ecology/
bfn.htm
**Contact:** Aleksei Zavarzin, Secretary

The foundation was formed to increase the activities of the St. Petersburg Society of Natural Scientists (SPSNS) in northwestern Russia and to aid joint projects in the Baltic Sea region between SPSNS and international organizations, such as the World Wildlife Fund.

The foundation worked with staff from the Russian Academy of Science to devise a strategic plan for protecting wetlands in southern Karelia, and performed field studies of coastal species in the Gulf of Finland for the Russian Federation's State Committee on Ecology. In addition, it has performed numerous field studies of flora and fauna in northwest Russia in conjunction with the World Wildlife Fund.

## CEC International Partners

St. Petersburg
**Tel/Fax:** 311-2198
**E-mail:**   cecstp@glasnet.ru
            cecstp@mail.spb.ru
**Web:**      www.cecip.org
**Contact:** Allison Pultz, Program
Coordinator

CECIP manages professional exchanges in museum work and arts organization management and projects

in contemporary visual art and ballet. Current activities center around St. Petersburg 2003, a multiyear celebration of St. Petersburg's tercentenary. The American Committee for St. Petersburg 2003 has been established in New York to promote participation by American cultural organizations in preparations for St. Petersburg's 300th anniversary celebration. CECIP headquarters are located in New York—see their profile in the North American Organizations section.

## Center for International Cooperation

Центр за Международное
Сотрудничество
Fontanka, 56-20
191002   St. Petersburg
**Tel:**       112-5368, 112-3952
**Fax:**      164-5775
**E-mail:**   Lena@len.usr.pu.ru
**Contact:** Elena Labkovskaia, Director

CIC was created in 1997 at the Department of International Relations of St. Petersburg Technical University, in collaboration with the Department of International Relations at San Francisco State University and the International Center for New Democracy and Social Change in Bishkek, Kyrgyzstan. The center's main objective is to study the experiences of developed countries, facilitate the transfer of new technologies and philosophies to the former Soviet Union, and develop a collaborative information network for research institutions within the NIS and abroad.

## Citizens' Watch

ul. Malaia Koniushennaia, 5
191186   St. Petersburg
**Tel:**       325-8916
**Tel/Fax:** 325-8915
**E-mail:**   citwatch@mail.wplus.net

**Contact:** Boris Pustintsev, President

Citizens' Watch was formed in 1992 by a group of Duma deputies, lawyers, human rights activists and academics concerned about the lack of civic control over state agencies and acts. The group organizes seminars and conferences to draft amendments to Russian laws that do not adhere to international legal standards and lobbies these amendments in parliament.

CW also publishes material and holds public conferences to stop the spread of fascism in Russia, which it considers a real danger in Russian society today. In 1995, the group led a seminar with the Russian-German Exchange entitled Neo-Nazism As an International Phenomenon: Common Danger. Recently, CW has focused on the issue of the right to privacy—a relatively new concept in post-Soviet law and society. It has held seminars in St. Petersburg on this topic, such as Legal Models of Personal Data Processing (1996) and Free Access to Information and Protection of Personal Data (1997). CW also publishes Russian translations of international human rights documents and Council of Europe documents for public use.

Since 1996, CW President Pustintsev has taken an active role in the public defense of Alexander Nikitin, the former Russian Navy officer charged with treason for his report on Russian nuclear hazards in the North Sea. As Chairman of the Public Committee in Defense of Alexander Nikitin, Pustintsev works with the Norwegian environmental group Bellona, Nikitin's former employer, to support Nikitin's defense.

## Crosses Charitable Foundation
Благотворительный Фонд
"Кресты"
Arsenalnaia nab. 7

195009  St. Petersburg
or
ul. Millionaia 5
North-West Polytechnical Institute
191186  St. Petersburg
**Tel:**      534-7298, 553-7289
**Contact:** Vladimir Korolev, President

This foundation helps prisoners obtain work skills and education to facilitate their return to society after release from prison. The Chance program offers prisoners training in professional farming through the cultivation of small garden plots and agricultural classes. The produce grown is also used as a valuable supplement to standard prison meals. The foundation also encourages prisoners to finish high school through a technical education program, Bachelors, which has been implemented by volunteer instructors of the North-West Correspondence Polytechnic Institute in two prisons over the past three years. Crosses also offers basic computer courses to inmates as well as events such as holiday celebrations and art exhibits.

## Foundation for International Professional Exchange
a/ya 377
196013  St. Petersburg
**Tel/Fax:** 312 6720
**E-mail:** itfipe@mail.wplus.net
**Contact:** Igor Tolochin, Ph.D.,
Resident Director for Europe and the NIS

See profile of FIPE in North American Organizations section.

## German-Russian Exchange
pr. Nevskii 104
191025  St. Petersburg
**Tel:**      273-9149
**Fax:**      272-2403

## Green World Environmental Association

a/ya 130
197371   St. Petersburg
**Tel:**       306-8883
**E-mail:**   fedorov@protection.spb.org
**Contact:** Alexander Fedorov
or
a/ya 68/7
188537   Sosnovy Bor, Leningrad oblast
**Tel/Fax:**  694-9481, 159-8437
**E-mail:**   greenwld@spb.org.ru,
            eugenia@teia.usr.pu.ru
**Web:**      www.spb.org.ru/greenworld/
**Contact:** Oleg Bogrov, Chairman;
Evgenia Makhonina, Assistant

Green World was founded in August 1988 as an environmental association in the city of Sosnovy Bor, located on the Gulf of Finland, 80 km to the west of St. Petersburg. It works to protect the marine ecosystem of the Baltic Sea region by disseminating information on the ecosystem and its environmental problems and lobbying for legal measures to save the Gulf of Finland coastline.

Green World monitors several environmental hazards in the Baltic Sea area, including a nuclear waste site in Sosnovy Bor. It also publishes the bulletins *Green World Baltic News* and *Nuclear News from Northwest Russia*. It plans to produce an analytical publication, *The Baltic Region—Our Habitat*. All publications are available in Russian and English.

## Innovations Center

ul. Dumskaya 1/3
191011   St. Petersburg
**Tel/Fax:**  310-0406
**E-mail:**   psp@mail.nevalink.ru
**Contact:** Dmitry Anashkin

The center organizes and supports projects that help neglected or disadvantaged children in the St. Petersburg area. The center's name, Innovations, refers to its goal of implementing creative, progressive methods in the social sector.

The group helped establish three clinics that offer medical, psychological and social assistance to disadvantaged youth and street children. One of the clinics, Lazaret, has aided over 400 children since opening in 1995. The center has also worked with a home for disabled children in Pavlovsk, helping to make bathrooms at the facility handicapped-accessible and renovating the home's physiotherapy area. Additionally, Innovations procured the volunteer services of a German physiotherapist who periodically visits the facility.

## Labor Confederation of St. Petersburg/Leningrad Region

Трудовая Конфедерация Санкт-Петербурга и Ленинградского Района
a/ya 189
192284   St. Petersburg
**Tel/Fax:**  314-5161
**E-mail:**   nerv@mail.wplus.net
**Contact:** Anatoly Savich, Deputy Chairman

The confederation unites 35 free trade unions from St. Petersburg and Leningrad oblast. It is a member of the Labor Confederation of Russia, which consists of the country's largest free trade unions.

The Labor Confederation bases its mission on complete independence from state management structures, and seeks to cooperate with all organizations that support the rights of workers. In February 1997, the confederation established the SST Information Center to support the information, publishing, and training needs of unions. The center organizes training seminars and publishes *The Independent Worker's Bulletin* as well as methodological manuals on trade union subjects.

## Mass Media Center
School of Journalism
St. Petersburg State University
1-ya Liniya, 26/606
199034  St. Petersburg
Tel/Fax: 323-0067
E-mail:  ruschin@DR2709.spb.edu
Contact: Dmitry A. Ruschin, Ph.D., Associate Professor

## Mass Media Laboratory
Faculty of Journalism
St. Petersburg State University
1-ya Liniya 26
199034  St. Petersburg
Tel:  218-4588
Fax:  218-3184
Contact: Julia Rakhmanova, Anna Sosnovskaya

The laboratory was founded at St. Petersburg University in 1994. It analyzes mass media and informational processes in northwest Russia, and has conducted several readers surveys for local newspapers, including *Natali, St. Petersburg Bulletin,* and *Business Chance,* in order to identify the interests, expectations, and advertising preferences of readers. The group also conducts marketing data and research for advertising firms.

## Memorial Society
Мемориал
ul. Razyeszhaya 9
St. Petersburg
Contact: Vladimir Shnitke, Board Co-Chair

See the profile of Memorial in the Moscow section.

## Nevsky Angel
Невский Ангел
ul. Gorokhovaia 5
190000  St. Petersburg
Tel:  312-1010, 315-5445
Fax:  315-2033
E-mail:  angel@mail.nevalink.ru
Contact: Vladimir Lukianov, Chairman

This organization provides social assistance, legal, and psychological consultations and training for social workers and NGO managers.

## NGO Development Center
Центр Развития Некоммерческих Организаций
a/ya 134 (postal address)
191186  St. Petersburg
ul. Malaia Koniushennaia, 5
191186  St. Petersburg
Tel/Fax: 325-8913, 325-8914
E-mail:  dra@infopro.spb.su, ndc@spb.org.ru
Web:  www.spb.ru/ptchela
Contact: Rosa Khatskelevich, Executive Director; Maria Fomchenko, Manager for International Contacts

The center was established in 1997 by the Russian-German Exchange to support the growth of third sector organizations in northwest Russia. It acts as a consultant for NGOs on legal, financial, and public relations issues and organizes seminars on such topics as NGO registration and how to set up a database. The center also advises organizations from abroad who are interested in starting projects in northwest Russia or in funding already existing programs.

The center publishes *Ptchela* (The Bee), a liberal-minded newspaper that focuses on social issues and organizations in the St. Petersburg area. Archived issues of *Ptchela* are available at the center's Web site. A library of third sector resources is available at the center's offices.

Under the auspices of the MANGO program (Methodological Assistance for NGOs funded by the European Union), the center is currently researching third sector development in Russia's northwest region by surveying existing groups as to their needs and challenges, establishing statistics on NGOs, and organizing working groups among regional NGOs.

The center has ten employees and cooperates with other resource centers in Novogorod, Pskov, Petrozavodsk, and Arkhangelsk.

### Nochlezhka Foundation
Фонд "Ночлежка"
ul. Pushkinskaia, d. 10
St. Petersburg
**Tel:**          119-2170, 273-9434,
                 119-2168
**Contact:** Valerii Sokolov

This foundation works with St. Petersburg's homeless population and in 1998 opened a homeless shelter in the city.

### Project Harmony–St. Petersburg
**Tel/Fax:** 274-5606
**E-mail:**  phstp@mail.nevalink.ru

### Psychological Crisis Center for Women
a/ya 604
191002   St. Petersburg
**Tel:**          375-0329
**Fax:**          315-9100
**E-mail:**  larisa@crisis.spb.su
                 sisters@sovam.com
**Contact:** Larisa Korneva, Alla Shoboltas

This center is committed to the eradication of violence against women. It provides a wide range of services, including education, training, counseling, and advocacy intervention in cases of sexual assault and domestic violence.

### Soldiers' Mothers Organization
Общественная организация
"Солдатских Матерей"
ul. Razyeszhaya 9
191002   St. Petersburg
**Tel/Fax:** 112-5058, 112-4199
**E-mail:**  smspb@iname.com
**Web:**     www.openweb.ru/windows/
smo/smo.htm
**Contact:** Ella M. Polyakova, Elena Villenskaya

Founded in 1991, Soldiers' Mothers provides practical assistance to military conscripts and their families. It assists people through the process of appealing for exemption from and/or deferment of military service for reasons of health, extreme family hardship, or conscientious objection. The group provides medical and legal consultation as well as moral support and education on legal rights and how citizens can exercise them.

Three times per week, Soldiers' Mothers holds receiving hours during which conscripts and their families can meet with volunteers experienced in the appeal process as well as lawyers and doctors willing to provide professional support for these appeals. The group provides access to the proper appeal forms and applications, often difficult to locate at official military or administrative offices. It also maintains files of all the people that receive assistance, including copies of their official appeals and complaints. In 1995, the Soros Foundation donated two photocopiers to the group in order to facilitate the appeals documentation process.

The group also maintains an up-to-date library of all legal texts pertaining to the rights of servicemen. It cooperates with a number of regional soldiers' mothers organizations in collective actions, information exchanges and participation in national conferences.

Soldier's Mothers publications include *The Defense of the Legal Rights of Conscripts: From Our Working Experience* (1995, St. Petersburg) and *The Rights of Conscripts and Servicemen in the Russian Army* (1995, St. Petersburg). The latter is a collection of photocopied newspaper articles addressing various issues of military service and the work of soldiers' mothers committees across Russia, produced with financial assistance from the European Union Phare/TACIS Democracy Program.

## Petersburg Center for Gender Issues

40/19 Vosstanija St. office 37
191123   St. Petersburg
**Tel:**   275-8722
**Fax:**   275-3753
**E-mail:**   pcgi@sisters.spb.ru
**Contact:** Olga Lipovskaia, Anna Kletsina

The center is an "educational, research, and political activity organization dealing with issues of gender inequality in Russian society." It is fully funded by the German Heinrich Böll foundation.

Since its formation in October 1992, PCGI has organized lectures and seminars on the following topics:

- Famous women in world history
- Contemporary status of women (sociological, political, personal aspects of women's lives in Russia)
- Feminist theory and methodology
- Feminist psychology and psychotherapy

- Cultural aspects of gender
- Health and reproductive rights of women

In 1994, PCGI held a Festival of Women's Art and organized an international conference, Feminist Theory and Practice: East-West, in 1995.. It also launched a public campaign and brought a legal suit against the Russian version of *Playboy*, and succeeded in stopping publication of pornographic images of female historical figures of Russia.

Current activities focus on:
- A campaign against trafficking of women
- A project to popularize gender and women's issues in the mass media
- Translation of women's studies classics into Russian (The center already has translated *Our Human Rights*, a women's human rights manual by Julie Mertus)
- A monthly newsletter *Posidelki* (the term means "get-togethers") for distribution to over 400 women's organizations throughout the NIS

Five women work in the center on a full- or part-time basis and about 25 others work as volunteers or on temporary contract.

## St. Petersburg Association of Scientists and Scholars (SPASS)

nab. Universitetskaya 5, k. 16
199034   St. Petersburg
**Tel/Fax:** 318-4124
**E-mail:**   root@spas.spb.su,
           didenko@spas.spb.su
**Contact:** Dr. Aleksandr Y. Vinnikov, Dr. Andrey L. Temkovskiy, Dr. Dilara K. Kambarova, Co-Chairs; Nellie I. Didenko, Secretary

SPASS was founded in 1989 by a group of researchers working to elect Andrei Sakharov for People's Deputy of the USSR. It currently unites approximately 700 scientists, scholars, educators, administrators, and policymakers from around Russia and the NIS. SPASS works to promote scientific freedom, open competition for funds, and collaboration with the government in the formulation of scientific policy. The group participates in national science policy and evaluates draft legislation pertaining to science. It also develops strategies for regional research and education. SPASS is the founder of a number of scientific institutes in Russia, including the European University in St. Petersburg, the St. Petersburg School of Religion and Philosophy, and the St. Petersburg School for Sociology of Science and Technology.

### "Strategy" Center for Political Science and the Humanities

Санкт-Петербургский
гуманитарно-
политологический центр
"Стратегия"
Ismailovskii per. 14, k. 411
198004  St. Petersburg
**Tel/Fax:**  112-6612
**E-mail:**  strateg@strateg.spb.su
**Web:**  www.glasnet.ru/~hronline/
ngo/strat/index.htm
**Contact:**  Aleksandr Sungurov, Director

Strategy works to promote the development of civil society, the growth of local government, and the strength of the electoral process in Russia. The group aims to foster cooperation among a variety of reformers, including academics, entrepreneurs, politicians, and social activists. Sungurov is the author of numerous scholarly publications on such themes as the role of scientists in developing democratic structures and the state of civil society in St. Petersburg today.

Much of Strategy's efforts are directed at encouraging the growth of local government structures. The center worked with St. Petersburg duma deputies on a legislation project in 1995 to increase the responsibilities of local government, and has acted as advisors to the St. Petersburg governor on this same topic. Together with the University of Birmingham, Strategy organized a series of seminars on decentralization of government power in 1995. In June 1997, the group hosted an international symposium in St. Petersburg called Local Government Controls in Post-Communist Countries.

### Transboundary Environmental Information Agency (TEIA)

Трансграничное
Экологическое
Информационное Агенство
a/ya 436
199000  St. Petersburg
**Fax:**  314-4128
**E-mail:**  teia@teia.org, editor@teia.org
**Web:**  teia.pu.ru/
**Contact:**  Elena Bakstova, Editor

TEIA promotes international nongovernmental cooperation by assisting in the distribution of information across border areas in the Baltic states, Finland, and northwest Russia. It publishes a biweekly electronic bulletin, *Transboundary and Environmental News*, on economic, environmental, and social issues impacting the region. The bulletin is available in English and Russian. The group is currently working on a project to increase Internet access for NGOs in northwestern Russia.

### Union of Journalists

Союз Журналистов
pr. Nevskii 70
191025  St. Petersburg

**Tel:**     273-4733, 273-2851 (library)
**Tel/Fax:** 272-4672
**E-mail:**  sprapic@glas.apc.org,
             annash@glas.apc.org
**Contact:** Anna Sharogradskaia,
Director; Irina Pyaro, Assistant
Director; Chris Hamilton, Freedom
Forum Librarian

The union is an affiliate of the National
Press Institute. See the profile of NPI in
the Moscow organizations section.

## "We Are Together" Mutual Assistance Club for Young Invalids

Клуб Взаимопомощи Молодых
Инвалидов «Мы Вместе»
ul. Zhukov 30, kor. 2, k. 430
198303  St. Petersburg
**Tel/Fax:** 153-0777
**E-mail:** kuzn@volspb.ru
**Contact:** Ravilya Fastova, Director

The club provides support to disabled
young people in the St. Petersburg area
by fostering friendships, sponsoring
excursions, hosting social events, and
providing job counseling and vocational training. The club recently started
a discotheque for disabled youth, the
first disco of its kind in the city. It
works with more than 150 disabled individuals ranging in age from 14 to 30.

The club also seeks to unite the
efforts of local groups for youth and the
disabled, regularly participating in a
Round Table Association of youth
organizations. In the summer of 1993,
the club represented Russia in a Peace
Assembly that took place in the former
Yugoslavia. It maintains close contact
with the Hungarian National Federation
of Disabled Persons.

## Wings Association for the Defense of Sexual Minorities

Ассоциация Защиты
Секуальных Меншеств
a/ya 108
191186  St. Petersburg
**Tel:**    312-3180
**E-mail:** krilija@ilga.org
**Contact:** Aleksandr Kykharsky,
President

When it registered in 1991 after much
legal opposition, Wings became the
first officially registered gay and
lesbian organization in Russia. The
group works to eradicate homophobia
and promote tolerance by educating the
populace about sexual minorities. It
also designs social support programs
and organizes cultural events for the
homosexual community.

## Women's Initiative Center

ul. Boiarova 16a
187020  Tosno, Leningrad region
**Tel/Fax:** (61) 29-403
**E-mail:** wic@neva.spb.ru
**Contact:** Irina Kniageva, President;
Nelli Bogachova, Public Relations

WIC was established in 1995 to help
women realize their personal creative
talents. The center runs the School of
Applied Arts and Crafts, which offers
two-month courses in traditional
Russian folk art such as ethnographic
dolls, traditional Russian lace, and
national dress.

Over 300 women have taken part in
these courses and have formed a
Masters Club, which organizes art fairs
and exhibitions for WIC graduates to
display their work. The center recently
established a Teenagers Business
Center, which provides teenagers with
vocational training.

### "Youth Association for the Hearing-Impaired" of the St. Petersburg Society of Disabled

Санкт-петербургская обществ.организация инвалидов с детства по слуху "Молодежная Ассоциация Слабослышащих"
a/ya 223
191194   St. Petersburg
**Tel:**      279-2023
**Fax:**     296-5426
**E-mail:**  spbmas@infopro.spb.su
**Contact:** Varvara Olshanskaia

The association was founded in 1996 to help hearing-impaired youth adjust to regular schools or attend institutes with special equipment. It arranges individual rehabilitation sessions for children with hearing problems, and provides advise and training to parents of deaf children. The group distributes literature about the medical, social, and psychological aspects of hearing disabilities to schools, parents, and youth.

## Samara (8462)

### Association for Social Support and Protection of the Disabled "Our Care"

Самарское общественное объединение социальной поддержки и защиты инвалидов "Наша Забота"
ul. Kuibyeshev 14, k. 1
443001   Samara
**Tel/Fax:** 15-04-09
**E-mail:**  flower@lib1.ssau.ru
**Contact:** Igor or Olga Sakharov

Our Care provides employment assistance to needy segments of the population, including families with many children, the disabled, and youth.

### "Center for Spiritual Culture" Interregional Public Organization

Межрегиональная общественная организация "Центр духовной культуры"
shosse Moskovskoye 16a
443056   Samara
**Tel:**      35-68-21
**Fax:**     35-86-08
**E-mail:**  root@rcdk.volgacom.samara.ru
**Contact:** Boris Oxmon, Director of External Relations

The center promotes education through cultural programs. It runs its own publishing house for cultural publications such as art books, albums, and posters. It also offers public access to short films and CD-ROM presentations on local and foreign artists and foreign cultures.

### Fund for Intellectual and Cultural Development

Фонд интеллектуально–культурного развития
ul. Leninskaia 137, k. 44
Samara
**Tel:**      33-29-58
**Fax:**     33-59-28
**Contact:** Irina Nikolaevna

This organization is involved in youth issues in the Samara region, and publishes the journal *Youth Bulletin of Samara*.

## International Association of Economics and Management Students (AIESEC)

Международная Ассоциация студентов економики и управоления
ul. Kubishevskaia 88
443099  Samara
**Tel:**      34-46-32
**Fax:**     00-02-33 (attn: AIESEC)
**E-mail:**  litv@samara.net
**Contact:** Maxim Sinelnikov

AIESEC arranges international internships for economics and business students, which range from one–six months in length. It also holds student discussion groups and conducts projects for youth involving practical management experience.

## International Information Bureau

Международное Справочное Бюро
ul. Uyanovskaya 19-23
443001  Samara
**Tel:**      33-55-30
**Fax:**     32-70-60
**E-mail:**  root@aded.samara.su
**Contact:** Olga Dovbysh

The bureau works to foster cooperation between nonprofit educational organizations around the world. It compiles and disseminates information about organizations, conferences, seminars and programs focusing on third sector issues and youth initiatives. The bureau also arranges exchanges for local youth and professionals with foreign organizations and helps local groups to locate foreign partners.

## Interregional Organization of Handicapped People

ul. Chernorechenskaia 50
443013  Samara

**E-mail:**  spider@transit.samara.ru
**Contact:** Vladimir Lasarev

## "Povolzhe" NGO Support Center of the Historical-Ecological and Cultural Association

Центр поддержки некоммерческих организациях–отделение исторически–экологическая культурная ассоциациая "Поволже"
ul. Tolstoi 47, k. 48
443010  Samara
**Tel:**      33-68-67
**Fax:**     29-51-79
**E-mail:**  povolzje@ssu.samara.ru
**Contact:** Natalia Bondarenko, Director; Olesia Chumak, Program Coordinator

*Povolzhe* (meaning "of the Volga region") was founded in 1996 to provide informational and technical support to local NGOs. The center offers consulting in accounting, taxation, management, project development, and relations with governmental bodies. It also maintains a database of nonprofit organizations in Samara oblast, other Russian cities, and abroad, as well as a library of literature on charitable organizations, nonprofit law, and European Council documents. The center has received financial assistance from the Eurasia Foundation, the British Know How Fund, and the BEARR Trust of the UK.

## Public Human Rights Center–Samara Region

Самарский региональный обшественный правозащитный центр
ul. Ventseka 38
443099  Samara
**Tel:**      33-76-93

The center began working in August 1997 to promote public awareness of human rights issues in the region. It sponsors educational programs on civil rights, democracy, law, and public life and holds a weekly consulting session for citizens seeking advice on specific human rights cases. In its first six months, the center worked with over 500 citizens. It also publishes a bulletin, *Pravozashitnik*, on regional human rights issues, and works with the local media to publish and televise information about human rights. The center is run primarily by volunteers, including local lawyers who provide free legal consultation.

## Research Group of Samara State University

ul. Maksima Gorkovo 61
443099   Samara
**Tel:**      32-39-50
**Fax:**      51-21-66
**E-mail:**  Kozina@glasnet.ru,
            p_romanov@yahoo.com
**Web:**      windoms/sitek.net/~soc
**Contact:** Irina Kozina, Pavel Romanov

The Research Group was formed in 1989 by sociologists at Samara State University to study problems related to secondary schools and national education, including such topics as socioeconomic challenges to students, adaptation of graduates to professional life, and urban culture. Projects have included Youth and Violence, Ethnic Relations in Samara, and the Culture of Childhood.

## Socio-Political Center of Samara

Общественно–полотический центр города Самары
ul. Ventsika 38
443099   Samara

**Tel:**      33-76-93, 32-35-07
**Fax:**      33-26-78
**Contact:** Viktor Ovsyanikov, Director

The center was founded in 1992 and provides office space and support services to political parties, social organizations, ethno-cultural centers, and other NGOs, working with an average of 30 organizations per year. It also acts as a referral service to groups requesting legal advice, program development, and technical consultation. The center gathers and distributes information about political and social organizations in the city and region and prepares analyses of the local political situation.

A recent study conducted by the center examined the behavioral patterns of various social sectors and age groups during a political campaign. The center has concluded from this study that reforms instituted "top-down," from government levels to the general public, are slow and insufficient. Its main goal, therefore, is to support and encourage "bottom-up" informational and educational activities that help society gain an awareness and appreciation of democratic institutions.

The center is currently developing a human rights education program for high school students and adults and is drafting new legislation on self-government in the Samara region, which it will propose to the regional administration. It has also developed a leadership training program on self-government, and established a leadership program for women in order to encourage their political activity.

## United Nations Association of Russia–Samara Regional Division

Русская Ассоциация Объединенных Наций–

Самарское региональное
отделение
ul. Maiakovskaia 19, k.5
443100   Samara
**Tel/Fax:** 32-89-54
**E-mail:** unarus@transit.samara.ru
**Contact:** Eugenia Kashouba,
Chairperson; Andrei Dolguikh, Vice
Chairperson

This division of the UN Association of
Russia conducts youth programs, provides consultation to the public on civil
issues through a Civil Advice Service
Bureau, and offers training programs
for local NGOs.

## Youth Palace of Samara
Самарский дворец детей и
молодежи
ul. Kuibyeshev 151
443010   Samara
**Tel:**       32-31-72
**E-mail:**   root@aded.samara.su
**Contact:** Tatiana Bodrova

This organization offers supplementary
education programs for youth.

## "Zabota" Society of Social Assistance and Employment for the Disabled
Общественное обсдипепие
социальной помочи и
занятости инвалидов
"Забота"
ul. Chapaevskaya 230
443010   Samara
**Tel:**       41-49-33
**E-mail:**   zabota@dionis.vis.infotel.ru
**Contact:** Natalia Usanova, General
Director

"Zabota" provides assistance to the
disabled and poor in the Samara region,
including job counseling and help with
employment searches.

## Saratov (8452)

## "Aid for Families and Children" Charitable Foundation
Благотворительный Фонд
"Помощь Семье и Детству"
ul. Radishcheva 72/25
410003   Saratov
**Tel:**       50-74-89
**E-mail:**   tatin@fachs.saratov.su
**Contact:** Tatiana Inozemtseva,
President

This charitable foundation was originally created by several women deputies from the Saratov Duma in 1992. Its
mission is to unite organizations from
the business, government, and nonprofit
sectors to work together on issues affecting children and families in Russia.

The foundation's accomplishments
include providing direct assistance to
200 needy families in the Saratov area,
publishing two reports on the third
sector in Saratov for use by the local
duma, and participating in a conference
on philanthropy and private charitable
giving in Russia, held in Moscow in
June 1998.

## The Eurasia Foundation
ul. Nemetskaia 54, etazh 2
410601   Saratov
**Tel:**       24-57-55, 91-01-59
**Fax:**       24-04-46
**E-mail:**   ef@saratov.su

See the profile for the foundation in the
section North American Organizations.

## Roundtable of Public Youth and Children's Organizations
Круглый Стол Молодежных и
Детских Общественных
Объединений города Саратова
Vishnevny pr. 9, k. 401
410040   Saratov
**Tel:**       17-07-87

**E-mail:** ngo@dirlin.saratov.ru
**Contact:** Dmitrii Kolchin, Secretary

This roundtable was established in
Saratov in October 1997, uniting 14
local groups concerned with issues
impacting young people. The goals of
the round table are:

- To disseminate information to
  Saratov youth organizations and
  promote cooperation between groups
- To encourage joint projects between
  the NGO and governmental sector on
  issues affecting children
- To participate in policymaking and
  legislative activity in the Saratov
  area, representing the interests of
  children and youth.

## Serpukhov (096)

### Serpukhov Society for the Monitoring of Penal Institutions

Серпуховское Общество
попечителей пенитенциарных
учреждений
ul. B. Kataninnaia, d. 14
142201    Serpukhov (Moscow Oblast)
**Tel./Fax:** 735-4470
**E-mail:** hrserp@glasnet.ru
**Web:** www.glasnet.ru/~hronline/
ngo/hrserp/index.htm
**Contact:** Irina Kotova, Vyacheslav
Zhuravsky

The society works to protect the rights
of the imprisoned by monitoring
conditions within Moscow oblast
penitentiaries and seeking legal redress
for rights violations. The organization,
however, strives to cooperate with local
government agencies whenever possible and work with—rather than
against—the authorities. It also strives
to educate prisoners and their families
on the rights of the imprisoned. The
group publishes a brochure entitled

*How the Convicted Can Protect Their
Rights*, which explains what constitutes
a rights violation within the prison
system. The brochure is distributed to
both prisoners and their families and is
also available on the group's Web site.

## Stavropol (8652)

### Southern Russia Resource Center

Южно-Российский Ресурс
Центр
ul. Dzerzhinskogo 116
355000    Stavropol
**Tel:**    35-66-70
**Fax:**    35-46-72
**E-mail:** srrc@avn.skeftel.ru
**Web:**    www.online.ru/people/srrc/

This is an affiliate of the Southern
Russia Resource Center in Krasnodar.

## Togliatti (8462)

### Fund "Development Through Education"

Фонд "Развитие через
образование"
bul. Lenina 3A, k. 4
445021    Samara
**Tel:**    26-94-67
**Fax:**    50-03-23
**E-mail:** def@is.tlt.ru
**Contact:** Vasily Efrosinin, Director

The mission of this organization is to
support and develop the educational
system of Togliatti.

## Tula (872)

### Orthodox Center of Spiritual Revival

F. Engelsa st. 135
300012   Tula
**Tel:**       31-04-36
**Tel/Fax:** 34-39-31
**E-mail:**   prcentr@tsu.tula.ru,
             ar@computerra.ru
**Web:**      prcentr.tulrci.edu.ru
**Contact:** Liudmila Romanovskaya,
President

The center was registered as a regional
public organization in mid-1996 and
has received the blessing of Serapion,
Metropolitan of Tula and Belev. "Charitable, spiritual, and enlightening
activities aimed at forming a Christian
consciousness" are the main goals of
the center. Members carry out their
activities in penitentiary institutions of
the Tula region (including one for
minors—there are 12 such establishments altogether). Since early 1997, the
center's representatives have been
visiting a prison camp near Tula and
reading katechizatorskie (catechism)
lectures. The center is forming Christian libraries in prison colonies and also
helping to build a church in one of
them.

Work among the "unprotected strata"
of the population (invalids, pensioners,
and indigent students and families) is
another sphere of the center's activities.
Center members read lectures about the
Christian faith and organise pilgrimages
to sacred places in the Tula region and
elsewhere in Russia when financial
resources allow. The center does not
have any regular financing and exists
only thanks to small donations.

## Tver (822)

### ONA Society of Independent Women Activists

Общество Независимых
Активистов–ОНА
ul. Novotorzhskaia 25
170000   Tver
**Tel:**       33-74-56
**Web:**      www.geocities.com/Athens/
2533/ona.html
**Contact:** Nadezhda Kruzhkova

ONA, meaning "she," was organized in
1995. It conducts a wide range of activities for women, including lobbying for
legislative change on pornography and
family law; organizing women's art
exhibitions, poetry readings and
medical/psychological lectures for
women; and publishing articles in local
papers about women's history in the
Tver region. Every March, ONA
organizes a week of women's cultural
and educational events to celebrate
International Women's Day.

### Tver Youth Film School

ul. Lunacharskogo 12-56
170003   Tver
**Tel:**       55-90-60
**Fax:**      57 00 00
**E-mail:**   kino@sch50.tmts.tver.su,
             school50@tversu.ru
**Contact:** Sergei Stepanov, Director

The school gives children the opportunity to learn about motion-picture
production. Stepanov is also the head of
a youth mime troupe that produces
silent films. The group won a prize for
one of their self-produced films in 1994
on the Russian television *program Sam
sebe rezhesser* (I'm the Director).

### Tver InterContact Group

Тверская группа
ИнтерКонтакт
a/ya 0565
170000   Tver

**Tel:**      42-54-19, 42-54-39
**Fax:**      42-62-10
**E-mail:**   inforuss@postman.ru,
              renyxa@redline.ru
**Web:**      www.volga.net/
**Contact:** Andrei Shkvorov, Director;
Dr. Marina Oborina, Director of
Academic Programs

Originally established in 1989 by a
group of students from the Department
of Modern Languages and Literature at
Tver State University, the InterContact
Group is currently active in the areas of
education, consulting, publishing, and
regional development. TIG offers a
Winter School for Applied Russian
Studies (two to seven weeks of intensive Russian combined with a cultural
program).

It also operates an Institute of International Education, a Translation and
Communication Center, and collaborates with the independent news
monitoring agency, What the Papers
Say (WPS), to produce the on-line
version of the WPS news digest.

### Women's Light Feminist Group
ul. Trekhsvyatskaya 31/11
170000   Tver
**Tel:**      34-33-73
**E-mail:**   val@usp.tunis.tver.su
**Contact:** Valentina Uspenskaya, Inessa
Obratsova

Women's Light is a research and
educational center aimed at educating
the public about women's history and
feminist studies. Founded in 1991, the
center prepares courses on gender/
feminist studies for university students,
presents public lectures on topics
related to gender, and produces a local
radio program.

Women's Light recently organized a
Computer Skills for Women program.
Volunteers from the center help unem-

ployed women and young girls learn to
use new technology, including e-mail
and word processing applica-tions. In
1997, the center began colla-bo-rating
with feminist groups in Moscow in
order to present training seminars on
women's rights and leadership in Tver.

## Ufa (3472)

### Human Rights Research Center of the Bashkortostan Republic
Исследовательский Центр по
Правам Человека Республики
Башкортостан
a/ya 11
450006   Ufa
**Tel:**      24-25-14
**Web:**      www.glasnet.ru/~hronline/
ngo/basckir/index.htm
**Contact:** Konstantin Potnin

The center is closely affiliated with the
Bashkortostan branch of the liberal
Yabloko party. It works to increase
public awareness of the rights and
responsibilities of citizens in a democratic society and to encourage the
development of rule of law and "legal
culture" in the republic. To that end, the
center publishes a quarterly newsletter,
*Know Your Rights*, and is developing a
civics curriculum for local schools. The
group also holds seminars to help
NGOs officially register.

### Women's Legal Defense Center of the Bashkortostan Republic
Центр правовой защиты
женщин Республики
Башкортостан
a/ya 105
450009   Ufa
**Tel:**      24-25-14
**Web:**      www.glasnet.ru/~hronline/
ngo/women/index.htm

**Contact:** N. Karavaeva

The center advocates equal rights and equal social status for women in the Bashkortostan Republic. It conducts sociological research on women in Bashkortostan society, and publishes a newsletter of rights violations and events of the both the local and world-wide feminist movement. Currently, the group is working to establish professional re-training courses for unemployed women and a program to encourage entrepreneurship among women.

## *Voronezh (0732)*

### "Grace" Interethnic Center of the Humanities
a/ya 327
394000  Voronezh
**Tel/Fax:** 49-99-49
**E-mail:** kim@vgasa.voronezh.su

### New View Association
Объединение Новый Взгляд
a/ya 212
394000  Voronezh
**Tel:**      78-51-19
**E-mail:**  kid@new_v.vrn.ru
**Web:**     ic.vrn.ru/~ppnew_v/
**Contact:** Katerina Tsetsura

New View is a volunteer-based organization seeking to empower children by developing new pedagogical methods and teaching networks. The group creates publications for school children and teenagers, and teaches children about computers and new technologies. New View is currently working on two projects: Children in the Information World and Children in the Computer World.

Children in the Information World includes such activities as:

- Children's Publishing Center
- Teen Press, a regional press agency designed to help adolescents stand up for their rights
- A newspaper for school children, *Pyatnitsa* (Friday)
- Internet access to resources for teenagers

As part of the Information World project, New View is providing regional schools with newspapers and periodicals and is currently working to establish an information center for dissemination of materials to children and teachers. The group believes that these initiatives will teach children and teenagers how to discuss important issues publicly and help them exercise their freedom of speech.

New View's second project, Children in the Computer World, includes:

- KidSoft, an annual spring festival that highlights the work of children in computing
- Creation of a home page on the World Wide Web
- Establishment of an electronic bulletin board for children in Voronezh
- Seminars and conferences for children interested in computers and programming.

### Society for the Protection of Women from Violence
ul. Liziukova 21, k. 127
394053  Voronezh
**Tel:**      73-83-19
**Contact:** Aida Kazminskaya

## *Yaroslavl (0852)*

### Center for the Formation of Sexual Culture
ul. Pionerskaya 19
150044  Yaroslavl

**Tel:**     55-66-91
**Fax:**    25-58-94
**E-mail:**  valya@cfsc.edu.yar.ru
**Contact:** Valya Shelkova, Director

In cooperation with Planned Parenthood of Northern New England, the center works to combat problems of high abortion rates, teen pregnancy, and the lack of information on sexuality, AIDS, and other sexually transmitted diseases in Russia.

## Yaroslavl Oblast Chamber of Commerce and Industry

Ярославская Областная
Торгово-Промышленная
Палата
Sovetskaya pl. 1/19
150000  Yaroslavl
**Tel:**     32-80-53
**Fax:**    32-88-85
**E-mail:**  tpp@hq.adm.yar.ru
**Web:**    www.adm.yar.ru/tpp/tpp.htm
**Contact:** Vladimir Lavrov

The chamber was created in 1992 and works in partnership with the Kassel Chamber of Commerce and Industry in Germany.

## Yaroslavl Distance Learning Center

a/ya 1063
Tsentralnaia Pochta
150000  Yaroslavl
**E-mail:**  world@dlc.edu.yar.ru
**Web:**    www.edu.yar.ru/
**Contact:** Yulia Belova, Deputy
Director; Larissa Zavylova, Education
Advisor

## Yaroslavl Regional Society of Pedagogy and Culture

Ярославское Областное
Общество Педагогики и
Культуры
ul. Respublicanskaya 108

150000  Yaroslavl
**Tel:**     30-40-32
**Fax:**    32-16-74
**E-mail:**  Nataly@yspu.yar.ru
**Contact:** Natalia Ivanova

The society develops new educational models for the Yaroslavl region and assists youth in their social growth and development. It also provides consulting in education and psychology, and has organized exchanges for teachers and students with schools in the Netherlands.

The group also established the Student's Psychological and Educational Club, in which students organize activities and workshops for disadvantaged youth, retired persons, and other members of the population suffering from the impact of transition.

# Russia: East of the Urals

## Country Code:  7

### Barnaul (3852)

#### Altai National Culture Center
Центр Национальной
Культуры
ul. Denisova 11, k. 2
Barnaul
**Tel:**     77-49-98
**E-mail:**  altai@yaj.dcn-asu.ru

The center is dedicated to reviving
public interest in the national culture of
the Altai through lectures, performances, and exhibits. It is currently
developing a project to produce and
market folk crafts (such as leather work
and perfumes) and local teas.

#### Civic Initiatives Support Center
Поддержка общественных
Инициатив
ul. Partizanskaya 41a, k. 4
656066  Barnaul
**Tel:**     36-75-52
**Fax:**     42-39-53
**E-mail:**  poi@alt.ru
**Contact:** Svetlana Churakova

This organization is a regional coordinator of the Siberian Civic Initiatives
Support Center. Established in 1997, it
serves as a resource center for NGOs of
Barnaul, Biysk, Rubtsovsk and Slavgorod. It provides local groups with
education and consulting services, and

works to develop links between the
third sector, the government, and the
media.

Since 1996, the center has conducted
26 seminars attended by approximately
540 third sector representatives. 1,040
hours of consultation have been provided to local NGOs and activists on
topics such as strategic planning, fund-
raising, tax issues, and marketing. Two
roundtables were held to encourage
cooperation between NGOs and the
government. The center has also held
two NGO fairs.

The center serves approximately 89
organizations in the city of Barnaul and
40 from the region as a whole. In May
1998, it received Eurasia Foundation
funding for the Altai Region NGO Resource Center. It has received additional financial support from USAID, the
Ford Foundation, the Mott Foundation,
and the Soros Foundation. Future plans
include projects to develop volunteerism and links with the private sector.

#### "Dream" Public Youth Organization
Молодежная Общественная
Организация «Мечта»
Pr. Lenina, d. 41, k. 4
646099  Barnaul
**Tel/Fax:** 24-18-60
**E-mail:**  mechta@yaj.dcn-asu.ru
**Contact:** Evgeny Lishin, Chairman

Dream was formed by a group of young
people striving to improve the conditions for youth in the Altai region. The
group's motto is "We dream of changing our lives for the better!" The goals
of the organization include creating
more job opportunities for college
graduates, protecting the rights of
young people, and encouraging civic
participation among youth.

In 1997, Dream formed a free legal consultation center for future draftees and current conscripts in the Russian military. Volunteers at the center advise conscripts as to their legal rights and obligations. Dream also publishes a monthly newsletter on draftees' rights that is distributed to the local branch of the Committee of Soldiers' Mothers and at draft offices.

## Ecological Club of Altai State University

Экологический Клуб Алтайского Государствен-ного Университета
ul. Dimitrova 66
656099   Barnaul
**Tel:**        36-86-41
**Fax:**        22-28-75
**E-mail:**   ecoclub@biogeo.dcn-asu.ru
**Web:**       arw.dcn-asu.ru/nko/ecoclub/index.ru.htm
**Contact:** Elena Repetunova, President

The club was established in 1994 by a group of students and professors from the Altai State University's biology department who were concerned about protecting the ecosystem of the Altai.

The club conducts a program to protect small creeks and rivers in the Altai. Volunteers study the flora and fauna surrounding creek and riverbeds and monitor water levels. Club members also conduct environmental education programs in local schools, teaching children about the importance of environmental protection and conservation.

## Student League of Altai State University

Алтайская краевая молодежная профсоюзная общественная организация "Лига студентов АГУ"
ul. Dimitrova 66, k. 411
656099   Barnaul
**Tel/Fax:** 22-23-39
**E-mail:**   chutchev@publish.dcn-asu.ru, kalinov@publish.dcu-asu.ru, shaidurov@publish.dcn-asu.ru
**Web:**       www.dcn-asu.ru/structre/index.ru.html
**Contact:** Vadim S. Chutchev, Chairman of the League; Aleksei V. Kokorin, Press Secretary; Vladimir N. Shaidurov, Deputy Chairman

Following the dissolution of Altai State University's student union in 1996, students formed a regional league in order to provide fellow classmates with social services, leisure activities, research assistance, and links with universities at home and abroad.

The league has helped to establish a grant program for ASU students. It provides the university's undergraduate and graduate students opportunities and financial support to participate in national and international conferences, find internships in leading Russian universities, and work in libraries throughout the former Soviet Union.

The league has its own student patrol and press club. It directed a theater group performance on St. Valentine's Day, and organized celebrations for the 25th anniversary of ASU. The group also organizes chess, basketball, paintball, and soccer tournaments for students. It plans to establish affiliates on ASU campuses in Rubtsovsk, Slavgorod, and Belokurikha in the future.

## Katun NGO Association

Ассоциация Неправительственных Организаций "Катунь"

pr. Lenina 66
656099 Barnaul
**Tel:** 22-09-08
**E-mail:** katun@glas.apc.org
**Contact:** Mikhail Shishin, Director

The association works to support the environmental movement in the Altai region by coordinating projects between ecological groups, working with staff of regional nature reserves and parks, and promoting ecological campaigns and events. It is currently working on a project to create a national park near the Katun River. The group is a regional affiliate of the Socio Ecological Union.

## "Luck" Public Charitable Foundation
Благотворительный
Общественный Фонд "Фарт"
Pr. Stroitelei 15-15
656015 Barnaul
**Tel:** 24-70-46
**E-mail:** fart@yaj.dcn-asu.ru
**Contact:** Svetlana Litvinova, Director

The goal of the foundation is to resolve societal problems through charitable works and volunteerism. Established in 1995, the foundation now has a bank of 30 volunteers who help carry out its projects.

In 1997, with help from the Eurasia Foundation, the Luck Foundation launched the Mercy School program, in which students from local schools provide assistance to elderly people in the community. The foundation maintains a list of 25 needy families in Barnaul and regularly donates food, clothing, and other assistance to them.

## Regional Foundation for the Development of Television and Radio in Altai Krai
Общественный Фонд
Развития Телевидения и
Радиовещания Алтайского
Края
656038 Barnaul
**Tel/Fax:** 42-14-87
**Contact:** Evgeny Semenikhin, Director

This foundation works to establish independent broadcast media in Altai Krai. It cooperates with local government to resolve freedom of speech issues and encourages cooperation between media groups at the federal, regional, and international levels.

## "Women's Alliance" Partnership
Некоммерческое парт-
нерство "Женский Альянс"
a/ya 1477
656066 Barnaul
**Tel/Fax:** 35-21-81
**E-mail:** women@barrt.ru
**Contact:** Natalia Sereda, Director;
Elena Shitova, Assistant Director of
International Affairs

Women's Alliance is a union of women's organizations of the Altai region. Formed in 1998, the union strives to create a strong and active sector of women's NGOs by engaging in social and legal advocacy programs for women. It has established a press center for women's NGOs, a crisis center for women, and a women's resource center. The group also conducts seminars on NGO development and conferences on women's issues. The partnership consists of 14 member organizations.

## Young Journalists of the Altai
Молодые Журналисты
Алтая
a/ya 661
656038 Barnaul (postal address)
pr. Sotsialisticheskii 68a, 3rd floor
Barnaul
**Tel/Fax:** 26-14-05
**E-mail:** yaj@yaj.dcn-asu.ru
**Web:** www.dcn-asu.ru/ic.projects/
journal/index.ru.shtml
**Contact:** Sergei Kanarev, Chairman

Young Journalists of the Altai was
formed in 1996 by a group of journalism students and professors from Altai
State University dedicated to the principle of a free press. The group operates an Info Center that serves the local
NGO community, providing Internet
access and training, access to databases
and relevant publications, and regularly
scheduled seminars on use of the media
to gain greater exposure for NGO projects and activities. Young Journalists
also offers specialized training and
seminars for journalists on topics such
as the Internet, unbiased election-
campaign reporting, and working with
the third sector.

The group serves as the regional
affiliate for the Moscow-based Agency
for Social Information, a news agency
that focuses on Russia's third sector.

## Chelyabinsk (3512)

## Chelyabinsk-Hanford Project
287 Pobedy
454021   Chelyabinsk
**Tel:**       33-44-47
**E-mail:** vs@chel-hanf.chel.su
**Contact:** Dr. Vyacheslav B. Sharov,

Chairman; Dr. Dimitry Ovsyanitsky,
Deputy Chairman

CHP began in 1992 as the result of
communication between Russian
physicians from the Chelyabinsk area
and members of the Washington state
chapter of Physicians for Social Responsibility (PSR). Both groups were
concerned about the health effects of
nuclear weapons production on local
populations surrounding the Chelyabinsk and Hanford sites.

Over $3 million in medical aid has
been sent to Chelyabinsk to help physicians treat patients with radiation-
related diseases. The group hopes to
educate the public on the health effects
of nuclear weapons production and
radiation exposure. There is an ongoing
exchange of physicians between the
two countries.

## Chita (3022)

## Agency of Public Ecological Expertise
Агенство общественных
экологических экспертиз -
АОЭЭ
ul. Chkalova 120
672000   Chita
**Tel:**       21-24-98
**Tel/Fax:** 21-26-05
**E-mail:** root@tasey.chita.ru
**Contact:** Irina Y. Malchikova,
Coordinator

The agency was created at the initiative
of the Baikal Foundation to promote
public environmental awareness and
conservation in the Chita and Aginsko-
Buryatsky regions. It conducts public
hearings, seminars, and consultations
on the environment, and seeks to in-

crease public activism to influence decisions of the local administration. It also promotes cooperation between the public and government in order to prevent environmental pollution and mismanagement of resources.

In 1996, the agency examined the results of a feasibility study for gold extraction on territory reserved for a national park. This territory has spiritual significance for Buddhists, as well as diverse fauna and flora. A licence for gold extraction had been issued in 1995 without consultation of the public.

As a result of the agency's activity and an accompanying enivornmental study conducted by the Baikal Foundation and Ecoline in Moscow, the license for gold extraction was revoked by local authorities and the territory remains intact.

The agency works in collaboration with Baikal Foundation, Baikal Watch, ISAR, Ecoline, and the U.S.-based Tahoe-Baikal.

### Baikal Foundation–Chita Office

Фонд Байкала–Читинское отделение
ul. Nedorezova 16 204
672014   Chita
**Tel:**      1-16-89, 1-24-98
**E-mail:**   chita@glas.apc.org
**Contact:** Tatiana Strizhova, Inga Zinoveva

The Chita branch of the Baikal Foundation works to protect the unique ecological makeup of the Lake Baikal region and to preserve the cultural traditions of local inhabitants. The group is currently working on establishing a program of volunteer caretakers to oversee local parks and nature reserves.

### Zabaikalsky Civic Development Center

Забайкальский Центр общественного развития
a/ya 279
672010   Chita
ul. Angarskaya 26
672007   Chita
**Tel:**      36-871
**E-mail:**   svetlana@dem.chita.su
**Contact:** Svetlana Bagina

ZabCDC was founded in November 1996 and established an NGO Resource Center in 1997 with support from Save the Children. A seminar ZabCDC conducted in 1996 in collaboration with local authorities resulted in the passage of a law on Provisions on Municipal Grants to NGOs in 1998.

Other projects of ZabCDC include a conference of Chita NGOs entitled Social Partnership: Government, Business, and NGOs, an NGO Leaders Club, publication of an NGO bulletin, and a roundtable, Charity in Chita: Traditions and Modernization. The center has provided services to over 69 NGOs and 355 people since its founding. It also serves as a regional coordinator of the Siberian Civic Initiatives Support Center.

## *Ekaterinburg (3432)*

### ACTR/ACCELS Ekaterinburg

American Information Center
ul. Mamina-Sibiryaka 193
620055   Ekaterinburg
**Tel/Fax:** 61-60-34
**E-mail:**   fsayekat@glasnet.ru
**Contact:** Susan Slivkin

See profile for American Councils for International Education in North American Organizations section.

## American Information Resource Center

ul. Mamina-Sibiryaka 193
620055  Ekaterinburg
**Tel:**        61-53-38
**Tel/fax:**  51-02-48
**E-mail:**   aic@irex.uraic.ru
**Web:**      irex.uraic.ru/airc
**Contact:** Natalia Shevchenko, Director

AIRC was opened in 1994 as a joint project of the United States Information Agency (USIA) and the Ekaterinburg Mayors' Library. The center provides access to information resources and supports the development of Russian professionals in the fields of business administration, economics, law, education administration, journalism/ communication, public policy and administration, and library and information science.

The center has a library, meeting rooms, and an Internet center with about 10 workstations. IREX's Internet Access Training Program is housed here (see IREX entry). The center also sponsors occasional exhibits and seminars.

## Army of Mercy

Армия Милосердия
pr. Lenina 52, корп. 2a, k. 1
620075  Ekaterinburg
**Tel/Fax:** 55-64-26
**E-mail:**  gif@dialup.mplik.ru
**Contact:** Ludmilla Dergunova, Manager

Army of Mercy was formed in reaction to the lack of material assistance for needy families and individuals in Ekaterinburg during the Soviet period. The group distributes to the disadvantaged basic humanitarian aid, such as food and clothing, donated by Western organizations.

## Center for Charitable Foundations and Organizations

Центр Благотворительных Фондов и Организаций
ul. Khokhryakova 104, k. 712
620063  Ekaterinburg
**Tel:**       22-30-39, 22-07-85, 22-34-17
**Fax:**      22-03-22
**Contact:** O. N. Chupakhin, President

This organization acts as a resource center for NGOs in the Ekaterinburg area. It collects and disseminates information on current legislation in Russia regarding the legal status and requirements for NGOs and helps new groups to register as official organizations. The center also holds training sessions and seminars for NGO leaders and staff to enhance their skills.

## Center for Environmental Education and Information

ul. Pushikina 9a, k. 402a
620219  Ekaterinburg
**Tel:**       51-02-11
**Fax:**      51-35-64
**E-mail:**  postmaster@ceti.mplik.ru
**Contact:** Larisa Strukova

The center is a regional support center for the ROLL project (see profile for Institute for Sustainable Communities, Moscow in Russia: West of the Urals).

## Center for Federalism Foundation

Фонд Центр Федрализма
ul. Komsomolskaya 37, k. 604
620219  Ekaterinburg

Tel: 49-44-03
Fax: 49-45-03
E-mail: fed@gentex.intec.ru
Contact: Andrei B. Franz, Vice Chairman

## Center for Social Support to Women

Центр социальной поддержки женщин
ul. Generalskaya 3, k. 301
Ekaterinburg
Tel: 65-87-41
E-mail: ekor@irex.uraic.ru
Contact: Elena Korotkih, Executive Director

This center was founded in 1997 with support from TACIS. It works to provide professional development and education services to women of Ekaterinburg and the Sverdlovsk region. The center offers computer training classes, job counseling, and individual consultations for women on interview techniques and self-image improvement.

## "Chance" Foundation for Children's Rights

Детский Правозащитный Фонд "Шанс"
ul. Bebelya 71
620034 Ekaterinburg
Tel: 45-55-33
Contact: Vera Strebizh, Director

The foundation acts as an advocate for children's rights by providing free legal consultations for children and parents and publishing materials on social issues that impact children. It has published booklets on the dangers of drugs and other problems faced by Russia youth.

## Ekaterina Charitable Foundation for the Development of Science and Education

ul. Frunze 76, pod. 3
620144 Ekaterinburg
Tel: 22-10-13
Contact: Valentin V. Korona

The foundation supports fundamental scientific research in biology, psychology, and archaeology. It provides support for scholars, innovative teachers, students, and others.

## Ekaterinburg Press and Information Center

Ural State University
K-83, Lenin Prospect 51
620083 Ekaterinburg
Tel/Fax: 55-59-05
E-mail: yuri.kotov@usu.ru
Contact: Ludmilla Shevchenko, Coordinator

This organization is an affiliate of the National Press Institute in Moscow.

## Free Research of the Urals

Свободные Исследования Урала
ul. Rodonitovaia 34, k. 57
620089 Ekaterinburg
Tel: 60-90-66
E-mail: explorer@online.ural.ru
Contact: Vladimir Ponomarev

Free Research of the Urals is a public organization that aids foreign individuals and groups interested in establishing projects in the Central Urals region. The organization will help with travel plans and accommodations, and can provide groups with the necessary information to start a project in the area.

## "Good Will" Charitable Foundation

Благотворительный Фонд
"Добрая Воля"
ul. Schmidt 44
620142   Ekaterinburg
**Tel:**      22-26-51, 22-26-56
**Fax:**      22-62-44
**E-mail:**  slk@etel.ru
**Contact:** Nikolai Geller, Director;
Elena Zirina, Assistant Director

Founded in 1994, Good Will works to
develop a sustainable and influential
nonprofit/NGO sector in the Ekaterinburg region. It has held a series of
seminars for leaders of local NGO and
organizations from other regions to
help develop interregional cooperation
between groups. It helped establish a
consulting service for NGOs, and also
organized a series of radio programs for
youth on ecological issues. Good Will
conducted some of the first independent sociological research on NGOs in
the Urals.

   In May 1997, the group sponsored
the All-Russia Conference of NGOs
Promoting Civil Society and Pluralist
Democracy. The conference brought
more than 30 NGO representatives
from 15 Russian regions to Ekaterinburg to discuss their experiences, share
knowledge, and develop joint projects.
The group is currently planning to
develop a training program to help
local NGOs learn vital marketing and
fundraising skills and thus become
more financially autonomous.

## Healthy Family

ul. Sheinkman 19, k. 154
62007   Ekaterinburg
**Tel/Fax:** 51-21-57
**E-mail:**  harbour@olga.c-burg.su
**Contact:** Olga Tsimerinova, President

This organization has worked with
Canadian Feed the Children on a
regional NGO development project.

## Legal Defense Regional Association of Sverdlovsk Oblast

Свердловское Региональное
Общественное Объединение
"Правовая Защита"
ul. Studencheskaia 51, k. 307
Ekaterinburg
**Tel:**      44-89-48
**E-mail:**  hrekat@glasnet.ru
**Contact:** Nellie Vovk, Chairperson

The association began in 1995 as a
public legal aid service working with
several human rights organizations,
such as the Committee for Soldiers'
Mothers, Memorial, and the Human
Rights Defense Center of Ekaterinburg,
that had no lawyers on staff to provide
legal consultation to clients. In 1997,
the association officially registered as
an independent organization to provide
legal consultations to NGOs and individuals in the Sverdlovsk region.

   Legal Defense also organizes roundtable discussions and seminars on legal
issues, advises other groups on establishing public legal consulting centers,
and has prepared draft legislation on
human rights issues at the local level.

## Memorial Human Rights and Information Center

Информационно-
правозащитной центр
"Мемориал"
a/ya 133
620102   Ekaterinburg
**E-mail:**  hrekat@glasnet.ru
**Contact:** Anna Pastukhova

The Memorial Human Rights Center serves as an informal "club" for various smaller human rights groups in the Ekaterinburg area. The organization helps groups obtain support for their projects, which includes finding partners for cooperative projects, informing groups of sources for financial aid, and providing them with needed publications and information resources. The center also sponsors Open University, a regularly scheduled series of public lectures on topics related to civic initiatives and democratic reform. Lecturers have included a legal expert who spoke about constitutional rights and an activist promoting alternative military service.

## "Open Society" Regional Center of Civic Initiative Support
ul. Vajner 16a
620014   Ekaterinburg
**Tel:**   51-42-27
**Contact:** Valdimir Popov, Vladimir Nevyantsev, Anna Pastukhova

## Ural Center for Social Adaptation of Military Personnel
Уральский Центр Социальной Адаптации Военно-Служащих
a/ya 960
620063   Ekaterinburg
**Tel:**   22-30-39
**Fax:**   22-03-22
**Contact:** Nikolai Khomets, Director

The Ural Center helps former military personnel and their families readjust to civilian life. The center works with non-governmental and state organizations to help their clients find employment, vocational training, housing, legal aid, and medical care. The group is a partner organization of the Center for Charitable Foundations and Organizations.

## Ural Foundation for Social Innovations
Turgenev St. 13, k. 148
620219   Ekaterinburg
**Tel:**   56-91-35
**Tel/Fax:** 56-90-98
**E-mail:**  ufsi@tehnec.ru
**Contact:** Andrey Vybornov, Chairman; Konstantin Kiselev, Executive Director; Elena Volynkina, Public Relations and Media Executive

UFSI was founded by a group of faculty, alumni and scientists from Ural State University, the Institute of Philosophy and Law of the Ural Branch of the Russian Academy of Sciences, and the Ural Academy of Civil Service of the President of Russia. It supports the development of projects in the fields of education, culture, science, economics, and media, and provides job placement and career development services to students and young professionals.

The foundation administers a training program, Open Governing, for the city administration of Nizhny Tagil. The program includes lectures and seminars presented by specialists of the regional administration and professors of local academic institutes. Short versions of the program are also offered in the towns of Rezh and Talitsa in Sverdlovsk oblast.

UFSI's project For a Free and Responsible Press provides educational seminars and roundtables for young journalists, publishes the magazine *STUDIO,* monitors the regional press to ensure that news events are covered fairly and without bias, and operates an independent television studio allowing young journalists to produce feature programs for use by local TV channels.

Another UFSI program focuses on assistance to drug addicts. Since 1997, the group has conducted a 24-hour crisis hotline, Telephone of Trust, for drug addicts and their families. The hotline provides psychological counseling as well as information about medical and legal services in Ekaterinburg. The project is supported by the Eurasia Foundation. UFSI also participates in the annual youth conference, Young Leaders of the 21st Century, held in Ekaterinburg since 1995, and publishes the newspaper *CAREER-Ural*.

In order to help finance its programs, UFSI has organized a commercial consulting service, the Marketing Research Center, which provides organizations and enterprises with evaluations of their operating environment and internal functions, including analysis of market conditions for specific sectors, strategic planning, marketing and public relations.

### Ural Region Ecological Foundation

Уральский Экологический Фонд
pr. Lenina 24/8, k. 428
620014   Ekaterinburg
**Tel:**      51-06-40
**Fax:**     55-72-27
**E-mail:**   postmaster@ecofond.intec.ru
**Contact:** Alexander Chernyaev, President; Gennadyi Rashchupkin, Executive Director

UREF was founded in 1989 by a group of scientists, journalists, academicians, and citizens concerned about environmental conditions in the city of

Ekaterinburg and Sverdlovsk oblast. The group gathers data and statistics on regional environmental issues and uses this information to lobby local government bodies and to raise public awareness. It estimates that its lobbying has resulted in the adoption by local authorities of six laws in 1996 on issues such as park use and animal control and three laws in 1997.

The group also publishes a monthly news bulletin that reports on environmental issues, activities of ecological groups in the Sverdlovsk region, and the relationship between ecological NGOs and the local government.

## Gorno-Altaisk (38822)

### Altai Children's Foundation

Детский Фонд Республики Алтай
a/ya 197  (postal address)
ul. Ulgasheva 13
659700   Gorno-Altaisk
**Tel:**      63-131
**E-mail:**   raisa@detfond.gorny.ru
**Contact:** Raisa Saimunova

The fund was founded in 1987 to promote the legal rights of children in accordance with the UN Convention on Children's Rights. It works to strengthen the status of children in society, and represents children's interests to legislative and executive bodies at all levels. It also conducts training programs and roundtables, fosters cooperation with government and business, and works to develop local volunteer initiatives.

The Fund has served as a regional coordinator of the Siberian Civic Initiatives Support Center (Novosbirsk) since 1995. In 1997-1998, it received a grant from the Eurasia Foundation for the project, Supporting NGOs in Altai Republic, and a grant from SCISC for the project, Legislation Concerning Housing for Orphanage Graduates.

## Irkutsk (3952)

### A. Luboslavsky Foundation for Human Rights and Freedom
Иркутский общественный благотворительный фонд А. Люьославского по защите прав и свобод человека
ul. Sukhe-Batora 10, k. 4-5
664011   Irkutsk
Tel/Fax: 33-32-92
Contact: Liubov Bashinova, Director

This human rights organization strives to provide social assistance to residents of Irkutsk. It is working to develop a network of local human rights services and organizations.

### Angara Women's Union of the Baikal Region
Байкальский региональный союз женщин "Ангара"
ul. Gogolia 75, k. 58
664074   Irkutsk
Tel:        34-24-19
Fax:        34-20-20 (attn: Shirobokova)
Contact: Albina Shirobokova, Director

Angara has been active in the Baikal region since 1992. It is associated with nearly 30 different organizations, providing consultation and support for women in a variety of areas. Angara organizes educational programs including computer courses and leadership skills training for women. The group also provides an anonymous telephone crisis line for victims of physical and

sexual assault. Angara's staff is aided by 30 volunteers.

### Baikal Center for Ecological and Citizen Initiatives
Байкальский Центр Экологических и Гражданских Инициатив
a/ya 1360 (postal address)
664000   Irkutsk
ul. Chaikovskogo 5
Museum of Irkutsk History
664000   Irkutsk
Tel:        38-17-87
Fax:        43-23-22
E-mail:   irkutsk@glas.apc.org
Contact: Irina Birnbaum-Diatlovskaia, Director; Zhanna Aseeva, Olga Moyiseeva

The center was founded in 1993 with help from the U.S.-based environmental organization Earth Island Institute. It serves as an information clearinghouse and supports local and international efforts to preserve Lake Baikal and restore the ecosytem of the Baikal region. The center develops environmental education programs on Lake Baikal's ecosystem for local schools.

   In 1996, the Baikal Center published a directory of individuals and groups involved with environmental activism in the Baikal region.

### Baikal Ecological Wave
Байкальская Экологическая Волна
a/ya 21
664033   Irkutsk
Tel:        46-75-47
Tel/Fax: 46-74-76
E-mail:   sutton@bew.sei.irk.ru
Contact: Jennie Sutton, Co-Chairwoman

In 1990, a group of Irkutsk citizens gathered to discuss ways in which they could work together to protect the Lake Baikal region. The organization resulting from this collaboration, Baikal Ecological Wave, disseminates environmental information in order to protect the lake and its ecosystem. The group also acts as a watchdog, performing independent monitoring and lobbying for further protection of the lake.

Baikal Ecological Wave developed an environmental education network of schools and youth organizations. It publishes a journal, *Wave*, that reports on ecological activities, issues, and projects impacting the Baikal region. The group helped to stop and reverse deforestation in the Vityaz nature preserve in 1992.

Currently, Baikal Ecological Wave is working with ISAR and Baikal Watch (part of the Earth Island Institute) on the Nerpa Project. Nerpa are freshwater seals that are found only in Lake Baikal. Project members will survey local people, hunters, and scientists to assess the state of the nerpa population at Baikal, as well as the impact of nerpa hunting on the local population, in order to make recommendations on how the hunting can be reduced or stopped.

## Baikal Foundation
Фонд Байкала
ul. Proletarskaia 7/18
Irkutsk
**Tel:**      46-49-68, 34-08-70
**E-mail:**   anatoli@bienru.irk.ru
**Contact:** Anatolii Vinober, Vladimir Molozhnikov

The Baikal Foundation was established in 1989 with a mission to preserve the unique ecosystem of the Lake Baikal region. It seeks to bring together various elements of society to resolve ecological and social problems impacting the Baikal region. Independent branches of the foundation are located in Ulan-Ude and Chita.

## Citizens' Information Initiative
ul. Ulan-Batorskaia 1, k. 120
664000   Irkutsk
**Tel:**      46-24-29
**Fax:**      43-45-36
**E-mail:**   citzinfo@irk.ru
**Web:**      www.teleport.com/
~citzinfo/grin.shtml
**Contact:** Maria Safonova, President

CII was formed in 1994 with funding from the Eurasia Foundation to establish a center for professional development in Irkutsk. Currently it also acts as an East Siberian representative for Interlegal, based in Moscow, and coordinates projects for the group Ecologically Sustainable Development, based in New York. CII helped Ecologically Sustainable Development realize two projects (one in Bolshoe Goloustnoe and another on Olkhon Island) promoting sustainable land and energy use in the Irkutsk oblast.

CII provides logistical, communication, and networking services for foreign and Russian organizations, businesspeople, and Irkutsk professionals such as scientists, doctors, and journalists. It offers consultations to local organizations on writing grant proposals and business plans and provides information about organizations and businesses in Irkutsk to potential partners abroad.

## Dialogue Information and Analytical Center
52-11 K-M-Stadt Prospekt
664057   Irkutsk

**Tel/Fax:** 43-57-96
**E-mail:** sutton@bew.sei.irk.ru
(indicate for Dialogue Center)
**Contact:** Rimma Dorozhkina,
Chairwoman

The center was formed by a group of journalists, teachers, psychologists and lawyers concerned about the deterioration of the family in contemporary Russia. The goal of the center's current project, The Institution of the Family in the Mass Media, is to inform and consult citizens of Irkutsk about issues concerning the family and to campaign for improvements in social policies affecting families.

Dialogue is also collaborating with the local Department of Education to open a "laboratory of family politics" that will collect and analyze information and issues affecting family relationships. This information would then be used to help create better state policies and procedures regarding families and children.

## EPRA Ecological Law Foundation

Фонд Экологическое
Правоведение
ul. Mamina-Sibiryaka 96
664058 Irkutsk
**Tel:** 46-19-26, 31-01-85
**E-mail:** root@epra.irkutsk.su
**Contact:** Nellie Romanova, President

EPRA was established in 1995 to develop the field of environmental law, provide legal advice to local environmental organizations, and promote the rational use of natural resources. The foundation's staff includes one scientist and several lawyers with backgrounds in environmental land use.

In 1996, EPRA established a legal consulting center for local groups involved in environmental projects. In July 1998, the foundation held a conference on human rights protection for environmental activists, attended by lawyers from Siberia and the Russian Far East. As a result of the conference, participants resolved to create a Siberian and Far East Lawyers Association.

## IREX–Irkutsk

Irkutsk State Pedagogical Institute
ul. Nizhnaia Naberezhnaia 6, k. 232
664053 Irkutsk
**Tel/Fax:** 24-05-59
**E-mail:** irex@irex.irkutsk.su

See profile of IREX in North American Organizations section.

## Project Harmony–Irkutsk

**E-mail:** phirkutsk@ic.isu.ru

See profile of Project Harmony in North American Organizations.

## "Revival of Siberian Land" Youth Charitable Fund

"Возрождение Земли
Сибирской" Молодежный
благотворительный фонд
a/ya 2144
ul. Kasianova 1a, k. 5
664048 Irkutsk
**Tel/Fax:** 26-70-13
**E-mail:** georn@rls.isu.runnet.ru
**Contact:** Georgii Gurullin

This organization began working in June 1994 to inform the local population about environmental and social issues and nonprofit sector development in the region. It promotes the rational use of natural resources and environmental protection in Siberia, with a particular emphasis on agriculture and land use. The group works with environmental organizations throughout Irkutsk oblast and abroad, including the Young Farmers' Union and the Future Farmers of America.

In 1997-98, the group provided 1,170 consultations for local groups and conducted 16 NGO seminars. It also held 17 meetings of the United Council of Nonprofit and Civic Organizations, two NGO Fairs, and six roundtables about democratization and third sector issues.

It has served as a regional coordinator of the Siberian Civic Initiatives Support Center (SCISC) since 1995, and publishes an NGO newspaper, *Nonprofit World,* in collaboration with SCISC. The group has received grants from Save the Children/SCISC.

## Society for Development of the Fur Trade
Общество поддержки развития скорняжных ремесел
ul. Timiryazeva 51
664011   Irkutsk
**Tel/Fax:**  25-16-08
**E-mail:**  skiner@irmail.ru
**Contact:** Vladimir Malinovich, President; Elena Ivanova, Deputy President

The society deals with legal issues of fur production and trade. It promotes the formation of a legal, regulated fur market in Russia, and is working to strengthen relations and trade with the Mongolian fur industry.

## Kemerovo (3842)

### Beauty Club
ul. Proletarskaia 18-84
650055   Kemerovo
**Tel:**        32-25-52, 21-30-50
**E-mail:**   beauty_club@hotmail.com
**Contact:** Tatiana Khobotskaia, Director

Founded in 1998, the club works with young men and women to help them develop positive self-images and professional skills. The club offers self-improvement seminars and encourages young people to pursue higher education. It also offers computer training.

### Civic Organization "Initiative"
Общественная организация "Инициатива"
ul. Nogradskaya 3, office 18
650099   Kemerovo
**Tel:**        36-48-67
**Tel/Fax:** 36-37-65
**E-mail:**   root@cmk.kemerovo.su
**Contact:** Irina Rondik

Initiative was established in 1997 as a regional representative of SCISC. The group provides consultation on grant writing and holds seminars on NGO development. It also has developed a fundraising center with financial support from the Eurasia Foundation. In 1998, Initiative organized two competitions for NGOs: The Most Socially Valuable Project and The Best NGO Sponsor. An NGO fair held by Initiative in the summer of 1998 included presentations of local NGOs and roundtables to discuss possible cooperation with the government and business sectors.

## Khabarovsk (4212)

### Business Women's Union
Некоммерческое парт-
нерство "Союз деловых
женщин"
ul. Gogolia 21, k. 41
680000   Khabarovsk
**Tel/Fax:** 23-44-92
**Contact:** Svetlana  Zhukova, Director;
Anastasia Blinkova, Coordinator

The union was created to provide support to professional women in the
Khabarovsk region. It conducts seminars, offers consultations, and organizes meeting with prominent businessmen and lawyers for local businesswomen. The union also publishes
articles about businesswomen in newspapers and magazines. It has received
support from the Eurasia Foundation.

### Center of Medical and Ecological Research
Хабаровская краевая
общественная организация
"Центр медико-
экологических проблем"
ul. Muravieva-Amurskogo 35, k. 341
680000   Khabarovsk
**Tel:**     32-88-78
**Fax:**    22-78-08
**E-mail:**   ryabkova@ecomed.
khabarovsk.su
kovalsky@ecomed.khabarovsk.su
**Contact:** Vlada A. Ryabkova,
Chairperson; Yurii G. Kovalsky

The center, which focuses on environmental problems of the Far East region,
conducted and publicized an
environmental study in the city of
Amursk. The center has about 70
volunteers and 10 employees.

### Center of Public Information of the Far East Academy of Sciences
Центр общественной
информации Дальневосточ-
ной Народной Академии
Наук
ul. Muravieva-Amurskogo 19, k. 305
680002   Khabarovsk
**Tel:**     32-56-10
**Fax:**    32-59-07
**E-mail:**   office@academy.khv.ru
**Web:**    www.ngo.khv.ru
**Contact:** Oleg S. Subbotenko, Director

This center coordinates the activity of
NGOs in regions of the Far East. It has
about 300 members, and conducts
research, organizes conferences, and
provides technical support for regional
groups. The center also created the
Union of Public Coordination in
Khabarovsk.

### Children's Arts and Crafts Center
Краевой детский центр
развития художественных
ремесел
ul. Zuparina 88
680002   Khabarovsk
**Tel:**     32-93-26, 32-60-72, 21-02 46
**Fax:**    32-60-56
**Contact:** Natalia V. Martynova,
Instructor; Viktoriia N. Khan, Director

The center provides resources and
instruction to children in order to
stimulate creativity at an early age. It
organizes exhibitions and seminars and
enrolls its members in international
competitions for children. The center is
the successor to the regional organization Kultura.

## Coordination Council on Public Health of the Interregional Organization of Economic Interaction "Far East and Zabaikalie"

Координационный совет по здравоохранению межрегиональной ассоциации экономического взаимодействия субъектов федерации Дальнего Востока и Забайкалья
ul. Muravieva-Amurskogo 19
680002  Khabarovsk
**Tel:**      32-45-71, 32-49-36
**Fax:**     32-59-07, 32-86-16
**E-mail:**  fema@online.fareast.ru
**Contact:** Vladimir A. Demenev , Executive Director; Stanislav V. Vavilov, Chairman; Aleksandr V. Kravets, Deputy Chairman

The council was created in January 1998 at the initiative of 14 regional governors of the Far East and Zabaikalie seeking to improve interregional coordination of public health care issues. The council has the following goals:

- To coordinate the activity of various committees, departments, and state agencies in order to improve health care services for local residents
- To compile a list of recommendations for improvement of health services and medical education in the region, and to participate in the drafting of health care legislation and insurance policies
- To establish the Far East Center for Medical Research
- To organize conferences of interregional health care associations, promote research on public health conditions, and arrange exchanges

and training for medical staff and researchers

Members of the council participate in parliamentary sessions of the Far East and Zabaikalie regions, where they discuss legislation on healthcare and develop public health programs.

## Creative Youth Center

Центр творческой молодежи
ul. Muravyeva-Amurskovo 19
Khabarovsk
**Tel:**      33-56-10
**Fax:**     32-59-07
**E-mail:**  office@academy.khv.ru
**Contact:** Oleg Ivutin, Director

The center created a Youth Parliament to involve young people in the public life of their region and develop their interest in legislation affecting their communities.

## Medical Association of the Khabarovsk Region

Медицинская ассоциация Хабаровского края
ul. Kransnodarskaia, 9
680009  Khabarovsk
**Tel:**      37-62-20
**Fax:**     37-29-92
**E-mail:**  hosp@dvmc.khv.ru
**Contact:** Mikhail I. Petrichko

Established in 1994, the association coordinates the efforts of regional medical workers, and works to protect their rights and promote public health care reform. It developed a system of medical standards, organized a number of international conferences, and conducted medical examinations in several criminal cases. The association has 456 members.

## Regional Association of Lawyers in Khabarovsk

Хабаровская краевая
ассоциация юристов
Amurskii bulvar 45
Khabarovsk
**Tel:** 21-19-69, 34-10-29
**Fax:** 34-20-97
**Contact:** Liudmila Gros, Chairman

The association was created in 1996 to provide lawyers with the opportunity to communicate with one another and help educate citizens on legal issues. It has conducted a number of conferences, established an arbitration tribunal, and helped submit several legal claims. Members of the association are professional lawyers who volunteer their services.

## Regional Public Association of Professional Psychologists in Khabarovsk

Хабаровская региональная
общественная организация
профессиональных
психологов
ul. Krasnorechenskaia 112, k. 307
680045 Khabarovsk
**Tel:** 36-48-42
**Contact:** Klara I.Vorobyova , Provost of the State Institute of Arts; Irina V. Pakhno, Executive Director of the Personal System School of Management

Created in 1997, the association strives to consolidate efforts of psychologists of the region to improve standards of counseling. It is divided into three divisions–pedagogy, social psychology, and medical psychology. Members of the association communicate with prominent psychologists of the Russian Federation and work in the children's rehabilitation center.

## Russian-American Education Center (RAEC)

ul. Serysheva 47, k. 205
680056 Khabarovsk
**Tel:** 34-37-34
**Tel/Fax:** 34-28-21
**E-mail:** arc@raec.khv.ru
**Web:** www.khv.ru/raec/
**Contact:** Tamara N. Silukova, Director; Marina Shesterkina, Administrative Manager

RAEC was founded in 1994 and is one of four centers organized by the American Russian Center at the University of Alaska, Anchorage. It is financed primarily by USAID. The centers— others are in Yuzhno-Sakhalinsk, Yakutsk, and Magadan—work in conjunction with local educational institutions. Their mission is to train Russian entrepreneurs, promote the development of Russian small business activities in the Far East, and foster linkages between Russian and US companies. The Russian co-founder of the Khabarovsk center is the Far East State University of Transportation.

Alaska is a particularly valuable source of expertise in fields relevant to Russia's Far East including resource extraction, cold weather construction, and infrastructure development. RAEC serves as a bridge over which Alaska's considerable expertise on northern technical, social and economic issues can be transferred to Russia in order to help the Far East region develop as a Pacific power.

To this end, RAEC provides training courses and seminars in business planning and management, individual consultations, Internet services, and specialized training courses for Russian business people in Anchorage. It also arranged meetings for alumni of the business club, and maintains a business library.

RAEC recently received a grant to create the Regional Universal Resources Center in support of regional NGO activities.

### Support Center for Cultural Heritage Organizations of the Khabarovsk Region

Координационный центр поддержки некоммерческих организаций, занимающихся сохранением и возрождением культуры народов, проживающих на территории Хабаровского края
ul. Zaparina 88
680002   Khabarovsk
**Tel:**       32-96-09
**Fax:**      33-96-09
**E-mail:**   sveta_stetskaia@hotmail.com
**Contact:** Svetlana Stetskaya, Chief Coordinator

The center was created in 1997 with help from the Eurasia Foundation. Its goal is to distribute information and assist ethnic-cultural clubs in Khabarovsk. It has provided office space to several such clubs, and filmed a documentary about organizations striving to revive local culture and traditions.

### Women's Union

Союз женщин Хабаровского края
ul. Frunze 69a
680000   Khabarovsk
**Tel:**       36-37-14, 21-02-96

**Fax:**       36-10-79
**Contact:** Galina Turkova, President; Ludmila Olshanova

The union was formed in 1995 to protect the rights of women in the Khabarovsk region and provide assistance to women in crisis situations and families with many children. It has organized a *Babie Leto* (Indian summer) fair for businesswomen. It organizes meetings, conferences, and roundtables to discuss assistance measures for local families. The union has 49 members.

## Krasnoyarsk (3912)

### Friends of the Siberian Forest

Друзья Сибирских Лесов
a/ya 26779
660036   Krasnoyarsk
**Tel/Fax:** 43-88-37
**E-mail:**   andrei@fsf.krasnoyarsk.su
**Contact:** Andrei Laletin

Friends of the Siberian Forest promotes sustainable forest use and the development of protected woodlands in Siberia. The group is a member of the International Network for Protection of the Taiga.

### Krasnoyarsk Center for Community Partnerships

a/ya 27027
660077   Krasnoyarsk
**Tel/Fax:** 55-33-73
**E-mail:**   echoal@krsk.ru

KCCP, the first school-based community resource center in Siberia, works to foster grassroots civic activism in Krasnoyarsk and Siberia. It assists in the formation of active, mutually beneficial school-community partnerships, and encourages the growth of volunteerism and the nonprofit sector. It is also involved in civic education projects in schools, providing teachers, parents and students with the information and skills to initiate community projects based on their own beliefs, interests, and ideas.

In 1998, KCCP worked with the U.S.-based organization ECHO to conduct a series of intensive training sessions for local teachers and administrators. The sessions focused on developing schools as community resource centers for grassroots activism and democratic change. In 1997, KCCP helped organize the first city-wide program on youth volunteerism in Krasnoyarsk.

Since its creation in 1996, KCCP has also provided citizens with legal and practical information on starting NGOs. It has offered "incubator" services such as access to meeting rooms, office machines, and the Internet to already established groups.

## Krasnoyarsk Regional Environmental Movement

ul. Lenin 41, k. 5
660049   Krasnoyarsk
**Tel:**      65-26-30
**Fax:**     27-54-19
**E-mail:**  kras@glas.apc.org
**Web:**     www.glasnet.ru/~kras/
**Contact:** Vladimir I. Mikheev, Chairman

KREM was founded in 1989 when it joined forces with the first ecological organization in Krasnoyarsk, Green World, to protest the expansion of nuclear activity and plutonium production in the region. The first plutonium production plant in the region, the Krasno-

yarsk Mining and Chemical Combine (KMCC), began operating in 1958. An underground facility, KMCC consists of three production reactors, only one of which is still in operation today. Plans are currently under way for construction of a reprocessing plant, RT-2, and a storage facility for nuclear warheads is already being built. More than four million cubic meters of radioactive waste and ten pounds of plutonium have already been injected into the ground water of the Enisey River.

Describing the local population's reaction to nuclear activity in the region, KREM chairman Vladimir Mikheev notes that "in the time of the Cold War, when this military facility was operated in full capacity, the public was not aware of the risk imposed to the environment and peoples' health by plutonium production in the region. Only under Gorbachev, and especially after Chernobyl, did it become impossible to conceal information about environmental damage from nuclear military facilities. Perestroika gave an impetus to environmental activism, and citizens began organizing themselves into public interest groups."

KREM is one of these groups and has played an active role in fostering public opposition to further construction at KMCC, publicizing information about the extent of radioactive contamination in the region. Expeditions with specialists on the Yenisey River allowed the group to gather critical facts about contamination of the river's watershed, and Green World and KREM collected more than 50,000 signatures of protest against construction of the RT-2 plant.

In September 1994, KREM and the SocioEcological Union held the Second International Radioecological Conference, entitled, After the Cold War: Disarmament, Conversion, and Safety, under sponsorship of the Center for Citizen Initiatives. It also conducted the Third International Radioecological Conference, The Fate of Spent Nuclear Fuel: Problems and Reality in 1996.

In 1997, the group collected 86,000 signatures in support of a referendum to ban construction of the RT-2 plant, although this referendum in turn has been banned by authorities. In 1998, KREM published the book *MCC: Independent View*, containing information about KMCC, its construction problems and environmental impact of the RT-2. It is planning to establish the Center on Nuclear Nonproliferation in Krasnoyarsk in order to expand its public education programs and citizen action against KMCC activity.

## Red Cross of Russia–Evenkiya Committee

ul. Surikova 42
660049   Krasnoyarsk
**Tel/Fax:**  26-59-52, 55-90-74
**E-mail:**  evenkiya@krsk.ru
**Contact:** Y. Altabasov, Chairman

The Evenkiya branch of the Red Cross of Russia is working to assist the native peoples of the Krasnoyarsk region, specifically in the Evenkiya and Taymir autonomous regions. It hopes to attract businesses, especially tourism to the region.

## Russian Women's Union– Krasnoyarsk Regional Branch

Красноярское региональное отделение Союза Женщин России
pr. Mira 110
660009   Krasnoyarsk
**Tel:**        49-32-41, 27-89-85
**Fax:**       27-89-77
**E-mail:**   root@legis.krasnoyarsk.su
**Contact:** Ludmila Krukova

The union began working in 1991 and became a regional representative of the Russian Women's Union in 1997. Its mission is to strengthen the status of women in society by steering public opinion in favor of equal rights and opportunities, involving women in public affairs, and protecting the interests of families and children.

As a regional coordinator of the Siberian Civic Initiatives Support Center (SCISC), the union has conducted six seminars, three roundtables, one press conference, and one NGO fair. The effects of these efforts are already evident; participation in the union's seminars increased from 10–12 organizations to 73 within the course of a year. Eighteen organizations participated in the union's First Regional NGO Fair-Presentation in the summer of 1998. At the fair, 38 organizations prepared and published an appeal to the Krasnoyarsk mayor and regional governor asking for help in establishing an NGO resource center.

In May and June 1998, the union participated in several conferences, including Children and Caring for the Future, Green Zone of Krasnoyarsk Day, and NGO and Mass Media Cooperation.

## *Magadan (41322)*

### "Living Arctic" Information and Public Awareness Organization
ul. Gorkovo 8a, k. 4
685000 Magadan
**Tel/Fax:** 23-289
**E-mail:** main@pilc.magadan.su
**Contact:** Victoria Matveeva, Executive Director

Living Arctic was founded in May 1996 with a mission to "promote a culture of open information for citizens, develop their creative and social activity, and support non-governmental organizations and citizen initiatives." The group acts as a resource and support center for the NGO community of Magadan, offering information and consulting services and technical support through seminars and training sessions.

Projects have included Shore of the Sea and Shore of Hope, involving environmental monitoring along the shores of the Okhotsk Sea; a Leadership Training School for local teenagers; an Effective Management seminar for NGO leaders; and assistance with the ISAR publication, *Public Associations of the Russian Far East.*

### Russian American Business Education Center
ul. Portovaya 16
Magadan
**Tel:** 3-53-44
**Fax:** 3-05-38

See the profile of Russian American Education Center under Khabarovsk.

## *Nizhny Tagil (3435)*

### Clean Home
Чистый Дом
ul. Frunze 15
622002 Nizhny Tagil
**Tel:** 24-63-46
**Fax:** 25-05-00
**E-mail:** luba@chome.e-burg.ru
**Contact:** Luba Fainentel, NGO Resource Program Director

Since 1994, Clean Home has been promoting environmental clean-up measures throughout the Nizhny Tagil and Sverdlovsk regions. It seeks to reduce public health risks posed by industrial pollution. Clean Home is currently working with the Institute for Sustainable Communities, based in Vermont, on the creation of a solid waste management plan for Nizhny Tagil. The group also conducts environmental education projects.

### Nizhny Tagil Human Rights Center
Нижнетагильский правозащитный центр
a/ya 169
622001 Nizhny Tagil
**Tel/Fax:** 24-47-38
**E-mail:** hrntagil@glas.apc.org
**Web:** www.glasnet.ru/~hrntagil/
**Contact:** Mikhail Zolotukhin

The center is a collective of several civic groups located in Nizhny Tagil, including the Ochishchenie Ecological Club, Renaissance Independent Committee, and the Free Professional Union of the Nizhny Tagil Metallurgy Plant. The center produces a radio program in conjunction with a local station, which features news from the human rights world and answers callers' questions on legal issues. Additionally, center members publish two newsletters, Human Rights Today and Worker's Word, and operate a video studio that tapes civic events throughout the Nizhny Tagil area and occasionally broadcasts films and documentaries.

### Nizhny Tagil's Disabled Soldiers Recovery Center
ul. Vostochnii Projezd 19
Nizhny Tagil
**Tel/Fax:** 24-19-21
**E-mail:** chome@ntag.e-burg.ru,
   luba@chome.e-burg.ru
**Contact:** Vera Sorokina, Executive Director

The center was established in January 1998 to provide medical, legal, social and psychological assistance to disabled veterans of regional wars.

## *Novokuznetsk (3843)*

### Agency for Ecological Information
Информационное Экологическое Агенство
ul. Tsialkovskogo 62, k. 3
654018   Novokuznetsk
**Tel/Fax:** 47-47-81
**E-mail:** oineca@nvkz.kuzbass.net
**Contact:** Elena V. Perfilyeva, Director; Olga Bezdenezhnykh, Executive Director

The agency, whose Russian acronym is "InEcA," was formed in 1993 and in September 1995 became a local coordinator of the Siberian Civic Initiatives Support Center (SCISC). Since its founding, InEcA has assisted 14 regional public organizations to register and six NGOs in Novokuznetsk and the south Kuzbass region to obtain grants. During 1995-97 it conducted 15 seminars, two discussion meetings and more than 800 consultations for NGOs. InEcA estimates that its services have been used by 116 different organizations. In addition, 19 newspaper articles and eight television stories have covered InEcA's activity.

InEcA maintains a database of environmental information, as well as a library with print information and video films. NGO representatives can access the Internet through the agency.

InEcA is a regional "Center of Public Environmental Examination" within the framework of a project organized by Moscow-based "Ecoline." I.e., it has a state license to carry out environmental examinations and audits.

In 1996 InEcA received a grant from SCISC for a project to expand the circulation of its publication, *Ecological Information Bulletin.*

The organization has a staff of eight.

### "Deep Ecology" UNESCO Club
ЮНЕСКО–Клуб "Глубинная Экология"
a/ya 3189
65080   Novokuznetsk
**Tel:**   45-58-35
**E-mail:** root@ecology.nkz.ru
**Contact:** Vladimir Kravchenko, Chairman

The club is a UNESCO-sponsored project dedicated to environmental education in Novokuznetsk. It has conducted seminars such as Leadership of NGOs, Sustainable Development, and Steps Towards Environmental Information–Regional Management, as well as numerous conferences on the environment and the NGO sector. The Save a Book–Save A Tree program involves the collection of old books and other printed material for donation to orphanages, libraries, and schools. The club also collects old clothes and household items for donation to the homeless and unemployed.

## Novosibirsk (3832)

### Adaptive Center for Disabled Children and Children with Cerebral Palsy

Центр адаптации детей-инвалидов и инвалидов детства с церебральным параличом
а/уа 315
630111   Novosibirsk
**Tel:**      28-88-97, 64-69-98

The center helps disabled children learn skills to function in society. It also provides assistance to families of disabled children, instructing them how to help their child live more independently.

### Ariadna
Novosibirsk
**E-mail:**   wariadna@finist.nsk.su, km@chc.nsk.su
**Contact:**  Larissa Tolkareva, Director; Katya Merkoulova

This is an organization of women with disabilities. It works with Planned Parenthood of Northern New England.

### Association for the Development of Sustainable Human Settlements (ADSHS)
Ассоциация Устойчивого Развития Населенных Пунктов (АУРА НП)
ul. Nikolaeva 8, k. 307

630090   Novosibirsk
**Tel:**      35-13-40, 35-76-29
**E-mail:**   ecodom@glas.apc.org
**Contact:** Dr. Igor Ogorodnikov, Director

ADSHS promotes environmental protection through the creation of ecologically-sound housing developments. The group works with another Novosibirsk organization, Ecodom, to build model "Natural Houses" that use renewable energy sources and building materials. ADSHS also seeks to raise public awareness about the importance of sustainable development.

### "Blokadnik"–Novosibirsk Voluntary Society for Victims of Leningrad Blockade
Новосибирское добровольное общество "блокадник"
ul. Kolkhidskaia 11, k. 84
630011   Novosibirsk
**Tel:**      41-94-31, 22-02-53
**Contact:** Maria Sorokina

This organization provides social protection and emotional counseling to pensioners in the Novosibirsk region, focusing on survivors of the siege of Leningrad (1941-1944) and the spouses and other relatives of its victims.

### Child Care Center "Joy of Childhood"
Центр Эстетического Воспитания "Радость Детства"
ul. Lenina 48, etazh 4
630004   Novosibirsk
**Tel/Fax:** 22-38-81
**E-Mail:**   helen@terra.nsk.su
**Contact:** Elena Kharitonova, President

Founded in November 1996, the center organizes activities for children to encourage their creative development and contribute to their social upbringing. It hosts a children's theater and classroom where it organizes plays and special events for schoolchildren, such as a "Young Leaders" program to encourage children to take an interest in community activities. In 1997-98, the center held a Young Miss Novosibirsk contest for children of the city.

The group also works to improve standards of prenatal care and children's health and nutrition in Novosibirsk oblast. Responding to what Director Kharitonova describes as an absolute dearth of information or support for pregnant women or new parents in Novosibirsk, the center conducts educational programs on prenatal car and child care for women, parents, and schoolteachers. It also distributes material on nutrition and pre-natal care to clinics, schools, and the general public.

### "Diplomacy Through the Family" Volunteer Association
Добровольнон общественное обьединение "Дипломатия через семьи"
ul. Zolotodolinskaia 33, k. 24
630090  Novosibirsk
**Tel:**     35-7235
**E-mail:**  kirichuk.v.s.@iae.nsk.su,
             gaponov@itam.nsc.ru
**Contact:** Irina Maslennikova

Founded in 1987, this association is an affiliate of the Agency for Social Information in Moscow and was among the first NGOs from the former USSR to "make bridges with the U.S." after the Cold War.

Since 1995, Diplomacy Through the Family has been developing informational programs for new NGOs in Siberia. It publishes a newsletter, *The Third Sector In Siberia*, which is distributed from the Urals to the Far East. It is also distributed electronically twice a month to more than 150 subscribers.

### Ecodom
Экодом
ul. Nikolaeva 8, k. 307
630090  Novosibirsk
**Tel:**     34-46-29
**Fax:**     23-83-44
**E-mail:**  ecodom@glas.apc.org
**Contact:** Dr. Igor Ogorodnikov, Director; Alexander Avrorin

Ecodom was established in 1989 to build energy-efficient, environmentally sound, and affordable housing for low-income people. It seeks to combine accumulated experiences from around the world with local technologies and traditions. Ecodom has developed a Natural House program, creating housing models that mitigate Russia's energy and environmental problems. One demonstration house has been built near Novosibirsk, and several others are under construction. The houses are single-family dwellings using renewable energy sources, such as solar and wind, and closed cycles of waste treatment and purification.

In 1998, Ecodom participated in a project to develop energy-efficient housing in Siberia with financial support from the United Nations Center for Human Settlements (Habitat). The goals of project were:
• To produce a design for energy-efficient production methods and housing construction

- To establish a training program for professionals and individuals in the construction industry
- To conduct a public education campaign on innovative and appropriate design and construction methods for reducing energy use in housing.

Ecodom works with Biointensive for Russia in Palo Alto, CA.

## Ecological Club of Novosibirsk State Pedagogical University– "Aves"

Экологический Клуб НГПУ–
"Авиес"
ul. Viliuskaia 28
Department of Botany and Ecology
Novosibirsk State Pedagogical University
630126 Novosibirsk
**Tel:** 68-01-15, 68-02-05
**E-mail:** aves@cip.nsk.su
**Contact:** Svetlana Gizhitskaya, President

Aves is made up of students from Novosibirsk State Pedagogical University's Department of Botany and Ecology. It seeks to promote environmental awareness among university students, schoolchildren, and the general public of Novosibirsk and Akademgorodok. Aves organizes an annual seminar and discussion series on environmental issues and "Inter-Institute Open Student Seminars," attended by teachers and students of Novosibirsk institutes. The group also runs the Environmental Olympics, a competition in environmental knowledge between student activists from across the region. Aves is a member of the Siberian Branch of the Union of Student Nature Conservation Groups.

## Ecological Club of Novosibirsk State University "EcoClub"

Экологический Клуб НГУ–
"ЭкоКлуб"
a/ya 547 (postal address)
630090 Novosibirsk
ul. Pirogova 20, k. 2
630090 Novosibirsk
**Tel:** 39-78-85
**F-mail:** shura@ecoclub.nsk.ru
**Contact:** Aleksandr Dubynin, Director

EcoClub was founded in 1990 by biology and botany students of Novosibirsk State University interested in protecting their region's biological diversity and promoting environmental education. The club conducts educational and city-cleanup programs for schoolchildren, presents seminars and slide shows on environmental protection, and coordinates an annual Earth Day in Akademgorodok. EcoClub also publishes a monthly newsletter on environmental issues in the region, *Siberian Ecological Bulletin Vestnik*, in collaboration with ISAR/Siberia. The bulletin offers news about the environmental movement in Siberia, highlighting the work of different organizations and publicizing books, conferences and financial opportunities. The club is one of the founding members of the Siberian Branch of the Union of Student Nature Conservation Groups.

## Foundation for the Support and Development of Education

Фонд поддержки и развития образования
ul. Kropotkina 130/1, k. 154
630111 Novosibirsk
**Tel/Fax:** 90-04-54
**Contact:** Nadezhda Silkina

This fund conducts educational and cultural research in Novosibirsk oblast in order to promote higher standards of education for local youth. It also researches adult education techniques for industrial workers of the region.

## ISAR–Siberia
Сибирское отделение американской неправитель-ственной организаций ИСАР
a/ya 130
630004   Novosibirsk
**Tel/Fax:** 21-48-95
**E-mail:**   isarsib@glasnet.ru
**Web:**      www.isar.org/isar/Siberia.html
**Contact:** Yuri Shirokov, Dawn Ng, Co-Directors

Established in February 1997, ISAR's Novosibirsk office provides information and technical support to environmental NGOs in Siberia. Its Search for Partners project seeks to foster cooperation, exchange and mutual support between international environmental organizations and Siberian groups with a similar focus.

ISAR constantly researches environmental grant programs in order to provide up-to-date information to local organizations. It also offers consultation on project development, proposal writing, and basic training on financial management.

In the fall of 1997, ISAR-Siberia initiated a small grant program in support of specific environmental NGO projects in Siberia. Twenty-nine grants of up to $1,000 for one-year projects were awarded to grassroots initiatives throughout the region. ISAR–Siberia also helped organize The Climate Train Project in collaboration with the UK organization Scientists for Global

Responsibility and the Siberian Environmental Fund. (See Siberian Environmental Fund in the Novosibirsk section below for more information on Climate Train.)

## National Press Institute
State Library of Science and Technology
630200   Novosibirsk
**Tel:**        66-17-96
**Tel/Fax:** 66-75-21
**E-mail:**   nskrapic@glas.apc.org,
              nsknpi@glas.apc.org
**Contact:** Sergei Vorobyov, Coordinator; Vladimir Panasenko, Larisa Benevalenskaya, Assistants

This is an affiliate of the National Press Institute in Moscow.

## "Obelisk" Association for Parents of Fallen Soldiers
Организация Родителей Военнослужащих, Погибших в Локальных Войнах "Обелиск"
a/ya 450
630117   Novosibirsk-117
**Tel:**        32-81-82
**Tel/Fax:** 32-83-02
**E-mail:**   grad@obelisk.nsk.su
**Contact:** Aleksandr Greblyuk, Chairman

The goals of the Obelisk Association are to publicly honor the memories of Soviet and Russian Federation soldiers who died in armed conflicts since1950 and to seek adequate financial support from the government for these soldiers' families. In many cases, soldiers died while serving in covert operations; consequently their deaths were not acknowledged by the Soviet government.

The group is currently creating a memorial book about soldiers from Novosibirsk and is gathering materials documenting military actions of the Soviet and Russian armies.

## Open Society Institute– Novosibirsk Branch

Институт "Открытое Общество"–Новосибирск Отделение
ul. Sovyetskaya 6
630007 Novosibirsk
**Tel/Fax:** 11-97-81
**E-mail:** michael@soros.nsc.ru,
tatyana@soros.nsc.ru
**Contact:** Michael Kaluzhsky, Executive Director; Tatiana Tkatchenko, Public Relations Coordinator

OSI has been working in Novosibirsk oblast since 1991, offering programs to support science, Internet development, education, third sector activities, culture, and art. During its first two years of operation, OSI worked primarily to support scientific researchers in Siberia after severe cutbacks in government funding levels for scientists. In 1993, Soros's International Science Foundation gave grants to 2,000 researchers in Novosibirsk through the Urgent Aid to Scientists program, followed by a three-year grant competition for scientists and researchers of the region.

Today, OSI emphasizes its Internet For Everyone project, providing Internet access to local organizations, institutes and individuals through a variety of support programs. Initiated in 1994, the project today links more than 50 research, education, culture and health-care organizations through the Novosibirsk Scientific Center Network. The network currently supports over 60

percent of the city's registered users, and provides links to a regional library and the Museum of Local Studies.

In 1996, Soros created Internet sites at Novosibirsk State University and the Institute of Automatics. In 1997, a public-access Internet hall was established at the Novosibirsk Regional Library, and an Internet center for students and professors was set up at the Novosibirsk Medical Institute. Soros funds for Internet development in Novosibirsk currently total around U.S. $2 million.

OSU has hosted an International Youth Forum Week in each of the past four years. OSI-Novosibirsk also hosted a documentary film festival in 1996 and the Soros Interjazz Festival in 1997.

## Public Committee to Save the Ob River

Общественный Комитет Спасения Оби
ul. Blukhera 54, 16
630073 Novosibirsk
**Tel:** 45-16-49
**Contact:** Galina Kuchina, President

The Public Committee to Save the Ob River was founded in 1992 as a community effort to restore the Ob River and watershed and protect it from further damage. The committee focuses its activity on curbing pollution of the river, reducing the amount of timber that is transported on the Ob, developing sand and gravel shores, and ecological education of youth and the population at large. The group has led numerous citizen demonstrations concerning the Ob to the city administration and mayor's office, such as protests against construction of an electrical plant on the river, construction of a bridge that would involve further forest clearing, and construction of houses in a protected zone of the watershed.

The committee has also submitted proposals to the city for cleaner drinking water. In 1996, the group held International Water Day in Novosibirsk to educate the public on the important health and medical benefits of clean, safe drinking water and the damaging effects of river pollution on the population. This event was attended by the general public, students, and other environmental NGOs. The committee also runs anti-pollution programs and River Clean-Up Days for school-children. It has also produced two films on the Ob River, which have been broadcast on local TV and shown in a number of schools.

## Russian Military Brotherhood–Novosibirsk Branch

Новосибирская областная общественная организация отделение "Российского Воинского Братства"
Krasnyi prospekt 59
630091　Novosibirsk
**Tel:**　　20-71-41
**Contact:** Viacheslav Mokritskii

This organization provides assistance, emotional support, and legal counseling to military service veterans and their families. It is a regional branch of the All-Russian Military Brotherhood.

## "Semipalatinsk Union" Public Association

Общественное объединение Союз Семипалатинск Новосибирской области
a/ya 355
630048　Novosibirsk -48

**Tel:**　　44-72-12
**Contact:** Elena Yakubovskaia

This group provides legal and medical assistance to refugees from areas of Semipalatinsk contaminated by the region's nuclear testing zone.

## Siberian Environmental Fund

Сибирский Экологический Фонд
pr. Universitetskii 4
Novosibirsk
**Tel:**　　32-91-81
**Contact:** Sergei Pashenko, Director

The fund works to promote environmental protection and public education in Novosibirsk. It is particularly active in researching the effects of aerosols and other pollutants on the atmosphere, as Director Sergei Pashenko is an expert in this field with the Russian Academy of Sciences.

In 1997, Pashenko led a Siberian delegation of six environmentalists on Climate Train, a train journey across Russia and China to participate in the UN Convention on Global Climate Change in Kyoto, Japan. Sponsored by the British Charity Know How Fund, ISAR-Siberia, and the UK organization, Scientists for Global Responsibility, 40 environmentalist activists from 14 countries made the trip on Climate Train. Train travel was chosen because it allegedly pollutes the atmosphere three times less than traveling by plane.

The journey started in Moscow and ended in Beijing before the final ferry trip to Japan. It involved discussion groups and exchange of information among the participants, as well as opportunities to promote environmental protection at stops along the way.

When the Climate Train arrived in Novosibirsk, the Environmental Fund and ISAR-Siberia held a two-day conference about the role of Siberia in the global climate dilemma. The conference was attended by 30 local environmental NGOs. Upon the Siberian delegation's return from Japan, participants gave presentations on Climate Train and the issues discussed at the Kyoto conference to schools, the media, and universitities of the region.

## "Sib-Novo-Center" Siberian Interregional NGO Support Center

"Сиб-Ново Центр" Сибирский Межрегиональный Центр Поддержки Негосударственных Организаций
pr. Dimitrova 4, k. 1003
630004  Novosibirsk
**Tel:**      20-71-00
**Tel/Fax:** 10-13-27
**E-mail:**  snz@sibnet.ru
**Contact:** Nadezhda Shpitalnaia, Executive Director; Elena Konovalova, Deputy Director

The Sib-Novo-Center was established to support the 1,000 non-governmental organizations that have officially registered in Novosibirsk. The goal of the center is to facilitate the development of the third sector in Western Siberia and to promote cooperation between Siberian NGOs and organizations in Western Europe. The center is funded directly by TACIS and German-Russian Exchange, an NGO based in Berlin.

The Sib-Novo-Center has undertaken several projects to support civic initiatives and NGO development in Novosibirsk, including:

- Leaders' School trains leaders of local NGOs in issues of effective leadership and how to run a public organization.
- Incubator Program helps potential groups organize, develop business plans, research sources for financial support and learn about the legal registration process for NGOs. In 1997, the incubator program helped 10 groups become official NGOs.
- Information Service Center provides access to the Internet, computer databases, and a library of reference materials. The service center also offers consultations on financial, legal, and administrative issues for NGOs.

## Siberian Civic Initiatives Support Center

Сибирский Центр Поддержки Общественных Инициатив
pr. Karl Marx 57, k. 702
630073  Novosibirsk
**Tel:**      46-45-32
**Tel/Fax:** 46 54-77
**E-mail:**  root@cip.nsk.su
**Web:**     cip.nsk.su
**Contact:** Anatoly Zabolotny, Executive Director

Founded in 1994 within the framework of the Civic Initiatives Program (CIP) and financed by USAID, SCISC provides support services to non-governmental organizations across Siberia. Its main programs include incubator services, training, information and Internet access to third sector groups. SCISC's main office is located in Novosibirsk, and the organization has a network of 11 affiliates in Tyumen, Omsk, Tomsk, Barnaul, Gorno-Altaisk, Kemerevo, Novokuznetsk, Krasnoyarsk, Irkutsk, Ulan-Ude, and Chita.

SCISC has worked to generate public awareness of third sector activities in Siberia and to improve relationships between government agencies and NGOs in the region. The center publishes an NGO directory (available on their Web site), has established NGO associations in almost all of the cities where it is active, operates a Volunteer Help Agency that promotes volunteerism, and has endeavored to increase local media focus on NGO events and activities.

Since its creation in 1994, SCISC has provided consultations to more than 15,000 people and conducted training seminars for more than 7,500 NGO activists. Media coverage of third sector activities in Siberia has also increased dramatically; by 1997, more than 700 print, television or radio pieces reporting on NGOs had been generated. A new "social marketing" project sponsored by SCISC will train NGOs on how to promote themselves better and work with the media to foster greater public support and awareness of their projects.

## Siberian Youth Initiative
Сибирская Молодежная Инициатива
ul. Pirogova 2
630090 Moscow
**Tel:**       39-74-34
**Fax:**      39-71-01
**E-mail:**   youth@iclub.nsu.ru
**Web:**      www.youth.nsu.ru/
**Contact:** Oleg Matuzov

The Siberian Youth Initiative was formed in 1990 by a group of students from Novosibirsk State University. The group coordinates youth conferences, seminars, and clubs that promote awareness of global problems and en-courage collaboration between organizations for young people. The initiative is responsible for organizing Interweek, an annual international youth forum held in May at Akademgorodok. Interweek brings together members of youth organizations from Russia and abroad to discuss international issues and to encourage youth initiatives. Interweek '98 focused on the theme "Sustainable Development: Myth or Reality?"

## "Smile" YMCA of Novosibirsk
Vokzalnaya magistral 41
630004  Novosibirsk
**Tel:**       22-06-47
**Tel/Fax:** 22-28-34
**E-mail:**   ymca@online.nsk.su
**Web:**      www.sibfair.itp.nsc.ru/firms/ smile/index_eng.html
**Contact:** Edward Shornik, Chairman of the Board; Vladimir Tropin, Executive Director; Igor V. Kushnir

The Novosibirsk YMCA was created in 1988 to provide educational, artistic, and recreational programs for local children and young adults. Current programs include an Aesthetical Center for 5- to 10-year-olds, a conversational-English camp, a drama and theater school, French language classes, participation in international festivals, a preschool program, math camp, and a Children's Fashion Center. Smile also offers a two-year TOEFL preparation class and the International Camp Counselor Program to prepare young adults between 19 and 30 years of age for work in summer camps in U.S. and UK.

## Soldiers' Mothers Committee–Novosibirsk Oblast

Новосибирский областной
комитет солдатских
матерей
ul. Koshurnikova 16, k. 62
630122  Novosibirsk
**Tel:** 79-49-48
**Contact:** Rimma Belik, President

The committee provides practical assistance, legal counseling, and emotional support to army conscripts and their families. It helps people appeal for exemption from and/or deferment of military service and also provides consultation on the legal rights of conscripts. It publicizes information about conditions in the armed services and the need for reform, including formation of a professional army. The committee prepares letters and documents regarding abuses on behalf of specific conscripts and submits them to the oblast administration on a regular basis.

## Union of Student Nature Conservation Groups–Siberian Branch

Сибирское Отделение
Движения Дружин по охране
природы
a/ya 547
630090  Novosibirsk
**Tel:** 39-78-85, 39-75-14
**Fax:** 35-52-37
**E-mail:** shura@ecoclub.nsu.ru
**Web:** iclub.nsu.ru/~eco
**Contact:** Aleksandr Dubynin, Director

The union is one of the oldest members of Russia's environmental movement. The organization was formed in 1960 and united student ecological groups across the Soviet Union. Today, the group continues to act as an umbrella organization for members of the nature conservation movement. In Siberia, the union is composed of two collective members; the Novosibirsk State University Ecological Club and the Aves Ecological Club (also affiliated with the university). However, the group collaborates with many different environmental groups from the Siberian region, including the Volgo-Ural Ecological Network Center in Tolyatti and the Altai State University Ecological Club in Barnaul.

The association is currently working on three projects:

- Program to Protect the Natural Heritage of Novosibirsk Oblast, in which union members conduct field studies to assess and document the state of the Novosibirsk ecosystem. A two-year study of the endangered black stork conducted under this program resulted in the discovery of 16 nesting sites.
- Information Service, in which members disseminate ecological information among regional NGOs and environmental activists. In collaboration with ISAR-Siberia, the group has published the *Siberian Ecological Digest* and the *Bulletin of the Steppe* and has helped local organizations establish e-mail accounts.
- An ecotourism program, which is conducted to promote greater ecological awareness among elementary and high school students. Union members have led educational excursions throughout the Novosibirsk and Gorno-Altai regions since 1997.

## West-Siberian Association of Economic Journalists

Западно-Сибирская ассоциация журналистов, освещающих экономические темы
pr. Dmitrova 4, kom. 807
630004   Novosibirsk
**Tel:**      20-75-60
**Fax:**     10-20-44
 **E-mail:**  root@wseja.nsk.su,
              tatyana@cis.ru
**Contact:** Tatiana Y. Tarasova,
Chairperson

The association was formed in 1994 by a group of journalists in order to improve the professional standards of the mass media and provide more accurate information on economic issues to the public. The 23 members of the association are journalists from newspapers, TV and radio across Western Siberia, and the majority of them write on economic issues both in Russia and abroad.

Together with the Federal Securities Committee, the association organized a series of seminars and a press conference for the Central Bank of Russia. It also published a collection of the best articles on economic issues in Western Siberia. Its members participate in TV programs and meet with representatives of the regional administration to discuss ways to improve relations and access to information on economic policy.

The association has received several grants from international foundations and organizations, but its regular source of funding is from membership dues. The association regularly publishes a press bulletin for its members.

## Women's Humanitarian Fund

Женский гуманитарный фонд
a/ya 205 (postal address)
ul. Trudovaia 1, k. 110
630107   Novosibirsk
**Tel:**      22-60-63
**Contact:** Natalia Demidova

The fund works to promote professional development for women in Novosibirsk oblast and encourage the participation of women in the private sector. It conducts research and offers educational training.

## Women's Creative Action Union "ZHITO"

Женское Инициативное Творческое Объединение "ЖИТО"
pr. Dmitrova 4, k. 1004
630004   Novosibirsk
**Tel:**      67-39-85
**Fax:**     32-61-21
**E-mail:**  woman@zubr.nsk.su
**Contact:** Natalia Stupakova

Zhito works to improve the situation of women in Novosibirsk oblast through educational and self-improvement programs, professional and career development seminars, and psychological counseling. The group is composed of approximately 50 women from the region who participate in discussion groups and seminars in an effort to foster civic participation of women in their local communities.

## Young Invalids Association

Новосибирская ассоциация молодых инвалидов
ul. Lavrentyeva 14, k. 113
630090   Novosibirsk
**Tel:**      23-63-47

**Contact:** Igor Gall-Savalskii

This association provides assistance to disabled children and young adults by researching new technologies and promoting employment opportunities for the disabled. It is run primarily by volunteers.

## Youth Information Business Center
Молодежный
Информационно-Деловой
Центр
Krasnyi pr. 26
630099 Novosibirsk
**Tel:** 10-12-04
**Fax:** 10-10-53
**E-mail:** root@jibc.sib.ru
**Contact:** Pavel Akimov, Chairman

The center promotes the study of business and supports students preparing for business careers. The group attends student competitions, conferences, and fairs to promote youth business activities; helps business students to network and find contacts both in Russia and abroad; and holds seminars in economics and law. It publishes the Business Notebook, a news bulletin that reports on issues in business education in Russia and provides information on various business careers.

## Omsk (3812)

## Civic Chamber of Omsk Region
Общественная палата
Омской области
ul. Krasny put 1, k. 104
644002 Omsk
**Tel:** 23-06-70
**E-mail:** ktv@palata.omsk.su
**Contact:** Zinaida Tikunova

The chamber was established in 1994 and is currently a regional coordinator of the Siberian Civic Initiatives Support Center (SCISC). It promotes relations between NGOs and government, and in 1997 held a conference, Omsk Third Sector: Problems and Perspectives, addressing such issues as NGO-government cooperation, NGO-media relations, legislative regulation of NGO activities, problems of youth and children's organizations, educational and scientific institutions, ecological and women's organizations, and ethnic centers. Leaders from 95 regional NGOs as well as government and media representatives participated in the conference. Ninety NGOs also participated in an NGO fair sponsored by the chamber.

## Tomsk (3822)

## Russian Children's Fund– Tomsk Oblast Division
Российского Детского Фонда
pl. Lenina 6, k. 282
634069 Tomsk
**TelFax:** 22-30-70
**E-mail:** detfond@trecom.tomsk.su
**Contact:** Galina Popova

The Tomsk branch of the Russian Children's Fund was established in 1988. Its mission is to protect children's rights by monitoring adherence to the UN Convention on Children's Rights, strengthening the authority of the family and its role in society, and representing children's interests to legislative and executive bodies.

For three years, the Tomsk branch has been a regional coordinator of SCISC. In 1997, it received grants from Save the Children and the Eurasia

Foundation and has conducted two NGO Fairs, one of which specialized in youth and children's organizations. In June 1998, it held a conference, Civil Society Establishment: Opportunities, Problems, Perspectives. Monthly events include seminars for NGOs, the government, mass media, and business representatives.

## Tomsk Resource and Informational Center
pr. Lenina 91
634050   Tomsk
**E-mail:**   andreev@tbsc.tomsk.ru
**Contact:** Gennady Andreev, Chairman

## Tomsk Human Rights Research Institute
ul. Altaiska 76/1, k. 105
634021   Tomsk
**Tel:**       22-29-35
**Contact:** Nikolai Kanduba

## *Tyumen (3452)*

## Tyumen Regional Association of Social Service Employees
Тюменская областная Ассоциация работников социальных служб
ul. Respubliki 83a, k. 403
625048   Tyumen
**Tel:**       36-52-57
**E-mail:**   social@diaspr.tyumen.ru
**Contact:** Vera Barova

TRASSE was founded in 1993 as a voluntary union of social service workers and a regional branch of the Interregional Association of Russian Social Service Employees. It also has served as a regional coordinator of SCISC since June 1997. In 1997-98,

the group developed an NGO resource center with funding from Save the Children and the Eurasia Foundation. It has held two NGO fairs and an NGO festival called Tyumen Meetings.

The association's Nonprofit Sector Development progam provides technical and informational assistance and educational seminars to NGOs, while the NGO Cooperation with Government program provides consultation to government representatives. Since 1995, TRASSE has directed an NGO Leaders Club, and recently began a Business and NGO Cooperation program.

## *Ulan-Ude (3012)*

## Baikal Foundation–Buryatya Office
Фонд Байкала-Бурятское отделение
ul. Tobolskaia 73-130
670036   Ulan-Ude
**Tel:**       27-72-45
**Contact:** Konstantin Karnyshev

The Baikal Foundation in the Republic of Buryatya provides expert ecological advice to local enterprises, reports on the state of the ecosystem of the Lake Baikal area, and recommendations to state agencies on environmental issues.

## Buryat Regional Association on Lake Baikal
ul. Kluchevskogo 40a
670042   Ulan-Ude
**Tel:**       21-02-88
**Fax:**       21-44-20, 33-37-06
**E-mail:**   shap@vsgtu.eastsib.ru
**Contact:** Vladimir Belogolovov

The association is a regional support center for the ROLL Project (see the profile of the Institute for Sustainable Communities, Moscow, in the *Russia: West of the Urals* section).

## Ecotourists' Club "Firn"
Экотуристский клуб "Фирн"
a/ya 2666 (postal address)
670033 Ulan-Ude
ul. Kommunisticheskaya 16
670000 Ulan-Ude
**Tel:** 21-49-55
**Tel/Fax:** 21-44-30
**E-mail:** firn@eastsib.ru
**Contact:** Liya Sandanova

Firn works to increase youth participation in ecotourism, the preservation of Lake Baikal, camping, and environmental educational seminars. It has been a regional coordinator of SCISC since 1997 and has conducted nine training seminars on NGO organizational development and three round-tables on state social order. Firn also fosters cooperation between the public and private sectors and among youth organizations. More than 400 people have received consulting services from Firn, and 32 NGOs as well as representatives from the Buryatia Republic, the Ulan-Ude administration, and the mass media attended an NGO fair in June 1998.

## Vladivostok (4232)

### CARITAS Primorye
22 Volodarskovo
690001 Vladivostok
**Tel:** 22-42-92
**Fax:** 26-96-16
**E-mail:** caritas@catholic.marine.su

**Contact:** Anastacia Potopenko, Director; Rev. Myron Effing

CARITAS Primorye was formed in 1992 as an affiliate of CARITAS International. It is an official charity of the Catholic Church in Russia and trains volunteers in humanitarian work. Currently CARITAS is caring for 200 dependent elderly in Vladivostok and is working to bring volunteer doctors to areas where medical services are inadequate or unavailable. The group has nine service points in Far Eastern Russia and maintains a paid staff of nine as well as 40 volunteers.

### Center for the Defense of Wild Nature
ul. Kirova 56A, k. 22
Vladivostok
**Tel:** 32-06-66
**E-mail:** zovtaigi@glas.apc.org
**Contact:** Vasily Solkin, Larissa Solkina, Larisa Kabalik

The center was founded by Vasily and Larissa Solkin, both journalists, wildlife biologists, and environmental educators in the Vladivostok region, to raise public awareness of the need for environmental protection in the Russian Far East. The Solkins helped coordinate an international campaign to save the Siberian tiger and organized several tiger research projects. The center publishes *Zov Taigi* (The Call of the Wild), dedicated to environmental issues in Primorsky krai, and distributes it among environmental NGOs throughout the Russian Far East.

The center also works with ISAR-Vladivostok to develop, translate and distribute publications on environmental education. It produces videos and television documentaries on Far

East nature protection issues. It also was awarded a grant from the W. Alton Jones Foundation for a program to monitor the development of environmental protection legislation in Primorsky krai.

## Eco-Logos Fund

ul. Chapaeva 14-107
Vladivostok
**Tel:**    31-49-24
**Fax:**    31-49-24
**E-mail:**    akub@glas.apc.org,
ecologos@online.vladivostok.ru,
leo@ecologos.marine.su

**Contact:** Andrei Kubanin, Victor Kitaev, Lev Kolonyets

Eco-Logos distributes information on environmental issues in Primorsky krai among regional environmental organizations. Their monthly bulletin *Eco-Alin* reports on regional environmental protection and NGO organizational development, programs, and events. The group also provides consultation to local NGOs on proposal writing and organizes seminars on fundraising.

## The Eurasia Foundation

ul. Abrekovskaia 8a
690001   Vladivostok
**Tel:**    300-063
**Fax:**    300-064
**E-mail:**    postmaster@eurasia.
marine.su
**Web:**    194.84.41.241/eurasia

See the profile for the foundation in the North American Organizations section.

## Far East Information Center (FEIC), Bureau for Regional Public Campaigning

ul. Uborevicha 17, k. 23

Vladivostok
**Tel:**    22-09-66
**Fax:**    22-53-98
**E-mail:**    swan@glasnet.ru
**Contact:** Anatoly Lebedev

FEIC seeks to provide an independent and professional source of information on Far Eastern political, economic, social and environmental issues. It distributes a weekly electronic information bulletin and gathers regional news through representatives in Khabarovsk, Sakhalin, Kamchatka and Magadan. FEIC is active in the fields of forestry, timber trade policies, biodiversity conservation, anti-poaching, and protection of Siberian tigers. It also monitors Sakhalin offshore oil and gas drilling and is involved in the creation of a World Heritage site on Sikhote Alin.

Director Anatoli Lebedev was a key leader of opposition against Hyundai when the company threatened to clear-cut deep into the old growth forests of the Upper Bikin River Valley. He is currently an active journalist, analyzing environmental issues and resource-use problems in the Far East. Lebedev leads the Russian Far East support group of Greenpeace and provides support for the USAID Project for Environmental Policy and Technology (EPT).

## Initiative Group for Monitoring the State of the Environment of Vladivostok

**E-mail:**    root@dpicnit.marine.su
**Contact:** Vyacheslav Borisov

## Institute for Marine Biology RAN

ul. Palchevskogo 17
Vladivostok
**Tel:**    31-09-05

**E-mail:** akub@glas.apc.org
(indicate "for Naydenko")
**Contact:** Tamara Naydenko

## IREX Office and Education Information Center

ul. Svetlanskaia 150, etazh 3
690005 Vladivostok
**Tel/Fax:** 26-97-09
**E-mail:** irexvlad@online.ru,
irexeast@glasnet.ru

## ISAR–Russian Far East

a/ya 91426
690091 Vladivostok
**Tel/Fax:** 26-06-94
**E-mail:** isarfe@glasnet.ru
**Web:** www.isar.org/isar/rfe.html
**Contact:** B. J. Chisholm and Yulya Fomenko, Co-Directors

ISAR has been working in the Russian Far East since 1993 with a mission to foster an active NGO sector that ensures citizen participation in biodiversity protection and sustainable natural resource use. The office provides information and technical support to environmental activists through a variety of projects, including a two-tiered small grants program for regional NGOs. The first tier, One Reaps What One Sows: Supporting the Grassroots Environmental Movement in the Russian Far East, provides grants of up to $1,500 to indigenous NGOs to work on environmental projects in their communities. The second tier of the grants program, Silver Web, is designed to support cooperation between environmental NGOs in the region with grants ranging from $8,000–$10,000.

ISAR-RFE conducts an environmental education publishing program, Listia v Ladoniakh, in order to increase the amount and quality of environ-

mental education materials in the Primorsky and Khabarovsky krais. It distributes an environmental education journal, *Notes from the Far East*, offering regional environmental news and articles by activists. In addition, the office coordinates information sharing among the NGO community through e-mail networking, database creation, and assistance to local groups in finding international and regional partners.

## Peace Corps Environmental Program

a/ya 323
Vladivostok
**Tel:** 31-04-63
**Fax:** 31-09-02
**E-mail:** nikolai_kazakov@pcrfe.marine.su
**Contact:** Nikolai Kazakov

The Peace Corps is creating an environmental education network for the Russian Far East, and is introducing non-traditional methods of teaching environmental education. It cooperates with ISAR, the Young Academy of Marine Biologists, the Departments of Education for Primorsky krai, Khabarovsky krai, and Sakhalinskaya oblast, and the Teacher Training Institute of Primorsky krai.

## Russian-American Far Eastern Center for Economic Development

ul. Mordovtceva 12
690600 Vladivostok
**Tel/Fax:** 26-67-74
**E-mail:** fecenter@online.marine.su
**Contact:** Irina Boiko, General Director

The center publishes an "informational-analytical journal," *Russian Far East: Economy, Investment, the State of the*

*Market.* It has also produced publications about such topics as the Far East economy, the financial crisis in the Pacific Rim, and the oil strategy of China. Articles are in Russian with summaries in English.

## "Tiger" Department of Primorsky Krai

ul. Pushkinskaia 93
690001   Vladivostok
**Tel:**       22-80-65, 22-03-02
**Fax:**      26-85-74
**E-mail:**  tigr@natura.marine.su
**Web:**     www.marine.su/tiger

Tiger reports that the biggest threats to Siberian tigers and leopards, both endangered species, are poaching, dwindling food sources, and deforestation. In fact, there are only 25 Amurian leopards left in Russia. The group engages in lobbying activity to combat poaching in the Russian Far East. It also conducts educational programs to increase the general public's interest and knowledge of the plight of Siberian tigers and leopards and the importance of protecting endangered species. Tiger receives funding from the World Wildlife Fund and the Global Network for Survival.

## Youth Academy for Marine Biology (MAMB)

ul. Nerchinskay 38, 9
Vladivostok
**Tel:**       25-68-74
**Tel/Fax:** 31-49-24
**E-mail:**  mamb@pub.marine.su,
                 akub@glas.apc.org,
                 faribm@visenet.iasnet.com
                 (indicate "for MAMB")
**Contact:** Liliy Kondrashova, Valentina Kubanina

## Yakutsk (4112)

## Public Environmental Center of Sakha Republic

ul. Bestuzheva-Marlinskovo 23/1
677001   Yakutsk
**Tel:**       45-04-95, 46-11-04
**E-mail:**  ecolog@gold.ru
**Contact:** Tatiana Kornilova, Liubov Yegorova, Chairpersons

The center was formed in 1989 by Yakutsk scientists and nature centers opposed to the government's industrial policies. The group studies the effects of Russia's space program activities in Yakutsk on the environment and the population's health and has held public demonstrations to oppose the expansion of space-related industry in the region. It also conducts research on the environmental effects of oil refineries and pipeline construction. The center's video-film on the regional environment has been presented on local TV.

## Sakha-American Education Center

ul. Kulakovskogo 46, k. 207, 208
Yakutsk
**Tel:**       26-08-39
**Tel/Fax:** 26-19-97

See the profile of this group's affiliate in the Khabarovsk section.

## Yuzhno-Sakhalinsk (42422)

## "Open World" Sakhalin Regional Organization in Support of Civic Initiatives
Сахалинская Областная общественная организация

по поддержке общественных
инициатив "Открытый Мир"
ul. Dzerzhinskovo 34, k. 42
693000  Yuzhno-Sakhalinsk
**Tel/Fax:**  30-983
**Fax:**       74-18-50
**E-mail:**  diva@sakhalin.ru
**Contact:** Irina Zin, Anna Romanova,
Co-Chairpersons

Open World was formed in 1997 by a
group of environmental activists interested in creating an active sector of
citizen initiatives in Sakhalin. The
group provides informational and
technical support to local groups and
works to foster cooperation between
social and government structures. Open
World published a directory *Public
Associations of the Far East*, and is
working to establish an NGO resource
center with funding from the Eurasia
Foundation. It recently participated in a
conference, Prevention of Corruption in
Government, with the Strategy Center
in St. Petersburg. The group currently
provides support to approximately 54
local organizations.

## Russian-American Business Training Center

296-1 Lenin St.
Yuzhno-Sakhalinsk
**Tel:**       32-985, 30-696
**Int'l Tel/Fax:** (50995) 18-75

See the profile of this group's affiliate
in the Khabarovsk section.

# *Ukraine*

## Country Code: 380

### *Kyiv (44)*

#### ACCELS Kyiv
Freedom Support Act Program Office
Kyiv Taras Shevchenko National
University, Red Building
vul. Volodymyrska, 60, Room 201
252033   Kyiv
**Tel:**      225-7182, 224-7356
**Fax:**      224-6960
**E-mail:**   aksels.kiev,
          accels@accels.freenet.kiev.ua,
          fsakiev@fsa.freenet.kiev.ua

See profile of American Councils for
International Education in North
American Organizations.

#### ACCELS Kyiv
Educational Information Center
Kyiv Taras Shevchenko National
University
vul. Volodymyrska, 60, Rooms 203-
204
252033   Kyiv
**Tel:**      244-3580, 224-3566,
          230-2371
**Fax:**      230-2672
**Tel/Fax:**  224-8549 (EIC)
**E-mail:**   ieac@accels.kiev.ua

#### Alliance for Enterprise Development
ul. Zankovetskoi 7, k. 21
252001   Kyiv
**Tel:**      228-1165
**Fax:**      229-2995
**E-mail:**   eileen_andersen@mail.iesc
.org

**Contact:** Eileen Andersen, Financing
Coordinator

The alliance is a consortium of four
U.S. NGOs (IESC, CDC, ACDI/VOCA
and MBA Enterprise Corps), which
assist Ukrainian and Moldovan enterprises (for-profit and non-governmental
organizations) looking for development
opportunities.

#### Association of Students—Plast (Scouts) Youth
Kyiv-Mohyla Academy
ul. Skovorody 2
254070   Kyiv
**Tel:**      416-4549
**E-mail:**   spykyiv@yahoo.com,
          plast@ukma.kiev.ua
**Web:**      www.ukma.kiev.ua/~plast
**Contact:** Bogdan Berezenko, Director

ASPY was founded in Autumn 1997 to
provide a forum for Plast members
(Ukrainian Scouts) studying in
Ukrainian universities. The association
organizes get-togethers, trips, and
summer camps for Plast. It also runs a
volunteer program, Scouts Introduce
You To Kyiv, offering free, English-
language tours of Kyiv's architecture,
parks, museums, and historical sites.
ASPY has 48 members and representatives in Poltava, Ternopil, and
Kolomyya.

#### The British Council
9/1 Besarabska Ploshcha
252004   Kyiv
**Tel:**      247-7235
**Fax:**      247-7280
**E-mail:**   Valentine.Boinitsky@
bc.kiev.ua
**Web:**      www.bc.kiev.ua/
**Contact:** Valentine Boinitsky, Project
Manager (Arts and PR)

The British Council, a registered British charity, is the United Kingdom's international network for education, culture and development services. The council was one of the first international agencies to establish itself in independent Ukraine in 1992. It now has an office, information center, and English Language Teaching resource center in Kyiv and centers in Lviv, Kharkiv, Odessa and Donetsk. These centers are "one-stop shops" for information from and about Britain. They also offer access to the Internet.

The British Council is responding to the huge demand for English language learning in Ukraine by—among other things:

- Working in partnership with the Ministry of Education to develop and strengthen teacher training and the teaching of Business English
- Supporting teachers of English by providing access to English teaching resources and a range of professional development activities
- Teaching English to the Ukrainian armed forces, under a contract with the British Ministry of Defense and Foreign Office.

It plans to open an English Teaching Center in Kyiv, which will offer courses taught by professional and experienced native-speaker teachers of English.

The British Council also supports projects of the UK's Know How Fund in Ukraine such as:

- Joint Industrial and Commercial Attachment Programme, which provides Ukrainian managers with training placements in British companies
- Regional Academic Partnerships Scheme, which funds partnerships between Ukrainian and British institutions of higher education

- Supporting Non-Governmental Organisations, which provides practical support to Ukrainian NGOs and their partners
- Joining the Global Information Society, in which the British Council is working with Ukrainian libraries and other information providers to support the development of the information society infrastructure in Ukraine.

## Center for Philanthropy
a/ya 53
253152  Kyiv
**Tel/Fax:** 550-2070
**E-mail:** CFP@philanth.relc.com
**Contact:** Svitlana Kuts, President

CFP works to promote philanthropy and people's involvement in the Ukrainian civil sector in order to more effectively solve community problems. CFP strives to introduce new forms and methods of philanthropy from democratic countries to Ukrainian culture. It hosts a library of literature on civil society and democracy, including journals on nonprofit management, legal issues, and the nonprofit movement worldwide. The group is working on a bibliography of philanthropy and civil society, as well as translations of foreign literature.

## "Compass Club" Youth Union
a/ya 128
253152  Kyiv
**Tel/Fax:** 553-7857
**E-mail:** taras@compass.freenet.kiev.ua
**Contact:** Taras Loginov, Director

Compass Club is a youth center for children in Kyiv, providing year-round educational and recreational programs in a spacious facility outside the city center. The club serves as a safe after-school gathering site for children of all ages. During the summer, the club runs a camp for children on a lake outside Kyiv. The camp offers programs in environmental education, theater, arts and crafts, and sports. Peace Corps and other international volunteers often serve as camp counselors.

## Counterpart Creative Center
Творчий центр Каунтерпарт
bul. Lesi Ukrainky 36b, kv. 43
252133   Kyiv
**Tel/Fax:** 295-9707, 295-9880
**Fax:**      230-2360
**E-mail:**  lyuba@cpkyiv.freenet.kiev.ua
**Contact:** Lyuba Palyvoda, Director

Formally registered in 1996, CCC extends work begun in 1993 when it began to function as a training and research facility for its parent organization Counterpart International, based in Washington, D.C. At this time, CCC has 20 local professional trainers; it has held 400 workshops in Ukraine and trained more than 6,000 leaders of NGOs in Ukraine.

The main goals of CCC are to support the development of the third-sector in Ukraine. It maintains a database with detailed information on more that 2,000 Ukrainian NGOs. The database serves as a research tool tracking the growth of the Ukrainian third-sector. It has recently published the third edition of its *NGO Handbook and Directory for Ukraine* in English and Ukrainian.

Over the past three years, CCC has organized training courses and developed materials for project, NGO, and financial management. It has established an NGO training and technical assistance resource center and organized three five-day training workshops for women entrepreneurs in Belarus and a similar workshop in Georgia.

CCC current projects include:

- Women's Enterprise Development program, which provides training and technical assistance to women entrepreneurs in Ukraine. It has conducted training sessions for more than 300 women in 13 cities, with an emphasis on the development of women's business associations
- Administration of a TACIS microproject facility in Ukraine to support NGOs
- Publication of a quarterly NGO bulletin.

## Economics Education and Research Consortium
National University Kyiv-Mohyla Academy
vul. Skovorody 2, dom 3, kom. 304
254070   Kyiv
**Tel:**      417-4174, 416-6936,
             416-6865
**Tel/Fax:** 417-7395
**E-mail:**  eerc@eerc.kiev.ua
**Contact:** Kenneth Gray, Acting Resident Program Director

This program is intended to develop a cadre of young Ukrainians with a two-year M.A. degree in economics, which they can then use to pursue further graduate study or enter a career of public service in Ukraine. Instructors are drawn from several Western countries and the curriculum is generally of a very high standard. Funding for the program comes from several foundations (Eurasia, Ford, Soros, Pew and Starr) as well as the Norwegian government and World Bank.

## Education for Democracy Foundation
National University Kyiv-Mohyla Academy
vul. Skovorody 2
254070   Kyiv

**Tel:** 416-4515
**Fax:** 463-6783
**E-mail:** riabov@rainbow.gov.ua,
riabovs@hotmail.com
**Contact:** Sergei Riabov, Chairman

EDF, a nonpartisan and nonprofit organization, was registered in Kyiv in February 1998. It was established by a group of scholars and educators as a resource center to improve the teaching of democracy and civics, and the formation of civil society in Ukraine. EDF conducts research programs and disseminates experiences and new forms of education based on democratic values. It provides resource support and training to local civic education NGOs.

Among the foundation's recent achievements are publication of a teaching manual, *Political Elections: Glossary-Reference Book*, which was distributed to voters, government officials, and NGOs, and *Polymath*—a series of competitions, quizzes, radio talkshows, TV, video materials, and articles in newspapers and magazines designed to foster interest and knowledge in young people on civic culture questions.

According to Riabov, a professor of political science at the Kyiv-Mohyla Academy, the foundation's activity has the support of the Ukrainian government. EDF cooperates closely in several projects with the Department of Political Culture, the Ministry of Education, and Ministry of Youth. Internationally, EDF collaborates with Center for Civic Education, the International Foundation for Electoral Systems, American Federation of Teachers, Centre for the Study of Democracy (Queen's University, Canada), Education Department of the Council of Europe, Center for Human Rights (Lithuania), and the Belarus Association of Think Tanks.

The foundation has a staff of four.

## The Eurasia Foundation– Western NIS Regional Office
bul. Lesi Ukrainky 26, k. 206
252133   Kyiv
**Tel:**   229-4359
**Fax:**   229-4359
**E-mail:**   eurasia@eurasia.freenet.
kiev.ua

Serves Ukraine, Belarus and Moldova. See the profile for the foundation in North American Organizations.

## Freedom House–Partnership for Reform in Ukraine
vul. Mala Zhitomirska 5, apt. 55
252001   Kyiv
**Tel:**   228-3128
**Tel/Fax:** 228-3845
**E-mail:**   freedom@carrier.kiev.ua
**Contact:** Marc Berenson, John Kubiniec, Program Officers

The Partnership for Reform in Ukraine program is a three-year, USAID-funded initiative to strengthen the effectiveness and sustainability of public policy institutes, or think tanks, in Ukraine. The PRU program provides financial training (in Ukraine and the U.S.), networking, and on-site technical support to think tanks and public affairs NGOs that are active in the research, development, advocacy, and implementation of initiatives that promote democracy and economic reform. The program places particular emphasis on improving the capacity of think tanks to inform public opinion and influence public policy.

To achieve its goal, PRU awards project grants to Ukrainian think tanks. In addition, the PRU program conducts training and networking programs in the U.S. and CEE countries through exchanges, internships, and study tours for the managers and researchers of

Ukrainian policy institutes. It makes a special effort to link Ukrainian think tanks with counterpart organizations throughout CEE, especially Poland, and the U.S.

Freedom House also implemented a program entitled Habits of the Heart from 1995-1998, providing support to indigenous public policy research institutions in Ukraine in the form of technical assistance, support for infrastructure and publications, and strategies for outreach to the media and government.

## Freedom Of Speech Center
P.O. Box 332
252001   Kyiv
**Tel:**      244-9176
**Fax:**     244-9175
**E-mail:**  bohdana@gu.kiev.ua
**Contact:** Roman Kukharuk, President; Bohdana Kostiuk, Roman Zinchenko, International Affairs Department

The center was organized and registered in 1996 with the aims of analyzing the Ukrainian mass media market, supporting journalists and talented youth, and producing works of culture. The center publishes books by young Ukrainian writers, organizes meetings for journalists with government officials, and maintains a database on the Ukrainian mass media. It has published a book about the mass media, *The Fourth Power in Ukraine*.

The center has representatives in all the regions of Ukraine. Its major offices are in Kyiv, Lviv, Chernivtsy, and Donetsk. It seeks partners abroad, especially in Central and Eastern Europe and the U.S.

## Gurt–Resource Center for NGO Development
Гурт
P.O. Box 126/7

252025   Kyiv
**Tel:**      228-5134
**Tel/Fax:** 416-2679
**E-mail:**  gurt@ngonet.kiev.ua
**Web:**     www.voiceinternational.org/gurt/
**Contact:** Bogdan Maslych, Director

"Gurt," which means "team," was founded in October 1995 with the goal to assist in establishing a civil society in Ukraine through development of the third sector. Gurt provides consulting and training, organizes seminars for NGOs, and publishes the newsletter *Nova Hromada*. It reports that it helps hundreds of NGO clients annually in Kyiv and the surrounding regions of Zhytomyr, Chernihiv, Cherkassy, and Kirivohrad.

In 1997, Gurt published two brochures, *Creating and Running an NGO* and *The Third Sector in Ukraine and Supporting Organizations*. Gurt is planning to publish a series of brochures on strategic planning, management, fundraising and legislation for NGOs.

Gurt's partners include the Foundation of International Civic Communications, AISEC, Ukrainian Youth Center, the Orpheus Civil Society Mutual Support Project, the European Foundation Center, the International Center for Not-for-Profit Law, VOICE International, the Conference of Ukrainian Students of Canada, Charities Aid Foundation-Russia, United Way of Belarus, and euroCom e.V. Gurt has five full-time staff and one full-time Peace Corps volunteer.

## Innovation and Development Center
Центр инновацій та розвитку
ul. Desiatynna 4/6, 2nd floor
252025   Kyiv
**Tel:**      229-1748, 228-8384
**Fax:**     229-1748, 220-6063

**E-mail:** idc@iopa.freenet.kiev.ua
**Web:** www.chat.ru/~ukr_case/
**Contact:** Oleksander Sydorenko,
Executive Director

IDC is dedicated to the design and
delivery of training courses, project
management, and project evaluation
services for Ukrainian clients in the
public sector and non-governmental
organizations, newly established
foundations, and international agencies
operating in Ukraine.

The founders of IDC are mainly
alumni of the Institute of Public Administration and Local Government who
received Western-style training.
Geographically, IDC activities occur all
over Ukraine and IDC specialists have
been invited to give workshops in other
countries of the former Soviet Union.

The center emphasizes the following
main areas of activity:

- Training for public sector and non-
  governmental organization personnel
  in the areas of communications,
  public relations, budgets and local
  finance administration, leadership,
  and strategic planning
- Project design and management,
  including case method and case
  writing
- Project evaluation, including evaluation of project execution, skills
  transfer, and long-term assessment of
  project impacts
- Creation of an appropriate
  environment for philanthropic
  activities in Ukraine.

IDC, together with various funders
and groups of authors, has undertaken a
number of publications concerning the
third sector, including: *Stability and
Integration in the Autonomous Republic
of Crimea: The Role of the
International Community*, *Ukrainian
NGO Directory*, and *Non-
Governmental Organizations of the
Autonomous Republic of Crimea
Handbook*.

IDC hopes to publish a magazine,
*Crossroads*, which will be devoted to
an exchange of views and activities
about philanthropic and charitable
activities. The magazine will be
distributed free of charge to donors,
charities and government officials.

## Institute of Statehood and Democracy

bul. Taras Shevchenko 37/122, k. 304
252032 Kyiv
**Tel/Fax:** 244-6409
**E-mail:** lozowy@gluk.apc.org
**Web:** www.freenet.kiev.ua/isd/isd-
home.htm
**Contact:** Ivan Lozowy, Executive
Director

ISD is a non-governmental, non-
partisan, public policy research and
educational institute, whose principal
aims are to propagate the idea of
Ukrainian statehood and assist in the
dissemination of democratic values, the
building of a rule-of-law society, and
the development of an independent
national policy. The institute was registered in June 1995 as a nonprofit civic
organization. Its ten founders include
five prominent politicians and five
businessmen. Although the institute
was created as an initiative by the
Popular Movement of Ukraine "Rukh,"
Ukraine's "largest national-democratic
political organization," it seeks to
engage all national-democratic activists
from Ukraine's eastern and southern
regions.

The institute's principal task is to
establish and run a program of study in
politics and governance in Ukraine in
order to promote the education and
skills of Ukraine's political leaders. The
institute regularly conducts seminars,
conferences, and symposia and holds

training courses for civic and political activists. Participants are chosen from all social strata, who have demonstrated a commitment to civic and political activism. The institute covers all expenses including travel and lodging.

ISD provides in-depth analysis of draft legislation and distributes analytical briefs to parliament members in order to encourage alternative legislation. In cooperation with the Conservative Party of Great Britain, the institute has conducted a number of seminars on organizing and managing publicity and election campaigns. Together with the Institute for Democracy in Europe, it organized a symposium on the rise of nationalism in the former Soviet Union.

The institute has published various books and brochures as well as an *NGO Newsletter* and an electronic bulletin, *The Rukh Insider*. A two-volume analysis of elections in Ukraine compiled by the institute is distributed free of charge.

The institute promotes the use of Ukrainian at its conferences and in its publications.

## International Biomedical Agency–Kyiv

ul. Pushkinska 22, kom. 304
252004   Kyiv
**Tel:**       224-7513
**Fax:**      229-1977
**E-mail:**  iba@iba.ukrpack.net,
           mrouga@iba.kiev.ua
**Contact:** Marina Mrouga, M.D.,
Director

IBA is an international network of independent, nonprofit organizations working to foster global collaboration in medical education. The agency was created in 1992 by U.S. and Russian medical educators and the Ukrainian

IBA office was opened in 1995 as a member of this international network.

As part of an international project conducted by the U.S.-based Educational Commission for Foreign Medical Graduates, IBA-Kyiv administered the Clinical Skills Assessment Project in Ukraine during 1995. It also created a Testing and Learning Center, with support from USAID and IREX. The center, which focuses on standardized test development, is currently recognized to be the technological and administrative model for the Medical Licensing and Examination Piloting Project, a national initiative to develop standardized quality control of medical education in Ukraine.

## International Center for Privatization, Investment and Management

vul. Eugene Pottier 20, etazh. 4,
kom. 407
252057   Kyiv
**Tel:**       441-7682, 446-1442,
           446-0117
**Fax:**      446-8277
**Contact:** Mr. Henryk Sterniczuk,
President

## International Management Institute–Kyiv

vul. Panasa Myrnoho 19
252011   Kyiv
**Tel:**       290-3352, 290-4330
**Fax:**      290-0495
**E-mail:**  imi@mcimi.freenet.kiev.ua
**Web:**     www.mim.kiev.ua/
**Contact:** Pavlo Sheremeta, at ext. 118

International Management Institute–Kyiv was established in 1989 as a joint venture between the Institute of Economics of the Ukrainian Academy of Sciences and IMI of Geneva, with the mission to educate professional managers for the Ukrainian economy. IMI's core activities include MBA programs, executive education, consulting services, a Ph.D. program in business administration, and research projects. It claims to have been the first institute in the NIS to offer a one-year MBA program based on a Western European model. By early 1995, IMI-Kyiv had graduated six classes with more than 300 MBA degrees. The IMI regularly hosts visiting faculty from abroad.

## International Media Center
vul. Shevtsova 1
252113  Kyiv
**Tel:**  446-0208, 446-4346, 446-5418
**Fax:**  446-1108
**E-mail:**  imc@sovam.com, mykol@sovam.com
**Contact:**  Mykola Kniazhytsky, Director

IMC supports the development of an independent broadcasting industry in Ukraine by lending studio facilities and production equipment to fledgling independent TV stations, holding seminars and workshops for local journalists with specialists from Ukraine and abroad, translating journalism education materials, and maintaining a reference library and information center for journalists.

## International Renaissance Foundation
ul. Artema 46
254053  Kyiv
**Tel:**  216-3307
**Fax:**  216-0166
**Pager:**  460-5460:17321
**E-mail:**  khmelevsky@irf.kiev.ua
**Web:**  www.irf.kiev.ua/
**Contact:**  Youry Khmelevsky, Ph.D., Chief Information Officer

IRF is the Open Society Institute office in Kyiv. It funds a wide array of initiatives in Ukraine. For more information, see the profile for Open Society Institute in North American Organizations.

## International Women's Right Center "La Strada Ukraine"
a/ya 246
252030  Kyiv
**Tel:**  224-7590
**Tel/Fax:**  224-0446
**E-mail:**  lastrada@fahi.gluk.apc.org
**Contact:**  Kateryna Levchenko, Olha Shved, Oksana Horbunava

La Strada Ukraine was established in 1997 in order to stop the illegal trafficking of women for prostitution in Ukraine, an underground business that has increased at an alarming rate in countries of the former Soviet Union since 1991. La Strada notes that, according to official data, 75 percent of unemployed Ukrainians are women, making them more susceptible to newspaper ads with attractive offers of overseas employment.

La Strada Ukraine has conducted 32 radio programs, 17 TV programs, 11 press conferences and roundtables, and 63 seminars and published 33 articles to shed light on this problem. Over 2,500 students have participated in La Strada seminars. It runs a telephone hotline to provide assistance to victims of trafficking and sexual abuse and offers consultations to women about working, studying, or vacationing abroad.

## Internews–Ukraine
P.O. Box 238
252032  Kyiv
**Tel/Fax:**  227-6223, 227-3511, 227-6036
**E-mail:**  inewsukr@internews.kiev.ua, sibel@internews.kiev.ua

**Contact:** Sibel Berzeg

Internews has been working in Ukraine since 1993 and reports it has trained more than 1,000 journalists. It produced the first independent, national, nightly news broadcast in Ukraine, *Windows*. It currently produces four television series, aired by independent stations around Ukraine, plus three weekly programs for broadcast by over 20 regional radio stations.

In mid-1998, Internews opened a Bi-Media News Room in Kyiv, which will allow it to augment lecture-based training with a live element, giving trainees experience in actual radio and television news broadcasts.

See profile of Internews in North American Organizations.

## IREX–Kyiv
Institute of Oriental Studies
vul. M. Hrushevskoho 4, kom. 301
252001   Kyiv
**Tel:**        229-3479, 228-8637
**Fax:**       229-3479
**E-mail:**   irexkyiv@irex.freenet. kiev.ua, staff@kyiv.irex.org

See IREX in North American Organizations.

## ISAR–WestNIS
a/ya 47
252006  Kyiv
**Tel/Fax:** 269-8542
**E-mail:**   isar@isar.kiev.ua
**Web:**      www.isar.org/isar/ West_NIS.html
**Contact:** Helena Gubar, Director; Dana Howard, Information Coordinator

A U.S.-based organization, ISAR's Kyiv office serves Belarus, Moldova and Ukraine. ISAR–WestNIS serves as an information clearinghouse for NGOs. It has developed an extensive database of regional environmental groups and, in 1995, published a directory of environmental NGOs in Belarus, Moldova, and Ukraine. The latest edition of this directory, entitled *Manual for Cooperation,* was published in September 1998. It also produces a monthly bulletin, which includes information about events of interest to local environmentalists. The bulletin is available in both hard-copy and electronic form.

ISAR–WestNIS focuses on three main programs:

- Environmental Networking. A network of specialists in specific areas of environmental study work to provide more effective information and facilitate cooperation among NGOs. The program includes a special focus on nuclear power issues.
- Small Seed Grants. ISAR's grant-making program offers support for environmental projects in fields such as media and public awareness, legal and legislative policy, alternative sources of energy, biodiversity protection, environmental education, community cleanup, pollution monitoring, "sustainable agriculture," and waste management.
- *Edinenie* (Joining Forces). ISAR's newest program seeks to assist the development of the third sector, to stimulate effective cooperation between NGOs, raise the image of NGOs in society, encourage their work with the mass media, and build relations with the government and business sectors.

## Kyiv Ecological and Cultural Center
ul. Radujnaia 31, k. 48
252218   Kyiv
**Tel:**       250-6701, 442-6434
**Fax:**      443-5262

**E-mail:** vladimir@kekz.freenet. viaduk.net
**Contact:** Vladimir Boreiko, Oleg Listopad

Founded in 1989, KECC is active in the fields of nature conservation, biodiversity protection, and support to environmental NGOs. Its main project, Love of Nature, seeks to promote the development of an environmental ethic in Ukraine and the former USSR, similar to the ideology that was developed in America by such writers as John Muir, Henry Thoreau and Ralph Waldo Emerson. It believes that environmental projects do not receive wide public support because they are presented in an overly scientific or economic manner. As part of the Love of Nature project, KECC has published and distributed a collection of books, including *Ethical and Aesthetic Approach in Nature Conservation*, *Nature and People of Kyiv Rus*, and *Environmental Traditions, Beliefs, and Religious Views of Slavonic and Other Peoples*, as well as translations of foreign literature. It has organized numerous seminars and workshops on environmental ethics for NGOs and schools and, in 1998, started publishing the e-mail bulletin *Love of Nature*.

KECC has also organized seminars for journalists and teachers, collected data on the environmental consequences of militarism, and started a program to promote public monitoring of acid rain. It has a staff of seven.

## League of Professional Women

per. Orlyka 2A, kv. 10 (postal address)
252024  Kyiv
ul. Tresvetitelska 4, k. 314
252001  Kyiv
**Tel:**  229-32-82, 293-90-32
**Fax:**  293-90-32
**E-mail:**  elen@mim.kiev.ua

**Contact:** Dr. Olena Lazorenko, President; Dr. Galina Kovadlo, Coordinator of Science and Educational Programs

LPW was formed in August 1997 on the initiative of Olena Lazorenko, Associate Professor at the International Management Institute, with the mission of transforming the social status of women by helping them with their professional careers. All of the members of LPW are volunteers, and presently the only sources of funds for LPW are membership fees and personal donations.

The league has focused on five main areas of activity: business, education and science, journalism, state administration, and youth. In April 1998, the league organized a consulting group, which unites top professionals in the fields of business, education and science, public administration, and mass media. It disseminates information regarding national and international projects, postgraduate education, training, workshops, and scholarships, fellowships, and internships. The league has conducted 22 consultations and organized job searches for its members. It intends to publish the magazine Gender in Science, which will contain articles written by women on politics, philosophy, law, culture, and management.

## League of Ukrainian Youth

Yaroslaviv Val, 9/4
252034  Kyiv
**Tel:**  224-4943
**Fax:**  274-8885
**E-mail:**  vyach@queen.ukma.kiev.ua.
**Web:**  www.ukma.kiev.ua/~plast/ lum/
**Contact:** Larissa Yolkina, President (tel: 243-6241); Vyacheslav Zapadnyuk, Secretary (tel: 430-2528)

The League of Ukrainian Youth was founded at the end of 1990 by students and teachers who had taken part in protest demonstrations and a hunger strike in Kyiv earlier in the fall. It was organized for the "development of democracy and realization of human rights in Ukraine; to support Ukrainian education; and to draw youth into scientific [professional] work."

The league organizes conferences and summer camps on such topics as: history, politics, philosophy, folklore, etc. Recently it collected and donated books to a Ukrainian school in the Crimea (a predominantly Russian area) and invited the students to come to Kyiv for lectures on Ukrainian history and literature. The league has a "theater studio" and a "literary studio." and began publishing a newspaper in 1998.

Besides Kyiv, the League of Ukrainian Youth has offices in Chernigiv, Cherkassy, Donetsk, Dnipropetrovsk, Bila Cerkva, Kharkiv, Lviv, Stryy, Odessa, Sumy, Ternopil, Vinnytsia, Berdychiv, Zaporizhia and Zhytomyr. Its staff of 164 is mostly volunteer labor. Total annual expenditures are about US$2,500.

## "Naturalist" League for Protection of Rights for Life and Balance in Nature

a/ya 189
252162   Kyiv
**Tel/Fax:** 474-6498
**E-mail:** nature@nature.freenet.kiev.ua
**Contact:** Nikolai Rud, President

The league was founded in 1996 as a union of young biology students and teachers. It offers educational programs on the environment and publishes a biology journal.

## NIS-US Women's Consortium

vul. Zankovetska 5/2, apt. 49
252001   Kyiv
**Tel:**       229-6543
**Tel/Fax:** 228-0685
**E-mail:**  consort@winrock.kiev.ua
**Contact:** Cara Galbraith, West NIS Coordinator; Lyudmila Bezsonova, Job Skills Training Coordinator

The first Kyiv Women's Center, co-founded jointly by five women's NGOs and the Kyiv City Administration, opened officially in August 1998. For a description of the broader program under which the Kyiv office operates, see NIS-US Women's Consortium in North American Organizations.

## Overseas Medical Aid Group

136 Krasnoarmeyska St., k. 43
252006   Kyiv
**Tel/Fax:** 268-3826
**E-mail:**  docdonald@worldnet.att.net
**Web:**     www.bandit.net/omag/
**Contact:** Donald Houston, M.D.

For a description of this project, which operates throughout the NIS and parts of southeastern Europe, see the profile in North American Organizations.

## PATH–Ukraine

29 Khreshchatik St., k. 50
252001   Kyiv
**Tel/Fax:** 462-0365, 462-0366,
                224-6189
**E-mail:**  kievpath@pathk.carrier.kiev.ua

See PATH in North American organizations.

## Project Harmony–Kyiv

**Tel/Fax:** 277-5348
**E-mail:**  phkievcc@inec.kiev.ua

See Project Harmony in North American Organizations.

## ProMedia Office
## Information and Press Center

Perchersky uzviz 3, 2nd floor
252023   Kyiv
**Tel:**      227-0160, 227-7761
**Fax:**     246-7939
**E-mail:**  info@ipc.kiev.ua,
tim@ipc.kiev.ua, gena@ipc.kiev.ua
**Web:**     www.ipc.kiev.ua/
**Contact:** Tim O'Connor, Resident
Advisor; Gennady Pochtar, Program
Coordinator

In late 1996, ProMedia asked newspapers in Ukraine what their biggest
needs were. One of the most common
answers from papers outside of Kyiv
was access to high-quality, timely news
photos. Whereupon ProMedia hired and
equipped Vasily Artyushenko, a
respected Ukrainian photojournalist.
His photographs were made available,
free of charge, via e-mail to private
newspapers across Ukraine.

Establishment of the ProMedia
Ukraine Internet Web site—on which
the photo service's current pictures and
archives are available—has allowed
newspapers to "window-shop" by
viewing thumbnail copies of the
available photos. By mid-1998, use of
the service had grown to include 80
newspapers in cities large and small
across Ukraine. According to results of
a survey, each of those newspapers
published, on average, about eight
pictures a month from the photoservice.

This is but one example of the many
creative programs that ProMedia—the
Professional Media Program, funded by
USAID and managed by IREX—has
been carrying out in Ukraine from
offices in Kyiv and the Crimea. Other
ProMedia activities support the development of a democratic legal and
regulatory framework for the media,
improve the quality of journalism,
promote more efficient business management, and assist in the development
of independent media associations and
NGOs. The ProMedia office in Kyiv
has a large library, meeting rooms,
computers connected to the Internet,
and an extensive, searchable database
of legal documents and past news
articles, which Ukrainian journalists
use to research stories.

## Pylyp Orlyk Institute for
## Democracy

Moskovska St. 40-A
252015   Kyiv
**Tel:**      290-7756, 290-6563
**Fax:**     290-6464
**E-mail:**  orlyk@orlyk.gluk.apc.org
**Web:**     www.elvisti.kiev.ua/orlyk/
**Contact:** Markian Bilynskyj, Director;
Valentina Telychenko, Deputy Director

Pylyp Orlyk (1672-1742), a Cossack
*hetman*, was chief author of the 1710
Bendery Constitution, alleged to be the
first constitution in the world to
embody the principles of separation of
powers and a democratically elected
parliament called the General Council.

The Pylyp Orlyk Institute was
founded 250 years after its namesake's
death with the assistance of the U.S.-
Ukraine Foundation. The institute is an
independent, public policy research
organization providing information to
Ukrainian policymakers, NGOs, academia, and media on issues pertaining to
the development of civil society. The
institute prepares analyses of legislation
and option papers, translates and publishes Western books, and provides
training and internship opportunities for
Ukrainian legislative staff. It also
cooperates with the U.S.-Ukraine
Foundation to implement a variety of
projects that support development in
targeted areas.

The Institute's Democracy Hotline
maintains an e-mail link between Kyiv

and Washington. It uses this link to give Ukrainian government officials the most up-to-date reports on how the U.S. media is covering Ukraine. A print publication, *The West: Window on Ukraine*, is distributed to 1,500 individuals in Ukraine and provides translations of select American Congressional hearings, U.S. government policy statements, and other important documents that relate to Ukraine. The institute also houses the U.S.-Ukraine Biblioteka Resource Center, which is a reference library for members of parliament. The Biblioteka holds over 1,500 volumes on public policy issues.

## Soros International House School

Kontraktova Square 4
254134   Kyiv
**Tel:**      417-7395
**Fax:**      416-2247
**E-mail:**   school@sihs.kiev.ua
**Contact:** Ms. Esfir Kotyk, Director

## Ukrainian Center for Independent Political Research

vul. B. Khelmnytsy 78, kom. 25
252030   Kyiv
**Tel:**        234-9315
**Tel/Fax:**  224-7742
**E-mail:**    kam@political.kiev.ua
**Contact:** Inna Pidluska, Foreign Relations Division; Dmitry Koublitsky, Post-Soviet Studies Division

The center was established in early 1991 as a non-partisan and non-governmental research institution. A group of young journalists and political analysts established this interdisciplinary, policy-oriented research institution outside the traditional university system. Its purpose is to enhance public understanding of democracy and to further the analytical research of

Ukrainian domestic and international politics and security.

UCIPR has hosted numerous conferences, workshops, seminars, and roundtable discussions and produces a number of publications, including *Ukrainian News*, *Military Bulletin*, *UCIPR's Notes*, *Ukraine in Documents*, and *UCIPR Daily News Report*.

The center is working to establish a network of similar offices throughout Ukraine. Through these offices, UCIPR plans to create a nationwide database of information on Ukrainian politicians, parties, public movements, enterprises, and major events occurring in Ukraine since 1991. There are also plans for a new, independent, foreign affairs quarterly, *The International Dimension*.

In 1998 UCIPR began publishing *Corruption Watch*, a monthly e-mail bulletin that reports on corruption issues in Ukraine. A recent issue included an analysis of a new "Presidential Decree on Fighting Corruption," the threat corruption poses in the military, and brief reports of corruption cases around the country. For subscription information, contact UCIPR at the e-mail address above.

## Ukrainian Conflict Resolution Association

a/ya 84
252128   Kyiv
**Tel:**       442-1842
**E-mail:**   hirnyk@bast.freenet.kiev.ua
**Contact:** Prof. Andrij M. Hirnyk, President

Established in 1995, the association directs the cooperative efforts of conflict resolution specialists in examining and predicting conflicts in ethnic, labor-management, national, and political arenas. It provides assistance in conflict analysis and resolution to government agencies, private organizations, and individuals. It also provides consulting in conflict management and organizes conferences and training sessions in conflict management skills, such as communication, mediation, and negotiation.

## Ukrainian Legal Foundation

vul. Saksahanskogo 41
252033  Kyiv
**Tel·**  227-2207, 227-2236,
227-2252
**Fax:**  227-2220
**E-mail:**  root@ulfl.freenet.kiev.ua,
chuck@chuck.ulfkiev.ua
**Web:**  rol.kiev.ua/ulf/ulf.html
**Contact:** Mr. Serhiy Holovaty,
President

ULF was founded in 1992 by members of the executive committee of the Association of Ukrainian Lawyers and lawyers from the Ukrainian Diaspora. In 1994, ULF played a critical role in the drafting and passage of Ukraine's Constitutional Accord and the Law on State Power and Local Self-Government, which helped break the constitutional impasse that had been blocking economic and political reform in Ukraine since independence.

ULF's projects include:

- Establishing the National Legal Library in 1994, the first such library in Ukraine
- Ukrainiain Center for Human Rights, which develops educational programs, monitors the human rights situation in Ukraine, and reviews legislation
- Ukrainiain Center for Legal Studies, which aims to establish a modern law school in Ukraine.

## Ukrainian Mediation Group– Search for Common Ground

Kyiv

**Tel/Fax:**  246-4813
**E-mail:**  sadams@gluk.apc.org
**Web:**  www.sfcg.org/mainukr.html
**Contact:** Scott Adams, Project Director

UMG is a network of independent, nonprofit organizations that provide conflict resolution services throughout Ukraine. The mission of UMG is to promote mediation and dispute resolution in Ukraine and, in the process, strengthen civil society and democratic reform.

In 1994, the Ukrainian Mediation Group formed a partnership with Search for Common Ground (see profile in North American Organizations), which has been supported with grants from private American foundations and USAID. The SCG-UMG collaboration has led to a series of professional exchanges, mediation training seminars, and projects, which have encouraged Ukrainians' efforts to influence the ways in which their society deals with conflict.

The Ukrainian Mediation Group has designed a training program to certify conflict resolution specialists. Graduates mediate labor, family, commercial, and consumer disputes. In the last year, the program has involved nearly 100 participants, including judges, lawyers, psychologists, teachers, and students.

UMG has been working with a core of Ukrainian judges who outsource cases to UMG mediators. In Donetsk and Odessa, UMG mediators have established a "noticeable presence" in the district courts and have gained the support of local judges. UMG hopes to expand its experience in court-annexed mediation in order to contribute to the legal reform process in Ukraine.

The challenges facing privatized and privatizing enterprises in Ukraine are enormous and conflicts between management and labor (and outside ownership where it exists) are inevitable. UMG has worked to provide consulting services for enterprises in various stages of the privatization process.

UMG has worked closely during the past two years with high schools to develop conflict resolution and peer mediation programs. In addition, there are programs focused on the mass media and the Crimea. For more about them, see UMG under Donetsk (below).

## Ukrainian Peacekeepers Veterans Association

ul. Volkov 20, k. 81
Kyiv
**Tel:**      519-4365, 244-1673
**Fax:**      228-9770
**E-mail:**  rauda@skyline.kiev.ua
**Web:**      infocenter.ukrpack.net/upva/index.html
**Contact:** Lt. Col. (Ret.) Yuri Donskoi

The association is a member of the Soldiers' Peace International Association (SPIA). It is a support center for soldiers and veterans who have served in peacekeeping operations abroad. Its current activity focuses on Ukrainian soldiers serving in Bosnia. The association has close contact with the UNDP office in Kyiv and takes part in international conferences of the SPIA, such as the International Assembly of Blue Berets in 1995, celebrating 50 years of UN peacekeeping activity. The association recently conducted a seminar, "Education in Human Rights for the Military of Ukraine."

## Ukrainian Society for Sustainable Development

USSD c/o "Lybid"
ul. Kutuzova 18/7, kom. 901
252133   Kyiv
**Tel:**      295-4337

**Fax:**      295-6618
**E-mail:**  enalt@ukrpack.net
**Contact:** Vadim Duikanov, Ph.D.; Nadia Sosonkina

USSD and the International Institute for Energy Conservation have a joint project to strengthen the role of NGOs in the sphere of national energy policy and to increase public awareness of energy conservation issues and the development of sustainable energy alternatives. Its other goals include exchanging information and forming coalitions with other NGOs and businesses, preparing informational materials and training seminars about energy conservation, and promoting alternative energy in the political arena.

The idea to establish USSD was born in 1994 during an international workshop on local environmental policymaking. NGO leaders and local and regional administration officials agreed on the need for an organization that could evaluate governmental policies, laws, and regulations to determine those most favorable for Ukraine's development.

In 1995, in collaboration with Kyiv National University, USSD began the Sustainable Ukraine project. Between 1995 and 1997, members of USSD published over 20 articles and research materials on the problems of sustainable development in Ukraine. Members of the organization designed new courses in environmental science and policies for graduate students at the Kyiv-Mohyla Academy.

USSD works with the International Institute for Energy Conservation and the People-Centered Development Forum.

## Ukrainian Student Association in the USA (USA/USA)

Poshtova Skrynka 15

254213 Kyiv
**E-mail:** vitaly@erc.kiev.ua
**Contact:** Vitaly Babych

The purpose of USA/USA is to recruit and advise a select number of Ukrainian students who are considering pursuing an American college education. Hundreds of Ukrainian students apply to USA/USA each year by submitting two essays written in English, a resume, a recommendation from a teacher, high school transcripts, and photos. The applicants are screened, and only a handful of students are chosen to take an English proficiency examination. Those who achieve the required score are then invited to attend a workshop in Kyiv. USA/USA hosts the week-long workshop, which explains the U.S. educational system to the students and gives them information on the TOEFL, SAT I, and SAT II tests. Students are advised on how to choose a college, apply for fee waivers and compete for scholarships. If students are unable to obtain fee waivers, USA/USA will provide the necessary funding. The selected students choose the universities and colleges, then fill out and send in their own applications.

## Ukrainian Youth Environmental League

a/ya 13
252030 Kyiv-30
**Tel/Fax:** 244-38-47
**E-mail:** liga@uyel.freenet.kiev.ua
**Contact:** Igor Kirilchuk, Chairman

The league was established in 1993 by members of the youth wing of Zeleny Svit, the Ukrainian Council of Student Groups for Environment Protection, and the Kyiv Eco-Cultural Center. It claims to be the only national, youth environmental organization in Ukraine. It promotes biodiversity protection and technology for "environmentally clean" products and runs education projects to involve youth in the environmental movement. The league has branches in 17 regions of Ukraine.

## Women's Information Consultative Center

vul. Saksaganskogo 12A/11
252033 Kyiv
**Tel/Fax:** 227-0704
**E-mail:** olena@wicc.kiev.ua
**Contact:** Olena Suslova, Chairperson of the Board of Directors

The main goal of WICC is to gather and disseminate information among the women of Ukraine about women's organizations (at home and abroad), their activities, and initiatives.

The center was founded in 1995. It is supported by its founders, various organizations, fees, and private donations. WICC provides information to individuals and organizations, consults on various aspects of women issues, participates in political lobbying, and organizes discussion groups and seminars. WICC has a library about women and women's issues; has collected statistical data on education, employment, and family life of women in Ukraine; and has compiled a Successful Women database.

WICC has issued the following publications: *Daughters of Ukraine* (1995), *Directory of Women's Organizations and Initiatives in Ukraine* (1996) , *Ms. Right Calendar* (about women's human rights, 1996), *We Are One Whole* (about the pilot project Empowering Education: Equal Rights and Equal Opportunities for Boys and Girls,1997). It also published a magazine, *Dawn*, for boys and girls who had participated in the Empowering Education project.

## Youth Congress of Ukrainian Nationalists

Yaroslaviv Val 9/6
252034   Kyiv
**Tel/Fax:** 228-7020
**E-mail:**  mcun@yahoo.com,
        root@andre.sumy.ua
**Web:**   www.grono.sumy.ua
**Contact:** Victor Rog, Chairman; Vasil Boyko, Secretary

YCUN works to facilitate the "consolidation of Ukrainian patriotic youth organizations." The organization was formed in June 1998, and it held its first summer camp in August near Ternopil, attended by 15 Ukrainian youth organizations. In October 1998 the first national convention of YCUN was held in Kyiv.

YCUN's current activities focus on (1) ecological actions against the building of the Tashlyk Hydro Power Station on the South Bug river, and (2) the startup of its new magazine, *Ukrainian Problems*. YCUN claims to have offices in every regional center (25 cities) and in 254 smaller towns. There are about 5,000 members in the congress, and its budget for 1998 was about 7,000 hryvnia (approximately US$3,000).

YCUN partners wirh 19 organizations in Ukraine and five Ukrainian diaspora organizations in Russia, Europe, the U.S., and Canada.

## Zeleny Svit (Green World)

Зеленый свит
vul. Mykhailivska 6, kom. 306
25200   Kyiv
**Tel:**     446-3435
**Fax:**     546-0073
**E-mail:**  fedoryn@grworld.freenet.kiev.ua
**Contact:** Serghyi Fedorynchuk, Information Center Director

Zeleny Svit was founded by a group of Kyiv writers and artists in December 1987 and established as a national organization at its first congress in October 1989. Its first chairman, Yuri Scherback, was later appointed Minister of the Environment and then Ambassador to the U.S.

Zeleny Svit is a federation of more than 100 local environmental groups with over 2,000 members across Ukraine. It is financed through dues, donations, and—more recently—grants from environmental funds. Much of its work is performed on a volunteer basis.

ZS and its local affiliates are engaged in a wide range of activities, including: environmental education, monitoring of enterprises, promoting environmental legislation and national funding of alternative energy, and lobbying for the creation of wildlife reserves. ZS affiliates have led successful campaigns to close polluting factories and construct water treatment facilities.

At the national level, Zeleny Svit has organized several referendums on nuclear power issues. Since 1996 it has organized a project to monitor water quality along the coast and in rivers in order to create a baseline of data which can be used to measure compliance with environmental regulations.

It has published the newspaper *Zeleny Svit* since 1990. In 1991 it became an Associate Member of Friends of the Earth International.

## *Berdyansk (615)*

## Sea of Azov International Ecological Foundation

Международный Экологический Фонд Азовское Моря
ul. Uritskogo 3
332440   Berdyansk

**Tel:** 33-24-47, 39-55-68
**Fax:** 33-23-06
**E-mail:** ariu@ariu.dnepr.net,
almag@ariu.dnepr.net
**Contact:** Mark Kotlyarevskii

The foundation works to protect the Sea of Azov and its environs, as well as to draw public attention to factors that threaten the sea's ecosystem and educate the populace about environmental protection issues. Foundation members compiled a report on the current state of the sea and its shores for use in public education. Additionally, the group has published ecological education materials that focus on the Sea of Azov for use in local elementary schools.

## Cherkassy (472)

### Ecological Education Publishing House
Экологическое образование
ul. Frunze 1
257002   Cherkassy
**Tel:** 47-43-83, 43-64-75
**E-mail:** zelsvit@zelsvit.freenet. kiev.ua

This group has published a collection of materials from the Second International Conference on Ecological Education held in Cherkassy in 1996. The collection includes curricular guides for teachers about ecological issues (in Ukrainian): one for high school classes on chemical processes and the environment and another for middle-school children on basic ecology issues.

## Chernihiv (462)

### City Organization of Large Families
ul. Kotsybynskogo 14
250034   Chernihiv
**Tel:** 95-35-06, 24-26-94
**Contact:** Nina Grigorieva, Lyudmila Shurik

This organization has about 400 members and was registered in 1995.

### Cossack Society
57 Shevchenka St.
Chernihiv
**Tel:** 95-42-24
**Contact:** Vitalii Bazhan

The society registered in 1995 and has about 150 members. It is funded by dues and donations. It organizes cultural, educational, and some commercial projects.

### Foundation for International Professional Exchange
October Revolution Ave. 117, suite 22
250038   Chernihiv
**Tel:** 27-22-27
**E-mail:** fipe01@elit.chernigov.ua
**Contact:** Natalia Zdanovich

See Foundation for International Professional Exchange in North American Organizations.

### Orthodox Brotherhood
40 Sverdlova St.
250000   Chernihiv
**Tel:** 24-15-47, 27-99-92
**Contact:** Inessa Vachnadze, Vyacheslav Login

The organization has about 25 members and engages in charitable, educational, and cultural activities. It was founded in 1995.

## Dnipropetrovsk (562)

### Educational Information-Consulting Center

Образовательный
информационно-
консультационный центр
ul. Gogolia 29
320044   Dnipropetrovsk
**Tel/Fax**: 453-578
**E-mail**:   malex@vidr.dp.ua
**Web**:      www.osvita-eac.dp.ua
**Contact**: Alexander Marchenko

The center offers preparation classes
and testing services for TOEFL, GRE,
GMAT, and other standardized tests. It
also offers Internet access to students.

### Pridneprovie Cleaner Production Center

Приднепровый Центр за чище
продукции
ul. Naberezhnaya Lenina 29-a, k. 505
320070   Dnipropetrovsk
or
a/ya 4159 (postal address)
320002   Dnipropetrovsk
**Tel**:       41-65-50
**Fax**:      41-65-90
**E-mail**:   ecofond@ecofond.dp.ua
**Contact**: Professor William M.
Zadorsky, President

The Pridneprovie Cleaner Production
Center was established in 1994 as a
joint initiative of the Pridneprovie
Ecological Foundation and the International Academy of Computer
Sciences and Systems. The center is an
association of enterprises, organizations, scientists and specialists committed to environmental protection and
the need for more environmentally
responsible industrial equipment and
standards. It offers educational programs and training to students, scientists, and engineers in the development

of resource-saving, environmentally
safe production techniques for such
industries as metallurgy, chemicals, and
power generation.

The center organizes regular meetings with representatives of local
environmental groups and promotes
environmental protection in the local
press. In cooperation with the Journalists' Union, the center recently held
a competition for the best publication
on the environment. The center is also
establishing an Environmental
Education Center to train industry
specialists and farming associations. In
1998, the center began publishing a
monthly magazine, *Constructive
Ecology and Business*, which focuses
on constructive ways to decide environmental issues in industry and agriculture within the context of a market
economy.

## Donetsk (622)

### American International Club of Donetsk

ul. Budjonogo 46, kv. 2
340053   Donetsk
or
c/o Michelle Ann Hanson, Peace Corps
P.O. Box 157
340000   Donetsk
**Tel**:       92-38-53
**E-mail**:   solnechnaya@hotmail.com
**Contact**: Lilia G. Shumatskaya,
Director; Michelle Ann Hanson, Peace
Corps Volunteer

The American International Club of
Donetsk was founded in August 1997
by Director Lilia Shumatskaya and U.S.
Peace Corps Volunteer Michelle
Hanson. The goals of the club are to
improve the members' spoken English,
to give young people a safe and com-

fortable place to gather, to provide members an opportunity to learn about different countries and cultures, and to share Ukrainian culture with foreigners. AICD conducts conversational English-language and environmental education programs and workshops on business, leadership, and career development—including resume-writing and inter-viewing techniques. It has recently started a training program for inter-preters and a conversational English program with local schools for club members who plan to be English teachers.

An executive committee of elected members organizes the club's activities, with the guidance of the director and local Peace Corps volunteers. The club currently has 50 members and a month-ly budget of US$300–$400. AICD has developed good working relationships in Donetsk with the British Council, Counterpart Resource Center, Follow Me (a private English school), and the Donetsk Iron and Steel Works.

## Center for Political Studies
ul. Universitetska 24
340055   Donetsk
**Tel:**      92-40-97
**Fax:**      92-60-67
**E-mail:**   greg@cps.donetsk.ua
**Contact:** Grigory Nemiria, Director

The center is an independent institute focusing on research into domestic and foreign politics in Ukraine and Eastern Europe. It also promotes reform of higher education.

## Donetsk Association of International Researchers
Office 43, Korp. 2,
Donetsk State University
24 Universitetska St.
340055   Donetsk

or
(postal address)
61 Kotzubinski St.
340048   Donetsk
**Tel:**      91-92-53
**Fax:**      92-71-12
**E-mail:**   charskykh@hotmail.com
**Contact:** Vitali Razumny, Project Coordinator

The association was founded by professors and students to promote democratization and to strengthen international ties in the Donetsk region by disseminating information about the history and current events of foreign countries. It has published several monographs and organized a couple of conferences. Its budget in 1996 was $18,000 and, in 1998, $10,500.

## Donetsk Christian University
p-t Ilicha 106a
340059   Donetsk
**Tel:**      97-22-10, 97-25-19
**Tel/Fax:** 97-25-26
**E-mail:**   uni@theologic.donetsk.ua
**Contact:** Alexei Melnichuk, Director; Yuriy Golovay, Assistant Academic Dean

The mission of Donetsk Christian University is "to work on behalf of the evangelical community of the former Soviet Union, to engage in theological as well as other scientific research and reflection, and to prepare people to fulfill the mission of the Church in both the spiritual and social spheres."

In 1989 the indigenous Russian/Ukrainian mission, Svet Evanglia (Light of the Gospel), was organized, with Sergei Tupchik elected president and Alexei Melnichuk vice president. The mission began mobilizing and sending missionaries throughout the Soviet Union with concentrations in Ukraine and the Far East.

In 1991, a pastor of a Svet Evanglia church in Makeevka, Ukraine, purchased an unused children's summer camp to be used as the location of a bible college. Alexei Melnichuk moved to Donetsk to work as director of the newly formed Donetsk Christian University. The university was organized under the Fund for Theological Education, a non-denominational, nonprofit entity. Classes began with 56 students in the fall.

A three-year Bachelor of Theology program began in 1993, when Alexei Melnichuk left for Denver Seminary to begin three years of study. Work also began on a new building to house staff and faculty. In 1994, an agreement was signed between the seminary, Conservative Baptists International, and International Teams to provide training and support for long-term professors.

In 1996, Melnichuk returned to Donetsk, and the first group of students graduated with Bachelor of Theology degrees. Since then, a computer lab has been installed, and work was completed on faculty housing and a student dorm.

The university has re-registered as a religious institution under the auspices of both the Union of Evangelical Baptists and the Autonomous Baptist Churches. This is the first time in Ukraine that a religious entity has been supported by two different denominations or organizations.

The university is one of the founding members of the EurAsian Accrediting Association. Its main partners overseas are Denver Theological Seminary and International Teams.

## Donetsk Environmental Council

Донецкий Городской
Экологический Совет
ul. Artema 9
340050   Donetsk

**Tel:**    35-35-50, 35-49-61
**Fax:**    35-24-19
**E-mail:**   evgenya@ekol.uvica.donetsk.ua
**Contact:** Marina Shafarostova

The Donetsk Environmental Council was formed in 1989 in response to worsening environmental conditions in Donetsk and the lack of any similar organization in the city. The organization works mainly in the sphere of environmental education. From 1997 to 1998, the council worked on a joint Ukrainian-British program to create environmentally oriented school materials. Members of the group also participated in an international effort to draft the Youth Charter to Protect the Environment, the focus of a conference in Istanbul, Turkey, in November 1997.

## Donetsk Regional NGO Service Center (RSC)

a/ya 25
Central Post Office
340000   Donetsk
**Tel/Fax:** 93-10-92
**E-mail:**   ngo@rsc.donetsk.ua
**Contact:** Natasha Sofyants, Director; Jason Berry, Peace Corps Volunteer

RSC was created in September 1997 to support the development of regional NGOs. The center investigates and analyzes Ukrainian NGO problems and activities; promotes collaborations between NGOs and the government and business sectors; and provides NGOs with technical assistance, information, training, and consulting in order to increase their professionalism. Training is offered in fundraising, financial management, public relations, conflict resolution, proposal writing, and strategic planning.

## Ukrainian Mediation Group

ul. 50-Letiya USSR 143
340100  Donetsk
**Tel/Fax:** 35-74-33
**E-mail:** drmg@ns.dc.ukrtel.net
**Web:** www.sfcg.org/mainukr.htm
**Contact:** Nikolai Borisov, Project
Director

UMG is a network of seven regional
centers that provide conflict resolution
services throughout Ukraine. The effort
to systematize practical approaches to
dispute resolution began in the 1980s
when Nikolai Borisov began mediating
between striking coal miners and
management in the Donetsk region.
Since that time, UMG has expanded
its repertoire. (See UMG profile under
Kyiv.) Many of the projects operate
without funding and succeed due to "a
seemingly endless supply of energy and
enthusiasm." UMG consists of 25 paid
staff members and over 100 volunteers,
including psychologists, lawyers,
judges, teachers, and students.

In order to build awareness about
alternative dispute resolution, UMG
has provided conflict resolution training
for journalists. In May 1998, a seminar
entitled Mass Media: Approaching
Conflict was held in Donetsk to encourage media professionals to consider
how TV, newspapers and radio can
affect and change conflict situations.

In Crimea, the regional Mediation
Groups have spoken about mediation
on local radio shows, and the organization is in the early stages of the Dialogue on Crimea project. Crimea is
threatened by tensions among national
and ethnic groups, most notably
Russians, Ukrainians, and recently
returned Crimean Tatars. With two
mediation centers in Crimea, UMG is
developing an inter-group dialogue
between civil society leaders representing each of the ethnic groups.

## Youth Center for Legal Studies

vul. Cheluskintsev 198A
340015  Donetsk
**Tel/Fax:** 35-80-49
**E-mail:** intdep@law.uvica.donetsk.ua
**Contact:** Sergey Khmara, Coordinator

The center is an NGO for young
lawyers and students at universities in
the Donetsk region. One of its main
activities is to provide students and
professors with information about
opportunities for internships, summer
schools, short-term courses, and law-
related graduate and post-graduate
studies abroad.

## Drohobych (03244)

### Ukrainian Association of Amnesty International

Maydan Rynok 6
293720  Drohobych
Lviv Region
**Tel/Fax:** 3-83-29
**E-mail:** officeai@amnesty.lviv.ua
**Contact:** Roman Hrechanyk, Chairman
of National Committee

Amnesty International began working
in Drohobych in 1991 and was founded
by Myroslav Marynovych, a former
Ukrainian prisoner of conscience.
UAAI consists of 28 groups across
Ukraine who collectively work for the
release of political prisoners and those
imprisoned as a result of ethnic, racial,
or religious prejudices. UAAI advocates fair trials for all prisoners and an
end to the death penalty and all forms
of torture.

## Ivano-Frankivsk (342)

## Small Business Economic Development Ivano-Frankivsk Business Center

26 Dnistrovska St.
284000   Ivano-Frankivsk
**Tel:**     25-20-22, 25-20-26
**Fax:**    25-9156
**E-mail:**   sbedif@sbedif.ivano-frankivsk.ua
**Web:**    www.sbedif.ivano-frankivsk.ua
**Contact:** Jerry Jaroslaw Kozubal, Director; Alexander Pasichnyk, Assistant Director; Roman Komarnitsky, Marketing Officer

The business center in Ivano-Frankivsk has been in operation since 1996. It is currently the largest project in Ukraine funded by the Canadian International Development Agency. It has a staff of 25, all residents of Ivano-Frankivsk. The director is a Canadian with over 25 years of management and consulting experience.

Ukrainian partners in the project include the oblast administration and city administration of Ivano-Frankivsk. The Canadian partners include Confederation College in Thunder Bay, responsible for overall project management, the University of Waterloo, the University of Saskatchewan, and Parkland Community Futures Corporation in Manitoba. The Canadian partners provide technical support and coordination to the various programs that are being delivered through the Business Center.

The project's objective is to train local entrepreneurs in the Ivano-Frankivsk oblast on how to enter and succeed in a market economy. The center offers a wide variety of programs and services to individual and business clients, including:

- Business Consulting. Four business consultants provide clients with

assistance in preparing business plans and advice on the legal and technical aspects of operating a business in Ukraine.

- Loan Fund. The center has a loan fund for small businesses. In the first year of operation, it approved 10 loans that created 65 new jobs. Loans can be up to a maximum of $10,000 and a 36-month term. All loans are fully secured by a lease agreement and the equipment is insured by a local insurance broker. Using capital of $350,000, the plan is to provide approximately 40 loans per year.

- Trade and Commerce Program. The center provides a service to encourage trade missions between Ivano-Frankivsk and other countries. The program matches Ukrainian and foreign companies wishing to explore new business opportunities. The center can provide information on company profiles and business opportunities and information on how to conduct business in Ukraine.

- Entrepreneurship Training Program. The center has developed training modules on starting a new business, marketing, financial planning, and youth and women in entrepreneurship. Training is provided by Ukrainian staff and occasionally supplemented by experts from Canada. The center can also design and deliver courses to meet the specific needs of business clients.

## Kharkiv (572)

### ACCELS–Kharkiv

pl. Konstitutsii 26, kom. 41A
Dom Nauki i Tekhniki
310003   Kharkiv
**Tel/Fax:** 12-74-37
**E-mail:**  fsakhkiv@fsa.kharkov.ua

See profile for American Councils for International Education in North American Organizations.

## Center for Educational Initiatives

ul. Sumskaya 37
310002   Kharkiv
**Tel:**      12-02-61
**Tel/Fax:** 47-16 32
**E-mail:**  ita@cei.kharkov.ua
**Contact:** Irina Pasisnichenko, Director

The Center for Educational Initiatives was founded by a group of Kharkiv scholars and educators in 1992 to support non-governmental groups working in the field of education and to promote new methods of teaching the humanities and social sciences. It creates new informational resources, organizes international conferences and workshops for university instructors, and establishes new educational institutions. CEI also provides technical training to local NGOs and has created a database of regional NGOs.

## EcoPravo-Kharkiv

a/ya 2050
310202   Kharkiv
**Tel:**      12-85-57
**Tel/Fax:** 23-40-47, 36-82-54
**E-mail:**  xleco@online.kharkov.ua
**Contact:** Aleksei Shumilo, President

Founded in 1993, EcoPravo offers legal services to citizens and non-governmental organizations on environmental law and represents individuals and organizations with cases involving environmental law in court. It is affiliated with the Environmental Public Advocacy Center in Lviv.

## Kharkiv State Institute of Culture

Bursatskii Spusk 4

**E-mail:**  denis@irex.kharkiv.net

## Kharkiv City Women's Club "Miroslava"

310023   Kharkiv
**Tel:**      47-97-73
**E-mail:**  tanya@mirslava.kharkiv.com
**Contact:** Tatiana Kononenko

Miroslava is one of the first women's volunteer organizations in Kharkiv. Its members include those who work in the spheres of science, culture, and education and also young people who share the goals of Miroslava. It works to improve the status of women in society and promote a better understanding of Ukrainian society at home and abroad.

Miroslava develops programs in many areas. It organizes educational conferences, seminars, and roundtables, at which priority is given to issues of equal rights, ecology and health, as well as spiritual issues. Miroslava's cultural activities include exhibitions, concerts, speaking tours, and art classes. With these activities, Miroslava intends to promote self-esteem, conflict resolution, and personal growth of women. The club also provides information services and organizes international exchanges, speaking tours, and opportunities to study abroad.

Miroslava receives organizational support and ongoing cooperation from the following organizations: Kharkiv Theater of Opera and Ballet, Kharkiv Art Museum, Administration for Domestic Businesses of Ukraine in the Kharkiv region, and Earth Action. Miroslava helps its partners plan public events and develop joint programs.

## Kharkiv "Human Rights Education Center"

Харківский "Освітній центр прав людини"

ul. Akhsarova 13, kv. 112
310204   Kharkiv
**Tel/Fax:** 37-08-11
**E-mail:** Oles@hrec.kharkov.ua
**Contact:** Oles Kusaikin, Chairman;
Nina Kusaikina, Director

The center was founded in 1996 by the Ukrainian branch of International Society for Human Rights, Kharkov Juridical Society, Human Rights Protection Group in Kharkov, and Center of Education Initiatives in Kharkov. In 1997, the center organized its second international conference on education and human rights. It has developed curricula on human rights for three kindergartens, six schools and one college. Activists from the center give lectures, organize seminars, publish articles, and make public appearances on radio and television. The center has received two grants from the TACIS program and the International Renaissance Foundation. The center is a partner of Amnesty International.

## Kharkiv Municipal Charity Union "Sintez"

Синтез
a/ya 8758 (postal address)
310002   Kharkiv
or
ul. Sokolova 46
210089   Kharkiv
**Tel:**      94-62-10
**E-mail:** syntez@mailbox.kharkov.ua,
fmah52a@prodigy.com,
muhoel@aol.com
**Web:**      www.geocities.com/Heartland
/Valley/7607/
**Contact:** Valeriy Ivanov, President;
Norman Berris, Consultant; Ganna
Dudukalova, Manager

Sintez is a charitable organization funded by contributions from individuals and the government. Its purpose is to help orphans, refugees, and homeless children of the Kharkiv region. Children under its care range from infants to 18 year-olds.

The instability of Ukraine's economy and budget deficits have had a disastrous effect on children's development and health in this region. Sintez has made attempts to ease the situation with the help of various commercial structures and international charitable organizations. According to official statistics, more than 1,000 children live in railway stations, commercial establishments, basements, and attics.

Sintez has been trying to open the first orphanage in the Kharkiv region for children aged 3 to 18, but it does not have sufficient funds to pay for food, basic equipment (beds, chairs, bookcases, etc.) and personnel. The orphanage would be open to orphaned children, children abandoned by their parents, lost children, and children removed from their families. Sintez seeks partners and sponsors to develop the orphanage and help the children of the Kharkiv region.

## "RAIX Group" Kharkiv City Public Organization

pr. Sadovyi 8/21
310128 Kharkiv
**Tel:**      14-24-52, 98-58-22
**Tel/Fax:** 14-24-27
**E-mail:** info@raix.kharkov.ua
**Web:**      raix@kharkiv.com
**Contact:** Andrei Ripka, President;
Natalia Vasilina

Founded in 1996, RAIX Group uses the Internet to collect information about world cultures to distribute to the people of Kharkiv and to provide details about Kharkiv to the world. It is interested in developing Internet usage in Kharkiv and offers technical and consulting services in using the Internet to local NGOs.

## Soros International House School

vul. Olmynskoho 11
310024   Kharkiv
**Tel:**       43-72-84
**Fax:**      47-82-84
**Contact:** Mr. Ihor Manko, Director

## Khmelnytsky (382)

### Podolsk Ecological Society

Родольское экологическое общество
ul. Kotovskogo 71
280000   Khmelnytsky
**Tel:**       29-13-75
**Fax:**      29-24-35
**E-mail:**   rusl@eco17.freenet.kiev.ua
**Contact:** Valerii Datskov, Chairman; Ruslan Belik, Deputy Chairman

The Podolsk Ecological Society was formed in 1997 to improve distribution of information related to the environment and environmental legislation. The society has developed an educational program to improve the "ecological literacy" of regional leaders. It served as a regional coordinator for the Unity program, a project sponsored by ISAR-Kyiv to establish a network of environmental organizations in Ukraine. The society has also designed a number of ecology courses for school curricula, organized eco-camps for children, and provided consultations on legal issues.

## Kirovohrad

## Information Center for Women in Kirovohrad

vul. Karla Marksa 24
316050   Kirovohrad
**Tel:**       22-65-06
**E-mail:**   oleg_volokhin@p14.fl.n46
43.z2.fidonet.org
**Contact:** Olena Garschenko

The center was founded in December 1996 by a group of women who work at the regional university's research library. It is doing research on the problem of domestic violence and organized a workshop on women's human rights in 1997. The center has been working on the database of women's organizations in the region. It plans to collect materials on women's issues and disseminate information throughout the region.

## Kolomyia (343)

### Veles Foundation in Kolomyia

Коломыйский фонд "Велес"
ul. Lysenka, 12/56
285200   Kolomyia
**Tel:**       33-46-04, 33-58-61
**Contact:** Vladimir V. Batiaikin, Chairman; Taras A. Gorodchuk, Program Coordinator

Veles was created in response to a worsening social and economic situation that has produced very negative effects for the region's environment. Founded in December 1996, Veles works in the following fields: education, eco-tourism, "rehabilitation" and protection of nature, and propagation of a healthy lifestyle. The foundation relies on volunteers and has no employees. Veles has organized expeditions on the Prut and Dniester rivers and in the Carpathians, cleaned a creek in cooperation with Zeleny Svit, and planted trees in the Carpathian national park. Volunteers from the foundation provide technical assistance to the Young Tourists Club on a regular basis.

Veles established a school for young parents and an eco-studio for kindergarten instructors in order to promote the idea of family tourism. It collaborates with the municipal department of education, municipal council, and the executive committee. Veles finances its projects through membership dues and donations.

## Lutsk (332)

### Center "Polissja"
ul. Griboedova 6
263005   Lutsk
**Tel/Fax:** 24-15-14
**Contact:** Volodimir Terletsky

The center was established in 1996 to monitor the environment in the Polessie region after the Chernobyl tragedy and to prepare recommendations for environmental protection and recovery in the area. It strives to introduce better control systems and to cooperate with the international community in Chernobyl-related research.

The center has conducted an expedition to the upper reaches of the Pripiat river and organized a study which supported the establishment of a new national park. It has mapped several river basins in the Polissie region, studied water balance in areas where marshes had been drained, and monitored stability, soil erosion, radiation levels, and biological diversity. The center has 20 researchers, new computer laboratories, several facilities, and vehicles for field trips. Center Polissja has the following partners: Wageningen

Agricultural University (Holland), Warsaw Agricultural University (Poland), and the Medicinal Herbs Institute (Moscow). The center published *Herbs of Polessie*.

## Lviv (322)

### ACCELS–Lviv
vul. 700-richia Lvova 57
Naukogo Technichniy Tsentr
Informatsii, kom. 509
290058   Lviv
**Tel/Fax:** 27-11-25
**E-mail:** fsalviv@fsa.lviv.ua

See profile for American Councils for International Education in North American Organizations.

### Counterpart Creative Center–Lviv
ul. Yuriia Drogobycha 8/12
290000   Lviv
**Tel:**      74-42-64
**Contact:** Galina Sabodash

Affiliated with the Counterpart Creative Center in Kyiv, CCC–Lviv operates a microcredit program in partnership with a local bank and Soyuz Ukrainok (SU), a national Ukrainian woman's organization. Loans range in size from US$500 to $5,000, interest rates are 17 percent (in 1998), and terms range from three months to one year. All borrowers must be members of SU in good standing.

### Counterpart Meta Center
vul. 700-richia Lvova 63, Fifth floor
290058   Lviv
**Tel:**      93-50-92
**Fax:**     93-50-93
**E-mail:**  meta@meta.lviv.ua

This three-year USAID-funded program is designed for entrepreneurs in the Lviv region. The center has modern office equipment and offers a range of services to small and start-up businesses, including small loans ranging in size from US$2,000 to $20,000. CMC is registered as a local, non-commercial organization but has partnered with Electron Bank to disburse approximately US$750,000 in loans. The goal is to help new businesses get off the ground and develop more small-business lending in Ukraine.

## Environmental Public Advocacy Center–EcoPravo

vul. Krushelnitska 2
290000  Lviv
**Tel/Fax:** 72-27-46
**E-mail:** epac@link.lviv.ua
**Web:** www.igc.apc.org/elaw/
europe/ukraine/ecoprav_lviv.html
**Contact:** Svetlana Kravchenko

The center is a joint project between EcoPravo–Lviv and the American Bar Association's Central and East European Law Initiative (CEELI). It is a pilot project of CEELI aimed at setting up a network of EPACs in Eastern Europe. It was founded in March 1994, and all of its members are lawyers.

The center's principal goals are:
- Raising the level of environmental and legal culture of citizens and NGOs
- Training a new generation of environmental lawyers
- Increasing awareness among lawyers and judges of environmental issues and the need for action
- Protecting citizens' environmental rights and raising the level of responsibility of government administrators

## The European Law Students' Association–Ukraine Branch

P.O. Box 10632
290000  Lviv
Tel/Fax: 79-47-58
**E-mail:** elsa@yep.lviv.ua,
andy@yep.lviv.ua
**Contact:** Andrew Shamryk, Secretary General

ELSA was founded in 1981 in Vienna, Austria, and today comprises 25,000 students from 180 university-based local groups, spanning 41 countries. ELSA–Lviv is the only member of the association in Ukraine. It conducts seminars and conferences for law students to broaden their knowledge of European and international law and runs a Student Trainee Exchange Program for law students to study and live abroad.

## Land O'Lakes–Lviv

10 Kopernika #6
290000  Lviv
**Tel:**      74-19-43
**Tel/Fax:** 27-19-11
**E-mail:**  jon@lol.lviv.ua,
dave@lol.lviv.ua
**Contact:** Jon D. Thiele, Country Manager, Western Ukraine Initiative; David Blood, Project Coordinator, Farmer-to-Farmer Program

Land O'Lakes is the largest dairy cooperative in the United States. Through its International Development Division and with support from USAID, it is involved in the development of the private economic sector in many countries of the world. Beginning in 1995, Land O'Lakes initiated programs to support private agribusiness in western Ukraine. These programs offer technical assistance, consultations, seminars, and business plan development to selected private farmers and small and medium-size private enterprises. Assistance is provided in various branches of the agricultural sector, including production and processing of grain products, fruits and vegetables, dairy, and meat.

In 1996, Land O'Lakes and ACDI (Agricultural Cooperative Development International) began the three-year Western Ukraine Initiative to accelerate the privatization process in the agricultural sector and increase trade between Ukraine and neighboring countries. Land O'Lakes and ACDI representatives provide training for business and banking professionals and promote economic ties between partners in Poland and other Western European countries.

## "Lion Society"
## Public Initiatives Center

Yuria Drohobycha, 8/12
290000   Lviv
**Tel/Fax:** 74-42-64, 72-68-33
**E-mail:** lev@lion.lviv.ua,
　　　　　　lion_society@mailcity.com
**Contact:** Igor Dobko, Deputy Chairman

The Lion Society was created in 1987 and was one of the first independent NGOs in Ukraine. Initially, the society organized projects aimed at the revival of national traditions and ecological actions, such as a yearly expedition on the Dniester River. The latter developed into a joint three-year German-Ukrainian project involving monitoring the Dniester for environmental damage.

In recent years, the Lion Society has focused on the development of the NGO sector. It established a West Ukrainian Resource Center, which supports NGOs in the region. Currently, the society is implementing a project to develop, train, and support NGOs in the Lviv, Ternopil, Ivano-Frankivsk, and Rivne regions. This project is supported by the PHARE/TACIS Democracy Program of the European Commission and includes production of a newsletter for NGOs of the region. The society has published several handbooks in cooperation with Polish and UK partners, which are available free-of-charge. The society has received support from ISAR, the International Renaissance Foundation, and the Eurasia Foundation, among others.

Among several new initiatives of the Lion Society is a plan to open a number of "citizen advice bureaus."

## Project Harmony–Lviv
**Tel/Fax:** 63-28-85
**E-mail:** phlviv@icmp.lviv.ua

See Project Harmony in North American Organizations.

## International Renaissance Foundation–Lviv

Международный фонд "Відродження" Львовское отделение
ul. Teatralnaia 17
290008   Lviv
**Tel:** 97-18-97
**Fax:** 97-17-94
**E-mail:** irf@link.lviv.ua
**Web:** www.irf.lviv.ua
**Contact:** Alexander Sofii, Director

This is a Soros foundation. See International Renaissance Foundation under Kyiv and the Open Society Institute in North American Organizations.

## SALUS Foundation

P.O. Box 320
290000   Lviv
**Tel:** 34-32-85
**Fax:** 72-57-38
**E-mail:** salus@icmp.lviv.ua

**Contact:** Olexandra Sluzhinska, Director

The SALUS Foundation deals with the problems of sexually transmitted diseases (STDs) and HIV/AIDS prevention in western Ukraine. It was established in Lviv in January 1996. The activities of the foundation cover a population numbering nearly ten million. During 1996–1997, five branches of the foundation were opened in cities of western Ukraine: Lviv, Ternopil, Ivano-Frankivsk, Uzhgorod, and Lutsk.

The foundation's director, Olexandra Sluzhinska, is a gynecologist, director of the Medical Diagnostic Center Astar, and the regional representative for Ukraine of the European Information Center Youth and AIDS.

The goals of the foundation include implementation of new technologies for diagnosing HIV/STDs and new therapeutic methods in the treatment of STDs and their complications.

The foundation has the following ongoing programs:
- Center for Sexually Transmitted Diseases. With financial assistance from the Open Society Institute, the center was established in December 1996, one of the first such centers in Ukraine.
- Rape Crisis Center. Established at the same time.
- Respect Yourself —Protect Yourself. With support from the Comité Catolique contre la Faim and pour le Developpement, the Salus Foundation developed this public information project. It has produced eight booklets on HIV, syphilis, gonorrhea, chlamydia, trichomoniasis, candida, herpes, and papillomavirus.
- Art Against AIDS. Established through the joint efforts of the Salus Foundation, Art Club Dzyga, and Scientific Medical Diagnostic Center Astar, the five-year Art Against AIDS program invites art students and artists to participate in a poster design competition, with the best posters used in a campaign against STDs.

Salus has also received support from the Counterpart Consortium and is pursuing a number of projects to expand its work in eight western Ukraine cities, including the establishment of telephone help lines.

## Soros International House School, Lviv

vul. Universitetska 1
290602 Lviv
**Tel:** 79-47-03
**Tel/Fax:** 72-68-54
**E-mail:** root@sihs.lviv.ua
**Contact:** Ms. Marianna Illina, Director

## West Ukrainian Charitable Foundation of Ecological and Tourist Educational Information

a/ya 6685
290005 Lviv
**Tel/Fax:** 72-35-52
**E-mail:** baten@iap.franko.lviv.ua
**Contact:** Josyp Tsaryk, President; Andriy Maksymov

This organization, known as WETI, was founded in 1995 by scientists, representatives of tourist organizations, and journalists from western Ukraine to promote Ukraine as an international tourist destination and to draw Ukrainian attention to achievements in tourism and ecology in other parts of the world. WETI produces unique books and videos about ecology and travel opportunities in and around Ukraine.

Promoting tourism in the Carpathians is one of WETI's main goals. Its book,

*The Carpathians: Pass After Pass*, consists of 400 photos, ethnographic materials, and discussions of the flora and fauna. It is working on a book and video about the Eastern Carpathians covering Ukraine, Poland, and Slovakia. WETI also plans to publish a book, *Carpathian Exotics*, about endangered plants in the region.

In the future, WETI hopes to publish a guide for tourists which will include brief information about places of interest in Western Ukraine, especially the Carpathian region. It will distribute the book outside of Ukraine free-of-charge. It is also preparing a data bank on the Internet with slides, travel information, and maps in Ukrainian and English.

WETI also educates the Ukrainian public on environmental and ecological issues. In collaboration with the Sabre-Svitlo Foundation, WETI founded a public ecological library in Lviv. It regularly supplies information to Ukrainian newspapers and magazines. In March 1996, it organized a seminar, "Ecology of the City," which drew many specialists from abroad. In addition, WETI has begun a video series on world ecology. The first film, *Ecology: Vienna's Experience*, acquaints the Ukrainian public with Austria's ecological experiences.

## Western Center of the Ukrainian Branch of the World Laboratory

ul. Mateiko 4
290000  Lviv
**Tel/Fax:** 35-33-84
**E-mail:** worldlab@ah.ipm.lviv.ua
**Web:** worldlab.lviv.net/
**Contact:** Petro Hrytsyshyn, Director

The center was established in 1992 as an independent branch of the International Center for Scientific Culture. The center focuses on environmental education, transboundary pollution prevention, developing an environmental resource center, and searching for alternative energy sources. In collaboration with the Environmental Research Institute of Connecticut, the center successfully completed development and publication of 15 university-level courses in environmental protection and pollution prevention. In May 1997, the center organized a workshop, sponsored by NATO, on the public health consequences of environmental pollution.

## Western-Ukrainian Center "Women's Perspectives"

ul. Bandery 32a
290013  Lviv
**Tel:**     74-33-81
**Fax:**     97-18-29
**E-mail:** Luba@incubator.lviv.ua
**Contact:** Luba Maksymovych, Director; Svetlana Belyaeva, Assistant Director

Founded in 1997, the center provides services for the social, economic and psychological adaptation of women. It also works to raise public awareness of gender issues and women and children's rights and encourages women's participation in the public sphere and business community. The center has branches in Ternopil, Kalush, Stryj and Sambir, and Gritsiv.

## Mikolayiv (512)

## DANA–Regional Women's Independent Association

P.O. Box 104
327 015  Mikolayiv
**Tel:**     41-65-78
**Tel/Fax:** 33-51-08
**E-mail:** elena@dana.mk.ua
**Contact:** Elena Kabashnaya, President

DANA was registered in September 1995 as a nonprofit organization. Its first activities were benevolent actions: helping the poor obtain clothes, footwear, and food products; helping children and invalids; organizing benefit concerts; and developing ways to help single mothers. Over time the members of DANA began expressing a desire for broader changes in Ukrainian society. They initiated new directions of activity and new ties and the organization drew new members with new ideas and plans. In the words of its president, "DANA is a living organism, she fluctuates and [adapts], lives and functions!"

In 1998, DANA created a crisis center for women who suffer from violence and started the How to Escape Violence program for women. Within a few months, 1,900 women had passed through the program.

DANA is currently focusing on civic education, emphasizing human rights, legislative activity, and a program directed against trafficking in women. It has raised public interest in this problem and created much press and TV attention on the issue. According to DANA, a compulsory course in human rights was introduced into Ukraine's schools as a result of its efforts.

DANA has 52 members and 874 volunteers.

## Ukrainian Cultural Foundation– Mikolayiv Branch

ul. Nilolska 54
327001  Mikolayiv
**Tel:**    35-04-26
**Fax:**    35-65-79
**E-mail:** clib@library.aip.mk.ua
**Contact:** Alla Myran, Director General; Lesya Boichenko, Associate Director General

In November 1987, representatives of 19 organizations gathered together and formed the constituent assembly at which the Cultural Foundation was created. The constituent assembly included members of public, cultural, and educational organizations, as well as representatives of major regional industrial and agricultural units and art museums. Initially the foundation obtained funds for its projects from sponsors, exhibitions, sales and auctions, book publishing, and events sponsored by regional industries. The foundation first became known for placing historical markers in the city of Mikolayiv in commemoration of Arkas Mikolayiv, a local historian and composer.

In 1989, the foundation moved into its first exhibition and office building, which has hosted over 300 art exhibitions of painters from Ukraine and other countries. It received a 10 percent commission on the sale of works of art. In 1991, tax legislation changed and the foundation had to establish some private businesses, which now support the foundation with limited funds.

From the beginning, the foundation has worked to coordinate and preserve the cultural heritage of the Ukrainian people. From 1993-98, the foundation sponsored scholarships for more than 30 gifted children in Mikolayiv to study music, art, writing, and folklore under the New Names scholarship program. On its 10th anniversary in November 1997, the Cultural Foundation and its 10 most active members received a special award from the Ukrainian government. To date, the accomplishments of the foundation include the House of Native Russian Art Theater, two public schools, a memorial to Arkas Mikolayiv, and development of a historical architectural plan of Mikolayiv.

Presently the foundation's main source of funding is an annual folk festival which it organizes in the streets of Mikolayiv. Musical and dance groups, artists, and potters from all over the region are invited to participate.

The foundation works in cooperation with the Art Union of Ukraine, the local administration and department of education, the scientific library, and a large number of colleges, museums, clubs, and cultural societies.

### "Zeleny Svit" Mikolayiv Regional Ecological Association

Зелений Звит
a/ya 158
327001   Mikolayiv
**Tel:**       35-33-85, 35-80-37
**Fax:**      35-31-12 (Attn: Zeleny Svit)
**E-mail:**   evgeny@ineco.comcentre.
nikolaev.ua,
anufr@nikgrpc.freenet.kiev.ua
**Contact:** Anatoly Zolotukhin, Chairman

"Preserve Nature for Future Generations" is the motto of Zeleny Svit (Green World), which has a rich history of citizen-based environmental advocacy work in the Mikolayiv region. It is a regional branch of the national organization, whose headquarters are in Kyiv. The group began working in 1988 to organize local protests of the Chernobyl disaster and expansion of the South Ukrainian Nuclear Hydropower Plant (NHPP), and the damage caused by the latter to the southern reaches of the Bug River. The group collected 210,000 signatures against plans to expand the NHPP and construct two reservoirs on the Bug River. In 1989, the Ukrainian Council of Ministers limited construction at

NHPP to 3 power units instead of 6, and suspended reservoir construction.

Over the past decade, the group has led numerous community demonstrations and programs against industrial and nuclear projects that pose a threat to the environment and health of the local population. In 1991, it collected 250,000 signatures to oppose further pollution of the Bug River and for the gradual replacement of three nuclear power units with gas turbines at NHPP.

In connection with the tenth anniversary of the Chernobyl catastrophe, the group conducted seminars on "Alternatives to Nuclear Energy" in Mikolayiv, Nikopol, and Zaporizhia in April 1996. The seminars were sponsored by local chapters of the Ukrainian Environmental Federation, Zeleny Svit, and two American NGOs, Center for Citizen Initiatives and Plutonium Free Future.

Today ZS focuses its activities on atomic power plant safety, alternative energy, environmental education, energy-efficient housing, developing Internet communications, and a bridge construction project on the southern Bug River to reduce air pollution in the city. The association has branches in the towns of Ochakov, Voznesensk, Bratskoe, and Berezanka in the Mikolayiv region.

## Odessa (482)

### ACCELS–Odessa

ul. Staroportofrankovskaya 26, kom. 60
South Ukrainian Pedogogical University
270020   Odessa
**Tel/Fax:** 32-15-16
**E-mail:**   fsa@accels.odessa.ua

See profile for American Councils of International Education in North American Organizations.

## Association of Realtors of Odessa and Odessa Region

Ассоциация риэлторов г. Одессы и Одесской области
a/ya 4 (postal address)
ul. Pushkinskaia 37, etazh 2, k. 217
270011  Odessa
**Tel:**     28-71-82
**Fax:**     28-71-23
**E-mail:** onb@tm.odessa.ua
**Contact:** Marinutsa Ruslan, President

The association was created in 1995 as a legal entity for real estate agents. The association established a school for professional realtors, the first such school to receive a license for professional training. In 1996, it began publishing a newspaper, *Birzha*. The members of the association founded the New Exhange in Odessa. In February 1998, the association changed its status and membership conditions and became a public organization, which re-registered in April 1998.

The association is now a non-commercial organization that unites individual real estate agents, as well as people interested in the real estate market. It strives to protect the interests of all market agents, develop legislative and economic tools for real estate regulation, define property rights, spread information, assist entrepreneurs who work in the real estate market, and cooperate with similar organizations.

The school for professional realtors trains real estate agents, real estate managers, and appraisers. Together with members of the association, the school has organized seminars for realtors and the public. The association is creating a unified database on the real estate market in Odessa, which will be available to the public. It also provides consulting services to members of association and their clients and has worked in cooperation with the East European Real Property Foundation and Development Alternatives, Inc.

## Association New Music

ul. Bazarna 48, kv. 1
270011  Odessa
**Tel:**     22-52-83
**Fax:**     26-16-89
**E-mail:** new_music@paco.net,
        alex@vidr.odessa.ua
**Contact:** Dr. Karmella Tsepkolenko, Head of the Board

Since 1996, ANM has represented Ukraine in the International Society for Contemporary Music. Two Days and Two Nights is ANM's annual international festival of modern art and music. The group also supports upcoming Ukrainian modern artists and produces CDs that contain work by contemporary Ukrainian composers. The association publishes literature and supports a Web page with information for contemporary musicians.

## Green Defense Association

ul. Bolshaya Arnautskaya 7/10
270012  Odessa
**Tel:**     24-99-55
**E-mail:** root@eco m.odessa.ua
**Contact:** Nataliya Levkovich

Founded in 1996, the association is an environmental law organization which focuses on the Northwestern Black Sea maritime region of Ukraine. Members of the association are professional lawyers and specialists in environmental protection and management. Goals of the Green Defense Association include:
- Raising public awareness of the environment

- Increasing public control over the implementation of environmental legislation for the Black Sea
- Improving current environmental legislation
- Reducing the negative influence of industrial and agricultural activity on the environment

## Odessa Charitable Fund "The Way Home"

P.O. Box 25
42, B. Arnautskaya St.,
270011 Odessa
**Tel:** 23-28-27
**Tel/Fax:** 42-93-26
**E-mail:** vestnik@te.net.ua
**Contact:** Sergey Kostin, Director

The Way Home was founded in 1997 to assist homeless people. Its establishment grew out of the experience of rendering charitable, social, and legal assistance to needy inhabitants of Odessa. After investigating the experience of homeless shelters in Moscow, St. Petersburg, and Kharkiv, the organizers of the fund prepared a comprehensive plan for a city program to assist homeless people, including a shelter. Experts from the law enforcement and medical communities support the fund. Volunteers working for the fund include members of the fund's trustee council, religious communities, and public organizations in Odessa.

Since its inception, 1,200 homeless people have registered with the fund. All have received medical, social, and legal assistance. Research by the fund's legal defense department has revealed numerous human rights infringements on the part of law enforcement bodies and medical establishments toward citizens who do not have proper registration. (Homeless people typically have lost their papers.)

The organization received small grants from the Dutch embassy and others totaling about US$15,000 in 1997. In 1998, it received a combined total of $50,000 in USAID funds through two Counterpart programs.

Kostin, the fund's director, is a 1984 graduate of Odessa Mechnikov State University. He currently manages the registration center and rehabilitation center of the fund, among other duties.

## Project Harmony–Odessa
**Tel/Fax:** 68-90-02
**E-mail:** pharmony@paco.net

See Project Harmony in North American Organizations.

## Public Association "Union"
Общественное объединение "Союз" сотрудников правоохранительных органов г. Одессы и Одесской области и участников ликвидации последствий аварии на Чернобыльской атомной электростанции
ul. Evreiskaia 11, GKB # 3
270001 Odessa
**Tel:** 25-70-19
**Tel/Fax:** 28-71-32
**E-mail:** union@tm.odessa.ua,
union@paco.net
**Contact:** Dmitrii Ruban, Chairman

Union was established in 1990 for all the "liquidators" of the Chernobyl accident: firemen, policemen, army personnel, etc. The association has branches in Izmail and Dneprovsk and 14 representative offices in other cities in Ukraine. It works on behalf of the victims of Chernobyl and their families: protecting their civil rights and benefits, improving living conditions, and providing legal counsel. The association established an information center for nonprofit organizations, which helps NGOs find partners abroad, conducts research on civil rights and medical rehabilitation, and organizes cultural exchanges.

The association created a database of foreign NGOs and worked in cooperation with the international organization Global Operations and Development to provide medical care to Chernobyl victims in the hospitals of Odessa.

## Scientific Center for Women's Research
Одесский Научный Центр Женских Исследований (ОНЦЖИ)
a/ya 97
270023   Odessa
**Tel/Fax:** 63-82-17
**E-mail:** ocws@tekom.odessa.ua
**Contact:** Svetlana Stefanenko

The center was founded in 1994 at Odessa State Academy of Technical Writers. It conducts research, conferences, and seminars on women's issues, such as "Ukrainian Women: Modern Status and Perspectives." Its publications include *The Past in the Name of the Future: Women's Movement in Ukraine in the 20th Century* and a directory, *Ukrainian Women in History and Today*.

## South Ukrainian Association "Svitlo"
ul. Hriboedov 8, kv. 2
270000   Odessa
**Tel:**      64-67-28
**E-mail:** karmella@paco.net
**Contact:** Dr. Karmella Tsepkolenko, Director

Svitlo deals with the trafficking of women in southern Ukraine. Members include psychologists and human rights workers who offer medical and legal

assistance to victims of the sex trade. The group hopes to end the trade by improving the economic and social status of women.

## Rivne (3622)

## Association for Legal Protection and Assistance to Local Entrepreneurs in Rivne
Ровенская областная общественная организация "Ассоциация защиты и содействия развитию предпринимателей" (РОАП)
ul. Zamkovaia 22-a., kv. 505
266028   Rivne
**Tel/Fax:** 22-06-81
**E-mail:** roman@roap.rovno.ua,
         roman@roap.vt.rovno.ua
**Contact:** Roman Kashinchar

The association was created in 1996 by individual entrepreneurs, whose goal was to support and develop businesses in the Rivne region. The association organizes seminars and educates local business owners on economic, financial, and legal issues. It represents local businesses in the Business Council, which was created on the initiative of association members as part of the governor's office in Rivne.

The association founded an analytical center, which conducts marketing research and distributes information to businesses throughout the region free-of-charge, thanks to grants from the Eurasia Foundation and USAID. It protects the rights of business owners in court, and was the first organization to take the mayor of Rivne to court. The association works with the Ukrainian parliament and regional mass media. Members of the association have regular columns in local newspapers, and they are currently working on installing modem connections everywhere in the region in order to distribute information more efficiently.

## Sevastopol (692)

### Society for Protection of Animals and Nature in the Crimea

pr. Ostrjakov 60, k. 29
335029 Sevastopol
**Tel:** 44-25-65
**Fax:** 44-44-77
**E-mail:** shadrn@fossil.ukrcom.sebastopol.ua
**Contact:** Dr. Nickolai Shadrin, Chairman

The society was registered in 1994 and works to involve the public in nature conservation activities. It has conducted a survey on the socioeconomic results of environmental damage in the Black Sea, led ecological expeditions along the Crimean coast, and held four "eco-camps" in 1998.

## Symferopil (652)

### Crimean Independent Consumer Association

Крымская независимая ассоциация потребителей
pr. Pobedy 4
333034 Symferopil
**Tel:** 25-46-90
**Fax:** 24-15-80
**E-mail:** knap@pop.cris.net
**Web:** www.veresk.net/knap
**Contact:** Alexander Altov, Chairman

The association was formed in March 1996. Its main focus is protection of consumer rights, which "are disregard-

ed despite the fact that the law on protection of consumer rights in Ukraine has existed for five years." With support from the Eurasia Foundation, the association established the Crimean Regional Center for Legal Protection of Consumer Rights in Symferopil, with branches in Alushta, Belogorsk, and Evpatoria. The association provides consulting to consumers, helps them prepare legal documentation, and participates in trials related to the infringement of consumer rights. During the last two years, the association has provided 4,000 consultations, prepared 3,000 documents for various cases, increased its membership by 2,500, and published 52 articles in three regional newspapers and three information bulletins. The association has a weekly show on local television.

### Crimean Independent Center of Political Researchers and Journalists

ul. Kirova 18/3, kv. 7
333011 Symferopil
**Tel:** 25-90-59
**Tel/Fax:** 27-69-65
**E-mail:** centr@kncpd.crimea.ua
**Contact:** Volodymyr Pritula, Director

The center was founded in March 1995 as the Crimean branch of the Ukrainian Center for Independent Political Research, based in Kyiv. It is a self-sufficient, nonprofit, non-governmental research organization. Its goals are to assist in the development of the Crimea, an autonomous republic of Ukraine, and to promote the integration of Ukraine and the Crimea, as well as the integration of Ukraine into the European and global family.

The center carries out research on Crimea and its ties to Ukrainian society. It prepares analytical reports concerning the social and political situation in the autonomous Crimean Republic and distributes it to the local and foreign press.

The center has organized a number of conferences, roundtables and seminars:

- July 1995, in cooperation with Freedom House, a roundtable on problems of national group representation in the power centers of the Crimea
- September 1995, a roundtable discussion on political realities and the future of the Crimea
- October 1996, a roundtable discussion on the new constitution of Ukraine and the constitutional process in the Autonomous Crimean Republic
- November 1996, a conference on the relations between powerful interests and the press in a society in transition

Leading political and nationalist activists from the Crimea and Kyiv have taken part in these roundtables, conferences and seminars. The center also organized internships abroad for Crimean-Tatar and Ukrainian journalists—at Radio Liberty in Prague in 1996, and at *Rzecspospolita,* a Warsaw newspaper, in1997.

## Crimean Initiative–Ecological Information Center
a/ля 35
333022 Symferopil
**Tel/Fax:** 27-79-39
**E-mail:** root@crin.wildwind.com
**Contact:** Tatyana Lysak

CI engages in a variety of programs to promote public education about environmental issues. It maintains a library of environmental resources and provides environmental information to the local media. CI also works to support the development of a range of NGOs by helping groups with organizational development issues, main-

taining an information exchange service, and helping organizations establish e-mail accounts. CI is interested in working with Western organizations and would welcome donations of educational materials for its library.

## Crimean Laboratory of Regional Researchers–"CrymLabri"
Крымская лаборатория региональных исследований
ul. Samokisha 30
333011 Symferopil
**Tel:** 29-72-65
**Tel/Fax:** 25-35-88
**E-mail:** lrr@simf.postbox.crimea.ua

CrymLabri is an independent scientific and research organization founded in 1996. The "laboratory" has several sections: a section on geopolitics, an analytical section, an international relations section, and a sociological laboratory. CrymLabri has its own computer center and issues an electronic magazine, *CrymLabri*. It provides organizations and media with the results of its research, copies of its latest surveys, and analytical data.

The laboratory has contacts with international political, research, and humanitarian organizations from more than 20 countries of the world. It hopes to broaden its scientific and social contacts with governmental and non-governmental organizations in Europe, America, and Asia.

## Crimean Noosphere Institute
Крымский Институт Ноосферы
ul. Gogola 9
Symferopil
**Tel:** 24-04-19
**E-mail:** valb@crao.crimea.ua
**Contact:** Viktor Tarasenko, Chairman;

Valentina Bobova, Coordinator

The noosphere is the part of the planet's biosphere that is impacted by human settlements and activities. The Crimean Noosphere Institute is a philosophical/academic organization, concerned with environmental conditions in the Crimea. It organizes periodic roundtable discussions about regional environmental issues and has prepared educational materials that introduce noospheric concepts. It is a partner of the California Institute of Noetic Science.

## Uzhgorod (312)

### Carpathian Agency for Regional Development

1 Myru St.
295800   Rakhiv
**Tel/Fax:**   (213) 22-14-06
**E-mail:**   office@card.uzhgorod.ua
**Contact:** Mr. Vasyl M. Khoma, Director; Juniper Neill, USPCV for English Assistance

CARD was formed in 1997 by the Rakhiv District Administration and Carpathian Biosphere Reserve to focus on sustainable development for the Rakhiv district. CARD has focused on improving the local economy through the promotion of eco-tourism. It has organized workshops to encourage villages to host visitors in their homes and has promoted homestay opportunities for tourists. CARD has also begun work on a youth center focusing on environmental education, established a business support center, produced publications, and organized conferences on sustainable development in mountainous regions. The office employs five paid personnel and six volunteers.

It works with organizations in Slovakia, Romania, and Hungary.

### Carpathian EcoClub "Ruthenia"

Карпатский экологический клуб "Рутения"
ul. Universitetskaia 25/506
294016   Uzhgorod
**Tel/Fax:** 24-38-28
**E-mail:**   ruthenia@cec.uzhgorod.ua
**Contact:** Vladimir Kricsfalusy, President

The organization works on environmental projects.

### Counterpart Creative Center– Uzhgorod

ul. Akademika Koroleva 3, kv. 4
Perechin, Uzhgorod Raion
**Tel:**      2-27-15
**Contact:** Andrii Vyshniak

See profile for Counterpart Creative Center in Kyiv.

## Vinnitsa (4322)

### Analytical Center "Ukrainian Spring"

ul. Pushkina 25, kv. 4
286000   Vinnitsa
**Tel/Fax:** 32-89-80
**E-mail:**   vsaci2@vsmu.vinnica.ua
             (attn: Pavel Moltshanov)
**Contact:** Pavel Moltshanov, President

Ukrainian Spring is a non-commercial, voluntary organization founded in 1997. It has offices in 14 Ukrainian cities. Its goal is to unite scientists, entrepreneurs, and members of the intelligentsia to provide analytical and intellectual support for the "spiritual, socio-economic, and scientific-technological" revival of Ukraine.

Ukrainian Spring has established a youth organization, Young Ukraine, composed of students from four universities in Vinnitsa. Other projects include an employment center and establishment of a publishing center for public organizations in the city. It would like to establish an Internet center and to establish contacts with foreign organizations in order to cooperate on these projects.

## Vinnitsa Region Jewish Community in Ukraine

P.O. Box 1993
286021   Vinnitsa
**E-mail:**   vinjew@sovamua.com
**Web:**   www.igc.apc.org/ddickerson/
podolia-vrjc.html
**Contact:** Igor Desner, Executive Director

The Jewish community in the Vinnitsa region supports elderly and sick Jews in the region, creates and implements educational programs, seeks to revive the Yiddish language and culture, strives to preserve Jewish historical artifacts, sites, and monuments in the region, and celebrates traditional Jewish holidays. The VRJC's archives in Vinnitsa contain documents pertaining to the Holocaust in Russian, Ukrainian, and German.

The VRJC has several ongoing projects. One of them is restoration of the synagogue in Vinnitsa. The community has eight Jewish schools, a lecture center, and musical groups, which perform Yiddish dance music.

## *Zaporizhia (612)*

## Association "Information Resources"

Ассоциация "Информационные ресурсы"
ul. Chuikova 24-148
Zaporizhia
**Tel:**   72-00-07
**E-mail:**   webman@reis.zp.ua
**Contact:** Victor Ostapenko, Project Director

The association was founded in May 1997 by former army officers, who wanted to provide consulting services, training, and help to small and medium-size businesses started by demobilized military personnel. The association was established after a three-year project to train ex-military personnel to start their own businesses was completed. Under the project, 21 businesses were registered by demobilized army officers and consulting services were provided to 200 clients.

The association is currently raising funds for its new project, 32nd of May, designed to create a consulting center to help businesses incorporate Web technologies in their activities. Under this project, expected to last five years, the association plans to provide services to 230 demobilized army officers, train 100 clients in using the Internet, and create 30 Web pages for customers. Partners of the association in this project include the Zaporizhia Military Commissariat, Regional Internet Service, and the youth club Vzlet-T. The association is looking for other organizations that would like to participate in this project.

## OLPO–Society of Individuals with Transplanted Organs

Общество лиц с пересаженными органами
а/уа 2152

bul. Shevchenko 51, kv. 10
330091   Zaporizhia
**Tel:**       34-12-15
**Fax:**     39-95-19
**E-mail:**   info@packet.zp.ua
**Contact:** Aleksei Arslanov, Chairman

OLPO is the first NGO in Ukraine to represent dialysis and transplant patients. It was founded in June 1994 by three patients at a kidney dialysis and organ transplant center in Zaporizhia. It came into being when the center was no longer willing to pay for treatments and the government was unable to finance them either. The objective of the society is to "represent this category of patients, facilitate their social rehabilitation, and provide medications for them."

There are about 80 members in the society, handicapped people from all parts of Ukraine. In May 1998, OLPO and the Transplantation Center in Zaporizhia organized an all-Ukrainian conference "Donors and Transplantation in Ukraine and Abroad." Conference participants came from Ukraine, Italy and Russia. Currently the society struggles to fulfill the "constitutional rights of citizens for medical and social help" as budget deficits prevent the authorities from covering medical expenses for patients with transplanted organs.

# *Internet Resources*

# Internet Resources

S till in its infancy, the Internet has already profoundly subverted the ability of powerful institutions (governments, newspapers) or economic/geographic factors (distance, costs of publishing and mailing) to control and shape the flow of information. Like the invention of the printing press, which Martin Luther used to erode the power of the clergy by printing the Bible in German so that ordinary folk could read the word of God, the Internet subverts the very premise of the media: that they must mediate information. For good and for ill, any individual, any small group, can now reach millions of others directly with a message, an ad, an image, a song, or a video. The economics of the distribution of information worldwide are becoming so inexpensive that media giants, which for decades could ignore competition or questions of user satisfaction, now sit on an obsolescing and costly distribution system and wonder whether they will survive the wildfire of Web-based small-scale news and information services the Internet has spawned. We are rapidly approaching the time when the power to reach others, even across oceans and international boundaries, will depend much more on one's imagination, message, and intelligence, than one's control of state power or a media empire.

To be sure, the media and especially television have also done a great deal to create the sense of global community that prevails today. So have the satellite, the jet airliner, and the multinational corporation. But until recently the set of concerns embraced by the concept of civil society has been thought of as being contained by national boundaries. Business was international, travel and entertainment was international, and diplomacy was, by definition, international. But issues of the voluntary sector of society—whether philanthropy, humanitarian concerns, or social and political reform movements—largely stopped at the water's edge.

There certainly are examples of institutions of civil society that extend across national borders and have been with us for a very long time. The Roman Catholic Church is one such example. In this century, organizations such as the Red Cross, the Scouts movement, and Rotary International are other examples of voluntary associations that bring thousands of people of different nationalities together to pursue common causes and interests.

But governments and corporations have always had bigger travel budgets than voluntary associations. Unless an organization in the nonprofit sector was fairly large and well funded, it was unlikely to have any kind of international program. The costs of travel and communications were too high, making face-to-face contact between people very difficult. These factors, in turn, helped to perpetuate the lack of knowledge and disinterest that many Americans exhibit about other societies.

The Internet is changing all of this, and dramatically. It includes several technologies that enable much smaller organizations and even individuals to participate in social, environmental, and other projects that are overseas and do not boast large budgets.

E-mail lists, or listservs as they are sometimes called, create "virtual communities" in the same way that a good printed magazine creates a sense of community among loyal readers and people who write letters to the editor. The advantage of the electronic version is that it can be supported by groups as small as 20 or 30 people, each living in a different nation or region of the world. There are no economies of scale that require a minimum subscriber base of thousands. As a result, today there are thousands of listservs and news groups. The Armenian, Azerbaijani, and Ukrainian communities in North America have all created vibrant e-mail lists by which they sustain a sense of national identity and remain informed about events in homelands thousands of miles away. This same sense of community is palpable on the Women-East-West list, where women worldwide meet to share experiences, expertise, and support with "sisters" in Eastern Europe and Eurasia.

The World Wide Web has allowed even the smallest organization to publish its materials and make them available to a potential audience of millions at virtually no cost. Already there are several hundred Eurasian NGOs that have their own Web sites, where you can read their newsletters and learn about their programs. A number of directories of NGOs in Eurasia are now available online. The Internet may already be the single best source of information about the development of civil society in the NIS.

Not only can you learn about civil society in another country with the Web, you can help support it. This directory includes dozens of Web sites that have uploaded excellent training materials and made them available to anybody online. Many of these materials were created for specific training projects, then shelved, thus reaching only a fraction of the people who could potentially use them. Today they are available to millions of people on the Internet, for free.

The Web's ability to "link" from one site to another is a very powerful tool for a global civil society. Consider the Web site known as Russian Feminism Resources. It is the personal creation of Elena Leonoff, who lives in Australia. Elena started her site in 1996 "in sheer disgust at the difficulty of finding information about Russian women online—the search engines were and still are swamped by porn and mail-order bride agencies." By putting in links from her home page to other sites, she has created an enormous library of information about the conditions women face in Russia and the community of women's organizations working in that country. For anyone interested in working on women's issues with women in Russia, Elena's page is the first place to go to start learning about how and where you can direct your energies with the most effect.

An innovative use of the Internet to support the growth of civil society internationally is the Virtual Foundation. It provides an opportunity for individuals and small organizations to participate in international philanthropy—a field previously reserved for governments and large charitable foundations. The Virtual Foundation is made up of a consortium of environmental organizations in the U.S. and Eastern Europe with extensive experience administering grants to NGOs. NIS NGOs submit project proposals to a local office of one of the consortium members, where the proposal is vetted. The proposal is then passed on to the foundation's board of directors in the U.S. for further review. If approved by the board, the proposal is uploaded to the Virtual Foundation's Internet site. People visiting the site can review a variety of proposals and either fund a project in its entirety or make a contribution that will be pooled with donations from others. Once sufficient funds have been raised for a particular project, a grant is made through the consortium member's local office in the region. That office assumes all the normal grant-making responsibilities to ensure that contributions are spent wisely. The Web also enables the NGO to keep its donors informed about their projects.

What will be the long-term effect of the Internet on civil society? The technology is so new that predicting even two-three years ahead is hazardous. It seems inevitable that voluntary organizations will continue to become more international and that this will have consequences for all national polities. Even before the advent of the Internet, organizations such as Amnesty International and The Nature Conservancy were mobilizing citizens from countries A, B and C to influence officials in country D. With the development of the World Wide Web, any government must be prepared to do battle with an army of Internet-based desktop publishers who can in a matter of minutes upload documents, photos, and even live interviews or videos to lobby for their causes or counter what they perceive to be official propaganda. The Internet's capacity to rapidly disseminate information widely and inexpensively represents a super-powerful impulse on the road to a global civil society.

## The Internet in Eurasia

Despite Eurasia's vast size and old telephone lines, the Internet has exhibited the same phenomenal growth there as has been experienced in other parts of the world. Because of its decentralized nature, it is difficult to know how many people are connected to the Internet in Eurasia. The Russian Non-Profit Center for Internet Technologies (www.rocit.ru) estimated that one million people were online in Russia in July 1998, up from 600,000 in October 1997. This figure probably underestimates the number of people, however, who share access to the Internet from their universities or jobs.

The chart below shows that the number of computers connected to the Internet in seven countries of the NIS increased by nearly two-thirds from mid-1997 to the end of 1998. Russia grew the slowest, perhaps because it started earlier than the others and already had a large installed base by mid-1997. Connectivity in some of the smaller countries doubled and tripled during this period.

To digress for a moment, it is interesting to note also the significant (nearly 3:1) difference in the size of the Internet in the United Kingdom and France, which are similar in terms of population and levels of economic development. To a large extent, the difference is explained by different national approaches to telecommunications regulation—France's Minitel being an example of a highly centralized and statist system. During 1998, Russia's FSB (the successor to the KGB) repeatedly talked about wanting to monitor all Internet traffic in Russia. Any efforts to try to centralize the Internet's development—whether by a Minitel trying to be a sole Internet service provider or by an FSB trying to ensure it can read all Internet traffic to and from Russia—will prove fatal to its growth. The reason the Internet has been such a wild success has been precisely because it has been allowed to develop outside of government control or intervention.

## *Number of Host Computers Connected to the Internet*

| Country | 30 Jun 97 | 31 Dec 97 | 31 Dec 98[*] | 18–Month Growth (%) |
|---|---|---|---|---|
| Armenia | 323 | 442 | 951 | *194.4* |
| Azerbaijan | 78 | 347 | 435 | *457.7* |
| Belarus | 379 | 708 | 1,052 | *177.6* |
| Georgia | 314 | 413 | 738 | *135.0* |
| Moldova | 147 | 245 | 613 | *317.0* |
| Russia | 112,827 | 152,619 | 182,680 | *61.9* |
| Ukraine | 10,275 | 13,996 | 19,775 | *92.5* |
| ***Total 7 NIS Countries*** | *124,470* | *168,898* | *206,244* | *65.7* |
| France | 304,028 | 355,031 | 511,193 | *68.1* |
| Poland | 73,645 | 88,454 | 130,554 | *77.3* |
| Spain | 169,534 | 196,403 | 306,559 | *80.8* |
| United Kingdom | 887,191 | 1,017,452 | 1,449,315 | *63.4* |

**Source:** Host counts performed by RIPE (Réseaux IP Européens, www.ripe.net). ".ru" and ".su" counts were combined for Russia. A "host" computer is, roughly speaking, one attached directly to the Internet system with a unique IP address. Any host computer may in turn "host" hundreds or thousands of Web sites and e-mail accounts on its own network.
[*] Actual count date was 5 January 1999.

Assisting the growth of the Internet in the NIS have been various programs based in the U.S. and other Western nations. Expansion of the Internet and e-mail access has been a major component of the assistance provided by the three most active Western funders in the NIS—the European Union's TACIS program, the United States Agency for International Development (USAID), and George Soros. Mr. Soros, for example, funded an Internet backbone—the laying of fiberoptic cable—in southwest Moscow in 1992. In 1994, he established the Regional Internet Program, which supports the development of user demand for e-mail and Internet access in Eastern Europe and Eurasia. In 1996, he pledged $100 million over five years to establish 32 University Internet Centers in cities throughout Russia. With support from USAID, American organizations such as IREX, ISAR, ECOLOGIA, Sacred Earth Network, American Development Foundation, Network for East-West Women, and many others have provided e-mail equipment, training, and access for hundreds, if not thousands, of NIS NGOs.

## Notes on the Following Sections

The Internet is already too vast for any guide such as this to be comprehensive. Instead we have tried to identify resources that are good starting points from which the reader can begin his or her search for further information. In selecting these resources, we have used several criteria. For e-mail lists, we have selected those that have a record of sustained activity (usually over a period of at least a year), or are sponsored by an organization that is likely to continue managing the list in the future.

Web sites can be divided into those that are updated regularly and those that are not. We have tried to select only those that are regularly updated and contain information beyond promotional materials about the organization that sponsors the site.

Within each section that follows we have described e-mail lists first, and then Web sites. In the description of an e-mail list, we include instructions on how to subscribe. Be aware that instructions to send the message, for example, *subscribe nuclear_rus your e-mail address,* intend you to type **your** e-mail address after *nuclear_rus*. Likewise, instructions to send the message, for example, *subscribe barents-l firstname lastname*, intend you to type **your** first and last names after *barents-l*.

Unless otherwise noted, all listservs and Web sites can be accessed free of charge. For some sections we have included the URLs of especially good links pages—pages with numerous links to other well-chosen Web sites. Many newspapers in the region have created Web sites. We have listed primarily those which are bilingual. There are many more newspapers online; in Russia alone, it is estimated that as many as 200 newspapers now have online editions.

CCSI welcomes all additions and corrections to this listing. We update the listing for all of these Web sites and e-mail lists in the Civil Society in Eurasia Resource Center on our own Web site: **www.friends-partners.org/~ccsi**.

## Contents of the Following Section

# *Clearinghouses*

## *E-mail Lists*

### CivilSoc

Sponsored by Center for Civil Society International, CivilSoc carries news related to the development of non-governmental organizations, democratic reform, and other civil society projects in the NIS. It includes announcements of conferences, grant opportunities, training programs, and job openings; reviews of electronic resources; and profiles of NIS non-governmental organizations and projects representing the third sector in the region. The list is moderated and messages are kept concise so as to reduce the cost of incoming e-mail for subscribers in the NIS.

List address: **civilsoc@solar.cini.utk.edu**

To subscribe, send the message: **subscribe civilsoc firstname lastname**
to: **listproc@solar.cini.utk.edu**

### Friends

This list is a companion to the innovative Friends and Partners Internet site established by Greg Cole in Knoxville, Tennessee, and Natasha Bulashova in Puschino, Russia. Friends is a good place to meet people and learn what is happening in a wide range of U.S.-NIS citizen activity. Unlike most other electronic mailing lists, which consist of single messages posted as they arrive on the list, Friends is a "digested" list. This means that messages are collected and posted together to the list in one large file, distributed to subscribers every few days.

List address: **friends@solar.cini.utk.edu**

To subscribe, send the message: **subscribe friends firstname lastname**
to: **listproc@solar.cini.utk.edu**

## *Web Sites*

### Center for Civil Society International
www.friends-partners.org/~ccsi/

As the authors of this guide, we don't want to appear too immodest, but we think that CCSI's Web site is the single best Internet resource related to the NIS. At the heart of our Web site is CCSI's Civic Action in Eurasia Resource Center, which includes profiles of hundreds of NGOs in the NIS, dozens of projects by Western organizations in the region, and an extensive list of electronic and print resources of interest to NGOs. All U.S. and NIS organizations are encouraged to add information about their work to the Resource Center by filling out an online form that is accessible from CCSI's home page or by simply sending information to CCSI at **ccsi@u.washington.edu**. CCSI's site also includes a very good list of grant, conference, and job announcements, archives of ASI's *Weekly Bulletin* (reports in Russian on third-sector developments in Russia), and a growing library of research and opinion about civil society.

### Friends and Partners
www.friends-partners.org/friends/

Friends and Partners began in January 1994 as a volunteer effort by Greg Cole in and Natasha Bulashova, mentioned above. Greg and Natasha used their computer expertise and equipment donated by their respective academic institutions and Sun Microsystems to create a place where others could collect and maintain information related to U.S.-NIS relations. Many, including CCSI, have taken up their offer, and the result is two servers, one based in Tennessee, the other not far from Moscow, which host numerous Web sites, with information in a wide variety of fields, including art, education, health, history, literature, science, space, etc. In essence, Friends and Partners has become a virtual meeting place for people interested in the NIS.

### REENIC: Russian and East European Network Information Center
reenic.utexas.edu/reenic.html

A project of the Center for Russian, East European, and Eurasian Studies at the University of Texas, REENIC is an extensive, regularly updated collection of links to hundreds of Web sites related to Eastern Europe and Eurasia.

# Agriculture

## E-mail Lists

### FADRnews

Sponsored by the Foundation for Agrarian Development Research, a Moscow-based nonprofit organization founded in 1993, FADRnews distributes bulletins in Russian about agricultural and environmental issues to nearly 500 subscribers. Archives are available at **fadr.msu.ru/win/mailserv/**

List address:   **fadrnews@fadr.msu.ru**

To subscribe, send the message:   **subscribe FADRnews**
                         to:   **majordomo@fadr.msu.ru**

## Web Sites

### Center for Citizen Initiatives
www.igc.apc.org/cci/

The Center for Citizen Initiatives has uploaded an extensive collection of Russian-language agricultural extension-type publications to its Web site (look under the link for "Russian pages"). Elsewhere on the site, there is a description of CCI's agricultural projects in Russia and links to other organizations active in the field.

## Foundation for Agrarian Development Research
fadr.msu.ru

The foundation is an independent organization dedicated to researching problems connected with the development of the agricultural sector in Russia. Its Web site contains a detailed description of the foundation's activities, announcements of upcoming conferences related to agriculture, an "electronic library" that consists of papers and articles published by foundation members, and a very good collection of links to other agriculture-related resources online in Russia.

# *Business*

## *E-mail Lists*

### *BISNIS Briefs*

BISNIS (Business Information Service for the NIS) at the Department of Commerce has a raft of e-mail publications for American companies active or interested in opportunities in the NIS. *BISNIS Briefs* is a biweekly bulletin that includes trade and investment leads, conference announcements, and general economic information about the NIS. BISNIS has similar bulletins for specific industries, e.g., defense conversion in Russia, and individual countries, e.g., Uzbekistan.

To be added to the biweekly *BISNIS Briefs* bulletin, send your name, company, postal and e-mail address, telephone and fax to: **bisnis@usita.gov**. To see (and sign up for) a complete list of the industry- and country-specific bulletins, visit BISNIS's Web site at **www.itaiep.doc.gov/bisnis/bisnis.html** and follow the link for "Subscribe to our Free Bulletin and Email Publications." Due to its congressional mandate, BISNIS's publications are available only to U.S.-based companies and companies based in the NIS.

### CERRO-L

CERRO is the acronym for Central European Regional Research Organization. The list is a combination of announcements and discussion on the general topic of economic reform in Eastern Europe and Eurasia. Archives of back messages are available at **ecolu-info.unige.ch/archives/**

List address:   **cerro-l@aearn.aco.net**

To subscribe, send the message:   **subscribe cerro-l firstname lastname**
                              to:   **listserv@aearn.aco.net**

## Web Sites

### American Chamber of Commerce in Russia
www.amcham.ru

The fastest growing American Chamber of Commerce in the world, the American Chamber of Commerce in Russia has more than 450 corporate members. Its Web site has quite a bit of information about the business environment in Russia and includes a series of white papers and the chamber's bimonthly newsletter.

### BISNIS
www.itaiep.doc.gov/bisnis/bisnis.html

BISNIS is the home page for the Department of Commerce's Business Information Service for the New Independent States. BISNIS includes a wealth of information about business opportunities, NIS companies seeking partners, analysis of market conditions and sectors, sources of investment financing, etc.

### *Business Central Europe*
www.bcemag.com/

A monthly magazine that covers business in Central Europe, Russia, and Ukraine. A few stories are available online each month.

### Business Collaboration Center
www.bcc.ru/

BCC is a USAID-funded project, managed by Citizens Democracy Corps, which provides informational assistance to projects and organizations that work to support business development in Russia. From the BCC home page, one can access home pages of 20 Western business training projects in Russia, an extensive electronic library of business training materials, and a calendar of business-related workshops and seminars.

### Cooperation Bureau for Economic Research on Eastern Europe
www.diw-berlin.de/Koop/english/

The bureau supports economic policy researchers and advisors dealing with economic reforms in Eastern Europe and Eurasia. Its Web site contains a regularly updated list of projects by researchers, with contact information, and a calendar of upcoming conferences in the field.

### Forum on Economic Freedom
www.cipe.org/

The Web site of the Center for International Private Enterprise, the forum contains over 800 documents, including a wide range of economic education materials. Among the highlights is *Economic Reform Today*, CIPE's quarterly journal, which has articles on such topics as "Business Views on Combating Corruption" and "The Lessons of Privatization." The site also includes information about CIPE's grant program and an online grant application form.

## Institute for the Economy in Transition
mac.www.online.ru/sp/iet/

Find out what Yegor Gaidar thinks! The Institute for the Economy in Transition is Gaidar's think tank, and its Web site usually has one or two speeches or articles by Gaidar on the issues of the day. IET's monthly newsletter, *Russian Economy: Trends and Perspectives*, is also available.

## Research on Eastern European Economies
www.bof.fi/env/eng/it/iten.stm

The Bank of Finland publishes research on the economics of the Baltic States and Russia and uploads some of it to its Web site. Each week, the bank publishes "The Week in Review," a brief synopsis of the week's major economic news. Also available on-line are abstracts of longer analytical pieces by the bank's staff.

## Russian Securities Market News
www.fe.msk.ru/infomarket/ewelcome.html

Available in English and Russian, this site contains information on the government agency that regulates the Russian securities market and analytical reports about the market by several firms.

## Strengthening Russian Chambers of Commerce and Industry: Case Studies
www.cipe.org/ruschamber/

An online publication prepared by the Center for International Private Enterprise in 1997 to provide chambers of commerce in Russia with ideas for new projects and suggestions on how they can be accomplished.

## Transition Newsletter
www.worldbank.org/html/prddr/trans/WEB/trans.htm

A monthly journal published by the World Bank, *Transition Newsletter: The Newsletter about Reforming Economies* has articles about countries making the transition to a market economy, plus an excellent section that keeps track of research, books, working papers, and conferences in the field. The Web site contains selections from the current issue and a complete archive.

# *Links Pages*

www.bcc.ru/links/

www.itaiep.doc.gov/bisnis/osin.htm

# Civil Society

## E-mail Lists

### Arnova-L

A forum for researchers of nonprofit organizations and philanthropy. Most of the discussion is related to the U.S., but the list includes researchers from Europe and Asia.

List address:   **arnova-l@wvnvm.wvnet.edu**

To subscribe, send the message:   **subscribe democracy_news**
                            to:   **majordomo@free.ned.org**

### ASI Bulletin

The Agency of Social Information (ASI) in Moscow publishes a weekly electronic bulletin that reports on a wide range of third-sector activities in Russia. Of special interest is its reporting on the interplay between NGOs and government agencies. Excerpts, translated into English, are sometimes posted to CCSI's CivilSoc list (see the Clearinghouse section above). An archive of the full Russian-texts is available at **www.friends-partners.org/~ccsi/asi/homepage.htm**

### Democracy_News

The countries of the former USSR are not the only ones which are in the process of trying to establish democratic forms of government and robust civil societies. *Democracy_News* is a monthly bulletin that carries news of conferences, Web sites, publications, book reviews, and other resources related to democracy-building efforts in Eastern Europe and the NIS, Africa, Asia, and Latin America. It is a publication of the National Endowment for Democracy, which funds hundreds of such projects around the world. Some issues include an essay on developments in a particular region or on a specific topic, such as corruption. To submit an announcement for inclusion in *Democracy_News*, send it to **democracy_news @free.ned.org**. The archives are available at **www.ned.org/page_8/exchange.html**

To subscribe, send the message:   **subscribe democracy_news**
                            to:   **majordomo@free.ned.org**

### ISTR-L

This e-mail list is sponsored by the International Society for Third-Sector Research (ISTR), which is a major international association promoting research and education in the fields of philanthropy, civil society, and the nonprofit sector. Most of the subscribers are academic researchers.

List address:   **istr-l@yorku.ca**

To subscribe, send the message:     **subscribe istr-l firstname lastname**
                            to:     **listserv@yorku.ca**


## *Web Sites*

### American International Development Organizations
www.pactworld.org/links.html
www.interaction.org/mb/members.html

Here are two sets of links to Web sites of the largest American organizations
working in the field of international development and humanitarian assistance.
Many of the groups listed have had active projects in Eurasia in the past few years.

### Antimilitarist Radical Association
www.glasnet.ru/~ara/

ARA's home page contains information about the issue of alternative forms of
military service and conscientious objection in Russia. The site includes a monthly
bulletin on draft issues in Russia and draft counseling resources for young people.

### Books for Russian NGOs
www.openweb.ru/windows/cip/book.htm

Fourteen books were produced during the course of the USAID-funded Civic
Initiatives Program, including *Taxation and Accounting for Noncommercial
Organizations in Russia* and *Marketing Research: A Social Marketing Tool for
Public Organizations*. The books are in Russian and the files are zipped.

### Centers for Pluralism Newsletter
sunsite.icm.edu.pl/home/idee/

The Centers for Pluralism, a project of the Institute for Democracy in Eastern
Europe in Warsaw, is an informal network of NGOs in Eastern Europe and the NIS
working in the general field of civic education. The CfP office in Warsaw publishes
a quarterly newsletter containing a great deal of information about NGO projects in
the region. Each issue has a section titled "Who is Who: Activities, Plans, SOS,"
which includes organizational profiles and project descriptions, and "Who is
Offering What," an annotated list of resources and foundations. At the back of each
issue is a list of contact information for several hundred NGOs in the region. A
Russian edition of the newsletter is available at **ngo.ryazan.ru/cfp/index.htm**. The
Institute of Statehood and Democracy in Kyiv publishes a Ukrainian edition. To
receive a copy contact Ivan Lozovy at **lozowy@gluk.apc.org**.

### CharityNet
www.charitynet.org/

CharityNet is the Web site of the Charities Aid Foundation, which provides many of
the same services in Great Britain that United Way and the Council on Foundations

provide in the U.S. The site includes a list of links to more than 2,000 NGOs and foundations in Great Britain and around the world and a searchable database of 90,000 NGOs in Great Britain with contact information. There is also an archive of a regular weekly section in a major London newspaper entitled "Charity Matters," which looks at the role of charities (the term the British often use for NGOs) in society (**www.charitynet.org/infostore/observer/index.html**).

## Civil Society and Governance Programme
www.ids.ac.uk/ids/civsoc/home.html

The program is a three-year research project of the Institute for Development Studies at the University of Sussex, which will analyze the character of civil society in 22 countries. The research will focus on the role of civil society in tackling poverty and promoting greater equality. The Web site includes a database of online articles about civil society and an interesting list of links to Web sites around the world that focus on civil society issues.

## Civnet
civnet.org/

Civnet is a large collection of resources related to civic education. It is sponsored in part by the United States Information Agency. Among the highlights is a bimonthly journal with articles that examine civil society in theory and practice within a range of cultural contexts. The Resources section includes civic education bibliographies, lesson plans, and even a couple of textbooks. There is also a listing of civic education organizations around the world.

## DemocracyNet
www.ned.org/

DemocracyNet is a project of the National Endowment for Democracy, a grant-making organization established and funded by the U.S. government to strengthen democratic institutions around the world through non-governmental efforts. DemocracyNet is an online library of democracy development resources. It includes a well-organized list of annotated links to organizations active in such fields as human rights, election observation, and conflict resolution and a searchable database of more than 4,000 projects that have been funded by NED, the Westminster Foundation for Democracy (Great Britain), the International Centre for Human Rights and Democratic Development (Canada), the Foundation Jean Jaurès (France), the Swedish International Liberal Centre (Sweden), and the Alfred Mozer Foundation (The Netherlands).

## Doors to Democracy
www.rec.org/REC/Publications/PPDoors/CEE/cover.html

This is an online version of "Current Trends and Practices in Public Participation in Environmental Decision-making in Central and Eastern Europe," published by the Regional Environmental Center (REC) in Hungary in 1998.

## Estonian NGO Database

www.ngonet.ee/

A database of more than 700 NGOs in Estonia compiled in 1996–97.

## German Charities Institute

www.dsk.de/

Information, including addresses, on more than 5,000 nonprofit organizations in Germany.

## Idealist

www.idealist.org/

Links to more than 14,000 NGOs on the Web, the vast majority of which are in the U.S.

## Issues of Democracy

www.usia.gov/journals/journals.htm

A quarterly electronic journal published by the United States Information Agency (USIA), which addresses topics such as "Advocacy in America" and "Law Enforcement in a Free Society." The journal is available in English and Russian. Other electronic journals available from this site (in English and Russian) include *U.S. Society and Values* and *Economic Perspectives*.

## Khabarovsk NGO Center

www.ngo.khv.ru/

An online resource center about and for NGOs in Khabarovsk. The site includes brief descriptions of some organizations in the region, information about grant opportunities, links to online resources, and an events calendar.

## Kyiv Freenet Yellow Pages

www.freenet.kiev.ua/FreeNet/ypngo.html

An e-mail directory of 250 NGOs that have their e-mail accounts on the Kyiv Freenet, a non-governmental Internet service provider funded by the United Nations.

## Moscow Libertarium

www.fe.msk.ru/libertarium/

One of the oldest World Wide Web projects in Russia—it started in 1994—this site is a resource center for libertarian issues. In 1998, the maintainers started to collect documents on the proposal by the FSB (formerly the KGB) to monitor Internet traffic in Russia, a project known by its acronym, SORM.

## NGO Cafe

www.soc.titech.ac.jp/ngo/

An excellent collection of links and documents by and for NGOs around the world maintained by Hari Srinivas in Japan. The site includes a selection of articles about how NGOs can use the Internet and a list of links to NGO directories around the world titled "NGO Bungee Jumps."

### NGO Scene in Japan
www.soc.titech.ac.jp/ngo/japan-ngo.html
A collection of links to NGO directories and reports about the third sector in Japan.

### NGONet
www.ngonet.org
An excellent collection of resources for and about NGOs in Eastern Europe. The site is maintained by Freedom House as part of its USAID-sponsored Democracy Network project to support the development of non-governmental organizations in Central and Eastern Europe. Of special interest are back issues of the *NGO News* newsletter, which focuses on such topics as "NGOs and the Corporate Community" and "Media Relations for NGOs."

### Nonviolence International–Newly Independent States
www.glas.apc.org/~ninis/
In addition to its materials about its own work, the NINIS Web site includes a database created in 1997 of over 150 organizations throughout Eurasia that work in the very broadly defined field of peace, conflict resolution, and human rights.

### OpenWeb
www.openweb.ru/
OpenWeb is a project sponsored by IREX in Moscow to teach NGOs how to create Web pages. The site hosts home pages for more than 20 organizations.

### Polish Non-Profit Center
www.nonprofit.org.pl/
An excellent gateway to the nonprofit sector in Poland maintained by KLON/JAWOR (**www.klon.org.pl/**). It includes a searchable database of NGOs and links to other Polish nonprofit resources. Most of the site is in Polish, but there is an in-depth 1997 survey of Poland's third sector in English.

### Ptchela
www.spb.ru/ptchela/
Includes brief descriptions and contact information in English, Russian, and German for 100 NGOs in St. Petersburg.

### Ryazan NGOs
ngo.ryazan.ru/
An extensive listing of NGOs in Ryazan, Russia.

### St. Petersburg NGO Directory
www.eurocomberlin.de/eurocom/StPetersburgRussia/NGO/Directory.htm

Compiled in 1997, this directory includes contact and membership information and brief descriptions of hundreds of NGOs in St. Petersburg.

### Ukrainian NGO Handbook
www.eurocomberlin.de/eurocom/Kiew/Articles/Handbook/index.htm

*How to Found an NGO and How to Manage It* is an online manual for Ukrainian NGOs published in 1997 by Counterpart Creative Center and GURT NGO Resource Center.

## *Links Pages*

ngo.ryazan.ru/links/index.htm

Links to dozens of NGOs throughout Eurasia.

www.ned.org/page_4/orginfo.html

Links to organizations engaged in democracy development work

# *Education*

## *E-mail Lists*

### CEEMAN-I

CEEMAN-L is managed by Internet guru Dennis McConnell for the Central and East European Management Development Association (CEEMAN) based in Slovenia. While the primary purpose of the list is to provide information for CEEMAN members, McConnell monitors so many information resources, electronic and print, that there is something for everyone on this list. He is especially good at finding information about academic exchange programs and funding opportunities. Archives of back messages are available at **ecolu-info.unige.ch/archives/**.

List address: **ceeman-l@maine.maine.edu**

To subscribe, send the message: **subscribe ceeman-l firstname lastname**
to: **listserv@maine.maine.edu**

## *Web Sites*

### IREX
www.irex.org

IREX (International Research & Exchanges Board) has administered academic and research exchanges between the U.S. and Eurasia since 1968. Since the early 1990s, IREX has been active in facilitating and promoting the use of e-mail and the Internet by scholars and non-governmental organizations. IREX's Web site includes information about all of its exchange programs and fellowship opportunities. It also includes information about its Internet Access and Training Program, with a list of more than 50 public access e-mail sites that IREX maintains around Eurasia.

## REDLINE
www.redline.ru/

The Russian Educational Line (REDLINE) offers access to online publications of curricular materials and reports on developments in the sphere of education. Also available is a growing online database of organizations, specialists, and projects that work in the field of education in Russia.

## Russian Links for Educators
www.glasnet.ru/glasweb/eng/educat.html

A list of links to schools and other resources related to education in Russia. Maintained by Glasnet, the list includes links to lists of Russian schools online, an education magazine, Web sites created by Russian schoolchildren, and more.

## Russian Schools on the Internet
www.imras.yar.ru/~korn/school

A list of Web sites and e-mail addresses for dozens of Russian (and some Ukrainian) K–12 schools that have Internet access.

## School Education Server of St. Petersburg
www.nit.spb.su/

This is the Web site for an e-mail network for secondary and vocational schools in St. Petersburg. So far more than 100 schools have joined the network. From the site, you can access home pages for various schools on the network and a list of e-mail addresses for St. Petersburg schools. There is also information about other Internet-related educational projects in Russia.

## U.S. Education Information Center
www.useic.ru/

This is the home page of the U.S. government–sponsored Education Advising Center in Moscow, established for students who want to attend a university in the U.S. The Web site includes all sorts of information for prospective students, including financial aid information. It also has a listing of all the Education Information Centers in Eurasia.

# *Environment*

## *E-mail Lists*

### BALLERINA-L

An online bulletin board for announcements related to the environment, natural resources, and sustainable development in the Baltic Sea Region. Messages are archived at **www.baltic-region.net/meetpoin/maillist.htm**.

List address: **ballerina-l@lists.grida.no**

To subscribe, send the message: **subscribe ballerina-l**
to: **lists@lists.grida.no**

### Baltic News

Baltic News is the e-mail newsletter of Green World, an environmental non-governmental organization near St. Petersburg. It reports on a variety of environmental events, projects, and resources from Green World and other organizations. The bulletin is available in English and Russian. Back issues are archived at **spb.org.ru/greenworld/**.

To subscribe, send the message: **subscribe nuclear_rus your e-mail address**
(Russian edition)
**subscribe nuclear_news your e-mail address**
(English edition)
to: **majordomo@teia.ru**

### Barents-L

Barents-L was started in late 1993 as a forum for discussions concerning the Barents Euro-Arctic region among researchers at Umea University in Sweden. Since then, the list has expanded to around 150 subscribers, most of whom reside in Scandinavia or northwest Russia. Back messages are archived at **ftp://ftp.umu.se/user/home/mao-ftp/public/BARENTS-L-Archive/**.

List address: **barents-l@listserv.umu.se**

To subscribe, send the message: **subscribe barents-l firstname lastname**
to: **listserv@listserv.umu.se**

### Ecostan News

An English-language monthly bulletin that carries reports on the environment and environmental movements in Central Asia. A good source of information on non-governmental organizations in the region. Back issues are at **www.ecostan.org/**

To subscribe, send a message asking to be added to the list to Eric Sievers at **esievers@igc.org**. A Russian-language version is available by sending a message to **catena@glas.apc.org**.

## EcoNews

A monthly Russian-language journal published by the Independent Ecological Information Center in St. Petersburg, EcoNews focuses on environmental issues in Northwest Russia and the Baltics. In contrast to other e-mail bulletins focused on the same topic, EcoNews tends to have longer, more philosophical essays. Back issues are available at **www.friends-partners.org/oldfriends/valery/econews/ econews.html**

To subscribe, send the message:   **subscribe econews**
                          to:   **majordomo@teia.pu.ru**

## EnvCEE-L

An excellent source for news and announcements related to the environment in Eastern Europe and the NIS. EnvCEE-L is sponsored by the Regional Environmental Center for Central and Eastern Europe (REC), a nonprofit organization based near Budapest, Hungary. Each month, EnvCEE-L includes a calendar of environment-related conferences and workshops. Searchable archives are available at the REC's Web site at **www.rec.org/REC/Databases/ENVCEE-L/** or **ecolu-info.unige.ch/archives/**.

List address:   **envcee-l@rec.hu**

To subscribe, send the message:   **subscribe envcee-l firstname lastname**
                          to:   **listserv@rec.hu**

## EnvEvents-L

A bulletin that lists conferences, exhibits, seminars, and workshops in Europe and North America that focus on environmental and public health issues. The list, which is sponsored by the Regional Environmental Center (REC), comes out once or twice a month. Back issues are archived in a searchable database at the REC's Web site at **www.rec.org/REC/Databases/Events/EventsFind.html**. To have events listed in an upcoming bulletin, send an announcement to **rec-info@rec.org** and put "Events Database" in the subject line.

To subscribe, send the message:   **subscribe envevents-l firstname lastname**
                          to:   **listserv@rec.hu**

## ISAR Kyiv Informational Bulletin

ISAR's office in Kyiv publishes a monthly bulletin for (mostly environmental) NGOs in Belarus, Moldova, and Ukraine. The bulletin includes information on upcoming conferences, conventions, and seminars; activity and event updates from organizations; requests for cooperation; opportunities for financial and technical support; and new publications. The bulletin is in Russian only and is distributed within the western NIS by postal mail and e-mail at the end of each month. Subscribers outside the western NIS can receive the bulletin by e-mail. The e-mail version uses Cyrillic fonts for DOS and arrives uuencoded and zipped. To be added to the print or electronic distribution list, send a message to **isar@isar.freenet.kiev.ua**

## Transboundary and Environmental News

TEN is a Russian-language biweekly compilation of environment-related news about the region composed of the Baltic states, Finland and northwest Russia. The news items are taken from national news agencies and cover such issues as energy, agriculture, environmental protection, and border issues. Back issues are archived at **www.teia.org**. To receive the bulletin via e-mail, send a message to **editor@teia.ru**.

## *Web Sites*

### BALLERINA
www.baltic-region.net/

BALLERINA is a project of the United Nations, the European Union, and the governments of Sweden and Norway to promote sustainable development in the Baltic Sea region by improving the availability and accessibility of relevant Internet-based information for decision-making at all levels. The Web site has a wealth of information about the Baltic Sea and links to intergovernmental and non-governmental organizations working on environmental issues in the region.

### EcoLine
cci.glasnet.ru/

EcoLine is the Web site of the Socio-Ecological Union, which serves as an umbrella group for more than 250 non-governmental environmental organizations in the NIS. This large site includes information about SEU, its members, a selection of news-letters published by SEU members, a searchable database of environmental NGOs from all over Eurasia, links to other Internet resources, and more.

### Environmental Technical Information Project
ecologia.nier.org/

A project of ECOLOGIA, which has been working in the NIS since the mid-1980s, ETIP is a collection of links to Internet resources and on-line databases that contain technical information about environmental issues. For each subject category (e.g., toxic chemicals, radiation, environmental legislation and education, etc.), ECOLOGIA has prepared a general introduction to the on-line resources available and how issues related to the specific category are approached in the U.S. For each Internet resource, ECOLOGIA has prepared an evaluation that describes the type of information provided and directions on how to navigate through the site. ETIP is available in English and Russian fonts.

### Eurasian Environmental E-mail Users Directory
www.igc.apc.org/sen/

An annotated directory of hundreds of Eurasian environmental organizations that have e-mail capabilities. Now in its fifth edition, the directory is published by the Sacred Earth Network (SEN), which has helped dozens of Eurasian NGOs get online. The directory is available at SEN's Web site, where there is also a good list of links to other environmental projects in the region.

### Regional Environmental Center
www.rec.hu

The Regional Environmental Center for Central and Eastern Europe was established in 1990 by the government of Hungary, the U.S. Environmental Protection Agency, and the European Commission to serve as a clearinghouse in support of environmental NGOs. Although its primary focus is on Central Europe, the REC does have some projects in the western NIS. The site administrators do an excellent job of finding environment-related Internet resources that are appropriate for NGOs and the region as a whole. The home page has the latest environmental news from the region. Inside there is a database of East European environmental NGOs, a searchable database of Internet resources, and a number of online publications for NGOs, journalists, and public officials.

### Transboundary Environmental Information Agency
www.teia.org

TEIA is a non-governmental organization that seeks to promote international cooperation by assisting in the distribution of information across border areas in the Baltic states and northwestern Russia. The Web site has a good selection of links to environmental organizations in the region. It also includes news of projects in northwest Russia that provide Internet access for NGOs in the region.

# *Funding*

## *E-mail Lists*

### Grants

Maintained by Marek Tiits of the Institute of Baltic Studies in Tartu, Estonia, Grants is of interest primarily to people in Eastern Europe and the NIS. The list consists solely of announcements about grant programs for which CEE and NIS residents can apply.

List address:   **grants@ibs.ee**

To subscribe, send the message:   **subscribe grants firstname lastname**
                              to:   **listserv@ibs.ee**

### Scientist

Sponsored by the American Association for the Advancement of Science, the list carries announcements about grants, fellowships, cooperative projects, and resources for scientists and engineers in Central Europe and Eurasia. Messages are archived at **www.aaas.org/international/scientist.htm.**

To subscribe, send the message: **subscribe scientist your-email-address**
to: **majordomo@aaas.org**

## *Web Sites*

### Database of Funding Sources for Environmental NGOs
www.rec.org/REC/Databases/Funders/FundersFind.html

A database of more than 100 funders that support environmental projects in Central Europe and, to a lesser degree, Belarus, Moldova, Russia, and Ukraine. The database is maintained by the Regional Environment Center (REC) in Hungary.

### European Foundation Centre
www.efc.be

EFC was founded in 1989 by seven of Europe's leading foundations "to build philanthropy in the New Europe by promoting foundations and corporate citizenship." Of special interest at EFC's Web site is the Orpheus Programme, which is a network of NGO resource centers in Western and Eastern Europe and Western Eurasia that have programs on civil society, education, environment, and philanthropy. Each program publishes a bulletin that reports on projects throughout the region with case studies of how organizations have tackled pressing issues.

### Funders Online
www.fundersonline.org/index.html

Funders Online is an online directory of 150 European foundations. It is European in the broadest sense, stretching from the Atlantic to the Urals. It includes information on the type of projects the foundations fund and where they are active. There is also a directory of NGO resource centers in Europe, with brief descriptions and links to their Web sites.

### Funding for Civil Society: A Guide to U.S. Grantmakers Giving in Central/Eastern Europe and the Newly Independent States
www.voiceinternational.org/fd/form.htm

A very useful guide to more than 50 U.S. organizations that fund civil society projects in Eastern Europe and Eurasia. The guide was compiled by VOICE International in 1997 and is regularly updated. Although the entire guide is available at the Web site, Western organizations are requested to pay a $30 fee if they download the guide.

## Grant Possibilities for Estonian Organizations and Individuals
www.ut.ee/grant/List1.htm

Don't be fooled by the title, this is an excellent resource for anyone from Eastern Europe or the NIS. The site consists of a table of 206 (mostly West European) grant and scholarship programs available to residents of Estonia (and elsewhere). The initial table includes the type of grant, the subject covered, and the grant institution. For each grant program there is a separate section that provides detailed contact information and basic information about the program, including eligibility and application deadlines.

## Grantmakers Online
fdncenter.org/grantmaker/contents.html

List of links to hundreds of U.S. private foundations and corporate grant-making offices compiled by the Foundation Center.

## Soros Foundations Network
www.soros.org

George Soros, through his family of Open Society Institutes in 26 countries in Eastern Europe and Eurasia, has contributed hundreds of millions of dollars to the development of civil societies in the region. It's no surprise therefore that the Soros Web site is a popular destination for people working with NGOs in Eurasia. The site includes information about dozens of Soros projects in the region, including annual reports for many of the Open Society Institutes. Many of the projects with home pages on the Soros site have uploaded resources and have links collections. The site has been designed to be useful to people who have slow Internet connections.

## Sources of Funding at Ecoline
cci.glasnet.ru/funds/

The Socio-Ecological Union's Center for Coordination and Information maintains a large Web site devoted to funding resources. In addition to grant and scholarship announcements, the site includes a database of several hundred Western foundations with descriptions of the type of projects they fund and links to their home pages. Unfortunately, many of the foundations listed do not fund projects in Eurasia. There is also a library of financial and tax information for NGOs in Russia.

## Sources of Funding in International Affairs
www.ned.org/page_4/funding/fundmain.html

Maintained by the National Endowment for Democracy, this site offers brief descriptions, contact information, and links to more than 75 U.S. and foreign foundations that fund international projects.

## TACIS
europa.eu.int/comm/dg1a/tacis/index.htm

TACIS is one of the European Union's largest aid programs in Eurasia, and has launched more than 3,000 projects in the region since 1991. A significant number of TACIS grants have been awarded for NGO projects. The Web site includes information about the TACIS grants programs as well as profiles ("case studies") of projects TACIS has supported in the past.

## Virtual Foundation
www.virtualfoundation.org/main.html

The Virtual Foundation is an excellent example of the way the Internet can be used to provide concrete assistance to someone who lives on the other side of the planet. The foundation is made up of a consortium of environmental organizations in the U.S. and Eastern Europe with extensive experience administering grants to NGOs. Organizations in Eastern Europe and Eurasia submit project proposals to a local office of one of the foundation's members, where the proposal is vetted. The proposal is then passed on to the Virtual Foundation's board of directors in the U.S. for further review. If approved by the board, the proposal is uploaded to the Internet. People visiting the Virtual Foundation's Web site can review a variety of proposals and either fund a project in its entirety or make a contribution that will be pooled with donations from other people. Once sufficient funds have been raised for a particular project, a grant is made by the consortium member responsible for that geographic region. The consortium member assumes all the normal grant-making responsibilities to ensure that contributions are spent wisely.

## Some Important Foundations That Fund Projects in the NIS

Charity Know How
**www.charitynet.org/charityknowhow/**

Charles Stewart Mott Foundation
**www.mott.org/**

Eurasia Foundation
**www.eurasia.org**

Ford Foundation
**www.fordfound.org**

John D. and Catherine T. MacArthur Foundation
**www.macfdn.org**

National Endowment for Democracy
**www.ned.org/**

Rockefeller Brothers Fund
**www.rbf.org/**

TACIS
**europa.eu.int/comm/dg1a/tacis/index.htm**

U.S. Civilian Research and Development Foundation
**www.crdf.inter.net**

# Health

## E-mail Lists

### Global Health and Environmental Bulletin

A quarterly bulletin, published by the Center for Communications, Health and the Environment, which has brief descriptions of projects, meetings, and resources related to improving health care in the NIS and around the world. Back issues are archived at CECHE's Web site at **www.igc.apc.org/ceche/**.

To subscribe, send a message saying you want to subscribe to: **ceche@igc.apc.org**

### NISHEALTH

NISHEALTH is sponsored by the American International Health Alliance, which manages hospital partnerships between health care institutions in the U.S. and Eurasia. The list carries announcements about resources, projects, and grants of interest to people engaged with health-related projects in the region.

List address:    **nis-health@igc.apc.org**

To subscribe, send a message saying you want to subscribe to: **mstorey@igc.apc.org**

### NISMEDINFO Bulletin

The NISMEDINFO bulletin is part of AIHA's project in Eastern Europe and Eurasia. The bulletin contains brief descriptions of a broad range of health care resources available on the Internet. Although it is intended for AIHA's partners in the region, anyone can be added to the distribution list. The bulletin is available in English and Russian and is archived at **www.friendspartners.org/~aiha/english/ health/ bulletin/index.htm**.

To be added to the distribution list, send a message to the bulletin's editor at: **dsturgill@igc.apc.org**.

## Web Sites

### American International Health Alliance
www.aiha.com
The American International Health Alliance (AIHA) manages a USAID-funded project to establish partnerships between health care institutions in the U.S. and their

counterparts in Eastern Europe and the NIS. In addition to information about AIHA's program, this site contains a wealth of information of interest to health care practitioners in Eastern Europe and Eurasia. The site includes a library of more than 400 documents that have been translated into various languages of the region. There is an excellent annotated guide, in English and Russian, to health-related Internet resources. AIHA has also assembled a list of links to other sites and resources that have information about health conditions in the region.

# Law and Human Rights

## E-mail Lists

### Huridocs

Huridocs was established as a means of facilitating contacts and the exchange of information between more than 250 organizations around the world that deal with the documentation of human rights violations. However, the list is open to others and is a good source of information about conferences, publications, organizations, and Web sites in the field of human rights work.

List address: **huridocs-gen-l@sonne.comlink.apc.org**

To subscribe, send the message: **subscribe huridocs-gen-l**
to: **majordomo@mail.comlink.apc.org**

## Web Sites

### AAAS Database of Human Rights Resources on the Internet
shr.aaas.org/dhr.htm

Many of the Soviet Union's most prominent dissidents were scientists, and the American Association for the Advancement of Science has long included a human rights component in its programs with the NIS. The AAAS on-line "Database of Human Rights Resources" includes a growing list of links to human rights Web sites and an index of Internet-based publications related to human rights and science.

### CIS Law Notes
www.pbwt.ru/cislaw.htm

An excellent quarterly bulletin published by the law firm Patterson, Belknap, Webb and Tyler. The firm's staff and prominent CIS lawyers and judges cover legal developments, with a special focus on commercial law in Russia, Central Asia, and the Transcaucasus.

### Express Khronika
www.online.ru/mlists/expchronicle/

*Express Khronika*, first issued in August 1987 as a samizdat newspaper, is a daily Russian-language bulletin/news service that reports mostly on human/civil rights events and organizations. *Express Khronika* has a network of correspondents in Russia and the former republics of the USSR. A weekly bulletin is available for free and the daily bulletin is available for subscribers.

## Human Rights Internet
www.hri.ca/

Long before most people had ever heard of the Internet, Human Rights Internet was a (non-electronic) clearinghouse for human rights organizations around the world. Originally based at Harvard Law School and now located in Ottawa, HRI maintains a vast library of information about human rights organizations and education materials. Recently HRI established its own Web site and has started to upload its materials. Already one can access a collection of human rights course outlines and syllabi, a directory of academic programs that offer human rights education courses, and a growing list of links to other human rights–related Internet sites.

## Human Rights Online
www.hro.org

Human Right Online is a virtual library of information about the human rights situation in Russia. The site includes a database of legal defenders/human rights organizations in Russia, a library of Russian and international legislation related to human rights, and several newsletters and publications published by Russian human rights groups.

## International Center for Not-for-Profit Law
www.icnl.org/

ICNL provides technical assistance to governments, courts, and NGOs around the world on the writing of laws and regulations that govern non-governmental organizations. Its Web site has articles discussing the basic elements of law needed for a vibrant NGO sector and archives of its quarterly journal.

## Internet Guide to the Law of the Caucasus and Central Asia
www.gtz.de/lexinfosys/

A project of the University of Bremen to help German companies expand to Eurasia, this is a database of over 200 laws available in German, Russian, and English. The university plans to expand the database to include all CIS countries.

## List of International Law Electronic Discussion Groups and Journals
www.lib.uchicago.edu/~llou/lawlists/international.html

Compiled and regularly updated by Lyonette Louis-Jacques, Librarian and Lecturer in Law at the University of Chicago Law School, this catalog is an excellent resource. It includes more than 150 e-mail lists and more than 70 online journals that focus on a wide array of international law topics.

## Memorial

www.memorial.ru

Memorial was founded in 1988 by leading elements of Russia's democratic intelligentsia to recognize the millions of citizens who passed through the gulag and to provide support for survivors and their families. Memorial's Web site includes online documents about human rights and the gulag, a map of the gulag, and links to regional chapters.

## Sakharov Foundation

www.wdn.com/asf

The Andrei Sakharov Foundation was organized in Moscow shortly after Sakharov's death in December 1989. The foundation's Web site includes information about Sakharov, his widow Elena Bonner, some of the projects she is involved in, a number of documents related to the work of the foundation in the fields of nuclear energy and human rights, and a list of links to other Web sites related to human rights in and around Russia.

## World Justice Information Network

www.justinfo.net/

At the heart of WJIN is a searchable database of thousands of links to organizations, universities, news sources, and government agencies around the world that relate in some way to the rule of law. The Web site is a project of the Rule of Law Foundation, headed by Sergey Chapkey, who worked for the procurator of the Odessa region in Ukraine for four years. The links reflect Chapkey's understanding of the broad range of resources that can be useful to attorneys, government officials, and law enforcement agencies in countries making the transition to democracy.

# *Media*

## *E-mail Lists*

### FSUmedia

FSUmedia focuses on the media in the former Soviet Union and efforts by Western organizations to support the development of an independent media in the NIS. It is a project of Internews and is moderated by Eric Johnson, who has also traveled extensively in Central Asia, Ukraine, and elsewhere in the NIS. Johnson does a good job of ensuring that FSUmedia does not become Russocentric.

List address: **fsumedia@sovam.com**

To subscribe, send the message: **subscribe fsumedia firstname lastname**
to: **listproc@sovam.com**

## Rjour-l

A Russian-language list for journalists and media professionals to discuss media-related issues, exchange information, and find out about new publications, conferences, and events in the sphere of print and television journalism. This is a good place to find out about Russian newspapers and magazines that are publishing online.

List address:   **rjour-l@irex.ru**

To subscribe, send the message:   **subscribe rjour-l firstname lastname**
to:   **listserv@irex.ru**

# *Web Sites*

### Committee to Protect Journalists
www.cpj.org/

The Committee to Protect Journalists was established in 1981 to monitor abuses against the press and promote press freedom around the world. The CPJ Web site includes its annual publication *Attacks on the Press*, which is a survey of press freedom in nearly 100 countries and a searchable Press Freedom Database of verified reports of journalists killed, imprisoned, attacked, or censored around the world. The links page has links to independent newspapers and radio stations, and a section titled "Sites Under Siege," which includes media outlets that are being harassed and are using the Internet to publish the news.

### International Center for Journalists
www.icfj.org

Founded in 1984, ICFJ has organized training workshops for more than 7,000 journalists and media officials from 172 countries. It helps establish newspaper exchanges, administers internships for foreign journalists in the U.S., and produces a variety of publications. ICFJ's Web site includes a listing of training, fellowship, and grant opportunities for the NIS and Eastern Europe and a clearinghouse of news about media assistance projects in the region.

### Internews Russia
www.internews.ru/

Internews helps to develop independent broadcasting institutions in Eastern Europe and the former USSR. The Web site is a good source of information about the media in the NIS, including profiles of organizations that defend the rights of journalists and freedom of speech, the text of media legislation, and media-related bulletins and newsletters.

### Moscow Media Law and Policy Center
www.medialaw.ru

Founded in 1995, the center works with legislators, the judicial system, and educational institutes to create a body of law and jurisprudence upon which a free and independent press can be built in Russia. The center's Web site includes the full text of ten books and reports, its monthly Russian-language publication, *ZiP*, which reports on media issues at the federal and regional level, and a selection of media laws.

### ProMedia Ukraine
www.ipc.kiev.ua

The Web site for an IREX-managed media project in Ukraine, the site has current news from Ukraine, links to Ukrainian newspapers and magazines, and information about media law.

## Online English-Language News

### E-mail Lists

### RFE/RL Newsline
Probably the best single source of news available, Radio Free Europe/Radio Liberty's daily bulletin contains news briefs about events in Eastern Europe and Eurasia.

To subscribe, send the message:  **subscribe**
                    to:  **newsline-request@list.rferl.org**

### Web Sites

### Directory of Russian Periodicals Online
rs.informika.ru/

Links to dozens of online newspapers, magazines, and bulletins in a wide variety of subject fields.

### Kyiv Post
www.thepost.kiev.ua

A number of news stories and Web links are accessible to anybody who visits this site, but for $95 one can have access to a year's worth (104 issues) of the full twice-weekly electronic edition of the *Kyiv Post*.

### Minsk Economic News
www.geocities.com/~minsknews/

Belarus's only English-language newspaper.

### Radio Free Europe/Radio Liberty
www.rferl.org/

RFE/RL was originally established by the U.S. government after WWII to serve as an alternative source for news about events in their own countries for the people of Eastern Europe and the USSR. RFE/RL has continued to broadcast news of the region with the support of regional leaders such as Vaclav Havel. RFE/RL's Web site is very large, with lots of news, including RealAudio files of RFE/RL's broadcasts, an archive of its *Newsline* daily news briefs, feature articles, special reports, and more. News reports are available in English and Russian.

### The Georgian Times
duggy.sanet.ge/gtze/

English-language bimonthly newspaper.

### The Moscow Times
www.moscowtimes.ru

One of Moscow's oldest and most respected English-language newspapers. Brief summaries of the top stories are available for free with the whole newspaper available to subscribers. Of special interest are the job announcements and classifieds, which are free.

### The St. Petersburg Times
www.times.spb.ru/

Published every Tuesday and Friday, with two or three top stories and opinion articles available for free and the rest available only to subscribers. Good classifieds and job and event listings.

### Ukraine Newsstand
www.brama.com/news/index.html

Part of the Brama.com Web site, the newsstand has links to six English-language newspapers that report on Ukraine and several dozen more in Russian and Ukrainian.

### Vladivostok News
vn.vladnews.ru

Current and back issues of Vladivostok's only English-language weekly newspaper.

# *Public Administration*

## *Web Sites*

### Local Government And Public Service Reform Initiative
www.osi.hu/lgi/

The initiative is a project of the Open Society Institute in Budapest to promote the sharing of expertise on local government between countries in Eastern Europe and Eurasia. The Web site has a number of case studies and innovative practices from different countries in the region on a whole range of local government issues, including programs for the elderly, economic development, financial management, and environmental policies. The documents are in a variety of languages, including Russian. There is also a growing list of links to other local government sites on the Internet.

## SIGMA
www.oecd.org/puma/sigmaweb/
SIGMA is a joint initiative of the OECD and the European Union's PHARE Programme to support good governance in Central and Eastern Europe. The SIGMA Web site includes its bimonthly newsletter *Public Management Forum* and a good collection of online policy briefs and longer papers on civil service reform and other topics.

## Transparency International
www.transparency.de
Transparency International works to curb corruption by mobilizing a global coalition of stakeholders in the integrity of national and international governance, including most importantly the institutions of civil society and the private sector. TI's Web site includes its annual *Corruption Perceptions Index*, which is a "poll of polls" measuring the public's view of the extent of corruption in their own country. In 1998, Denmark was ranked as the least corrupt, and the U.S. tied with Austria for 17th place. The Web site also includes the *TI Source Book*, which is a collection of best practices from around the world in the effort to combat corruption.

# *Region-Specific*

## Belarus and Moldova

## *E-mail Lists*

### Belarus
The Belarus list is the main place for people who are interested in Belarus to meet one another on the Internet. The list is a mix of news stories, announcements, and discussion.

List address:   **belarus@solar.cini.utk.edu**

To subscribe, send the message:   **subscribe belarus firstname lastname** to:    **listproc@solar.cini.utk.edu**

## Belarus Update

Belarus Update is a biweekly bulletin published by the International League of Human Rights (ILHR) as part of its Belarus Human Rights Support Project. The bulletin carries news reports about the human rights situation in Belarus and the activities of social movements that oppose President Alexander Lukashenko. Back issues and other information about ILHR's Belarus project are available at **www.ilhr.org**.

To be added to the mailing list, send a mesage to: **belarus@ilhr.org**

## *Web Sites*

### A Belarus Miscellany

solar.cini.utk.edu/~kasaty/miscellany.html

Regularly updated by Peter Kasaty, this modestly titled site is the first place you should visit if you want to find something related to Belarus. In addition to providing links to dozens of other sites focused on Belarus, Kasaty has provided contact information for Belarusian government offices, universities, non-governmental organizations, media, and Internet providers. He also profiles the work of other individuals interested in Belarus and provides some kind of contact information (usually an e-mail address).

### Belarusian.com

www.belarusian.com/

Belarusian.com is maintained by Sergei Polevikov, a Ph.D. student in economics at Rice University whose mother is president of Nadzeya, a prominent women's political party in Belarus. Polevikov has collected quite a bit of interesting information about the political opposition to Belarusian President Alexander Lukashenko.

### Belarusian Association of Journalists

www.baj.unibel.by

The Belarusian Association of Journalists was founded in 1995 and by 1998 had 450 members representing around 100 state and private media organizations. The BAJ Web site has weekly news bulletins about Belarusian events prepared by Radio Racija, information about a human rights press center in Belarus, and periodic reports that monitor violations of Belarusian laws on the mass media.

### Belarusian Chronicle

chronicle.home.by/

Wire service articles and other news from and about Belarus.

## MoldNet
www.moldnet.md/

MoldNet is the Academic Internet Network for Moldova, which started as a Soros Foundation project in 1995. Under the heading "Civil Society" on the home page, you will find a link to the Contact Center, an NGO resource center in Chisinau, which also hosts Web sites for other NGOs. Also under "Civil Society" on the MoldNet home page, there is a list, with contact information, for 25 NGOs in Moldova.

## Virtual Guide to Belarus
www.belarusguide.com/

This site is a collaborative project among Belarusian scientists abroad. The site has a variety of sections such as history, culture, politics, geography, and travel, which are maintained by different people on different computers around the world.

# Caucasus

## *E-mail Lists*

### Annotated Daily Headlines of the Georgian Press
Compiled by the Caucasian Institute for Peace, Democracy and Development in Tbilisi, this bulletin contains the headlines and synopses of the major stories of the day from a variety of Georgian newspapers.

To be added to the list, send a message to: **Bruno.Coppieters@vub.ac.be**

### Georgia's NGO Sector News
A weekly bulletin published by the Horizonti Foundation in Tbilisi, which reports on the activities of NGOs in Georgia, conferences, workshops, funding opportunities, and the issues affecting NGOs in the region.

To be added to the list, send a message to: **presscenter@horizonti.org**

### Groong
Groong is the unofficial on-line network of the Armenian-American community. It has extensive news of events in Armenia and announcements of events, conferences, and projects of various Armenian-American organizations. The list is for announcements only. More information is available at groong.usc.edu

List address:   **groong@usc.edu**

To subscribe,
send the message: **subscribe groong your-email-address firstname lastname**
            to: **groong-request@usc.edu**

## Habarlar-L

Habarlar-L is an electronic mailing list that focuses on Azerbaijan and Caucasia. The list is moderated and consists only of news postings from wire services, government ministries, regional newspapers, and NGOs.

List-address:   **habarlar-l@usc.edu**

To subscribe, send the message:   **subscribe habarlar-l firstname lastname**
                                         to:   **habarlar-l-request@usc.edu**

## Right to Speech

The weekly electronic newsletter of the Public Interest Protection League, based in Zugdidi, Georgia. The newsletter contains news of Georgian NGOs, announcements about seminars, conferences, and grant opportunities, and advice for NGOs. More information about PIPL is available on the Web at **attend.to/pipl**

To subscribe, send the message:   **subscribe RS**
                                         to:   **pipl1@hotmail.com** or **upleba@hotmail.com**

## Transcaucasus: A Chronology

A monthly summary of significant social, economic, and political events in Armenia, Azerbaijan, Georgia, and Nagorno Karabagh as reported by local and international media and selected sources in the region. It usually consists of paragraph-long news briefs. Back issues are archived at **www.anca.org/tcc.html**.

To be added to the list, contact the editor, Richard Giragosian, at: **giragosi@msn.com**

## Turkistan-N

Turkistan-N is an electronic newsletter that reports on the "Land of the Turks," which includes Central Asia and the Caucasus. It includes information about the culture, history, and news of Turkic peoples in this region. An archive of old messages is available at **www.euronet.nl/users/sota/turkistan.htm**

List-address:   **turkistan-n@vm.ege.edu.tr**

To subscribe send a message to: **sota@euronet.nl**

# *Web Sites*

## Azerbaijan International
www.azer.com/

*Azerbaijan International* is a quarterly print magazine. Each issue focuses on a special topic such as cinema, independence, refugees, or youth. Its Web site includes more than 500 articles from past issues and more than 1,000 photographs.

### Azerbaijan Society of America
www.azerbaijan-america.org/

The society works to deepen the public's knowledge about Azerbaijan's history and people and to promote economic and cultural ties between the U.S. and Azerbaijan. Its Web site has a good collection of links to news about Azerbaijan and organizations and people with an interest in the region. It also has a repository of Azeri fonts for personal computers.

### AzerWeb
www.savechildren.org.az/AzerWeb/Index.html

Sponsored by the United Nations and maintained by Save the Children, AzerWeb is an online resource center about and for international organizations with development and humanitarian assistance projects in Azerbaijan. The Web site includes a directory with extensive program information on more than 60 Western organizations active in Azerbaijan. There is also a directory of local NGOs with contact information and brief descriptions.

### Central Eurasia Project Resource Page
www.soros.org/central_eurasia.html

One of the sections of the Soros Foundation Web site, the Central Eurasia Project Resource Page has a page for each country in the Caucasus and Central Asia. The country pages have an excellent collection of links to other sites, news sources, and articles on the country's history, government, business, human rights, media, environment, etc.

### Horizonti Foundation
www.horizonti.org/

The Horizonti Foundation is an NGO resource center in Tbilisi. The foundation's Web site has information about all kinds of NGO projects, as well as announcements of funding and training opportunities for organizations in the region, and analysis of the NGO sector in Georgia and the laws that regulate it.

### Parliament of Georgia
www.parliament.ge/

The official Web site of the government of Georgia contains information about the government, press releases, and links to news services and other Web sites in Georgia.

### Virtual Azerbaijan
www-scf.usc.edu/~baguirov/azeri.htm

An extensive list of links to Azerbaijan-related Internet resources, including current events, history, Web sites in Azerbaijan, Western organizations and businesses with a presence in the country, sports, and more.

# Russia

## *E-mail Lists*

### Johnson's Russia List

Johnson's Russia List is a daily e-mail newsletter with news and analysis of all aspects of contemporary Russia. Managed by David Johnson, the list carries an eclectic collection of wire service and foreign newspaper reports, translations from the Russian press, and analytical pieces by Russian and foreign academics.

To be added to the list, send a message to: **davidjohnson@erols.com**

## *Web Sites*

### Moscow Online Magazine and City Guide
www.moscowguide.com/

A monthly online magazine intended as a survival guide for expatriates living and working in Moscow. Includes information on such subjects as visas, medical care, transportation, shopping, and doing business in Moscow. The guide is a great resource for tourists visiting Moscow.

### Rusline
www.rusline.com/

A megalist of links to sites related to Russia, with an emphasis on business-related sites.

### Russian Government Internet Network
www.gov.ru/

The Internet home page of the Russian government, it includes links to government agencies and official decrees.

### Russian Government Online
www.gov.ru/

An extensive list of links to federal government agencies and regional governments, in Russian and English.

### Russian Story
www.russianstory.com/

This site has to be seen to be believed. For around $1, you can download the current issue of more than 25 of Russia's biggest daily and weekly newspapers, including *Argumenty i Fakty*, *Nezavisimaja Gazeta*, *Pravda* and *Kommersant Daily*. The files are in Adobe Acrobat format, which means you see a picture of the entire page. It also means they are pretty big files. You can download the front page for free. Also available are summaries of the top story in each paper and a searchable archive of articles.

### Ryazan Online
ngo.ryazan.ru/

This site allows you to visit Ryazan virtually and learn about its history, meet local artists, and find contact information for local government officials, schools, newspapers, medical clinics, and more. It includes an extensive database of local NGOs.

### St. Petersburg Web Home Page
www.spb.su/

One of the first Web sites in Russia, the St. Petersburg Web is a great way to visit the city built by the first Romanov czar nearly 300 years ago. SPW hosts the electronic version of several newspapers and magazines. There is a map of the city and subway system, an entertainment guide, information about the business climate, and more.

## Links Pages

weblist.ru/

www.ru/

personal.msy.bellsouth.net/msy/s/h/sher07/bll-link.html

# Ukraine

## E-mail Lists

### Corruption Watch
*Corruption Watch* is a biweekly bulletin published by the Ukrainian Center for Independent Political Research, which reports on instances of corruption by national and local government figures in Ukraine and efforts to combat corruption. Stories are excerpted from Ukrainian newspapers or are written by staff members.

### Rukh Insider
The *Rukh Insider* is a monthly news bulletin that carries "in-depth information on political events in Ukraine, including behind-the-scenes coverage of significant current issues, the positions of policymakers, and tactics and strategy information on Ukraine's ongoing political struggle to leave behind its Soviet, communist past." Originally published by the secretariat of Rukh, one of Ukraine's first and largest democratic political parties, the *Rukh Insider* is now compiled by the Institute of Statehood and Democracy, a non-governmental, non-partisan research and

educational institute in Kyiv. An archive of past issues is available at
**www.freenet.kiev.ua/isd/isd-home.htm**. To be added to the electronic mail
distribution list, send a request to **lozowy@gluk.apc.org**.

## Ukrainian Announcements

An online bulletin board for the Ukrainian–North American community, the list
includes announcements of Ukrainian events in the U.S. and Canada, news and
discussion of current events in Ukraine, and questions from subscribers. Archives
are available at **www.infoukes.com/lists/**. The computer that hosts the announcement
list also hosts other Ukrainian mailing lists that focus on such topics as arts,
business, history, politics, sports, and travel. There is even a list devoted to
"flaming" where subscribers can insult one another in a variety of languages.
Information about these other lists is available at the Web site cited above.

List address:   **announce@infoukes.com**

To subscribe, send a message with the word **subscribe** on the Subject line
to:   **announce-request@infoukes.com**

## *Web Sites*

### BRAMA–Ukrainian Gateway
www.brama.com/

Similar in style to Yahoo, BRAMA contains hundreds of annotated links to
Ukrainian-related resources on the Internet. The major subject categories include:
Arts and Culture, Business, Entertainment, Law, News and Media, About Ukraine,
and In the Ukrainian Diaspora. The last category is a directory of more than 100
(primarily) Ukrainian–North American organizations that can be browsed either by
field of activity or location. The Law category has dozens of links and the News and
Media section includes excerpts from *IntelNews*, a daily and weekly English-
language newspaper in Kyiv.

### Infocenter Chornobyl
www.ic-chernobyl.kiev.ua/

Maintained by the Chornobyl State Regional Center of Scientific and Technical
Information, the site has information about the accident at Chornobyl and conditions
today as well as links to other Chornobyl Web sites.

### InfoUkes
www.infoukes.com/

Another megasite for Internet resources related to Ukraine. The WWW Links
section has links to dozens of Web sites around the world that have Ukrainian
resources.

## Institute of Statehood and Democracy

www.freenet.kiev.ua/ISD/ISD-HOME.HTM

The institute is a non-governmental public policy research institute in Kyiv. The Institute's Web site includes contact information for the central and oblast governments and ministries, the Verkhovna Rada (parliament), political parties, and the current situation in Ukraine.

## Tryzub

www.tryzub.com/

The tryzub (trident) is the official coat of arms of Ukraine, which dates back to Kievan Rus' around the turn of the millennium. The site contains a variety of information about Ukraine and also hosts the home pages of several Ukrainian organizations, including the Shevchenko Scientific Society, the oldest scholarly society in Ukraine, and *Suchasnist'* (Contemporary Scene), a Ukrainian literary journal.

## Ukraine FAQ+

www.sabre.org/UKRAINE.html

An on-line library of information about Ukraine including the country's history, culture, current events, bibliographic resources, business information, and more. The site is a project of the Sabre Foundation.

## Ukrainian Weekly

www.ukrweekly.com/

*The Ukrainian Weekly* newspaper has been serving the Ukrainian–North American community since 1933. Its Web site has an excerpt from the current issue and all the stories from 1997 and 1996. There are also excerpts from the special year-end dition going back to 1976 and a section on the Ukrainian famine in the 1930s.

# *Religion*

## *Web Sites*

## FSU Monitor

www.fsumonitor.com/

Online news and advocacy on human rights and Jews in the former USSR. The site is a project of the Union of Councils for Soviet Jews, which has been an active defender of human rights in Eurasia for several decades.

## Keston Institute

www.keston.org

Keston Institute is a research and information center dealing with religion in communist and post-communist countries. Keston's Web site includes select articles from its e-mail bulletin, *Keston News Service*, which reports on religious liberty issues in Russia and Eurasia. There is also information about other, more scholarly journals published by Keston.

### Russian Christian Home Page
www.bethel.edu/seminary_academics/international/russian/russian3.htm

A good list of links to Christian resources in Russia, including religious texts and writings and home pages of churches and schools in Russia. The list includes Orthodox, Catholic, and Protestant links.

### Russian Orthodox Church
www.russian-orthodox-church.org.ru/en.htm

The official Web site of the Moscow Patriarchate contains official statements by church officials, a history of the Orthodox Church in Russia, and an overview of the role of the church today.

### Russian Religious News
www.stetson.edu/~psteeves/relnews/

A collection of articles, interviews, and statements about religion in Russia from a wide variety of sources. The site is maintained by Dr. Paul Steeves of Stetson University. Most of the articles concern Protestant denominations.

# Women

## *E-mail Lists*

### Women-East-West

Women-East-West is sponsored by the Network of East-West Women, which works to promote the formation of independent women's movements in Eastern Europe and the NIS. The list includes discussion and announcements. To be added to the Russian-language sister of this list, contact Irina Doskitch at **neww@glasnet.ru**.

List address:   **women-east-west@igc.apc.org**

To subscribe, send the message:   **subscribe women-east-west**
                          to:   **majordomo@igc.apc.org**

## *Web Sites*

### Network of East-West Women
www.neww.org/

NEWW's On-Line project has provided modems and e-mail training to women's organizations in Eastern Europe and the NIS. Its Web site contains announcements of grants, conferences, and jobs related to promoting women's organizations in Eastern Europe and the NIS and home pages for organizations in the region, which NEWW hosts for free.

## Open Women Line
www.owl.ru

OWL is a project of Zhensky Innovatsionny Fond "Vostok-Zapad" (Women's Innovation Fund "East-West") to provide easy access for women to the new information resources on the Internet and to develop information exchanges between women's organizations within Russia and on an international level. Although the site was only created in 1998, it already includes several databases of women's organizations in Eurasia, a very useful set of links to Internet resources of interest to women, documents on women's rights, and an online magazine.

## Russian Feminism Resources
www.geoclties.com/Athens/2533/russfem.html

An extraordinary collection of resources about women's organizations in Eurasia. It includes profiles of organizations in English and Russian, links to other sites, and a good selection of interviews and reports about the conditions women face in the region. Believe it or not, this is the personal Web site of Elena Leonoff in Australia.

## Women's Human Rights Resources
www.law-lib.utoronto.ca/diana

An extensive list of annotated links to Internet sites and documents on women's human rights compiled by the Bora Laskin Law Library, University of Toronto.

## Women in Business
www.bcc.ru/WIB/

A project of the Business Collaboration Center in Moscow, the Women in Business Web site hosts home pages of women's business organizations. It also hopes to include newsletters, publications, and news related to women in business.

## Women in Business
www.cipe.org/women/

Another Web site devoted to women in business, this one is sponsored by the Center for International Private Enterprise, which funds and organizes business development projects around the world. The site contains back issues of CIPE's newsletter *Organizing for Success: A Newsletter for Women Entrepreneurs* and has a list of links to major American women's business associations.

## Women's Information Network
www.owl.ru/win/winet/index.html **(Russian)**
www.owl.ru/win/winet/English/English.html **(English)**

A database of over 1,300 women's organizations in Russia and the other countries of the NIS.

# *Miscellaneous*

## E-mail Lists

### EE-Jobs

Graciously sponsored by the Civic Education Project, EE-Jobs only carries job announcements for positions related to Eastern Europe and the NIS. While it is a very good resource, it would be even better if more people remembered to post their job announcements to EE-Jobs.

List address:   **ee-jobs@cep.yale.edu**

To subscribe, send the message:   **subscribe ee-jobs your-email-address**
to:   **majordomo@cep.yale.edu**

### Expat

If you are looking for a nanny in Moscow or the ATM machine with the lowest user fee, then the Expat list is for you. Expat is a forum for the community of expatriates in Moscow to share tips for living, working, and shopping in Moscow. Commercial advertisements are strictly forbidden.

List address:   **expat@irex.ru**

To subscribe, send the message:   **subscribe expat**
to:   **listserv@irex.ru**

### Info-Russ

Info-Russ was started by Alex Kaplan, a professor of electrical and computer engineering at Johns Hopkins, to help the academic community of emigres from the former USSR adjust to their new environment and communicate with one another. The list started with 40 of his friends and has since grown to over 1,000 subscribers. Messages to Info-Russ often consist of people seeking or providing information about job openings, visa and immigration requirements, etc. However, Info-Russ also carries important news items, especially in the field of human rights. Back messages are archived at **psi.ece.jhu.edu/~kaplan/IRUSS/inforuss.html**.

List address:   **info-russ@smarty.ece.jhu.edu**

To subscribe, send your e-mail address and name to: **info-russ@smarty.ece.jhu.edu**

### Quick Dispatch

Quick Dispatch is a monthly bulletin of announcements about conferences, education and fellowship opportunities, and Internet resources related to academic research about Eastern Europe and the NIS. Most of the conferences listed are held in Europe. The bulletin is prepared by the Cooperation Bureau for Economic Research on Eastern Europe at the German Institute for Economic Research in Berlin (**www.diw-berlin.de/Koop/english/**).

Send a message asking to be added to the list to **coopq@diw-berlin.de** or **dbowen@diw-berlin.de**.

## RusTex-L

A technical discussion group that focuses on how to print and display Cyrillic on computers and send Cyrillic text across the Internet. Many RusTex-L subscribers are computer experts, and the level of discussion is often beyond intermediate-level computer users. However, collectively RusTex-L subscribers are the single best source of information on how to use Cyrillic on computers, and some of them will usually respond to specific questions with clear and helpful answers, especially if the questions are about a nonstandard Cyrillic problem.

List address: **rustex-l@listserv.acsu.buffalo.edu**

To subscribe, send the message: **subscribe rustex-l firstname lastname**
to: **listserv@listserv.acsu.buffalo.edu**

# Web Sites

## Access Russia

www.arussia.com/

Access Russia acts as an agent for INION (Institute for Information on Social Sciences of the Russian Academy of Sciences), which maintains a library of more than 13 million books, journals, and conference proceedings on a wide variety of subjects, including economics, politics, law, history, philosophy, and sociology. Through Access, Russia scholars, journalists and others can search through abstracts of the INION collection and order articles that will be delivered electronically.

## Accessing the Internet by E-Mail

www.cis.ohio-state.edu/hypertext/faq/usenet/internet-services/access-via-email/faq.html

Even if you only have access to e-mail, you can still access the World Wide Web, Usenet, FTP, and the other Internet technologies. *Accessing The Internet By E-Mail: Doctor Bob's Guide to Offline Internet Access*, now in its 7th edition, provides step-by-step instructions for navigating the whole Internet and retrieving documents. The only caveat we would add to Dr. Bob's guide is that the computers he lists for retrieving World Wide Web documents sometimes become overloaded and are shut down by their administrators. It's important, therefore, to have the most recent edition of Dr. Bob's guide.

To receive the document via e-mail, send an e-mail message to **mail-server@rtfm.mit.edu**. Leave the Subject line blank. In the body of the message, write **send usenet/news.answers/internet-services/access-via-email**

To receive a Russian translation of the 6th edition of Dr. Bob's guide, send an e-mail message to **BobRankin@MHV.NET**. In the Subject line write **send accmail.ru**

### Emancipation of Labor
www.geocities.com/CapitolHill/Lobby/3198/trud.htm

Articles and links related to labor unions and the difficulties workers face in Russia.

### Eurasia Bulletin
www.census.gov/ipc/www/eb.html

The *Eurasia Bulletin* is a quarterly publication of the International Programs Center of the U.S. Bureau of the Census. Recent issues have included reports on "Ethnic Reidentification in Ukraine" and "Demographic Developments in Eastern Europe and the former Soviet Union: Present and Future."

### European Roma Rights Center
www.errc.org

The European Roma Rights Center (ERRC) is an international public-interest law organization that monitors the situation of Roma in Europe and provides legal defense to victims of human rights violations. EERC's Web site contains reports of the situation facing Roma in various European countries, its quarterly newsletter, and a very good list of links.

### GlasNet
www.glasnet.ru/

GlasNet is an Internet service provider in Russia that is used by many non-governmental organizations. The GlasNet home page has a nice collection of links to other Russia-related Web sites, online news sources, search engines, etc. The site hosts home pages for a growing number of GlasNet subscribers, both individuals and organizations.

### Kirim Tatarlarinin Evi–Home of the Crimean Tatars
www.euronet.nl/users/sota/krimtatar.html

On May 14, 1944, all Tatars in Crimea were rounded up and deported to Central Asia and Siberia. It comes as a surprise to many people—even those with a strong interest in the human rights movement in the USSR—to learn that it was the Crimean Tatars who engaged in the largest continuous mass protest movement in the USSR. Home of the Crimean Tatars includes several extensive histories of the people, information about Tatarstan, background on the Crimean Tatar National Movement, and more.

## Sister Cities International

www.sister-cities.org

SCI's Web site includes an online directory of all the U.S.-NIS sister city associations and links to their Web sites.

## The Jamestown Foundation

www.jamestown.org/

The Jamestown Foundation is a think tank that works "to monitor the evolution of the republics of the former Soviet Union (FSU); to provide information about, and analysis of, trends there that affect the vital interests of the United States and the West; and to encourage the development of democracy and free enterprise in that part of the world." The foundation produces daily, weekly, and analytical bulletins about events in the former USSR, which are distributed to government officials, journalists, the academic community, and subscribers. Non-current issues (usually older than a month or two) of some of these publications such as the *Monitor*, *Prism*, and *Commentary* are available for free from the foundation's Web site.

## Transitions

www.ijt.cz/transitions/

*Transitions* is a monthly print publication that seeks to examine and provide a forum for the discussion of the political, economic, social, and cultural transitions occurring in Eastern Europe and the former Soviet Union. The successor of OMRI's biweekly magazine, *Transition*, the new publication is published by the Institute for Journalism in Transition, a non-governmental organization in Prague. Select articles are available online from the current issue, and the full text of the magazine is available three months after it appears in print. Be sure to look at the collection of political cartoons.

## United Nations Development Program

www.undp.org/undp/rbec/

Each year the UNDP's Regional Bureau for Europe and the CIS publishes a report titled "Human Development Under Transition: Europe and CIS," which describes human development trends in the region. The compendium covers areas such as governance, the economy, poverty, social trends, and human settlements. The full report along with several other UNDP publications on the region is available from this site.

# Telnet, or, How to Check Your E-Mail
# When You Are Away from Home

Suppose you are traveling and want to access your e-mail, but your e-mail provider does not offer local dial-up access worldwide. What do you do?

In these circumstances, if you have access to any computer with an Internet connection, the odds are that it has a useful little program on it called Telnet. This helpful Internet utility allows one to access a remote server (computer) on the Internet, from any other computer on the Internet, and give it commands just as if you were logging in back home.

Here's a real-life example of how Telnet was recently used. Dr. O. Ataniyazova, head of a public health and environmental nonprofit based near the Aral Sea in Uzbekistan, was in Seattle recently. She had been on the road for nearly four weeks and knew there was important e-mail waiting for her in her Glasnet account.

How to access it? Making a long-distance call through her laptop back to the Glasnet number in Nukus, where she had her account, would be difficult, expensive, and the connection would probably be of poor quality. The solution: She "telnetted" back to her account using a computer in Center for Civil Society International's Seattle offices. It cost her nor us anything to do this. Here's what was involved:

1.  First, using a CCSI computer, she connected to the Internet through our local service provider.
2.  Then she launched Telnet from Windows. In most computers, the Telnet program resides in the Windows directory (c:\windows\telnet.exe)[1]
3.  Once Telnet was launched, she got a toolbar offering these choices:

### Connect    Edit    Terminal    Help

She clicked on "Connect" and her first menu choice was "Remote System…"
4.  Here she entered **glasnet.ru**  This was the name of her Internet service provider's host computer. (It was also the domain name of her Internet address—the part of the address after the "@" symbol.)
5.  Now she got a screen that looked just like the screen when she logged in to Glasnet from her computer back in Nukus. It prompted her for a login name and password, which she gave. That's all there was to it! While she was in Seattle, Dr. Ataniyazova was able to open her mailbox in Nukus and read her e-mail—just by knowing her login name, her password, and her host computer name…and knowing how to use Telnet.

---

[1] It is also possible to launch Telnet directly from an Internet browser. In the area where you normally type a URL, instead of typing "http://…", type "telnet://…"; the characters after the "//" must be the name of your server. In the above case, the server name was "glasnet.ru," so the line would have read, "telnet://glasnet.ru"

# Cyrillic Fonts and the Internet

T he requirements for communicating in Cyrillic on the Internet can vary depending on which computers and software are being used at each end. The good news is that in a couple of years technology will have advanced to the point that your computer will automatically shift fonts so that you can read a document with Cyrillic fonts or any other language with ease. The latest versions of Netscape Navigator and Microsoft Internet Explorer already shift automatically to the correct font for many Cyrillic documents. The bad news is that a single standard does not exist today that allows anybody on the Internet, using a few simple keystrokes, to switch from Latin to Cyrillic characters and back.

The challenge of using Cyrillic on the Internet breaks down into two separate problems:

- Being able to read documents that were written with Cyrillic characters
- Being able to compose a message in Cyrillic and send it to Eurasia

## Reading Cyrillic documents

To be able to read a document in Cyrillic you need to have Cyrillic fonts installed on your personal computer. "Installing" simply means copying the fonts to the correct folder or subfolder on your hard drive. (Windows has a Fonts subfolder under the Windows folder.) There are four main families of Cyrillic fonts:

- **Windows** fonts are the standard used for Microsoft Windows applications. This font family is also called Code Page 1251.
- **KOI-8** fonts are the standard used for UNIX machines in Eurasia. A lot of e-mail messages composed in Eurasia are formatted in KOI-8 fonts.
- **AV** (*Alternatyvni' Variant*) is the standard for computers running DOS. These are also referred to as DOS fonts and Code Page 866,..,and they are rapidly becoming obsolete.
- **Macintosh** fonts are used on Apple Macintosh computers.

To be able to read documents in Cyrillic at a Web site, you need to change the "Document Encoding" or "Fonts" (try both) in your Web browser. To read an e-mail message written in Cyrillic, you need to either change to a Cyrillic font in your e-mail program, if it is a Windows program or download a message, open it in your favorite word processor, and then apply Cyrillic fonts.

## Composing and sending Cyrillic messages via e-mail

In order to compose a message in Cyrillic, you not only need Cyrillic fonts, you also need a keyboard driver for your computer. The driver "maps" each Cyrillic character to a button on your keyboard. Windows 95 comes with a Russian keyboard driver, which you can activate easily. (Open Control Panel, then Add/Remove Programs, then Windows Setup, then choose Multilanguage Support.) There are also shareware Cyrillic keyboard drivers available on the Internet, as well as commercial software packages. The shareware versions require changing some of the default settings in the Windows operating system and so are not for the faint of heart.

After you have composed a message in Cyrillic, you need another kind of software to be able to send it to someone. Because Western e-mail systems do not recognize the code in which Cyrillic characters are sent, you need to enclose your message in a "protective envelope" before e-mailing it. The simplest way to do this is to send it as an attachment, e.g. as a Word document composed in Cyrillic letters.

Another way to do it is to code the document first, using a software known as UUENCODE. Knowing how to use this software can be helpful, since e-mail sent from the NIS to the West sometimes comes "uuencoded," requiring you to "uudecode" it before you can read it. Uuencode/uudecode capabilities are sometimes included in software that "zips" files, such as WinZip. Uuencode/uudecode programs are also available on the Internet as Shareware. One of the simplest to use is called "UUCode Version 2.0," which is available at:

**www.mecheng.asme.org/database/WIN_GEN/3621.html**

Below is an example of what a uuencoded one-line message looks like when it arrives in your e-mail inbox:

```
begin 644 WHATSNEW.TXT
M6$9%4E!23R!V97)S:6]N(#$N,2XQ('=A<R!R96QE87-E9"!I;;!!-87D@,3DY
end
```

The key to recognizing this as a uuencoded message is that the first line will always start with the word "begin" followed by a three-digit number. The most common first lines are "begin 644" and "begin 666." The next bit of text, in this case "WHATSNEW.TXT," is the name that the original sender gave to the file. Browse through some of the sites below, and you should find what you need in order to be able to send and receive e-mail in Cyrillic fonts.

## Obtaining Cyrillic Fonts and More Information

Below are some Internet sites that contain Cyrillic fonts that can be downloaded and installed in a personal computer. Some of them also contain keyboard drivers and instructions.

### American Association of Teachers of Slavic and East European Languages
clover.slavic.pitt.edu/~aatseel/

Information and fonts for Cyrillic and East European languages. On the home page, scroll down to "Slavic fonts and keyboard drivers."

## Belarusian Language
solar.cini.utk.edu/~kasaty/bel-ling.htm

Information about the Belarusian language and fonts.

## Fingertip Software
www.cyrillic.com/

A commercial vendor of Cyrillic fonts and keyboard drivers. Some of the software is available for a free 45-day trial period.

## Friends and Partners
www.friends-partners.org/friends/cyrillic/cyrillic.html

A collection of links to other Internet sites that contain Cyrillic fonts for all types of computers and directions on how to use them.

## How to Make Russian Windows
www.kiarchive.ru/pub/cyrillic/windows/

A large collection of fonts and keyboard drivers assembled by Relcom, one of the major Internet service providers in Russia.

## Russification of the Macintosh
www.friends-partners.org/partners/rusmac/

A well-organized collection of documents that explain how to use Cyrillic fonts on Macintosh computers.

## Smart Link
www.smartlinkcorp.com/

Another commercial vendor of Russian fonts, keyboard drivers, and converters.

## Sovinform Bureau
www.siber.com/sib/

A good collection of fonts and software utilities for using Cyrillic. Click on the link "Russify Everything."

## Ukrainian Server
www.brama.com/compute/index.html

Maintained by Max Pyziur, who does a good job of explaining the myriad of issues involved with using Cyrillic fonts and provides links to fonts for DOS, Windows, and Macintosh. Of special interest is the information available on getting Cyrillic fonts for Ukrainian.

# Internet Training Centers and IREX Internet Resources

## IREX Internet Programs

Since 1993, IREX has been active in establishing non-commercial Internet access throughout the former Soviet region. Since 1995, IREX has administered the USIA-sponsored, Internet Access and Training Program (IATP). This program provides e-mail and Internet access and training for alumni of U.S. government–sponsored exchange programs, higher educational institutions, and non-governmental organizations in the NIS. IATP covers five regions in Russia, two regions in Ukraine, Armenia, Georgia, Kazakstan, Kyrgyzstan, and Uzbekistan. More than 65 public access Internet sites have been established for non-commercial use, and they are open to the public.

IREX also administers a NATO Infrastructure Grant to establish the first non-commercial Internet exchange in St. Petersburg, Russia. The purpose of the Open Internet Exchange is to create a high-speed Internet ring linking eight institutions, including universities and libraries, in the St. Petersburg region.

Information on the following centers was provided courtesy of IREX. Most of the centers were established under the IATP program with USIA funds, but some were also funded by USAID, the Carnegie Corporation of New York, or the Soros Foundation.

## 1. Internet Access and Training Centers

### *Armenia*

**National Library of Armenia**
72 Teryan St.
Yerevan
**Tel:** +374 (2) 563-587
**Contact:** Nesres Hayrapetyan, Tamara Sargissian

**American University of Armenia**
40 Baghramyan Ave.
Yerevan
**Tel:** +374 (2) 271-173
**Contact:** Nonna Sachiyants, Andranik Balasanyan

**Erevan Institute for Architecture and Construction**
105 Teryan
Yerevan
**Tel:** +374 (2) 580-177
**Contact:** Marineh Melikyan

**State Technical University of Armenia**
Gyumri Educational Complex
Gyumri
**Tel:** +374 (6) 936-832
**Contact:** Khoren Mamikonyan

## English Centre and Library

Vanadzor
30a Tigran Mets
**Contact:** Artak Asloyan

# Georgia

## ACCELS

4 Takaishvili St., 2nd floor
Tbilisi
**Tel:**     +995 (32) 22-01-53
**Contact:** Eric Johnson
**E-mail:** accels@access.sanet.ge

## Georgian Technical University

Institute of Public Administration
(GIPA)
77 Kostava St., GPI, 6th bldg., 2nd
floor
Tbilisi
**Tel:**     +995 (32) 94-07-71, 33-61-20
**E-mail:** ipactr@access.sanet.ge
**Contact:** Nugzar Sikharulidze

## Library Automation Association of Georgia (LAAG)

The National Library
7 Gudiashvili St., Room #1
Tbilisi
**Tel:**     +995 (32) 98-75-61
**E-mail:** nplg@access.sanet.ge
**Contact:** Temuri Chichenkeli

## Academy of Sciences Library

Sarbutalo District
1 M. Aleksidze St., Bldg 4
Tbilisi
**Tel:**     +995 (32) 99-88-23, 33-01-35
**E-mail:** root@library.acnet.ge
**Contact:** Irakli Garibashvili

# Russia

## Altai State Polytechnical University

ul. Lenina, d. 46, kom. 242
Barnaul
**Tel:**     +7 (3852) 26-14-14
**E-mail:** ikar@agtu.altai.su
**Web:**     oasis.altai.su

## Bryansk Regional Scientific Library

ul. K. Marksa, d. 5
Bryansk
**Tel:**     +7 (0832) 46-36-50
**E-mail:** zdnr@libr.bitmcnit.bryansk.su

## Cheliabinsk State Technical University

prospekt Lenina, d. 76, kor. 3b, 2nd
floor, kom. 254
Cheliabinsk
**Tel:**     +7 (3512) 65-42-92
**E-mail:** helen@urc.ac.ru
**Web:**     www.urc.ac.ru

## American Information Center

ul. Mamina-Sibiriaka, d. 193
Ekaterinburg
**Tel:**     +7 (3432) 51-02-48
**E-mail:** olga@irex.uraic.ru
**Web:**     irex.uraic.ru

## Belinski Regional Library

ul. Belinski 15
Ekaterinburg
**Tel:**     +7 (3432) 51-53-53
**Contact:** Valeri Kugler
**E-mail:** valery@library.uraic.ru
**Web:**     library.uraic.ru

## State University at Mari El

ul. Krasnoarmeiskaia, d. 71, kor. V
Ioshkar-Ola
**Tel:**     +7 (8362) 12-34-17

## Irkutsk State University Scientific Library

bul. Gagarina, d. 24
Irkutsk

**Tel:**     +7 (3952) 33-55-59
**E-mail:**  foxkit@irex.irkutsk.su

## Ivanovo State University
Main Auditorium, kom. 321
Ivanovo
**Tel:**     +7 (0932) 30-02-42
**Fax:**     +7 (0932) 32-66-00

## Kazan State University
Department of International Relations
ul. Lenina, d. 18
Kazan
**Tel:**     +7 (8432) 38-73-21

## Khabarovsk State Technical University
ul. Tikhookeanskaia, d. 136, kab. 424
Khabarovsk
**Tel:**     +7 (4212) 72-84-98
**E-mail:**  ddos@main.dvags.khv.ru
**Web:**     www.khstu.khabarovsk.su

## Far Eastern Academy of Government Service
ul. Muraveva-Amurskogo, d. 33, kom. 13
Khabarovsk
**Tel:**     +7 (4212) 33-50-45
**Fax:**     +7 (4212) 22-47-48
**E-mail:**  valery@main.dvags.khv.ru,
            colobok@main.dvags.khv.ru

## International Pedagogical University of Magadan
Magadan
**Tel:**     +7 (4132) 23-42-37
**E-mail:**  admin@ipu.magadan.su

## K.D. Ushinski State Scientific Pedagogical Library
Moscow
**Tel:**     +7 (095) 231-05-85
**E-mail:**  ushinka@glasnet.ru
**Contact:** Aleksandr Yevgenievich Zaichik

## The Library of Foreign Literature, American Center
ul. Nikolo-Yamskaia 1, 2nd floor
Moscow
**Tel:**     +7 (095) 915-36-36
**E-mail:**  internet@irex.ru
**Web:**     www.irex.ru

## Library of Natural Sciences of the Russian Academy of Sciences
ul. Znamenka, d. 11
Moscow
**Tel:**     +7 (095) 291-17-85
**Web:**     ben.irex.ru
**Contact:** Boris Glushanovski

## State Public Historical Library
Starosadskii Pereulok, d. 9, kom. 311
Moscow
**Tel:**     +7 (095) 928-70-60
**E-mail:**  webmaster@openweb.ru
**Web:**     www.openweb.ru

## Novgorod State University
ul. Bolshaia Sankt Peterburgskaia, d. 41
Novgorod
**Tel:**     +7 (8162) 22-35-12
**Web:**     www.novsu.ac.ru

## Novosibirsk State University
Vychislitelnyi Tsentr (Computing Center)
prospekt Akademika Lavrenteva, d. 6, kom. 441
Novosibirsk
**Tel:**     +7 (3832) 35-05-79
**E-mail:**  andy@sicnit.ru

## Penza Technological Institute
proezd Baidukova, d. 1a, kom. 236
Penza
**Tel:**     +7 (8412) 55-95-40
**E-mail:**  ayt@vmis.ptiac.ru
**Web:**     www.pti.ac.ru

## St. Petersburg Library of the Russian Academy of Sciences

Birzhevaia liniia, d. 1
St. Petersburg
**Tel:**     +7 (8123) 27-73-77
**E-mail:**  natasha@ban.spu.ru

## Russian Museum Library

pl. Iskusstv, 1
St. Petersburg
**Tel:**     +7 (8122) 18-35-92
**Fax:**     +7 (8122) 18-74-36
**Contact:** Irina Soldatenkova
**E-Mail:**  rml@spb.org.ru

## St. Petersburg State University

Telecommunications Center
University Nab. 7/9
St. Petersburg
**Tel:**     +7 (8123) 25-87-51
**Fax:**     +7 (8123) 25-87 50
**E-mail:**  Ivch@hq.pu.ru
**Web:**     www.spbu.ru
**Contact:** Valeri Lovchikov

## Smolensk State University

ul. Kirova, d. 22 B
Smolensk
**Tel/Fax:**  +7 (0812) 26-06-20
**Contact:** Valeri Markovich Balk
**E-mail:**  balk@shu.smolensk.su

## Tomsk State University

prospekt Lenina, d. 36, kor. 2, kom. 206
Tomsk
**Tel:**     +7 (3822) 41-02-95
**E-mail:**  alex@public.tsu.tomsk.su,
            public.tsu.tomsk.su

## Tula State Pedagogical University

prospekt Lenina, d. 125, kor. 4, 3rd floor, kom. 307
Tula
**Tel:**     +7 (0872) 25-14-88
**Fax:**     +7 (0872) 25-40-60

## Ulianovsk State Technical University

ul. Severnyi Venets, d. 32
Ulianovsk
**E-mail:**  ron@ulstu.ru

## Far Eastern State Technical University

ul. Pushkinskaia, d. 10, kom. 105
Vladivostok
**Tel:**     +7 (4232) 26-76-28
**Fax:**     +7 (4232) 26-98-60
**E-mail:**  diana@pub.marine.su

## Voronezh State Pedagogical University

ul. Lenina, d. 86, kom. 428
Voronezh
**E-mail:**  scr@vgpi.voronezh.su
**Web:**     www.vspu.ac.ru

# *Ukraine*

## Kharkiv State University Central Scientific Library

pl. Svobody, 4
Kharkiv
**Tel:**     +380 (572) 45-72-24
**E-mail:**  sasha@irex.kharkiv.net

## Kharkiv State Polytechnical Institute

ul. Frunze, d. 21
Kharkiv
**E-mail:**  ben@kharkiv.net

## Kharkiv State Institute of Culture

ul. Bursatskii Spusk, d. 4
Kharkiv
**E-mail:**  denis@irex.kharkiv.net

## Institute of Oriental Studies

vul. M. Hrushevskoho 4, kom. 209, 210

Kyiv
**Tel:**    +380 (44) 229-0772
**Fax:**    +380 (44) 229-1593
**E-mail:**  artur@orient.freenet.kiev.ua

**Donetsk State Polytechnical University Library**
ul. Artema, d. 58
Donetsk
**Tel:**    +380 (622) 35-87-83
**E-mail:**  cats@irex.kharkiv.net

**Donetsk Oblast Library**
ul. Artema, d. 84
Donetsk
**Tel:**    +380 (622) 93-35-00

## 2. IREX Internet Resources

### IREX-L

This is an electronic mailing list that distributes information about IREX's activities in Central and Eastern Europe, the New Independent States, Mongolia, and China, as well as in the United States. Postings include announcements and brief updates on conferences and policy forums, new grants and programs, and a monthly calendar of events.

List address:    **majordomo@info.irex.org**

To subscribe, send the message:    **subscribe irex-l**
                            to:    **majordomo@info.irex.org**

### IREX

www.irex.org

Established in 1995, IREX's Web site contains extensive information about the programs and projects administered by IREX, including downloadable application materials for grants and host opportunities for U.S. universities. In addition to its main site, IREX has more than 35 field office and affiliate Web sites containing training materials and resources for scholars and professionals in the Unites States and in IREX's overseas program regions. A list of links to other Web sites can be found at **www.irex.org/ontheweb/**.

### Frontline

www.irex.org/publications/frontline/

IREX's quarterly newsletter *Frontline* can be read on-line or downloaded. Frontline contains news and articles about American field research and training programs in Central and Eastern Europe, the New Independent States, Mongolia, and China.

### Handbook for Working Journalists

www.irex.org/publications/directories-resources/jourhandbook.htm

*A Handbook for Working Journalists in the Baltics and Other Emerging Democracies* was published in 1995 by IREX as the final phase in a two-year project to strengthen business and economic journalism in Estonia, Latvia, and Lithuania.

## IPP Training Materials Database
www.irex.org/ippdatabase

Contains materials created by 22 Russian and Ukrainian partnerships under the Institutional Partnership Project (IPP). The IPP products range from educational curricula and training materials to CD-ROMs and videocassettes in the following spheres: agricultural reform, business development, the development of civil society and NGOs, and health care reform. These materials were disseminated to more than 200 repositories throughout the NIS, Ukraine, and Mongolia. The database provides information about the holdings, location, and hours of operation for each repository. In addition, 85 of the most popular products can be downloaded directly from the database.

## Library and Archival Resources
www.irex.org/publications/directories-resources/

Materials include library assessment reports describing libraries and archives in Central and Eastern Europe and the New Independent States.

## Media Resources
www.ipc.kiev.ua

The Web site of the Professional Media Program (ProMedia) in Ukraine contains a host of media resources in Ukrainian, Russian, and English. (Not all information is available in all languages.) The site includes information on current and upcoming ProMedia activities; instructional handbooks for journalists on a variety of topics; archives of ProMedia/Ukraine's Media-Law Bulletin; lists to Ukrainian newspapers; some current news items of interest to the media; copies of Ukraine's laws affecting media; and links to Ukrainian, CIS, and world media-assistance organizations, newspapers, broadcasters, wire services, and other sites of interest or use to Ukrainian journalists.

## On-line Alumni Journal
www.irex.org/alumni/journal/

This semiannual on-line journal contains scholarly and non-scholarly articles written by or about alumni from Central and Eastern Europe and the New Independent States.

## Open Web Project
www.openweb.ru

The Open Web Project provides free Web sites and training to non-governmental organizations in the New Independent States. The project is housed at the Internet Access and Training Program site in the Historical Library in Moscow.

## Polemika

www.irex.ru/acad/journal/

Each issue of this semiannual on-line journal focuses on a specific topic, such as foreign policy, economics, media development, and legal reform. The articles are written and edited by alumni of the USIA-sponsored Regional Scholar Exchange Program and Freedom Support Act Fellowships in Contemporary Issues.

## Policy Papers and Conference Reports

www.irex.org/publications/policy-papers/

These proceedings and reports resulting from IREX policy forums and conferences address current issues of transition in Central and Eastern Europe and Eurasia. Recent topics have included education reform and conflict resolution in the Balkans.

## Training-of-Trainers Material

members.tripod.com/~IATP_SAKARTVELO/

The Web site of the Internet Access and Training Program (IATP) in Georgia offers a comprehensive list of on-line training materials for training-of-trainers courses. These training courses continue to increase the number of knowledgeable local Internet trainers. They provide participants with special training and Internet skills that teach them how to develop and teach interactive Internet courses.

# *Print Resources and Indexes*

# Print Resources

*The annotated list of resources below is a selective and eclectic one. Many of the items cited were consulted by the authors in developing this revised edition of **The Post-Soviet Handbook**. Since the first edition was published in 1996, a number of specialized directories and databases were produced by organizations working in the NIS. Some of these are specific to a country, region, or city. Some correspond to a special interest, e.g., women's organizations or business associations. A great number of excellent training resources have also been produced, which await their own catalog. For reasons of space, we regret not being able to describe all such resources here.*

### Access Russia Catalog

RIS Publications
89 Main Street, Suite 2
Montpelier, VT 05602
**Tel:** (802) 223-4955,
(800) 639-4301 (sales)
**Fax:** (802) 223-6105
**E-mail:** paul@rispubs.com
**Web:** www.rispubs.com
**Contact:** Paul Richardson

This catalog is produced by RIS Publications, formerly Russian Information Services. It first came out in 1990 and it gets better every year. It is not a large publication (about 14 pp.), but it offers a wide-ranging and well-chosen selection of books, maps, videos, software, and periodicals related to Russia, plus the Baltics, Central Asia, the Caucasus, and

Ukraine. The selection of books in Top New Titles and General Interest and History is one you will find in few other places. Likewise the selection of Travel Guides and Books for Children. There are three pages of resources for Russian-language learners. You can even get Russian telephone adapters for a laptop through *Access Russia*.

### Armenian International Magazine

P.O. Box 10793
Glendale, CA 91209-3793
**Tel:** (818) 246-7979
**Fax:** (818) 246-0088
**E-mail:** aim4m@well.com

Armenian International Magazine is 64 high-gloss pages of news articles, commentary, and photos concerning Armenia, the Caucasus, and the Armenian Diaspora. Each monthly issue contains important news from around the world, book reviews, interviews, and information on the arts. Photo essays capture Armenian society in transition. One issue reported on the 100th delivery flight of humanitarian supplies from the United Armenia Fund. Kirk Kerkorian (a wealthy American who owns the MGM Grand Hotel and is of Armenian descent) was in Yerevan on his first visit to Armenia and greeted the flight. Another article profiled Vano Haritunians, an architect with the firm of Frank Gehry and Associates, who worked on the celebrated Guggenheim Museum in Bilbao. Subscriptions are $45/year in the U.S.

### Azerbaijan International

P.O. Box 5217
Sherman Oaks, CA 91413
**Tel:** (818) 785-0077
**Fax:** (818) 997-7337
**E-mail:** ai@artnet.net
**Web:** www.azer.com

**Contact:** Judith Scott, Circulation

This quarterly magazine began publication in January 1993 and describes itself as "the only English-language magazine about Azerbaijan that is systematically distributed to subscribers internationally." It also states that it is the "only publication officially representing SOCAR (State Oil Company of Azerbaijan) to the international business community." Issues are glossy and in color and cover themes such as natural resources, environment, literature, health care, science, refugees, and youth. Subscriptions are $28/year in the U.S.

### The BEARR Trust Newsletter
*Information about UK NGO Links with the former Soviet Union*
The BEARR Trust
Chichester House
278 High Holborn
London WC1V 7ER
**Tel:** (44 171) 404-7081
**Fax:** (44 171) 404-7103
**E-mail:** bearr@gn.apc.org

BEARR stands for British Emergency Action in Russia and the Republics. The trust is a registered British charity formed in 1991 to act as a bridge between the welfare and health sectors of Britain and those of the former Soviet Union. It operates a small grants program in the NIS, serves as a clearinghouse, and publishes this quarterly newsletter, which costs £20/year in the UK.

### Belarusian Non-Governmental Organizations
United Way Belarus
3-30 Uralskaya ul.
220038   Minsk
**Tel:** 30-32-76
**Fax:** 30-80-54

**E-mail:** uwb@user.unibel.by
**Contact:** Yelena Kuzminich, Executive Director

The publisher of this directory hopes it will come out annually. This 1997 edition, in English and Russian, contained more than 1,000 entries for NGOs in Belarus.

### Belarusian Review
P.O. Box 10353
Torrance, CA 90505
**Fax:** (310) 373-0793
**E-Mail:** BelReview@aol.com
**Contact:** Joe Price, Editor

Launched in 1989, *Belarusian Review* is an independent, English-language quarterly. Individual subscriptions are $40/year for North America, $60/year for overseas (overseas includes airmail and handling). For institutions, add $20 to above rates. Single copies can be ordered for $10/copy. Back issues are available at 150 percent of the original price. To subscribe, send check/money order, payable to "Belarusian Review," to above address.

### Centers for Pluralism Newsletter
Institute for Democracy in Eastern Europe
2000 P Street, NW, Suite 400
Washington, DC 20036
**Contact:** Irena Lasota
or
Institute for Democracy in Eastern Europe
P.O. Box 311
00-950   Warsaw, Poland
**Tel:** +48 (22) 620-8344
**Fax:** +48 (22) 620-8358
**E-mail:** idee@pingwin.icm.edu.pl
**Contact:** Anna Jakowska

This quarterly newsletter is a valuable resource for hundreds of individuals and organizations throughout Europe, the NIS, and North America. The first issue, published in 1993, had 14 pages. Current issues run to more than 100 pages and link hundreds of people in more than 30 countries. Every issue describes in detail the work of scores of NGOs active in the post-Soviet world, both indigenous and international, and provides complete contact information. It is published in separate English and Russian editions and offered free-of-charge to individuals and groups in the "East." Those who live in countries with freely convertible currencies and for whom "$30 does not represent a week's salary" are asked to pay $60/year —$30 for a subscription for themselves and $30 for an organization in a country where these conditions prevail.

## Charities Aid Foundation

per. Yakovapostolskii, 10
103064 Moscow
**Tel:** +7 (095) 928-05-57
**E-mail:** lenay@glas.apc.org,
cafdavis@glas.apc.org

CAF–Russia is a rich source of publications and reference materials for those involved in third-sector work in the NIS. Most are in Russian, but some are in English. One good example of each:

- Paul Legendre's *The Non-Profit Sector in Russia* (1997), 56 pp.
- Эффективность работы некоммерческих организаций в регионах России (*Effectiveness of Non-Commercial Organizations in Russia's Regions,* 1997)

The latter report, in Russian, contains the results of a research project conducted by CAF regarding the state of NGOs outside of the Moscow–St. Petersburg area. CAF surveyed NGOs in Arkhangelsk, Nizhnii Novgorod, Togliatti, and Chelyabinsk on questions of finance, organizational structure, leadership, and program goals.

## *Contemporary Caucasus Newsletter*

The Berkeley Program in Soviet and Post-Soviet Studies
University of California
361 Stephens Hall, #2304
Berkeley, CA 94720-2304
**E-mail:** bsp@socrates.berkeley.edu
**Web:** socrates.berkeley.edu/~bsp/caucasus/caucprog.html
**Contact:** Marc Garcelon, Executive Director

The essays in this newsletter are based on lectures given at Berkeley or on books and articles that scholars at the university—usually on visiting fellowships from the region—are in the process of completing. Each newsletter contains four or five essays.

## *CSCE Digest*

Commission on Security and Cooperation in Europe
234 Ford House Office Building
Washington, DC 20515-6460
**Tel:** (202) 225-1901
**E-mail:** csce@mail.house.gov
**Web:** www.house.gove/csce/

The Commission on Security and Cooperation in Europe, created in 1976, "monitors and encourages progress in implementing the provisions of the Helsinki Accords." The *CSCE Digest*, which comes out monthly, is one way to keep informed on the activities of the Organization for Security and Cooperation in Europe (OSCE), the 52-nation institution that arose from the Helsinki Accords. OSCE missions in places such as Tajikistan, Chechnya, or Bosnia and Herzegovina have helped to expose human rights violations, monitor elections, and perform other tasks that ultimately support peace and democracy in the region.

### Directory of Environmental Electronic Mail Users In Northern Eurasia, 5th edition

The Sacred Earth Network
267 East Street
Petersham, MA 01366
**Tel:** (978) 724-3443
**Fax:** (978) 724-3436
**E-mail:** sacredearth@igc.org,
**Web:** www.igc.org/sen/
**Contact:** Claire Mandeville, Susan Cutting

The directory lists 875 environmental e-mail stations in the 15 nations of the former Soviet Union and has maps showing their locations. Over 370 of these entries include more detailed information about the organizations' environmental work, and 92 point to Web sites for further information. Most entries include complete contact information.

Sacred Earth Network has provided equipment and training that has directly enabled approximately 400 Eurasian environmental groups to communicate via electronic mail. E-mail is vital to the efficient development and imple-mentation of collaborative international environmental programs.

The 160-page directory may be purchased for $35 by organizations and $25 by individuals. Prices include domestic shipping. International orders require additional postage, and pay-ment must be made by wire transfer.

### Directory of Human Rights Protection Organizations, 1995
*Справочник правозащитных организаций СНГ*

Moscow Helsinki Group
bul. Zlatoustinskii 8/7, kv. 93
101000  Moscow
**Tel:** +7 (095) 206-8507
**Fax:** +7 (095) 921-1209
**E-mail:** hrn@glas.apc.org

This is the first directory of non-governmental, human-rights protection organizations on the territory of the former USSR (with the exception of Baltic countries). The directory is divided into four parts:
- Organizations that cover all aspects of human-rights protection (Helsinki committees, branches of the Inter-national Human Rights Protection Society, etc.)
- Organizations working in one particular area, such as a Center for Promotion of Prison Reform or Independent Psychiatric Association
- Organizations offering legal assis-tance free-of-charge
- Charitable organizations

### A Directory of Non-Government Environmental Organizations of St. Petersburg
*Негосударственные Экологические организации Санкт-Петербурга, справочник*

Transboundary Environmental Information Agency
Box 436
190000  St. Petersburg
Russia
**Tel:** (812) 325-6293 (cell, 2124)
**Fax:** (812) 312-4128 (box 275)
**E-mail:** sasha@teia.org
**Web:** www.teia.org
**Contact:** Alexander Shkrebets

This directory, printed by Notabene Publishers in1998, describes 160 environmental NGOs in St. Petersburg as well as 12 broadcast and print resources in the city. Entries are in Russian and English. There are organizational title indexes in each language, and an index by focus of activity. Organizational information from the directory is also on the Web at: www.spb.org.ru/eco/

Project director for the publication was Nathaniel Trumbull, now a graduate student at University of Washington, and data compilers were Elena Kobets and Erna Lahti.

### Directory–NGOs and Ecology: Belarus, Moldova, and Ukraine, 2nd edition
*Общественные организации и экология, Беларусь, Молдова и Украина, справочник*
ISAR-Kyiv
a/ya 47
Kyiv
**Tel/Fax:** +380 (44) 269-8542
**E-mail:** isar@isar.freenet.kiev.ua
**Contact:** Helena Gubar, Director

The second edition was published in the spring of 1996. It contains entries in both Russian and English; an index and a list of organizations supporting public organizations in Belarus, Moldova, and Ukraine; and a list of publications by ISAR.

### Directory of Programs in Russian, Eurasian, and East European Studies
American Association for the Advancement of Slavic Studies
8 Storey Street
Cambridge, MA 02138

**Tel:** (617) 495-0677
**Fax:** (617) 495-0680
**E-mail:** aaass@hcs.harvard.edu
**Contact:** Carol R. Saivetz, Executive Director

Published biannually. Includes information on academic departments, faculty and their research interests, summer language programs, and overseas programs at over 300 North American institutions of higher education. Cost is $30 prepaid for non-AAASS members, plus $3 for postage and handling.

### Directory of Public Associations of Siberia
*Общественные объединения Сибирского региона*
Siberian Center for Support of Public Initiatives
pr. Karla Marxa, 57, kom. 702
630073  Novosibirsk
**Tel:** +7 (3832) 46-45-32, 46-54-77
**E-mail:** root@cip.nsk.su

This directory, published in late 1998, contains information about public associations of Siberia (Altai, Irkutsk, Kemerov, Krasnoiarsk, Omsk, Novosibirsk, Tomsk, Tiumen, Chita regions, and the republic of Gornyi Altai and Buriatiia). The cities and the organizations in these cities are listed first in alphabetical order. In the second part of the book, the organizations are listed under their sphere of activity and referenced by location. The publication was financed by USAID.

### Directory of Trainers and Consultants for NGOs in Russia, Counterpart, 1997
*Справочник тренеров-консультантов для*

*некоммерческих организаций в
России*
Counterpart International
910 17th NW, # 328
Washington, DC 20006
**Tel:** (202) 296-9676
**Fax:** (202) 296-9679
**E-mail:** info@counterpart.org
**Web:** www.counterpart.org

This directory, in Russian, lists individuals, their employer/ organization,
and their training/ consulting
specialty—e.g., economic development, social aid, etc. The directory
contains contact information and very
brief descriptions of individual skills
and education. It can be found on the
Internet at www.ort.ru/book.htm.

## Directory: Public Associations of Entrepreneurs

*Справочник: Общественные
Объединенуя Предпринимателей
центр делового сотрудничества*
ul. Lyusinovskaya, 36, 11th floor
113093   Moscow
**Tel:** +7 (095) 931-9660
**E-mail:** all@bdp.cbi.co.ru

This directory, in Russian, was produced
in 1996 under a program funded by
USAID and managed by Deloitte
Touche Tohmatsu ILA Group, Ltd. It
describes 64 organizations, from the
Russian Association for the Support of
Small Businesses to a number of
professional and trade associations. All
are located in Moscow.

## Directory: Ukrainian Non-Governmental Organizations

Counterpart Creative Center
39 Pushkinskaya St., 14
252004   Kyiv, Ukraine
**Tel:** (380 44) 225-6272

**Fax:** (380 44) 230-2360, 295-9880

This large directory is 192 pages long
and provides contact information and
brief descriptions for more than 1,000
organizations throughout Ukraine. A
useful appendix identifies 26 NGO
resource and service centers in Ukraine.

## East European Constitutional Review

Constitutional and Legislative Policy
Institute
Nador utca 11
Budapest, 1051-Hungary
**Tel:** +36 (1) 327-3117
**Fax:** +36 (1) 327-3103
**E-mail:** rosea@osi.hu
**Contact:** Alison Rose

*EECR* is published quarterly by New
York University School of Law and
Central European University. The
Constitutional and Legislative Policy
Institute in Budapest provides facilities,
resources, and funding for *EECR*'s
network of correspondents and
affiliates in Eastern Europe.

The regular departments in *EECR* are
Constitution Watch, a country-by-
country "update on constitutional
politics in Eastern Europe and the ex-
USSR;" special reports; five or six
feature articles; and book reviews. The
writing in *EECR* is generally excellent
and covers a very wide range of topics.
Articles submitted and accepted for
publication receive a $500 honorarium.

*EECR* is also available in Russian (as
*Konstitutsion-noe Pravo:
Vostochnoevropieskoe Obozrenie*) at
the Moscow Public Science
Foundation, Prospekt Mira 36, rooms
200-201, Moscow 101000. Fax: +7
(095) 280-3515. Contact: Olga
Sidorovich, e-mail: olga@glas.apc.org.

## East-West Church and Ministry Report

Institute for East-West Christian
Studies
Wheaton College
Wheaton, IL 60187-5593
**Tel:** (630) 752-5917
**Fax:** (630) 752-5916
**E-mail:** iewcs@wheaton.edu
**Web:** www.wheaton.edu/bgc/iewcs
**Contact:** Mark Elliott, Editor

This quarterly newsletter is available in
print ($44.95 per year includes free
electronic subscription) or in electronic
form only ($19.95 per year). It is a
product of the evangelically oriented
Wheaton College, and therefore its focus
is on non-denominational Christian
activity in CEE and the NIS, but the
newsletter combines well-researched and
sober analytical essays (e.g., "Cults and
New Religious Movements in the
Former Soviet Union") with some very
practical information (e.g., Web sites of
embassies that give visa information).

## East → West Links

*Directory of Information Sources in
the former Soviet Union and Central-
Eastern Europe*
Turpin Distribution Services Ltd.
Blackhorse Road
Letchworth
Herts SG6 IHN
United Kingdom
**Tel:** (44 1462) 67-2555
**Fax:** (44 1462) 48-0947
**E-mail:** turpin@rsc.org

Formerly the *Directory of Libraries and
Book Agents in the former Soviet Union
and Eastern Europe*, this directory is
invaluable for locating publications from
the region. Full contact information is
given and the data is taken from the
addresses used by the Slavonic Acqui-
sitions department of the British Library
Document Supply Center. Their Web
site is www.portico.bl.uk/dsc

## Guide to Foreign Affairs Research Organizations in Russia

IREX
1616 H Street, NW
Washington, DC 20006
**Tel:** (202) 628-8188
**Fax:** (202) 628-8189
**E-mail:** irex@info.irex.org
**Web:** www.irex.org

The *Guide to Foreign Affairs Research
Organizations in Russia* (April, 1995.
85 pp.) was produced by IREX and the
Carnegie Endowment for International
Peace and lists 87 different organizations. The guide "is intended to serve as
a tool for all institutions and individuals attempting to establish contacts
with partners in Russia." In selecting
organizations, the authors did not
restrict themselves to organizations
primarily focused on foreign affairs.
They included some institutes with
different fields of primary concern—
e.g., economics, ethnography, and
nuclear physics—that were deemed
important or relevant to issues of international relations. Thus the guide profiles not only the Center for Strategic
and Global Studies but also the Institute
of Economic Transition (founded by
Egor Gaidar, a former Prime Minister
of the Russian Federation), the Public
Opinion Foundation, and the International Charitable Foundation for Political and Legal Research (Interlegal).

All the information in the guide is
available electronically at IREX's Web
site. Carnegie and IREX also plan to
publish expanded and updated versions

of the guide in the future and they encourage users of this guide to submit updates and information for future editions.

## Journal of Democracy

The Johns Hopkins University Press
Journals Division
2715 North Charles Street
Baltimore, MD 21218-4319
**Tel:** (410) 516-6987,
(800) 548-1784
**Fax:** (410) 516-6968
**E-mail:** jlorder@jhunix.hcf.jhu.edu

The journal, started in 1990, is a program of the National Endowment for Democracy's International Forum for Democratic Studies. Each quarterly issue carries articles by leading scholars of democracy as well as by activists who are or have been on the frontlines of the fight for freedom and civil society somewhere in the world.

## NGO Handbook for Ukraine, 1997

Counterpart Creative Center
ul. Pushkinskaia, 39-14
252004 Kyiv
**Tel:** +380 (44) 225-62-72
**Fax:** +380 (44) 230-23-60,
295-98-80

This publication is the second version of the first handbook published by Counterpart Foundation in June 1996 with financial support from USAID. It lists Ukrainian non-governmental organizations by location and has an appendix, which contains NGO information from Counterpart's database.

## NGO News: A Regional Newsletter for Non-Governmental Organizations

Freedom House
Menesi ut 18
1118 Budapest, Hungary
**Tel/Fax:** +36 (1) 185-3108, 185-0985,
166-9879
**E-mail:** fh@freedomhouse.hu
**Web:** www.ngonet.org,
www.freedomhouse.org
**Contact:** Robert Muraskin, Editor

*NGO News* is distributed to several thousand NGOs in Central and Eastern Europe, Western Europe, and the U.S. The first issue was in December 1995. The focus is on projects and sources of funding for NGOs in the CEE region and the Baltic states, but much in the pages of this professional-quality newsletter will be of interest to those working in countries farther east.

## OSCE Newsletter

Organization for Security and Co-operation in Europe
Department for General Affairs
Karntner Ring 5-7
1010 Vienna, Austria
**Tel:** +43 (1) 514-36-196
**Fax:** +43 (1) 514-36-105
**E-mail:** wkemp@osce.org
**Web:** www.osce.org

This newsletter, like the *CSCE Digest* above, has to do with the work of the Organization for Security and Co-operation in Europe, the institutional child of the 1975 Helsinki Accords. There are now OSCE centers in most of the nations of the former Soviet Union, and the newsletter generally reports on subjects involving those centers or the mandates of the three General Committees of the OSCE:
- Political Affairs and Security
- Economic Affairs, Science, Technology and Environment

- Democracy, Human Rights and Humanitarian Questions

For example, a recent newsletter reported that the OECD and OSCE set up a permanent joint Web site after a conference in Paris on the topic of "National and International Approaches to Improve Integrity and Transparency in Government"(www.oecd.org/daf/cmis/bribery/pariscon.htm). It also reported on the monitoring of Ukrainian elections by the OSCE's Office for Democratic Institutions and Human Rights.

## Outreach News

OECD Centre for Co-operation with Non-Members (CCNM)
2 rue André-Pascal
75775 Paris Cedex 16, France
**Tel:** +33 (1) 45-24-83-60
**Fax:** +33 (1) 45-24-91-77
**E-mail:** ccet.contact@oecd.org
**Web:** www.oecd.org/sge/ccnm/news/outreach

The OECD (Organisation for Economic Co-operation and Development) is one of the world's major, multilateral, economic development agencies. It exists to enable its 29 members "to consult and co-operate with each other in order to achieve the highest sustainable economic growth in their countries and improve the economic and social well-being of their populations."

The OECD evolved from the Organisation for European Economic Co-operation established in 1948 to administer the $13-billion Marshall Plan. Membership originally consisted of the countries of Western Europe and North America, but it has expanded in recent years to include Japan, Korea, Mexico, and other countries.

Among formerly communist nations, only Poland, Hungary, and the Czech Republic are today members of the OECD. The Centre for Co-operation with Non-Members (CCNM) is the focal point for the development of policy dialogue between the OECD and non-member economies—such as the economies of the NIS. Established in January 1998, it takes over the work of the Centre for Co-operation with Economies in Transition (CCET).

The CCNM publishes monographs and periodicals, diskettes, and electronic books, some at no charge to the user and many in more than one language. In a recent issue of the quarterly *Outreach News,* all the articles on the CNNM Web site were in both English and Russian. Not all articles deal with economic issues, and of the economic-related articles few are technical. For example, a recent edition of *Outreach News* carried articles such as "Strengthening the Rule of Law in Russia" and "Polish EcoFund a Model for Other Funds."

## Religion, State and Society

Keston Institute
4 Park Town
Oxford OX2 6SH
United Kingdom
**Tel:** +44 (1865) 31-10-22
**Fax:** +44 (1865) 31-12-80
**E-mail:** keston.institute@keston.org
**Web:** www.keston.org
**Contact:** Rev. Michael Bourdeaux

This excellent quarterly is available for an annual subscription of £35/$53. Keston Institute is a research and information center dealing with religion in communist and post-communist countries. It is ecumenical in approach, reporting on all denominations and faiths. It is funded by donations from a wide range of individual supporters, churches, missions, trusts, and foundations.

Keston also has an extensive archive at its headquarters in Oxford, publishes a bimonthly newsletter, *Frontier*, and offers an e-mail Keston News Service.

### Teacher's Gazette
Учительская Газета
Vetoshnyi per. 13-15
103012   Moscow
**Tel:**       928-8253
**Fax:**      924-2927
**E-mail:**  ug@ug.ru
**Web:**     www.ug.ru/
**Contact:** Petr Polozhevets, Editor-in Chief

*Teacher's Gazette* is a well-respected newspaper for elementary and secondary school teachers in Russia. The publication celebrates its 75th anniversary in 1999. Along with news on education in Russia and abroad, the publication promotes education reform in Russia. It provides teachers with weekly supplementary lesson plans on civics and new teaching methodologies.

### Transition: The Newsletter About Reforming Economies
The World Bank
Room N11-039X
1818 H Street, NW
Washington, DC 20433
**Tel:**       (202) 473-7466
**Fax:**      (202) 522-1152
**E-mail:**  books@worldbank.org, jprochnowwalker@worldbank.org
**Web:**     www.worldbank.org
**Contact:** Richard Hirschler, Editor; Jennifer Prochnow-Walker, Research Assistant

This newsletter comes out six times a year and is produced by the Macro-

economics and Growth Group of the Development Research Group at the Bank. Articles are not technical and more varied than one might think—e.g., a recent issue had an article titled "Looming AIDS Epidemic in Transition Economies: Can It Be Avoided?" Each issue includes a calendar of upcoming events, interesting charts and graphs, and reviews of other resources.

### Transitions
Institut novinarstvi transformachnich zemi (IJT)
Seifertova 47
130 000 Prague, Czech Republic
**Tel:**       (420 2) 627-9445
**Fax:**      (420 2) 627-9444
**E-mail:**  transitions@ijt.cz
**Web:**     www.ijt.cz/transitions
**Contact:** Mark Schapiro, Editor at Large; Kees Schaepman, Executive Editor

IJT is a nonprofit organization created to support "dialogue and debate on societies in political transition" and to provide assistance to the independent media. It is funded by the Open Society Institute (Soros Foundations) and the German Marshall Fund of the United States. *Transitions* is published monthly and subscriptions cost $65/year. Each issue is about 100 pages. Well-written articles printed in elegant typefaces are graced by photos of extraordinary quality.

### The Ukrainian Weekly
2200 Route 10
P.O. Box 280
Parsippany, NJ 07054
**Tel:**       (973) 292-9800
**Fax:**      (973) 292-0900
**Web:**     www.ukrweely.com
**Contact:** Roma Hadzewycz, Editor-in-Chief

Founded in 1933, this newspaper is a premier, inexpensive source of information about events both in Ukraine and in the U.S. that affect U.S.-Ukrainian relations. An annual subscription costs $50 ($40 for members of the Ukrainian National Association).

### Writing Tools from Russia Catalog

Smartlink Corporation
4695 Macarthur Court, Suite 230
Newport Beach, CA 92660
**Sales:** (800) 256-4814
**Tel:** (714) 552-1599
**Fax:** (714) 552-1699

This is a catalog of fonts and drivers, proofing tools (spelling and grammar checkers), OCR software, translation software, electronic dictionaries, and CD-ROM-based language learning aids for Russian and other languages of the NIS. The ParaType Library of fonts offers a collection of typefaces developed by Russian type designers over the past 50 years and furnished by the highly regarded Paragraph Company in Moscow. There is also a set of Windows-based fonts and drivers for Turkish and East European languages.

### Yevshan Ukrainian Catalog

Yevshan Corporation
Box 325
Beaconsfield, Quebec
Canada H9W 5T8
**Tel:** (800) 265-9858
**Fax:** (514) 630-9960
**E-mail:** info@yevshan.com

Yevshan Communications describes its catalog as North America's "#1 source of Ukrainian books, music and videos." In addition, the catalog offers maps, flags, holiday cards, Cyrillic font programs for computers, subscriptions to popular Ukrainian newspapers and periodicals, and even a food parcel service to Ukraine. Yevshan's specialty is Ukrainian music production and distribution.

# Index of North American Organizations

# Index of NIS Cities

# Notes

# *About Center for Civil Society International*

C enter for Civil Society International (CCSI) supports activities by American voluntary organizations and independent associations—our so-called "third sector"—that strengthen institutions of pluralism, law, and market economies worldwide. The focus of CCSI's activities is on publishing resources, both in print and electronically, that foster contacts and relationships between America's third sector (professional associations, charitable organizations, mutual aid societies, special interest groups, educational and health organizations, etc.) and the third sector that has emerged in recent years in Russia, Ukraine, and other states of the former Soviet Union. CCSI maintains an extensive World Wide Web site containing more than 3,000 documents and operates a free electronic mailing list, named CivilSoc, whose subscribers number more than 1,400.

On the Board of Advisors of CCSI are Elena Bonner, Greg Cole, Gulmira Dzhamanova, Herbert J. Ellison, John Miller, Yale Richmond, S. Frederick Starr, Sharon Tennison, and Elena and Andrei Topolev. Members of CCSI's Board of Directors are Ronald S. Bemis, John Harner, Richard Greene, Catherine A. Fitzpatrick, Dennis McConnell, Vladimir Raskin, and Daniel C. Waugh.

CCSI is a private, nonpartisan educational organization, based in Seattle, Washington, USA. It is registered as tax-exempt under section 501 (c)(3) of the U.S. Internet Revenue Code and receives its funding from voluntary donations and foundation grants.

Principal staff of Center for Civil Society International are Holt Ruffin and Richard Upjohn. For more information, contact:

> **Center for Civil Society International**
> 2929 NE Blakeley Street
> Seattle, WA 98105-3120 USA
>
> **Tel:**　　(206) 523-4755
> **Fax:**　　(206) 523-1974
> **E-mail:**　ccsi@u.washington.edu
> **Web:**　　www.friends-partners.org/~ccsi/